THE COMPLETE HOME IMPROVEMENT MANUAL

CONSULTANT EDITOR
RICHARD WILES

THE COMPLETE HOME IMPROVEMENT MANUAL

DRAGON'S WORLD

Dragon's World Ltd
Limpsfield
SURREY RH8 0DY
Great Britain

Editorial and design concept by Richard Wiles

Hardback: ISBN 185028 009 6

Printed in Spain by Cayfosa. Barcelona.
Dep. Leg. B-18003-1986

CONTENTS

HOUSE CONSTRUCTION   8

CHAPTER 1   ADAPTING YOUR LIVING SPACE   13

CHAPTER 2   DAMP, ROT AND INSECT ATTACK   80

CHAPTER 3   PLUMBING   90

CHAPTER 4   ELECTRICS   118

CHAPTER 5   HEATING & INSULATION   146

CHAPTER 6   DECORATING   154

CHAPTER 7   HOME SECURITY   210

CHAPTER 8   MAKING MORE OF YOUR GARDEN   216

CHAPTER 9   PROJECTS   242

Contributing authors

Mike Lawrence
Ian Penberthy
John Sanders
Jason Steger
Jane Taylor
Mike Trier

Photographers

Jon Bouchier
Simon Butcher
Simon de Courcy Wheeler

Illustrators

Kuo Kang Chen
Steve Cross
Paul Emra
Pavel Kostal
Janos Marffy
Sebastian Quigley
Laurie Taylor
Brian Watson

HOUSE CONSTRUCTION

Depending on when they were built, houses can be constructed in a number of different ways, and the method of construction may well affect the way in which you carry out any improvements or it may actually make certain improvements necessary to make the building more habitable.

Although it is often said that older houses are better built than their modern counterparts, this is not always the case. True, old houses can be solidly built and their solid walls offer good sound insulation. But often older houses lack good thermal insulation and water-proofing. Modern houses on the other hand are much better protected against damp and are often built with thermal insulation included.

Whatever type of house you own or may own in the future, it is unlikely that you will leave it exactly as it was when you bought it – you will want to change it, to improve it, to make it meet your needs more closely. Having an understanding of its basic structure will help you see where improvements can be made and give you an idea of just what is possible and what is not.

The following pages show some typical house constructions – they are by no means exhaustive but are typical of the types of construction you are likely to come across.

THE MODERN HOUSE

The modern house shows great improvements over its older counterparts in the areas of damp-proofing and thermal insulation. A major contributing factor to these improvements is the cavity wall. All the external walls of the house comprise two separate 112mm (4½in) thick leaves, the outer one being invariably brick and the inner one of brick or more often these days of lightweight concrete blocks. The two leaves are set about 50mm (2in) apart from top to bottom, galvanised metal wall ties linking the two so that they provide mutual support and won't lean away from each other. The inner leaf supports the weight of the floors, ceilings and roof.

The cavity between the leaves of the wall stops any damp penetrating through from the surface of the wall and it provides a slight degree of thermal insulation which can be improved by filling it with an insulation foam or by installing styrofoam plastic slabs during building.

A felt or metal flashing prevents damp rising up through the wall and this is linked to a thick plastic waterproof membrane which is incorporated in the solid concrete floor slab. The floor itself may be clad with tiles, wood blocks or have a wooden floor built on top.

The foundations for the walls are likely to be deep trenches filled with concrete, the walls themselves beginning just below ground level. This is a much more effective and much quicker way of doing the job and is typical of modern methods of construction which are much more efficient than earlier practices.

Ease of construction is carried through to the roof, which is built up from a series of ready-made wooden trusses which do away with the ridge bar. One disadvantage of this system is that it does not lend itself to attic conversions. The roof will be clad with interlocking concrete tiles.

Upper floors will almost certainly be clad with particleboard sheets rather than wooden floorboards and these provide a much flatter and more rigid surface. The ceilings will be clad with drywall as will be any non-loadbearing internal partitions which will have a wooden internal framework. Loadbearing internal partitions may be of brick but more likely concrete blocks.

interlocking concrete tiles

Cavity walls built on a concrete slab foundation, and trussed roof.

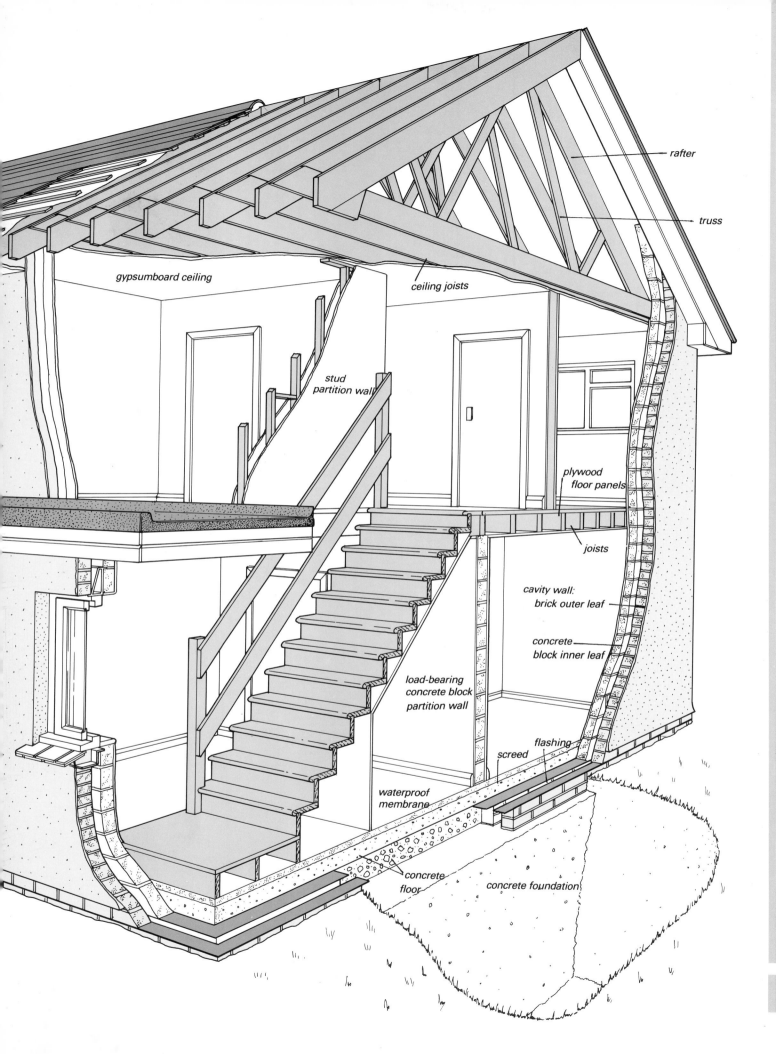

rafter

truss

gypsumboard ceiling

ceiling joists

stud
partition wall

plywood
floor panels

joists

cavity wall:
brick outer leaf

concrete
block inner leaf

load-bearing
concrete block
partition wall

flashing

screed

waterproof
membrane

concrete
floor

concrete foundation

THE COUNTRY COTTAGE

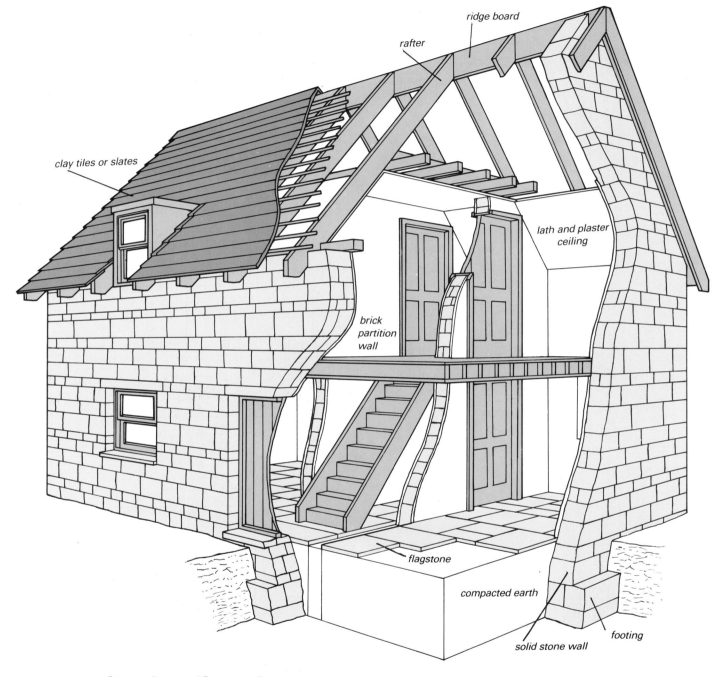

ridge board

rafter

clay tiles or slates

lath and plaster
ceiling

brick
partition
wall

flagstone

compacted earth

footing

solid stone wall

Stone walls; ground floor on earth.

Usually a hundred years or more old, the typical country cottage is small and may be built with brick or stone walls, depending on the area in which it is sited and the sort of materials that would have been readily available at the time.

The walls will be solid between 225mm (9in) and 300mm (12in) thick with no cavity as in a modern house and no flashing to prevent moisture rising up through the wall from the ground. The thickness of wall should be enough to stop damp penetrating from the outer surface, but old age may well have reduced the effectiveness of the wall. The ground floor may be flagstones laid directly on to a compacted earth below.

Many houses of this type have very shallow foundations to the walls which should be borne in mind if digging anywhere near them.

Internal walls may be brick faced with plaster or lath-and-plaster; ceilings will also be of lath-and-plaster construction. Often the rooms in these cottages will be quite small with low ceilings. The upper rooms are usually partly in the roof, reducing headroom still further. The roof may be clad with clay tiles or slates, or in some cases even thatch.

VICTORIAN VILLA

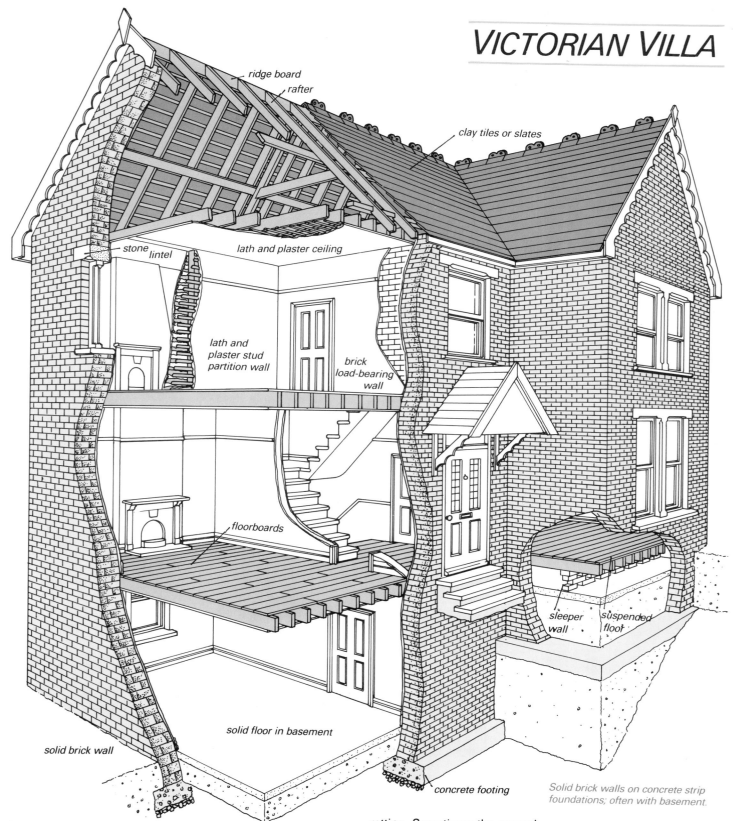

ridge board

rafter

clay tiles or slates

stone lintel

lath and plaster ceiling

lath and plaster stud partition wall

brick load-bearing wall

floorboards

sleeper wall

suspended floor

solid floor in basement

solid brick wall

concrete footing

Solid brick walls on concrete strip foundations; often with basement.

Often quite large, this type of building still has solid brick walls which can lead to penetrating damp and are not good from a thermal insulation point of view. However the walls have substantial footings. Basements are common as are attic rooms, providing a lot of space ideal for a growing family or if hobby rooms are required. Some have flash-

ings in the form of layers of engineering bricks around the foot of the walls, and suspended wooden ground floors are usual. These may be supported by brick 'sleeper' walls or simply rest on bricks laid on the ground below; some form of water proofing is usually laid between the wood and its supports to prevent

rotting. Sometimes the ground below the floor is covered with a layer of concrete. Floors will be decked with 100mm (4in) or 150mm (6in) wide boards and ceilings will be lath and plaster. The same construction will be used for nonloadbearing partitions. However, any that carry the load of the floors or roof above will be brick. Generally rooms will be very tall and quite

large and the steeply pitched roofs are ideal for attic conversions. The roof will be built in the traditional manner with sloping rafters linked to a central ridge bar. This structure is clad with clay tiles or slates. The walls above windows and doorways may be supported by stone lintels or bricks arranged on end to form 'soldier arches'.

11

WOOD-FRAMED HOUSES

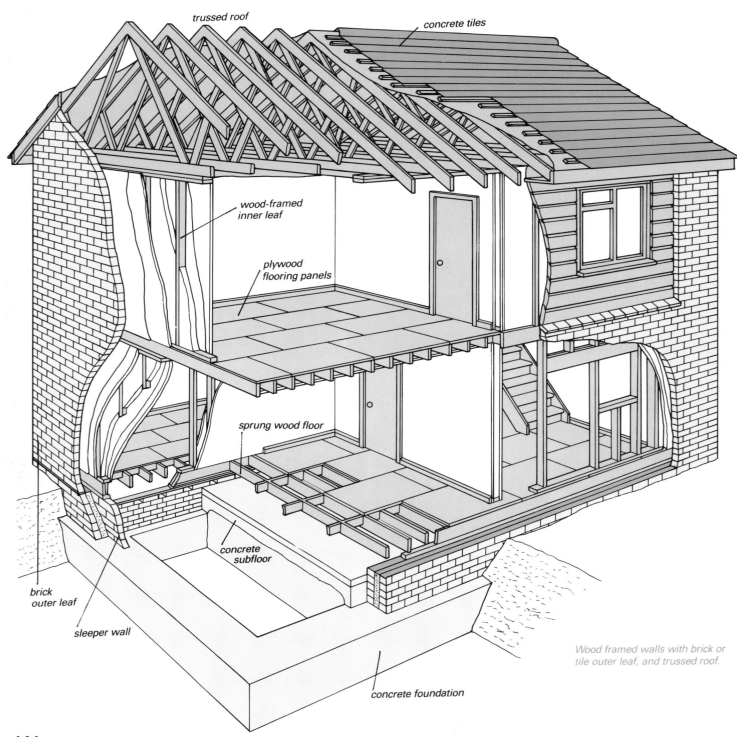

trussed roof

concrete tiles

wood-framed
inner leaf

plywood
flooring panels

sprung wood floor

concrete
subfloor

brick
outer leaf

sleeper wall

Wood framed walls with brick or tile outer leaf, and trussed roof.

concrete foundation

Wood framed houses are built in a similar fashion to a cavity-walled house in that the outer walls comprise two leaves with a gap in between. The outer leaf provides weather protection and may be of brick or possibly tiles but usually is wooden siding laid over a plywood skin. The inner leaf is a strong wood frame work

that supports the loading of the floors, ceilings and roof. All the internal partitions are also of wood construction.

Obviously, since wood is susceptible to rot, steps must be taken during construction to protect it as much as possible. All the wood will be treated with

preservative and vapor barriers are incorporated to prevent moist air entering the framework of the walls.

The foundations of the walls will be concrete filled trenches and the inner wood frame is supported on a low 'sleeper' wall which rises to floor level. The

ground floor itself may be sprung wood, the ground below being covered with a layer of concrete. Floors generally will be clad with plywood and ceilings and walls with drywall. The roof is likely to be made from pre-fabricated trusses and clad with ashphalt shingles.

ADAPTING YOUR LIVING SPACE

Choosing a home to live in inevitably involves compromise. Your decision is influenced by where you want to live, how big a house you want (and that usually comes down to the number of bedrooms), how much you can afford and whether or not you can get a mortgage. Coming a long way down the list of priorities is the arrangement of the space inside the house. Whether the rooms are the right size and shape for your own particular needs is often not even considered. In any case, it is extremely unlikely that you would be able to find a house where the interior arrangement was exactly right, unless you had the house designed and built for you, or you built it yourself.

Even if, by some miracle, a house provided just the sort of layout you needed when you moved in, needs change, families grow, possessions increase, and keeping pace with fashions in the home may leave you dissatisfied with what you have. This is usually overcome by moving to another house where the process of compromise begins all over

again. However, not everyone is able, or may even want to move: the availability of work, children settled in school, and nearness of relatives and friends, and the considerable upheaval caused by a move must all be taken into account.

Rather than accept that moving is the only solution to the problem of improving your accommodation, consider making more of and adapting what you already have; you should even do this when you first move in. By adapting your home to keep pace with your needs, you will be much happier living there and will get much more satisfaction from your home.

Remodeling

Room size, shape and number are often particular problems — a growing family may mean you could do with more bedrooms, or an additional bathroom to ease that early morning traffic jam, perhaps even separate dens for the older and younger elements of the family. Many people have to look after elderly or infirm relatives, in which case an extra

powder room or bathroom and bedroom can be very useful.

Extra rooms can be provided by partitioning off larger ones with wood framed walls complete with access doors. In the same way, large open-plan rooms can be divided into smaller, cosier rooms if that is what you prefer. In the latter case, a partial or half-height partition would provide an effective division between, say, the dining and living areas of a room while retaining the spacious, airy feel of an open-plan layout.

Adding Rooms

If you need more rooms and there is simply no way you can get more from the existing layout, it is often possible to add an extension to your house. If you don't want to go to the trouble of having such an extension designed for you, there are some prefabricated types to choose from.

Of course, you may feel that your house has too many small, cramped rooms and you would rather have a few, large open-plan rooms. In a case like this, it

is usually a simple matter to remove a dividing wall between two rooms, having first taken steps to support any wall or floor above.

Dealing with Doors

Access routes between rooms are important, if you are to get the best from your home. Very often doors are not placed in the most convenient locations, there is no reason why you shouldn't reposition doors, or make new doorways between adjoining rooms where none existed before; or block off redundant doorways where, say, two rooms have been joined into one. Using similar skills, you can improve the light of gloomy rooms by installing larger windows.

The methods for carrying out all of these alterations are covered on the following pages, together with ways of correcting defects in the fabric of the house so that whether you are just moving in or have lived in your house for many years, you can bring it right up to snuff.

DIVIDING THE SPACE

Partitions can be used in most homes to make best use of available space, turning large or awkwardly-shaped rooms into more manageable or more sensible accommodation.

The large, L-shaped room is common to many homes, yet it is not the most convenient of shapes to furnish or heat. By building a partition with an access door across one of the legs of the 'L' you can produce two smaller, rectangular rooms which are much cosier and more easily heated.

Long, narrow rooms also produce their own particular problems, such as giving the impression of being like tunnels or causing difficulties in positioning furniture. Everything tends to be put round the walls, leaving a large bare area in the center of the room. By building a partition that spans, say, only half of the room's width, you can create two distinct areas (for living and dining perhaps) without completely losing the feeling of being in one large room. Furniture can then be grouped more effectively. You can achieve the same effect by building a waist-high partition across the room, but in this case there would be much more of an open-plan feel to the room. Such a partition would also provide some useful shelf space along the top, or a tier of shelves could be arranged between the top of the partition and the ceiling.

Obviously, if you are using a partition to make two rooms out of one, you will have to arrange access to the new room. The easiest way is to build a door in the partition. However, this means that you must walk through one room to reach the other and that might not always be convenient, especially if the rooms are used as bedrooms. To overcome this problem you can either make a new doorway through one of the original walls of the room or build a second partition at right angles to the first to form a small lobby, from which both rooms can be entered separately.

Providing Daylight

An important point to consider when partitioning a room is the availability of daylight in both new rooms. You may find that the only suitable position for the partition means that one room has no window at all. In this situation, you can provide a fair degree of natural light by incorporating panes of glass (clear or frosted depending on the purpose of the room) along the top of the partition. You could even include a glass door.

Creating Storage Space

Partitions can be very useful for creating storage space as well. By building what is effectively a false wall across the end of a room, you can use the space between it and the original wall for inset shelving, cabinets and even walk-in closets. This can be particularly handy if there is a very small room next to a large one, since by cutting an opening in the original dividing wall and arranging the internal divisions of the storage space carefully, you will provide a storage facility for both rooms.

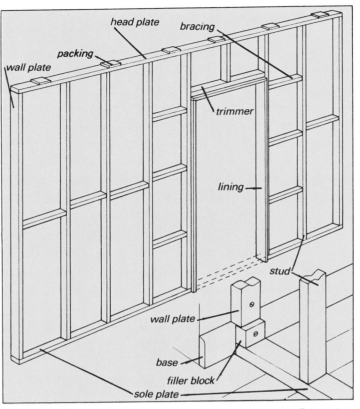

Build a stud framework, except for the wall plates and bracing, flat on the floor; lift and wedge it into position, fit the bracing and wall plates and cut out the threshold of the door. Fit a block baseboard (inset) so that the drywall edge is fully supported.

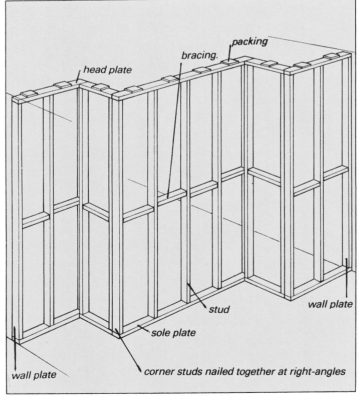

By building the partition wall in angled sections, alcoves are formed which can be used to incorporate built-in storage in both rooms.

A bathroom formed by partitioning off a larger room. The confined space is visually enlarged by the overall tiling of the walls and bath platform, and light is admitted through a glass block wall.

The easiest form of partition to build is the wood frame variety — it is ideal for dividing one bedroom into two, making an extra powder room or bathroom, or splitting a dining area from a kitchen or living room. The wood frame is simply nailed together and faced with drywall on each side; it is easily adapted for doorways, pass throughs or windows. Being essentially hollow, it can also be used to conceal electrical wiring and water pipes.

The framework comprises a number of uprights called 'studs' fitted between lengths of wood spanning the width of the ceiling and floor. These are called the 'head plate' and 'sole plate' respectively. Short horizontal lengths of wood are fixed between the uprights to brace them and support the cladding. In most cases 75 × 50mm (2 × 3in) rough sawn softwood is ideal for the studs and bracing, with 75 by 38mm (1½ × 3in) for the head and sole plates. If the partition is to carry a lot of weight such as shelves or cupboards, a larger size of wood should be used, say 100 by 500mm (2 × 4in).

Planning the Partition

Deciding where to put the partition is the first thing to do so that you end up with two usable rooms. If possible arrange things so that each new room gets the benefit of a window, but don't be tempted to set the partition so that it divides a window in two. Not only does this look dreadful, but in some cases it is illegal. If you cannot provide a window for each room, glaze the upper portion of the partition so that you can 'borrow' some natural light from the room with the window. Similarly, if you cannot provide an opening window for each new room, install some form of mechanical ventilation.

Important considerations are the layouts of floor and ceiling joists since the head and sole plates will be attached to these. Ideally, the partition should run at right angles to the joists so that its weight is spread across them. If this is not possible, it must be directly above a joist. If the floor is a solid one, this is not a problem.

If the head plate does not span the ceiling joists and does not come immediately below a single joist because the ceiling joists do not line up with the floor joists, you should nail lengths of 50mm (2in) sq blocking between the ceiling joists and attach the headplate to these.

Before you begin work, check under the floor and above the ceiling for any cables or pipes that might be damaged by nails or screws. It is also a good idea to check with your local Building Code before carrying out any structural work.

Erecting the Framework

Begin by cutting the head and sole plates to length; whenever possible buy wood long enough so that you can span the room with one piece. Nail the sole plate to the joists through the floorboards using 100mm (4in) long common nails or fix it to a concrete floor with 100mm (4in) long No. 10 woodscrews and wall plugs or with masonry anchors or masonry nails. Screw the head plate to the ceiling joists.

Cut the studs for each end of the partition, leaving them a fraction over-length so that they will be a tight fit between the head and sole plates, and screw them to the wall. Use 100mm (4in) long No. 10 screws and wall plugs.

Then mark off the positions of the other studs along the sole plate, making sure their centers are 400mm (16in) or no more than 600mm (24in) apart. They should be positioned so that the edges of the cladding material will meet along their center lines (standard sheets of drywall are 1.2m/4ft) wide. If the partition is to have a door in it, the stud positions on each side of the opening must be adjusted to allow for the door width and the thickness of the lining (see page 16).

Measure and cut each stud individually since there is no guarantee that the head and sole plates will be parallel.

Set each stud in place, making sure it is vertical with a level, and fix it by driving 75 or 100mm (3or 4in) common nails at an angle through the side of the stud into the head and sole plate (known as toe-nails).

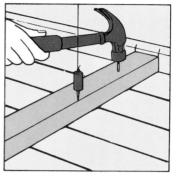

Nailing the sole plate to the floor joists; mark the line of the wall on the ceiling and hang a plumb-line to give the position on the floor.

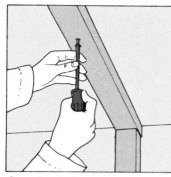

Screwing the head plate to the ceiling joists through countersunk clearance holes; prop the wood in postion with one of the studs.

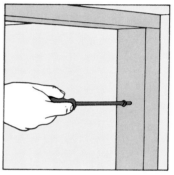

Fixing one end stud to the wall with screws and wall-plugs, after tapping it into position; repeat for the other end stud.

Marking the position of a stud on the sole plate, using an offcut; the studs are usually spaced at 610mm (24in) centres.

After setting the foot of the stud on the squared marks, tapping into the vertical position; check that the foot is still on the marks.

Toe-nailing the stud using an offcut for support; drive in two more nails on the other side and repeat at the top of the stud.

Trick

FINDING CEILING JOISTS

First tap the ceiling and listen for a 'flat' sound to indicate the presence of a joist. Then make a series of holes across the joist position with a bradawl, feeling the resistance to the blade as it enters the wood.

BRACING THE STUDS

With all the studs in place, the next job is to fit the bracing. If you intend cladding the partition with standard 2.4m (8ft) sheets of gypsumboard, the bracing should be placed in a row 1.2m (4ft) from the floor. If the partition is taller than 2.4m (8ft), a second row of bracing should be fitted to support the upper edges of the drywall panels and the lower edges of the panels above them.

For strength, stagger the bracing above and below each other — this makes fitting easier, too — but if they are to support the edges of two sheets of drywall they must all be in line. In this case, the center line of each brace must coincide with the edges of the panels. Mark the brace positions on the studs with a pencil and level to make sure they are all horizontal.

Cut the bracing so that it is a close fit between the studs but not over-length, otherwise it will push the studs out of true, which may present problems when you clad the framework.

Begin fitting the bracing at the wall end of the partition and work in towards the center. A block of wood nailed to the wall stud will support the end of the first brace while you nail through the second stud into the other end of the brace. Use two nails. Then toe-nail the inner end of the brace to the wall stud. If the

Toe-nailing in-line bracing; the block below, temporarily nailed to the stud, provides support during nailing.

Fixing an extra stud over a door-opening; the bracing here is the lintel for the doorway and must be set into the stud each side.

bracing is to be fitted in line, repeat this procedure for each one; if it is to be staggered, simply drive nails through the studs into the ends of the brace.

The bracing over a doorway is called a 'lintel' or 'header' and its

Nailing into the ends of staggered bracing; this method of construction is stronger and easier to erect.

Screwing the lining to the stud; the side linings are rebated into the head lining and should be flush with the gypsumboard.

ends must be fitted more securely in 13mm (½in) deep slots cut in the sides of the adjacent studs. Cut down the side of each slot with a back saw and remove the waste with a 25mm (1in) bevel-edged chisel, working inwards

from each end of the slot. Alternatively use a double stud at the header ends to support the header.

Trimming the Doorway

Having completed the framework, you can remove the section of sole plate from the threshold of the doorway. Simply saw through each end level with the studs on each side. Then clad the framework with gypsumboard (see opposite), trimming the panels round the doorway flush with the studs and header.

The door opening should be trimmed with lengths of 100 × 25mm (4 × 1 in) planed softwood that fit flush with the faces of the gypsumboard panels on each side (use wider lumber if thicker studs were installed). Cut a length to fit snugly between the studs at the top and screw this to the header. Then screw two longer pieces to the studs on each side of the door opening.

Finally, cut pieces of molding to fit round the door opening, mitering their corners at 45°, using a miter box as a guide for the saw. Nail the molding to the edges of the trimming pieces with 25mm (1in) finishing nails, driving their heads below the surface so they can be filled before painting.

Trick

DRY PARTITION

For a lightweight partition, you can use a ready-made dry partition system. One proprietary version comprises sandwich construction panels of two sheets of drywall bonded to a cellular core of card.

Installation is simple: you nail narrow battens to the walls, ceiling and floor and slot the edges of the panels over them, nailing through the panels into the battens to fix them. Panels are joined by nailing into battens fitted between them. Baseboards are fixed in the same way.

Trick

PLASTER-BOARDING

Plasterboard is a sandwich of gypsum plaster between two layers of thick paper, which hold it together. You can plaster over it or paint or paper it to match the other walls in the room. It is ideal for cladding a timber framed partition, the panels being simply nailed in place.

When buying plasterboard, choose the tapered-edge variety; the long sides of each panel are narrowed so that when butted together the joint can be filled without the filler standing proud of the surface. Always handle plasterboard carefully; it is easily broken. If you intend plastering it, fit the grey side outermost, but if you want to paint or paper over it leave the ivory-coloured side showing.

Fix all the full-size panels to the framework first then cut smaller pieces to finish off, completing one side at a time. If the partition doesn't span the room completely, work from the outer end towards the wall.

Cutting

To cut plasterboard, use a sharp knife and steel straightedge; you won't be able to cut through in one go, so after cutting through one side, stand the board on edge and snap the waste back to break the plaster. Then cut through the remaining paper layer. For right-angle cuts you must mark both sides of the panel and cut through from both sides. Trim full panels to be about 25mm (1in) less than the floor-to-ceiling height; this will allow you to push them up tight against the ceiling with a 'foot-lifter' before nailing. (You can make your own footlifter from a couple of timber offcuts, balancing one across the other like a see-saw.)

Nail the board to the frame, using 30mm (1¼in) galvanized plasterboard nails, spacing them at 150mm (6in) intervals and working outwards from the centre of the panel. Keep the nails at least 13mm (½in) from the edge of the panel to prevent them breaking the edge. Drive the nails in so that their heads just pinch the surface but do not break through the paper covering. This is just enough to allow for a thin skim of filler.

To fill the joints, apply a layer of proprietary joint filler then press in a length of paper jointing tape. Apply more filler up to the level of the surrounding plasterboard, feathering the edges with a damp sponge. When dry, apply one or two thin layers of joint finish, again feathering the edges with a sponge.

Lifting a sheet of drywall with a foot-lifter; the gap at the bottom will be covered by the baseboard.

Nailing the drywall to the wooden framework; nail at 150mm (6in) intervals and at least 12mm (½in) in from the edges.

Measuring from the last full-width sheet to the end wall; measure at top, middle and bottom and use the largest dimension.

Scribing against an uneven wall; cut the board to shape with a fine-toothed general-purpose saw.

Cutting drywall; score through the paper on one side with a sharp knife and snap the board smartly backwards.

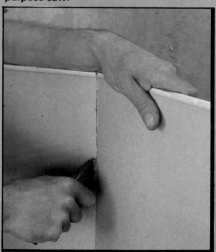

Separating the two pieces; bend the board slightly to give a cutting guide and cut through the other paper layer.

CONSTRUCTING A BLOCKWORK WALL

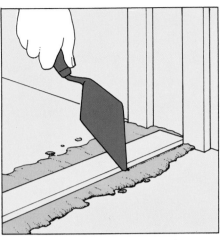

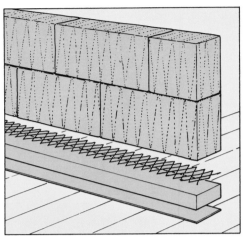

On a solid floor, spreading a mortar bed on the floor between vertical guide battens.

Scribing a guide line in the mortar for one face of the wall against a straight-edge.

On a timber floor, build on a sole plate with metal lath; underfelt beneath absorbs sound.

Although a wood-framed partition is easy to build, it will not provide really effective sound insulation and it will need extra strengthening if it is to carry shelves or cabinets. In situations such as this, a partition built from lightweight concrete blocks is much more suitable. However, you cannot build such a partition on an upper floor, since even a reinforced concrete floor is unlikely to be strong enough to carry the load of a concrete block partition. A concrete first floor

makes an ideal foundation and even a suspended wood first floor will do if a full-width wood sole plate is put down first, but check with your local Code beforehand.

Before starting work, the floor, walls and ceiling should be stripped of all coverings and any coving and base cut away with a chisel to clear the blocks. The easiest way to mark the position of the partition is with a chalked plumbline, snapping it against the floor to leave two

parallel chalk lines the width of the blocks. Continue these lines up the walls and across the ceiling. The bob weight on the line will make sure the marks on the walls are vertical.

For strength, it is best to tie the partition to adjacent walls by cutting recesses in them to accept the end blocks of alternate courses or by using galvanized metal ties screwed to the walls and buried in the blockwork mortar joints. Nailing a guide batten to the wall against

one of the chalk lines is also a good idea.

Trowel a 150mm (6in) wide layer of mortar (1 part masonry cement: 6 parts soft sand) across the floor to span the chalk lines on it, levelling it out to about 9mm ($\frac{3}{8}$in) thick. Then scribe a guide line through the mortar in line with the chalk marks on the end walls, using the point of your trowel and a long straight-edged plank. You will lay the blocks up to this line.

Trick

PRODUCT

AERATED BLOCKS

There are many different types of concrete block to choose from, but the best types for building an internal partition are known as 'aerated' blocks. These are light in weight, so they're easy to handle — an important quality since they're twice times the size of a normal brick; this fact also means that you can build a full-height partition relatively quickly. You can drill them, knock nails into them or even cut channels in them to conceal electrical cables and pipework. Sound won't pass through them as easily as it would a woodframed partition, nor will heat. Aerated blocks should be laid in the same manner as bricks in a 'stretcher' bond pattern with mortar joints. Their normal size is 440 × 215 × 100mm (17 × 8½ × 4in). For finishing, you can either plaster them directly or nail on battens and fix a gypsumboard cladding to the battens.

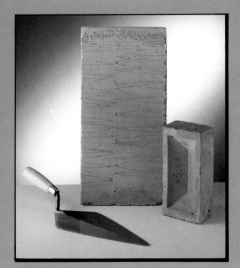

The size of a lightweight block makes construction much faster than when using bricks; the weight of the wall is less.

Cutting a notch from the corner of a block to fit round an obstruction, using a general-purpose saw.

Dry-laying to check for fit; allow a finger-thickness between blocks for mortar. Vertical battens give support until the mortar hardens.

Spreading the mortar bed on the floor; scribe the line of one face of the wall in the mortar with the point of the trowel.

'Buttering' one end with mortar before laying the block; place this end against the previous block.

Laying the block on the mortar bed, flush with the scribed line.

Tamping the block level with the adjacent block using the trowel handle; check each block as it is laid with a spirit-level.

Alternatively, stretch a string line between vertical joints and hold it in place with a brick.

Securing a metal frame-clamp to the side wall; tie alternate courses in this way.

Checking the face of the blockwork for alignment; use a long spirit-level or straight-edge and check in a number of directions.

Before laying the blocks it is as well to carry out a dummy run on the first two courses, so you will know how best to arrange them to keep the number of cut blocks to a minimum. Set them out along the layer of mortar in line with the scribed mark, keeping the spacing between them equal to the thickness of your index finger.

If the partition is to have a door in it, now is the time to position the frame. Nail battens across the corners of the frame and across the bottom to hold it square and prop it up with another batten nailed to the top.

Once you have sorted out the first two courses, you can begin laying the blocks properly. It is best to build up about four courses of blocks at each end of the partition first and then stretch a stringline between them as a guide for the blocks in the middle.

Trowel a layer of mortar on to the original thin layer and 'butter' the end of the first block with more mortar. Set the block in place against the scribed line and against the wall to form a neat mortar joint. Tap the block level and upright with the handle of the trowel. Repeat the procedure for the next block in the course and lay two or three more before working back towards the wall with the second, third and fourth courses. Collect the mortar that is squeezed out from between the blocks for reuse.

As you work, make sure the blocks butt up to the guide batten and check them every now and again with a mason's level to ensure you are keeping the courses upright and level. Tie each alternate course to the wall by either inserting the end blocks in the cut-outs made previously or with galvanized metal wall ties. Secure the door frame to the blockwork with the same ties. Then build up the center of the partition.

If you need to cut any blocks to make them fit, do this with a bricklayer's chisel and a light sledge or heavy duty hammer. Measure up the block and scribe a cutting line on all four sides with the end of the chisel. Then tap gently all the way along this line with the chisel. Finally, lay the block face up, set the chisel in the centre of the cutting line and strike it a sharp blow which will separate the two halves of the block.

It's also easy to saw blocks to size and shape using a masonry saw — ideal if you have to notch a block, say to fit over one corner of a doorway.

A ceiling-height door frame makes the wall more stable; fill the gap above the door with wired glass, or a gypsumboard or wooden panel.

A door-height opening needs a lintel above it to support the blockwork; a course of bricks on top will align with the blockwork.

Nail temporary 'strainer' battens across a door-frame to keep it square and support it upright with a plank nailed to the top.

FITTING SERVICES IN A PARTITION WALL

Careful planning is essential when arranging a partition and this extends to working out what cable and pipe runs you may need to pass through it and installing them as you build.

Services in stud partitions

The time to put either cables or pipes into a stud partition is when you have just completed the framework or finished the cladding of one side. With the studs and bracing still exposed you can fit the cables and pipes in place with little trouble.

One important point to remember whenever installing cables or pipes in any kind of wall, is that they must always run vertically or horizontally directly to or from each fitting. That way if ever you, or future occupants, want to drill holes in the wall you will know the likely danger areas.

Electricity

Running cable through the framework of a stud partition is easy. First, bore a 19mm (¾in) hole through either the head plate or sole plate into the ceiling or floor void as appropriate and depending on the direction from which the cable is to come. Drill similar holes through the centers of any bracing that cross the cable route.

Feed in the cable, leaving plenty of excess. Then cut a hole in the drywall at the fitting's position and feed the end of the cable through this as you fit the drywall in place.

Plumbing

Pipework in a stud partition can be tackled in the same way, making sure the holes you drill through the framework are larger than the pipe's diameter. This will make manouevring them into place easier and allow them to expand and contract as the temperature fluctuates. Try to keep the number of joints inside the partition to the bare minimum and make sure you test any plumbing system before you finish the cladding; that way if there is a leaking joint you will

be able to do something about it before it does any real damage. Copper pipe is flexible enough for you to be able to spring quite long lengths into place and, if the pipes are to drop down from the ceiling you could remove a floorboard in the room above and feed it down through the partition from there. If you use modern flexible plastic pipe, the job will be even easier.

An alternative method to pushing the pipes through holes drilled in the framework is to clip them into notches cut in the edges of the bracing and studs. Make the notches with a back saw and bevel-edge chisel, cutting them wide enough to accept a pipe clip of the right size and deep enough so that the pipe does not touch the drywall cladding.

Services in Blockwork Partitions

Concealing cables and pipes in a blockwork partition is also easy, provided you set them in place before you finish off the surface with plaster or gypsum board cladding.

Electrical cables can be run across the surface of the blocks in pipes and held in place with clips.

Pipes need a bit more work since they may be too large in diameter to conceal within the layer of plaster. In this case, use a light sledge hammer and bricklayers chisel to chop out a channel (called a 'chase') across the face of the blocks, making it wide enough to accept the appropriate size of pipe clip and deep enough that the pipe will be flush with the surface.

Hot Water Pipes

It is best not to bury hot water pipes in this way as expansion of the pipes may cause the plaster to crack; this is not so serious with gypsumboard cladding provided there is some space around the pipes. If you really want to bury a hot water pipe, it would be best to run it through another pipe of the next size up, which would act as a sleeve and allow expansion.

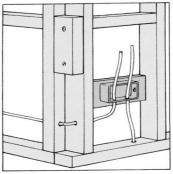

Mount an outlet box in a stud wall on a brace nailed between two studs; drill holes for cables, allowing plenty of clearance.

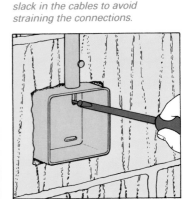

Mount switch boxes on boards nailed to the studs; leave plenty of slack in the cables to avoid straining the connections.

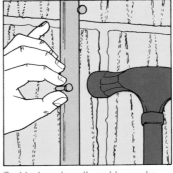

On blockwork walls, cable can be run through conduit nailed to the blocks; this will be concealed when the wall is plastered.

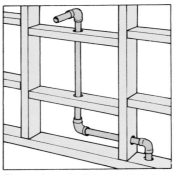

An outlet mounting-box is partially recessed into blockwork, and then plugged and screwed in the recess.

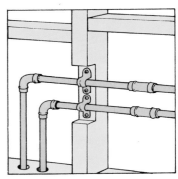

Pipework can be fed through holes drilled in the studs and bracing; this will provide adequate support within the wall.

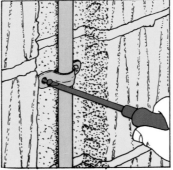

Alternatively, cut notches in the framework and secure the pipe with saddle-clips.

Bury cold water pipes in blockwork by cutting a chase and securing the pipes within it with saddle-clips plugged and screwed to the blocks.

Hot pipes may be boxed in with wooden battens or run within an outer pipe in a chase to allow for expansion and contraction.

Plaster is an excellent and inexpensive material for giving a smooth, hard surface to an internal wall so that it is ready for painting or wallpapering. The tricks lie in getting the consistency of the plaster right and perfecting the use of the plasterer's trowel.

There are many types of plaster, but they can be divided into two basic types: gypsum-based and cement-based. The former are used solely for indoor work, whereas the latter are mainly used outdoors for rendering walls. Cement-based plasters do have a use indoors, however, and that is to finish external walls that might be subject to damp penetration: damp will attack a gypsum plaster and cause it to crumble.

Modern plasters come premixed with lightweight fillers such as perlite or vermiculite, which give a higher degree of thermal insulation and fire resistance. Other ingredients slow down the setting time and generally make the mixture more workable. All that is necessary is to mix the plaster with clean water.

Plaster is normally applied to

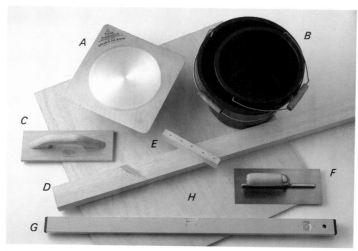

Plasterer's tools: hawk, bucket, float, straight-edge, scratcher, metal trowel, spirit-level and spot-board (beneath).

the wall in two layers. The first, called a 'floating' coat, is intended to even out the irregularities in the wall surface, so it is kept fairly thick — about 10mm (3/8in) being usual. The second, finishing coat is spread much thinner 3mm (1/8in) or so — and carefully trowelled off to a smooth finish.

Different types of building materials absorb water at different rates and if too much water is absorbed from the fresh plaster,

it will dry too quickly and crack.

For example, bricks and lightweight building blocks absorb water quickly and are termed 'high suction' surfaces. On the other hand, materials such as concrete and gypsumboard do not absorb water that quickly and are termed 'low suction'. You must choose a plaster to match the surface; if in doubt, the best thing to do is coat the entire wall with a bonding agent which will make a low suction

surface.

Browning plaster should be used for the floating coat on high suction surfaces and Bonding plaster on low suction surfaces. Finish plaster can be used for the finishing coat in both cases.

Only buy plaster as you need it since it has a limited shelf life. A 10kg (22lb) bag of Browning or Bonding plaster should cover an area of about 1.5m² (1.8yd²) at a depth of 10mm (3/8in). The same quantity of Finish plaster, spread thinly, should do about 5m² (6yd²).

In addition to a couple of clean buckets and a long level, you will need some special plastering tools: a spot board about 1m (3ft) square and supported on trestles or an old table to hold the mixed plaster while you work; a hawk for carrying small quantities of plaster to the wall; a rectangular metal plasterer's trowel; a wooden float for producing flat surfaces (with a few nails knocked into the end it can double as a 'scratcher' for scoring the floating coat before applying the finishing coat); and a 1.5m (5ft) length of 75 × 25mm (1 × 3in) planed wood for levelling the plaster surface.

Trick

PLASTERER'S

Cleanliness is essential when mixing plaster, since any dirt present in the mix will affect the drying time. Always use clean tap water for mixing and have a separate bucket of water for cleaning the tools.

Mix the plaster and water in equal volumes in a clean bucket, adding the plaster to the water by sprinkling it on top and breaking up any lumps between your fingers. When the water has soaked into all the plaster, use a thick piece of wood to stir the plaster into a smooth consistency, (Finish plaster should resemble runny ice-cream), make sure there are no lumps.

Wet the spot board and turn out the plaster on to it, kneading it with the trowel. If the mix appears too wet, sprinkle on a little more plaster and mix in with the trowel.

MIXING PLASTER

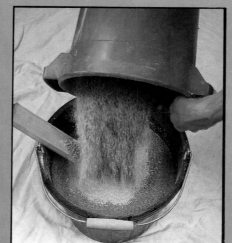

Mixing equal volumes of plaster and water by pouring the plaster on to the water; break up any lumps of plaster.

Kneading the plaster with a trowel after pouring it on to a wet spot-board; add more plaster if it is too runny.

SETTING OUT FOR PLASTERING

One problem the beginner faces when tackling a plastering job is that of producing a floating coat that is uniform in thickness and level over the entire wall surface. It would be a hopeless task to try to do this without some form of thickness guide to work to. The answer is to divide the wall into small sections or bays and use the dividers as depth guides.

You can space the dividers as close together or as far apart as you like, but a suitable distance is about 1m (3ft). As you gain in experience of plastering, you may find that you can space them further apart, reducing the total number of bays and getting the job done quicker.

Dividing the Wall

There are various methods for dividing the wall into bays, and a traditional way is to trowel narrow strips of plaster from floor to ceiling. Known as 'screeds', these strips of plaster are allowed to harden, then more plaster is spread on the wall between them and brought up to their level, using a long straightedge place across the screeds to check.

The problem with the screeding method is being able to get the plaster strips to the right thickness in the first place. Small blocks of wood, known as 'dots', can be fixed to the wall at the top and bottom of the screed position and used as thickness guides by setting a straightedge between them.

A much easier way of dividing the wall into bays, which also provides accurate thickness guides for the overall floating coat, is to use wooden 'grounds'. These are lengths of planed, 10mm (⅜in) thick by about 50mm (2in) wide softwood, which are fixed to the wall with masonry nails. Since you only plaster one bay at a time, you only need two grounds per wall as you can move them along as you work.

After setting out the first bay, you can apply a floating coat between the two wooden grounds, striking it off level with a long wooden straightedge called a 'rule'. Then, having let the plaster harden off for a while, you

should carefully pull one ground from the wall and nail it back on further along the wall to make a second bay.

Plaster the second bay using the wooden ground and the edge of the plastered bay as thickness guides. Continue applying the floating coat in this way, moving the wooden grounds along the wall until you have completed the job.

When fitting wooden grounds it is essential that they are set vertically, otherwise the plaster surface will be out of true. Use a long masons level to check that they are upright and, if necessary, slip small wooden shims as packing pieces behind the grounds to bring them into line.

Using Metal Lath

An alternative to using wood grounds is the metal screed bead which you can buy from your builder's supply house. It does the same job as the ground but is designed to be left in place on the wall; it 'disappears' under the finishing coat of plaster.

The center of the bead is formed into a raised, inverted U-shape, the depth of which is equal to the depth of the floating coat, and on each side there is expanded metal mesh. You can cut it by snipping through the mesh with metal snips then sawing through the bead with a hacksaw.

Beading is fixed to the wall with plaster 'dabs' — blobs of plaster trowelled on to the wall. Push the beading into the dabs then check with a level. You may find it easier, however, to spread a complete vertical strip of plaster on the wall and push the beading into this. Or you could nail it in place with galvanized masonry nails.

Allow the plaster to harden off and then use the beads as thickness guides for the floating coat. Similar beading is available for plastering external corners where it has the added advantage of providing a hard 'nose' to the corner to resist damage (see page 25).

Setting up guide battens (grounds) before plastering; pack out any low areas with card or plywood and fix to the blockwork with masonry nails.

Checking the level of the front faces of the grounds; use a straight-edge to ensure a uniform distance from the blockwork.

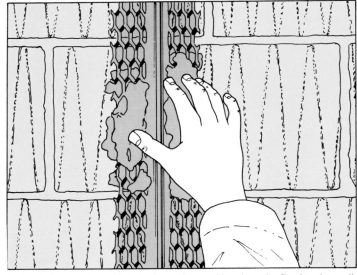

Instead of grounds, a galvanized metal screed bead can be fixed to the wall on dabs of plaster; this is left in the plaster.

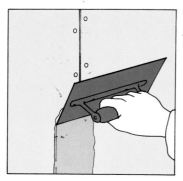

Spreading a 100mm (4in) wide band of plaster, from bottom to top, over the join between sheets of tapered-edge gypsumboard.

Bedding joint tape into the plaster with a trowel, working from top to bottom; this reinforces the plaster and stops it cracking.

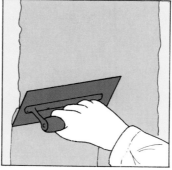

Spreading plaster in thin vertical strips in the bays between taped joints; work from bottom to top and avoid forming ridges.

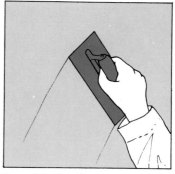

Spread the finishing coat over the entire area with long, sweeping strokes to remove any ridges which were formed in the first coat.

Wallboard gives a much smoother finish to a wall than bare masonry such as bricks or blockwork. Consequently, when it comes to putting a plaster finish on a drywall-clad wall or partition, there is no need for a floating coat to even out any irregularities in the surface. You need only apply two very thin finishing coats directly over the drywall.

The plaster needed for the job is sold ready mixed or in a powder form requiring only the addition of water before use. It is mixed in the same way as other plasters, but you will find that it will have a much creamier texture than normal floating coat plasters.

Because you are only applying a finishing coat to the drywall board there is no need for wood grounds or other types of thickness guide, except at any external corners (these are dealt with on page 25).

It is a good idea to practice scooping the plaster from the hawk on to the trowel first, using a spare piece of drywall to try your hand at spreading the plaster and making it stick to the board. The technique is to hold the hawk in your left hand (or right if you are left handed) so the top is level and set the trowel blade on edge, so it is at right angles to the top of the hawk. Use the trowel to push some plaster towards the edge of the hawk, scooping it off at the same time as tilting the hawk towards you. The whole is done in one smooth movement.

Dealing with the joints

The first job is to seal the joints

between the individual panels of gypsumboard, reinforcing them with perforated paper tape or nylon tape to prevent the plaster cracking. The standard paper tape is available in 2″ wide rolls of 15-150m (50-500 feet).

Cut strips of tape to run the length of each joint, including any horizontal ones, before you begin plastering. They must be exactly the right length and should not overlap or be folded, otherwise the plaster won't grip the wall properly.

To seal the joint, spread a thin layer of plaster, about 100mm (4in) wide, along it from bottom to top. Hold the trowel so that the blade is at an angle of about 30° to the wall, reducing it as you move up the joint and the plaster on the trowel thins.

While the plaster is still wet, press the tape into it. The easiest way to do this is by draping one end over the blade of the trowel and pressing this into the plaster at the ceiling. Then gently slide the trowel down the plaster, positioning the tape with your other hand. Once the tape is in place, run the trowel carefully up the plaster to make sure it is bedded properly. Treat all the other joints between the panels in the same way.

Finishing the Wall

When the taped joints have dried — which should take about 1½ hours — fill in the areas between them with more plaster. Work upwards from the floor, spreading the plaster in thin vertical strips and being careful not to build up ridges at the joint positions. Stop just

short of the ceiling and work downwards from there to get a nice, sharp angle.

Unless you are working on a very small area, by the time you have finished putting on the first coat, the area you started on will be ready for the second coat. This should be about 3mm (⅛in) thick and applied with long, sweeping strokes to eliminate ridges. Start at the bottom corner of the wall and work upwards

and along to make one continuous coating.

Allow the plaster to set slightly and then go back over it with a clean trowel to smooth off the surface. Finally, when it has hardened fully, 'polish' the surface by splashing clean water on to it with a paintbrush (about 100mm/4in wide) then sweep the trowel back and forth lightly. This will give a smooth, matt finish ready for decoration.

Self-adhesive drywall joint tape eliminates the need for pre-plastering between sheets of plasterboard board.

Available in 90m (295ft) rolls, it consists of a fine glass-fibre mesh coated with adhesive which has a delayed cure rate to allow for repositioning and provide good adhesion.

Ensure that the boards are free from dust and grease and apply the tape from top to bottom, pressing firmly as you go; avoid overlaps at intersections by butt jointing.

Apply a coat of Finish down the joint and scrape off excess so the mesh is visible; apply a second coat when the first is dry. The edges may now be tapered with a wet sponge or the whole area given a finishing coat of plaster. The tape is also ideal for ceilings.

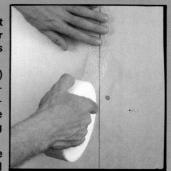

PLASTERING MASONRY

If the wall you intend plastering has been newly built, you probably won't have to do any preparation work to it at all before you fix wooden grounds or metal lath in place. However, if you are replastering an old, existing wall because the original plaster was in poor condition, a considerable amount of preparation may be required.

Preparing an Old Brick Wall

If you haven't already done so, hack off all the old crumbling plaster, using a bricklayers chisel and a heavy duty hammer. Use a wire brush to remove any remaining traces from the brickwork then inspect the mortar joints. If they appear soft or crumbly, rake them out with a chisel and repoint them with fresh mortar.

To help the plaster to grip the wall, it is a good idea to coat the exposed masonry and the edges of any remaining original plaster with a bonding agent. Smooth surfaces like concrete or wood must also be treated, or 'keyed', by nailing on expanded metal mesh.

At this stage, you can fix the grounds or beads. Then all types of masonry, whether old or new, should be dampened by splashing on clean water with a paintbrush. This will help slow down the rate at which the wall absorbs the moisture from the plaster, preventing it drying out too quickly and possibly cracking.

Applying the Floating Coat

It is a good idea to practice scooping plaster from the hawk and applying it to the wall before you attempt the job for real. When you're satisfied that you can get the plaster to stick to the wall and spread it out evenly, scrape it off, discard it, then make a start for real. The method of scooping plaster from the hawk is the same as that used when plastering plasterboard, but the technique of applying it to the wall is slightly different.

Set the loaded trowel against the wall so that the bottom corner of the blade rests on the ground or bead and the blade itself is at an angle of about 30°

Scooping plaster from the hawk on to the trowel; put into the plaster and scoop forwards and upwards.

Practising applying plaster to the wall; work upwards from waist-height, starting with the trowel at 30 degrees to the wall.

As you apply the plaster, tilt the trowel more parallel to the wall surface; keep the hawk close to the wall to catch droppings.

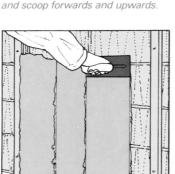

Applying the plaster in vertical strips; at the end of each stroke, press the lower edge of the trowel to firm the plaster onto the wall.

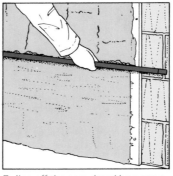

Ruling off the completed bay; use a straight-edge with a sawing motion to lower any high spots and show up areas with too little plaster.

Scoring the surface to provide a key for the finishing coat; the nails should protrude 3mm (⅛in) through the float or batten 'comb'.

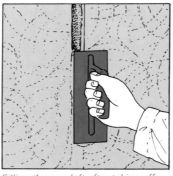

Filling the gap left after taking off the ground batten; level off with the trowel, flush with the hardened plaster on each side.

Applying the finishing coat; work from bottom to top and cover the floating coat with a thin layer, then apply a second coat.

Polishing the finishing coat; wet the surface sufficiently to remove ridges and marks and polish firmly with a perfectly clean, flat trowel.

to the wall surface. Move the blade upwards to spread a vertical strip of plaster next to the thickness guide, keeping the blade resting on the guide and gradually reducing its angle as the plaster spreads.

Apply more strips of plaster in the same way, always working upwards from the bottom of the wall and across the bay. There is no need to worry too much about an uneven surface, so long as you get a good thickness of plaster on the wall.

When the bay is finished, use the long wooden rule to strike it off

level with the thickness guides. Place it across the guides and draw it upwards, moving it from side to side in a sawing motion as you go. This will level off the high spots and accentuate the dips. Add more plaster to the latter and strike it off again until the entire bay is level.

Finally, before the plaster sets, key the surface for the finishing coat. You can do this by passing a wooden float with nails knocked through its face over the plaster to leave a pattern of score lines, or you can use a 'comb' made by tapping several

nails along the edge of a piece of scrap wood.

When the plaster has set, do the next bay.

Applying the Finishing Coat

When the floating coat has hardened (it should take about two hours), you can apply the finishing coat. This is done in exactly the same way as plastering wallboard, applying two thin coats of Finish plaster and polishing the surface to produce a flat, hard surface.

PLASTERER'S

DEALING WITH CORNERS

The main problem when plastering corners, whether external or internal, is getting a good, sharp angle. You will face a similar problem at the junction between the wall and ceiling. However, the techniques for dealing with both types of corner are not difficult to master.

Dealing with External Corners

There are two forms of guide you can use for forming an external corner: a timber batten or purpose-made metal beading.

The wooden batten is used as a thickness guide for the floating coat then the finishing coat on each wall. Nail it on to one wall so that it projects by the right amount beyond the other and use as a ground for that wall. Then, when the plaster has set, move it round the corner and repeat the process. Any sharp ridges on the apex of the corner should be sliced off with the trowel blade and then the corner rounded off with a block plane or rasp. With wallboard you must tape the angle first.

Two depths of metal beading are available to deal with masonry or gypsumboard-clad walls and they can be fixed in place with plaster or galvanized nails. On wallboard, nails must be used. The beading acts as a ground for the floating coat on masonry walls. Before this hardens, cut back its level to allow for the finish coat. Trowel off flush with beading, leaving the nose exposed to provide a knock-resistant corner.

Dealing with Internal Corners

For dealing with internal corners, you need a long wood rule. Use this to rule the floating coat outwards from the corner.

After keying the floating coat, cut out the angle by running the corner of the trowel blade up and down it, holding the blade flat against each wall in turn. This will produce a sharp angle. The finish coat should be treated in the same manner. The final job is to hold the short side of the blade against one wall so the long side is just touching the fresh plaster. Hold the blade at 30°-40° and gently run it down the corner.

For finishing corners where both walls have been plastered, use a special V-shaped angle trowel. This produces a constant right angle in the fresh plaster. Load a small amount of plaster onto the angled blade of the trowel and run it lightly down the angle.

Reinforcing the external corner of a masonry wall with angle-bead; set it into blobs of plaster, 30cm(12in) apart.

Plastering one wall; work away from the corner, using the nose of the bead as a thickness guide.

Plastering the adjoining wall in the same way; leave the nose just visible. Score the surface of both walls.

Applying the finishing coat, this time covering the nose; round off the corner by running a wet finger along the bead.

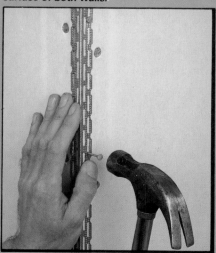

Securing angle-bead to the corner with galvanised nails; nail through the drywall into the stud.

Applying a coat of finishing plaster, working away from the corner; the nose should be left visible in this case.

OPENING UP THE SPACE

In this through living/dining room, the stubs of the original dividing wall have been left to support a steel girder and to provide an alcove next to the fireplace which has been fitted with shelves.

The archway in this wall provides a focal point and leads the eye from the dining area through the living room to the garden.

Rather than wanting more rooms in your house, you may find that you would prefer fewer, larger rooms. Some rooms may be too small for their intended use, while others may be too large.

Kitchens are commonly too small for comfort, particularly in older houses, which were not designed for all the equipment we take for granted today. Bathrooms too can often be cramped. Or the rooms generally may feel claustrophobic, and can often be gloomy if they have small windows or are on the shady side of the house.

Many problems of this kind can be overcome by removing part of or even the entire wall between two rooms. For example, a kitchen and dining room or a dining room and living room could be combined. Removing the wall between a bedroom and small room, or even making an opening in it will provide more closet space or room for a shower.

Of course, the problem might not be one of having insufficient space in any one room, but rather poor access between rooms. It's not unusual for there to be no direct access between a kitchen and dining room, the route between them being via a hall. Making a doorway in the dividing wall, or even a pass-through, will make life much more bearable and will prevent cooking smells drifting through the house.

Whether you are making a simple pass-through or taking out an entire wall, the method is basically the same. Before making the opening, a steel, concrete or wooden beam is inserted in the wall to span the opening and support any load on it from above. Then the opening is cut out below this beam and the floor, walls and ceiling are refinished.

Planning the Job

The most important aspect of this type of job is planning, since the wall you intend breaking through may contribute to the overall strength of the house and without it, the building may come crashing about your ears. Walls fall into two categories — load-bearing and non-load-

bearing — and you must identify which it is before starting work (see opposite).

If you are in any doubt about this stage of the job, consult a structural engineer or architect. You may have to submit plans of the job to your local building department. They will be concerned that you don't breach the Building Code (see page 251) and will pay particular attention to how you intend supporting the wall above the opening and also — in the case of through rooms — to the amount of light and ventilation the new room will have. If you intend making an opening in one of the exterior

An opened-up kitchen/diner, the dining area defined by boldly contrasting wall and ceiling covering.

walls, you generally must apply for a building permit. Always check your local code before beginning any job.

Other points to bear in mind when considering this kind of work are that you will need to completely redecorate the new large room and you will also have to do something about heating. Previously you could heat two small rooms separately, now you will have to heat one large one and so you may need to uprate any heating appliances.

Pipe and cable runs in the wall you are to work on should also be dealt with by rerouting them before work begins. If you are only making a doorway or hatch, moving its position slightly may avoid the need to reroute the services.

The job involves a lot of dust and debris, even if you are only making a small opening, so if at all possible remove all of the furnishings from the rooms affected. Cover anything else with dust sheets and lay a thick plastic sheet on the floor on which the debris and rubbish can be collected.

The way you tackle the job of making an opening in a wall or removing the wall completely, depends on the type of wall it is and its construction.

A load-bearing wall contributes to the strength of the house by supporting some of its structure: a floor/ceiling, an upstairs wall or part of the roof.

A non-load-bearing wall is simply a dividing partition and its complete removal will have no effect on the rest of the house. Inspect the floor space above it for signs that it supports the joists, or an upstairs wall. Look in the attic, too, to see if any of the roof framework rests on it.

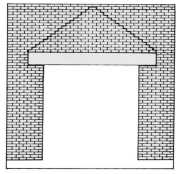

In a narrow opening, the brickwork outside the triangle is self-supporting; a lintel is needed to support the masonry within the triangle and the structure above.

All external walls are load-bearing and in general any wall at right-angles to the joists will be load-bearing too. Walls that run parallel to the joists are probably non-load-bearing.

Walls may be of brick, concrete blocks or be wood framed. All three types of construction are used for both load-bearing and non-load-bearing walls.

When you make an opening in a wall, no matter how narrow or wide, you must insert a supporting beam or lintel across the opening to take the load of the structure above, even if it is a non-load-bearing wall. The problem is that even removing a narrow row of bricks or blocks to make room for the beam will put the structure at risk.

For a narrow opening like a door, the bonding pattern of the bricks or blocks will tend to make the wall above the opening self-supporting (or self-corbelling) and only a small triangular section of masonry will be at risk. This can be removed, the lintel

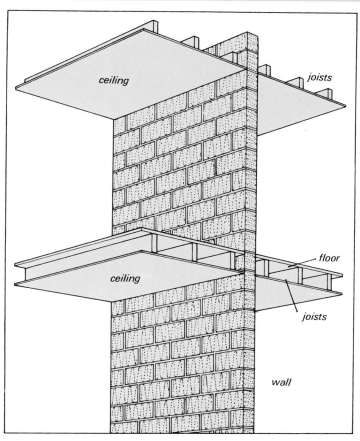

Non load-bearing wall – joists run parallel to the surface.

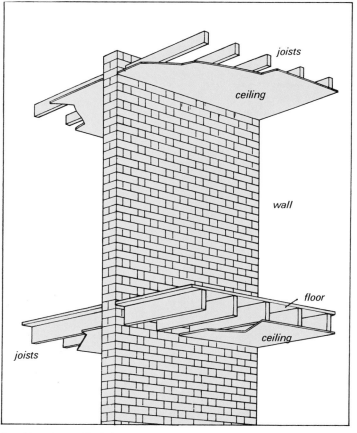

Load-bearing wall – joists run at right-angles to the wall, and the floorboards will be parallel to the surface.

fitted and the masonry replaced.

With a very wide opening, the self supporting tendency will disappear and a wide area of the wall will be liable to collapse. To prevent this happening, you must support the wall (and sometimes the ceiling on either side) temporarily with heavy wood and adjustable props.

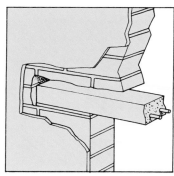

A reinforced-concrete lintel set into a brick wall. To support and distribute its load, a lintel must rest on a bearing at both ends; slot it 225mm (9in) into the masonry, bed it on a 3:1 mortar mix and fill above and at the ends with mortar.

Types of Beam

Openings in walls may be spanned by lengths of concrete, steel or wood. Those for fitting over small openings like doors and windows are called lintels; those for spanning wider gaps are called beams. The following are common: Steel Joist — a heavy I or L-shaped girder for spanning very wide gaps in load-bearing walls; Reinforced Concrete Lintel — for internal or solid brick external walls in spans up to 3m (10ft). Heavy to lift, often cast on the job site, Pre-stressed Concrete Lintel — lighter than reinforced concrete lintels. Not suitable for load-bearing walls, except in upper floors. For spans up to 3m (10ft), wood lintel — for use in wood framed walls.

MAKING A NEW DOORWAY

As with all jobs of this type, making a new doorway requires a considerable amount of planning before work begins. You should also check the requirements of your local building code.

A lintel must be chosen to match the type of wall being cut into (see page 27) and you must select a position for the door that, if possible, won't interfere with existing cable and pipe runs and which should be at least 450mm (18in) from any corner.

It is possible to buy doors and ready-made frames in a range of standard sizes, and unless you really want to make the frame from scratch, it is best to buy the door and frame first, making the opening to fit it. Make sure its height leaves enough of the wall above the opening for fitting the lintel and the temporary wood supports.

Providing Temporary Support

With a masonry wall, you must provide temporary support for the wall above the opening and the load it carries while you cut

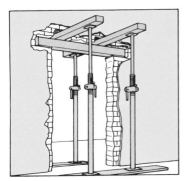
A new wall opening supported by metal jacks bearing on to wooden needles within the opening; stand the jacks on strong planks.

out a slot for the lintel. If the wall supports the joists of the ceiling above, you must support the ceiling on both sides of the wall as well.

Support the wall with 1.8m (6ft) lengths of 100 × 75mm (3 × 4in) sawn wood called 'needles' — on top of adjustable metal props, which work like an automobile jack (you can rent these), spaced at 1m (3ft) intervals. With a normal sized doorway, you would need only one set centrally above the opening.

To support the ceiling, lengths of 100 × 50mm (12 × 4in) wood are used across the tops of more

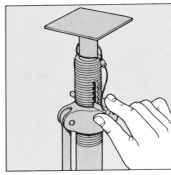
Adjusting a metal jack; with the pin removed, raise the inner tube to the required height, insert the pin and tighten with the handle.

props. None of the props should be more than 600mm (2ft) from the wall, and if they are to stand on a wood floor, the feet should be placed on another length of 100 × 50mm (2 × 4in) wood to spread the load.

Marking out the Opening

Before marking out the doorway on the wall, use a bricklayers chisel to remove patches of plaster roughly where the edges and top of the opening will be. This will allow you to adjust the position of the opening to coincide with the mortar joints, to reduce

the number of bricks or blocks you have to cut through.

Measure up the door frame, adding 50mm (2in) to its width and 25mm (1in) to its height to allow for positioning. Using these dimensions, draw an outline of the opening on the wall. Then measure up the lintel — which should be at least 300mm (1ft) wider than the opening — and add a further 50mm (2in) to its width for fitting. Draw the outline of the lintel on the wall above the door opening.

Finally, draw the outline of the wood needle centrally above the needle outline. Repeat the outlines on the other side of the wall.

Fitting the Needles

Cut the hole for the needle with a light sledge and bricklayer's chisel. Slide the needle through so it protrudes equally on both sides of the wall and fit the props beneath it, tightening them to take the load. Both props must be adjusted simultaneously to ensure even support, so you'll need assistance. Fit the ceiling supports at the same time.

Trick

OPTIONS

A hatchway between a kitchen and dining room can be extremely useful. Plan its position carefully so that it coincides with a work surface in the kitchen and something like a worktop or or small table in the dining room so that there will be somewhere to place dishes, plates, etc.

The method for making a passthrough is basically the same as that for making a doorway, except that the opening is not continued to the floor. In a wood framed partition, a wood sill piece is needed between the studs on each side of the opening.

The passthrough can be left open with pastered edges and a wood sill, screwed across the bottom or a wooden lining frame can be fitted to take hinged or sliding doors, or some form of roller blind.

MAKING A HATCHWAY

A new doorway set in an existing door to form a pass through between kitchen and dining room.

A pass through between living room and kitchen/dining room, set into a wall and closed off with a roller blind.

Fitting the Lintel

Chop away the plaster from within the lintel outline to expose the masonry below. Remove the bricks or blocks by cutting through their mortar joints and lifting them out. If any above the slot should drop, remove these and keep them for replacement later.

Lift the lintel into place, bedding it on mortar (3 parts soft sand: 1 part masonry cement) laid on the 'bearings' at each end of the slot. Make sure it is level and, if necessary, pack out below the ends with tiles or slates.

Fill any spaces around the lintel with more mortar and replace any bricks or blocks that have dropped out. If the wall is of blocks, bring the lintel up to the height of the adjacent blocks by laying a course of bricks on top.

Cutting the Opening

Leave the mortar to set for at least 24 hours, and preferably 48. Then remove the needle and wood supports. Fill the needle holes with brick offcuts and mortar. Lever off the base board and place it to one side for cutting down later.

Remove the plaster inside the opening's outline to expose all the masonry below. Chop this out by cutting through the mortar joints, working down the wall one course at a time. Because of the bonding pattern used, you will find that on alternate courses you will have to cut through bricks at the sides of the opening. Do this as you come to them, driving the chisel into their faces and levering them out from below.

Trim off the masonry flush with a solid floor, or just below a wooden one. In the latter case, join the two floors by screwing battens to the joists then fit a piece of plywood or short pieces of floor-board on top.

Fitting the Frame

The frame can be held in place with either galvanized metal ties mortared into the wall, or by screws and wall plugs. If ties are to be used you need three per side. Cut recesses in the sides of the opening for the ties. If you intend screwing the frame to the wall, drill screw clearance holes in it and offer it up so these can be marked on the wall. Drill and plug the holes.

Set the frame in place, packing out the sides as necessary with wood offcuts to set them vertical. Then either fill the tie recesses with mortar and brick offcuts or insert the screws.

Fill in the gaps round the frame with more mortar and offcuts and trowel a thin layer of mortar over any exposed masonry at the sides and top before refinishing the plaster.

Finally, nail lengths of molding round the frame, mitering the corners, and trim and refit the base boards to the base of the wall.

Doorways in Stud Partitions

To put a doorway in a stud partition, first expose the framework below the partition's skin. Find the stud positions on each side of the proposed opening by tapping the surface and probing with a bradawl. Draw in the stud positions on the surface and another line between them to mark the height of the door frame plus an allowance for the wood lintel.

Cut along this outline with a keyhole saw continuing the cut through the skin across the top of any studs or bracing you come across. Lever off the skin to expose the framework and the back of the other skin. Remove the latter in the same way.

Cut out all the framework within the opening and then make up two short 'trimmer' studs to support the lintel. Nail the trimmer studs to the original studs on each side of the opening and the lintel to the tops of the trimmer studs. Nail through the lintel into the base of any cut stud.

If the door frame is narrower than the distance between the trimmer studs, fit an intermediate between the lintel and sole plate, linking it with short braces to one of the trimmer studs.

Cut out the section of sole plate across the bottom of the opening and fit the door frame as described on page 19. Finish the partition by nailing on gypsum-board and putting a skim coat of plaster over the top.

Removing a brick to enable the prop needle to be inserted above the position of the lintel.

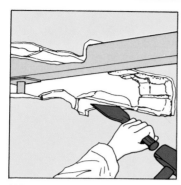

With the props in place to support the brickwork above, removing bricks to make way for the lintel.

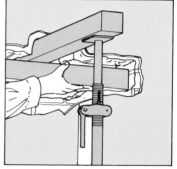

Lifting the lintel on to its bed of mortar; ensure that it has a bearing of 23cm (9in) each side of the opening.

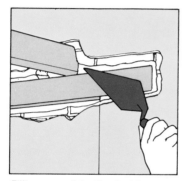

Filling around the lintel with mortar; this must be allowed to cure for at least 24 hours before removing the props.

Chipping away the plaster within the marked lines beneath the lintel.

Removing the brickwork to form the opening; chop at right-angles through any protruding bricks to leave a clean edge.

Screwing a metal frame-tie to the door-frame; six ties are needed in all and must lie between mortar joints in the sides of the opening.

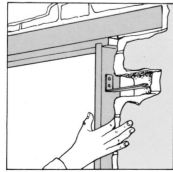

Fitting the frame tie into a pocket cut in the brickwork; set the tie in mortar and fill the gap above it with brick fillets and mortar.

BLOCKING OFF A REDUNDANT DOORWAY

There are two methods you can use for blocking off a redundant doorway: you can fit a wood framework around the inside and panel it with wallboard on both sides, or you can use bricks or lightweight building blocks. In each case, plaster is used to finish it off. Using bricks or blocks is only really feasible if the floor is solid.

Another point to consider when faced with a redundant doorway is whether you can put it to some other use such as panelling in the back and filling the recess with shelves.

Removing the Old Frame

Before work can begin, you must remove the old door and frame. Unscrew the door hinges, lift the door away and lever off the molding. The lining frame may be fixed by masonry nails, screws or metal ties cemented into the brickwork. You should be able to lever it free, but if you have difficulty (or if you want to try to save the frame for reuse) you should cut through its fixings. To do this, work a saw blade down between the back of the frame and the wall and cut through any obstruction you meet.

Panelling with Wallboard

If you are filling an opening in a stud partition, the supporting framework should be made of wood to match the partition's framework — usually 75 or 100 × 50mm (2 × 3 or 4in) sawn softwood. On the other hand, if panelling a masonry wall, you might need two separate frames of something like 50mm sq (2in sq) wood to panel each side flush.

The frame should comprise a head plate, sole plate, two upright studs and a central brace. Toe-nail these together and to the insides of the opening, making sure the frame is set back from the face of the wall sufficiently to allow for the thickness of the wallboard and its skim of plaster.

Nail a panel of wallboard to each side of the frame, and to prevent the skim coat shrinking back from the edges, nail lengths

Glass shelves form a light barrier.

of metal lath around the join. Apply a skim coat of finish in the normal manner (see page 24). When the plaster has hardened, fit a length of new base board across the opening.

Filling in with Masonry

If you choose to fill the opening with bricks or concrete blocks, you must tie the new masonry to the old in some way. The easiest method is to hammer 150mm (6in) masonry nails half-way into the side of the opening to correspond with the mortar joints of alternate courses of the new bricks or blocks. As you lay the courses, they will be buried in the mortar.

Lay the bricks or blocks in the normal overlapping fashion and point all the mortar joints flush with the face of the masonry when finished.

Finally, apply floating and finish coats of plaster as described on page 24, using the surrounding original plaster as a thickness guide.

Two methods of filling a doorway.

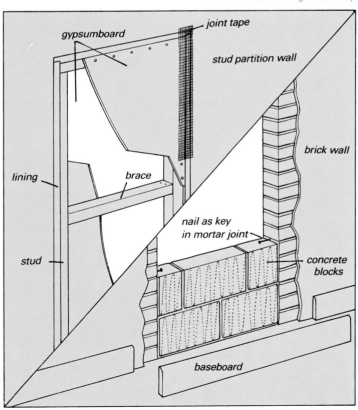

gypsumboard
joint tape
stud partition wall
lining
brace
brick wall
stud
nail as key in mortar joint
concrete blocks
baseboard

Many of the techniques used in making an opening in an internal dividing wall are applicable to cutting an opening for an external door. However, there are some extra points to consider.

There is normally no limitation on where you position internal doors, but the positioning and installation of external doors is subject to the requirements of your local building code, so you may have to make the necessary applications to your local building department and building inspector first (see page 251).

Depending on the age of your house, you may be faced with cutting through a solid 225mm (9in) thick wall made up of two layers of bricks bonded together, or a 275mm (11in) thick cavity wall where there is a gap between the inner and outer leaves of brickwork. In the latter case, the inner leaf only is load bearing, but even so you must support both leaves while making the opening and when it is finished.

You could, of course, convert an existing window into a doorway, in which case the job would be quite straightforward, since there would already be a supporting lintel across the opening. For a new opening, however, you must fit a lintel (see page 27).

Fitting the Lintel

Temporary support for the wall must be provided by 75mm (3in) sq needles on top of adjustable metal props. To fit the needles, remove a whole brick from the outer layer and drill through the inner layer at the corners of the opening. Use the holes as a guide for chopping out the masonry from the inner layer. Insert the needles and tighten the props.

Draw the outline of the lintel on the inside wall and chop out the plaster and masonry from within the outline. Drill the corners of the outer layer and remove the masonry between the holes to allow the fitting of the lintel. This should be set on mortar bearings and packed out with tiles or slates to set it level. Fill all round the inner portion of the lintel with mortar and rebuild any brickwork above it. Rebuild the outer brickwork in the same fashion, either continuing the bond of the adjacent courses or standing the bricks on end to form a 'soldier arch'.

Cutting the Opening

When the mortar has set, remove the needles and brick up their holes. Then cut out the opening for the door frame. Frames come in standard sizes, so you must make the opening to fit the frame.

Remove the bricks down to floor level, cutting through the protrud-bricks of the inner layer, on solid walls but removing whole bricks from the outer layer to give a toothed appearance.

Square up the toothed outer layer by fitting cut bricks in place so that their 'finished' ends are outermost.

Fitting the Frame

Toe-nail the frame together before inserting it in the opening. Tack a length of flashing material to the underside of the sill, covering the nail heads with a bituminous sealant.

The easiest way of fixing the frame in the opening is with screws and wallplugs, packing out the sides to make them truly vertical. Fill any gap on the inside with mortar, and apply caulking around the frame on the outside to keep out water.

The door sill should overhang the brickwork slightly and is best fitted with a metal weather bar, which is set in caulk to prevent water penetration. Once the frame is in place, you can hang the door and finish the internal surfaces with plaster.

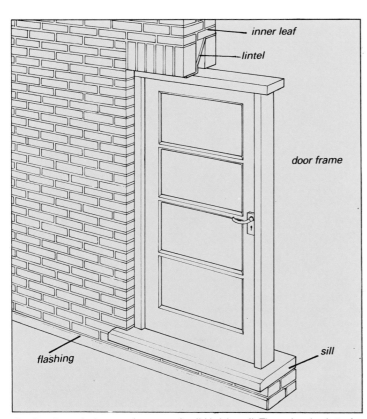

Section through doorway in external solid brick wall. The galvanized steel lintel must be installed so that it slopes downwards towards the outer leaf of the wall. The DPC under the sill should link up with the DPC in the wall at each side of the doorway opening.

Cutting out bricks to form the opening; unlike internal doorways, the bricks are not cut flush at the sides.

Filling the gaps with half-bricks; spread mortar on top of the whole brick and butter the end and top of the half-brick.

After recessing and screwing one leaf of the hinge to the door, mark, recess and screw the free leaf to the door-jamb.

Fitting the door-frame to the wall; drill through the frame into the brickwork and secure with frame-fixing plugs and screws.

MAKING A THROUGH ROOM

The techniques for removing a wall between two rooms to turn them into one large, through room are essentially the same as those needed to make a new doorway or a pass-through. However, if the wall is load-bearing much more of the structure of the house will be at risk from collapse, so you must take particular care to ensure that you provide temporary support for any loads carried by the wall before you start to remove it and that there's adequate permanent support when finished. This means finding out if the floor joists of the room above rest upon it and also if the wall continues upwards to form a dividing wall on the floor above.

If there is no continuation wall above and the floor joists simply rest on top of the wall, you can remove it completely, using stout wood planks and adjustable props to bear the weight of the joists from below while the supporting beam (see page 27) is set in place. However, if there is a continuation of the wall to cope with, you must leave a margin at ceiling level to allow the insertion of wooden needles at 1m (3ft) intervals.

Choosing a Supporting Beam

As already mentioned, it is normal for wide spans of this sort to be supported by a steel beam but long beams can be very heavy and you might find it easier to use a steel angle instead. This will be lighter and only good for shorter spans depending on the size.

You could also use a reinforced concrete beam or a pre-stressed concrete beam (the lighter of the two). But both will only cope with spans of 3m (10ft) so they're only really suitable for narrow rooms.

In any event you may have to gain approval from your local Building Inspector for the way you intend to tackle the job, and this includes your choice of beam. If you are not sure of the best type to use always take professional advice or check with your local Building Code.

Whatever type of beam you choose, it will still be heavy and you will need helpers to lift it into position. You will also need

enough extra adjustable props to support it at 1m (3ft) intervals while you mortar it in place.

Creating the Bearings

The ends of the beam must rest on bearings that are 150 to 225mm (6 to 9in) wide, and because of the heavy loads carried it is usual to support the beam on concrete 'padstones' (concrete blocks are ideal). This helps spread the load evenly across the bearings.

As an alternative to a concrete padstone, you could use a heavy steel plate, or one or two courses of a strong brick; normal facing bricks would crumble under the weight.

The bearings must have substantial support below them to cope with the loads imposed on them from above and the way you arrange this support can take several forms. It is something that the Building Inspector will pay particular attention to.

A common method of supplying support for the bearings is to build brick columns or piers at each end of the span, toothing every second course into the brickwork of the adjoining walls.

Such piers must have substantial foundations of their own and this usually means digging down into the ground below, putting in a layer of well compacted gravel and pouring a thick layer of concrete on top. The exact requirements will be specified by your local Code.

Once the foundation has hardened, you can begin building the footings of the piers, remembering to set flashing in one of the mortar joints level with the flashing of the existing walls. This should be just below the level of the floor. If the floor is solid concrete, it should have a damp-proof membrane in it and you must take steps to see that your new flashing and the membrane are sealed together.

In some cases you may be allowed to use a course of engineering bricks as a flashing.

When the pier has been built, it is topped with mortar and the padstone set in place and levelled.

If the wall you are breaking through is a solid 225mm (9in) thick wall comprising two leaves of bricks, you may be able to

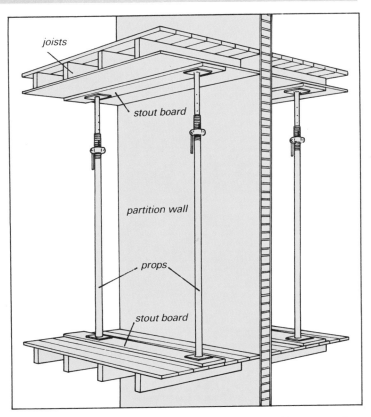

Ceiling joists at right-angles to the wall must be supported by props under planks, spaced at 1m (3ft) intervals.

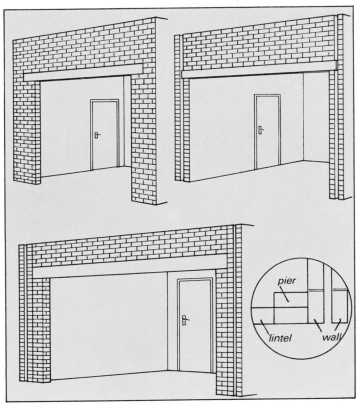

Lintel supported on stubs of original wall (top left), and on piers adjacent to wall (bottom left). Inset: section down on to a lintel showing how it rests with its front face flush with the padstone and supporting pier.

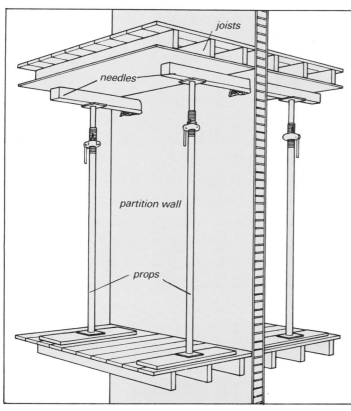

Ceiling joists parallel to the wall are propped with needles passed through the wall above the level of the lintel.

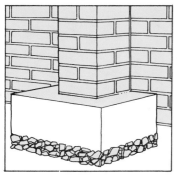

Piers are supported on concrete padstones, cast on top of compacted gravel.

Wear stout gloves, overalls, facemask and goggles when knocking down masonry; and a helmet if there are bricks overhead.

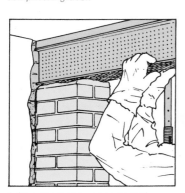

Lifting the lintel on to a bed of mortar on top of the supporting brick pier; assistance will be needed for this operation.

Wedging the lintel on the pier with a tile; slate or brick slips of brick may equally be used.

leave short stubs of the wall projecting into the room to act as piers for the ends of the beam. However, you will need to check with your local Building Code to be satisfied that the original wall has substantial enough foundations. Remember, the weight carried by the wall, which was spread evenly along the length of its foundations will, on removal of the wall, be concentrated on two much smaller patches.

The mortar of the old wall should be in good condition, too. If it is loose or crumbly you will have to rake out all the joints and repoint them with fresh mortar.

If the walls running across the ends of the beam are load-bearing, it may be possible to cut directly into them to form bearings. In this situation a longer than normal padstone should be used to spread the load sideways, or it may be necessary to add some extra strengthening by toothing-in a shallow pier.

If you decide to construct piers, you can save some of the cost of renting adjustable jacks by building the piers before the bulk of the wall is removed. Chop out enough masonry from each end of the wall to allow room for the piers to be built, leaving enough of the wall in place to carry the load without risk of collapse. Then when the piers have been completed and hardened off, you can rent the necessary equipment and begin demolition.

Removing the Wall

Having arranged temporary support with planks, needles and props and decided how you are going to tackle the job of providing bearings, start to remove the masonry from the wall.

First draw the outline of the opening on the wall with a pencil and long straightedge. Remove the plaster from within the outlines using a light sledge and bricklayers chisel. This will be very dusty work, so it's essential to empty both rooms of all furnishings and seal any doorways by pinning thick plastic sheets or old blankets over them. This will prevent the dust spreading to the rest of the house. Sprinkle the debris with water from a houseplant sprayer to settle the

dust. Wear safety goggles, a facemask, thick gloves and stout boots when hacking off the plaster or removing the masonry.

With the masonry of the wall exposed, begin chopping out the bricks or blocks by cutting into their mortar joints and levering them upwards with the blade of the chisel. Try to keep as many bricks as possible in one piece because they are always useful to have around for other jobs.

Nevertheless there will still be a massive amount of rubble to dispose of and one way is to put it into stout plastic sacks as you go and take these to a local dump when the job is finished. Alternatively, you could rent a small rubbish container, which is much more convenient. If you intend leaving it in the road, check with your Sanitation Department since many will not allow this unless they have given you prior authorisation. You may also have to ensure it is properly lit at night to avoid accidents.

Unlike making a new doorway, where you cut a slot for the lintel first, fit it and then remove the masonry below, when making a through room with its associated heavy beam this is not really feasible, since it would be very difficult to lift in place and support. You must make the complete opening while the load above is still supported by the temporary props. It's essential to have all the necessary tools, equipment and materials to hand so that you can proceed quickly with the job.

At floor level, either trim the masonry off flush with a solid floor, or just below a wooden one. In the latter case, take care not to break through any water proofing.

If there is a difference of level between the floors of the two rooms, either build a wooden step or cast a concrete one in situ.

Positioning the Beam

With the masonry removed, you can make the bearings. Lifting the beam into place will be heavy work so it is as well to do a little preparation beforehand. To avoid the need for lifting the beam from floor level to the

MAKING A THROUGH ROOM

A floor-standing structural brick arch. A semicircular framework is used to support the bricks during construction and as a template for the shape. The bricks may be cut to wedge shapes and laid with uniform mortar joints, or be uncut and with tapered joints (a rough arch). At the sides of the arch, where the headroom is limited, cabinets have been used here to form a central passageway.

well, using battens or special beads to form the corners as described on page 25. (Beading is probably best since the piers project into the room slightly and

Plastering over a steel box beam with metal lathing plaster; when this has hardened, complete the job with a coat of Finish plaster.

are, therefore, more likely to be knocked.)

Finally, cut base boards to fit round the base of each pier.

Dealing with a Non-Load-Bearing Wall

If the wall is of the non-load-bearing variety, the job will be much simpler since there is no need to fit a beam.

With a masonry wall, simply hack off the plaster and remove it brick by brick or block by block from the ceiling down. Chop out any metal ties holding the partition to the end walls, or cut through any bricks or blocks that have been toothed into them. At floor level, trim the masonry off flush — it may just sit on top of the floor anyway.

Replace the ceiling, if necessary by cutting back to the nearby joists and nailing on a fresh strip of gypsumboard. Finish it off with a skim coat of plaster and repair any damage to the walls.

If the wall is a wood-framed stud partition, simply lever off the cladding and prise apart or unscrew the frame. Fill any holes in the adjoining walls and redecorate.

ceiling in one go, support it on trestles or pairs of stepladders, setting it so that you can get hold of it easily.

Set the coarse adjustment of the jack posts that will support the beam so that they can be set in place quickly and the fine adjustment made without fuss.

Lift the beam into place on the capstones and check that it is square across the room by taking measurements from nearby fixed points. Set the jack posts in place and tighten them until the beam comes up tight against the joists or masonry above. Check that the beam is level and make any fine adjustments with the posts.

At this stage you can remove the posts holding the joists, but leave any needles in place.

Finishing the Bearings

Trowel a layer of mortar between the top of the capstone and the underside of the beam

and then tap pieces of slate into place to wedge the beam tightly upwards. You may need to insert two or even three pieces. Do the same at the other bearing, making sure it forms as tight a wedge as possible.

Finish off by pointing more mortar round the ends of the beam and capstone. If it is set on bearings cut into the end walls, fill the cavities around the ends of the beam with whole bricks or offcuts and more mortar, pointing it neatly.

With the bearings finished, check along the top of the beam to make sure it is supporting the joists or masonry above fully. If there are any gaps they must be wedged out too. In the case of masonry, use mortar and more slate wedges. If it is a wood floor, drive slates between the beam and any joists that are not supported.

Finishing Off

Allow the mortar to harden for at least two days before removing the jack posts from below the beam together with any needles and their posts. Fill the needle holes with brick offcuts and mortar, then make good the ceiling, adjacent walls and floor.

If you have used a steel beam, clad this in a material that will protect it from fire: do not leave it exposed. The usual method is to clad the beam with gypsumboard on a wooden framework nailed to wedges hammered into the sides of the beam.

The corners of the gypsumboard should be taped or fitted with metal corner beads and finished as described on page 25.

Concrete beams can be directly plastered over, their surfaces being rough enough to provide a key for the floating and finish coats.

When the beam has been plastered, finish the piers as

MESH ARCH FORMERS

One of the problems with taking out a wall between two rooms to make a through room is that the beam and its supporting piers remain as clear evidence of what has been done. The same applies if you remove a door and frame from their opening to make an open plan access point between two rooms. These functional pieces of the structure can be a necessary evil if you are to make the most of the space available to you. However, they can be disguised and made to look more decorative by forming them into curved archways. With clever decoration and finishing they can even become features in their own right.

Construction

There are many ways in which you can construct archways from scratch, using a basic framework of sawn wood clad with hardboard, plywood, drywall or imitation bricks, but probably the easiest is to use prefabricated galvanised steel mesh arch formers. These are fixed in place at the top of the opening and plastered to match the adjoining walls.

Mesh arch formers usually come in four pieces, each piece being half of the face of one side of the arch and half of the associated area of soffit. In this way they can be trimmed down to fit narrow walls, or widened by the addition of extra soffit strips. They are available in a variety of shapes and sizes for spans of up to 3m (10ft). Some one-piece versions are available, too.

The faces of the prefabricated mesh panels are usually extended at the edges to form mounting flanges which sit flat against the face of the wall. The formers are secured by driving galvanized masonry nails through the flanges into the wall or by pushing the flanges into dabs of plaster.

If you intend disguising a newly fitted beam with arch formers, they should be installed before you plaster either the beam or the piers. If you want to improve the look of an existing opening, you will have to cut away a margin of plaster so that the mounting flanges of the formers will sit back flush against the wall.

Instead of using Bonding plaster for the floating coat, the mesh arch formers should be given a backing coat of Metal Lathing plaster. This hardens to leave a rough finish ready for the application of thin layers of Finish plaster. Rule the finish off level with any surrounding original plaster.

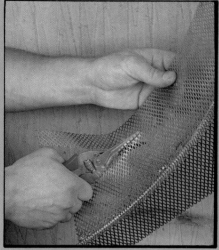

Cutting the soffit of an arch section to width after holding it in position and marking the wall thickness on the soffit.

Fixing the arch section to the wall with masonry nails; fix expanded metal to a wooden lintel before plastering.

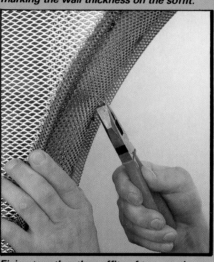

Fixing together the soffits of two sections with twists of galvanized wire passed through the mesh.

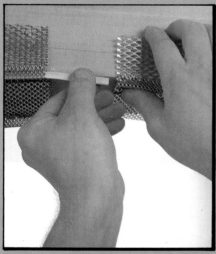

Joining adjacent sections with plastic strip pushed into the angle of the mesh and secured with self-tapping screws.

Applying metal lathing plaster to the face of the arch and adjoining masonry where the plaster has been cut back.

Applying plaster to the soffit; rule off flush with the surrounding plaster and apply a finishing coat.

ENLARGING A WINDOW

Despite advances in the use of metals and plastics for window frames, by far the majority of window frames are made of wood. However, one of the drawbacks of wooden window frames is that unless they are scrupulously maintained, they very quickly succumb to rot and other forms of weather damage. Repairs can often be made since wood is a versatile material, but if you've left it too long you will have no option but to replace the window completely.

Of course there may be nothing wrong with the window frame and you may want to replace it for some other reason: to let more light into a gloomy room, or more ventilation by fitting an opening window instead of a fixed one; you might have rearranged the interior of the house by removing a wall or adding one, making a bigger window necessary or perhaps its repositioning. You may feel that the existing window does not really fit in with the character of the house, which is quite often the case when older properties have been modernised by previous owners.

Although you may actually want a larger window for reasons of getting more light or ventilation, there is another reason why you might not be able to avoid increasing its size. Window frames are made in a standard range of sizes and you may not be able to buy a frame that exactly matches the size of the old one. Again, this is particularly true of older properties where the builders and joiners of the day did not work to standard size window openings.

You could, of course have a window made specially but that could be expensive. Or you could fit the next smaller size and make the opening smaller by adding more brick courses at the sill and toothing in extra bricks at the sides. But this is hardly a satisfactory solution unless the existing window was very large and you wouldn't be losing an appreciable amount of light.

Window Types and Materials

Modern windows come in a wide choice of styles in wood metal or plastic. They can be simple fixed panes or they can be opening with top-hinged, side-hinged, pivotting, horizontally-sliding or vertically-sliding portions. The tendency is to go for large, uninterrupted panes of glass, but if your house is old you can still buy windows with lots of small panes to give it a period look.

Despite the fact that it needs regular maintenance, wood is still the most popular material for. window frames and it offers the widest choice of styles and sizes. Wood also provides better heat insulation, cutting down on the amount of heat lost through the window — an important point in these energy conscious times.

Steel windows are functional in appearance but can suffer considerably from rust if not looked after. Aluminum windows, too, can suffer from corrosion due to the atmosphere, especially in coastal areas.

On the face of it, plastic would seem to be ideal for window frames, being largely maintenance free. However, it is not easy to paint (and is intended not to be), which means you are stuck with the manufacturer's color, and if this is white you may find it yellows with age.

How Frames are Fixed

Wooden window frames are normally held in place by galvanized metal ties cemented into the brickwork at the sides of the opening, by nails or screws driven into wooden wedges set in the brickwork, or by screws and wallplugs. Metal-framed windows may be held by metal brackets or be fitted to hardwood frames, which in turn are screwed into the opening. Plastic frames are treated in the same way.

What the Job Involves

Assuming you are going to fit a larger window frame in place of

Apart from increasing the area of view and the amount of light which enters a room, a picture window or patio doors can add an extra dimension to a room. In this example the square floor tiles and paving slabs make the garden feel like an extension of the dining room.

Cutting through the metal frame ties of a window with a hacksaw blade held in a handle after cutting away the caulk beading.

Remove sashes, or casements, and fixed glazing from the frame before easing it out; cut and remove in pieces if necessary.

the original, you must provide temporary support for the wall (with needles and jack posts) while you remove the old frame and lintel and fit a new, wider lintel. This should be either concrete or steel so that both leaves of the wall are supported. If the wall is solid, you can fit a concrete lintel to the inner leaf and form a curved soldier arch over the top of the window in the outer leaf.

With the lintel in place, cut out the brickwork for the larger frame. Prepare the edges of the opening, prop the frame in place and nail, screw or cement in place. The final job is to seal round the edges with mortar and caulk.

Removing the Old Frame

To make the frame lighter and easier to handle, unscrew any opening portions and remove all the glass.

Chop out the mortar seal at the edges of the frame with a flat chisel and run a thin-bladed tool such as a screwdriver round the gap to find where the fixings are. If they're screws you can attempt to remove them, but it's probably easier to cut through them with a saw inserted in the keyhole.

Having cut through or released the fixings, lever the frame out with a stout bar or knock it out with a length of wood and a light sledge hammer.

Packing up with piece of tile while assistant supports the weight of the lintel; leverage from a masons chisel assists in this operation.

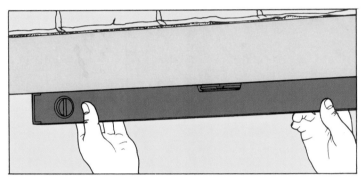

Checking for horizontal with a masons-level held against the lower face of the lintel.

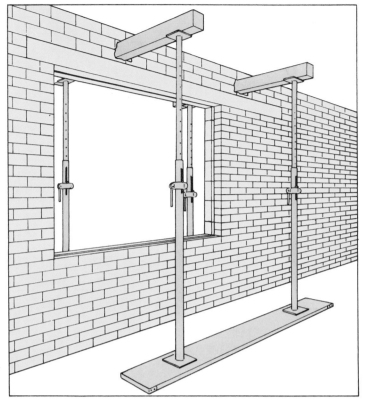

New longer lintel installed in outer leaf of cavity wall, using props and needles to support the brickwork above the opening.

With the wall above the window opening supported by one or more stout wooden needles and adjustable jacks, and with the old window frame out of the way, you can remove the old lintel and brickwork from above the opening.

Remove bricks from the outer layer first. These may be laid in horizontal courses across the lintel or they may be set vertically. If the house is old, the bricks might be formed into a curved, self-supporting segmental arch.

Cut through the mortar joints with a bricklayers chisel to remove the bricks, making a gradually tapering, stepped opening up to the level of the wooden needle above. This will prevent any brickwork falling while you are working on other parts of the opening. Try to break as few bricks as possible, especially the weathered outer ones since you will be able to use these later to finish round the new window. In this way the new brickwork will be indistinguishable from the original so that the window will blend in with the appearance of the house.

Removing the bricks from the outer leaf of the wall will expose the face of the load bearing lintel which will be set in the inner leaf. You should remove this next.

From inside the house, hack off the plaster above the window opening to expose the inner face of the lintel and the brickwork above it. Again, chop out the bricks to form a stepped opening up to the level of the needle. Then chop into the mortar joints at each end of the lintel, working along the top, ends and underneath. Use a stout bar to lever the ends of the lintel upwards to finally release them. Then get some help to lift the lintel from its bearings in the wall.

One point to watch when doing this job is that you must not allow any rubble to fall into any cavity within the wall's thickness. It may lodge and form a bridge for moisture to cross from the outer skin to the inner and cause damp patches on the inner face of the wall.

Fitting the New Lintel

Measure up the new lintel and draw its outline on the inside of the wall centered over the new window position. Remember, the new lintel should be at least 150mm (6in) wider at each side than the window opening itself to provide decent-size bearings. When you draw out the position of the lintel, allow an extra 25mm (1in) at each end and on the depth to provide enough space to manoeuvre the lintel into position.

Cut straight down through the plaster along the outline with the bricklayers chisel blade to provide a cutting guide and then hold the blade flat to the wall to hack off the plaster within the outline.

Go on to remove the bricks exposed by the removal of the plaster, again chopping through the mortar joints in an effort to keep as many bricks in one piece as possible. Clean up the bearing openings and make sure their surfaces are flat and level.

Whether you are using a steel or concrete lintel, it will be heavy and you will need some help to lift it into place. You can make the job easier by positioning it close to the opening on a pair of trestles so you don't have to lift it so far.

Trowel a layer of mortar on to each bearing and lift the lintel into place, setting it centrally over the opening. Check that the lintel is flush with the inner face of the wall and, is not projecting beyond the outer layer.

Hold a level against the underside of the lintel and check that it is horizontal. If necessary, correct this by packing pieces of tile or slate beneath the ends. When you are satisfied, fill the gaps round the ends of the lintel with more mortar and brick offcuts, pointing the joints neatly flush with the surrounding brickwork.

Then replace the brickwork of the inner layer above the lintel, working upwards towards the needle and copying the original brick bond

ENLARGING THE OPENING

Marking the outline of the new opening on the wall; allow 25mm (1in) fitting tolerance above the frame dimensions.

Chipping off the plaster using a masons chisel and light sledge.

Chopping out the brickwork to the new width of the opening; work from top to bottom and do not cut any bricks.

Toothing out the brickwork at the sides of the opening (on the inner leaf of a solid wall, cut the bricks to leave a square edge).

Removing the concrete sub-sill (if present) after cutting back the sides of the opening.

Building up the base of the opening to within one brick-height of the frame; copy the original bond and fill in the edges with half bricks.

Building a soldier course of bricks above the opening; a temporary wooden former supports the arch shape until the mortar has set.

Filling in above the soldier course with saved whole bricks; some wedge-shaped cut bricks will be needed directly above the arch.

Having set the new lintel in place and re-finished the brickwork of the inner leaf above it, you can chop out the brickwork at the sides of the opening and, if necessary, across the base. First, draw the outline of the new opening on both sides of the wall, making it about 25mm (1in) wider and deeper than the actual frame dimensions to give a fitting tolerance.

Removing the Brickwork

All external walls, will comprise two layers of bricks. Treat each separately, working in from each side of the wall.

If the wall is a solid one produce a square edge along the opening outline on the inner layer by chopping through bricks where necessary. Always remove complete bricks even if they project beyond the outline. This will give a toothed appearance to the edge.

If the base outline runs through the center of a course of bricks, remove the course completely; you can make up the difference later.

Finishing the Opening

Replace the outer layer at the sides of the opening by mortaring cut bricks into the toothed sections so that their cut ends are innermost.

Next, replace the area of wall above the window, laying the bricks on the lintel and copying the original brickwork bond for strength and appearance. In a solid wall, you can create a curved, self-supporting soldier arch by setting a wooden framework in the opening on which the bricks of the arch are laid. Then the surrounding courses are fitted round the arch and the mortar left to set for a couple of days before removal of the formwork.

Fitting the Frame

The frame must sit squarely in the opening; if it is twisted, you may have problems in opening and closing the window and the glass will be under stress and may shatter at the slightest vibration.

In a solid wall you can set the frame: flush with the outer face with its sill overhanging the edge; in the center of the opening with narrow reveals on each side; or flush with the inner face with a sub-sill at the bottom to throw water clear of the wall.

When set forward in the opening, the sides and top of the reveal are plastered and a wooden or tiled window board set across the bottom. When set at the back, it is normal to trim round the inside with molding.

Fixing the Frame

The simplest method of securing the frame is with frame fixings (see opposite) but you can also use conventional wallplugs and screws, wooden wedges or metal frame ties. With each type, you should wedge the frame in the opening with wood offcuts so that it is set squarely in place, while the fixings are marked and made.

With screws and plugs, clearance holes must first be drilled in the frame and the hole positions on the wall marked through these. The holes are drilled and plugged and the frame fitted.

Wooden wedges are tapped into slots cut in the mortar joints and the frame nailed to the wedges. Metal frame ties also fit into slots in the joints, being screwed to the frame and mortared in place.

In all cases, you must leave a 3mm ($\frac{1}{8}$in) gap between the top of the frame and the underside of the lintel to allow for any settlement of the structure.

Leave the packing pieces in place and fill the gaps at the sides with mortar, leaving it about 3mm ($\frac{1}{8}$in) below the level of the frame face. Fill this gap with caulk when the mortar has set. Use caulking to fill the gap between the lintel and frame also.

If there is a gap below the frame, fill this with bricks and mortar, splitting the bricks lengthways if necessary.

Making a Sub-Sill

You can make a sub-sill from wood screwed or nailed in place, or a double layer of tiles set on a sloping bed of mortar.

Another way is to cast a concrete sill in situ, making up a wooden formwork 'tray' nailed to the wall. The sill should overlap the edge of the bricks by no more than 25mm (1in) and you can form a drip channel (to prevent rainwater trickling under the sill) along the bottom edge by pinning a length of waxed cord (sash window cord will do) in the bottom of the tray. The top of the lintel should slope downwards so angle the sides for this. Also provide reinforcement by setting steel rods in holes drilled in the brickwork.

Mix the concrete from 4 parts sand: 1 part cement and pour it into the form. Agitate the mix to compact it and remove air bubbles and draw it off level with the top of the form. Leave the concrete for at least 24 hours before removing the formwork.

Fitting a timber wedge into a slot cut in a mortar joint; fit wedges near the top and bottom, and in between for tall windows.

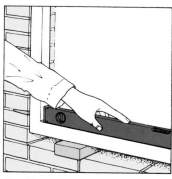

Wedging the frame in position with wooden blocks; leave 3mm (⅛in) gap between the frame and the lintel and later fill with caulking.

Checking that the sill is horizontal using a level; make any necessary adjustment by moving the wooden packing.

Checking that the frame is vertical; adjust by tapping with the handle of a hammer.

Securing the frame by hammering 100mm (4in) cut-nails through the frame into the wedges; recheck levels after each fixing.

Bricking up under the frame after completing the fixings and removing the timber packing; use bricks split lengthways if necessary.

Trick

OPTIONS

Developed from the conventional wall plug and screw fixing, the frame fixing is much simpler to use and ideal for securing wooden members to masonry. It comprises a hefty screw and a long plastic wallplug.

To use, wedge the frame in its opening and drill holes for the fixings right through it and into the wall. Without removing the frame, tap the plug and screw combination through the frame and into the wall, finally tightening the screw for a secure fixing.

Frame fixings are supplied in various lengths to hold wood thicknesses up to 85mm (3⅜in). Another development of this is the hammer fixing, which is used in the same way, but set by driving a ridged, countersunk pin into the expanding plug.

FRAME FIXINGS

Drilling through clearance holes in the batten into the wall; countersink the holes so that the plug sits flush.

Passing the plug, with screw partially inserted, through the batten into the masonry before screwing up.

While the upper floors of a house will always be constructed of wood, the ground floor may be made of wood or it may be of solid concrete.

Suspended Wooden Floors

All wood floors are based on the same method of construction with minor differences. They have a supporting framework of wooden beams called joists to which are nailed wooden boards or plywood panels.

The joists of wooden ground floors are supported at their end — and sometimes at one or two points in between — or additional wood beams known as 'wall plates'. These, in turn rest on the tops of low brick 'sleeper' walls. These are not solid, but are laid in honeycomb fashion with spaces between the bricks to allow the air to circulate below the floor to prevent condensation and rot forming (see page 79). For the same reason, vents are usually fitted at the base of the external walls and must always be kept clear. Slates or strips of flexible flashing material are laid between the wall plates and sleeper walls to prevent damp attacking the wood.

Sometimes the joists are laid on top of individual bricks set on the ground. Upstairs, the joists are also supported by wall plates but these are held by metal brackets called joist hangers, which are cemented into the walls. Sometimes the joist ends may be set in sockets between the bricks, with a metal plate below to spread the load through the wall.

Solid Concrete Floors

Most modern houses have solid ground floors. These comprise layer of compacted gravel on top of which is a 100mm (4in) layer concrete called the subfloor. Damp-proof membrane bitumen or thick plastic comes next and it carried up and down the wall to link with the flashing around the base of the house.

A thin layer of mortar can be laid on top of the membrane to provide a level surface for the floorcovering.

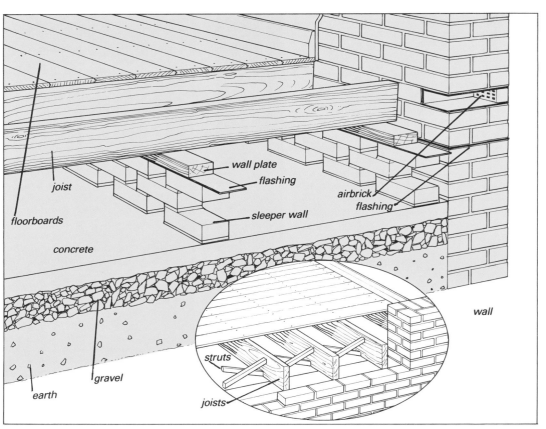

Suspended wooden ground floor; the joists are supported on wall-plates which in turn rest on flashing over open-structure sleeper walls. Inset: upper floor joists are stiffened with herringbone struts.

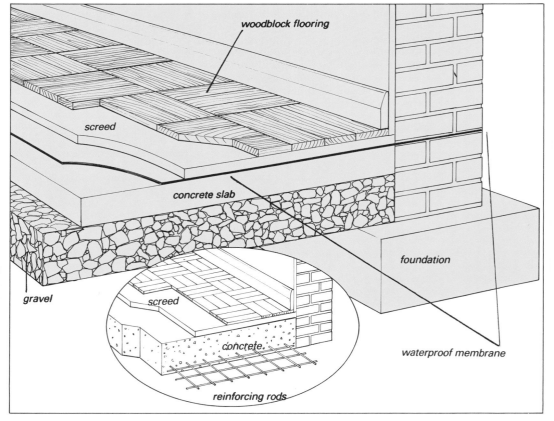

Solid ground floor consists of concrete slab on gravel, and flashing covered by concrete screed on which the flooring is laid. Inset: solid upper floor has screed on top of reinforced concrete slab.

Wood as a building material has a lot to offer: it's readily available, cheap, light and easily worked — and it's ideal for flooring. However, wood has its drawbacks, due mainly to the fact that it was once a living material and is affected by damp or dry atmospheres, by insect attack and by rot (see page 80).

Over the years a wooden floor can suffer considerably from wear and tear. The joists may warp or sag, boards may shrink to open up gaps through which draughts whistle, or they may become loose or damaged. The whole structure may be weakened by woodworm or rot. Fortunately, many of the minor problems can be cured easily, although serious rot or insect attack may mean complete replacement.

Creaking Floorboards

Probably the most common fault with a wooden floor is creaking floorboards due to the fixings working loose. The cure is simple: either drive the nails back in or replace them with longer nails or screws. Punch nail heads below the surface and countersink the screw heads.

Curing Gaps between Boards

Gaps may open up between square edge floorboards if the wood shrinks after it has been laid. A few narrow gaps can be filled; if, however, there are fairly wide gaps between all the boards, it may be more satisfactory to lift them all and relay them (see page 43) closer together, adding a narrow filler board at one side of the floor.

Gaps of less then 6mm (¼in) can be filled with papier-mâché, which you can make yourself. Half fill a bucket with small pieces of torn, soft white paper, adding boiling water gradually while you pound the paper into a thick paste. Allow it to cool and stir in cellulose wallpaper paste, adding plenty to make a thick mixture. You can also add wood stain at this stage to match the colour of the boards.

When the papier-mâché is cold, force it between the boards with a filling knife, leaving it slightly proud of the surface.

FILLING NARROW GAPS

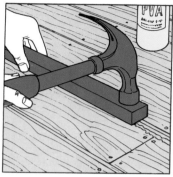

Filling the gap between square-edge floorboards with a glued wooden fillet hammered into position; use papier mâché for gaps below 6mm (¼in).

Fixing the fillet to the center of a joist with a 38mm (1½in) panel-pin; hammer gently and punch the head below the surface of the wood.

Planing the raised edge of the fillet flush with the boards using a smoothing-plane; allow the glue to set before planing.

PACKING OUT THE JOISTS

Correcting a sagging floor by first lifting the boards in the affected area; a wooden batten adds leverage when pulling out the nails.

Measuring the depth of sag from a straight-edge placed across the joists; this measurement is the thickness of the packing needed.

Nailing the packing piece to the top of the joist after planing to the required thickness; avoid the nailing positions of the boards.

Leave this for at least 48 hours then sand it smooth.

Fill wider gaps with softwood fillets: cut the fillets fractionally wider than the gaps they are to fill, using a circular saw if you have one, if not a backsaw. The fillets should be fractionally deeper than the floorboards: that is, about 25mm (1in). Plane the fillets so that they taper slightly at the bottom then tap them into the gaps with a hammer and block of wood. Use a plane to shave the top edges of the fillets flush with the tops of the floorboards. Make sure the ends of fillets meet on a joist: secure them to the joists with brads.

Damaged boards

Damaged sections of boards should be cut out and replaced, or a new board fitted if the damage is substantial. First check that there are no pipes or cables running below the damaged section, otherwise you will have to remove the entire board in case you cut into them by accident.

To cut out a section of board, first find the edges of the joists at each end. Do this by sliding a knife blade along the gap between the boards. If the boards are tongued-and-grooved, you will have to cut through the tongues by drilling a starting hole and using a keyhole saw or with a circular saw set to the depth of the board.

Drill a starting hole for the saw just in from the edge of each joist and cut through the board at each end in line with the joist edges.

Lift out the damaged section; if it is nailed to intermediate joists, lever it free using a bricklayers chisel and a stout length of wood. Lever the board upwards at the fixings with a chisel until you have lifted the end enough to be able to slide the wood below it, while resting it on the tops of the boards on each side. Pushing down on the end of the board will spring the fixings from the joist. Continue in this fashion until you have freed the board. A complete floorboard can be removed in the same way.

Screw or nail lengths of 50mm sq (2in sq) batten to the sides of the joists flush with the undersides of the old boards. Then nail a new section of floorboard to the tops of the battens.

Sagging Joists

On wide, unsupported spans, the joists may sag in the centre of the floor, giving it a slightly 'dished' surface. To overcome this, add packing pieces to the tops of the affected joists.

Lift the floorboards and place a straightedge across the joists at several points. Measure any gap between the tops of the joints and the straight edge and use the measurements to mark out lengths of softwood batten. These must be the same width as the joists. Plane the battens to size and nail them to the tops of the affected joists. Finally, re-lay the floorboards.

RENEWING FLOOR JOISTS

The first indications you might get that there is something amiss with the supporting joists of a floor are an unevenness in the level of the boards, movement or even partial collapse. Wooden first floors are particularly prone to attack by rot and insects, both encouraged by the damp conditions that can occur if the void below is not properly ventilated or if the wood has come into contact with moisture rising through the surrounding masonry or through a build up of debris below.

Lever up one or two floorboards and have a look with a flashlight. You may find that the problem is simply due to one or two joists having become twisted and this can be cured by toe-nailing tight fitting wooden struts between them. However, if the wood is being eaten away by insects or rot, you will have no option but to replace every piece affected.

Removing the Old Joists

Lever up enough floorboards to get at the affected joists, using the method described on page 41. Pull all their nails out and stack the boards so that you can replace them in the same order.

If only a small section of a joist is damaged, the affected area can be sawn out and replaced. Make sure, though, that the cuts are at least 600mm (24in) beyond the damage.

Removal of a complete joist will mean levering it from its wall plates at each end, and also any intermediate wall plates. If the ends are set in sockets in the wall, cut through the joist just short of the wall and pull the stubs out. Brick up the sockets, cementing metal hangers into the top joints.

Fitting the New Joist

If only a section of joist has been removed, cut a new piece of wood of the same size as the old joist so that it is long enough to overlap the ends by at least 450mm (18in). Bolt this to the old joist with two carriage bolts at each end.

If a complete joist is to be fitted, trim back its ends to a taper so that there is no chance of it touching the external walls. Toe-nail the joist to its wall-plates.

If the wall plates themselves are in a bad way, replace them at the same time, simply laying them on top of the sleeper walls. Make sure you prevent contact with the masonry by laying a strip of flexible flashing along the wall first (it's sold in rolls by a building material supplier).

Treat all the wood with preservative, paying particular attention to the porous endgrain of all sections. Before replacing the floorboards (which should also be checked and replaced if necessary — see opposite), remove all rubbish and bits of wood from the underfloor area as this can cause a reccurence of the problem. Check that all the vents and airbricks are unblocked, too.

Something to watch out for are pipe and cable runs below the floor. Pipes are usually set in notches in the tops of the joists and cables pass through holes drilled in them. Cut notches in replacement joists as shallow as possible to avoid weakening the wood.

Always remove the fuse controlling any underfloor electrical circuit before beginning work. You can cut the cable out of the old joist by making two saw cuts down to the hole. Make similar cuts in the new joist and glue the offcut back for added cable protection. Alternatively, disconnect the cable from the nearest fitting and thread it through the holes.

Upstairs Floors

Replacing joists in upstairs floors is much more involved because they support the ceiling of the room below. Fortunately, they are less susceptible to rot than ground floors, but they still may suffer from insect attack.

In addition to lifting the floorboards, you will have to remove a section of ceiling, replacing it later with a drywall panel. It is a complicated job which will make two rooms uninhabitable at once.

Sawing through a rotten floor joist to one side of the wall-plate; new joists overlap the existing one and are bolted to them.

With the wall-plate removed renewing the flashing on the sleeper wall; the flashing should overlap both edges of the wall and at joins.

Laying a new wall-plate on the flashing; take care that there is no dirt on the flashing so that the plate is supported along its whole length.

If the thickness of the wall-plate is greater than the original, it may be necessary to notch the joists to maintain the existing floor-level.

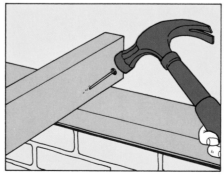

Fixing a joist to the wall-plate by toe-nailing; a heavy object held firmly against the back of the joist will prevent it from moving.

Coating the end of a joist with preservative paste, smeared thickly on to the end grain; the paste soaks in over the years.

If you are going to lay a new floor, make sure you buy the boards at least two weeks before starting work and stack them in the room in which they will be laid. This will allow them to dry out properly, preventing shrinkage later. Ideally, choose tongued-and-grooved boards, but if you're just replacing odd boards, square-edged ones would be better. In the latter case, make sure you get the right size: 100mm (4in) and 150mm (6in) are common widths and the usual finished thickness is 19mm (¾in), but thicker boards are available.

Removing the Old Boards

Lift the second board in from the wall, using the method described on page 41. Then use a length of stout wood to lever up the others. Take care along the walls, since the boards are likely to be tucked under the baseboard.

Tidy up the joists by pulling out any remaining nails and fitting packing strips if necessary (see page 41).

Lifting a floorboard with a claw hammer and flat chisel; lift first with the chisel until the claw can be inserted under the end of the board.

Fitting the Boards

Fit four or five boards at a time, keeping any end joints between them to a minimum. Where joints cannot be avoided, make sure the boards meet at the centre of a joist and that their ends are cut square. Use up offcuts when you can and stagger the end joints so they don't all fall in a line.

Mark and cut the first board to clear any obstructions and fit it up against the wall. Force a chisel blade into the top of the joists and use it to lever the board tight against the wall while you drive two nails through it into each joist. Use cut floor brads at least twice the length of the depth of the board.

If you are using boards, the groove of this first board should face away from the wall and be nearer the joist than the top. Set the next four boards in place and push them tightly together using wooden wedges or floor cramps. In the former case, nail a length of wood temporarily across the joists and fit pairs of opposing wooden wedges between it and the boards. Tapping the wedges together will force the boards tight up against each other. Floor cramps clamp to the joists and when tightened exert great force against the edges of the board, (you should be able to get them from a good tool rental company).

In both cases, cut short offcuts of floorboard to fit between the edges of the boards and the wedges or cramps to protect the board edges.

With the boards cramped tight, nail the outermost one down. Then remove the wedges or cramps and nail the remainder.

Continue in this way across the room. Where there are pipes or cables below the floor that you might want to reach in the future, screw the boards down. Cut off the tongues of tongue and grooved boards to make lifting easy.

The Final Boards

Stop within two boards' width of the far wall since you will not be able to cramp these last boards. To fit the final boards, first lay a full board up against the last one to be nailed down. Lever it tight up against this board with a chisel. Next, take a short offcut of floorboard and hold it against the base so that its other edge overlaps the full board. Hold a pencil against the edge of the offcut and run it along the full board to mark the profile of the wall on it.

Cut the board along the pencil ine and then refit it, but this time along the wall, springing in a full board between it and the others at the same time. Nail both boards down.

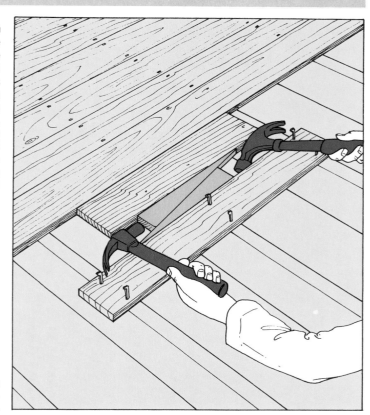

Using folding wedges to pack boards tightly; nail an offcut temporarily across the joists for the wedges to bear on and tap the ends inwards.

Compacting boards using a flooring clamp; position it on top of a joist and, with scrap wood as packing, force the boards together.

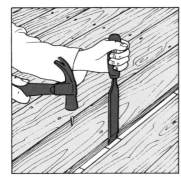

Levering boards together with an old chisel; hammer it vertically into the top of a joist and pull towards the board while nailing.

Fitting the last T & G boards: plane off two tongues, position one board against the previous groove and scribe along the second board.

After cutting the first board along the line and placing the cut board against the baseboard, pressing the two planed boards into position.

CARPENTER'S

Trick

LEVELLING A FLOOR

Wooden floors are notorious for becoming worn and having warped and uneven boards that make laying floorcoverings like carpet, linoleum and vinyls difficult. The uneven surface of the boards causes ridges in the covering which wear very quickly, putting them in need of early replacement.

If you have wooden floors which are uneven, a simple way of levelling them out is to cover them with sheets of hardboard. This provides a smooth, even surface to extend the life of the floorcovering, and it has the added advantage of insulating the floor slightly by preventing cold draughts from blowing through any gaps between the boards. If you want a level surface for tiles, use a thicker material such as plywood or particle board (see opposite).

Before you begin the job, go over the entire floor, punching down all the nail heads, refixing loose boards and replacing any missing sections. If there are any vital pipes or cables below the floor, make up access panels by cutting out short lengths of floorboard and screwing them back to battens nailed to the sides of the joists. Each panel can be covered with hardboard individually.

Hardboard comes in 2.4m × 1.2m (8 × 4ft) sheets, which you can use whole or cut in half to make more manageable. Buy the hardboard few days before you intend using it and stack it on edge in the room where it is to be used so that any stretching or shrinking due to the atmosphere takes place before you nail it to the floor.

Making an access panel; nail 38mm (1½in) sq batten to the side of the joist and screw the cut end of the board to it.

Punching nail heads below the surface of the floorboards with a nail punch before laying hardboard sheets.

Nailing down handboard with 19mm (¾in) annular nails (ring-shanks) every 15cm (6in); hold with long-honed pliers.

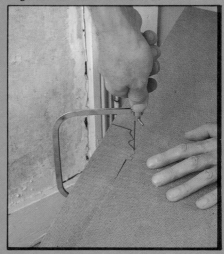

Starting the second row of boards with an offcut to stagger the joints; lay at right-angles to the run of floorboards.

Laying the Hardboard

Start in one corner of the room, laying down a complete sheet rough side uppermost and butting it up to the base skirting board. Nail the sheet in place using 19mm (¾in) annular nails (which have ridges around their shank for better grip), spacing them at 150mm (6in) intervals and setting the outer rows no closer than 13mm (½in) to the edges of the sheet. Making a mark on your hammer handle will help in spacing the nails accurately and quickly.

Continue along the wall, laying whole sheets until you have to cut one to fill in at the end. Take the offcut back to begin the second row of sheets, thus ensuring that the joints between the boards are staggered. This is essential.

Use an offcut of wood and a pencil to scribe awkward shapes, such as the molding at door openings, on to the hardboard and cut them out using a jig saw or coping saw. Cut straight lines with a circular saw or back saw.

Using a contour gauge to form a template of a door architrave; trace round the rods on to the hardboard.

Cutting out the shape of the architrave with a coping saw; support the board firmly whilst cutting.

Floorboards are quite expensive and when you're using them it takes a long time to cover a large floor because you're only doing a small strip at a time. Flooring grade plywood, on the other hand, is much cheaper and it comes in standard 2.4 × 1.2m (8 × 4ft) sheets which means that you can quickly cover a large floor area. And even though you have to screw it down, you only fix the screws round the edges of the sheets so there is much less fixing work to do.

Flooring grade plywood is normally 18mm (¾in) thick (thicker sizes can be obtained) and you can even buy sheets with tongued-and-grooved edges. When screwed down to the original joists it provides a strong, rigid surface that is ideal for all types of floorcoverings, including quarry tiles (see page 193).

You can also use thinner grades of ply directly over the top of a boarded floor to provide a sound surface for tiling, although you would have to refit the base boards higher up the wall to accommodate the extra thickness on the floor.

Despite its cheapness and convenience, plywood does have disadvantages when used for flooring. It can't be used in a bathroom since if it gets wet it will swell up, and the large sheets present difficulties if you want to lift them again. You may also have to cut out large sections to fit around obstructions in a room, and you must make special arrangements to reach cable and pipe runs below the floor in the form of access panels which can be removed if necessary.

Planning the Job

Because plywood comes in such large sheets, it is important that you plan the job carefully to keep the number of sheets you buy and the amount of cutting to a minimum. The edges of adjacent panels should always meet on the centrelines of joists, so the first thing to do is find the joist spacing to see if a standard size panel will fit exactly between joists without trimming. A joist spacing of 400mm (16in) would be ideal, but other spacings would mean trimming down to size.

Draw up a floorplan of the room and draw on the joist centrelines (you can find them from the positions of the original board fixing nails). Then use this plan to work out the number of full boards and part boards needed. You may be able to buy narrow offcuts of plywood to fill in gaps round the edges of the room.

You will also need to support the edges of the sheets between the joists and for this you need lengths of 75 × 50mm (2 × 3in) sawn softwood. You can work out the quantities from the plan. These battens are known as trimmer joists.

Preparing the Joists

Remove all the old floorboards and pull out any remaining nails from the joists using your claw hammer as a lever. Brush the joists down so their tops are clean.

Next cut and fit the trimmer joists, toe-nailing them between the joists and being careful to set their positions accurately. Make sure their top edges are level with the tops of the joists. Also fit trimmer joists where you want to make access panels to reach pipes or cables beneath the floor — these panels must be supported on all four edges, by the joists and trimmer joists.

Fixing the Plywood Sheets

Start in one corner and slide the first sheet under the base (with the grooved edges outermost if using T & G board). Drill countersunk pilot holes for 50mm (2in) fixing screws at 300mm (12in) intervals all round the edge of the sheet and into the joists. Screw the sheet down, making sure the screw heads are recessed well below the surface.

Continue fixing the sheets in the same way, cramping them together as you would floorboards before fixing (see page 43). Scribe the boards to fit at the edges and make any cutouts with a power jig saw or a coping saw. Straight cuts can be made with a power circular saw or a back saw.

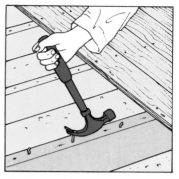
Pulling up old floorboard nails which have pulled through the boards, using a claw hammer.

Hammering a trimmer joist into position between the joists; the trimmer must be a tight fit.

Nailing into the end of a trimmer. One end of each trimmer can be fixed in this way; the other end will have to be toe-nailed.

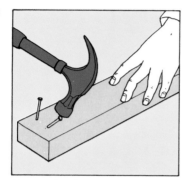
Hammering the toe-nails into the trimmer before putting it into position between the joists.

Toe-nailing a trimmer joist against a wall; ensure that the top of the trimmer is flush with the top of the joists.

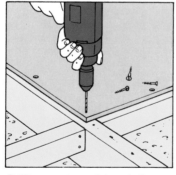
Drilling countersunk bored pilot holes through the plywood, into the joist; a combination countersink and drill bit saves time.

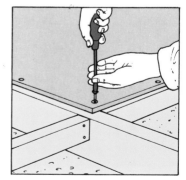
Partly driving in screws round the edges of the plywood; no fixings are required in the center of the panel.

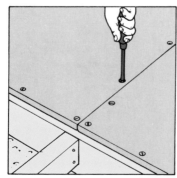
Fully tightening the screws; panels should meet over the centre of a joist and the screws in adjacent panels should be staggered.

SOLID CONCRETE FLOOR

Solid concrete floors in modern houses are usually made up of a layer of gravel, topped by a layer of concrete (the subfloor), on top of which there's a waterproof membrane linked to the flashing in the base of the surrounding walls and finally a screed of mortar, which provides a smooth, level surface for your floorcovering. This type of construction is very tough, but even so, defects can occur: cracks, uneven surfaces and damp patches due to a faulty waterproof membrane are all common problems.

Damp can be a particular problem in very old solid concrete floors, since they were often laid with no membrane at all.

In many cases localized damage can be repaired quite simply, but if it is widespread the only real solution is to dig up the floor and replace it.

Rotten wooden floors can also be replaced with solid concrete ones relatively cheaply and they have the added advantage of providing a much more stable surface for laying something like quarry tiles or wood blocks. In this instance, however, you must incorporate pipework air ducts to link any ventilation holes or grilles in the external walls with the suspended wooden floors in adjacent rooms.

Repairing Cracks

Provided a crack in a concrete floor is no more than 6mm (¼in) wide you can repair it with mortar, since it probably won't extend down beyond the surface screed. However, anything

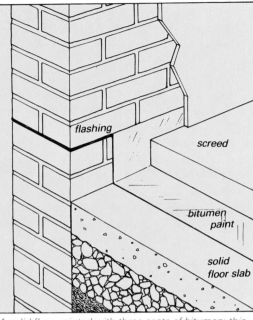

A solid floor painted with three coats of bitumen; this is taken up the wall to the flashing, and a 50mm (2in) screed laid on top.

If the flashing is below floor-level, a groove must be cut and the bitumen emulsion taken down the groove to the flashing.

wider than this will probably affect the subfloor slab as well, which will mean a new floor.

To repair a surface crack, first open it up with a cold chisel to a depth of about 13mm (½in), undercutting the edges so the mortar will hold fast. Brush out all the dust and debris and paint the surface of the crack with a solution of one part PVA adhesive and one part water.

Make a fairly dry mortar mix of 3 parts sand: 1 part cement and equal quantities of water and PVA adhesive. Trowel this into the crack, levelling it off with the surrounding floor. Allow to harden before laying any floorcovering.

Uneven Floors

If the surface of the floor is uneven you can smooth it with a self-levelling floor screed. Supplied in powder form for mixing with water or latex, depending on which it's based, the screed provides a smooth 3mm (⅛in) layer on which you can lay floorcoverings.

Pour small amounts of screed onto the floor at a time and trowel roughly level. There's no need to work out trowel marks, since they gradually settle out. Before you apply the screed you must remove the base boards and make sure there are no major cracks or depressions in the floor — fill these as previously described. Nail a batten temporarily across the threshold of any interconnecting doorway to provide a positive edge to the screed. When it has set, remove the batten and trowel a narrow sloping fillet of mortar along the edge to blend it into the adjoining floor.

Water-proof membranes may be thick plastic sheet, PVC, butyl rubber or painted-on bitumen emulsion, and to be effective they must provide a continuous layer across the floor and be joined to the wall flashing if the waterproof membrane becomes punctured, damp patches will appear on the floorcovering.

If you're not sure if damp is rising

through the floor, tape a sheet of polythene over the floor and leave it for a few days. If damp is rising, water droplets will appear on the underside of the sheet.

Small areas of damp can be treated by breaking through the surface screed and coating the damaged area of waterproof membrane with bitumen emulsion, then rescreeding with mortar.

If the problem is widespread, or if the floor has no waterproof membrane at all, the real solution is to dig it all up and lay a new floor. However, a cheaper alternative is to remove the base and remove a strip of plaster to find the flashing. Paint the floor with two or three layers of bitumen emulsion, (each one at right angles to the one below it for maximum coverage) taking it up the walls to the level of the flashing. If the flashing is below floor level, hack out a groove in the floor next to the wall until you can reach the flashing, paint on the emulsion and refill the groove before continuing the emulsion across the floor. Finally, lay a 50mm (2in) mortar screed on top. This will mean cutting down doors, and making steps for ramps between rooms. You should also check with your local Building Department since it will reduce the height of the room, which may contravene the Building Code.

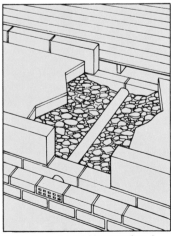

A ducting pipe laid in gravel and terminating at an air-brick provides ventilation for a suspended floor.

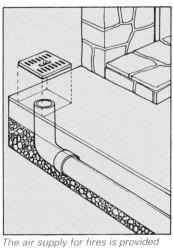

The air supply for fires is provided by ducting from an outside wall airbrick to a floor-mounted ventilator.

The first job is to remove the old floor and dig out the ground below to at least 300mm (12in) below the final floor level. Lever up an old wooden floor and saw through the joists for easy removal. Then demolish the dwarf walls. Break up a concrete floor: the best way is with a rented jack hammer. Keep the rubble for use as a bed for the concrete later. The work will be dirty and dusty, so wear stout boots, thick gloves, overalls and safety goggles.

Preparing the Site

Find the flashing in the walls; it may be a layer of slate or bitumen, or one or two courses of engineering bricks. If necessary, chop off plaster to find the flashing.

If the floor in the next room is of suspended wood, lay plastic drain pipes between any airbricks and the inter-connecting door threshold, setting them in place with bits of stone or brick: this is vital to provide ventilation throughout the floor. Build a retaining wall across the threshold with concrete building blocks.

Next make up some datum pegs from 50 × 25mm (2 × 1in) sawn softwood marked with the depths of the bed and concrete subfloor layers: 150mm (6in) and 100mm (4in) respectively. Cut a point on one end of the pegs then drive a peg into the ground near a given reference point, to indicate the surface of the floor. Drive the other pegs in at 1m (3ft) intervals, checking that their tops are level with the first.

Constructing the Slab

Put down the brick and stone bed, levelling it with the marks on the pegs and compacting it well with a sledge hammer or purpose-made tamper. Spread a layer of damp builder's sand over the top as a 'blinding layer' to fill any voids.

The concrete for the subfloor should be of 1 part cement: 2½ parts concreting sand: 4 parts gravel. You can either rent a mixer and batch it up yourself, or order it pre-mixed. In the latter case you might not be able to have it discharged directly to the floor and will have to be ready

Driving in the reference datum peg, marked with levels for gravel and concrete; the top should be 50mm (2in) below the flashing.

Level the second datum peg with the reference peg. Use a level on a straight-edge. Space pegs at 1 metre (3ft) intervals.

Blinding the compacted gravel layer with damp builders' sand to fill any voids in the surface.

Laying concrete; spread it out evenly then compact and level with the peg tops using a stout beam. Work backwards to the door.

Tacking plastic waterproof membrane to wall above flashing; make neat folds at corners, overlap sheets by about 300mm (12in).

Dividing the floor into bays with 50 × 25mm (2 × 1in) battens on edge, held with blobs of mortar; level with packing if necessary.

Levelling off the tamped mortar in the first bay by drawing a straight edge along the tops of the dividing battens.

Filling the channels, left after removing the dividing battens, with mortar; level the mortar flush with the adjoining surfaces.

Smoothing over the surface with a metal trowel; when the mortar is stiff, go over it again with a wetted trowel to polish it.

with sturdy builder's wheelbarrows.

Lay the concrete so that it is level with the tops of the pegs, tamping it down well and drawing a stout batten across the tops of the pegs to level it. Fill any hollows with more concrete then tamp again.

When the concrete has cured, lay the cleavage membrane. With bitumen emulsion apply about three coats, taking it up the wall to the flashing. If plastic sheet is used, tack it to the walls above the flashing. Make folds at

the corners rather than cuts and overlap the sheets by 200 to 300mm (8 to 12in), sealing the join with tape or building adhesive.

Finally, use 50 by 25mm (1 × 2in) battens to divide the floor into 1m (3ft) wide bays for the finishing screed. Set the battens in place with dabs of mortar and level them if necessary by packing offcuts underneath: check with a spirit level.

Fill the bays with a 3:1 mortar mix and draw it off level with a straight-edged batten held

across the tops of the dividing battens. When two bays have been completed, lift out the batten in between and fill the resulting slot with more mortar. Then trowel both bays smooth with a metal trowel. When the mortar has stiffened, give it a final polish with a wetted trowel.

REPLACING AN OLD CEILING

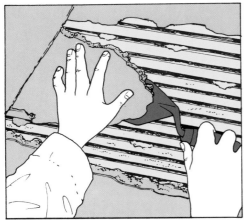

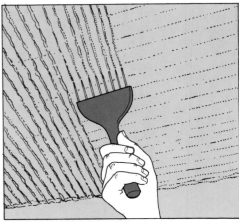

Levering off the damaged plaster from the laths with a trowel; clear the area within the marked lines and undercut the edges.

Applying a coat of bonding plaster across the laths after brushing on PVA adhesive; press the plaster well into the laths.

Keying the plaster with a scratch comb, working across the laths to avoid knocking out any plaster.

Applying a thicker second coat of bonding plaster over the first, taking it on to the edges of the original plaster.

Ruling off the second coat using an aluminum darby to flatten high spots and make low areas show up.

After keying the second coat, applying two thin coats of finishing plaster; give a final polish with a wetted metal trowel.

There are two types of ceiling construction, depending on their age. Early ceilings were made by nailing thin strips of wood (laths) to the joists so that there were narrow gaps between them. Plaster, often reinforced with animal hair, was then spread over the laths and forced through the gaps in between. The ridges so formed are called 'nibs' and these hold the ceiling together.

The more modern method of constructing a ceiling is to nail sheets of gypsumboard to the joists and coat them with a thin skim coat of plaster.

Damage can occur to a ceiling for all sorts of reasons: you might put a foot through it while working in the attic or a leaking water pipe might weaken it, settlement of the structure of the house and even old age can also take a toll.

Dealing with Cracks

Cracks are the most common form of damage found in a ceiling and if they are only fine they can be filled with a filler compound. However, if they are wide and cover a large area of the ceiling the structure will be dangerously weak and should be replaced.

Coping with a Sagging Ceiling

Sagging can occur in lath and plaster ceilings if the nibs become broken, but if the area affected is not too extensive you can repair the nibs by pouring on quick setting plaster while you support the ceiling from below.

To do the job you'll need a prop made from a panel of plywood fixed to the end of a stout batten. This is wedged between the floor and ceiling to hold the latter against the laths. Then, after

vacuuming the area above the ceiling and moistening it with water from a plant sprayer, pour on the plaster and allow it to set.

If a plasterboard ceiling sags it's probably because the fixing nails have pulled loose. Refix the affected portion by renailing with 50mm (2in) drywall nails spaced 150mm (6in) apart.

Patching Damaged Areas

If plaster has fallen away from the laths but they appear to be in good condition, replaster them after cutting back the original plaster to make a regular shape and reach sound plaster. Undercut the edges of the plaster and make sure there is no old plaster left between the laths. Then treat the area with an adhesive.

When plastering always work across the laths, spreading on a thin coat of bonding plaster first and keying it with a 'comb' made

by knocking a row of nails into the edge of a short batten. Apply another coat of bonding plaster and key this with a devilling float, pressing it down to allow for two thin finishing coats. Polish these when hard with a wetted steel trowel.

If the laths are broken or the ceiling is of gypsumboard, you can patch any damage with a panel of gypsumboard. Simply cut back the old ceiling to the nearest joist centerlines, and if the damage covers a large area fit 50mm (2in) sq timber bracing between the joists to support the ends of the panel.

Make sure the panel is a tight fit and nail it in place with 30mm (1¼in) gypsumboard nails. Spread a layer of bonding plaster over the patch, working it into the joints and finish off with two thin coats of finish plaster, ruling them off level with the surrounding ceiling and giving them a final polish with a wetted steel trowel.

Taking down an old lath-and-plaster ceiling is an extremely dirty and dusty job, so before you start you must take the necessary action to protect both yourself and the other rooms in the house from its effects.

Protective clothing is essential and you'll need to wear overalls, safety goggles, a facemask and thick gloves. Most important is a construction worker's 'hard hat', which you can rent or buy. Hopefully the ceiling will come down under your control, but it's as well to be prepared for unexpected falls.

Safety clothing; if you suspect the presence of asbestos, buy a special mask – this type is not adequate.

Because so much dust will be flying about, strip the room of all furnishings and seal the connecting doors to other rooms with plastic sheets or old blankets. It's a good idea to spread a large, thick plastic sheet across the floor to make collecting the debris easier, and you should have a good supply of thick plastic sacks to hand for bagging up the rubbish. If the ceiling is very large, it may be worthwhile renting a small container to dispose of the old ceiling.

Sprinkling water on the dust will keep it damped down and stop it billowing about too much.

Providing Access

You need to be able to reach the ceiling easily so that you can lever sections of it away from the joists. For simplicity, place a scaffold board between two step ladders so that your head will be about 150mm (6in) from the ceiling — a ladder on its own is not suitable. An alternative is to rent sections of scaffold tower to

make small access platforms, but this is probably only worthwhile if the job is large.

Any ceiling-mounted lighting fittings must be removed (after turning off the power at the panel or removing the appropriate fuse: see page 138). Pull the supply cable back above the ceiling if you can get to it; if not tape up the ends and leave it hanging.

If the ceiling is immediately below the roof space, go up into the attic and check that there are no other electricity cables lying across the top of the ceiling which you may snag as you remove it. Clip these out of the way along the joists.

You will find that there is a lot of dirt and dust above the ceiling and this should be removed with a vacuum cleaner.

Many attics are insulated with various materials laid across the top of the ceiling and obviously, these must be removed. Roll up glass fiber mat insulation and put into plastic garbage bags stacked in an unaffected part of the attic until it can be replaced. Loose-fill insulation is more difficult to handle, since it is so light: try scooping it up with a plastic jug and pouring it into garbage bags or, if you have an industrial vacuum cleaner, you may be able to suck it up and empty the vacuum into the bags.

Removing the Ceiling

You can use a large claw hammer or a flat chisel and hammer to remove the old ceiling, although you might find the former easier as the latter will mean holding both arms above your head, which can be very tiring.

Hack into the plaster, levering pieces away until you have exposed a large area of laths. Prise these from the joists, always working away from yourself so that any falls will not be on top of you.

Continue working across the room until you have removed the entire ceiling. Then go back along each joist with a pair of pincers and pull out all the lath-fixing nails. Finally, work round the edges of the ceiling with a chisel to clean up the plaster of the walls.

Prising away laths from the joists using a claw hammer, after levering off a section of plaster; work away from you for safety.

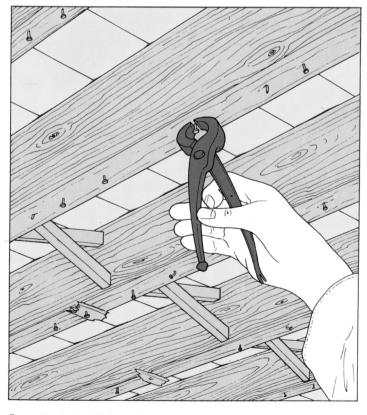

Removing the lath-fixing nails with a pair of pincers; make sure that none remain so that the new ceiling will fit tight against the joists.

FITTING A NEW CEILING

Cladding a ceiling with gypsumboard is quite a straightforward job, but because the boards are so large they're awkward to handle and you'll need one or two helpers to get the job done.

Gypsumboard for ceilings comes in two thicknesses: 9.5mm (⅜in) and 12.5mm (½in), the former being suitable for use where the joist spacing is no more than 450mm (18in) and the latter where the joists are up to 600mm (2ft) apart. The standard sheet sizes are 2.4 and 1.8 × 1.2m (8 and 6 × 4ft). You may find the smaller sheets are easier to handle and you can cut them in half to make them even more manageable. The edges should meet on the joist centrelines, so you'll probably have to trim them slightly anyway.

When you buy gypsumboard make sure you get the tapered-edge variety, as it is much easier to produce 'invisible' joints with this. Store it on edge in a dry place until you need it.

Preparing the Joists

The first job is to nail lengths of 50mm (2in) sq or 75 × 50mm (3 × 2in) wood along the walls parallel with the joists so that its lower edge is level with the undersides of the joists. Then fit more short lengths of wood to the walls between the ends of the joists. These will provide support for the edges of the boards.

The sheets of gypsumboard must be fitted with their long edges at right-angles to the joists, so you should also toe-nail more lengths of batten to act as bracing between the joists so that the inner edges of the sheets will fall on their center lines. A length of batten marked with the board width will help position them accurately.

Finally, mark the position of each joist on the walls as a guide for nailing the sheets in place.

Trimming the Sheets

If you need to cut sheets to size, use a utility knife and wooden straightedge. Cut down through one face of the board, snap back the waste against a batten and run the knife blade down the

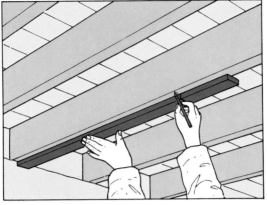
Marking the center line for the bracing on the joists using a batten marked with the width of a board as a guide.

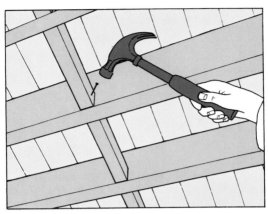
Toe-nailing the bracing in line between the joists; cut it to a tight fit and tap them in flush with the joists.

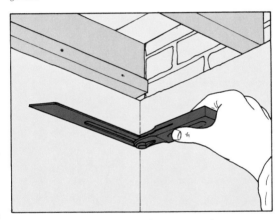
Using a sliding bevel to transfer the angle between walls to the gypsumboard; continue the line across with a straight-edge.

Propping the gypsumboard while nailing it; the edges of the board should be on the center lines of the joists and bracing.

crease from the other side.

It's unlikely that the walls of the room will meet squarely, but you can scribe the sheets to fit by setting a profile gauge in each corner and using this and a straight-edged batten to transfer the angle to the gypsumboard.

Fitting the Gypsumboard

Remember, if you intend plastering the ceiling, to fit the gypsumboard grey side downwards. If you intend just filling the joints and either painting or papering directly over the top, leave the ivory-coloured side showing.

Holding large sheets of gypsumboard against the ceiling for nailing can be difficult so, to make it easier for your helpers, nail lengths of 50 × 25mm (2 × 1in) batten together to form T-shaped props with which they can support the board while it is nailed in place.

Offer up the first board and nail it in place, working from the centre outwards and spacing the nails at 150mm (6in) intervals. Drive them home so that they just dimple the surface; the recess can be filled later.

Use 30mm (1¼in) gypsumboard nails for the thinner sheets and 40mm (1½in) for the thicker kind.

Continue in this way, working across the ceiling. Try to keep any cut edges up against the wall, but if this is not possible make sure they meet on a joist with a slight gap in between for filling. Stagger the joints, too.

When you have clad the entire ceiling, seal the joints between the sheets and, if you prefer, apply a thin skim coat of plaster (see opposite).

Alternative Ceilings

Of course, you don't have to install a gypsumboard ceiling; there are other possibilities.

In an old cottage property, you could leave the joists exposed and either leave the floorboards above visible or nail gypsumboard strips between the joists, finishing with a thin skim coat. The joists could then be painted or stained. If the boards were left exposed, however, you should seal the floor above with hardboard to prevent dust and dirt falling through.

You might consider installing a suspended ceiling. These normally have a steel or aluminum supporting grid, which is screwed to the wall at the edges of the ceiling and supported by brackets or wire hangers attached to the joists in the center. The grid can carry fiber tiles or even translucent plastic tiles with fluorescent lights behind to make an illuminated ceiling.

Another possibility is to clad the underside of the joists with tongued-and-grooved boarding and finish it with stain and varnish.

Finishing a gypsumboard ceiling with a coat of plaster is carried out in a similar manner to finishing off a drywall partition (see pages 23 to 25). However, the mere fact of having to work above your head presents difficulties of its own. It's best to apply small amounts of plaster at a time to avoid tiring your arm too much.

Deal with the joints first, spreading a thin layer of plaster down the center of each and pressing lengths of 50mm (2in) wide nylon mesh or paper tape into the wet plaster with your trowel blade. Trowel lightly over the tape then apply another thin layer of plaster over the top.

This will divide the ceiling into handy bays. Fill in each bay with a thin layer of plaster, but don't go over the taped joints. Hold the trowel blade at about 30° to the surface of the ceiling with the back edge about 2mm ($\frac{1}{16}$in) clear of the wallboard to provide an even layer. Reduce the blade angle as the plaster spreads and pinch the back edge in as you complete the stroke to stop the plaster falling off. Work away from you to avoid flicking plaster into your face.

When you have filled in all the bays, go over the entire ceiling with another thin layer of plaster. Rule it off with a long metal straightedge — the correct tool is called a 'darby' although a strip of aluminum threshold strip will do — to remove the worst of the high patches and show up the low spots which should be made good.

How you treat the angle between the ceiling and walls depends on whether you are replastering the walls at the same time or not. If not, simply run the corner of the trowel blade along the angle from the ceiling and wall sides to cut out the angle neatly. If you are replastering the wall as well, lay on the floating coat then tape the joint between wall and ceiling before applying the finish coats. Finish the corner as normal (see page 25).

Finally, polish the hardened plaster with a clean, wetted trowel blade.

Bedding jointing tape into wet plaster over the joint between two sheets; press it into one end of the joint with the trowel and feed it along.

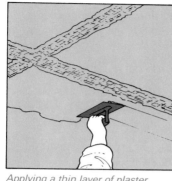

Applying a thin layer of plaster between the taped joints; hold the trowel at 30° to the surface, gradually reducing the angle.

Ruling off with a darby after applying a second layer of plaster over the entire area; work outwards from one of the wall angles.

Finishing off the angle between wall and ceiling with an internal angle trowel to leave a gently curved join.

Trick

FILLING THE JOINTS

If you intend papering or painting directly over the drywall, the joints must be made to 'disappear'. For this you will need drywall joint compound paper jointing tape and joint finish.

First spread a layer of compound down the seam and press the tape into it with a taping knife to bed it. Apply another layer of compound over the top, feathering the edges by going over them with a damp sponge.

When the compound has dried, apply a finishing layer, feathering its edges in the same way. Treat the nail head depressions with compound and finish in the same manner.

At the angles between wall and ceiling, fill large gaps with compound; then apply compound to both wall and ceiling and press a creased length of tape into it. Apply two more layers of compound to wall and ceiling, feathering the edges of each.

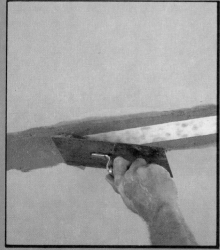

Bedding paper jointing tape into joint compound cover with more compound, feather the edges, after it dries apply another coat.

Applying a layer of joint finish compound over the folded paper jointing tape at the wall angle; joint finish compound is used at all stages.

Trick

ATTIC ACCESS

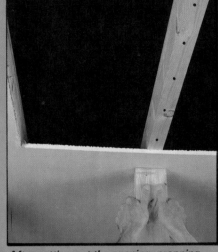

Cutting along a joist with a keyhole to form the opening; continue with a panel saw. Locate the joists with a bradawl.

After cutting out the opening, propping beneath the joist which is to be cut, using a strong length of wood.

Cutting through the joist, the thickness of the trimmer back from the opening; you will need a short panel saw for this job.

Nailing the trimmer joist to the end of the cut joist; nail through the outer joists into the ends of the trimmer.

Nailing the wood lining to the joists with oval nails; the bottom edge should be flush with the ceiling.

After fixing architrave round the opening, screwing the hinged trap-door to the lining.

Being able to get into the roof space of your home is important, not just because of the extra storage capacity it offers but also to be able to deal with emergencies like leaking roofs and burst pipes, and also to be able to install extra lighting fittings (see page 122).

Most houses already have some form of hatchway providing access to the attic but it may not always be in the most convenient place, and in some instances there may be no access to the attic at all. In both situations you can make a new opening with little trouble.

The usual position of an attic hatchway is in a hall or over a landing, but in the latter case make sure it is not over the staircase itself. Don't put it near an external wall either if this meets the eaves of the roof, as there wont't be enough headroom above the opening.

Another important consideration when positioning an opening is the space needed in the roof and in the room below for any attic ladder you intend fitting.

Having decided on the approximate position, locate the adjacent joists by tapping the ceiling and probing with a bradawl, or mark through from the loft if you can reach it by some other route.

Break through the ceiling between a pair of joists and open up the hole until you can make a saw cut alongside one of them. Then mark out the opening on the ceiling from this baseline. It's size will be determined by the joist spacing and since this will be too close to make the opening between a pair, it will have to span three. This means cutting through the centre joist and linking it to the joists on each side with short 'trimmer' joists. The wood used must be the same size as the original joists.

Before you cut through the intermediate joists, support the ceiling on each side of the opening with stout planks and wood or adjustable metal props (see page 32).

Line the opening with 25mm (1in) thick planed wood the same depth as the joists and nailed in place flush with the ceiling. The corners of this can be simply butted together.

Then make up a plywood trapdoor for the opening, hinging it to the bottom of the lining and either fitting a magnetic catch on the opposite side or an automatic catch such as that supplied with an attic ladder.

Finally, nail lengths of mitered molding round the opening, driving the nails into the joists so that the molding holds the edges of the ceiling firmly in place.

When you want to get into your attic there's no reason why you shouldn't use an ordinary ladder, provided it's secured to the opening in some way — by hooks and eyes perhaps, but whatever you do, never use a pair of step ladders. In trying to climb out of the attic and groping for the top of the steps with your foot, you could easily knock them over, leaving you stranded, or worse you might fall with the ladder.

One drawback of using a normal ladder is that you'll need somewhere to store it and you'll have to go to the trouble of digging it out of storage every time you want to get into the roof space. A much more satisfactory solution to the problem of climbing into your attic is the proprietary extendable attic ladder. This sits just above the trapdoor on hinges or pivots screwed to the inside or top of the opening frame and can be pulled down whenever you need it. Such a ladder makes your attic much more usable.

Types of Ladder

Purpose-made attic ladders are usually produced in aluminum with 50 or 75mm (2 or 3in) wide treads. Most have two or three sliding sections with a safety catch that must be released before they can be extended. Some are linked to the trapdoor by a special bracket so that they come immediately to hand when you open it up.

When closed, the ladder lies across the tops of the joists next to the trapdoor, but it swings upwards over the opening before it can be pulled down, so it is essential that there's enough height above the opening for this.

Another important factor is the size of the opening itself which must be large enough to allow the ladder to pass through. This is not usually a problem if you are making a new opening, but if you want to fit the ladder to an existing opening, you will have to take some careful measurements. You will also need to know the distance from the floor of the attic (not the ceiling) to the floor of the room below.

For really limited attic space, there's a concertina attic ladder that folds up compactly rather than sliding.

Attic ladders can be quite simple in design or complex with risers and balustrades just like a proper staircase, and most come with some form of automatic trapdoor catch operated by light pressure on the door itself.

Installing an Attic Ladder

Obviously, the method of installing an attic ladder varies from one make and model to another, but usually it is quite a simple procedure. Often all that is necessary is to screw the hinges or pivots to the framework of the opening (on the same side as the trapdoor hinges) and fit the automatic catch to the other side of the opening. There may also be travel stops to adjust on the ladder and a bracket to fit to the trapdoor to hold the ladder so that it is easily reached.

Springs and levers on this attic ladder push it forwards as it is lowered and counteract the weight for ease of operation.

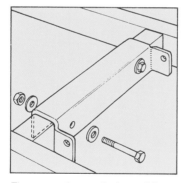

The supporting cradle for a sliding attic ladder hooks over the trimmer joist at the hinge end of the access door and is screwed in place.

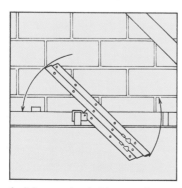

A sliding section ladder must have sufficient clearance below the roof rafters to swing up into the raising and lowering position.

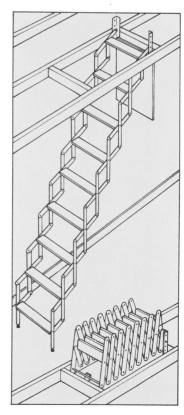

A concertina attic ladder in the extended and stowed positions.

A sliding section attic ladder in the raised and lowered positions.

ROOF TYPES

They break down into two basic types: flat and pitched (sloping). In the main flat roofs (which still slope a little so that rainwater will run off) are restricted to small extensions and garages. It is unusual for a flat roof to be used on a house; the pitched roof is the norm.

Flat Roofs

A typical flat roof will have wooden joists spaced at 400–450mm (16–18in) intervals supported by the walls at each end of the extension. Narrow wedge-shaped slats of wood called 'firrings' are nailed to the top of the joists to produce a 'fall' towards the gutter.

The joists are clad with square-edge or tongued-and-grooved boarding or possibly exterior grade plywood or particle board (sometimes with roofing felt bonded on). Triangular battens are nailed along each edge to stop water running off at the sides and the exposed edges of the roof are protected by wide fascia boards. A wooden batten is nailed along the top of each board as a drip rail.

The entire roof is covered with three layers of bituminous roofing felt, the first nailed in place and the others bonded on with bitumen adhesive. Where the roof meets a wall, a seal is made by laying a strip of felt up against it and setting its top edge into one of the mortar joints. Final protection is provided by scattering chippings over the top to reflect heat.

Pitched Roofs

Pitched roofs come in three basic styles: mono-pitched, duo-pitched and hipped. The mono-pitched roof has a single sloping side and is usually only found on lean-to extensions, sheds and garages. A duo-pitched roof has two sloping sides joined along the top, the open ends being filled in with a wall called a gable end. This is probably the most common form of roof. If the end of the roof is also sloping it is termed hipped.

Sometimes the shape of the building will make two sections of roof necessary, the two meeting at right angles. In this case, the junction between the two roofs is called a valley.

The pitched roof structure comprises angled supporting members called rafters attached to a ridge board or bar at the top and resting on wallplates along the tops of the walls at the bottom. Sometimes the rafters are notched over the wallplates, at others they rest on top.

This type of construction can impose considerable loads on the side walls, tending to push them outwards, so it's common to link the rafters with horizontal joists which may also support a attic floor and ceiling below.

The length of the roof and its span also present other problems such as sagging rafters or joists, so extra bracing is sometimes added to support these. It may take the form of simple timbers laid across both at right angles or the installation of intermediate load-bearing walls and complex structures of wooden beams running horizontally, vertically and diagonally through the roof space.

Generally the ends of the rafters overlap the side walls and it is usual to fit fascia boards to cover them and sometimes horizontal boards — soffits — along the gap underneath. At a gable end, the edge of the roof is sealed with bargeboards.

The supporting structure of the roof is normally covered with roofing felt nailed to the rafters. Then narrow battens are nailed across this at right angles to the rafters. These support the roof cladding which may be of slate, concrete or clay tiles, or for light structures corrugated materials like steel, asbestos or plastic. Rectangular cedar shingles or even felt tiles may be used.

Slates, tiles and shingles are all nailed to the battens in an overlapping pattern with staggered joints to keep out the water. Tiles get extra support from projections along their top edges called nibs, which hook over the battens.

Corrugated materials may be held by long screws with special cupped heads that fit against the curves of the sheets or hook bolts which fit under the supporting framework. With this material there would be no felt underlayer.

Felt tiles come in strips for nailing in an overlapping pattern.

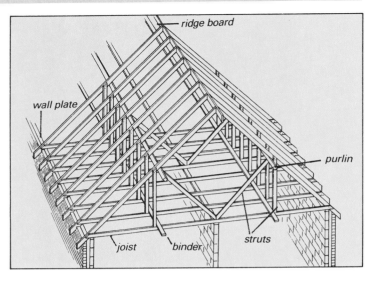

One form of traditional duo-pitch roof structure. The short, vertical hangers may be absent and the tops of the angled struts may be joined by horizontal collars.

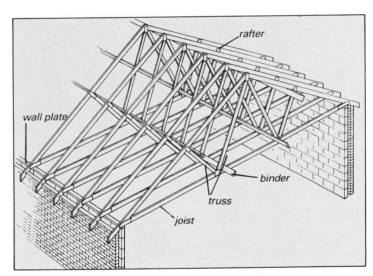

Modern trussed-rafter construction. No structural horizontal members are present; the trusses and rafters are joined by metal fasteners and braced upright by horizontal planks.

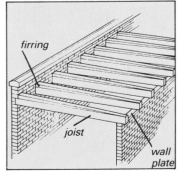

Flat roof: the horizontal joists are supported at both ends by load-bearing walls and tapered furrings on top provide a drainage slope.

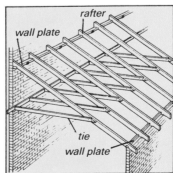

Mono-pitch roof: depending on the span, the rafters may be tied halfway up to the inner wall to give extra rigidity.

Trick

ACCESS TO THE ROOF

Because roofs are so far from the ground you must make sure you have both a safe means of reaching the roof and a safe working platform once you get there. You can reach the roof by a normal extending ladder, but you must take steps to prevent it toppling over. Always set the feet so that they're about a quarter of the ladder's length away from the wall against which it is leaning. On concrete you can prevent the feet slipping by standing them on a piece of sacking. On soft ground, set them on a board with a batten nailed on the edge as a stop. Drive stakes into the ground to stop the board moving. You can also tie the feet of the ladder to stakes driven into the ground.

Tie the top of the ladder to a screw-eye fixed to the fascia board or even to a batten spanning the inside of a window opening, and make sure it extends beyond the eaves by at least 1m (3ft). Don't rest it on the guttering, which could break under the weight; rent a ladder stay to hold it away from the gutter, propped against the wall below the fascia.

If the work you are doing means carrying up bulky materials, you'd be better off renting a scaffold tower which will provide a platform at roof level for stacking materials. These are sectional in construction and often have wheels at the bottom for manoeuvring them into position.

If you use a scaffold tower always make sure it is set on firm ground (with boards under the feet if necessary), level, that any wheels are locked up and that it is fitted with outriggers or tied to the building to stop it toppling. Construct a platform at the top from stout boards, making sure there are toe boards round the edges and a handrail. Always climb up inside the tower and not on the outside, and don't lean ladders against it.

Traversing the Roof

Roof tiles and slates are easily broken, so you must have some means of spreading your weight as you climb across them. The best way is with a roof or 'cat' ladder. This has a large hook, which locates over the ridge of the roof, and usually a pair of small wheels. The wheels allow you to run the ladder up the roof before turning it over to engage the hook over the ridge of the roof.

While you can do many jobs working from a roof ladder, for any major work on a chimney, it's better to build a scaffold tower round it, supporting the feet on boards to spread the weight.

Tying the bottom of a ladder to pegs driven into the ground; rest the base on a thick board with a batten nailed to it.

Using a ladder stay to support the top of the ladder away from the guttering; it is tied to a batten inside the window.

Locking the wheels of a scaffold tower by depressing the handle; the wheels must rest on strong level boards.

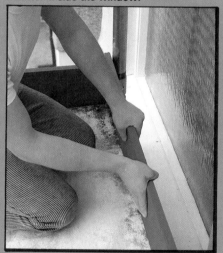

At the top of the scaffold tower, slotting in the toe-board round the boarded platform.

Pushing a roof-ladder up to the ridge on the wheels attached to it; the wheels prevent damage to the roof covering.

When the end of the roof-ladder is over the ridge, turning it over to hook on the ridge, leaving the rungs uppermost.

REPLACING A SLATE

Sliding the clawed end of a slate-ripper under a damaged slate; hook the blade round the fixing nails and pull to cut them.

After removing the damaged slate; nailing a strip of lead to the exposed batten with a galvanised clout nail.

After sliding a new slate into the gap, bending up the strip of lead over the bottom edge to hold the slate in position.

One of the problems with slate is that it is very brittle and deteriorates with age, the surface flaking (called 'delamination') and becoming powdery or cracked as a result of weather damage. Slates are much lighter than concrete tiles and can often be lifted by a high gust of wind.

Loose or missing slates may also be the result of 'nail sickness', whereby the nails corrode and break.

You can buy new slates from a building material supply house or lumber yard, but it's cheaper to pick up used slates from demolition sites. Provided you inspect them carefully for signs of damage to the surface edges or nail holes there's no reason why they should not be used. You must make sure they are the same thickness as the ones being replaced and, for aesthetic reasons as close a colour match as possible. It doesn't matter if you can't get the right size, just get the next size up, as cutting them down is quite easy. In general, the sizes available range from 225 × 150mm (9 × 6in) to 610 × 355mm (24 × 14in).

To remove the old broken slate you'll need a tool called a slate ripper, and unless you intend doing a lot of roofing, it's best to rent one of these rather than buy it. The ripper has a thin, barbed blade for cutting through the slate fixing nails, which are hidden by the slates above.

Slide the ripper up under the broken slate, feeling for the fixing nails. Hook the blade over one and tug downwards sharply to slice through it (you may have to strike the ripper's handle with a light sledge hammer). Then repeat for the second nail. The slate may be nailed along its top edge (head nailed) or at the center (center nailed). Slide out the old slate.

Fitting the New Slate

If you have to cut the slate to size, scribe the size on its face and set it over the edge of a wooden batten. Then chop along the line with the heel of a trowel. After cutting along half of the line, turn it round and finish the cut from the other end.

You won't be able to nail the new slate in place because of the slates above. Instead, it's retained by a lead strip measuring 225 × 25mm (9 × 1 in). Nail this to the batten visible below the two exposed slates with a galvanized nail.

Carefully lift the slates above and slide the new one into place so that the bevelled edge along the bottom is uppermost. Bend up the end of the lead strip to retain it then make a second bend for extra strength.

If the slate is at the gable end of the roof you'll also need a horizontal clip to stop it sliding off the edge.

Trick

CLIP FROM INSIDE

Using a lead strip to retain a single slate has its drawbacks: it may be bent open by a heavy load of snow and, of course, it's clearly visible. To overcome both problems you can use a special concealed clip. Two are fitted to each slate to be fixed, but they can only be used where the slates are nailed to battens fixed across the rafters.

The clips incorporate toggles which drop down over the batten to provide a secure, invisible fixing.

To fix the clips to the slate, first drill holes through it at the centre for the clip retaining tags. Push the tag through the hole and bend the clip round the edge of the slate until a hole in its end fits over the protruding tag at the back of the slate. Bending the tag over secures the clip.

To secure the slate, simply slide it under the ones above until the toggles drop over the batten.

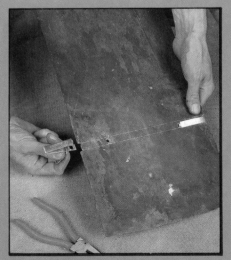

After drilling, and notching the edges of the slate, sliding the proprietary clip on to the slate.

From inside the roof, sliding the slate back into position so that the toggles on the clips hook over the battens.

If several slates are damaged in a relatively small area, it may be worthwhile reslating that area rather than trying to replace slates individually. With care, you may then be able to use some of the existing slates again.

Slates are fixed to the roof in rows, or courses, each course overlapping the one below by at least half a slate length and sometimes by more. In addition, the joins between slates in adjacent courses are staggered: in this way the joins are always covered by the slates above or below to ensure a water-tight construction.

Where the roof has a gable end, wider than normal slates are fitted to the ends of alternate courses to produce a square edge to the roof (these are known as 'slate-and-a-half' slates). In addition, the edge slates at a gable end may be bedded on mortar laid on stacks of narrow slate strips known as creasing slates. These tilt the edges of the slates upwards so that rainwater runs down the roof to the gutters and not off the edge.

To ensure a water seal at the eaves, a course of shorter than normal slates is laid first then covered completely by the next course, which overlap the slate joints.

When you fit the new area of slates, you must copy the original overlapping/staggered joint pattern exactly otherwise you will have problems later.

Preparing the Slates

Buy sufficient slates to do the job with a few extras in case of breakages. In addition to cutting them to size as described opposite, you will also have to make nail holes in them, and you must reproduce the hole positions as well — either along the top edge of the slate or at sides in the centre. Make sure the nail hole positions are no closer to the edge than 25mm (1 in) however. You can often use an old slate as a template for marking the hole positions.

You can make the nail holes either by drilling them or by simply driving a nail through while supporting the slate on a block of wood. For safety and ease of working, do all the cutting and drilling on the ground and carry the finished slates up to the roof. You will need 30mm (1¼in) copper, zinc or aluminium roofing nails to hold the slates in place.

Preparing the Roof

Remove the old slates from the roof using the slate ripper as before and starting with the upper courses of the area to be renewed. You will find that as you remove these upper slates, you will expose the heads of the nails holding the slates below. Cut these off with a pair of pincers rather than using the ripper (or withdraw using the claw of a slater's hammer).

Collect the slates and lower them to the ground with a bucket and rope, taking particular care with whole, undamaged ones, since you'll be able to refit them. A bucket can also be used to carry the new slates to the roof.

Having stripped off the old slates, inspect the battens below and if any are broken or rotten cut them out with a saw. Make the cuts over the centre lines of the supporting rafters and angle them outwards. By cutting the ends of the new sections to match, the old battens will provide a certain amount of support to the new sections, helping to bear the load of the slates attached to them.

Make sure the new battens are the same size as the old, treat them with preservative and nail them in place.

Fitting the New Slates

Begin fitting the new slates, starting at the lowest course and nailing them to the battens to recreate the overlapping pattern of the rest of the roof. Use two nails per slate and make sure it is fitted with the bevelled lower edge uppermost to aid drainage.

Work your way up the roof, nailing the slates in place until the surrounding original slates make this impossible. Then fit the other slates with lead clips or toggle clips (see opposite) to complete the repair.

Starting above the eaves, nailing the first row of short slates to the battens using two nails per slate (one for the first slate).

Sliding a full slate in the next course under the slate above; make sure the tapered lower edge of the slate is uppermost to aid drainage.

At the top of the repair, where it is not possible to nail the slates, using strips of lead (or toggle clips) to secure them.

At the verges of the roof, two lead strips are needed, one vertical, and one horizontal to prevent the slate from slipping sideways.

OPTIONS

Where you have to replace an area of slates it's useful to rent the correct tools as used by slaters:
• Slate ripper (A) is invaluable for slicing through the nails securing the slates.
• Slater's hammer (B), with a flat head at one end and a pointed end opposite; use the former for knocking new nails; the latter for punching new nail holes in the slates.
• Chopping iron (C) or stake, which has a spike for temporarily fixing it to the roof surface while you rest the slate on top and hole it with the slater's hammer.
• Slate cutters (D) like a large pair of scissors; simply mark the slate for cutting then snip along the line.

REPLACING A TILE

Despite the fact that tiles appear much more substantial and are certainly heavier than slates, they're almost as brittle and can suffer from the effects of severe weather conditions in the same way, becoming cracked, broken or even coming away from the roof completely. So it is just as important to check a tiled roof regularly as it is a slated one.

Types of Tile

Traditionally, tiles were made of clay but this material has been largely superseded by concrete, which is cheaper and more durable. A wide range of shapes and finishes is available, so when replacing one or more tiles it's essential that you get the right type and finish if the repair is to blend in with the rest of the roof.

Tiles may be plain or interlocking (see below), the former being basically flat and the latter usually ridged. Most have a very slight curve formed in them to make sure they bed firmly on the tiles below them. Sometimes tiles are curved across their width as well as their length.

Most tiles have two or three lugs formed along their top edge — called nibs — which fit over the tile battens to hold them in place. In addition, holes are usually provided for nails, and it's common to nail the third or fourth course of tiles to the battens to provide extra strength

to the roof structure. Otherwise, the weight of the tiles above will hold each in place.

You can also obtain special shaped tiles such as the pantile, which has an S-shaped profile. These may be plain or interlocking and are usually nailed in place.

Laying Tiles

Plain tiles are laid in much the same way as slates in an overlapping pattern, the tiles of one course overlapping the ones below by at least half a tile's length and sometimes more. The joints in adjacent courses are staggered to ensure a good water seal.

Extra-wide tiles are available for finishing alternate courses at gable ends, and shorter than normal tiles for making up an eaves course and also for fitting below the course immediately below the ridge.

Interlocking tiles only need shallow overlaps because of their design, but special sizes are still available for finishing off at the eaves and gable ends.

Replacing a Tile

Because the tile you want to replace will be hooked over the batten, you need some means of lifting the adjacent tiles sufficiently to be able to lift the broken one from the batten. The best method is with wooden wedges which you can cut from lengths of 50 × 25mm (2 × 1in)

Raising the tiles above a broken one by sliding wooden wedges under the bottom edges; an adjacent tile must also be raised if interlocking.

Prising out the remains of the broken tile using the point of a bricklayers' trowel to lift the nibs over the batten.

If the tile was nailed to the batten, cutting through the fixing nails with a hacksaw blade held in a padsaw handle.

Sliding the replacement tile into position; use the trowel blade again to lift the nibs over the batten. No nailing is necessary.

batten, making them about 150mm (6in) long. You will need at least two of these and possibly more if the tiles are of the interlocking type.

Push the wedges beneath the tiles of the course above the broken one so there is a big enough gap for the nibs to clear the batten. Lift the tile up and

remove it. If you can't get hold of it because the end has broken off, slide the blade of a bricklayer's trowel underneath the remaining portion and use this to lift it clear.

If you can't lift it away because it is nailed in place, try wiggling it from side to side, which may pull the nails free. If this doesn't work, you will have to cut through the nails with a slate ripper (see pages 56–57), a pair of pincers or a hacksaw blade, whichever is easiest.

If the tile is of the interlocking type, you will have to wedge up one of its neighbours as well to free it completely.

You can fit the replacement tile by lifting it into place with the trowel blade, hooking the nibs over the batten. Even if the original was nailed in place, there's no need to worry about the replacement since the tiles above will hold it down.

Finally, remove the wedges carefully to lower the surrounding tiles, making sure any interlocking ridges are properly engaged and that all the tiles are sitting flat.

INTERLOCKING TILES

Modern concrete interlocking tiles come in a variety of styles and finishes.

They have interlocking ridges along the sides and often the top as well. These ridges provide a watertight seal between tiles and do away with the need for such large overlaps.

Mostly they have nibs and nail holes for fixing, but some are held by special clips nailed to the top edge of the tiling battens.

If several tiles are damaged over a relatively small area of the roof, it's probably just as easy to re-tile that area than attempt to replace tiles individually. Buy enough tiles to do the job with a few spares in case you break any. It is always useful to have a few spare tiles to hand to make odd repairs, as you may not always be able to buy matching tiles for your roof when you want them.

Always stack the tiles out of the way, since they are easily broken and always carry them on edge rather than flat on top of each other — that way they are less likely to break under the weight.

As with renewing an area of slates, you must recreate the original overlapping pattern of the tiles to ensure that the roof retains its strength and also is waterproof. In some instances, you may not be able to obtain tiles of a direct colour match to the ones on your roof, particularly if they are very weathered. In this case, if the repair is in a conspicuous position, you can fix it using tiles from another part of the roof where fitting the new ones will go unnoticed.

Unlike slates, you can't cut tiles to size, so you must make sure you get the right number of special tiles for finishing off courses at gable ends and for making up the eaves course. You will also need a supply of 30mm (1 ¼in) copper, zinc or aluminium roofing nails for fixing the tiles to the battens. If the tiles are of the interlocking type held to the battens by clips and nails, you must buy sufficient clips as well.

Wooden wedges, as described opposite, will be needed for lifting the tiles surrounding the repair so that the old tiles can be lifted from underneath them and the new ones hooked in place.

Removing the Old Tiles

Begin at the top of the damaged area, working downwards and removing tiles as described opposite. Once you have removed a few from the upper courses, you will expose those below so that you can simply lift them off. If they are nailed down, cut off the nail heads with pincers. Continue until you have removed all the tiles.

Removing damaged tiles, again using wedges to lift the tiles above; save any whole tiles which have to be removed for access to re-use later.

Brushing debris from the remaining tiles and any exposed roofing felt and battens; check the battens for signs of rot.

Replacing the tiles, working from the bottom of the damaged area upwards; nail every fourth course as an extra security measure.

The tiles will be heavy and brittle, so handle them with care and lower them to the ground with a bucket and rope. There are bound to be perfectly good tiles among the damaged, so keep these separate and handle them carefully so you can refit them.

Preparing the Roof

Once the tiles have been removed you can inspect the roof structure below. This will comprise the tile battens and in most cases below them a layer of roofing felt. Brush off any dirt and dust and pull any remaining nails from the battens with pincers or a claw hammer.

Fitting the New Tiles

Begin fitting the new tiles along the bottom of the repair area, working your way up the roof. Hook the nibs of the tiles over the battens and nail every third or fourth course down for extra security.

As you work, use the wooden wedges to lift the surrounding tiles so that those below can be lifted into place. Make sure any interlocking types are properly linked together and if these are normally held to the battens with clips and nails make sure you fit these to every course.

Continue until you come to the last tile, fitting it in the same way as described opposite. If retaining clips are used on the tiles you won't be able to fit a clip to the last tile, but the weight of its neighbours will hold it down.

If the repair involves replacing tiles along a gable end, you will find that there are gaps between the overlapping tiles at the edges of the roof. These should be pointed with mortar. First coat the edges of the tiles with a bonding agent and then mix some more into the mortar before you use it.

Trick

REPAIRING BATTENS

Examine the tile battens for signs of damage or rot, cutting out any affected sections and fitting new ones. If the roof has a layer of felt under the battens, this must be protected while they are cut. To do this, prise the nails holding the battens to the rafters free with pincers and slide a piece of hardboard below the batten. Make the cuts above the rafter centre lines and at an angle so they will support the ends of the new piece which should be cut to match.

Cut a new piece of batten of the same size and nail it in place after treating it with pre-

servative.

Also inspect the felt layer for tears or holes. If you find any, they must be patched before replacing the tiles, and if necessary you must remove sections of battens as described above to do the job.

To patch damaged roofing felt, cut out the damaged portion to make a regular shaped hole. Then cut a patch of new felt about 50mm (2in) larger all round than the opening. Stick this in place with bitumen adhesive.

RIDGES, EAVES, VERGES, VALLEYS, HIPS

Ridge Tiles

At the apex of the roof, the tiles on each side are sealed by a row of half-round or angled ridge tiles. These span the upper courses on each side and are bedded on mortar.

Replacement is carried out by chiselling out the old mortar and levering the old tile off. Then a new one is fitted on a fresh bed of mortar. Slate roofs are treated in the same way although sometimes they may have lead sheet wrapped over the ridge bar instead.

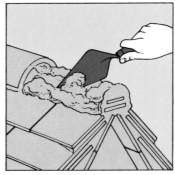

Chiselling out the old mortar from beneath a damaged ridge tile using a light sledge and masons chisel; work carefully to avoid damage to tiles.

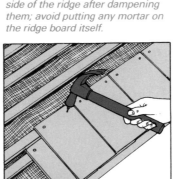

Applying mortar to the tiles each side of the ridge after dampening them; avoid putting any mortar on the ridge board itself.

Bedding the new ridge tile into the mortar after soaking the edges in water; butt it up to the adjoining tile and check that it is level.

Fixing the eaves-tile batten just below the lowest full-tile batten by nailing into the rafters (in line with the nails above).

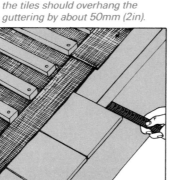

Nailing the eaves tiles to the batten using two rustproof nails per tile; the tiles should overhang the guttering by about 50mm (2in).

Nailing the first course of full tiles in position; the lower edges should be flush with those below and the joints staggered.

Eaves Tiles

Water is prevented from running through the joints between tiles or slates because just over half of each joint is overlapped above and below by the tiles in the neighbouring courses.

To ensure this overlapping pattern continues at the eaves, a course of shorter tiles or slates is nailed in place so that their ends are flush with the course immediately above, but their joints are staggered by half a tile's width.

Gable Tiles

The staggered joints of alternate courses of tiles or slates means that when a gable end is reached there would be a toothed pattern to the edge of the roof. To avoid this, special extra-wide tiles and slates are made which are one-and-a-half times the normal width, allowing a square edge to be produced.

As an alternative, it's sometimes possible to buy half-width tiles which do the same job.

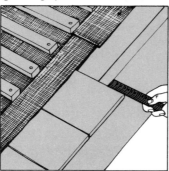

Measuring the projection of the gable-end tiles; bed the undercloak tiles face down in mortar and tuck the inner edges under the felt.

Setting the end tiles in to mortar on the undercloak; use alternate full-width and width-and-a-half tiles to give a level edge.

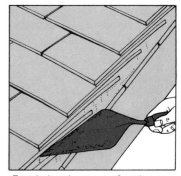

Repointing the verge after the mortar has hardened; a pigment added to the mortar will make the pointing less obtrusive.

Checking the size of a cut tile adjoining the valley; this must allow the valley tile to be firmly bedded down beside it.

Working from the bottom of the valley upwards, aligning the bottoms of the valley tiles with the adjacent cut tiles.

Bedding the first hip tile into mortar; this will have to be shaped to prevent it overhanding and is supported by a hip-iron.

Valley and Hip Tiles

Where two roofs meet there must be some means of joining the courses of tiles to ensure a watertight seal. Rather than trying to run the courses into each other, it is usual to form a gutter along the angle of the join which will carry water away. This may be formed from zinc sheet, but an alternative is to use valley tiles which are nailed to the roof members and often interlock with the adjoining courses.

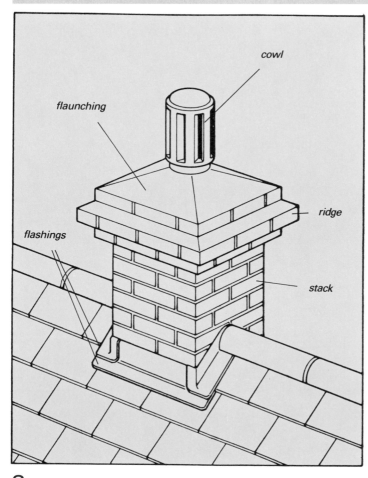

Labels: cowl, flaunching, ridge, flashings, stack

A Chimney's Weak Points

A common problem with chimneys is a defective seal with the roof, allowing water to run inside. Mortar and tile fillets can crack and crumble; flashings can tear or pull out of their mortar joints. The mortar joints of the brickwork can become eroded and if the chimney is rendered the mortar covering may crack, crumble or be forced outwards from the masonry.

At the top, the flaunching may become cracked, letting water in, or even begin to break up if the frost gets in. Pots, too, may become dislodged or broken.

Making Repairs

Very often minor cracking in mortar fillets or flaunching can be sealed with roofing cement, and flashings that have come away from their joints can be mortared back in place. Tears in flashings can be dealt with using a self-adhesive flashing material.

Crumbling mortar can usually be raked out and the joints repointed; mortar fillets round the base of a chimney can also be remade. Patches of bad render can also be hacked off and renewed.

If the flaunching is in a bad way, or the pot needs renewing, first tie the pot to the chimney with a rope in case it should fall as you work. Sometimes they are of smaller diameter than the flue and may actually fall down it. Hack off the old flaunching collecting the pieces in a bucket for lowering to the ground.

If the pot is smaller than the flue, it must be supported on pieces of slate laid round the top of the chimney. Then trowel on a one part cement: four parts sand mix to make the new flaunching. Make sure it has a good 'fall' from the center to the edges so that water will run off. You can always build up the center with bits of brick.

If the chimney is no longer in use, it's a good idea to seal its top. To do this, remove the pots and old flaunching, replacing two of the bricks in the top course with airbricks. Then trowel mortar on top and set a paving slab over the opening. Finally, add more mortar to form flaunching on top.

Set high up on the roof, exposed to the elements, the chimney can suffer a considerable amount of damage over the years, weakening it and often allowing the rain to enter to cause further damage to the structure of the roof and rooms below. You should regularly check your chimney for signs of damage — damp patches on the ceilings and chimney breasts of upstairs rooms are a good clue that something is amiss, and if you are unable to get on to the roof itself to have a look, you can always check it over from below with a pair of binoculars.

A chimney is a shaft which runs up through the house to take away the combustion gases from heating appliances. It is usually built from brick or stone and has a lining of mortar, clay pipes or sometimes metal to prevent the corrosive gases eating into the masonry (older chimneys have just bare brick insides). The chimney breast is part of that shaft.

The chimney may run up the gable wall of a house or pass through the middle and out through the roof — either at the ridge or one of the sides. A watertight seal is made at the junction with the roof in one of three ways: by laying a triangular fillet of mortar round the base of the chimney; by laying small tiles up against the base; or by mortaring zinc or lead sealing strips known as flashings into the joints of the brickwork. Flashings are by far the most efficient type of seal and are often assisted by further strips of metal, called soakers, below the tiles.

The chimney above the roof may be exposed brickwork or may be rendered with mortar. The upper courses of bricks are usually arranged to produce an overhang so that rainwater running off the top is thrown clear of the sides.

On top of the chimney will be an earthenware pot set in a sloping bed of mortar called flaunching. The flaunching slopes so that rainwater will run off it. The pot may also have a metal or earthenware cowl or cap to prevent water running down inside.

To remove damaged chimney pots chip away the cement flaunching with a bolster and club hammer; tie the pot securely to the stack.

Reduce chimney opening with strips of slate laid across the top of the brickwork to support a pot of smaller diameter than the original.

Trowel on new flaunching cement after thoroughly wetting brickwork and base of the pot; slope downwards towards edges.

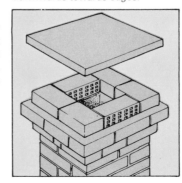

Capping off a disused chimney stack; replace two of the bricks in top course by airbricks. Cover with a paving slab bedded in mortar.

REPAIRING A FLAT ROOF

The felt covering of a flat roof is easily damaged and may become cracked, split or blistered, or joints may lift to let water through to the ceiling below. Fortunately, repairs are easily carried out, even if this means refelting the roof entirely.

Repairing Cracks and Blisters

A common problem with a flat felted roof is blistering where a pocket of air forms beneath the felt and under the heat from the sun will eventually stretch and split the covering.

To repair a blister, first make an X-shaped cut across it with a sharp knife. Fold back the sections of felt and let the area below dry out for a while. Then spread bitumen roofing cement over the area and press the felt back down. Spread more roofing cement over the top and reinforce the repair by setting a piece of glass fiber mat in the mastic followed by another layer.

Cracks in the felt can be treated in the same way, and any small holes can be patched with felt and roofing cement. However, if the damage is widespread, it is better to refelt the roof completely.

Refelting a Flat Roof

Begin a stripping off the old felt with a strong scraper or even a spade. When felt flashing is laid up against a house wall, chisel out the mortar joint and pull it free. Clean up the wood below, driving down any protruding nail heads and replacing any rotten wood.

Cut the felt to length a day or so before you do the job and lay it out flat so that it loses its tendency to curl up. You will need enough underfelt for two layers and enough coarse-grit felt for a final layer or 'capsheet'.

Lay the strips of new felt parallel to the fall of the roof, nailing the first layer to the roof with 19mm (¾in) extra-large-head galvanized nails spaced 150mm (6in) apart. Take the first layer up over the drip rails and nail it to their sides. Where strips have to be joined, make sure they overlap each other by at least 50mm (2in) and seal the joint with a layer of bitumen

cement.

Lay the second layer in the same way, but bond it to the first with cement only, making sure the seams between strips are staggered in relation to those below. You can spread the cement with an old broom, rolling up the strips and pressing down half at a time with a rounded batten.

Before applying the final layer, cut a strip of felt and nail one edge along the drip rail at the end of the roof. Fold this back on to the roof and fix it with cement. Fit the capsheet, sticking it down with cement so that it overlaps this strip. Then cut more strips and nail them to the side drip rails, folding them back over the capsheet.

To seal the roof to the end wall, cut another strip of felt and mortar its top edge in the chased out joint between the bricks. Stick the felt to the wall and over the capsheet with roofing cement.

The final job is to spread roofing cement over the entire roof and spinkle on a layer of 13mm (½in) chippings.

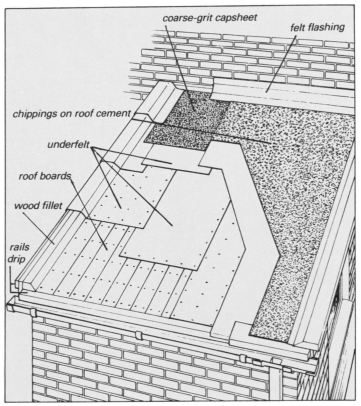

Covering layers of a flat roof. Overlapping strips of felt are laid parallel to the fall to the gutter and drip battens prevent drainage off the edges; the first nailed felt layer is covered by two layers held by roofing cement and topped with chippings. A felt strip seals it to the wall.

Nailing down the first strip of underfelt using a batten to flatten the felt and start the nails; nail at 150mm (6in) intervals.

After spreading cement along the 50mm (2in) overlap, nailing down the second strip along the join; press it down into the cement.

Coating the completed first layer with cement; bond the first strip of the second layer to it so that it overlaps the drip batten.

Smoothing down the second layer of underfelt using a length of thick dowel or an old rolling-pin to remove any air bubbles.

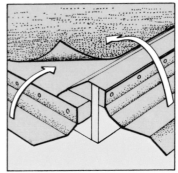

To protect the eaves and verges, welted aprons are tacked to the edges and folded over the second underfelt and capsheet respectively.

Using a trowel to spread the layer of gravel chippings over the felt capsheet after coating it with bitumen cement.

Wherever a roof — either pitched or flat — meets a wall, or a chimney, or something like a roof window, there is the problem of making a really watertight joint. This is done by sealing it with a flashing.

Flashings may be triangular fillets of mortar, small tiles set in mortar, or zinc, lead or roofing felt strips set in the mortar joints of the brickwork and overlapping the roof. Although lead and zinc flashings are the most efficient, all types can suffer the effects of time and weather, cracking, corroding or breaking up to let water in — and this can have serious consequences if not attended to immediately.

In most cases repairs can be made fairly easily, particularly if a self-adhesive flashing material is used. This is an aluminium foil, coloured grey to give the appearance of lead, with a very strong, waterproof bitumen adhesive on the back. It can be used to cover old cracked mortar and tile flashings, repair tears or splits in metal flashings or even replace them completely. And it is useful for sealing the felt of a flat roof to the end wall.

Raking out the defective mortar joint with a chisel before replacing the flashing; brush out any loose debris and coat with PVA.

If mortar or tile and mortar flashing is crumbling, hack away all the loose material with a cold chisel, paint the area with a bonding agent and trowel in fresh mortar to make good the triangular shape, resetting any tiles as necessary.

Sometimes metal flashings will spring from their mortar joints and in a case like this it is a simple matter to chase out the joint with a cold chisel, roll up some strips of lead to make wedges and jam the edge of the flashing back in place. Then repoint with fresh mortar.

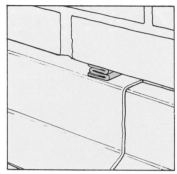

Use folded strips of lead to wedge back the flashing; tap in just far enough to prevent it from springing out, as they will be removed later.

Repointing along the joint with new mortar; bevel it outwards at the bottom, and, when hardened, remove the wedges and point the gaps.

Degreasing a torn metal flashing with steel wool (use a damp cloth in the case of felt) before applying flashing-strip primer.

Pressing on a cut patch of self-adhesive flashing strip when the primer has dried; an old wallpaper edge-roller ensures a good seal.

Trick

USING SELF-ADHESIVE FLASHING

If a metal flashing is badly corroded, fitting a new one from lead or zinc can be quite a difficult job because of the complex shape of the flashing. It is better to remove it by chiselling out the mortar joints and fit self-adhesive flashing instead. You can use the material to give added protection to a repaired mortar flashing too.

Soakers

Sometimes metal flashings have extra pieces which run under the tiles. These are called 'soakers' and should be left in place for added protection.

Bitumen Primer

The flashing is applied in conjunction

with a bitumen primer which should be painted along both sides of the joint and allowed to dry. Cut strips of flashing to fit, peel off the backing paper and press them gently into place with your fingers, trying not to crease the material too much otherwise you may not get a watertight seal. A really good seal can be achieved by pressing the flashing flat with a wallpaper seam roller.

If overlaps are necessary always make sure the upper strip overlaps the one below by at least 50mm (2in) to prevent water seeping in.

If you are replacing the flashing round a chimney, treat the lower joint first, trimming the ends with a knife to fit round the corners of the brickwork. Then do the sides and finally lay a piece along the upper joint.

INSTALLING A ROOF WINDOW

A roof window is a relatively cheap and straightforward way of admitting natural light to an attic room with very little structural work.

In many houses the attic is unused space and even if use is made of it, often that is only for storing possessions not in daily use. But frequently the attic can be the answer to many families' needs for extra living space, providing one or more rooms at a lower cost than that of selling and moving to a larger house.

An important step in making an attic really usable is to admit natural light by installing windows in the roof. These can take the form of pivotting windows flush with the roof surface, or much more elaborate (and more expensive) dormer windows which stand vertically and have their own small roofs and cheek pieces (see pages 66 to 68).

Pivotting roof windows are straightforward to install (the job should take about a day) and convenient, too. Their opening panes are hinged in the centre so they can be reversed completely to allow cleaning from inside the attic. Various wooden and aluminum-framed versions are available in sizes ranging from 700 × 550mm (28 × 22in) to 1400 × 1340mm (55 × 53in), and if larger areas are required there's no reason why they should not be fitted side by side or one above the other.

When choosing the size of a roof window, bear in mind that your local Building Code may specify that the total window area must be a certain percentage of the floor area. The actual figure varies according to your location, always consult your local code before beginning any job. Obviously, a job of this kind will form part of an attic conversion and as such is subject to approval by your local building department.

Roof windows are normally double glazed as standard and you can usually specify special types of glass, too. These include wired or toughened, opaque and anti-sun. It is usually possible to fit them with cord-operated blinds as well since they do not lend themselves to conventional curtains.

Positioning the Window

Ideally the window should be positioned so that you can reach its top-mounted catch easily (some may be cord-operated, however) and be able to see out of it when sitting. However, the roof structure may impose certain limitations on this.

Unless the window is very narrow, you will have to cut through at least one rafter to fit it and possibly more, but you must not cut through any horizontal beams running across the rafters. These are called purlins and are a vital part of the roof's strength. If you cut through them the roof may sag or even collapse completely.

If possible, get a size that will fit neatly between two existing rafters, but if this is not possible, set one side against an original rafter and fit a short trimmer to the other side between the trimmers securing the cut rafters.

Another limitation is the fact that the bottom of the frame must be just above a full course of tiles or slates even though those at the sides and across the top will have to be trimmed to fit.

Installing the Window

If you feel that installing a roof window is too big a job to tackle, the supplier may be able to put you in touch with a local contractor who will be able to do it for you. However, the job is fairly straightforward, requiring an opening to be made in the roofing felt, a section of tiles or slates removed and then the battens and appropriate sections of rafter cut out. Timber trimmers link the cut rafters to those on each side. Then the window frame is screwed in place, flashings fitted and the tiles or slates replaced.

Fortunately most of the work can be done from inside the roof, but you will still need a scaffold tower and roof ladder so that you can haul the window frame up and also refix the roofing.

Begin in the attic by cutting out a section of roofing felt about 100mm (4in) smaller all round than the window, but slit the corners so this material hangs down. This will expose the backs

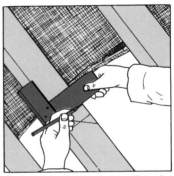

After cutting through the roofing felt where the window will be, sliding out the tiles to form the opening.

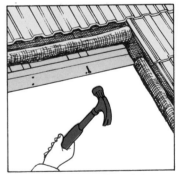

Squaring lines across the rafters for the position of the trimmer, so that the lining will be horizontal with the minimum amount of planing.

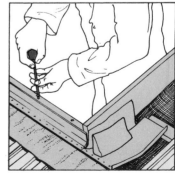

Nailing the trimmer through into the ends of the cut rafters; also nail through the side rafters into the ends of the trimmer.

After laying the bottom flashing across the tiles, screwing on the bottom profile section to the frame; this will secure the flashing.

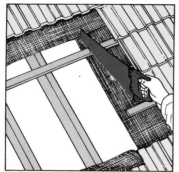

Cutting through the tile battens after gauging the position of the window (one side against a rafter) with a measured batten.

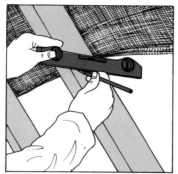

Marking the position of the upper face of the top lining; allow the recommended clearance between the lining and the frame.

Propping the rafters above and below the trimmer positions; these are nailed square to the cut rafters, outside the horizontal linings.

Cutting through the intermediate rafters at the top and bottom of the opening, following the squared lines of the trimmer positions.

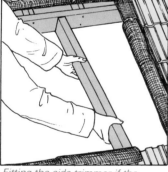

Fitting the side trimmer if the window does not fully span the gap between rafters; nail into the ends through the horizontal trimmers.

Screwing the metal fixing brackets to the rafters; gauge the distance of the window above the tiles with spacer battens.

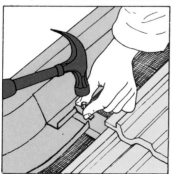

Nailing through clips to fix the side flashings (or directly to the rafters in the case of slates) after fitting the bottom flashing.

Lifting window pivots into the supports – the top of the window is outside the frame; screw out stop-screws attached to the pivots.

of the tiles or slates, and if tiles are simply hooked over the battens you may well be able to remove them from inside the roof. If they are nailed (and slates certainly will be) you will have to remove them from the outside as described on page 56. Remove all the tiles or slates from within the window area together with those in the courses immediately above and below.

Cut through the battens and knock them free of the rafters from behind. Next mark the rafters for cutting. This is a little complicated since you must make allowance for the planed wooden lining pieces which fit round the finished window opening, covering the sides of the rafters and trimmers. The side pieces simply fit to the rafters, but the top and bottom pieces should be horizontal and vertical respectively to tidy up the installation and improve air flow over the glass to prevent condensation forming. Allowance must also be made for the thickness of the trimmers.

Begin by marking the bottom cut on each intermediate rafter. The fitting instructions will specify a clearance between the bottom of the window frame and the tops of the tiles below. Mark off this distance along the top edge of the rafter from the tile batten and use a spirit level to draw a vertical line from this point to the bottom edge of the rafter. Then square a line back from this point to the top edge. It should come out in line with the top edge of the tile batten. If it is further down the rafter than this, adjust the window frame mark accordingly. Finally measure down from the squared line a distance equal to the thickness of the trimmer and square another line. This is the cutting line.

Measure the window frame and mark its height along the top of the rafter. From this point draw a horizontal line across to the lower edge and square back from this point to the top again. Now measure further up the joist the thickness of the trimmer and square a cutting line at this point.

Fit stout planks and adjustable jack posts between the tops of the rafters and the joists below

and cut through the rafters with a saw. Cut trimmers from the same size wood and nail them in place, measuring for each individually in case the rafters are not parallel. Add a vertical trimmer if necessary to suit the window width.

Remove the opening light from the window frame and paint or stain and varnish it as appropriate. When dry, screw on the fixing brackets and screw the frame in place to the rafters. Make sure it is mounted squarely by measuring the diagonals (which should be equal).

Replace the course of tiles or slates below the window followed by the lower section of flashing. This is usually retained by a metal capping piece screwed to the frame. On a tiled roof any lead flashing must be 'dressed' down, or flattened, to fit into the ridges of the tiles by gently tapping it with a rounded block of wood.

Next come the side pieces which may be nailed directly to the window frame or held to the tile battens by special clips and nails. If the roof is slated, the flashing pieces are actually interleaved with the slates on each side. Finish off by fitting any metal capping pieces then the top section of flashing, which may need extra support in the form of battens nailed across the rafters. On a tiled roof a triangular 'tilting fillet' is fitted across the top of the window to preserve the slope of the tiles above.

Tiles and slates at the sides and across the top of the window will almost certainly have to be cut to fit. Cutting slates is covered on page 56, but cutting tiles is much more difficult and you will need to rent an angle grinder with a masonry blade to do the job. The tiles or slates at the top corners of the window will have to be cut into L-shapes.

Narrow slates at the sides of the window can have nail holes punched in them and be hung as normal, but tiles will have to be set in place on strips of mortar.

To finish off the window, refit the opening light to its hinges and check its operation.

FITTING A DORMER WINDOW

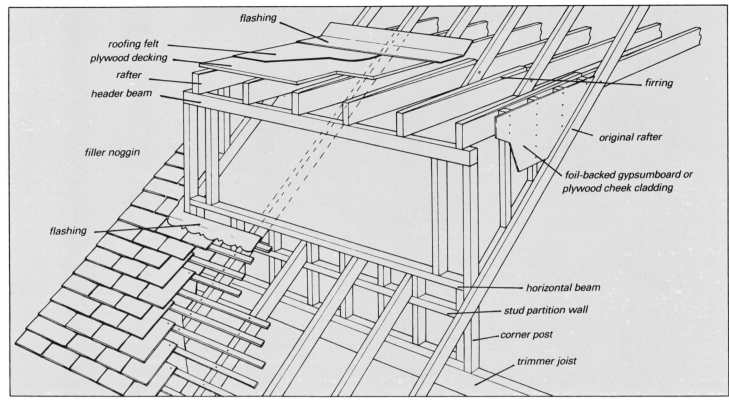

Framework structure of a dormer; apart from being rigid itself, it must also support the roof above and below. The corner posts are supported on a original trimmer joist, and the rafters rest on a header beam and are bolted to the rafters. A stud framework in the cheeks and front wall is clad with foil-backed drywall or plywood and the roof is decked with plywood, set to a fall with firrings. The window is fitted between filler bracing set between the corner posts and is supported on a horizontal beam.

One of the problems in converting an attic to usable living space is that because the roof slopes, a large proportion of its floor space does not have enough headroom. If the roof slopes steeply there may be enough space along the center to make a room, but if the pitch is shallow most of the floor area will be of no use at all. The problem can be overcome by the installation of one or more dormer windows. These not only provide essential natural light but also increase the headroom over areas of floor that were previously unusable.

A dormer window is fitted to a strong wooden framework built out from the side of the roof, so unlike the sloping roof, window it is upright just like the windows in the walls below. The top of the window framework is linked by long joists to the rafters on each side of the roof, and these joists also provide support for the ceiling of the dormer and part of the attic room. The sides of the structure are clad with some form of building board and often tile hung or sometimes covered with overlapping boards. The roof is usually flat and felt covered, but versions with tiled pitched roofs may also be seen.

Dormer windows can be quite small or they can extend almost from the ridge to the eaves of the roof, depending on how much extra space you need and the size of the original roof. There's no reason why you should not have dormer on both sides of a pitched roof, or even on all four sides if it is hopped — provided you have the space and can obtain the necessary approval.

In addition to providing windows and extra floor space inside the attic, a dormer can also be useful when it comes to positioning the stairs to the new room. With a dormer built up from eaves level, you can site a staircase immediately below it fixed to the external wall of the house, whereas normally it would have to run through the centre for there to be enough headroom at the top.

Supporting the Structure

Since several rafters will have to be cut through to make the dormer, the framework must be strong enough to support the load previously borne by the cut rafters. It must also have support at floor level unless it is possible to set the framing directly on top of a loadbearing wall. The original attic joists would certainly not be strong enough. However, since a dormer will be put in as part of an attic conversion (see page 69) this is not really a problem. A strengthening framework and extra joists will have to be put in for the new attic floor and this can be made to support the dormer framework as well. This new framework is built directly on to the house load-bearing walls and is completely independent of the original attic joists and ceiling below.

Calculating the loads involved and designing the supporting framework is specialist work and must be undertaken by an architect, engineer or an attic conversion company.

Building the Framework

The construction of the dormer framework would follow on from constructing the floor support structure. Once the dormer is complete, the rest of the conversion work can be carried out.

As with the installation of a sloping roof window, access to the roof will be needed so that bulky materials can be a carried up and passed through from the outside after removing a few tiles or slates and cutting an opening in the roofing felt. An access tower and roof ladder are essential.

The first job is to build the framework of the dormer, making sure it is secure before cutting through the original rafters and removing them.

The first sections of framework to be erected are the two corner posts for the outer end of the dormer. There is no need to strip off all the roofing within the dormer area for this initial construction work; remove only small sections of tiles and pass the framework through. In this way the roof can be kept reasonably weathertight for most of the time.

The corner posts stand on the supporting floor joists or trimmer below and are linked immediately below rafter level by a horizontal beam or purlin. Additional short wooden studs are nailed between the purlin and the supporting floor beam. The purlin has two purposes: to tie the bottoms of the corner posts together and to support the lower ends of the original rafters when they are cut through. All of the construction is toe-nailed together.

Next, nail a horizontal beam across the tops of the corner posts this is sometimes known as a 'header'. The joists for the top of the dormer can then be fitted: nail their outer ends to the top of the header and pass them right through the roof and bolt to the rafters on each side for stability. In some cases they may rest on top of a structural wall if one is available.

If the roof of the dormer is to be flat, tapered wooden slats, called firring pieces, are nailed to the tops of the joists so that the roof will have a fall to the front for drainage.

If the dormer is to have a pitched roof, a ridge board and additional rafters are installed above the joists.

Before removing the area of roof from within the dormer framework, fit additional trimmer rafters between the corner posts and the roof ridge bar (or hip rafter if the dormer is a wide one on a hipped roof). Cut shallow notches in the sides of the corner posts to take the ends of these trimmers, which are nailed in place.

To complete the framework, the roofing must be stripped off. Lift the tiles or slates from the battens, cut out the felt and saw through the battens to expose the joists: cut these off flush with the undersides of the dormer joists and level with the inner face of the new supporting purlin.

Nail vertical studs between the trimmer rafters and the joists above to provide support for the side 'check' cladding of the dormer, spacing them to take account of the width of the cladding sheets so that their edges always fall on the centerline of a stud.

Complete the framework by adding a wooden subframe to support the window itself. This is usually a horizontal beam set between the corner posts and supported below by short studs nailed to the top of the new purlin, and possibly to the sides of the cut rafters as well. The window will be narrower than the distance between the corner posts, so nail additional studs between the horizontal beam and header to support it at the sides.

That completes the basic framework; now work can commence on cladding the framework and making it weatherproof.

Cladding the Framework

The roof is covered first and if it is flat, it is decked with exterior grade plywood, butting the sheets together and nailing them to the supporting joists. To provide support for the flashing, slip a narrow strip of board under the roof at the junction with the dormer and nail it to the original rafters. To provide a certain degree of protection until the job is completed, you can add the first two layers of felt at this stage, taking them up under the original roof and leaving overlaps at the sides and front for finishing off.

Next the sides and front of the framework on either side of the window opening can be panelled in: you can use foil-backed gypsumboard for the cheeks. Nail it to the outside of the framework with the foil side outermost to prevent moisture penetration and cut down on condensation.

Fit lead soakers beneath the tiles on each side of the dormer at this stage; it may actually be easier to do this before cladding the sides, since they will slip in from the ends of the courses without the removal of the tiles.

Further protection can be provided by nailing sheets of building paper to the outside face of the gypsumboard.

Before finishing off cladding the sides, add flashing to the front of the dormer below the window opening, taking it over the top of the frame-supporting

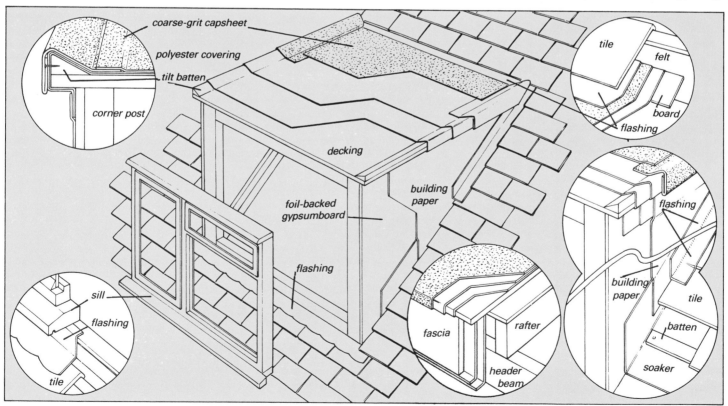

Weather proofing the dormer; tilt-battens on the side edges of the roof direct rainwater on to the felt which is laid from side to side. Roofing material, laid first on the roof then on the sides, is covered on the roof with gritted roofing felt. The tiles or slates above the dormer rest over the self-adhesive flashing strip which in turn covers the roofing felt along the back edge. Flashing strip below the window frame covers the roof beneath. The cheeks and front panels are finally clad with a matching roof-covering material.

FITTING A DORMER WINDOW

Passing the dormer rafters into the roof-space; they rest on the header and are attached to the rafters at the front and back of the roof.

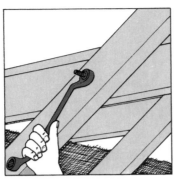

Bolting the dormer rafters to the main roof rafters; use hexagon-headed bolts and place a washer between the nut and the wood.

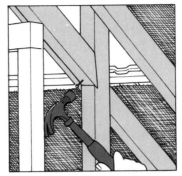

Toe-nailing the trimmer rafters to the notched corner posts; these support the framework for the cheeks of the dormer.

Tapping vertical bracing into place between the front purlin and the horizontal beam which will support the window frame.

Sliding metal flashing under tiles adjacent to the dormer cheeks to form a drainage channel; the short side of the flashing is vertical.

Nailing foil-backed waterproof drywall to the cheeks after cutting to shape; slide it down inside the flashing and nail through into the noggings

Cladding the sides with tiles hung on battens; work upwards, and outwards from the corners, staggering the joints.

Screwing the window frame to the filler noggins after levelling it and checking that the diagonals are equal to ensure that it is square.

beam and down over the roof tiles or slates below.

Then the dormer can be clad. If tiles are to be used, nail narrow battens horizontally round the dormer (the spacing being dictated by the tile size). If boarding is used as cladding, nail the supporting battens on vertically. Both tiles and boards are nailed to the battens in an overlapping pattern to keep out rainwater.

Then comes the window frame. The best type of frame to fit to a dormer is one made of wood.

A gutter is fixed along the front fascia board with a short down-pipe at one end which can be led down the corner of the dormer to discharge its contents over the roof below.

Finishing Off Inside

Having clad the outside of the dormer and glazed the window, it is possible to finish it off inside, and this will probably be done at the same time as building the interior of the attic room.

While the framework is still exposed, however, glass fiber or polystyrene insulation can be fixed between the various frame members at the sides and in the roof before they are clad with drywall or whatever internal wall cladding is being used.

OPTIONS

PVC WINDOW FRAMES

Wood and steel window-frames need regular painting if they're to keep their good looks, and if wood isn't looked after properly it will rot (even aluminum can suffer from corrosion — see page 160). The problem with a dormer window is that it's difficult to reach for painting, which is why a plastic frame may be a sensible choice, so long as it doesn't clash with the overall style of the house. It is self-colored (commonly white, sometimes brown or green) and largely maintenance-free (although the white version can be prone to yellowing).

The frame itself is screwed to a wooden linen nailed round the inside of the window opening. The panes of glass are set on rubber gaskets and held in place by snap-in glazing beads. However, this job is best left until the rest of the work is complete.

With the window frame in place, the roof can be finished off. Battens are nailed round the edge and either wood or plastic (preferable as no painting is needed) fascia boards nailed to them at the sides and front. Triangular fillets of wood are nailed along the tops of the side fascias to direct rainwater to the front and then the felt roof covering taken over on to the fascias.

When space becomes cramped at home, it's not always necessary to move to a larger house to solve the problem. Often, more usable space can be arranged using the resources already at your disposal — and usually at a lower cost than that of moving.

There are two ways in which you can gain a substantial amount of more living space in your existing home. One is to extend the house physically (usually with a single-storey, ground floor extension) and the other is to make use of what is normally wasted space in the attic. Of the two, the latter is often preferable since it won't make your garden smaller and it is likely to be more acceptable to your neighbours who won't be faced with sheer walls looming over the garden fence.

Very often an attic conversion can be carried out without the need for filing with your local building department, whereas a separate extension to give the same amount of usable living space may need a permit. It varies in different locations so allways check with your local building code (see page 251).

How much Space is Available?

There are many points to consider before you go ahead and convert your attic to living space, but the first thing to do is have a good look around it inside and around the floor below to get some idea if a conversion is possible or not.

First of all you should check whether there's enough potentially usable space available — and there may not be anywhere near as much as you think. The problems arise because what you will be trying to do is create a roughly rectangular shape within a triangular one. On the face of it an attic has a vast floor area — equal to the area of the floor below — but because the roof slopes inwards the amount of that floor area which is of any real use can be quite small.

The design of the roof also has an effect on the space available without making structural modifications to it. For a roof of any given size, a gable-ended design will have more im-

mediately usable space than one with a gable at one end and a hip at the other. A roof with both ends hipped will offer even less room. This situation can be improved upon considerably by the addition of dormers, but knowing just what you have to start with will give an idea of how much work might be involved and whether it will be worthwhile.

The pitch of the roof also has an effect, a low shallow pitched roof offering less space than a tall steeply-pitched one because of the need for a reasonable headroom over most of the floor. The Building Code usually stipulates a minimum headroom, but this only applies to a percentage of the floor area, so the rest of the floor area can have a lower headroom. This allows you to push the outer walls of the rooms out into the eaves a bit, which can be very useful.

You may find however, that the height of the ridge of the roof above the attic joists isn't sufficient even for this.

The method of construction of the roof can present its own problems and some types don't lend themselves to conversion at all. Really heavy vertical posts supporting the ridge with heavy cross-pieces below and diagonal struts cannot be removed and they may be spaced too closely to allow rooms in between. Some modern houses have roofs made of prefabricated lightweight trussed rafters with no ridge bar at all, and these can't be altered either.

How will you reach the Attic rooms?

Having the space available either as the roof stands or with the addition of dormers is one thing, being able to get into the attic easily is another. You must fit a proper staircase to the attic — an attic ladder is usually not allowed, nor would it be very convenient. So you should work out roughly where you could install it.

Ideally, the new flight of stairs should be fitted over the existing stairwell, but to do this you may have to break through the wall of an adjoining room with a consequent loss of space in that room. In this situation you would want to be sure that the space

Some of the original wooden members have been retained in this attic room to provide an open-plan division with no loss of light or space and to break up the expanse of wood cladding on the ceilings and walls.

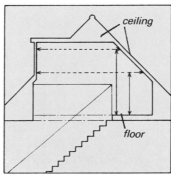

Usable floor area occurs where the headroom is at least 7'-0", check your local Building Code.

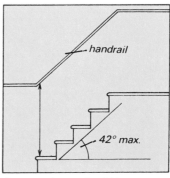

A new staircase should have: max pitch 38°, min. headroom 6ft 11in; handrail 34in high. Check your local building code.

lost at the foot of the stairs would be regained together with a lot more space in the attic.

You should also take into account where the staircase will break through the ceiling into the attic. It will need quite a large opening and this may interfere with essential roof supports, chimneys, cisterns and pipework.

You must have ample headroom at the base of the stairs, on

the stairs and at the top of the stairs, although the latter can often be provided by building out a dormer to the eaves.

If the house is a two storey building, the conversion of the attic will make it three storeys high and here you may run into another snag, with your local building code. The door that opens to the stairwell of a three-storey building may have to be self-closing and the walls, floors

CONVERTING AN ATTIC

and door frames may need to offer half-to one-hour fire resistance. Often the floors and walls will be built to this standard anyway, but there are still the doors to take care of. The local Codes vary so widely that you should allways check with your local Building Codes before any building project.

Other Considerations

There are other things to think about as well, such as what type of windows you will fit and where you will fit them. How will you supply electric light and power, heating and a water supply (if one of the rooms is to be a bathroom or powder room)?

Your lighting and power accessories will almost certainly need new circuits, which means having sufficient spare fuseways or breakers at the electric panel, or extending the existing service panel. And if you intend extending your central heating system you may find that the boiler doesn't have the extra capacity.

In general, you will probably have to re-route pipes and cables already in the attic.

Handling the Paperwork

All the work done to convert the attic into living space must comply with the requirements of the Building Code, and before work can begin plans must be drawn up and submitted to your local Building Department for approval. They will be able to advise you on any aspects of the work about which you are unsure, and he will probably want to make several checks on the work as it progresses.

The Codes vary so greatly across the country that what may need approval in one area does not need approval in another. If you feel unsure it is allways best to check with your local Building Department or consult with a local professional Architect or Engineer before starting any job.

Attic conversion work should not be undertaken lightly since major structural alterations to the roof are inevitable. If carried out in the wrong way they could bring the roof down. That is why

Installing a new attic floor; after setting the front trimmer across load-bearing walls, checking that it is absolutely level.

Hanging a central cross trimmer between the side trimmers to support a partition wall; pack it out over supporting walls below.

Hanging new joists between the side trimmers; lay a straight-edge across the front and central trimmers as a guide to level.

Laying side trimmers perpendicular to the front trimmer and resting across the original joists; attach them with metal joist hangers.

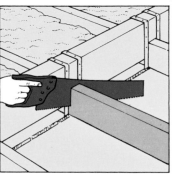

After installing a stairwell trimmer between the side trimmers to support the existing joists, cutting through to form the well.

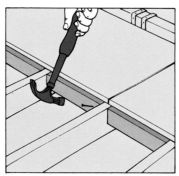

Toe-nailing bracing between the joists to support the edges of the plywood flooring panels; stagger the joints between panels.

it is essential to employ professionals to carry out at least all the initial design work, loading calculations and the necessary structural alterations. Then, if you want to save some money, you can carry out the less critical parts of the job yourself: building the dividing partitions, cladding the floor and ceiling, installing the electrical circuits and pipework.

There are two routes you can take to getting professional help: you can either employ an archi-

tect to design the conversion and then get him to supervize the builder who does the work, or you can approach a specialist attic conversion contractor, who will both design the conversion and carry out the work. In the first instance you'll get something that suits your needs exactly, whereas in the latter you may get a variation on one of several standard plans. However, there may be quite a difference in price, and with any work of this kind it is essential to get

two or three quotes from different companies for comparison.

In many cases the architect or conversion company will handle the Building Code side of the job for you, relieving you of a considerable headache. Both will also be able to tell you if the structure of the roof makes a conversion possible at all. Sometimes it is possible to remove major supporting members which are in the way and support the load they carried by making one of the internal partitions load-bearing or by inserting strong wooden beams in the framework of the walls or floor. In other areas, essential supporting framing may be left in place and the internal partitions built off them.

What the Job Involves

The weight of the floor, partition walls and ceiling of an attic conversion can be quite considerable and that's without the loading imposed by the framework for a dormer and, of course, the furnishings added to the completed rooms. So the very first job that is done when converting the loft is to build a supporting structure that will be able to carry this loading and also provide partial support to the roof if parts of its original framework have been removed.

Strengthening the Floor

It is most unlikely that the original attic joists will be up to the job of providing the necessary extra support, unless you're very lucky. There are two ways in which a strong floor frame can be made: either extra joists of the same size as the originals are fitted between them, or a completely separate structure is built over the top of them, being supported directly by the load-bearing walls. Of the two, the latter is preferable, since it will tend to insulate the rooms below from noise and vibration from the rooms above. It will also prevent damage to the ceiling during the construction stage. However, it does mean that the available headroom will be reduced.

Constructing a stud framework for partitioning off the roof space at the eaves; nail into the end of the bracing then toe-nail to the studs.

Nailing through the top of the framework into a headplate fixed to a purlin; apply cladding after the structure has been inspected.

Framing the sides of the stairwell with bevel-topped posts nailed to the rafters above and the ends of the joists below.

Dividing up the attic space into rooms with intermediate partition walls; these should be levelled and fixed to rafters where possible.

Insulating the roof with panels of styrofoam pushed between the rafters; use two thicknesses to make up the necessary depth.

Nailing lining timbers round an access hatch after cutting through the framework and inserting a trimmer over the opening.

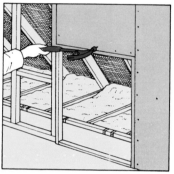

Cladding the partition with foil-backed gypsumboard nailed to the studwork, foil side outwards, and butting up to the lining.

Cladding the ceiling of a dormer with foil-backed gypsumboard after pushing styrofoam slabs between the dormer rafters.

The separate framework will consist of strong wooden beams called trimmers around the edges and in certain strategic points with the joists fitted between them on metal hangers. Where the trimmers and joists pass over intermediate loadbearing walls they are packed out with wood blocks to provide extra support.

Once this framework is in place, the necessary modifications can be made to the roof itself — adding extra support struts, dormer frameworks and even, in some cases, load-bearing wood-framed partitions.

The floor is normally clad with tongued-and-grooved plywood sheets, which provide a quickly-laid and flat floor.

The Stairs

It is possible to buy standard size flights of stairs, either of the closed or open tread type, and if at all possible these should be chosen to save on the expense of having stairs specially made to fit. It may be necessary to add a trimmer joist to the floor at the foot of the stairs for extra strength; another trimmer will be needed in the attic floor to support the top. The opening for the stairs will be quite large, requiring several original attic joists to be cut through. Their ends must be supported from the new framework either with trimmer joists or metal hangers.

The staircase itself may need cladding along the underside with gypsumboard, unless it is of the open-tread variety.

The Ceiling and Walls

Joists for the ceiling can be nailed between the original rafters, and if a dormer is fitted they are bolted in place and carried through to support the dormer roof.

The internal walls can be lightweight stud partitions. The frames should be nailed together flat on the floor and then lifted into position where they can be nailed to the floor joists, the ceiling joists and to the rafters or other parts of the structure. Always notch the frameworks to fit over the existing roof members, not the other way round or you will weaken the roof.

Doorways

Doorways can be made in the usual fashion and a useful tip here is to save the section of sole plate cut from the opening and use it as a lintel above the door.

While the ceiling and partition frameworks are bare, you can fit all the electrical accessory mounting boxes to battens nailed in place and run in all the cables and any pipework. Then cut insulation material to fit between the studs and bracing of the walls, the joists of the ceiling and the original rafters.

Wall Cladding

Clad the walls and ceilings with foil-backed gypsumboard This will help insulate the rooms and prevent moisture passing through the walls into the roof space. The final job is to plaster the walls and decorate.

You need to be able to get to the rest of the roof for repairs and maintenance to water tanks and pipework, in addition to using it for storage purposes.

To this end, hatches should be built into the partition frameworks. They can be fitted with plywood panels held by magnetic catches and trimmed with molding.

An additional handrail attached to the wall ensures safe ascent or descent for the left- or right-handed on wide stairs.

case has no risers and is completely exposed.

In a closed tread staircase the treads are about 25mm (1in) thick and will overhang the risers by a similar amount, their leading edges or noses being rounded off. A decorative molding is often fitted below the nose. An open tread staircase will tend to have thicker treads because they are not supported by risers, although sometimes a batten will be set on edge immediately below them to stiffen the tread.

All staircases must have at least one handrail and if wide they must have one on each side, depending on the requirements of your local code. The handrail forms part of the balustrade, the other parts of which are the newel posts and balusters.

The newel posts fit at each end of the stairs with the handrail running between them. Not only do they support the handrail but often the strings as well which will be slotted into them and fixed with wooden dowels. Further support for the handrail is provided by the balusters which fit between it and the strings. Often they are turned for a decorative appearance.

Staircase Styles

Though straight staircases are common, where space is limited it is often necessary for the stairs to change direction on the way up. A small quarter landing is used to provide a 90° change of direction and a half landing will turn the stairs back on themselves in a dogleg.

If there isn't room for a half or quarter landing a turn can be put into the stairs by inserting triangular treads called winders. Winders are also used in spiral staircases which can be great space savers. Unfortunately they are not very practical since carrying furniture and other bulky items up them is difficult.

Staircases are often taken for granted yet they are complex pieces of carpentry which give many years of trouble-free use. They rarely need replacing: just as well, since they're often tailor-made to fit. Even so you can buy ready made versions, which cater for common storey heights and these can often be adapted slightly to fit exactly.

Staircase Construction

A staircase comprises a number of steps fixed between two long boards which are fixed to the joists of the floors they connect. These boards are called strings. the horizontal surfaces of the steps are called treads and sometimes they have vertical boards between them known as risers.

Strings can be in two forms: closed and cut. With the former the ends of the treads and risers are housed in shallow slots cut in the face of the string and held there by wedges driven in from behind and below. The risers are fixed to the treads below with housing joints or screws, and to the treads above by triangular blocks glued and nailed in place. The top edge of a cut string is shaped to provide horizontal ledges to which the treads are fixed. Sometimes both forms of string will be used in the same staircase, the closed string being fixed against a wall with the cut string on the outside.

Further support for the steps can be provided by a beam that runs below the treads and risers parallel to the strings. This is known as a carriage.

There are two basic types of staircase: the closed tread and open tread. Of the two, the former is most common, having treads and risers in a boxed-in construction. The underside of the strings are usually clad with lath and plaster or gypsumboard or there may be a closet below the stairs. The latter is preferable since it allows easy inspection and repair. The opentread stair-

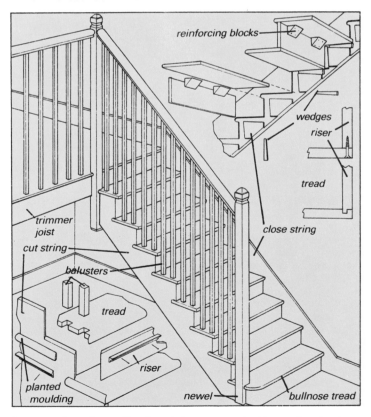

Anatomy of a staircase. Treads and risers ar enotched into a closed string (top) and held in place by wedges; risens may be screwed to, or recessed into treads. Treads rest on top of cut strings (bottom) and balusters are set into the ends, covered by mouldings.

REPAIRS TO TREADS

Actual physical damage to stair treads is rare and will probably be limited purely to split or broken nosings. These can be repaired by cutting them off flush with the riser below with a chisel and pinning on a new molding.

A much more common problem is creaking as a result of the treads becoming loose. The ease with which this can be fixed depends very much on whether you can get to the underside of the stairs or not. If you can, simply pin and glue 50 × 50mm (2 × 2in) triangular blocks of wood between the treads and risers below, and drive screws up through the tread into the riser above. This is the only way you can fix a staircase with closed strings.

Cut Strings

If the staircase has one or two cut strings, you can make the repair from above. First prise off the molding from below the tread nose and the molding holding the foot of the baluster in place, using an old chisel. Run a hacksaw blade along the gap between the back of the tread and upper riser, cutting through any fixings. Alternatively, cut through the riser itself with a backsaw. Drive a chisel blade between the tread nose and riser and lever it free. Then you can remove the risers if damaged.

If necessary, cut a new tread and riser from wood of the same size as the originals.

Closed Strings

If one of the strings is closed, glue and pin supporting blocks to it for the ends of the riser and tread. Use offcuts of the tread and riser wood as positioning guides to ensure a tight fit. Then glue and pin the riser in place.

Pin and glue more blocks to the top of the lower riser and then glue the tread on top, strengthening the bond by driving screws or nails down through the ends into the cut string or strings. Don't drive any screws or nails through the leading edge of the tread as they may become exposed as the tread wears.

Refit the baluster, pinning it to the handrail and then pin the retaining moulding to the end of the tread. Finally, refit the moulding beneath the tread nose.

If you can reach the underside of a closed string staircase, you can replace treads or risers by removing their retaining wedges with a chisel and sliding the damaged parts out. Slot the new pieces in and fit new wedges. If a carriage runs down the centre of the stairs, however, the work is best left to a joiner or builder.

Replacing a tread: prising off the planted molding with an old chisel and mallet to free the balusters.

If the soffit prevents access from beneath, cutting between the riser and tread with a hacksaw blade.

Prising up the open end of the tread from the string; remove the tread by wiggling it free from the closed string.

Nailing and gluing a reinforcing block to the riser below; also nail a batten below the groove in the closed string.

Shaping the nosing of the new tread with a spokeshave; keep the curve uniform and ensure that the front edge is straight.

After applying adhesive to the edges of the risers and battens, screwing the new tread to the batten on the closed string.

REPAIRS TO BANISTERS

Of all the sections of the staircase likely to suffer damage, the handrails come top of the list. Yet they play an important safety role by preventing people from falling from the stairs and so must be kept in good repair.

The balusters are the most vulnerable part of the assembly and may become loose or broken.

A loose toe-nailed baluster can be simply tapped free with a mallet and block of wood, the nails removed and the holes opened out with a drill to accept countersunk screws. You then glue and screw it back in place.

If the ends of the baluster are held by mortise joints, you can stop the baluster rattling about by driving narrow wedges into the gaps around the ends, having first smeared them with glue. Cut the ends of the wedges flush with the surface of the string or handrail as appropriate. Sometimes, the balusters are held by thin strips of wood nailed in place betwen the ends of adjacent balusters. In this case, carefully prise off the strips on each side of the loose baluster and replace them with slightly longer ones.

If the baluster is actually broken, you can either replace it with a new one (assuming you can get one to match) or glue it back together, reinforcing the joint with dowels or screws.

Toe-nailed balusters are easily removed as described above, as are those held by nailed-on capping pieces. However, if they are mortised into the string and handrail, you may have to saw through the ends to remove the baluster. Then glue blocks of wood into the mortises, plane them flush, cut the new baluster to fit and glue and screw it in place as you would a skew-nailed version.

If a section of handrail is broken, you can make a simple repair by screwing a metal plate underneath across the break. Alternatively, you can cut out a section and fit a new piece, using special handrail bolts or screws. These need matching holes in the ends of the old and new rail, and the easiest way of marking them is with a paper template that matches the profile of the rail with the hole centre marked on it. Hold the template over the end of each piece and mark the hole centre by punching through with a nail. Additional holes must be drilled or cut with a chisel into the underside of the rail so that the nuts securing the bolt can be tightened.

Newel posts are unlikely to break, but if they do, they must be replaced completely. To remove it, you will have to lift the adjacent floorboards and unbolt the base from the joists. Then

Removing a loose baluster by tapping it away from the handrail; use a hammer or mallet wood with a block to protect the wood.

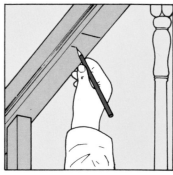

Marking the position for refixing the baluster on the underside of the handrail; drill and countersink the baluster before fixing.

Screwing the baluster back to the handrail; clamp a stop to the handrail to prevent the baluster from sliding out of position.

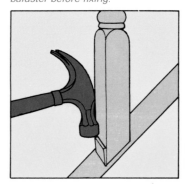

Wedging the bottom of a baluster into its notch; tap wedge between baluster and string after applying woodworking adhesive.

drive out the dowels holding the handrail and string to it. Finally, tap the newel post free — it may help to cut it into sections with a saw.

Use the old post as a guide for marking out the new one, making sure the mortises and dowel holes are all positioned correctly. Treat the base of the post with preservative and refit it, glueing the string and handrail in place and reinforcing the joints with fresh dowels.

Trick

STAIRCASE KITS

Whether you are installing a new staircase or simply repairing an existing one, the range of components available in kit form makes the task much easier.

The stairs may be ready-assembled and consist of 12 or 14 treads for a full flight or six treads for a half-flight; they are available with or without risers, and bullnose steps allow extra versatility at floor-level.

The newels, baluster spindles, rails and fittings are manufactured in a wide variety of styles, from traditional to contemporary, allowing great freedom of choice. The timber, which includes mahogany and hemlock, is usually sanded ready for varnishing or staining.

Wood is used in large quantities in the construction of houses, not just for supporting the roof, partition walls and floors but also for more decorative, yet practical, trimming jobs. These trimming pieces are known collectively as 'joinery' and include the baseboards, picture rails and cornices between walls and ceiling.

Repairing and Replacing Baseboards

Over the years the baseboards can take quite a hammering from being knocked by brooms, vacuum cleaners, furniture legs, children's toys and so on. In fact, that's what they're there for — to protect the plaster of the wall, which would soon fall apart under this treatment. Eventually, the base will become scruffy and you will want to repair small sections or even replace complete lengths.

Various base board profiles are available from lumber yards and hardware stores and it's quite possible that you will find a match for the existing boards, allowing short damaged sections to be replaced. However, with some older properties you may not be able to match the base trim and you will have to replace it all, or put up with one wall having a different base to the rest.

In most cases the base will be nailed in place, which makes removal and replacement easy. However, always make a check for screws first and release any you find from the affected area.

To replace just a section of base, drive a flat masons chisel down behind it to prise it from the wall, then drive in wooden wedges on each side of the damage. Cut out the damaged piece with a saw, making the cuts slope inwards at an angle. Cut a new piece of board to fit the gap and, if necessary, nail wooden spacer blocks to the wall so that they just fit under the cut ends of the original board. Use masonry nails if fixing to brickwork.

Cut a new section of board to fit, sloping the ends to match the cuts in the original board, and nail it in place. Drive the nail heads down with a nail set and fill the holes before painting.

Remove entire lengths of base by prising them from the wall with a flat chisel and wooden wedges, starting at an external corner or where the base meets a door frame molding. If the base runs between two internal corners you may have to cut through it to pull it away as its ends may be trapped behind the ends of the abutting base.

If the base was nailed to wooden wedges set in the mortar joints of the wall or to short wooden slats (called 'grounds') make sure they are in good condition; replace them if necessary.

In older properties the plaster will stop at base level, whereas in modern houses it will continue to floor level. In the former case you may have to nail wooden spacer blocks to the wall to set the base out far enough; you may also find that the new base is not as deep as the old and the resulting gap between it and the old plaster must be filled with fresh plaster.

Where boards meet on external corners, miter their ends at 45°. At internal corners, cut one board end square and fit it tight into the corner; cut the end of the adjacent board to fit the profile of the first. Use an offcut of base for drawing the profile on the back of the board and cut it out with a coping saw.

Dealing with Picture Rails

Picture rails were a common feature of older houses, but during modernisation they are often torn out — often a shame since they can be an interesting and useful decorative feature in their own right but more importantly complement the proportions of the room.

Sections of picture rail can be repaired in much the same

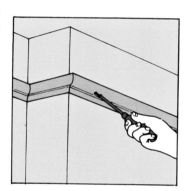

Where a picture rail is to be used for hanging pictures, a stronger fixing will be obtained using screws and the correct wallplugs.

manner as base, cutting through it at an angle, levering it out with a chisel, and cutting a new piece to match. This can be nailed in place, driving the nails through the plaster and into the wall or wooden frame behind.

Entire lengths can also be replaced in the same way, but you must make sure they are level. The quickest way to mark a guideline is with a chalked line and level. Stretch the line out across the wall at the right height, check it is horizontal with the spirit level, then snap the line against the wall to leave a chalk line on its surface. Treat the ends of the picture rail in the same manner as base and either nail or screw it into place.

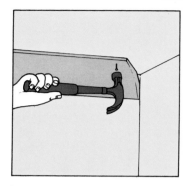

Nailing plaster cornice in position as temporary support while the adhesive dries; fill holes and gaps with surplus adhesive.

Fitting Cornices

Cornices may also be made from materials other than wood; for example, plaster, gypsumboard, various plastics and fiberglass. Their purpose is to tidy up the angle between the walls and ceiling, and they can be very plain in appearance or quite ornate. Although you may be able to obtain matching patterns for repairing damaged cornices, cutting out a short section is quite difficult and it would be easier to replace a complete length. Cornices are normally only stuck in place so you can remove them by driving a flat chisel behind from both the wall and ceiling sides.

Before fitting new lengths of cornice, the wall and ceiling should be prepared by removing any paper, filling cracks or holes and roughening the surface with wire brush.

Cut the cornice to length using a fine-toothed saw, mitering the ends and cutting down from the face so that the edges don't break away.

The type of adhesive used to stick cornices in place will vary with the material they are made from and full instructions will be supplied by the manufacturer. Spread the adhesive on the cornice and stick it into place, driving a few nails through the edges to provide temporary support while the adhesive sets. Any adhesive that oozes from the joints or from behind the cornice should be wiped away.

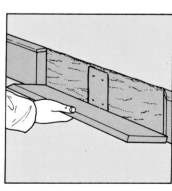

Offering up the new length of baseboard, with one end mitered, to mark the position for the second miter.

Pinning a length of matching bead or molding to the top edge after nailing the base to the blocks fixed to the wall.

BUILDING AN EXTENSION

An extension room should blend in well with the main building and should be carefully planned to ensure that it fulfils its requirements.

The reasons for needing extra space in your home have already been discussed on previous pages together with some of the methods of obtaining that extra space without having to move to a larger house. However, there are occasions when none of these methods provide the answer.

Enlarging individual rooms by removing dividing walls or making extra rooms by erecting partitions are good ideas provided the internal layout of the house lends itself to this form of alteration. There may not always be enough total floor area to make this a viable proposition. And attic conversions are fine so long as you can really make use of the extra space at the top of the house; this may not always be so, particularly if you need, say, a larger kitchen or a downstairs bathroom for an invalid unable to cope with stairs. In many cases the answer to the space problem is to build on an extra room or rooms at the side or rear of the house.

Types of Extension

Most extensions take the form of a single-storey addition to the ground floor, but it is sometimes possible to extend the first floor out over a garage or for the really ambitious to add a two-storey structure.

The ground floor extension can be purpose-designed and built to suit your needs exactly, or it can be constructed from a number of standard prefabricated components from an extension manufacturer. Which type you choose depends very much on what you will use it for. The former is ideal for bathrooms, kitchens, bedrooms, living rooms (space you need all year round); the latter is more suited to laundry rooms, sun rooms, children's play rooms, work-shops and the like, and includes simple metal-framed, fully-glazed conservatories.

A purpose-built extension will be more expensive than a prefabricated version of the same size, but it will be more durable and can be made to match your house exactly which may be a requirement in some areas. On the other hand, the prefabricated extension is easily and quickly assembled.

Code Requirements

As with an attic conversion (see page 69), you may not actually need a building permit for an extension, but it is as well to check with the local Building Department just in case. In some areas the Building Code requires that any addition is built in the same style and in matching materials as the main part of the house. In this situation, even if the extensions within the permitted size and did not project above the roof line or beyond the front of the building, you would still need a building permit.

Regardless of the Building Code situation, all the work must comply with the Building Code, so early contact with your local Building Inspector is essential. He will want to see plans of the extension, being particularly interested in the foundations and will advise you on the requirements for your specific situation. He will also want to inspect the work as it progresses.

With a purpose built extension you should employ an architect to design it and take care of the Building Code matters. He will also supervise the building work. This should be done by a competent builder, but you may be able to reduce the cost if he will agree to you doing the less critical parts of the job.

A standard contract should be taken out with the builder that defines his responsibilities, specifies starting and completion dates and gives details of how payment will be made.

Prefabricated extensions are often designed for assembly by the purchaser, although the manufacturer can send his own erection team to do it for you; he may even insist on this if the extension is above a certain size.

Obviously, any extension will be costly and you should give considerable thought to how you will pay for it. In some cases you may qualify for a guaranteed loan through the federal Government. You may be able to extend your mortgage, or get a loan from a bank or finance company. It's worth shopping around to get the best terms.

The most important parts of the structure of your new extension are the foundations, which support the walls and spread the load evenly across the ground. Consequently, their design is quite critical and should be carried out after consulting your local Building Code which will specify the type of foundations required for the job and the depth to which they must be dug, based on local ground conditions.

To be effective, foundations must lie on firm, stable sub-soil, and depending on the soil type this may mean digging to a depth of 1m (3ft) or more. The type of soil will also dictate the type of foundations needed, as will the method of construction of the extension.

Types of Foundation

For a purpose-built extension with brick or block walls, it is usual to lay concrete in a trench and build the walls on top, but for lighter constructions like prefabricated buildings a slab of concrete known as a 'raft' is more common.

Strip Foundations

The most common form of foundation is the 'strip' type. With these a layer of concrete at least 150mm (6in) thick is spread along the bottom of the trench, levelled off, then the walls built on top. Normally, a width of 450mm (18in) is quite adequate, but at depths below 1m (3ft) or on certain types of

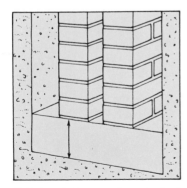

Strip foundations require a depth of 150mm (6in) and a width of 450mm (18in) on normal subsoil; no reinforcement is needed.

weak soil a width of 750mm (30in) or more is preferable — often with steel reinforcement added.

Trench-fill Foundations

A disadvantage of the strip foundation is that it can involve quite a lot of brick laying to bring the walls up to ground level — a time consuming job during which the sides of the trench are always at risk of caving in. A

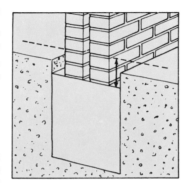

Saving time on bricklaying, using a trench-fill foundation. Excavate at least 660mm (26in) deep, and 150mm (6in) wider than the wall.

much quicker method, and a cheaper one, is to use the trench-fill foundations. With this, the trench is filled with concrete to within 150mm (6in) of the final ground level then the walls begun.

The concrete for this type of foundation should be at least 500mm (20in) deep and about 150mm (6in) wider than the width of the wall. The sides of the trench must be vertical to prevent any possibility of the load above causing the foundations to topple.

Dealing with Sloping Ground

Where foundations are laid in sloping ground they should be stepped down the slope, the depths of the steps being equal to a complete number of brick — or block courses. The strips of concrete should overlap by at least 300mm (12in) or by an amount equal to the depth of the concrete if this is greater. The concrete of trench-fill foundations should overlap by at least

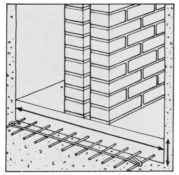

On soft subsoils a wide strip foundation is needed to spread the load ; reinforcement is needed if it projects more than its thickness.

1m (3ft), or double the step height, whichever is the greater. Regardless of ground slope, the concrete should always be level and this is achieved by driving depth pegs along the center of the trench and levelling their tops.

Concrete Raft Foundations

Suitable for light structures, the concrete raft is a large slab of concrete at least 200mm (8in) thick at the edges to support the walls and about 100mm (4in) thick in the centre over a 100mm (4in) layer of compacted gravel or broken brick hardcore. Sometimes steel reinforcement is called for as well.

This type of construction provides both support for the walls and a floor inside. It often works well on soft, loose soils since it spreads the load over a wide area.

Concrete rafts are cast with wooden formwork, and the method is described on page 224.

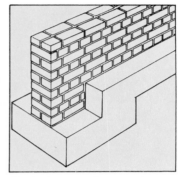

On sloping ground a stepped trench-fill foundation is used; the height of the steps should be an exact number of brick courses.

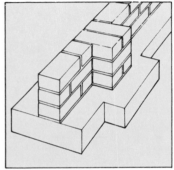

Where the wall will have projections, the foundations must follow the shape, keeping the same distance outside the wall.

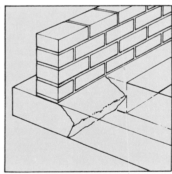

To join on to an existing foundation, cut back the joining edge to a V-shape to provide a good key for the new concrete.

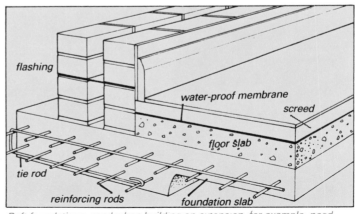

Raft foundations, used when building an extension, for example, need careful design; consult your local Building Inspector or Engineer.

flashing

water-proof membrane

screed

floor slab

tie rod

reinforcing rods

foundation slab

CONSTRUCTING THE WALLS

Unlike garages and similar outbuildings, the walls of a habitable extension to your house must be of cavity construction; that is comprising an outer leaf of bricks and an inner leaf of bricks or, more usually, lightweight concrete insulating blocks with a 50mm (2in) air gap in between. This gives a nominal wall thickness of 275mm (11in), although sometimes the cavity may be 75mm (3in) wide to accommodate polystyrene slab insulation and still leave an air gap.

The cavity wall construction is designed to prevent water penetrating the wall to the inner surface by keeping the two leaves separate. Many older houses have solid 225mm (9in) outer walls made up of two leaves of bricks but with no cavity between them and if of poor construction this can allow penetrating damp which will ruin interior decoration and damage the plaster (see page 80). Even if the main part of your house has solid outer walls, your extension must still be of cavity wall construction.

Catering for Drain Pipes

An important consideration when building an extension is the position of any drainage pipe run — either an existing one from the house or any new waste pipes from fittings in the new extension. You must sort out the route the pipes will take before the

Positioning a plastic cavity-wall tie, sloping down towards the outer leaf. The ribbed ends ensure high pull-out strength, and drip rings prevent water from crossing the cavity; the flexible plastic accommodates uneven courses.

walls are built since they will pass through them below floor level and openings must be left in the walls as they are built. Lintels will need to be incorporated to support the wall above the openings. If the extension is to have trench-fill foundations, ducts should be made in the concrete to allow the passage of pipes. A simple method is to set slightly larger pipes in the concrete as it is poured and then run the pipes through these round openings later. Alternatively rectangular openings can be made with wooden formwork.

Marking Out

The positions of the inner and outer leaves of the walls should be marked on to the concrete of the foundations with chalk, making sure the gap between the two is uniform and of the correct width. The wall as a whole must be positioned centrally on the concrete strips, the centre lines of the wall and foundations being within 25mm (1in) of each other.

As the walls are built, stringlines are stretched between the corners to make sure each course of bricks or blocks is laid in a straight line.

Cavity Wall Construction

Although you can use brick for both inner and outer leaves of the wall, in practice it makes more sense to use lightweight concrete blocks for the former since these will provide a certain amount of insulation — a requirement of the Building Regulations. Otherwise you would have to provide some other form of insulation: by fixing 50mm (2in) polystyrene slabs against the inner leaf with special ties or by filling the cavity after the wall was built with an insulating foam.

With this type of construction, the inner leaf is the load-bearing part of the wall, carrying the weight of any floors and ceilings so lintels must be fitted across any openings in it, such as doorways and windows. Steel boot lintels are the best choice since they are relatively light in weight and their shape ensures that any water that does

Laying a batten, with strings attached for later removal, across the wall ties to prevent mortar from falling into the cavity.

Building up the inner leaf; lay a bed of mortar along the blocks below; butter the end of the block with mortar and tap into position.

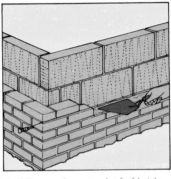

Building up the outer leaf of brick; build up the corners first, stretch a string-line between and fill in the middle up to the line.

Closing the cavity at window and door openings; turn the inner leaf and insert a vertical DPC between it and the outer leaf.

penetrate the outer leaf of the wall is prevented from reaching the inner leaf and channeled back out over the toe of the boot.

The two leaves of the wall should be constructed simultaneously, laying a few courses of each at a time. As construction proceeds, the two leaves must be linked together with metal or plastic wall ties to prevent them leaning away from each other. The ties are designed to prevent water running across them to the inner leaf but they must still be set in the mortar joints so that they slope downwards slightly towards the outer leaf. Ties should be set about 450mm (18in) apart vertically and 900mm (3ft) apart horizontally, the positions in each horizontal row being staggered when compared to those above and below. At door and window openings, the ties should be set one above the other at 300mm (12in) intervals.

Water penetration must also be prevented from below and this is achieved by inserting a flexible bitumen damp-proof course (DPC) in a horizontal

mortar joint around the base of each leaf, at least two courses of bricks above ground level. When the floor is laid (see page 45), a damp-proof membrane (DPM) is taken up the walls and tucked in under the DPC.

Strips of DPC must also be fitted in the vertical mortar joints where the inner leaf is turned to close off the cavity at windows and door openings, and also below the threshold of the door, linking to the DPC in the outer leaf.

The most convenient bond for laying bricks for an extension is ordinary stretcher bond where the bricks in one course overlap those of the course below by half a brick's length. Certainly the blocks of the inner course are best laid in this manner. However, if your house is old and has character, it may be worth the trouble of copying the original brick bond so that the extension blends in.

As with the construction of a blockwork partition (see page 18), the walls must be toothed into the existing house walls at alternate courses to ensure stability.

The most common form of roof for a single storey extension is the flat type; it is easily and cheaply constructed and, depending on the method of covering, should be good for at least 20 years before it needs recovering. Often a flat roof is the only viable proposition, for the simple reason that the upper windows of the house would get in the way of a pitched one.

However, if the space is available there is no doubt that a tiled pitched roof is much more attractive and offers the additional advantage of a small amount of attic space which can be used for storage purposes. It would, of sourse, be much more expensive than a flat roof.

Flat Roof Construction

The method of construction of a flat roof is the same as that outlined on page 54, the joists usually being laid along the length of the extension from the house to the end wall. At the house end, the joists may either rest on top of a wooden wall plate, being toe-nailed in place, or be nailed to metal hangers nailed to the wall plate. The ends

of the wall plate are set in sockets built into the extension side walls.

At the end of the extension, the joists can simply rest on top of the end wall and be nailed in place or, if there is a window in the end wall, a second wooden beam can be fitted to span the opening and support the joists.

Tapered firring pieces are nailed to the tops of the joists to create the right fall. If a felt covering is chosen this should be 1 in 60. However, a flat roof may also be covered with asphalt, in which case the fall should be 1 in 80.

In some cases with a particularly long roof, it may be more convenient to set the roof joists across its width, resting their ends on the side walls and nailing the firring pieces across them at right angles.

Sheets of exterior grade plywood or particle board are used to provide a roof decking and are nailed down through the firring pieces into the joists. Tongued-and-grooved boarding could also be used, but the sheet materials provide a much flatter surface which is better suited to the types of covering material. The

sheets should be staggered so the joints between their short edges do not coincide.

Covering with Asphalt

Although a felt-covered roof is the cheapest and easiest to construct (see page 62), a much more durable finish can be obtained by having it covered with asphalt. This material is heated until it melts and is then spread over the roof to provide a solid, impervious layer when it cools. It is a job that requires skill and is not one you should attempt yourself.

Before the asphalt is applied, a layer of sheathing felt is laid on the roof and aluminum extrusions added along the sides to act as finishing strips. A lead flashing is nailed in place across the end above the gutter.

A narrow band of asphalt is spread on to any walls the roof meets and then two layers are spread on to the roof, being smoothed out with a wooden float. Then the joint between roof and wall receives an extra fillet of asphalt to ensure a watertight seal.

Finally, sand is rubbed into the

surface and a layer of white chippings spread on top to reflect the heat of the sun.

Preventing Condensation

Flat roofs can often suffer from condensation when moist air passes through the ceiling from the rooms below and cools on contact with the underside of the roof. This is a particular problem if the extension is used as a bathroom or kitchen where there is a lot of moisture present.

Leaving ventilation gaps behind the fascia and insulating the roof will help, but the best idea is to either use foil-back gypsumboard for the ceiling — which will stop the moist air passing through — or staple a separate polyethelene vapor barrier to the underside of the joists before nailing the gypsumboard in place. Once the extension has been weather-proofed by glazing the windows and fitting the doors, the room can be finished. Before plastering the walls and ceiling, lay in the necessary electrical cables, mount accessory boxes and run in any pipework for hot and cold water or central heating.

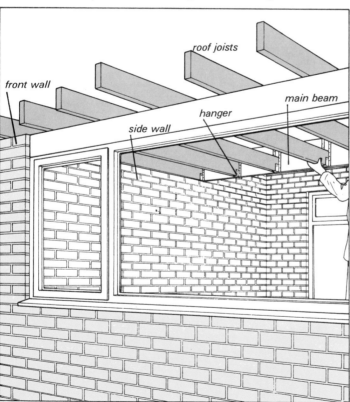

Resting the roof joists between the front wall and main beam which has been set into the side walls of the extension.

Nailing the roof joists into hangers attached to the main beam; toe-nail through the top of the roof joists into the main beam also.

Nailing furring pieces (narrow end over the front wall) to the tops of the roof joists to set a 1 in 80 fall for the roof covering.

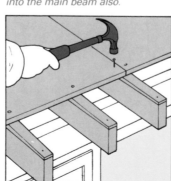

Nailing the plywood roofing sheets over the furrings; stagger the joints between the short edges.

After pouring hot asphalt on to the roof, smoothing it out to a layer about 10mm (⅜in) thick.

DAMP, ROT AND INSECT ATTACK

Dampness in the home is more than just a nuisance. It can make the place difficult and expensive to heat; uncomfortable and unhealthy. And it can be positively destructive. If you're lucky it will merely ruin floorcoverings, decorations, and furnishings. If you're not, you could face crumbling plaster indoors, crumbling brickwork outdoors, and a running battle against wood-devouring insects and fungii. So, how can it be prevented? How can it be cured? It helps to think of it as either 'rising' or 'penetrating' damp.

Rising Damp

Rising damp is simply the result of walls and solid floors soaking up moisture from the ground. All buildings do this to some extent, but in most, the process is kept under control. In modern homes this is achieved by building an impervious layer called a flashing — into the walls a little way above ground level. Made of slate, lead, copper, aluminum, zinc, roofing felt, or waterproof 'engineering' bricks, this simply stops the rising moisture reaching floor joists and any other part of the house structure that might be damaged by it. A similarly impervious sheet plastic or bitumen waterproof membrane does the same job in solid floors at ground level and,

in theory, this combination should protect the house against rising damp forever. Unfortunately, it doesn't always work out that way.

The most likely cause of a failure is that part of the flashing or waterproof membrane has ceased to be impervious. This may be because it has been physically broken, say, in the course of building work, or by subsidence, or because it has become porous with age — metal and felt flashings are prone to this. In the latter case, a completely new damp-proofing system may be needed; elsewhere, repairs should do the trick.

What's called 'bridging' can also lead to trouble. Here, moisture by-passes the flashing or waterproof membrane via, say, a pile of contractor's debris heaped against the wall. Garden walls and flowerbeds can also act as 'bridges', as can porches and extensions built, either without damp-proofing, or with flashings and membranes that don't link up with those of the house.

Paths and patios present a twin threat: even if they don't form a physical bridge across a flashing, they can still help dampness get at the wall above. The paving may have been irresponsibly laid so that rainwater drains towards the house, caus-

ing flooding and, if this rises above the flashing, rising damp. Less obviously, rising damp can be caused merely by raindrops bouncing off a paved surface that finishes less than 150mm (6in) — or two bricks depths — below the flashing.

From that, it may sound as if rising damp is a problem no matter what you do, but, in fact, flashing and membrane failures are rare. Serious rising damp is far more likely in older houses, because these were usually built without any sort of damp-proofing at all. Instead, they relied on the fact that, so long as a wall or floor lost moisture by evaporation as fast as it took up from the ground, rising damp wouldn't be a problem. And it works — most of the time. The snag is, the balance can be so easily upset. Laying a vinyl floorcovering, or paint-ing the walls of the house could do it. So, if you live in an old house, even if it does not suffer from rising damp now, have damp-proofing installed as a precaution.

Penetrating Damp

The second type of dampness — penetrating damp — can usually be traced back to an obvious fault: a leaking pipe, a hole in the roof, gaps around window and door frames, or a faulty gutter. Repair the cause and the

dampness should disappear. However, there is one form of penetrating damp that's harder to identify and cure, and that is dampness soaking through the very fabric of exterior walls.

Again, this is most likely in older houses: it's relatively easy for dampness on the outside of their solid walls to soak through to the inside. Even so, the problem is usually triggered by a definite fault. If the pointing (the mortar between bricks) is sound, it may be that the bricks themselves have become damaged or porous with age, and in this case, all you can do is waterproof the surface with cladding, rendering, paint, or a chemical sealant.

In modern homes, walls consist of two skins of masonry with an air gap in between. Any moisture in the outer leaf of this cavity wall stays there, but bridge the gap and penetrating damp appears. In new work, it's likely to show as regularly-spaced patches. This usually means that moisture is getting in via dirt or mortar, caked on to the metal 'ties' holding the leaves of the wall rigid and together. Where the dampness is widespread, check for cavity wall insulation that has been badly installed. In both cases, have the builder or insulation installer put things right.

Curing damp that has penetrated through the wall's fabric is more complicated and the first step is to decide what kind of wall you're dealing with by inspecting exposed brickwork. If it contains 'headers' (bricks laid at right-angles to the wall's face) it's solid. If the brickwork is rendered, or clad in some way, the age of the house is a good guide: if it was built before 1945, the walls are almost certainly solid.

Having identified the type of wall, what next? With a solid wall, there's a lot you can do to help yourself.

Pointing Pointers

Start by hacking out old, unsound pointing with a small cold chisel and light sledge hammer, aiming to cut back to a depth of about 10mm (⅜in). Brush out any loose debris, then splash in clean water to help the new mortar to stick (the porous masonry would otherwise suck the moisture from the new mortar). Use a 1:4 mix of cement and sand; for small areas buy this dry ready-mixed in bags. Make a 'hawk' from a square of plywood with a dowel handle nailed in the centre and use to hold a small amount of mortar close to the wall. Mold the mortar into a small mound shape then cut off a sausage-shape on the back of a small pointing trowel. Press this firmly into place between bricks, then continue until you've covered about one square metre (one square yard), then go back and apply a pointing profile to match the surrounding wall.

● **Flush pointing** Smooth the mortar level with the face of the wall using a wad of sacking or coarse hessian. Use for

sheltered walls only, or where the surface is to be painted.

● **Rounded pointing** Indent the mortar using a length of 10mm (⅜in) diameter dowel or plastic tube to give it a delicate half-round profile.

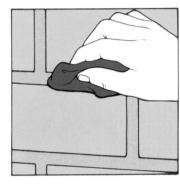

● **Weather-struck pointing** For exposed walls. Use the trowel to shape the mortar into a neat sloping bevel: use a long, straight wooden batten held against the wall to steady your hand as you

work. With either pointing profile, tackle the vertical joints before the horizontals.

Wall Faults

With the pointing completed, check the masonry. Moisture penetrating a cracked brick may freeze in winter, expand and

literally 'blow' the face off the brick: this 'spalling' allows more moisture to soak in to the extent that rain often appears to pour through the wall. Cracked or spalled bricks should be hacked out with a cold chisel and hammer and replaced. Chop around the brick to free it or drill into it many times with a large masonry bit then attack the brick and remove the fragments.

If bricks aren't badly spalled, make a repair with a little car body filler with brick dust sprinkled on to match the surrounding brickwork.

If so many are affected that this is not practical, merely cut out the unsound material, make good with mortar and render the entire wall.

To replace a brick, try to find a second-hand one to match the rest of the wall. Clean up the inside of the hole, dampen it, then line the bottom and one end with a stiff mortar mix. Butter the top and one end of the replacement brick by scraping the mortar off the trowel. Form a wedge-shape and furrow the mortar to aid suction. Insert the brick in the hole, buttered end to clean end, tap in place and point the joints.

Where the damage is less extensive, rake out cracks and small holes, undercutting the surrounding sound material to form a ledge for the filler material to grip to. Fill with a 1:5 mix of cement and sharp sand or a proprietary exterior filler.

'Blown' or blistered areas of render that have come away from the brickwork should be cut away with a hammer and chisel and filled with mortar to within about 25mm (1in) of the surface. Allow this to stiffen, then scratch the surface with the edge of a steel float or trowel to provide a key for the finishing coat. This

can consist of plain mortar or mortar mixed with fine aggregate — depending on the texture of the original; try to match the surrounding surface. Once applied, saw it off level with the surrounding wall by drawing a straight-edged timber batten across the surface.

If damp continues to penetrate despite repairs (it can take months for the original dampness to dry out) consider sealing the wall. Having it rendered and/or painted with an exterior wall paint is one possibility. Shielding the wall with some form of cladding is another. But either will obviously alter the look of the house.

To avoid that, use a colorless silicon-based water repellent. This is brushed or sprayed on to the surface of the wall (you can rent suitable spraying equipment) normally in two coats, and should provide effective protection for up to five years. All you do then is apply a further coat.

But do remember the problem with old houses and the evaporation of rising damp: anything you do to keep moisture out of a wall, will, to some extent, also keep moisture in, so you must have flashing installed before you start.

Finally, there's the old problem of penetrating damp in basements and cellars. You'll never cure the damp problem — the water is under tremendous pressure from the surrounding ground — but you can conceal its effects.

If the dampness isn't too bad, you may get away with sealing the wall using a black bitumen-based paint designed for the purpose. The wall can then be lined with plasterboard mounted on preservative-treated timber battens screwed to the wall. There is, though, a surer method, which involves lining the wall with proprietary bitumen-impregnated corrugated lathing, on top of which you can fix plasterboard or plaster direct.

Trick

Pointing takes practice and you'll discover that the sausages of mortar either fall out of the joint or off your trowel: to help you get it to stick, hold the hawk directly under the joint and scoop the sausage into place using the trowel. This way, if it falls out again, you won't drop the mortar, and can try again.

CURES FOR RISING DAMP

Given that the only sure way to prevent rising damp is to insert both a flashing and a waterproof membrane, you might think it's asking a lot to carry out the work successfully in an existing building. And using traditional building methods, so it is. Putting in a flashing, for example, involves literally sawing right through the house walls, then inserting a suitably moisture-proof sheet material into the resulting slot. That's a job for professionals and as you might expect, it's not cheap. But there are easier ways to provide the protection of a flashing.

Choosing a Flashing

Perhaps the oddest flashing system designed for use in existing building is the version that works by 'electro osmosis'. This involves simply girdling the house in a band of copper, which is then connected to a metal rod sunk into the ground: it sounds unlikely, but it does actually work. The rising moisture is helped on its way by the tiny electrical charge naturally present in all walls. By providing an efficient electrical ground, this charge is removed and the dampness stays in the ground.

Porous ceramic tubes are another possibility. Set into holes drilled deep within the masonry and capped with grilles to stop them playing host to unwanted wildlife, these improve the wall's ability to lose excess moisture through evaporation and thus keep the wall effectively free from damp.

The cheapest, simplest, and most commonly used system, however, is the chemical flashing. Here a waterproof chemical — normally a silicon-based liquid similar to that used to seal a wall's surface — is pumped into the brickwork under pressure until the courses at flashing level are saturated. This renders the wall at that level waterproof and thus converts it into an effective mechanical flashing.

Which is best? Well, they all work, so your choice will probably be based on cost and the appearance of the finished product. So far as looks are concerned, a chemical flashing is undoubtedly the least conspicuous. The holes drilled to ensure that the chemical gets right into the brickwork are fairly small and easily plugged with mortar once you've finished. These mortar plugs can then be concealed behind rendering — a simple mortar 'skirt' around the base of the house is all that's needed.

Chemical flashings also tend to be the least expensive to install, particularly so if you rent the necessary equipment and do the work yourself: the others are best installed by specialist contractors. But a word of warning. If you're installing a flashing because it's a condition of your mortgage, your bank or building society are unlikely to accept a do-it-yourself effort. Their interest lies as much in a long guarantee for the work, as in the quality of the damp-proofing and so, even though a chemical flashing is still probably the best bet, you must have it put in by a reputable specialist company.

Hacking off the plaster to just above the rising damp using a light sledge and masons chisel; remove the baseboard, and set aside if sound.

Drilling 75mm (3in) deep holes in the second course of brickwork, angled downwards; drill two holes per stretcher, one per header.

Inserting the short injection nozzles into the drilled holes; tighten the wing nuts to expand the nozzles and form a seal.

Turning on the control valves of the two nozzles inserted in the wall; switch on the pump to circulate the injection fluid.

Installing a Chemical Flashing

Assuming you've decided to install a chemical flashing yourself, you need to start by doing a little homework. Most tool rental shops will supply you with the heavy-duty masonry drill, pumping equipment and chemicals you need, but both prices, and the amount of guidance you can expect on their use, vary considerably, so shop around.

For a typical semi-detached house, the damp-proofing itself should take two or three days, allowing yourself a fair margin for error, and you can reckon on a further couple of days to make good the holes and conceal them behind a rendered plinth, if necessary. It's therefore worth taking a week's vacation for the purpose, though a couple of long weekends would do just as well. Having worked out your dates, book the rental equipment in advance and ask if you can take away the instructional literature so you can study it before you actually have to start work.

Take a note of the length of wall you wish to treat, so that the supplier can make sure he has enough chemical in stock. Exactly how much you need depends on the thickness and porosity of the masonry, so you'd do well to take more than you think you need — hopefully on a 'sale or return' basis. As a rough guide, allow 3 litres per metre (8 pints per 3ft) of wall.

Before you Start

If your house walls are showing

Pressure-injection equipment in use.

Bleeding air from the system via the third nozzle; turn off the valve when the fluid flows freely.

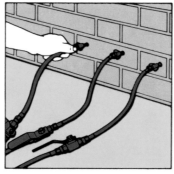

Inserting the third nozzle into the next hole; open the valve so that all three nozzles are injecting.

As the bricks become saturated, closing the control valves and moving along to the next hole.

With the first injection completed, repeating with the longer nozzles after drilling out to 190mm (7½in).

signs of rising damp — stained, wet wallpaper and plasterwork to a height of about 450mm (18in) — hack off the plaster to just above this level, using a light sledge hammer and masons chisel. Prise off the base board and save for refitting later. Also remove any radiators, pipes and electrical accessories.

Before taking charge of the rented equipment, check that it is in good working order and make sure you know how it works. If you damage it through ignorance you may lose your deposit. Typical machines comprise a pump, and injection nozzles. The latter consist of three or more short probes for a 112mm (4½in) wall and three or more long probes for a 225mm (9in) wall. The machine may have an integral reservoir for the fluid, or you may need to pump it from a drum via a suction nozzle.

Start by drilling 10mm (⅜in) diameter holes two thirds of the way into the wall, at 112mm (4½in) intervals along the line of the chemical. You can drill inject from one side of a 112mm (4½in) wall using the short nozzles; from both sides of a 225mm (9in) wall; or from one side in two stages using short then long nozzles. There's been some dispute as to whether it's better to drill into the mortar or into the bricks, but most experts now agree that it's better to drill into the mortar above and below a brick course that is both 150mm (6in) above ground level and below the level of internal floor joists. If you'd prefer to inject the bricks, drill holes at a downward angle: one per header; two per stretcher.

With the holes drilled, the next step is to insert the 'probes' through which the chemical waterproofing agent is injected — normally they're secured with butterfly nuts which expand them against the sides of the holes. It's usual to insert all but one nozzle in the holes, then bleed off a little fluid from this to dispel air from the system, before inserting it and switching on again. Switch on and wait, checking both the wall and the level of chemical from time to time. Eventually, you should see the surface of the wall begin to 'sweat', and that's your cue to switch off, withdraw the probes and move on to the next section of wall.

The chemical you've injected will begin to cure fairly quickly but, to make sure, it's best to leave the wall overnight before filling the holes you've drilled with a mortar mix of sharp sand and cement in the proportions 5:1. Leave this to dry out thoroughly, then brush over the surface of the wall above and below the new flashing with an exterior masonry sealer of the sort used for curing penetrating damp. Leave this to cure before covering the mortar plugs with a rendered plinth. This should stop the rendering acting as a bridge for rising damp and thus defeating the object of the exercise.

Re-Plastering Indoors

It's best to wait until the dampness has disappeared from the internal walls before you replaster — and this can take about one month per 25mm (1in) of wall thickness. If this isn't acceptable, use a render containing a waterproof additive after about three days.

Damp-Proofing Floors

Damp-proofing an existing floor is a little more complicated. The correct method — and the only one guaranteed to succeed — is to dig up the floor, put down a layer of either hot bitumen, brush-on bitumen, or plastic sheet, making sure this is keyed into the flashing in the walls, then top with a 50mm (2in) thick screed of concrete.

It doesn't take a vivid imagination to see that this is a difficult, messy, time-consuming and expensive job. If your floor is beyond repair, this could be your only course of action. See page 46 for full details on how to lay a new solid floor.

Where the deterioration of the original floor is minimal, treat the surface with a coat of bitumen, applied by brush, then cover it with self-levelling flooring compound (see page 46) to leave a surface ready for any flooring. This is quick, simple, and will certainly stop damp rising through the floor. Unfortunately what it may also do is increase the risk of dampness rising through the adjacent walls, by-passing their flashing in the process. If this leads to an outbreak of rot in the base boards, you've got trouble. Seek expert advice if you're unsure.

One possible exception to this is where the floor is below ground level. Here, so long as you are careful to continue the damp-proofing up the walls to a little above flashing level, all should be well.

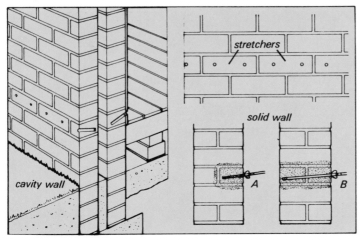

In solid walls, drill 75mm (3in), then 190mm (7½in) holes.

cavity wall

stretchers

solid wall

PROBLEMS WITH ROT

If the obvious effects of moisture were all you had to contend with, outbreaks of rising and penetrating damp wouldn't be too bad. The trouble is that dampness can give rise to all sorts of other problems, and the most serious of these is wood rot.

Wood rots are merely fungii; part of nature's waste-disposal system, and in fields and forests they do a valuable job eating up dead trees and other plant matter and returning its goodness to the soil. The trouble is, the average home is just full of dead trees in the form of rafters, joists, floorboards and other structural members. The only reason that all wood is not disposed of as a matter of course is that it's far too dry. Dry, that is, until it has been exposed to rising or penetrating damp for more than a couple of weeks. At that point, certain species of fungus that don't like their food too soggy get to work and your home starts to fall apart. These are commonly referred to as simply wet rot, and dry rot.

Wet Rot

Of the two, wet rot — in particular rot caused by the so-called cellar fungus — is the most common and the most fussy. It tends to like wood that is fairly moist and won't touch anything else, so it's effects are mercifully confined to areas of obvious dampness. What's more, if its habitat is allowed to dry out, the fungus usually dies and that makes it relatively easy to get rid of. Remove the source of dampness, replace the rotten wood and the problem is solved.

How do you identify wet rot? To begin with, affected wood looks and feels like most people's idea of rotten wood and it is likely to be fairly localized. Surrounding dry wood will be totally unaffected. Of the fungus itself, you are unlikely to see very much at all: it may show as a yellowish-brown skin on the timber surface, or as a vein-like covering of dark brown thread-like strands.

Of the other wet rots, the only common one that looks markedly different is one called *Poria vaillantii*. It's normally found where the dampness has

Wood affected by dry rot; it is cracked along and across the grain.

been caused by water dripping from plumbing and gutter leaks and tends to cover the surface with cord-like white strands.

Dry Rot

Dry rot is a far more formidable opponent. Although, in spite of its name, dry rot needs a relatively damp piece of wood to get started, once established, it is quite capable of spreading right through the house: it has even been known to work its way along an entire street, invading one town house after another. If dry rot encounters wood that is too dry for it to consume, it produces its own water and makes it damp. If it meets a barrier of solid masonry (brick, stone; even coarse concrete) it manufactures acid and eats through it.

As if that were not bad enough, dry rot also has the ability to bide its time if conditions are not particularly favorable. It can establish itself in a small way within a house and go completely unnoticed for years, only to run through the place like wildfire as soon as the environment is more to its liking. This, of course, means that merely removing the source of dampness and replacing affected wood will not get rid of the rot. The remnants of the fungus left in the masonry and the apparently unaffected surrounding woodwork will simply take a rest — if you're lucky — then start again.

And there's another tricky thing about dry rot: because it dislikes extremely wet, cold conditions, it may only become a serious problem after you have cured the cause of dampness

and have begun to dry the place out. Unless you provide plenty of ventilation as well as warmth, far from denying the fungus a habitat, you may actually create precisely the warm, humid conditions in which it thrives.

So, how do you combat this menace? The short answer is that you must remove every scrap of wood that might possibly contain traces of the fungus — and that means a lot of timber that seems quite sound — and treat everything else in the vicinity (wood or masonry) with a suitable chemical fungicide. And you have to be thorough about it. Although it may seem, at the time, as if the cure is more destructive than rot, take half measures and, before you know it, you'll have another outbreak on your hands.

It's therefore obviously an advantage to be able to identify dry rot as early as possible. Unfortunately, the bulk of the fungus is made up of microscopic 'roots' called *hypae*, running invisibly through wood and masonry. By the time signs visible to the naked eye appear, they will already have done a lot of damage. In fact, very often, dry rot does not become apparent until it is sufficiently mature to produce fruiting bodies which discharge millions of spores into the atmosphere and accelerate the spread of the fungus (they're sometimes mistaken for brick dust).

To complicate matters, visible signs of the fungus tend to vary according to conditions. If it has established itself in a secluded spot — behind panelling, in cellars and so on — you may see the hypae on the surface as a cottony mass of fibers. You might also discover the fruiting bodies, emerging through cracks such as those between the base boards and floor, or even outdoors in a quiet corner. These are small, rubbery, whitish growths at first, developing into rusty yellow honeycomb structures between 50 and 500mm (2in and 20in) across. On vertical surfaces, these stand out like shelves. Elsewhere they lie flat.

But if the fungus itself varies in appearance, the look of badly affected wood does not. It will be so soft and powdery, you can easily push a screwdriver straight through it. It will also have an almost charred appearance in that the surface will be badly cracked both along and across the wood's grain.

Dry rot fungus; the spores look like rusty coloured brick dust and, if discovered, the source should be investigated immediately.

The first, and absolutely essential step in the treatment of wet rot is to remove the cause of the dampness that produced the conditions under which the fungus was able to thrive. Whether it was rising damp, penetrating damp, leaking plumbing, or whatever: fix it.

If the outbreak of rot seems unconnected with an obvious source of dampness — and this is most likely in little-used attics and in the space beneath a suspended wooden floor — it could be that the moisture necessary for the survival of the fungus is being provided by condensation. Condensation can be caused by a number of factors, but in this sort of situation, poor ventilation is almost certainly at the root of the problem. In attics, check that the eaves are clear. Elsewhere, make sure that there is enough ventilation and that this has not become clogged or blocked in any way.

With the source of dampness taken care of, the next step is to survey the damage. As well as finding out just how far the rot has spread, concentrate on checking the extent to which the strength of affected wood has been reduced. Unless there are other factors to be taken into account, such as difficulties in redecorating partially rotten wood, any wood that is still strong enough to do its job, allowing a fair margin for safety, can be left in place.

Getting Down to Work

Once you've decided how much wood needs to go, you can start removing it. Depending on the location of the rot, you should be prepared for a fair amount of mess, as much of the worst-affected wood will break up as you take it out.

If you are removing floor joists, roof members, or anything else with a structural role, take care to provide adequate support, using adjustable props and so on, until the work is complete. And do dispose of the rotten wood sensibly. Burn it. Put it on the compost heap if you must, but don't leave it lying about where it can contaminate anything else with the fungus.

Next, replace whatever you've

After marking angled lines with a combination square, cutting out the rotten wood with a backsaw; chisel along the back edge.

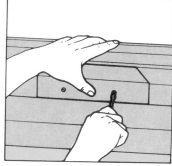

After applying waterproof give to the mitered replacement wood, screwing it with countersunk screws to the sound wood behind.

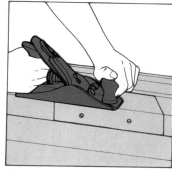

Planing flush with the adjacent wood surface; fill any gaps with filler, prime the wood and paint thoroughly.

removed with new wood. Use preservative-treated wood this time, preferably the pressure-treated type; this vacuum impregnation saturates a far deeper layer than can be achieved by merely brushing or spraying on the preservative (deeper even than soaking) and therefore provides much greater protection. Remember, though, that if you breach this layer of chemically-treated wood, rot may find its way into the heart of the wood in the future. So, if you have to cut, chisel, plane, or work the wood in any way, treat the newly-exposed surface with preservative before fitting the wood into place.

Make Sure with Preservative

A liberal dose of wood preservative should also be applied to nearby woodwork and in particular to any partially rotten wood you may have seen fit to keep. So far as killing off wet rot is concerned, this is not strictly speaking necessary. As the area dries out, the fungus should die anyway. However, it doesn't hurt to make sure. Wood that has endured fungal attack once, tends to be prone to it forever and as the area dries, there's just a chance that dry rot will take over where wet rot left off.

There are a number of preservatives you can use, but go for a solvent-born type that will also give protection against insect attack. This can simply be brushed on, but for the best results, apply it using spraying equipment. This can be rented from any good tool or hardware store, but be sure to tell them

exactly what you want to spray, and obtain a protective mask and goggles while you're about it — wood preservative is dangerous if inhaled.

If it proves impossible to treat some sections properly, consider using one of the new 'dry' preservatives on the market as insurance. These are pellets, which you insert into holes drilled in the wood and cover with filler. They will stay there until the wood becomes damp, then slowly dissolve to kill any fungus that may try to gain a foothold.

Drying Out

The final job is to let the area dry out completely. As already described, there's some risk here of initiating an attack of dry rot while you're doing this, so take care.

The trick is to provide enough warmth to draw the moisture out into the air and enough ventilation to remove the resulting very humid air as quickly as

possible. It will almost certainly take several weeks; perhaps several months if a damp wall is involved. But it is essential not to give up and leave the job half done.

You must also beware of slowing the process down by sealing damp surfaces with inappropriate decorations. Putting up wooden cladding is just asking for trouble. Go for thin wallpaper rather than washable wallcoverings or tiles (which can hold in moisture); latex paint rather than enamel for the same reason. And the cheaper the better: whatever you put up will almost certainly be ruined by the moisture passing through it. Incidentally, don't worry if you discover a white powdery substance on the walls. Called efflorescence, it's simply mineral salts drawn from the masonry. Brush it off with a stiff-bristled hand brush but don't wash it off: this merely redissolves the salts and slows up the drying-out process.

Trick

When spraying, try to cover every bit of exposed timber, bearing in mind that the object of the exercise is to impregnate a sufficiently deep layer of timber to provide long-term protection. Pay particular attention to cracks, holes, joints and any other nooks and crannies, because it is in these, more than anywhere else, that fresh outbreaks of rot and insect attack are likely to begin.

TREATING DRY ROT

The main difference between the treatment of dry rot and wet rot is that the former has a nasty habit of making comebacks. The only way to stop that happening is to be ruthlessly efficient in erradicating it from your home. Don't even be tempted to take shortcuts in order to save money, because however much you may have spent already, it will be money down the drain.

What's the Damage?

As soon as you realize there is dry rot in your home, set to work as quickly as possible. The longer you wait, the more damage will be done.

The first step is to assess the scale of the disaster and decide whether you want to tackle the repair work yourself or call in a specialist contractor. Obviously, the latter won't be cheap, but it is probably the best option where the dry rot is so extensive as to have threatened important structural members such as those in the roof. It is also advisable to have the work carried out professionally if it is a condition of a mortgage. Any reputable firm will provide a good guarantee against renewed attack and it is to this that the bank or building society will look in order to protect their investment.

Assuming you do decide to tackle the job yourself, it's best to start by finding a fairly badly affected piece of wood. If you cannot tell what's damaged and what's not simply by looking, perhaps because the rot has been hidden under decorations, poking about with a screwdriver will soon reveal it — the screwdriver will go straight through. Just one word of warning. Watch your step if floorboards and/or joists are involved, particularly if searching out the rot involves moving heavy furniture. They may be too rotten to take the weight.

Having found a likely place to start, strip out the infected wood, providing temporary substitute structural support as necessary, and keep going until every bit of rotten wood has been removed. But don't stop at the obviously affected wood. Everything within at least 450mm (18in) or better still one metre (3ft) of the last visible signs of rot, must be regarded as contaminated and disposed of.

You can use your discretion to decide whether to remove the whole of a partially rotten wood, or to cut it and salvage whatever remains. If the wood is in contact with soil or masonry along its length, however, don't try to save anything, even if only part of it is visibly

Setting a ceramic air brick into mortar in a solid wall after chiselling out a whole brick with a masons chisel.

Fitting a telescopic air brick; fit the louvres (angled downwards) to the liner and adjust to length with the inner liner.

damaged.

All infected wood should be taken out into the garden and burned. Plastic garbage bags are useful here for transporting the smaller crumbly bits, and it's vitally important that you clear up thoroughly as you go. Dirt, sawdust, odd bits of wood, nails, wallplugs; nothing that has been, or may have been, in contact with the fungus must be allowed to remain.

The spores may even invade electrical socket outlets and as you can't wash them off these fixtures, replace with new sockets; if the spores have been in contact with any cables, renew these too. You'll soon recognise attack: the plastic sheathing will be discolored.

Don't miss the Masonry

Once the infected wood is out of the

way, turn your attention to any soil and masonry in the vicinity. A blowtorch can be used to burn off much of the surface growth in situ. When you've done that, remove any crumbling plaster, brush off any trace of fungus that remains and dispose of the debris as carefully as you did the infected wood.

Even after that, masonry and soil may still harbor remnants of the fungus and should be treated with a suitable water-soluble fungicide, according to the manufacturer's instructions. It's particularly important not to skimp on the recommended dosage and to ensure that the fungicide penetrates right into the wall. You'll need to rent pressure-spraying equipment for this and if the masonry is more than 100mm (4in) thick — the thickness of one brick — in addition to spraying the surface of the wall, it's necessary to inject the fungicide into the interior through suitably drilled holes. Spaced roughly 230mm (9in) apart, these should slope downwards at an angle of about 45 degrees and reach to within 50mm (2in) of the other face of the wall.

This treatment should be carried on all masonry within 450mm (18in) of the affected area. On party walls, and external walls where there is evidence of fungal growth on the outer face, it is also well worth treating the wall both from sides. And once again, clean up as you go. The infected brick dust from drilling the wall is enough to start another outbreak of rot.

Next, if you find bare soil beneath affected floors, remove it to a depth of 150mm (6in) over an area at least one metre (3ft) greater all round than that apparently contaminated. Shovel it into bags and move as far from the house as possible. The newly exposed soil should then be sprayed with fungicide in the same way as the masonry.

Mopping Up

Run a final check to make absolutely sure that nothing which might harbor the fungus or its spores has been missed. That includes wallpaper, carpets, furniture, insulation, and so on within about one metre (3ft) of the obvious damage.

Every bit of wood within about two metres (6ft) should now be thoroughly sprayed with solvent-borne preservative. Take as much trouble over this as over the rest of the job. Be sure to dose the wood according to the manufacturer's instructions, paying particular attention to nooks and crannies.

Cut back floor joists to 1m (3ft) outside the affected area; or replace whole joists. Clean up, spray the subsoil and remaining wood.

Levering rotten base board away from the wall; this is a favorite place for dry rot which may first show as fungus.

Chiselling off plaster from brickwork within, and up to 1m (3ft) outside the affected area.

Drilling at an angle of 45° downwards into the brickwork; space the holes at intervals of about 230mm (9in).

Pressure-injecting the wall with a water-soluble fungicide; always wear suitable protective clothing.

Ready for Repair

Having got thus far, it should be safe to start rebuilding and replacing all the woodwork you've stripped out. As with wet rot, though, do use preservative-treated lumber and remember to re-treat any bare wood that may have become exposed due to sawing, chiselling and so on.

And don't forget to take care of whatever it was that caused the dampness which triggered the attack of dry rot, be it penetrating damp, rising damp, or condensation. Unless the rot took hold while the house was locked up and uninhabited for some reason — and that is usually what sets off the worst outbreaks — you should also take another look at the way in which your home is ventilated. If there is one thing dry rot loves, it's a piece of wood in a warm, still, humid environment.

Additional air bricks are easily fitted: just chop a hole through the wall in the appropriate place (avoiding breaking through the flashing if the air brick is to go beneath a floor), slide in the air brick and mortar it in place. In other poorly ventilated corners of your home, some sort of ventilator grille may be more appropriate and you will find a range of these available at any good lumber yard or hardwood store.

Finally, remember that furniture, particularly things like built-in closets, can create poorly-ventilated areas even in an otherwise well ventilated room. In such cases, free-standing furniture should be kept just a little way away from the wall, and built-ins should be fitted with ventilation grilles: drilling a series of holes will do.

Replacing a rotten door frame with preservative-treated wood; first coat the wall with a waterproof sealant.

INSECT INVADERS

Another problem commonly, though by no means exclusively, associated with damp homes, is invasion by insects and other pests. These may be anything from bees to owls, but by far the most common and most destructive intruders are wood-boring beetles and termites.

The upper surface (top) of a floorboard may show no signs of attack from the common furniture beetle, but the underside (bottom) reveals its presence.

The common furniture (or woodworm) beetle, Anobium punctatum; the first sign of its presence may be small piles of fine sawdust. Well-polished furniture is relatively safe.

Woodworm

It's actually the larvae of the beetle rather than the adult insect which does the damage, so it's not surprising that the most widespread species (the Common Furniture Beetle) is popularly known as woodworm.

Its life cycle begins when the adult — a beetle only a few millimetres long, varying in colour from reddish yellow to dark brown — lays its eggs on a suitable piece of wood. Cracks, endgrain and joints are favourite sites, generally in areas where the air is still and where the timber is moderately damp, but not wet. The interiors of cabinets, together with the backs of drawers and freestanding units are all likely candidates, as are floor joists, exposed floorboards and roof structural members.

As the larvae hatch from the eggs, they begin burrowing into the heart of the wood, where they remain happily munching until the time comes to pupate and transform themselves into adults. Once this metamorphosis is complete, the adult eats its way to the surface of the wood, and flies off to mate and find a likely spot to lay its eggs.

All this makes the woodworm fairly difficult to spot: you have to be lucky to see either the larvae or the adult beetles. However, the holes through which the adult emerges — the flight holes are generally just over one millimetre (1/16in) in diameter — are a sure sign that the insects have been at work, and if you find traces of fine, powdery 'bore dust' in the vicinity, you can be pretty sure that adults have only recently left, and that the wood is still at risk.

Other Woodborers

Another wood-boring insect is the Death Watch Beetle, a pest similar in many respects to the Common Furniture Beetle; the main difference being that at about 6mm (1/4in) long, it's larger and therefore produces larger flight holes, typically about 3mm (1/8in) in diameter. The adults are also not good at flying, and so you may well see them on the floor around affected wood. The adults can often be heard tapping their heads against the woodwork in a quiet room.

A further significant difference is that the larvae are far more agile than ordinary woodworm, and will wander over the surface of wood on hatching, searching for just the right spot to burrow in. Being fairly large — up to 12mm (1/2in) — once in the wood they create a lot of debris, identifiable to the naked eye as bun-shaped pellets.

Their favourite habitat is wood that is already under attack from fungus and attacks are largely confined to fairly old housing, so the Death Watch Beetle is becoming less common in the home.

The same applies to the Powder Post Beetle. This woodborer will only eat hardwoods such as oak, and so (although you may find it in old furniture) it is unlikely to cause major problems.

The House Longhorn Beetle is another fussy eater — its diet consists solely of softwood. Unfortunately, it's big (the larvae can be up to 24mm/1in long and over 6mm/1/4in across) so it's capable of doing a lot of damage. To make matters worse, it tends to specialize in roof members, so its a serious pest indeed.

Other Uninvited Guests

Of course, not all of the creepy-crawlies one finds indoors are there to eat you, literally, out of house and home. Many will have simply strayed in from the garden. Others are usually content to do no worse than eat a bit

Damage to a wallplate caused by woodboring weevils; these insects lay their eggs on wood already infested with wet rot.

The death-watch beetle, Xestobium rufovillosum , and its flight holes; it is normally seen near the rotting wood which it infests.

of wallpaper adhesive. And some, notably spiders, actually do good by preying on the insect population.

There are, however, quite a number of undesirables which you may encounter, ranging from nuisances such as ants, wasps, and bees — check for nests of the last two in the attic – through destructive individuals such as the Common Clothes Moth, to wholly unsavoury types such as cockroaches and fleas. Thanks to modern insecticides, these, and many other insect pests are fairly easily controlled, but if you are in any doubt about exactly what you're dealing with, the local library can probably help out with one of the many specialist books on the subject.

Modern poisons will also take care of warm-blooded invaders such as rats and mice, though here if the situation gets out of hand, you would do well to contact the local Health Department and ask for their help.

GETTING RID OF WOODWORM

Where woodworm has attacked roof members, it's vital to establish just how much damage has been done and to decide whether or not the woodwork has been so weakened as to warrant its replacement. The resistance offered by the wood when you drill into it will give some guide, as will signs of structural weakness such as sagging in the roof as a whole. If in doubt, seek expert advice. The replacement of structural roof members is, in any case, no job for amateurs.

Having replaced any badly affected wood, the next step is to clean up. On partially affected wood of no structural importance, obviously unsound material can be chiselled away and replaced with suitably shaped patches. The surface of all wood should then be thoroughly brushed, or better still, vacuum-cleaned, to remove all traces of dirt and dust.

All that remains is to treat the wood with a preservative containing a long-lasting insecticide, and you will find several of these on the market. They are best sprayed on — that way you can be sure to get the preservative right into cracks, gaps and flight holes — and pressure-spraying equipment is widely available for hire.

Make sure that you treat every bit of wood thoroughly according to the preservative manufacturer's instructions. If that means stripping off roofing, insulation and so on, then that's what you must do. It takes only a small gap in the wood's preservative 'armor' to allow this tiny, but highly destructive pest to return.

Other Indoor Woodwork

Most other interior woodwork can be treated in exactly the same way as timber in the attic. The only difference is that you will probably have to do quite a lot of preparatory work to gain access to all the relevant surfaces.

For example, if you need to treat a suspended wooden floor, you will have to lift enough floorboards to allow you to spray affected joists, wallplates and other concealed lumber. Similarly, when treating staircases, you may have to remove plasterwork to get at the underside of the enclosed type. And don't forget structural members hidden behind architraves and other decorative joinery: although woodworm can't enter painted wood, the unpainted back is a likely point of attack. So, for a

Pressure-spraying roof members with woodworm preservative; thoroughly clean up first to ensure complete coverage. (Inset) Spraying floor members; lift every fifth or sixth board for access and spray the joists, wallplates and under the boards.

really thorough job, these too should be exposed and sprayed.

Treating Furniture

Spray-treatment with preservative is also suitable for some woodworm-infested furniture. However, for small scale work, it's generally preferable to merely inject the chemicals into the wood through the flight holes: you'll find numerous preservatives ready-packaged in aerosol container/dispensers designed for the work. The dispenser may include a slim tubular nozzle which you can poke into the flight holes for deepest penetration.

This method of treating woodworm is also worth considering for small-scale outbreaks in painted interior woodwork. It saves having to strip off the paint to expose bare wood — a must if you intend spraying.

Injecting the individual flight holes of the common furniture beetle in a chair rail; wickerwork can also be affected.

PLUMBING

Plumbing is work that many do-it-yourself enthusiasts will fight shy of — the mere thought of the possible damage caused by gallons of water cascading through the house should anything go wrong is enough to give many people nightmares. But domestic plumbing systems are not complicated and modern plumbing materials and fittings are not difficult to use. Although you can't hope to match the skills of a professional plumber, provided you approach each job with care, there is no reason why you should not handle most of the plumbing work around the home.

Making Changes

Apart from regular maintenance and essential repairs, there are many plumbing jobs that you might want to tackle yourself which could cost quite a lot if you were to employ a plumber.

The basic water supply/drainage systems in many houses are often inadequate for the needs of those who have to use them,

and if the house is old, the fittings are likely to be ugly and showing the effects of age. In the bathroom, a ceramic basin may be chipped or stained, the bath's enamel coating may be worn or chipped, and the toilet may have a noisy, inefficient tank. In the kitchen there may be a battered glazed earthenware sink or utilitarian steel item with chipped and stained enamel finish; neither lending itself to the installation of smart kitchen units. All can be replaced with modern stylish and efficient fittings in a wide range of colors to brighten up these purely functional rooms.

You may want to extend the systems to take account of a growing family or simply to make life easier. You put in extra washing/bathing facilities, an extra toilet and, in the kitchen, you can make permanent connections for washing machines, dishwashers and the many other labor-saving devices that need a water supply. You can tackle all these jobs without professional assistance.

Obtaining the Necessary Permission

Depending on the type of work you intend carrying out, you may have to obtain permission before you start. Your local Building Inspector will be particularly concerned that any work you do does not lead to the water supply being contaminated, and he may not allow the use of some plumbing fixtures or fittings. Your Local Building Department will want to know that the work is carried out in accordance with the local Building Code, which lays down certain requirements for the way you arrange water supply and drainage from an appliance.

If you are simply replacing a fitting with a similar but more up-to-date item and you are not moving its position, it is most likely that permission will not be required. However, if you are using an unconventional fitting, or extending or modifying a drainage system, then you will almost certainly need approval. If you are in any doubt at all about

this, it is best to check with your local Building Code before starting work — it could save you a lot of wasted time and money.

Easily Worked Materials

Most modern plumbing systems are made with copper pipes with copper or brass fittings (although lead or galvanized steel pipes may be found in very old systems) and this material is easily cut, bent and joined, making alterations to the existing pipework a straightforward process.

Recent developments in plastic pipe and fittings have led to the availability of plastic hot and cold water supply systems. With their simple push-together or glued joints, these systems make plumbing jobs even easier. Plastic waste pipe systems have been in use for some years and are just as easy to assemble.

Most repair work and all modifications or extensions to your plumbing system will make it necessary to drain part or all of the pipework. You should familiarize yourself with the system so that you know where all the stop-valves and drain-cocks are situated and also which faucets and appliances are fed directly from the rising main, the cold water storage tank if any, and the hot water cylinder.

Draining Parts of the System

It's not often that you will need to drain the system completely to do a particular job; it's usually only necessary to drain the affected circuit, keeping the rest of the system in commission and minimizing disruption.

Connections to the rising main or repairs to the various circuits within the house may mean turning off the main stop-valve fitted to the main just after it enters the house. If you're lucky there will be a drain-cock immediately above the stop valve. Simply push a hose on to the valve's outlet, lead it outside and open the valve to drain the pipe. If there is no drain-cock open the kitchen faucet until the water stops flowing.

When working on hot faucets, you can prevent too much hot water going to waste by shutting off the cold water main stop valve (which keeps the hot water cylinder topped up) first, then opening up the relevant hot faucet. This will keep most of the heated water still in the cylinder.

If the cylinder itself needs draining, turn off the immersion heater or boiler first. Close any stop-valve on the supply pipe from the cold water main and use the drain-cock which should

be fitted at the base of the pipe to empty the cylinder. If there is no drain-cock, the only way you can empty the cylinder is to disconnect the vent and draw-off pipe at the top of the cylinder and siphon out the water with a hose, connect the vent and draw-off the hot faucets to keep spillage to a minimum.

If a boiler circuit needs draining, turn off the boiler, tie up the float arm in the heating circuit's feed and expansion tank in the basement and drain the circuit from the drain-cock next to or inside the boiler. If the boiler is part of a central heating system, this will need draining, too.

Draining the Complete System

In an emergency you may need to drain the complete system. To do this, turn off the main stop-valve and open up all the faucets and drain-cocks. Once the trouble has been pinpointed, you can reinstate any unaffected circuits while you make repairs.

Refilling the System

In most cases all you need to do to refill the system is close any drain-cocks, open up any stop-valves or free any ball-valve float arms and close the faucets when water flows from them.

If you have drained a heating system, you will have to open the radiator bleed valves (see page 146) to allow air to escape as they fill with water, closing them when water appears.

Air locks can be overcome by connecting a hose between the kitchen cold faucet and the faucet of the affected circuit. Open the latter then the former; pressure will force the air bubble out of the system.

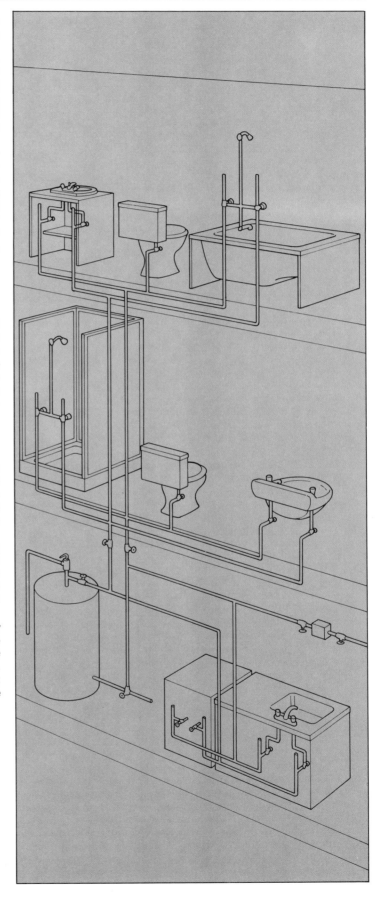

Water supply piping in a typical house. The supply pipe enters the house from the municipal supply or from a private well. A branch pipe feeds the hot water cylinder which is the beginning of the hot water supply system. Other branches feed to the individual fixtures and appliances.

WORKING WITH PIPE

The most common material used in modern plumbing systems is copper pipe; it is easy to cut, bend and join. All copper pipe used for plumbing systems comes in metric sizes, the most common being 15mm (½in), 22mm (¾in) and 28mm (1in). The apparent difference in sizing is explained by the fact that metric pipe dimensions refer to the external diameter, whereas Imperial pipe sizes refer to the inside diameter. Luckily, there are joint fittings available which allow modern metric pipes to be connected into older Imperial systems.

Measuring Copper Pipe

Lengths of copper pipe are joined by separate copper or brass connector or joint fittings, the pipe ends being inserted into them. Therefore, it is important when measuring up for a pipe length to make allowance for the margin of pipe inside the joint. Often the positions of the pipe stops inside the joint are marked on the outside but if they are not, it is simple to find out how much pipe fits inside. Just insert an off-cut of pipe into the joint and mark on it where the end of the pipe socket comes. Pull out the offcut and measure from the mark to the end. Incorporate this measurement in the overall length of pipe to be cut.

Cutting Copper Pipe

One of the most important skills to master when carrying out plumbing work is that of being able to cut a square end on a piece of pipe. A square end is essential if the pipe is to fit tightly against the pipe stop inside the joint, helping to form a watertight seal.

There is a simple way of marking a square cutting line round a pipe. First take a strip of thick paper with a straight edge and wrap it round the pipe so that the ends overlap and the edges are aligned. Then run a pencil around the edge of the paper; this will give you a square cutting line.

You can cut the pipe with a fine bladed hacksaw after first setting it in a vise. Don't overtighten the jaws of the vise as copper pipe is quite soft and easily distorted. Carefully saw through the pipe, keeping to the marked line. Then remove the burrs around the outer and inner edges with a half-round file. Make sure you shake out all the filings as they could cause damage to faucets or ball valves if left inside. Devices are available for debuffing both the inside and outside of a cut pipe.

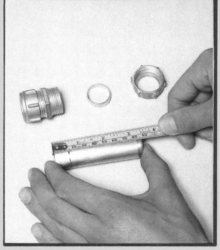

Measuring the depth of the pipe-stop in a fitting using an offcut; above, left to right: fitting, olive and capnut.

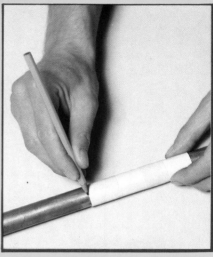

Marking a cutting line round the pipe against a piece of thick paper wrapped round it, to ensure a square end.

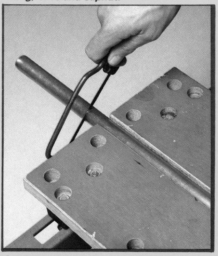

Cutting copper pipe with a fine-toothed hacksaw; a portable workbench is useful for holding the pipe without scoring it.

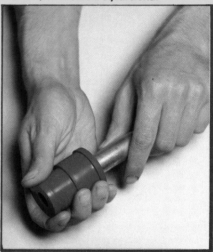

Using a de-burring brush to clean up simultaneously the inside and outside of a sawn end of pipe.

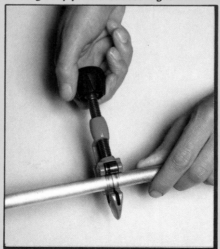

Cutting copper pipe with a wheel tube-cutter; rotate the cutter round the pipe, gradually tightening the screw-handle.

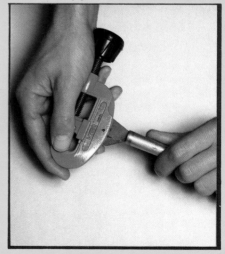

Reaming the cut pipe with the attachment on the cutter; wheel-cutters only leave a burr on the inside.

Trick

Bending copper pipe with an internal bending-spring; overbend slightly, bend back and pull out with the attached wire.

Using a pipe-bender; insert the pipe and the correct size of former and close the handles to give the required angle.

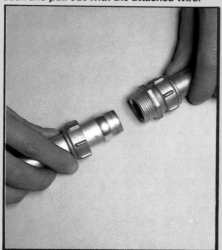

Joining copper pipe with a compression fitting; slip on first the capnut, then the olive, and screw into the joint body.

Tightening the capnuts with two wrenches grip the joint body with one and give each capnut 1½ turns from finger-tight.

Applying soldering paste to the end of the pipe after cleaning with steel wool; use the correct soldering paste for the fitting.

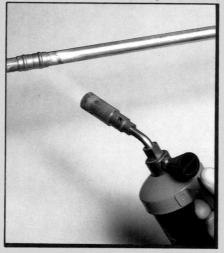

Heating a capillary fitting with a blow; heat the whole fitting until rings of solder appear at the ends.

If you have a lot of pipe to cut, rent or buy a wheel tube cutter. This ensures a square cut every time. To use it, all you do is insert the pipe between its jaws, and tighten up the adjuster. Then rotate the cutter round the pipe, tightening the adjuster as the cutting wheel bites into the pipe. The tool produces a burr-free outer edge to the cut and usually incorporates a 'reamer' (a hardened steel cutting edge) for scraping out the internal burr.

Bending Copper Pipe

Although you can buy angled joints for changing the direction of pipe runs, these are only limited to certain angles and they could work out expensive if you had to use a lot in a pipe run. It is cheaper and neater to bend the pipe itself.

You will need a special tool to prevent the pipe kinking as you bend it. For 15mm (½in) and 22mm (¾in) pipes you can use a bending spring. This is pushed inside the pipe and positioned at the point where it is to be bent. Then you simply bend the pipe over your knee, the spring supporting the walls of the pipe. A length of stiff wire attached to the end of the spring allows its removal.

With 28mm (1in) pipe, you'll need a bending machine. The pipe is inserted between the machine's formers and the handles pulled together to form a bend.

Joining Copper Pipes

There are two types of joint used for joining copper pipes: the brass compression joint and the copper capillary joint. Compression joints are easy to fit and may be dismantled and remade at will, whereas capillary joints are soldered permanently in place; however, they are cheaper than compression joints.

The compression joint has a central body with a threaded collar or capnut at each pipe socket. A watertight connection is made by tightening the capnuts which, in turn, compress brass or copper rings (called 'olives') between the body of the joint and the pipe.

A watertight seal is made with a capillary joint by melting solder between it and the pipe end. Some capillary joints have integral rings of solder and need only be heated with a blowtorch until the solder melts and flows round the pipe. Others, known as 'endfeed' fittings, have to be heated then fed with solder separately. The latter are cheapest, but the former are easiest to use.

INSTALLING A NEW SINK

The kitchen sink will probably be the first item you want to replace when modernising a kitchen; there is now a very wide selection of kitchen sinks to choose from. They can be stainless steel, enamelled steel, ceramic or glass fiber and come in a wide range of colors to match any decorative scheme. You can buy single or double bowl sinks, sinks with single or twin drainers, individual bowls and drainers, bowls for waste disposal units, sinks that act as tops for kitchen units and others for setting into worktops. All can be installed in the same basic manner, with slight alterations to the way they are mounted, the faucets fitted and wastes installed.

It is important for the sink to be out of commission for the least amount of time possible during the alteration work. To ensure this, assemble the new sink with its faucets and waste outlet before removing the old one. Likewise assemble any base unit but don't fit the sink top to it until it is in position. If you are fitting a new worktop to an old sink base unit for an inset sink, you can make the cutout for the sink before fitting the top. Use a powered jig saw or saber saw for the job.

Assemble the waste outlet to the new sink first, bedding it on a layer of plumber's putty if no rubber or plastic gasket is provided with it. Some sinks may have an overflow duct formed integrally, but others will have a separate overflow assembly. In the former case make sure the slot in the waste outlet is aligned with the duct. In the latter, the overflow pipe has a 'banjo' fitting at its end which fits over the outlet tail. Make sure the hole in this is aligned with the slot in the outlet before securing it with the outlet's backnut.

Fit the faucets in place, applying a layer of plumber's putty round the base of each if no gasket is provided. If you decide on a mixer valve, make sure it is for kitchen use only. These don't allow cold mains water to mix with stored hot water within the body of the faucet, avoiding the possibility of contaminating the mains supply.

It may be necessary to fit 'top hat' spacer washers to the faucet tails before the backnuts can be tightened fully. To aid connection to the supply, fit lengths of flexible copper pipe with a swivel connector at one end to each faucet tail. These should be 15mm diameter.

Removing the Old Sink

First turn off the water supply to the hot and cold faucets and open the faucets to drain the pipes.

You may find difficulty in reaching the faucet tails to disconnect them and it will be easier to cut through the supply pipes as close to the faucets as possible. If the pipes are buried in the wall, chop out the plaster round them to make the cuts. Unscrew the waste trap from the outlet or disconnect it from the waste pipe.

Break any seal between the sink and wall with a hammer and chisel and lift the sink away if it rests on metal brackets. Alternatively unscrew it from its base unit and lift it out. Remove any brackets with a hacksaw.

Installing the New Sink

Move any base unit into position and set the sink top in place. Mark and cut back the supply pipes so that the flexible pipes can be connected without too sharp a bend. You can use either compression or capillary joints to make the connections, but some Building Codes may insist on capillary joints for any pipes carrying mains water.

Screw on the trap, either using the original or a new trap depending on whether the waste pipe is horizontal or vertical. It must have a 75mm (3in) deep water seal.

If the original waste pipe won't line up with the new sink, or if it is of lead, install a new plastic pipe of 38mm (1½in) diameter, making sure it has a fall of 18–45mm per metre (¾–1¾in per yard) towards the drainage point. Use either push-fit connectors or solvent-weld fittings.

The waste pipe should discharge into a soil stack; wherever possible connect up to the original pipe. If you have to cut a hole through the wall for the pipe, you can rent a masonry core drill to cut it in one operation. Seal round the pipe with a non-setting caulking, restore the water supplies to both faucets.

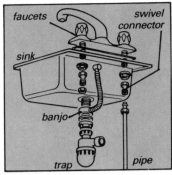

Install new sink needs: faucets; 15mm (½in) swivel connectors and pipe; 38mm (1½in) slotted waste outlet, trap, banjo fitting and waste pipe.

Smearing jointing compound over the sealing washer before placing it on the waste outlet; the slot on the outlet faces the back of the sink.

Tightening the backnut with an adjustable wrench after aligning the hole in the banjo fitting with the slot in the waste outlet.

Screwing the overflow grille and plug stay to the free end of the banjo hose; sinks with an integral overflow do not need a banjo.

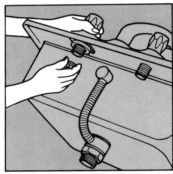

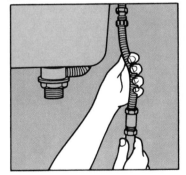

Securing faucets with backnuts after sliding on top-hat washers; position any sealing gasket between the faucet body and the sink top.

Using a corrugated faucet connector for ease of bending; conect it first to the faucet tail, then to the end of the supply pipe.

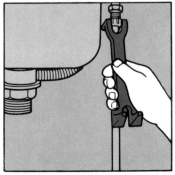

Tightening the compression joint with a basin wrench; this allows access to the right corners often encountered behind sinks.

Connecting trap to waste pipe after screwing to the outlet; double sinks should have a fall from each trap before teeing together.

FITTING A WASTE DISPOSER

A waste disposal unit is a useful appliance to have in a kitchen; it contains a set of hardened steel blades driven by a powerful electric motor which will grind up most forms of kitchen waste. The ground waste is mixed with water inside the unit to make a slurry which can be flushed down the drain. The waste disposal unit is suspended directly below the sink, fitting between the waste outlet and the trap. Some sink units have a small separate bowl specifically for waste disposal.

Practically all waste disposal units need a larger than normal waste outlet in the bottom of the sink — about 90mm (3½in) in diameter — and this may mean buying a new sink with this size outlet. However, some stainless steel sinks can have their outlets enlarged by a special hole saw which you may be able to rent Ceramic or enamelled sinks cannot be cut and must be replaced. Another point to consider if you are thinking about enlarging the existing outlet hole is whether you will still be left with a circular depression large enough to bed the outlet flange in; it must be below the level of the sink bottom otherwise the sink won't drain properly.

After installing the new larger outlet fitting in the sink, the waste disposal unit grinding compartment is mounted beneath it by an assembly of circular plates which ensure a watertight seal with the outlet and support the weight of the unit. An angled outlet pipe is attached to the side of the grinding compartment and a normal P or S trap connected to this. A bottle trap should not be used since it takes too long to discharge its contents.

As with other kitchen sinks, the waste pipe should be of 38mm (1½in) diameter and it should have a fall of about 15° to the drainage point.

Once the waste pipe has been run in, the motor compartment can be fitted beneath the grinding compartment and the wiring connections made in accordance with the manufacturer's instructions.

Bedding the 89mm (3½in) waste outlet into the sink on a ring of plumbers' putty; some units will fit on a standard waste.

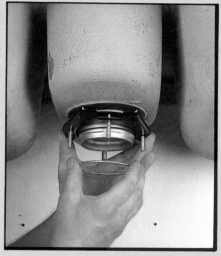

Assembling the suspension; top to bottom: rubber washer, pressure plate, suspension plate and circlip.

Tightening the Allen screws with the key provided; these lock the suspension plate against the pressure plate.

Attaching the waste disposer to the suspension after fitting the waste elbow; the unit hinges forwards for servicing.

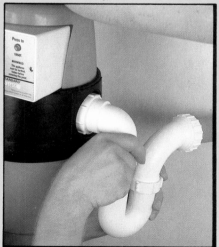

Tightening the swivel connections on the trap after connecting to the elbow and waste pipe; do not use a bottle trap.

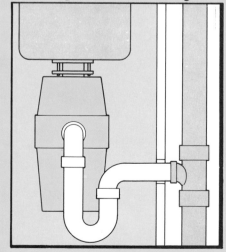

The disposal must have its own connection to the stack and not be interconnected with the sink drain because of the possiblity of the drain becoming blocked and backing up the sink.

Trick

Clamping the baseplate of a plumbing-in kit to the supply pipe; the baseplate hinges open to pass round the pipe.

Screwing the stop-valve body into the baseplate; a cutter bores into the pipe as the stop-valve is screwed in.

Attaching a conventional stopcock to a branch pipe after breaking into the supply with a tee fitting.

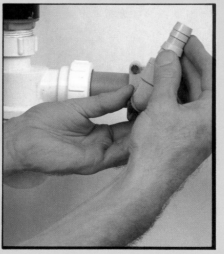

Attaching the trap to a washing-machine standpipe; the hose from the machine hooks into the top.

Connecting into the kitchen sink waste pipe using a sanitary-tee; the curve should point towards the stack.

Screwing a waste connector into the strap, clamped round the sink waste pipe; a tool is supplied to bore into the pipe.

WASHING MACHINE/ DISHWASHER KIT

Making permanent connections to the supply and waste pipes is a much neater and more efficient way of installing a washing machine or dishwasher than pushing the machine's hoses on to the kitchen faucets and hooking the waste hose over the edge of the sink. Fortunately, there are plumbing kits available that make this job extremely simple.

Some machines need both a hot and cold water supply whereas others may only need cold water. It doesn't matter, the method of connection remains the same. It is fairly common to take the cold supply from the kitchen cold faucet supply pipe, but check the machine's instructions first as it may not always be suitable.

Water Supply

To supply the machine with water you simply break into the nearest supply pipes with compression or capillary T fittings, or use an automatic connector such as that supplied with a plumbing-in kit. This allows the connection to be made without draining the pipes. Then run lengths of 15mm (½in) pipe to the machine's position. Each pipe should terminate in a combined stop-valve and washing machine hose connector. Screw the hoses to the connectors and the supply side is complete.

Waste

For the waste you can use a conventional washing machine standpipe kit comprising a vertical length of 38mm (1½in) waste pipe with an integral P trap at the bottom. This should be connected to a waste pipe that passes close by or is connected to the kitchen sink waste pipe with a T fitting. Then hook the waste hose into the top of the standpipe.

Alternatively, you can use a washing machine waste pipe connector. This clamps round the existing kitchen sink waste pipe and a tool supplied with the fitting is used to bore a hole in the pipe. A hose connector is then fitted over the hole and the machine's waste pipe pushed on to its end.

Kitchen sink traps with integral waste hose connectors are also available, but not all machine manufacturers or plumbing codes approve of them. The Code in your area may have specific requirements. Allways consult your local Plumbing Codes before installing any new fixture or fitting.

If you are updating an old bathroom or remodelling it, one of the jobs you are likely to do is replace the hand basin.

Modern basins may be made in ceramic, enamelled steel or glass-reinforced plastic. They come in a variety of shapes and colors, usually designed to match in with a range of other bathroom fittings. Basins may be wall-mounted, recessed into the wall, let into flat surfaces or mounted on pedestals; even double basin units are made.

Arrange this so that the basin is out of action for the minimum of time. To do this you can prepare the new basin by fitting its faucets and waste outlet before removing the old basin. You will find it easier, too. If necessary, use top-hat spacers on the faucet tails to allow the backnuts to be tightened fully and bed the outlet on plumber's putty or the gasket provided. To aid connection to the supply pipes, attach lengths of flexible pipe to the faucet tails.¯

Removing the Old Basin

Turn off the water supplies to the faucets and open them to drain the pipes (see page 91). Unscrew the faucet connectors and waste trap, having a bowl ready to catch any water that may spill out. If you can't undo the faucet connectors, cut through the pipes just below them. If you are moving the basin's position, you may prefer to cut the pipes below floor level and make up new extensions to the new position. If the pipes are lead, you should replace them completely.

With the pipes disconnected, unscrew the basin from the wall and lift it away, then remove the brackets or pedestal.

Installing the New Basin

Mark, drill and plug any wall fixing holes for the new basin and its brackets, making sure the basin is at a comfortable height, (although you can't alter this with a pedestal basin). Fix the basin to the wall and cut back the supply pipes so that the flexible copper pipes can be connected to them with a smooth radius.

If the basin is pedestal-mounted, you can fit much longer pipes to the faucets before positioning the basin, running them down the inside of the pedestal for concealment

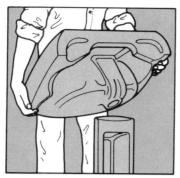

Lifting a basin on to its pedestal to measure the length of the supply pipes and the height of the waste outlet and fixing holes.

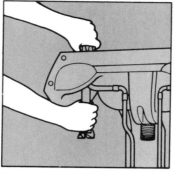

Connecting the supply pipes to the faucet tails using a basin wrench; bend or joint the pipes to run neatly within the pedestal.

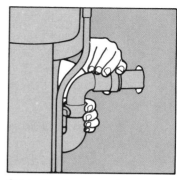

Connecting the trap to the waste pipe after moving the basin and pedestal into position and securing the basin to the wall.

and connecting them to the supply pipes near floor level.

If you're lucky, the original trap can be screwed to the outlet of the new basin, however it may not align exactly in which case you could fit a telescopic version. If you are renewing the waste run completely, use a P or bottle trap and 32mm (1¼in) waste pipe (unless the waste run is over 1.7m (5 feet) long in which case it should be 38mm (1½in) pipe). The pipe should have a gradual fall and discharge into a soil stack.

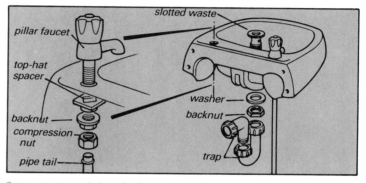

Components needed to plumb in a basin: faucets, connectors and pipe; 32mm (1¼in) waste outlet, trap and waste pipe.

Labels: slotted waste, pillar faucet, top-hat spacer, backnut, compression nut, pipe tail, washer, backnut, trap

Fitting a vanity unit: After fixing the outlet spout, checking that the connecting pipes on the water inlet are the correct length.

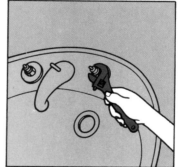

Fixing the water inlet assembly to the unit; ensure that all washers supplied are fitted as instructed, or the inlet will not be secure.

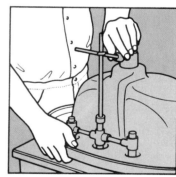

Attaching the pop-up-waste operating rod to the underside of the water inlet; adjust the length of the rod according to the depth of the unit.

Applying a gasket to the opening in the base unit before inserting the basin, to ensure a watertight seal.

Attaching the pop-up watse plug after pressing the basin gently on to the gasket.

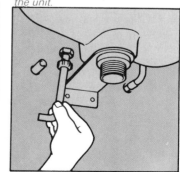

Connecting the supply pipes after attaching the angle bracket, between washers, to the waste outlet and screwing it to the wall.

REPLACING AN OLD BATH

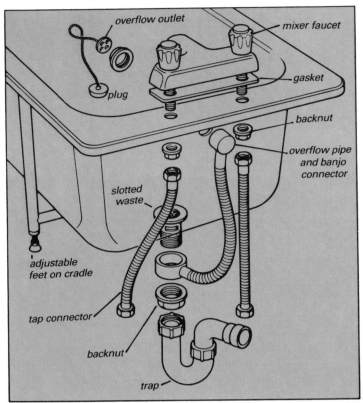

Components needed to plumb in a bath: faucets; 22mm (¾in) corrugated pipes; 38mm (1½in) waste outlet, P-trap and banjo fitting with overflow pipe. You will need a slotted waste outlet unless the overflow is attached directly to the trap; a shallow trap may be needed if height is limited.

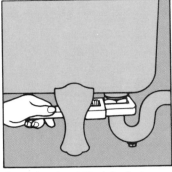

Removing the old bath by first disconnecting the trap using an adjustable wrench.

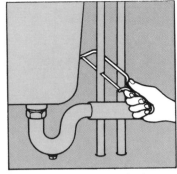

Cutting through the supply pipes with a hacksaw; leave sufficient length to attach flexible pipes.

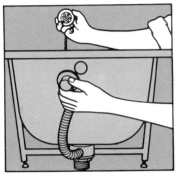

After fitting the waste outlet and banjo to the new bath, connect overflow pipe to plug holder; remember to fit the sealing washers.

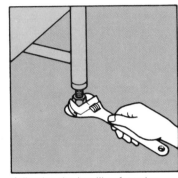

Adjusting the levelling feet; the bath should be level crossways and lengthways, as a drainage fall is built into the bottom.

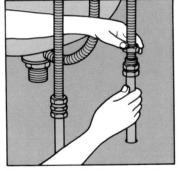

Connecting the flexible pipes to the supply pipes; use compression types to avoid the possibility of scorching the bath.

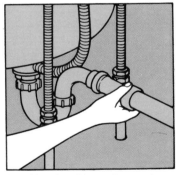

Attaching the slip coupling on the trap to the drain pipe, check for leaks before finally closing up the tub.

Replacing an old bath with a new one is carried out in much the same way as fitting a new hand basin; connections have to be made to the hot and cold water supply pipes and to the waste pipe, or new pipes installed (particularly if the old ones are lead). You will probably find that the connections at the faucets and waste outlet are difficult to reach, and this may mean some careful preplanning before sliding the new bath into place.

Choosing a New Bath

Gone are the days of the old cast iron bath with white enamel finish; baths nowadays come in all shapes, sizes and colors. The oblong bath is still most popular, but you can also buy triangular baths for fitting in corners, oval baths and short, deep tubs for use where space is limited. Faucets can often be fitted at the side of the bath or at a corner, as well as in the traditional end position.

Although you can buy enamelled, pressed steel baths, the most popular type now (particularly for handyman installa-

tion due to their light weight) are plastic baths. These usually have a non-slip finish molded into the bottom and come with a steel and wood supporting cradle with attachments for pre-molded trim panels.

One point to watch with a plastic bath is that you can't make soldered capillary joints anywhere near it because there is a danger of the blowtorch melting the plastic.

Removing the Old Bath

Cut off the water supplies and remove the trim panels. If you can reach the faucet tails, disconnect the supply pipes from them; if not cut through the pipes as close to the faucets as possible. Treat the waste pipe in the same way and also cut through any overflow pipe which will pass out through the wall. The latter won't be needed any more since all modern baths have an over-flow assembly similar to that used on a basin.

Carefully break any seal between the bath and wall with a cold chisel and pull the bath away.

Because a cast-iron bath will be too heavy to manhandle down stairs, break it into smaller pieces with a sledge-hammer after first draping a thick blanket or tarpaulin over it to prevent splinters flying about.

Fitting the New Bath

Assemble the faucets, waste outlet and trap to the bath in the same manner as fitting out a basin. Because of the lack of space below the faucet, lengths

of flexible pipe will really come into their own if you connect them to the faucet tails before locating the bath. Note that the pipes should be 22mm (¾in) size.

Fit the supporting cradle and move the bath into position, making sure it is level from end to end and side to side. Connect the flexible pipes to the supply pipes using compression joints, and the trap to the waste pipe.

Finally, turn on the water and check for leaks before installing the side and end trim panels.

One of the first things you will want to get rid of when modernising a bathroom is an old toilet with a high level tank. Made of cast iron, these tanks tend to be noisy in use, prone to corrosion and unattractive to say the least. Fortunately, modern plumbing fittings make the job much easier than it would first seem.

Modern Efficiency

Modern tanks have much more efficient and quieter flushing mechanisms than their high level predecessors; modern toilet pans, too, are of a better design. Older examples simply relied on the force of water pouring in from the tank to carry away waste, whereas the latest versions incorporate valves which produce a strong siphonic action to suck the contents through the trap aided by the flow of water from the tank.

There are several different toilet/tank layouts to choose from: the tank can be wall-mounted and connected to the pan by a short vertical flush pipe, it can be concealed within a partition so that only the flush handle shows, or it can be mounted directly to the back of the pan (known as a close-coupled suite).

If you just want to change a high level tank to a low one, you can get a special slim 'flush panel' that will fit to the wall behind the pan and still allow the seat and lid to be lifted — a conventional low level tank would project too far from the wall for this.

Removing the Old Tank and Pan

Turn off the water supply, flush the tank to empty it and disconnect the pipework, cutting it if necessary. The flush pipe should simply pull from the back of the pan.

Unscrew the tank from the wall and lift it from its brackets; take care since it will be very heavy.

The pan may incorporate a P trap connected to a waste pipe passing through the wall or an S trap connected to a pipe rising vertically from the floor. It may be screwed or cemented in place. Carefully break the seal

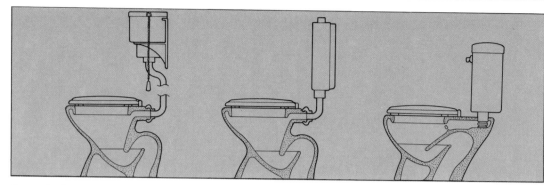

Types of toilet pan and tank; (left to right) high-level tank; low-level flush-panel tank and S-trap wash-down pan; low-level conventional cistern wash-down pan; close-coupled tank and siphonic S-trap pan. With the exception of the close-coupled suite where the connection is made through a rubber gasket, the cistern and pan are connected by a flush-pipe.

with the pipe and remove the pan, clearing any old mortar from the floor. Then carefully chisel out the mortar from the pipe socket.

Fitting the New Pan and Tank

Connect the pan to the waste pipe with a wax ring connector and screw it to the floor using brass screws with lead washers under their heads. Don't cement

it in place as this may cause the pan to crack as the mortar dries.

Use the flush pipe to determine the tank position (unless you are installing a close-coupled suite) and screw its brackets to the wall. Check that the tank is level, packing it out beneath if necessary, and screw it to the wall.

Next, connect the flush pipe and assemble the flushing mechanism according to the instructions supplied.

Either make up a 15mm (½in) pipe extension from the old supply pipe to the tank, or run in a new pipe from a more convenient source. Fitting a stop-valve just before the cistern will make maintenance easier in future. You will find that most modern tanks and flushing services include an integral overflow pipe.

Finally, turn on the water and check that everything works without any leaks.

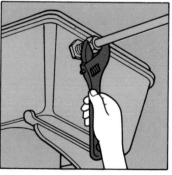

Disconnecting the supply pipe to the tank after turning off the supply and flushing the tank; some water will still be inside.

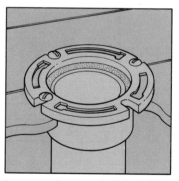

Loosen and remove the bolts holding the bowl to the floor, rock the bowl to loosen the seal and then lift the bowl away from the floor.

Clean off the old gasket material and install new flange bolts into the floor flange.

Fit new wax gasket to new bowl and lower bowl onto floor flange, press down to compress the sealing gasket and then tighten flange bolts.

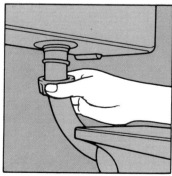

With a separate cistern, after mounting it on brackets, connecting the flush pipe; the other end fits into a rubber boot on the pan.

Attaching the water supply pipe to the ball-valve inlet; assemble the flushing mechanism following the manufacturer's instructions.

Trick

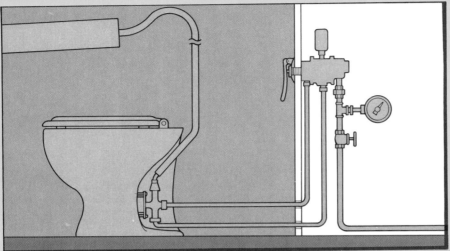

Water enters flushing system through a double acting flush valve. Upon flushing, water is sent to unit first via a small pipe connected to a disintegrating jet which breaks up contents of bowl. The valve then switches to a flushing jet which forces contents of bowl upwards to soil stack.

REMOTE AUXILIARY TOILET

It can often be useful to install an extra toilet — as part of an attic conversion, room extension or alteration to a basement, or if you have an elderly or infirm person living with you. Unfortunately, you are often limited in your choice of sites for the appliance because of its need for a bulky 100mm (4in) or 75mm (3in) soil pipe. The position of the existing soil stack or underground drain effectively dictates where you can put a new toilet, unless you go to the expense of installing complete new drainage runs.

Freestanding Pump and Shredder Unit

Fortunately, there is a piece of equipment on the market that can overcome these problems. It is a freestanding pump and shredder unit, which fits behind the toilet pan and is connected to its outlet by a rubber sealing collar. When the toilet is flushed the waste flows into the unit where a pressure switch turns on a set of grinding blades which reduce all solid waste to a slurry. This is then pumped through narrow bore pipes to a soil stack up to 30m (97ft 6in) away. It will even pump vertically up to a height of 2m (6ft 6in).

The waste pipe can be of copper with soldered capillary joints or plastic with solvent-weld joints and needs a minimum bore of 18mm (¾in). Being so much smaller than conventional soil pipe, it can be run under floors, through partitions and along base boards to make an inconspicuous installation. The unit also has a vent pipe which must be taken outside, and this should be considered when making a final decision on positioning.

The device is electrically operated, needing its own fused supply.

Because the unit is rather unconventional, you must have the approval of your local Building Department before going ahead with the installation; some may now allow it, so check with them before you buy.

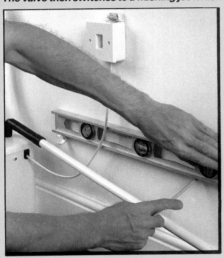

Marking the level of the pipe clips on the wall to give a fall of 1 in 200; clip regularly to avoid sagging.

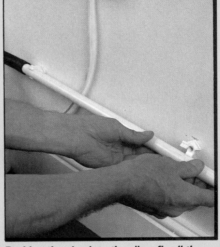

Pushing the pipe into the clips; fix all the clips to the wall before inserting the pipe.

After cutting into the waste stack, solvent-welding a 32mm boss outlet to it, to take the waste pipe.

Connecting the waste pipe to the stack; a 32 to 22mm reducer is solvent-welded into the boss to accept the pipe.

Although many appliances can be installed by connecting short lengths of pipe to adjacent supply pipes, sooner or later you will be faced with the job of installing longer pipe runs. A certain amount of pre-planning is needed if you are to avoid problems after installation.

Obviously, it is essential to keep the pipe runs as short and direct as possible, reducing the amount of work and time needed and also keeping costs down. It will help if you draw up a floor plan and sketch the pipe runs on

Feeding pipe through access holes cut into a stud partition wall; drill oversize holes through bracing as squarely as possible.

Clipping a pipe in a chase cut in a solid wall; use saddle clips of the size to match the pipe and screw into wallplugs.

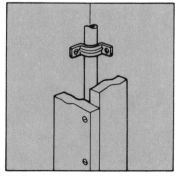

Surface mounted pipes, secured in a corner with angled saddle clips, can be boxed in with two pine battens fixed through the edges.

it. Keep the changes in direction to a minimum together with the number of joints used. Joints are expensive and they are a potential source of leaks.

When you do have to change direction of the run, try to bend the pipe rather than using a right-angled joint, keeping a gentle radius as this won't restrict the water flow so much.

Pipes can run horizontally or vertically, but avoid inverted loops of pipe as these are potential sources of air locks.

You must support pipes at regular intervals with proper pipe clips; this prevents any strain on the joints and stops water hammer caused by the pipes vibrating as it flows through them. Install the clips at 1.2m (4ft) intervals.

Running Pipes Under Floors

In suspended wooden floors, pipes can be clipped to the sides of joists, or if the run is at right angles to the joists, the pipes can pass through notches cut in the joist tops or through holes drilled in them. Notches should be about 12mm (½in) wider and 6mm (¼in) deeper than the pipe, and holes 6mm (¼in) larger in diameter to allow for expansion. Don't make them any larger in case you weaken the joist. Site the notches and holes clear of any floorboard fixing nails.

If you are installing the pipes below a wooden first floor, you may be able to clip them to the undersides of the joists, but make sure they are well insulated otherwise they may freeze up in winter (see page 151). Similarly, pipes can be run across the tops of joists in the attic, but here too they must be well-lagged.

Although you can bury pipes in concrete floors, installation is best done when the floor is laid or by casting a pipe channel in the floor which can be used later. Cutting a channel in an existing floor would be hard work and you run the risk of breaking through the water proof membrane layer. It is probably better to clip the pipes round the walls at base board level.

Pipes in Walls

Hollow stud partition walls are

Feeding pipe through oversize holes drilled 50mm (2in) below the tops of joists and central to boards; assemble fittings first if possible.

Clipping a pipe run parallel to a joist with plastic screw-on clips; fix the clips at 450mm (18in) intervals and push in the pipe.

Feeding pipe parallel to joists by lifting a floorboard at each end of the run; intermediate boards will have to be lifted for clipping.

ideal for concealing pipe runs. If you are building the partition at the same time as installing the pipework, drill holes through the various frame members and feed the pipe through before completing the cladding (see page 151).

If the partition already exists, you can drill through the head plate from the room above and remove small squares of drywall to be able to cut notches in the framework for the pipes. Then nail the squares back and fill the joints. You may be able to drill the

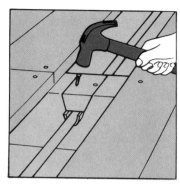

Nailing back the wedge-shaped offcut from a notch cut in the top of a joist; felt below the pipe prevents expansion noise.

sole plate from below after lifting a floorboard or two, or by running a long bit down behind the base.

In solid walls you can chisel a channel, or chase in the plaster deep enough to accept the pipe — special machines are available for rent to ease this chore — then clip it in place before plastering over the top. However, this is not recommended for hot pipes since their contraction and expansion may cause the plaster to crack. It is better to clip them to the surface of the wall; this should always be done with both hot and cold pipes if they run on an outside wall as they will be less likely to freeze up in winter than if they were buried.

When running a pipe through one side of a wall and out the other, it is best to mortar a sleeve made from pipe of the next size up into the wall. This will then allow enough room for the pipe to expand without cracking the plaster. The sleeve should be cut just long enough so that its ends are flush with the plaster on each side.

Nailing a supporting batten to blocks nailed to the sides of the joists where pipes cannot be fixed to the joists themselves.

Trick

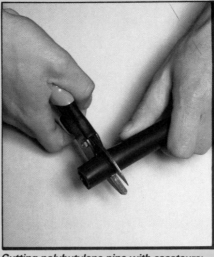

Measuring to the line marked on a plastic push-fit fitting; this is the distance to the pipe-stop within the fitting.

Cutting polybutylene pipe with secateurs; this method is quick and leaves no burr. A hacksaw may be used instead.

Pushing a stainless-steel sleeve into the end of the pipe to provide extra support where lengths are joined.

Smearing silicone lubricant round the end of the pipe to prevent chafing when it is pushed into the fitting.

Pushing the pipe into the joint; the knurled rings are pre-tightened and need no adjustment, except if dismantling.

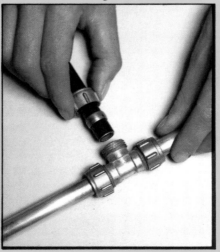

Joining to copper pipe with a standard compression fitting; slip on the capnut and olive before inserting the sleeve.

USING PLASTIC PIPES

Plastic pipes have long been used for waste systems and for some time it has been possible to buy flexible polythene pipe for use with cold water supply systems; however, plastic pipe systems are also produced for both cold and hot water supplies, bringing the all-plastic plumbing system into reality.

Plastic pipework offers many advantages: it is light in weight, easily cut and joined, is a poor conductor of heat so less heat is lost from hot water and there's less likelihood of pipes freezing up. Also, it does not corrode, which can be a health hazard in some metal systems.

There are two types of plastic supply pipe available, but most common and easiest to work with is polybutylene pipe, a brown flexible material produced in 15 and 22mm sizes to match copper pipe. It can be used for any domestic hot or cold supply work with one exception — that is, it must not be connected directly to a boiler; you must fit short lengths of copper pipe first.

Polybutylene Pipe

Polybutylene pipe is sold in 3m (10ft) lengths or 50m (195ft) coils and is flexible enough to be fed below floors or round obstructions. You can bend it by hand to a minimum radius of four times its diameter, provided you clip it on each side of the bend. It should also be clipped more frequently than copper as there may be a tendency for it to sag; 400mm (16in) is the recommended spacing for the 15mm size and 600mm (24in) for the 22mm size.

Polybutylene pipe can be connected with normal brass compression fittings, making it easy to connect to existing copper systems. Or you can use the joints developed with the pipe. These look like plastic versions of compression joints, but there's no need to dismantle them to make the connection; you simply push the end of the pipe into the fitting until it comes up against the pipe stop. A toothed metal grab ring prevents the pipe pulling out again and a rubber O-ring provides a watertight seal. Joints can be disconnected by unscrewing the capnut.

Unfortunately, this form of pipe is not approved by all Plumbing Codes (although it's increasingly finding favor), so you must check with yours before you use it. Also, if your plumbing system was used to ground the electricity system (it is in many older houses) inserting plastic pipes will mean re-arranging the grounding; seek the advice of a qualified electrician.

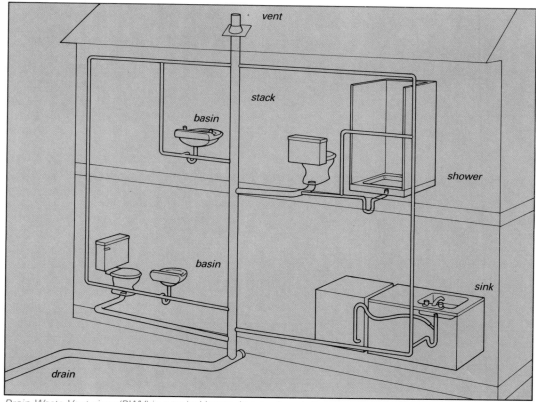

Drain-Waste-Vent pipes (DWV) in a typical house. In a modern drainage system all toilets discharge directly into the stack via a closet bend. Other appliances which may have longer drainage runs to the stack are also connected to a vent pipe, which protects the trap in case of a partial vacuum in the drain. The vent pipe rejoins the stack in the attic before continuing on through the roof to the outside air.

Installing new appliances should not cause any major problems if you are replacing existing fittings and simply re-connecting to the original supply and waste pipes. However, if you intend changing the position of an appliance or installing an extra one, the problems begin. The supply side of the job is quite straightforward, but the way you tackle the waste system is more complicated. Actually installing the pipework is not difficult, but waste systems must comply with the Building Code.

Before you tackle the job you must draw up a set of plans to show the pipe runs and submit them to the local Building Department for their approval. They will probably want to come and see the installation when it is complete.

Single Stack and Two Pipe Drainage

Your house may have a modern single stack drainage system in which a large diameter pipe connected to the underground drain, runs up an outside wall or, more likely in modern houses, through the house inside a duct.

All the waste and soil pipes from the upper floor appliances and fixtures will be connected to the stack, and some ground floor appliances may also be linked to it. However, it is quite possible that a downstairs toilet will be connected directly to the underground drain.

On the other hand, your house may have an older two-pipe waste system where the soil pipe from any upstairs WC is connected to a vertical pipe on the outside, and any fittings such as basins, baths and showers discharge into a funnel-shaped hopper at the top of a second pipe. This, in turn, discharges over a trapped gully at ground level.

The type of system fitted determines how you go about connecting up the wastes of new installations.

Running Waste Pipes

Waste pipes are larger in diameter than supply pipes, particularly soil pipes which measure 100mm (4in), and nowadays are nearly allways made of either plastic or hubless cast iron with slide fitting con-

necting clamps.

Because of their size, waste pipes are much more difficult to conceal than supply pipes. Keep the pipe runs short by siting appliances as close as you can to the stack position and on an outside wall so the pipes can go straight outside. You can, of course, box in waste pipes and even run them between the joists of a wooden floor. However, you must never cut the joists to allow a pipe (even the smallest diameter waste pipe) to pass across them as this will seriously weaken the floor. In this situation you have no alternative but to run the pipe along the wall, clipping it at regular intervals just as you would a supply pipe.

Waste pipes must also have a positive fall towards their discharge point —about 30mm for every metre of length (1¼in per yard).

Choosing the Pipe Size

You will find several sizes of waste pipe in use: 32mm, 38mm, 50mm, 75mm, 10mm, (1¼in, 1½in, 2in, 3in, 4in) are common, and possibly 150mm

(6in). The larger sizes are for use with toilets and for vertical waste stacks only. The only appliances that use 32mm (1¼in) pipe are a hand basin and, a bidet and then only if the pipe run is less than 1.7m (5ft 7in) long; above that figure, up to a maximum of 2.3m (7ft 6in), use 38mm (1½in) pipe. The waste pipes from baths, showers and sinks must all be in 38mm (1½in) pipe.

Making the Connections

Where possible, avoid making direct connections to the soil stack; rather, connect new appliances to existing waste pipe runs using T connectors.

However, the positions of existing appliances may not always make connection to their waste pipes possible, in which case you have no option but to connect to the soil stack, provided it is plastic. Basin and bath wastes can be solvent-welded to a spare entry boss on the stack after cutting out the circle of plastic inside, or joined to it with the aid of a 'strap boss' fitting.

If you have to connect an extra toilet to a soil stack you may need to replace the existing single branch fitting with a double branch — complicated, since it means cutting out the old one and making up the missing pipe sections before solvent-welding the new one in place.

If the stack is of cast iron a section can be removed and replaced with a hubless cast iron T fitting, using the slide fitting connecting clamps, merely position the new fitting, mark the pipe and cut it out, slide the connectors over and tighten. Two other points to consider are that you must not connect any waste pipe any closer than 200mm (8in) below a soil pipe that joins the stack on the opposite side; and all connections to the stack must be at least 450mm (18in) above the point where it bends to join the underground drain.

WASTE PIPES AND FITTINGS

Waste pipes come with internal diameters of 32mm and 38mm to match the old imperial 1¼in and 1½in bores respectively. The smaller size is only used for short runs from hand basins and bidets otherwise all waste systems are in the larger size. Soil pipes come in 75mm (3in) and 100mm (4in) sizes, although you may find that older cast iron pipes are slightly larger; fortunately, you can buy special push-on adaptors.

It is not a wise idea to try to bend plastic waste or soil pipes but since there is a wide range of straight connectors, bends of various angles and T-junctions this isn't a drawback. It is worth having a good look at the systems available before you start to see which has the fittings that will suit you best.

There are two methods of joining plastic waste pipes: solvent-welding and push-fit connectors, tors. The former makes a permanent seal between pipe and connector by means of a special solvent, which is brushed on to both pipe and connector, melting and fusing the plastic together. The latter has simple rubber O-rings to make a water-tight seal and can be dismantled and remade if required.

An advantage of the push-fit system is that an allowance can be made at each joint for thermal expansion caused when hot wastes flow down the pipes; this cannot be done with solvent-welding, so on long runs special expansion joints must be incorporated.

Making Solvent-weld Joints

As with connecting copper or plastic supply pipes, it is essential to cut the ends of pipes squarely so that they butt up evenly against the pipe stops inside the connectors. Measure each length of pipe, making an allowance for the amount inserted into the connector, and use the same method to mark a square cutting line as that described for copper pipe on page 93; that is, use a straightedged strip of paper wrapped round the pipe with the ends overlapping and the edges aligned. Butt a pencil up to the paper and run it round the pipe.

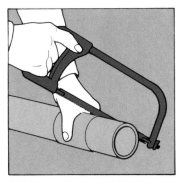
Making a solvent-weld joint in waste pipe: cutting the pipe to length using the edge of a piece of paper as a cutting guide.

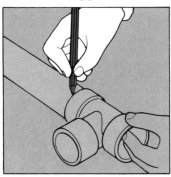
After wiping with a rag to remove all loose particles, and inserting fully into the fitting, marking round the socket as a guide.

Having marked the line, you can cut the pipe with a fine-bladed hacksaw. File off any burrs and, to aid insertion, use the file to bevel the edge of the pipe. Push the end into the joint socket as far as it will go and mark the pipe with a pencil so you will know how much of the end to prepare.

Remove the pipe and use a file or steel wool to roughen the end of the pipe up to the pencil mark. Similarly, treat the inside of the joint socket with steel wool until you have removed the 'glaze' of the plastic's surface. Then wipe the end of the pipe and inside the joint socket with the appropriate pipe cleaning fluid (as recommended by the manufacturer).

Make sure you have the correct solvent-weld cement for the type of pipes you have; different plastics use different cements. Then, using the brush supplied with it, or a small clean paintbrush, apply the cement to the end of the pipe and the inside of the joint socket.

Push the pipe into the socket until it comes up against the pipe stop, twisting it slightly as you do

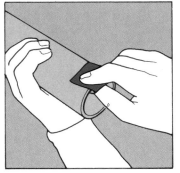
Removing burrs from the cut end with fine abrasive paper held lightly; alternatively use a fine metalworking file.

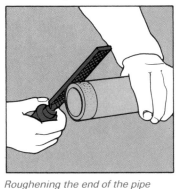
Roughening the end of the pipe within the marked line; use a fine file or wire wool, and roughen inside the socket also.

so to spread the adhesive. Then hold the pipe and joint together for 20 to 30 seconds to give the adhesive a chance to make the bond. Wipe off any excess, and make sure that the connector points in the right direction for the next length of pipe. If the pipe is to carry hot waste water, leave it to set for 24 hours before using the system.

Push-Fit Connections

Push-fit joints are easily made. Bevel the pipe end with a file and apply a coating of vaseline to lubricate it. Push it into the joint socket and then pull it out again by about 10mm (¾in) to allow for thermal expansion of the pipes.

Many old houses may still have copper or lead waste pipes and traps running from their baths and basins, together with cast iron soil pipes from the toilets. However, these days, plastic is the universally accepted material for both waste and soil pipes, and this is much easier to work with than its metal counterparts.

Various types of plastic are used for waste and soil systems:

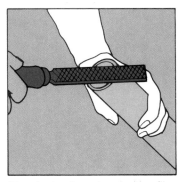
Chamferring the cut end with a file to make it an easy fit in the fitting; make sure that you do not file the end out of square.

Applying an even layer of cement to the pipe after cleaning; apply to the fitting also and push in the pipe with a twisting motion.

polyvinyl chloride (PVC), acrylonitrile-butadiene-styrene (ABS) and polybutylene (PB). All are suitable for domestic use so it doesn't matter which you choose with the proviso that you use the same material and brand throughout the system. Different types of plastic won't be compatible with each other, and different makes may vary slightly in size so that they cannot be connected together to guarantee a watertight seal.

Making a push-fit joint; push in pipe fully, mark round mouth of socket, then withdraw pipe 10mm (⅜in) to allow for expansion.

Perched up in the attic, or down in the basement the cold water storage tank tends to be out of sight and out of mind; fortunately, they give very little trouble and, apart from the occasional check for corrosion in metal tanks and possible repair or replacement of a faulty filler valve, need little maintenance. However, there may come a time when you want to replace the tank you have; a common reason is that the old one does not have the capacity to meet your needs (most likely if you have installed extra appliances, particularly a shower). Or a galvanized steel tank may be badly corroded.

Choosing a New Tank

Most modern tanks are made of plastic which is a much more suitable material than anything used previously. The ideal capacity for domestic use is 227 litres (50 gallons) and such a tank may be round or rectangular. However, before you buy, check the dimensions since the only way into the attic may be through the normal access trap and you must be sure you can get the tank through. Plastic tanks can be flexed quite a bit to pass through narrow openings, but if it looks as though there just isn't enough room, buy two smaller units and connect them together in the attic with a length of 28mm pipe. Fit the valve in one tank and take all the outlet pipes from the other to ensure a through flow.

Removing the Old Tank

Turn off the water supply and drain the tank by opening all the bathroom cold faucets. You will need a jug and bucket to scoop out the remaining water in the bottom of the tank.

Disconnect the pipework by unscrewing the connectors, but if they are difficult to remove, cut through the pipes and extend them later to meet the new tank.

Slide the old tank out of the way; if it is a metal one you may find it easier to leave it in the attic rather than attempt to man-handle it through the trap since it will be extremely heavy.

Installing the New Tank

An important point to remember when carrying out any plumbing work in the attic is to always use compression joints or the newer push-fit polybutylene connectors, not capillary joints — the flame from a blowtorch could ignite dust in the attic with disastrous results.

A plastic tank, being quite flexible, must be stood on a firm base and this can be made by laying a few stout boards across the joists or using a sheet of 19mm (¾in) thick plywood.

Holes will have to be drilled in the sides of the tank to take the connectors for the various outlet and inlet pipes, and their diameters should match the size of the connectors as closely as possible. The job is made easier by using a special hole saw or tank cutter fitting in an electric drill.

Fit the tank connectors, wrapping their threads with teflon tape for a watertight seal. Then join the old pipes to them with short extension pieces. It is a good idea to take the opportunity of fitting gate-valves in the outlet pipes if none were fitted before, which will make repairs to the appliances they feed that much easier in future.

Fit the valve in the same way — either re-using the old one or a new one if it is unserviceable. Then add a plastic overflow pipe.

Turn the water back on and check for leaks as the tank fills. Finally, fit a lid, or make one from exterior grade plywood, and wrap the installation and pipes with a suitable lagging material (see page 151).

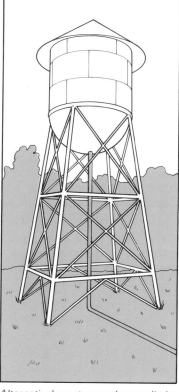

Alternatively, water may be supplied from a public or municipal reservoir. Some houses and supplied from local storage cisterns.

Removing the old cistern: baling out the water remaining below the feed pipes after draining the cistern by opening the bathroom cold taps.

Cutting through the feed pipes with a hacksaw; carefully remove any burr so that it does not fall into the pipes and cause blockages.

Installing the new cistern: cutting the outlet holes with a hole saw 50mm (2in) above the bottom, to prevent sludge from flowing in.

Fitting gate valves; a short length of 22mm pipe is needed to connect them to the tank connectors, using compression joints.

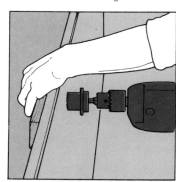

Drilling the hole for the supply pipe to the ball valve; support the wall of the cistern with a block of wood held behind the drilling point.

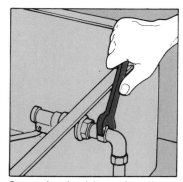

Connecting the rising main to the ball valve after wrapping PTFE tape round the ball-valve tail; clip the pipe firmly to prevent vibration.

INSTALLING A NEW HOT CYLINDER

The supply of water to the hot faucets in your home will come from a copper storage cylinder. The water in the cylinder may be heated by an electric immersion heater or by a boiler.

There are two ways a boiler can heat the water in the cylinder: directly or indirectly. In the former, water is taken from the base of the cylinder, passed through the boiler and returned to the top of the cylinder where it is drawn off by the faucets. In the latter, there is a heat exchange inside the cylinder linked by a closed pipe circuit to the boiler. The water in this circuit is continually heated and circulated between boiler and heat exchanger which, in turn, heats the water in the cylinder. An indirect system is much better than a direct one since there is less chance of a build up of scale or corrosion in the boiler.

A hot water cylinder is unlikely to need much attention, but you may want to replace it with one of greater capacity or change a direct cylinder for an indirect one, or perhaps fit a cylinder with provision for installing an electric immersion heater. If simply installing one of larger capacity, make sure it has the same connections (that is, direct or indirect) as the old one. The way to tell is that the boiler pipe tappings in a direct cylinder are almost allways female whereas those in an indirect cylinder are usually male.

Removing the Old Cylinder

Turn off the immersion heater or boiler and allow the system to cool down before draining the cylinder, hot pipes and boiler circuit (see page 91).

Disconnect the pipework from the cylinder by unscrewing the various connectors and spring the pipes out of the way. If an immersion heater is fitted, isolate the circuit at the fuse panel. If you intend re-using the heater, you will need to buy or rent an immersion heater wrench to unscrew it.

Slide the old cylinder out of the way; being copper, it may be worth some money in scrap value which will help towards buying the new one.

Fitting the New Cylinder

You may well find that the old pipes no longer match up to the connectors of the new cylinder, in which case you will have to cut them back and make up extension pipes, connecting them with capillary or compression joints.

Prepare the connectors for the cylinder by wrapping teflon tape round their threads and screw them in tightly. The pipes are connected with compression fittings; fit the draw-off pipe to the top, the cold feed pipe to the bottom and the boiler pipes to the connectors in the side. Note that the feed pipe from the boiler is attached to the top connector and the return pipe to the boiler to the lower of the two.

If you are not fitting an immersion heater but the cylinder has a boss for one, it should be closed off with a special plate — seal the threads with tape. Similarly treat the threads of a heater unit, spread jointing compound over the faces of its sealing washer and screw it down tightly with the correct wrench. Then fit the thermostat and adjust its temperature setting.

Refilling the Pipework

Refill the pipework and cylinder from the bottom upwards by connecting a hose between each drain-cock and the kitchen cold faucet in turn. This will prevent air locks. Check for any leaks.

Make the connection between the immersion heater and its fused circuit and turn it on — or start up the boiler — to heat the water. Check again for leaks; some may occur as the metal expands. If you find any, tighten the connections further.

Finally, if the cylinder does not already have molded-on or prefitted insulation, fit a lagging jacket.

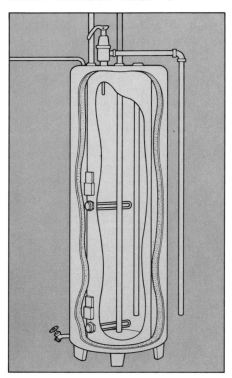

Electric hot water heater.

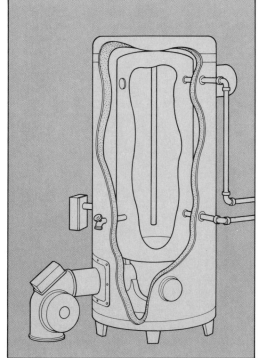

Oil fired hot water heater.

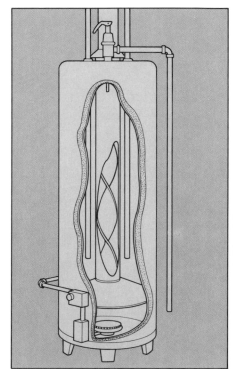

Gas fired hot water heater.

There is much to be said for installing a shower — either instead of, or in addition to a bath. A shower is a very hygienic and quick way of washing, it's refreshing and what is more to shower well you will use but a fifth of the water needed for a bath. This provides real savings in the cost of heating water since you will be using less.

Where space is at a premium, a shower can be installed over an existing bath; even so, a free-standing or built-in shower cubicle takes up very little space — about 1m (3ft) square is all you really need — and it is ideal for putting in a bedroom, on a landing or in any spare corner — even under the stairs.

Installation of a shower is not at all difficult, provided you have carried out plenty of pre-planning and matched the arrangement to the existing plumbing system. Obtaining a good, stable pressure of water at the shower head is essential and this requirement will determine the type of fitting you use and how you arrange the pipework and connections. If this is not done properly, you may well end up with a dribble of water rather than the strong, invigorating spray you hope for. If the connections are made incorrectly, you also run the risk of water temperature fluctuations which could lead to discomfort and at worst scalding.

A Good Pressure Head

Conventional showers work on a gravity principle, taking their supplies of cold and hot water from the cold water storage tank and the hot water cylinder. Since the hot water cylinder is supplied by the cold water tank, the pressure in both sets of pipes is directly related to how high the cold water tank is above the shower rose. The higher it is the greater the pressure and vice versa. A conventional shower will only work if the tank is at least 1m (3ft) above the rose and preferably 1.5m (5ft).

The need for this pressure head of water may cause problems in low buildings, which may not have a cold water storage tank at all, other than to provide a supply for topping up the hot cylinder. In this situation all

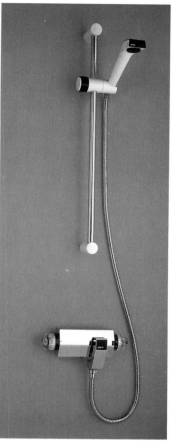

(Left) Thermoscopic mixer which controls temperature to ±1°C and breaks up water scale before it can deposit; ideal in hard water areas. (Centre) High wattage electric unit with low setting for summer economy and fine temperature control.
(Right) Thermostatic mixer with maximum temperature stop and dual controls for flow and temperature; can be flush or surface mounted.

the cold faucets will be supplied by the mains. Since it is generally not allowed by most Plumbing Codes to mix mains pressure water and storage tank water in the same appliance, an extra cold water storage tank would have to be installed to feed the shower only, possibly with a pump to provide a sufficient pressure. An alternative would be to install an instantaneous electric shower which only needs connecting to a mains cold water supply.

Pressure Temperature Fluctuation

Another reason for not taking the cold supply from the mains and the hot supply from the cylinder is that mains pressure can fluctuate at different times of the day. It will tend to overpower the stored water pressure anyway, making it difficult to get a sufficiently hot shower, but if the pressure was to drop suddenly the temperature would go up and could get dangerously hot.

For the same reason, you should arrange to take the hot and cold feed pipes for the

shower directly from the draw-off pipe at the hot water cylinder and from the cold water tank or mains. This will ensure that the pressure in the pipes is even and unaffected by someone else in the house flushing a toilet, or turning on a tap.

The only way you could connect into existing feed pipes and be sure that someone using the shower would not be scalded would be to install a thermostatic shower mixer which automatically adjusts the pressure of the hot and cold supplies to maintain a constant termperature.

Types of Shower Unit

The simplest form of shower fitting is the old rubber hose accessory for pushing on to the bath faucets. The temperature of the spray from its rose is controlled by opening or closing the two faucets, but it is difficult to balance them properly. Many frown on this accessory, too, since it could easily fall into the bath water, allowing the supply to become contaminated.

An improvement is the com-

bined bath/shower mixer which is similar in appearance to a normal bath mixer faucet except that a flexible or rigid pipe runs from it up the wall to a head. To operate it, you adjust the hot and cold controls until the water flowing from the spout is the right temperature. Then you pull a small plunger to divert the water up to the head.

Unfortunately, this fitting still has the drawback of being connected to a supply that may also feed other fittings and pressure fluctuations may occur when they are used.

A better idea is the manual shower mixer which fits to the wall above the bath or in its own shower cubicle and has its own hot and cold water supply pipes. Most have two controls: one to vary the water pressure and the other to balance the hot and cold water for the desired temperature.

A thermostatic mixer will be similar in appearance and work in a similar way, but it automatically compensates for a drop of pressure in one supply pipe by reducing the flow of water from the other. In this way, the temperature set by the user is maintained, even though the overall water pressure from the head may drop. If a drastic drop in pressure from one pipe occurs, it will turn itself off completely.

Where it is impossible to connect to a cold water storage tank, you can fit an electric instantaneous shower which takes a mains supply and heats the water as it flows through, using powerful heating elements.

SHOWER SET-UPS

If a shower is to be of any use at all it must be provided with decent and constant water pressure. This need determines the way in which you connect up the pipework and also the extra equipment you may have to install. Just what you have to do will depend on the existing water supply network in your home and also on the type of home it is.

The Conventional Shower

Simple in design, the conventional shower relies on gravity to provide a decent water pressure at the head. The controlling factor is the cold water storage tank or reservoir and its height above the rose. This supplies the bathroom cold faucets as well as the hot water cylinder (where the water is heated) which in turn supplies the bathroom hot faucets. Therefore both cold and hot faucets are under the same water pressure — the higher the tank the greater the weight of water above any one point and the greater the pressure.

Since a conventional, manually controlled shower takes its cold supply directly from the cold water tank and its hot supply directly from the hot water cylinder, the cistern must be far enough above the shower head to provide a sufficiently strong flow of water. The minimum distance is 1m (3ft) but a greater height is preferable.

Pipe connections are straightforward: just run a feed pipe from the base of the cold water cistern and another pipe from the hot water draw-off pipe attached to the top of the hot water cylinder (neither pipe should be connected to a branch already supplying a faucet). Take the new pipes to the shower mixer, connecting them to the relevant inlets.

Lack of Pressure Head

The problems occur when the tank is less than 1m (3ft) above the rose. This may occur if the tank is installed below ceiling level (in an airing cupboard above the hot cylinder perhaps) or where the ceilings themselves are low, both situations

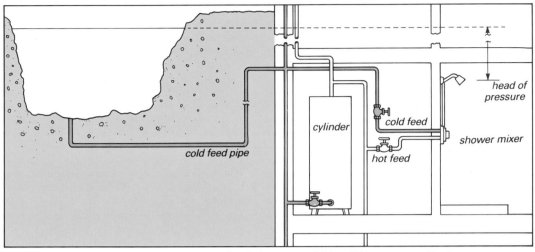

A gravity operated shower requires a minimum head of pressure of 91cm (3ft) to operate effectively

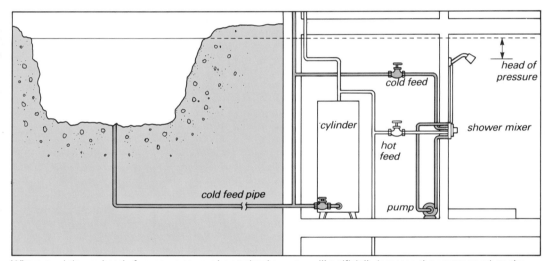

Where a minimum head of pressure cannot be attained a pump will artificially increase the pressure when the shower is turned on.

being common in older properties.

The obvious solution is to raise the cistern higher, either taking it into the loft or setting it on a wooden platform built in the loft. Then the existing pipes can be extended and the new shower pipes put in as before. In a house where the upper rooms are partly in the roof, you may also need to move the cistern sideways so that it can be raised high enough under the apex.

However, it may not always be possible to move the cistern higher: your house may have a flat roof with no attic space or you may live in an apartment with someone else on the floor above. In this situation the only solution (unless you fit a more expensive electric shower operat-

ing on mains water) is to provide an electric shower pump to boost the water pressure at the shower head. Various types are available, some of which have water-proof casings making them suitable for installation in the shower cubicle itself. However, most will need positioning clear of the cubicle so that there is no possibility of them getting wet.

Depending on the design, the pump may need fitting in the pipe between mixer and rose, or it may be arranged to force water through the feed pipes to the mixer. Some operate automatically as soon as you turn the shower mixer on; others have to be powered manually via a ceiling-mounted pull-cord switch.

Some houses may have combined cold water tanks and hot water cylinders, the former being mounted on top of the latter. In the main, the cold water tank is intended to supply the hot cylinder only and would not have the capacity to feed a shower as well. In this case, you would have to install a separate cold tank to meet the needs of the shower, making sure it is level with the existing cold tank to ensure an equal pressure in both hot and cold feed pipes.

Since such a set-up is unlikely to be high enough to supply the correct water pressure for a shower on the same floor, pumped assistance will also be needed.

As with all major plumbing jobs, installing a shower, whether it is to be fitted over a bath or in its own purpose-built cubicle, requires a certain amount of pre-planning if all is to go as it should. You have to work out just where you will fit the shower head and the mixer and how you will run the pipes between the mixer and the hot and cold water supplies. Fortunately, the use of a thermostatic mixer will reduce the need to run completely new pipes from the cold supply and the hot water

Screwing a shower runner to the wall after sliding the rose-holder on to the tubular runner.

Marking the pipe positions for a surface-mounted mixer after fixing the backplate to the wall.

Screwing a fixed shower rose into its holder; connect the pipework to the back of the holder.

cylinder. However, you should try to do this if you can.

Choosing a Thermostatic Mixer

There is quite a range of thermostatic mixers available and it is really a case of finding one that suits your budget and one that you like the look of. Some may be surface-mounted, which makes for easier fixing, particularly if you are mounting it over a bath; others are intended to be recessed into the wall and are more suitable for fitting into a purpose-built cubicle where this can be arranged or into a false wall specially built for the job.

Running In the Pipes

Invariably the supply pipes will have to be connected to the rear of the unit regardless of whether it is surface-mounted or recessed. If the mixer is to be fixed to a false wall, this should not be too difficult to arrange since the pipes can be positioned before the wall is finally clad; the same applies if you are building a complete cubicle. However, if the wall is of masonry, it is a little more difficult.

One way is to run the pipes down the reverse face of the wall, then pass them horizontally through it to the back of the mixer. Of course, this means that the pipes will be exposed in the adjoining room, although this may be acceptable if it is, say, a closet. On the other hand you could box them in neatly.

Setting Pipes in Channels

Setting the pipes in channels cut in the wall, which are then plastered over is not a good idea, since the hot pipe will expand and contract as its temperature varies and will crack the plaster. However, you may be able to get round this by running the pipes through sleeves made of pipe buried in the wall.

When laying in the pipes, work back from the mixer position to the points where you intend breaking into the existing plumbing system. That way you will only have to turn off the water for a short time while you

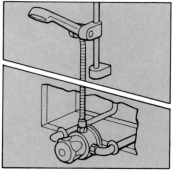

An adjustable-height rose is fed from the mixer via a reinforced flexible hose screwed on to the mixer outlet.

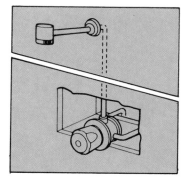

Hidden pipework is better for a fixed rose; run it up behind, or inside larger pipe within the wall.

make the final connections.

If possible, take the cold feed directly from the cold water supply and the hot feed from the draw-off pipe at the hot water cylinder immediately above the main branch for the hot faucets. If these connections would make for particularly tortuous pipe runs, you can connect into branches supplying the bathroom hot and cold faucets but *only* if you are using a thermostatic mixer. This will compensate for any drop in pressure in one pipe (caused when a fawcet is turned on) by reducing the flow from the other pipe.

Installing the Mixer

The way the mixer is attached to the wall will vary from one model to another. However, surface-mounted versions will probably have a baseplate that screws to the wall and recessed versions will fix to the wall's framework with screws. They have a bezel that seals to the wall to prevent water seeping behind and into the wall.

Attach the pipes to the inlets of the mixer using the compression fittings provided, making sure they are tight.

Fitting the Rose

Various types of shower heads are available: some are fixed permanently to the wall, others are part of a handset which can be slotted into a wall-mounted holder. In some cases the holder will slide up and down a vertical rod to allow height adjustment. The latter is probably the most useful.

If the head is fixed perman-

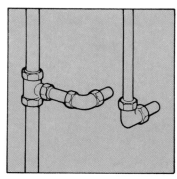

The hot supply can be teed into a convenient hot pipe, using a 22×22×15mm reducing tee if connecting into 22mm pipework.

ently it will be connected to the mixer by a rigid pipe; either concealed behind the wall or run across the surface. If the head is part of handset, it will be connected by a flexible pipe. In each case, the connections are made with capnuts and rubber seals.

Installation is straightforward: simply screw the bracket or brackets to the wall so that the head will be at a comfortable height. Fit the head in place and connect up the supply pipe between head and mixer.

FITTING A SHOWER TRAY

Available in a variety of colors to match other bathroom fittings, shower trays can be acrylic plastic or ceramic. The latter are more expensive but much harder wearing.

Because a shower tray will be close to the floor, it should be fitted with a shallow 50mm (2in) seal P-trap and a (1½in) waste pipe. Even with a shallow-seal trap it will be necessary to raise the tray slightly above the floor to gain the necessary clearance for the waste run. Some manufacturers supply brackets for this purpose, but if not you can set the tray on a wooden platform or on bricks.

The gap round the bottom of the tray can be filled in with tiled panels to match the cubicle and at least one should be removable to provide access for clearing blockages in the trap. You could run the trap and pipe below floorboard level but only if the pipe run is parallel to the joists.

Assembly of the trap to the tray is the same as assembling a bath waste.

After bedding the waste outlet into a ring of plumber's putty and wrapping teflon tape round the thread, tightening the backnut.

Screwing the shallow-seal trap to the waste outlet; check that the O-ring is in place and that the trap points towards the waste pipe.

Levelling the tray on a plinth of bricks using packing pieces after connecting the waste pipe to the trap outlet.

Lowering a shower tray with its own plinth on to the adjustable feet. First locate their position and screw them to the floor.

After levelling the tray on its feet, screwing the fixing bracket to the wall; recess it into the plaster and tile over it later.

Fitting the removable side panels of the plinth after making the waste connections by pushing them up under the lip of the tray.

OPTIONS

ELECTRIC SHOWERS

If installing a conventional gravity fed or pumped shower seems too complicated, you could install an instantaneous electric shower instead. This takes its water supply through one 15mm (½in) branch pipe connected to the rising main. It also needs connecting to a 30A electrical supply controlled by a ceiling-mounted pull switch.

Electric showers are housed in self-contained water-tight casings so they can be installed inside the shower cubicle or over the bath. The supply pipe and cable are fed in through the back of the unit so you will need to chase the wall or run them in from the other side of the wall.

Break into the main with a T fitting and use a threaded connector to link the pipe to the shower's inlet. It is essential that the switch is pull cord operated for safety. As with any new fixture or fitting check with your local Electric and Plumbing Codes to see if it is allowed in your area — or if there are any special requirements needed before installation.

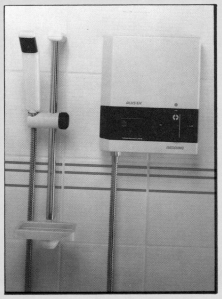

8kW unit with automatic on/off water valve permits a good flow of hot water even under very cold conditions.

Microchip control of temperature and flow; dial selection of flow and push-button stop/start and hot/cold.

FITTING A CUBICLE

Because a shower head is fitted high up on the wall, you must take particular care to prevent water spraying out into the room where it will damage flooring and decorations. If the shower is fitted over a bath this is easily arranged; all that is necessary is to screw a rigid shower screen to the wall so that it projects along the edge of the bath, or to install a plastic shower curtain so that it hangs inside the bath. The job is slightly more complicated if you have installed a seperate shower tray, since it must be enclosed on all four sides.

There is no reason why you should not build your own cubicle, erecting wooden framed panels round it and cladding them with tiles or a similar waterproof finish, and using a shower curtain for the door. However, it is probably easier to use one of the many ready made shower kits currently available, and it would certainly be much quicker.

Cubicle Format

Shower cubicle kits come in three basic forms to match the position of the tray within the room. If you have put the tray in the corner of the room so that two sides of the cubicle are already formed by the existing walls, you will need a corner kit with two upright panels. If the tray simply backs on to a wall, you can use a freestanding kit of three panels, and if the tray is in an existing alcove, all you need is a single panel kit to close it off.

These shower cubicle kits usually comprise adjustable aluminum frames (allowing different size trays to be accommodated) glazed with either patterned safety glass or, more likely, plastic acrylic sheets. One or two of the panels will incorporate sliding or bi-folding doors and you should be able to position these to give the easiest way of stepping in and out.

Securing the Panels

Installation is straightforward: vertical channels are screwed to the adjoining walls, the upright panels are secured to them and the whole cubicle is held rigid by channel sections around the top and bottom which are held together at the corners by plastic blocks. A watertight seal is provided at the walls and around the tray by applying a bead of flexible caulking.

Inside the cubicle, the existing walls of the room should be tiled to prevent water seeping into the plaster and damaging the structure.

Joining the mitered corners of the bottom track by attaching the angle bracket with self-tapping screws.

Installing the bottom track on the tray after appylying a bead of caulk to the underside; ensure the angle is square.

Marking the positions for fixing the upright channel (panel spacer) to the wall; check that it is vertical.

Fitting the rollers and guide pegs to the sliding door by tapping them into the end of the door channel.

Securing the fixed panel to the panel spacer; insert the panel into the spacer and drill holes for the fixing screws.

Hanging the sliding door; position the bottom guide pegs in the bottom track and feed the top track on to the rollers.

PLUMBING IN A BIDET

Considered by many to be a luxury, a bidet is nevertheless a useful appliance to have in a modern bathroom. Those available come in shapes and colors to match other bathroom fittings so a co-ordinated look can be maintained.

There are two types of bidet: the straightforward over-rim bidet and the more complicated rim-supply and ascending spray types.

The over-rim bidet is very similar to a normal wash basin in that it is fitted with individual pillar faucets or a mixer, the spout of which discharges over the rim and into the bowl of the bidet. It is plumbed-in in the same way as a basin, too.

The rim-supply and ascending spray type is rather more complex. The controls allow hot water to flow through the hollow rim to warm it and make it more comfortable to sit on; they are then used to divert the flow to a vertical spray in the base of the bowl. The spray outlet will be covered with water when in use and to prevent to likelihood of the water supplies being contaminated by back-siphonage, the feed pipes must be taken directly from the cold water mains supply and the hot water cylinder just as they would with a shower, but via a vacuum breaker device that prevents back siphonage and possible contamination of the drinking water supply.

Both types normally have a pop-up waste fitting which should be connected to a waste pipe and P-trap if the waste run is no longer than 1.7m (5ft 6in) or 38mm pipe if it is longer than that up to a maximum of 2.3m (7ft 6in). The waste pipe can run directly to a soil stack. A 75mm (3in) deep seal trap is needed.

Installing The Bidet

With an over-rim type, assemble the faucets and waste to it as you would a normal hand basin. Since it will be set against the wall, flexible copper pipes with swivel connectors will make the connections to the 15mm (½in) supply pipes much easier. Run these pipes back to the most convenient break-in points on the bathroom hot and cold faucet supplies. Note that if the cold faucets in the bathroom are supplied direct from the mains, you must have separate hot and cold faucets on the bidet and not a mixer. The latter can only be fitted if both supplies come from storage tanks. It is illegal to mix mains and stored water in one fitting, to prevent contamination of the drinking water supply.

The ascending spray type of bidet is somewhat more complicated to install because of its control mechanism which must be assembled to the bowl first. All the necessary parts will be supplied with the bidet and it is just a case of putting it together in accordance with the manufacturer's instructions, but always check with your local Plumbing Code before plumbing in any new device or fixture. Then flexible copper pipes are linked to the faucet tails as before. The cold water supply pipe must run from the base of the cold water storage tank (no connection to the mains is allowed) and the hot water pipe from the draw-off pipe above the hot water cylinder.

Connect up the waste pipe and screw the bowl to the floor.

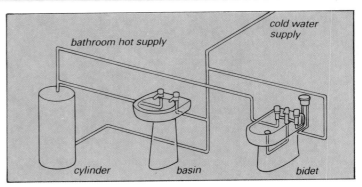

An ascending spray bidet must be connected to the supply from the hot water cylinder and the cold water supply via a vacuum breaker valve.

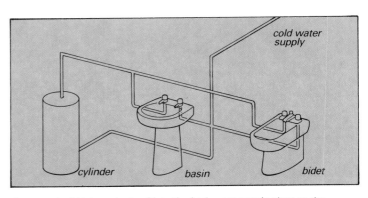

An over-rim bidet can be teed into the bathroom supply pipes to the washbasin or bath; use 22×22×15mm fittings in the latter case.

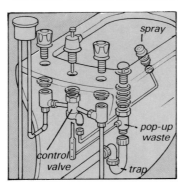

To connect ascending spray bidet: faucets; spray; vacuum breaker valve; control valve mixer; 32mm pop up drain and trap; 15mm pipe.

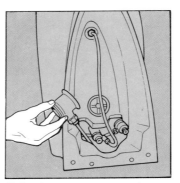

Fitting the pop-up waste to the outlet after connecting the spray supply pipe between the spray and the mixer.

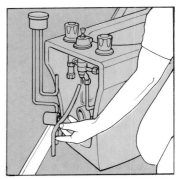

Connecting the bidet to the waste and supply pipes; corrugated connectors are useful here as the bidet fits against the wall.

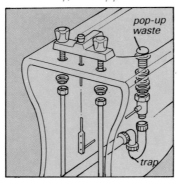

Components needed to connect an over-rim bidet: faucets; 32mm pop-up waste and trap; 15mm supply pipes.

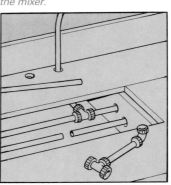

Connecting into the washbasin supply pipes; use slip-tee fittings which can be slid along the pipe after cutting.

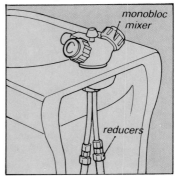

15 × 10mm or 15 × 12mm reducing connectors are needed to connect to the 10 or 12mm tails of a monobloc mixer faucet.

FAULT FINDING

Faults	Causes	Action
Faucet can't be turned off fully Constant dripping from tap spout.	Worn faucet washer or seating.	Replace faucet washer or regrind seating.
Water flows from around faucet spindle. Faucet handle easily turned. Juddering or knocking sound from plumbing system when faucet turned on.	Worn gland packing in old faucet; worn O-ring seals in more modern types.	Replace gland packing with wool soaked in vaseline; fit new O-ring seals.
Water flows from toilet or storage cistern overflow pipe; can be heard running constantly through cistern ball-valve.	Leaking ball-valve float keeping valve open. Incorrectly adjusted float arm keeping valve open. Particle of grit jammed in valve keeping it open. Worn ball-valve washer, preventing it closing fully. Worn ballvalve.	Unscrew float and fit a new one. Bend float arm so that valve closes. Work float arm up and down to free grit; if this doesn't work remove valve and clean. Remove piston and replace valve washer. Replace valve.
Toilet tank flush handle needs operating several times before toilet will flush.	Worn siphon washers or flap valves in cistern. Wear and corrosion in an old high level tank.	Fit new siphon washers or flap valves. Replace tank.
Water flows constantly into the pan from an old high-level toilet tank.	Worn or badly corroded 'Burlington' cistern.	Replace tank.
Juddering or knocking sound from plumbing system when any appliance is used.	Ball-valve float in storage or toilet tank 'bouncing' on ripples caused as water flows in. Long unsupported pipe runs, particularly if under mains pressure. See also second cause above.	Dampen float arm movement by suspending a small plastic pot from it with galvanized wire so that pot is submerged in water. Clip pipe run securely to walls and roof members.
Waste water won't flow away from a sink, basin, bath, or other fitting.	Waste outlet blocked by materials such as soap, hair or food debris. Waste trap blocked.	Clean waste outlet. Clear blockage with a sink plunger or dismantle trap, remove blockage and flush through.
Toilet pan won't clear when flushed, water level in pan higher than normal.	Blocked toilet trap. Blockage in soil stack or underground drainage run.	Clear blockage with proprietary toilet plunger, or work it free with a length of flexible curtain wire. Clear blockage with drain rods through stack clean out or access chamber.
Water flows from around a manhole cover.	Blockage in underground drainage run.	Clear blockage with drain rods through access chamber.
Gutter overflows.	Leaking gutter or downpipe joint. Sagging gutter run.	Scoop debris from gutter and flush through; clear down-pipe with a wad or rags on the end of a long rod. Remake joint. Reposition gutter brackets to ensure a constant fall towards the outlet.

Trick

Removing the headgear of a bathroom faucet after unscrewing the cover; grip the spout to prevent it from turning.

Fitting a replacement washer to the headgear after unscrewing the retaining nut to remove the old one.

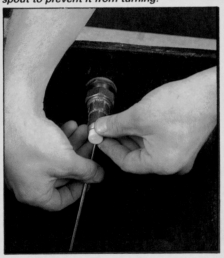

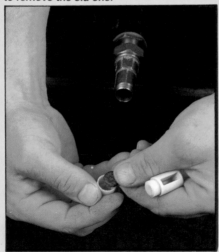

Prising the piston from a ball valve, using a screwdriver in the slot beneath, after removing the float and piston cap.

Inserting a new washer into the piston after dismantling the piston by unscrewing the two halves.

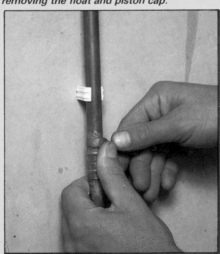

Repairing a pipe with a two-part epoxy compound; tear off enough to cover the leak and roll between the fingers to activate.

Stopping a leak with a repair clamp; clip the two halves of the clamp together round the pipe and tighten the wing-nut.

LEAKS, BURSTS

Faucets

Faucets which can't be turned off fully or which drip constantly need re-washering.

Turn off the water supply and open the faucet to drain the pipework. Depending on the type of faucet, either unscrew the protective cover and lift it up, or remove the shrouded handle by removing the retaining screw. This may be under the indicator button in the top or at the side. Or the handle may just prise off.

Hold the faucet spout to stop it turning and unscrew the head gear nut. Lift out the head gear and unscrew the nut holding the rubber washer underneath. Discard the washer and fit a new one. Then re-assemble.

Ball-valves

If an overflow pipe drips constantly, it indicates a problem with the ball-valve in the tank concerned. First check the float for leaks or bend the float arm so that it closes the valve fully. If this doesn't work, rewasher the valve.

Turn off the water and drain the pipework. Disconnect the float arm and unscrew the cap from the end of the valve. Push out the piston.

Hold the piston body with a pair of pliers and unscrew the cap from the end. Prise out the rubber washer and fit a new one.

Re-assemble the piston, lubricating it with vaseline. Then re-assemble the valve and float arm. Restore the water supply.

Bursts

A burst pipe requires quick and effective action to both minimize the damage done by escaping water and to get the system back in use as soon as possible.

Turn off the water supply to the affected pipe immediately and pack thick cloths round the damage to staunch the flow while you drain it down. If the pipe is damaged because you have driven a nail through it, leave the nail in place until the pipe is drained.

Once the pipe is drained, cut out the affected section and fit a new piece. You can buy a repair kit comprising a length of flexible copper pipe with two push-fit polybutylene connectors to allow a quick replacement to be made.

Your roof presents a very large flat surface to the sky and during a rainstorm the amount of water flowing off it can be quite considerable. If nothing was done to collect this water, it would simply cascade down the walls of your house, seeping into the brickwork and doing untold damage. It would not be very pleasant for anyone walking underneath either. That is why every house has a rainwater collection system.

The rainwater system comprises gutters which run along the roof at eaves level to catch the water as it runs off and channel it to vertical downpipes. The downpipes either discharge the water into a trapped gully at ground level or are connected directly to an underground drainpipe. This, in turn, may direct the water to a storm drain running under the road outside, or to a soakaway in the garden.

Rainwater System Materials

Early rainwater systems were made of cast iron and many houses still have such systems. However, cast iron is not the best of materials to use for something that is in constant contact with water and the air; it can suffer badly from rust if it is not protected by regular painting, and it is very heavy—which proves awkward when putting it up or taking it down.

Asbestos was used as a replacement for cast iron rainwater systems, but this material is bulky and quite brittle. It is realized now that asbestos is a health hazard as well, so it has no place in the home.

These days plastic is the most common material for rainwater pipes and gutters: it is light in weight, unaffected by corrosion, requires virtually no maintenance and is easily installed.

Plastic systems offer a choice of three basic gutter profiles: half-round, semi-elliptic and square, and common sizes are 75mm (3in), 100mm (4in) and 150mm (6in), these being measured across the widest part of the gutter. They are available with matching downpipes and a wide range of accessories that allow even the most complex arrangements to be duplicated.

Connectors are available to allow modern plastic systems to be linked to original cast iron guttering, which is particularly useful if you live in a semi-detached or terraced house and need to connect to a neighbour's system. Unfortunately, no adaptors are available to join plastic systems from different manufacturers, even though nominally they may have the same dimensions. For this reason you should always try to match existing plastic systems with components of the same make — and this is usually stamped on the gutters and fixings.

Another material used for rainwater systems is extruded or cast aluminum which, more expensive than plastic, can be used to give the appearance of cast iron if you want to maintain a period look.

Potential Problems

The most common problem with any rainwater system is a blockage, either in a gutter or downpipe. This will cause an overflow so the trouble is easily spotted. The remedy is simple: scoop out the debris and flush the gutter through, or push a wad of rag through the downpipe with a long rod to move the blockage. If this is not possible because the pipe incorporates an offset bend, you may have to dismantle it to reach the blockage. This should not be too difficult since the sections of pipe usually just slot into each other.

A sagging gutter may also cause an overflow and to cure this it might be necessary to reposition the brackets to ensure a steady fall towards the downpipe. Or you may need to reposition just one bracket.

Leaks may occur at the joints in cast iron systems and a repair can be made by removing the securing bolt (sawing through it if necessary) scraping out the old sealant and applying a fresh layer of mastic before bolting the sections back to gether.

Surface rust should be cleaned off with a wire brush and then the metal primed and painted — coat the inside of the gutter with bituminous paint. Rust holes can be repaired with glassfiber, but if a system is this bad it is better to replace it.

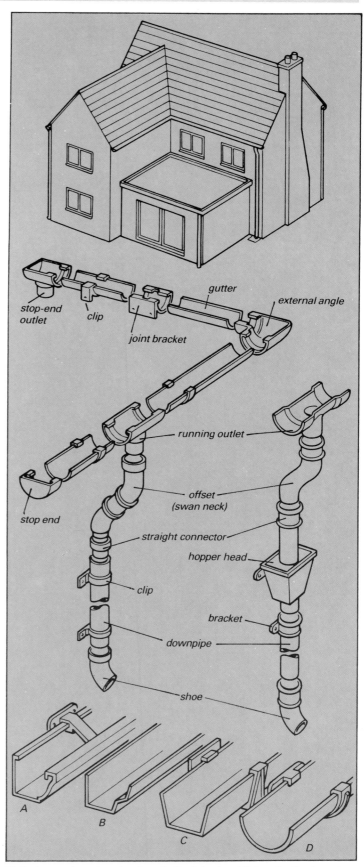

Guttering carries rainwater, from both pitched and flat roofs, direct, or via a hopper head to a downpipe and thence to a drain or soakaway. It is available in various sections: (left to right) moulded (often ogee); ogee; square; half-round. It may be screwed or clipped to the fascia.

FITTING A PLASTIC SYSTEM

If your existing rainwater system needs replacing, the easiest material to use is plastic. Get hold of a catalogue from your local supplier and inspect the existing system, noting the number and type of plastic fittings you will need. Measure the length of the guttering and of the downpipe, allowing a bit extra for trimming.

You should also measure the size of the gutter between the rims and buy the equivalent size; in this way you will be sure that your new system will be able to cope with the amount of water coming off the roof. However, if you intend extending the system for any reason, it may be worth choosing the next size up.

Plastic systems come in various brands, but there is little to choose between them, so stick to the one that is most readily available. The guttering, pipes and fittings are obtainable in grey, black or white plastic, but they are easily painted if none of these colors fits in with your exterior color scheme.

Safe access is essential when you are replacing guttering and the best thing to do is rent a scaffold tower. However, if you have no choice but to use a ladder, make sure its feet cannot possibly slip and that the top is tied to an eye screwed into the roof fascia board or house wall.

Removing the Old System

If the old guttering is cast iron, the sections will be bolted together with a caulk seal in between. It is most unlikely that you will be able to unscrew the bolts holding the sections together, so for quickness simply cut through them between the nut and underside of the gutter, using a hacksaw. Then tap out the bolt with a drift or a narrow scrap bolt. Break the caulk seal with an old chisel.

The gutters may rest in brackets screwed to the fascia board or be screwed directly to the board. In the former case, lift out the sections of gutter and either unscrew or saw off the brackets. In the latter case, get someone to support the gutter while you unscrew it. Each section will be very heavy and rather than attempt to carry it to the ground, lower it on a rope. Don't simply throw it down since cast iron is very brittle and will shatter when it lands.

The outlet section of gutter should simply lift out of the top of the downpipe. Then remove the downpipe; unscrew or saw through its mounting brackets and lift each section clear.

You can remove asbestos guttering and downpipes in the same manner, but before you start spray the entire system well with water to prevent any dust or fibres flying about. For added protection, wear a face mask and thick gloves. Try not to break any of the pieces, rather saw them up with a hacksaw, damping them down.

Essential Preparation

Once you have removed all the old system, you can inspect the fascia board for signs of damage or rot. If it is in bad condition, it should be levered off and a new board nailed to the ends of the rafters. Otherwise, clean it off with a stiff brush, fill any old screw holes with a good quality exterior filler and paint it with primer undercoat and finish coat.

Similarly, brush down the wall behind the downpipe, fill the old pipe bracket screw holes and, if the rest of the wall is painted, treat it with the same color.

Installing the New Guttering

The new guttering must have a steady and gradual fall towards the downpipe end if the water is to flow away efficiently. This fall should be about 5mm (¼in) in

Levering away an old cast-iron downpipe; if it is fixed securely, cut through the bolts with a hacksaw, close to the wall.

Lowering an old section of guttering on a rope; make sure you have a firm foothold as the sections are very heavy.

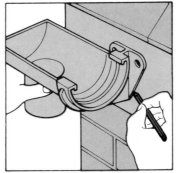

Positioning the new outlet; fit it low down on the fascia as the water must drain down to this point.

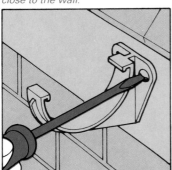

At the far end of the run, screwing the fixing bracket high up on the fascia to give a minimum fall of 5mm (¼in) per metre (3ft).

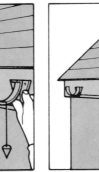

Stretching a string line between the outlet and other bracket; check with a spirit level that you have the necessary fall.

With the string line still in place as a guide to height, fix the intermediate brackets at the recommended intervals along it.

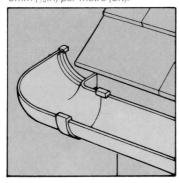

Clip in the guttering along one run before fitting a corner piece, followed by the guttering on the other side of the corner.

Fitting a stop-end to the end of the guttering; if the outlet is not at one end of a run, fit a running outlet and two stop-ends.

Fitting a square-to-round adaptor to enable the run to be continued in guttering of a different section to the original one.

every metre (three feet) and it is arranged by positioning the gutter brackets progressively lower along the fascia.

Begin by screwing one bracket to the end of the fascia furthest from the downpipe and as close to the eaves as possible (bearing in mind that the gutter must be slipped into it). This bracket should be 150mm (6in) in from the end of the fascia. Drive a nail into the fascia level with the top of the bracket and tie a length of string to it. Take the string to the other end of the fascia and pull it taught while someone else checks that it is horizontal with a spirit level. Lower the string enough to match the required fall and tie it to another nail hammered in place. Fit another bracket to the fascia at this point, its top level with the string and 150mm (6in) in from the end of the fascia.

Working towards the down-pipe end start fitting the lengths of gutter into the brackets, spacing the latter at 1m (3ft) intervals and setting extra brackets on each side of any joints. Use galvanised screws to hold the brackets in place and line up each with the string line.

The first length of gutter should have a stop end clipped to it to close it off; the end of the gutter should project 50mm (2in) beyond the end of the fascia.

The method used for joining lengths of gutters incorporates a rubber seal which is held to the plain end of the next length by a plastic spring clip. In other systems both ends are plain and a completely separate clip-on jointing piece is used. Sometimes this joint doubles as a support bracket.

You will have to trim at least one length to size. Measure for this very carefully, making sure it overlaps the rubber joint seals fully. In some cases, where the gutter is to run round a corner, it is easier to fix the corner piece in place first and then measure up to it for the gutter pieces on each side.

You can cut the guttering with a hacksaw, taking care to keep the cut square. Clean off any burrs with a file. Some types need notches cut in their edges to accommodate the securing clips and these can be made with a hacksaw and file, or you

Hanging a plumb-line from the outlet to mark the position of the leader.

Fitting a swan-neck to guttering on overhanging eaves; two-part swan-necks allow sideways adjustment of the leader position.

Marking the position on the wall of the top leader bracket; this should be a little distance below the outlet.

Fixing the bracket block of a two-part pipe bracket to the wall; this type permits all wall fixings to be made without the pipe in position.

Sliding the pipe clips on to the pipe to coincide with the bracket blocks; the wedge-shaped connector should taper downwards.

Screwing the pipe clip to the block after connecting to the swan-neck; the pipe socket, whether integral or separate, should be uppermost.

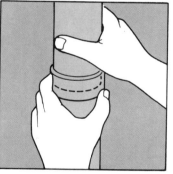
Connecting lengths of pipe; joints are not solvent welded, and an expansion tolerance of 10mm (⅜in) should be left between lengths.

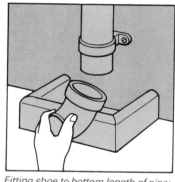
Fitting shoe to bottom length of pipe; angle it away from the wall, 50mm (2in) above the ground or splash block and solvent-weld it to the pipe.

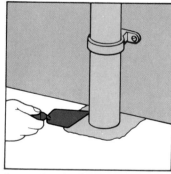
Connecting the downpipe to a drain; fit a caulking bush into the drain socket, solvent-weld the pipe and mortar in place.

can hire a proper tool.

When you reach the down-pipe end, fit the outlet section and another stop end so that it projects 50mm (2in) beyond the end of the fascia.

Fitting the Downpipe

If the downpipe needs an offset bend at the top to set it out from the wall so that it will connect with the gutter outlet, this should be made up first. Then you can offer it up to the gutter and determine the downpipe

position. You may be able to buy a one-piece offset bend; if not, you can make one up from two offset connectors and a short length of straight pipe. In this case, the pieces must be solvent welded together to ensure a watertight assembly. The top socket of the offset bend fits over the top of the gutter outlet.

Use a plumbline to mark a vertical guide line on the wall for the pipe bracket positions. Then assemble the pipe, working downwards and screwing the brackets to plugged holes drilled in the wall. The bottom of each

section pushes into the wider socket of the section below.

If the downpipe is to discharge over a gully, a 'shoe' fitting is solvent-welded to the bottom of the pipe. This deflects the water away from the house wall. It should terminate about 50mm (2in) above the gully grid to prevent water splashing up the wall. If a direct connection to an underground pipe is needed, the last section of pipe is solvent welded into a socket which closes off the top of that pipe.

Finally, test the system by pouring water into the gutter.

4

ELECTRICS

If you stop to consider how advanced today's electrical appliances and light fittings have become, it's rather surprising how primitive the electrical system is in many homes. Even new homes are seldom built with enough power points or anything more adventurous than a single centre light in each room, and many older houses have electrical systems that are quite incapable of coping with modern demands. Yet the fittings and the know-how needed to provide a thoroughly up-to-date wiring system are freely available, and improving your home's electrical systems can be a very rewarding job. You could save yourself a lot of money too — a professional electrician is an expensive person nowadays.

Safety First

Many people shy away from doing their own electrical work out of fear — fear that if they make a mistake the results could be fatal. This is perfectly true, but the skills involved in do-it-yourself electrical work are easy to master, and furthermore you can always see what you are doing and double-check that you've done it properly ... unlike plumbing, for example, where you can only tell if your joints are watertight when you turn the water back on. So provided that you are able to work methodically and are prepared to check everything twice, there is no reason to be afraid that the end result will be dangerous. You will probably have taken a great deal more care than the average electrician, simply because it's your home and your family that is involved.

The other quality you need is respect: electricity can be a wonderfully willing servant so long as you treat it properly. Take sensible precautions all the time when you are carrying out electrical work, and you will be at no risk. This means never

attempting any electrical job unless you know exactly what you are doing, never working on any part of your electrical system unless you have isolated it from the mains supply, and always double-checking everything before restoring the power.

Last of all, teach your children about the dangers of electricity, so that they will understand it and not take chances with it when they grow up.

Local Codes

All electrical work whether done by an electrician or not must be carried out according to your local building code. The codes vary greatly from one location to the next. Always check the proposed work with your local Building Department to make sure that it complies with local practices and procedures. Many different things can vary, the type and size of wire required in a particular location, the number of circuits, outlets or lighting points

— also you may be required to have your work inspected by either a licensed electrician or a building inspector before switching on.

Never begin any work you know or think may not comply with your local electrical code.

Always use U.L. listed materials, anything else may create a fire hazard.

Always follow manufacturer's instructions supplied with any materials, fixtures or appliances.

Simple Improvements

The best way of working out how you can improve your existing system is to take a tour round the house. Look out for areas where there are a lot of electrical appliances and too few electrical outlets; extension cords trailing across the floor are the tell-tale signs here. Some appliances might benefit from being permanently hooked up to the power supply instead of just being plugged in; examples are freezers, waste disposal units and extractor fans, to name just three. Ask yourself whether outlets are conveniently sited; some may be too low to reach easily, or may be hidden behind furniture.

Look at the lighting too. If you have just a central fixture in each room, anything would be an improvement, and even if you are happy with what you've got, replacing some of the fixtures could change and improve the lighting in the room concerned. Adding more lights, or altering the positions of existing ones, could be the answer. If it's ideas you need, keep your eyes open in public buildings — hotels, restaurants, banks and the like; you will often be able to see quite advanced lighting ideas in practice far better than by visiting a lighting showroom.

As you work your way round the house, note down what you've got and an idea of what improvements are needed on a rough floor plan. This will be a great help in future when you come to plan and carry out the improvements you need.

Major Alterations

If you have an out-of-date system — or your initial survey shows up really serious shortcomings, you will have to consider some major rewiring work. It's often easier to plan and install completely new circuits that go exactly where you want and provide all the facilities you need than to spend hours tracing existing circuits and working out how to modify them. Of course, it will often be possible to use parts of the existing set-up if they are in good condition, but this is best looked upon as a bonus.

Apart from improvements to your existing lighting and power circuits, you may want to install extra circuits to major appliances such as waste disposal units, washing machines and clothes dryers, or to provide power to outbuildings. All this may well entail fitting a new service panel to cope with the extra circuits — a chance to ensure that this too is able to cope with all your needs.

Electricity reaches your home via an underground or overhead supply cable — usually the former, except in rural areas. This is tapped off the local supply from a nearby substation, a supply called 'three phase' because it has three phase or live cables and one neutral. The voltage difference between any pair of live cables is 240 volts — the voltage normally supplied to heavy current users such as factories — while that between any of the live cables and the neutral is 120 volts — the normal voltage for household use. Factories and the like draw current from all three phases, while the household supply is normally 2 phase, three conductors — two live or 'hot' wires and one neutral.

With 120 volts available between either hot wire and the neutral and 240 volts between the two hot wires this provides the home owner with enough electricity to operate normal household circuits and also heavy appliances which generally require 240 volts.

The Service Panel

When the supply cable enters your house, it passes first of all to the utility company's service head and from there to the electricity meter, which records how much electricity you use. Up

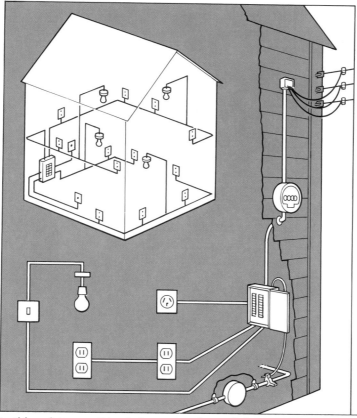

1. Non-metallic cable (Romex)

2. Armored cable (BX)

3. Conduit

Wire sizes

to this point, everything belongs to the local utility company, and must not be tampered with in any way; the service head and meter are fitted with special seals so any interference can be readily detected.

From the meter, two more cables called meter tails run to your main service panel. In older homes there may be several fuseboxes, all linked to a main disconnect to which the meter tails are connected; in a modern house there will be a one-piece service panel which may also contain a main breaker switch as well as the individual circuit breakers.

Distribution

The service panel controls the distribution of current to the various circuits in the house. The live meter tails are connected to strips called busbars along which are mounted a number of individual fuses or circuit breakers of different ratings, depending on the type of service panel. Their purpose is to protect each circuit from receiving too much current — either because the consumer tries to take too much, or if an electrical fault occurs — the fuse will 'blow' (or the breaker will trip)

and cut off the supply to that circuit. The fuse may be the replaceable screw-in type containing a length of fuse wire, or may contain a cartridge fuse with the wire concealed in a small metal-capped ceramic tube. On the most modern installations the fuses may be replaced by small electro-mechanical switches that trip to off if excess current is drawn by the circuit. In addition the main supply circuit bringing power to the service panel is also protected by either a main fuse or circuit breaker. Removing the fuse or shutting off the breaker turns off the power supply to the whole house.

The other end of each fuse or circuit breaker is connected to the live wire of the circuit cable. The returning neutral wires of all the circuit cables are linked to a neutral terminal block to which the neutral meter tail is connected. Within the service panel you will also see that the ground wires from each circuit are also attached to the neutral busbar, from there a single grounding wire runs from the neutral busbar to the house's grounding point — either it is attached to the incoming cold water supply pipe or to a grounding rod driven into the earth beneath in the house.

Individual Circuits

From the fuses or breakers in the fusebox or service panel individual cables run out to supply the various circuits in the house. All circuit wiring is color coded — the neutral wire is always white, the grounding wire may be either green or bare without any covering, the 'hot' or live wire in a 120 volt circuit is usually black or another color, but not white or green. To obtain 120 volts at an outlet requires connecting one black wire and one white wire. To obtain 240 volts requires connecting two black or colored wires — however the two black wires must be fed from opposite supply phases at your service panel. Circuits carry different loads depending on the job they are required to do, ranging from 15 or 20 amps for a normal domestic circuit up to 50 amps for, say, a stove or central air conditioner. The wires making up each circuit are sized according to the load that they carry; number 12 wire and number 10 wire are the most common in residential work — (wire sizes get smaller as the gauge number increases) — number 14 gauge wire is the minimum size wire for residential work.

Trick

ELECTRICIAN'S

RUNNING CABLES

Running underfloor cables parallel to the joists; a flat-section sprung-steel coil helps to feed the cable through.

Running cables across the joists; drill clearance holes at least 50mm (2in) below the top and central to the floorboard.

Plastering over plastic conduit, chased into the wall, through which the cable has been threaded.

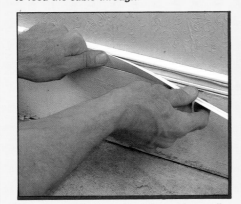

Running cable through mini-trunking; nail or stick the channel to the wall, feed in the cable and snap on the cover.

Nailing a covering channel over cable buried in a chase in the wall to provide some protection against stray nails.

Fixing cable to a door frame with plastic cable clips; these are available in sizes to match the various cable sizes.

Two kinds of wire are available: Non-Metallic Sheath Cable (Romex) which is a flexible cable covered in plastic, or Metal Armored Cable (BX) which has a flexible steel spiral covering. For any project that you plan it is always advisable to use the same type of wire and equipment as already exists in your home, as this has most likely been determined by your local electrical code. In addition to these two wiring systems, individual insulated conductors can be run in galvanized steel pipe or conduit. Conduit can be obtained in a variety of sizes and comes in 10 foot lengths — it must, however, be bent by using a special tool called a "hickey." The code requires that conduit be used in certain situations. It is not the easiest technique for the average homeowner to become involved with.

If you have wooden floors, you can run circuit cables underneath them — or in the void between the floor and the ceiling above. Under first floors you can simply let the cable rest on the concrete slab, although it's better to clip it to the sides or bottom edges of the joists if there's enough room to crawl under the floor. At second-floor level you can let the cable rest on the ceiling surface if it runs parallel with the joists; if it crosses the joist line you have to drill small holes in the joists — ideally at their mid-depth point — and thread the cable through the holes. In this case you need lift only one floorboard and you can run the cable right across the room; with cable runs parallel to the joists you have to lift a board at each side of the room and 'fish' the cable through the void.

Solid Floors

If you have solid floors, you can cut out a channel and run in the cable, which should be protected by conduit, but it is generally a lot simpler to run the cable in plastic raceway mounted on top of the skirting board or even behind the base board itself.

In attics you should clip the cable to the joists above the level of any insulation. There's no need to thread it through joists except where there are walkways.

Cables In Walls

If you have masonry walls, you can bury the cables in shallow channels (called chases) cut in the wall surface with a mason's chisel and light sledge hammer or a rented chasing machine. You can lay the cable in without any further protection, but it's better to either thread it through protective conduit or cover it with pin-on protective channeling, even though both methods mean you need a wider chase. The chase is simply plastered over when the cable is in place.

With stud partition walls, you can thread the cable down between the sheets of drywall on either face, but you will have to drill through the head and sole plates and also expose any bracing so you can cut a small section away and allow the cable through.

If you're surface-mounting your cable, either clip it to the wall, the base board and door and window frames by running it in a metal or plastic raceway. This has a base you pin, screw or stick to the wall and a snap-on cover that conceals the cables inside.

Trick

ELECTRICIAN'S

PREPARING CABLE

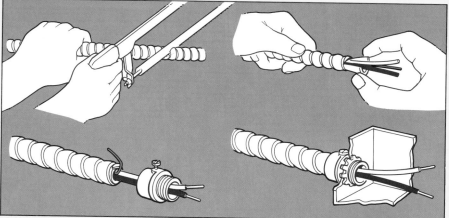

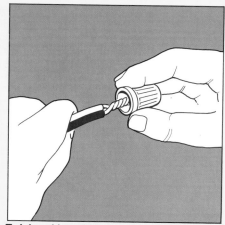

To join BX: 1. Cut an 8in length of the armor from the end of the cable and remove the paper wrapping from around the wires. 2. Insert a plastic anti-short bushing. 3. Slide over a BX connector and tighten the clamping screw. 4. Insert the connector into the junction box and tighten the locknut.

To join cables within a junction box, twist together the ends of the two wires, screw on a wire nut and tighten until no bare wire is visible.

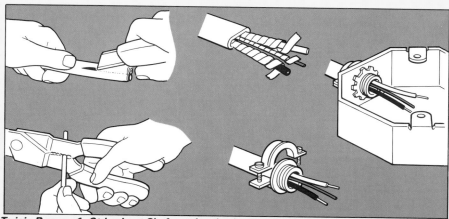

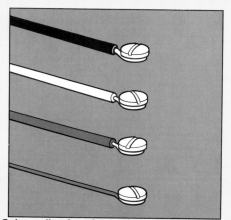

To join Romex: 1. Strip about 8in from the plastic covering. 2. Remove the paper wrapping. 3. Strip off about ¾in of the insulation on each conductor. 4. Slide over a Romex cable connector and tighten the clamp. 5. Insert the connector into a junction box and tighten the locknut.

Color coding for wires and terminals.

To join Romex cable, split the plastic covering about 8 inches from the end with a blade, being careful not to nick any of the conductors. Remove any paper wrapping from around the conductors, snip about ¾ inch of the insulation on each wire with a pair of electrician's wire snippers. Insert the end into a connector made for plastic cable and tighten up the clamping screws, so that the cable is secured to the connector. Push the connector into the junction box and tighten the lock nut.

To join BX cable, use a hacksaw to cut 8 inches from the metal armor. Hold the cable securely and cut the armor across — not with — the spiral. It is not necessary to cut completely through the armor. When the cut is nearly through grab the armor above and below the cut and twist sharply: this should break the remaining armor without the need for the saw blade to reach the conductors. Insert a plastic bushing around the wires into the end of the cable to protect the wires from the sharp edges of the armor. Pull

the grounding wire away from the others and wrap it around the armor (in this system the armored covering to the cable acts as a ground). Attach a BX connector onto the end of the cable, push it back firmly and tighten the screw. Push the connector into the box and tighten the locknut.

Junction Boxes

All connections between the circuit wiring and any switch, outlet or fixture, or any splices in the circuit wiring must be made within a junction box. Under no circumstances must electrical wire be spliced with tape and left exposed. Junction boxes come in 3 shapes, octagonal, square, and outlet boxes. The three shapes of box come in a variety of depths and a variety of types depending on the proposed location. The outlet box is used for switches and receptacles, the box can be ganged by removing one side and joining it to another outlet box to make a double box or more if necessary.

Outlet boxes are most often attached directly to wall studs by means of a flange, or set into panelling or drywall between the studs by use of clamps or clips. The hexagonal box is most often used for hanging electrical fixtures and is attached directly to the studs or ceiling joists. The square box is most often used to splice wire together. Individual wires to be spliced are held together with a wire nut, which locks and twists the wires together.

As mentioned above, all white wires are neutral, green or bare copper wires are ground. Wires with black or red (or any other color except white or green) are 'hot' or live wires. In addition when attaching any wire to an outlet such as a switch, receptacle, or light fixture, the following color coding applies:

The white wire attaches to the silver (or chrome) terminal.

The green wire attaches to the green terminal.

The black wire attaches to the brass terminal.

EXTENDING LIGHTING CIRCUITS

If you want more lighting points around the house, or you want to move existing lights to new positions, you can do so simply by extending one of the existing circuits.

All circuits are wired up as radial circuits, with one circuit cable leaving the fuseway or the circuit breaker in the service panel and running out, feeding points along the way, until it reaches the most remote point on the circuit. With a 15 Amp fuse and a supply voltage of 120 volts, such a circuit can in theory supply $15 \times 120 = 1800$ Watts of power; each lighting point is rated nominally at between 60–150 Watt, so up to 12 points can be supplied. In practise this is usually reduced to eight, to avoid overloading if light fixtures with more than one bulb are used. So the first step you have to take is to find out how much load you already have on each circuit.

To do this, turn off the main switch at your service panel and remove one of the 15 or 20 Amp circuit fuses (or trip off the circuit breaker). Then go round the house and check how many lights and electrical outlets fail to work on that circuit. The next step is to determine the total wattage of all appliances and fixtures normally used on that circuit. This can be done by checking the information plate on each appliance or light fixture. The reserve capacity can then be found by deducting the present circuit wattage from the maximum circuit capacity (1800W for a 15A circuit or 2400W for a 20A circuit). If by adding an extra fixture the circuit wattage comes up to within 20% of the maximum circuit capacity — the circuit would be close to fully loaded and it would be better to check for other circuits with a larger reserve.

What Type of Circuit?

Assuming that you find you can extend an existing circuit, your next job is to work out what type of wiring practice has been used to wire it up, so you can decide how to carry out the extension work.

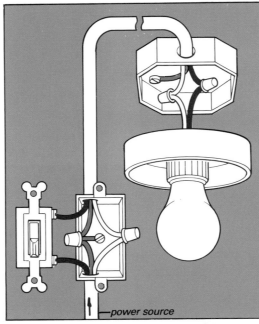
Wiring for end-of-the-run fixture, middle-of-the-run switch.

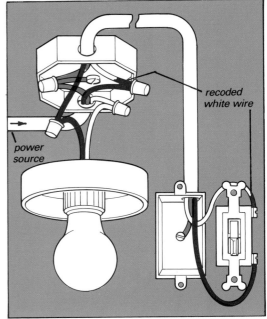
Wiring for middle-of-the-run fixture, end-of-the-run switch.

The New Light Position

You now have to decide on where the new light is to be positioned, so you can plan the best point at which to connect its power supply into the existing circuitry. If you are installing a new ceiling light downstairs, you may have to lift one or more floorboards in the room above so you can see where the circuit cables go and to enable you to run in the cable to the new light; the exception to this is if your new light is between the same pair of joists as an existing one, in which case you may be able to feed in the new cable between the existing and new light positions simply by fishing it along between the two holes in the ceiling. Fitting new ceiling lights upstairs is much easier so long as you have an attic above, since the existing cables will be run across the attic floor.

Once the position for the new light and switch has been determined, any convenient outlet will do as a source for the power to the new switch and fixture.

There are several possible power sources, a middle-of-the-run outlet or an end-of-the-run outlet, a middle-of-the-run switch or fixture (see page 134).

Wiring a New Light

Once a source of power has been identified, merely run a 2 conductor cable to the nearest of the two new boxes — either the switch box or the fixture box, then run cable between the two new boxes. Two situations can occur:
1. The power feeds into the fixture box. In this case the fixture is said to be wired in the 'middle-of-the-run' and the switch is wired at the 'end-of-the-run'.
2. The power feeds into the switchbox. In this case the switch is said to be wired in the 'middle-of-the-run' and the fixture is wired at the 'end-of-the-run'.

Middle of the Run Fixture, End of the Run Switch

Three connections are necessary.
1. The incoming neutral white wire is connected to the white wire from the new fixture.
2. The incoming 'hot' wire is connected to the outgoing white wire on the switch loop; however, this white • wire must be recoded by wrapping it with electrical tape to show that it is now a hot wire.
3. The returning black wire on the switch loop is connected to the black wire on the new

fixture.

Cut a short length of grounding wire and splice together with all the other ground wires; attach the loose end to the fixture by means of a metal screw. At the switch box, recode the incoming white wire to show that it is a 'hot' wire. Connect both wires to the switch terminals. Attach the ground wire to the switch box by means of a metal screw.

End of the Run Fixture, Middle of the Run Switch

Two connections are necessary at the fixture, three at the switch.

At the fixture box splice black to black and white to white and again cut a short length of ground wire and splice together with the other ground wires, attach the loose end to the fixture by means of a metal screw.

At the switch box three connections are necessary:
1. Splice together the two neutral white wires.
2. Connect the two black wires to the switch terminals.
Cut a short piece of ground wire and splice it together with the other ground wires, attach the loose end to the switch box by means of a metal screw or clip.

WARNING
Allways turn off the power at the service panel before beginning any work. Double check that the circuit is dead by means of a voltage tester.

FIXINGS TO CEILINGS

Trick

Whatever type of light fixture you are installing, you must make a firm fixing for it to the ceiling — you can't just drive screws into the ceiling surface and hope for the best. What you do depends on the type of light you're fitting.

Other Fittings

Depending on their type, you may have to make provision for a special mounting method within the ceiling. Generally any fixture likely to weigh over 30–40 lbs should not be supported by the box alone. Many of today's ceiling lights are supplied with just a length of cord attached, and you have to connect this up to the circuit (and possibly the switch cable) using the correct size wire nuts. The Electrical Code requires this connection to be made within an electrical box, that is set with its open end flush with the ceiling surface. The cables enter the box and are connected, the plate of the light fixture then covers the box when it is screwed into place. To fit the box you must cut a circular hole in the ceiling and fix a bearer between the joists just far enough above the ceiling to allow the box to be mounted with its rim flush with the underside of the ceiling surface. (Some boxes come complete with adjustable metal bearers that are screwed to the adjacent joists). Screw the box in place and repair if necessary with filler round its rim. Then feed in the circuit cables through the knock-out in the side of the box and make the connections to the fixture. You will need to make three connections if the fixture is in the middle of the run – two if it is at the end of the run. Make sure too that you make all the ground connections before securing the fixture in place.

With some light fixtures the holes in the baseplate are at the same spacing as the threaded lugs at each side of the box, and you can mount the fitting with small machine screws driven into the lugs. Otherwise you must secure the fixture using an adaptor plate which is usually supplied with the fixture itself. Check the manufacturer's instructions supplied with the fixture for the exact method of installation.

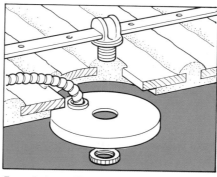

For existing ceilings, mark around the box, carefully cut a hole, fish through the wires. Insert a hanger bar then attach the box to the bar.

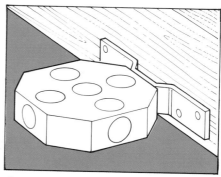

Box with a flange for attaching to the side of a joist.

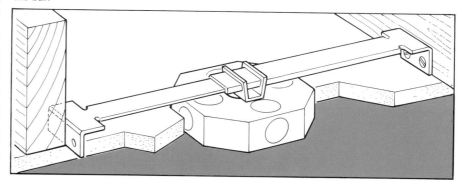

For positioning fixture between joists, use a box with an adjustable hanger bar.

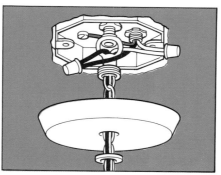

Typical ceiling fixture mountings: 1. Fixture supported on chain attached to nipple screwed on to a stud within box, a common method for hanging heavy fixtures.

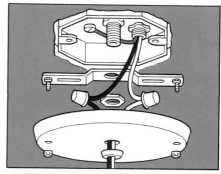

2. A steel bracket is attached to the stud within the box. The canopy or fixture is then screwed on to the bracket.

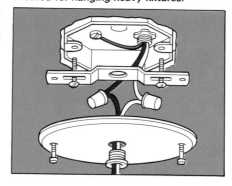

3. The bracket may be attached to the box by two screws. The canopy or fixture is then screwed to the bracket.

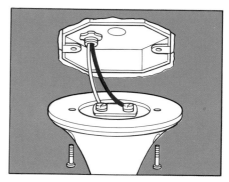

4. The fixture may screw directly into the box.

MOVING OR ADDING A PENDANT LIGHT

One of the simplest jobs you can do is to move a pendant light from one position to another — for example, so its new position is precisely over the center of your dining table. Start by deciding on the precise position of the light, and make a hole in the ceiling at that point. If you don't mind leaving the old box in place (minus its pendant, of course) you can simply use it as a junction box, and run cable on to the new light position, where you will have to fit a new box. However, you will probably prefer to remove the box altogether and to repair the hole in the ceiling. In this case you need to fix a junction box above the ceiling at the site of the old fixture and run extra cable from there to the new fixture position. This is only possible if the junction box is to remain easily accessible — junction boxes must not be covered over permanently. In the case of a plaster ceiling this is obviously not possible so the choice is to leave the box in its position and cover it with a special cover plate or to disconnect the wiring to the old box completely before plastering it up.

In either case you will have to gain access to the existing wiring — by lifting first-floor floorboards to move a light in a ground-floor room or by gaining access to the attic above upstairs rooms. If you're leaving the old box in position, simply disconnect its fixture, feed in the prepared end of the new cable and connect its live and neutral wires to the same two wires that held the original fixture connections; splice the cable ground to the other ground wires. Then run the cable — parallel to or across the line of the joists, depending on how the floor is constructed — to the new fixture position and connect it up to the new box, making sure that it is compatible with the type of mounting bracket supplied with the new fixture. Attach the incoming ground wire to the box by means of a metal screw. Secure the mounting bracket in position before splicing the wires black to black, white to white. Finally screw the fixture into place.

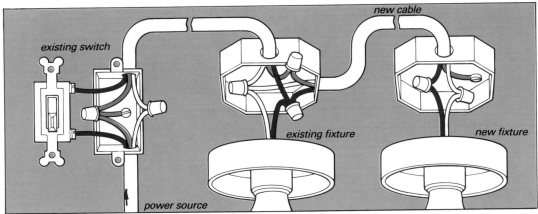

Addition of a new fixture to an existing end-of-the-run fixture. Both fixtures are operated by the existing switch.

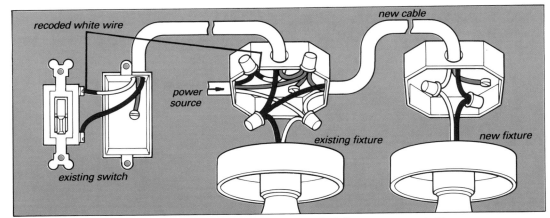

Addition of a new fixture to an existing middle-of-the-run fixture. Both fixtures are operated by the existing switch.

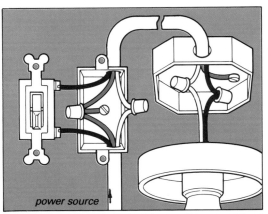

New fixture and switch. End-of-the-run fixture, middle-of-the-run switch. For locating power source, see p. 134.

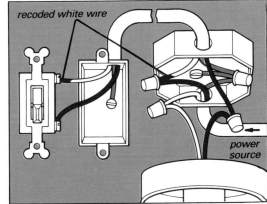

New fixture and switch. Middle-of-the-run fixture, end-of-the-run switch. See p. 134 for locating power source.

Adding an Extra Light

If you want an additional light on the circuit, as opposed to just moving an existing one to a new position, the main decision you have to make is how to take the power supply from the existing circuit. You can either connect a branch cable into an existing fixture or cut the circuit cable at a convenient point and install a junction box.

In the first case, connect the black wire of the new cable under the wire nut containing the 'hot' black wire and the neutral white to the other neutrals. Link the ground to the other ground wires.

In the second case, cut the circuit cable at a convenient point. Fit a 4 × 4 junction box, connect all the black wires together, connect all the white wires together and connect all the ground wires to-

gether. Run the new cable to either the switch box or the fixture box and connect as already described.

WARNING

Allways turn off the power at the service panel before beginning any work. Double check that the circuit is dead by means of a voltage tester.

Installing wall lights involves little difference from adding ceiling fittings, except that you have to chop a cable chase and a recess for a mounting box in the wall surface. Wall lights are usually supplied with a short length of cord emerging from the body of the fitting, and so as with certain ceiling fixtures you have to connect it to the fixed wiring using wire nuts. You must house these in a box set in the wall as opposed to the ceiling.

Once you have decided on the position of the new light, mark round its baseplate on the wall surface. Drop a plumbline from the ceiling above it and mark the line of the cable chase. Draw round the box you intend to use, making sure that it is wholly within the baseplate outline, and chop out the chase and the box recess. When the recess is deep enough, offer up the box and mark the positions of its fixing screws. Drill and plug the holes and fix the box in place.

Next, run in the cable drop to the light from the ceiling void, and run in the switch cable too if the light is to be controlled from a nearby switch. You can use round conduit to protect the cable if you wish, or just plaster over it after securing it in the chase with cable clips.

Connect the light (and switch) cable(s) to the light as described (the fixture will be either middle-of-the-run or end-of-the-run) and tuck the wire nuts neatly into the mounting box. Finally fix the light baseplate to the wall to conceal the box.

On stud partition walls you can drop the cable down inside the partition (you will have to drill a hole in the head plate first, and you may have to cut away a little gypsum board to expose the horizontal bracing if any get in the way). If possible, try to mount the light close to the stud; you can then select an electrical box that can be mounted on the stud which will also provide a firm fitting for the new fixture.

WARNING

Allways turn off the power at the service panel before beginning any work. Double check that the circuit is dead by means of a voltage tester.

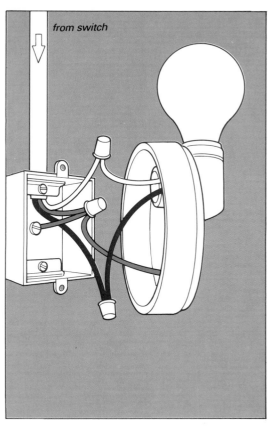

Middle-of-the-run wall fixture.

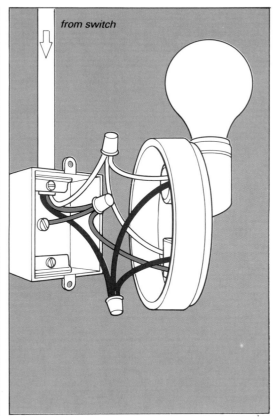

Middle-of-the-run wall fixture with integral outlet. Fixture controlled by the switch outlet always live.

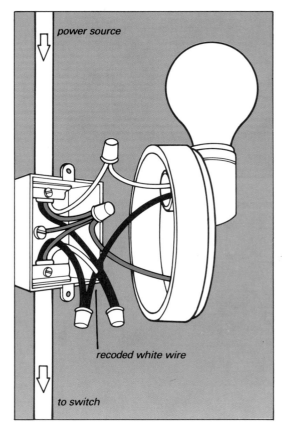

End-of-the-run wall fixture.

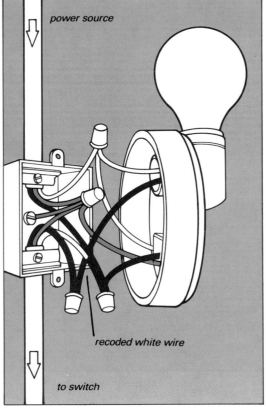

End-of-the-run wall fixture with integral outlet. Fixture and outlet are controlled by the same switch.

125

FITTING SWITCHES

Most lights — ceiling or wall fixtures — are controlled by a separate switch, mounted on the wall at a convenient position. The usual site is next to the room door at about 1.2m (4ft) above the floor. The switch cable from the light itself (or from the junction box providing the switching connection) runs down to the switch position, where it is connected to the switch terminals.

Wall switches can be surface- or flush-mounted and need a mounting box depending on the type. The metal flush boxes are screwed into a recess cut in the wall; the plastic surface-mounting ones are just screwed to the wall surface, and are often used in conjunction with surface wiring in plastic or metal raceways.

The most common type is called a toggle switch; each switch usually has two terminals labelled L1 and L2, to which the wires of the switch cable are connected (the cable ground core usually goes to a ground terminal in the mounting box). Such switches are called single pole switches.

Three-way switches have three terminals each, two traveller terminals and one common. These switches operate in pairs to provide control of one light from two different switch positions — known as three-way switching — and in this case are linked by special three-core and ground cable. The three cores are color-coded red, black and white for identification. Switching from three (or more) positions is possible using one or more special intermediate switches between two three-way switches; these have two pairs of terminals and are called four-way switches.

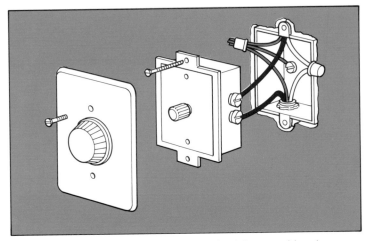
How to connect a dimmer switch, with middle-of-the-run wiring shown.

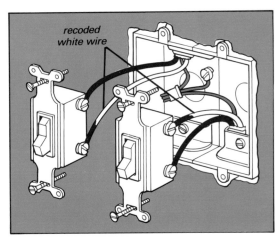
recoded white wire

A pair of end-of-the-run wired switches.

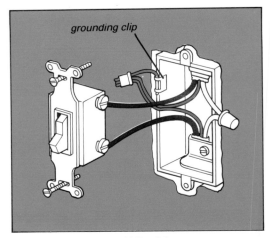
grounding clip

A switch wired in the middle of the run.

Trick

FITTING A DIMMER SWITCH

Dimmer switches are light switches that enable you to raise or lower the intensity of the light they are controlling as well as providing the usual on/off switching. There are several styles: some have separate on/off switches and rotary dimming controls; some combine the rotary dimming control with a push-on/push-off action; the most sophisticated are controlled just by finger pressure on the faceplate, or even by remote control. Most models are one-gang versions, often capable of three-way switching, but some include models with up to four gangs. Many include a small fuse to protect the delicate dimming circuitry from the effects of current surges.

You can fit a dimmer in place of an existing switch simply by removing the old faceplate, disconnecting the switch cables and reconnecting them to the dimmer faceplate. The manufacturers usually include instructions that indicate which terminals should be used, so the job is quite straightforward.

There are two points to note. Firstly, many dimmers have a minimum operating wattage as well as a maximum, and some models may not control a single bulb very well. Secondly, some need a deeper-than-usual mounting box, so check before you buy.

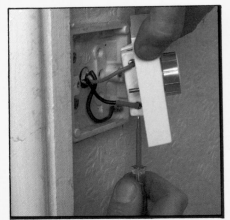
Connecting a dimmer switch in place of a plateswitch; if for a fluorescent tube, check first that the switch is suitable.

There are two areas of the house where three-way switching is particularly useful — in the bedroom, where you may want to turn out bedside lights without having to get out of bed, and on the stairs, so you can control both hall and landing lights from top or bottom of the stairs. The hall/landing set-up is a classic example of three-way switching at its most useful.

For full control of both lights from both locations, you need a pair of three-way switches on the landing and another pair in the hall. The left-hand of the two switches is linked by one three-wire and ground cable; another similar cable links the two right-hand switches. The final wiring depends on the location of the fixtures and of the power source. There are several possible situations. The power supply can be at the beginning of a run while the fixture is either at the beginning, middle or end of a run or the power and the fixture can both be in the middle of the run (see diagrams).

Another advantage of this arrangement is that if the landing and hall lights are on different circuits you will always have light on the stairs (vital to prevent falls) even if one lighting circuit fuse blows. You must remember, though, that if one circuit blows, the other may still be live, so you must isolate both by removing

the circuit breaker if you want to work on the switches or any of the wiring.

If you have partial three-way switching (it's quite common to find installations where the landing light has three-way switching but the hall light does not) it is quite a straightforward job to upgrade it to full three-way control.

In bedrooms, several three-way switching options are possible. The simplest arrangement is to have switches to control the main light both by the room door and by the bed. The switch drop from the light goes to one switch or the other (usually whichever is nearer to it) and the two switches are linked as usual with three-wire and ground cable.

More common is the set-up where a main ceiling light is switched by the door (via a single pole switch) while two individual bedside lights are controlled by switches at the door and at each side of the bed. This offers the maximum flexibility, since each bedside light can be switched on or off from door or bed quite independently — a boon when one partner is a late reader!

Such a set-up is obviously quite involved to wire up, and could in principle use a great deal of cable, especially the more expensive three-wire and ground variety.

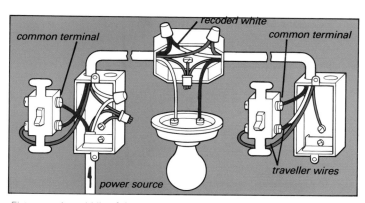

Power source and fixture at the beginning of the run.

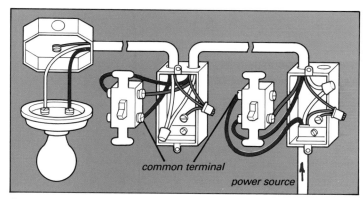

Fixture at the middle of the run.

Fixture at the end of the run.

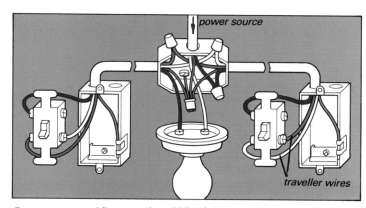

Power source and fixture at the middle of the run.

Before commencing any work:

Make sure that you are completely familiar with the relevant requirements of your local Electrical Code. Remember that electrical codes vary from one location to the next.

Allways make sure that the power is turned off.

If ever you are in any doubt consult a licensed electrician or your local Building Inspector.

Check your home owner's insurance policy — some are invalidated if any electrical work is carried out by anyone other than a licensed electrician.

When carrying out any work:

Double check that a circuit is shut off by using a voltage tester.

Use only U. L. listed and approved parts and materials and install them in accordance with the requirements of your local Electrical Code.

Use proper insulated tools and as a precaution stand on a rubber mat. Use a wooden ladder not a metal one.

Allways double check your work before restoring the current.

Have your work checked by your local Building Inspector or a licensed electrician if required by your local Code.

127

PLANNING LIGHTING SCHEMES

Effective and attractive lighting schemes are even more difficult to plan than color schemes, and this probably explains why most homes are distinctly unadventurous in this department. Yet this need not be the case: there is such a wide range of versatile and inexpensive light fixtures now on the market that anyone can afford to have a go at creating some unusual and highly decorative lighting effects in the home. To do so, it helps to know some of the basics about light outputs, light levels and the types of bulbs and fittings you can choose.

Outputs and Light Levels

Electric lamps (the proper term for light bulbs and tubes) are rated in watts (W). This measurement tells you how much electricity the lamp is using, but is not necessarily a very good indicator of how efficient the lamp is at producing light, and it certainly tells you nothing about how much useful light it produces or in what direction it emits it. The unit used for measuring light output is the lumen, and some lamps emit more lumens per watt (in other words, burn more efficiently) than others. Amongst filament lamps, coiled-coil pear-shaped lamps are generally the most efficient, single-coil lamps the least, and efficiency increases with lamp wattage. Fluorescent tubes are far more efficient emitters of light than filament lamps — on average, a tube gives out about four times as much light as a filament lamp of the same wattage.

The next thing you need to know is how much light to provide to light up a given room area. Obviously this depends to a certain extent on the type of light fixture chosen, whether the surface being illuminated is lit directly or indirectly, even the colour of the surface, but as a rough guide for general lighting work you need to provide about 20W per sq m (2W/sq ft) of room area. This is for minimum overall lighting; regard any additional local lighting in the room as being supplementary to this.

Light Fixtures

Light fixtures come in five main types, and the characteristics of each will affect the quantity and direction of the light emitted (this will also depend on the type of bulb fitted — see page 130).

Pendant fixtures include simple pendant with one bulbholder and mutli-light units suspended from a ceiling-mounted rod and chain. They emit light either generally or in a mainly upward / downward direction, depending on the type of shade that's fitted.

Close-ceiling fixtures are actually mounted on the ceiling surface, and so emit light only in a downward direction.

Wall-mounted fixtures include simple brackets (with or without shades) as well as spotlights and uplighters (which can also be freestanding).

Concealed fixtures are usually recessed into the ceiling void, and include downlighters, eyeball fixtures and 'wallwashers' — fixtures that cast a diffuse wash of light down a wall surface.

Lastly, **freestanding lamps** include the wide range of table- and floor-standing models offering general or local lighting according to type.

Light and Shadow

Avoiding glare and hard shadows are two of the most important factors in lighting design, and answers are best given with reference to particular lighting requirements. For example, a center light in the living room is no good for reading (unless you sit right underneath it); what you need is a lamp behind you, casting light onto the page. In dining rooms you should avoid low fixtures where the naked bulb is close to eye level; use a rise-and-fall fixture over the dining table with a directional shade. In workrooms, you need a concealed bulb above your work surface to light up the work without dazzling, while in bathrooms concealed lighting above the mirror actually leaves your face in shadow; fixtures at each side of the mirror give better illumination.

Generally speaking, a good lighting scheme provides a balance of light where it is needed and soft shadow where it isn't. Over-bright lighting is cheerless and severe, while dark shadows simply strain the eyes. In particular, fluorescent lights give a curious flat lighting effect with no shadows — fine for a kitchen, for example, but not very relaxing in the living room.

Always aim for an acceptable overall level of lighting, even when local lights (for reading, spotlighting a picture and the like) are providing extra illumination. The overall effect is then one of contrast, yet with no hard shadows or areas that are starved of light when they need it.

Downlighters used to illuminate work surfaces and pick out plates on wall.

A rise-and-fall fitting is useful for changing the mood of a room.

Downlighters

Once the province of restaurants, hotels and offices, recessed light fixtures are now widely available for use in the home too, and one of the most popular types is the downlighter. This is a can-like fixture that is installed within the ceiling void so that its bottom edge sits flush with the ceiling surface. You can also get semi-recessed downlighters, useful where the ceiling void is comparatively shallow, and also fixtures where the bulb is housed on its side — again taking up less vertical space.

Downlighters are usually fitted with internal silvered bulbs which cast a fairly wide beam, but various other lamp types can be fitted too. Installation is comparatively simple. Once you have decided on the position of the fixture, check that it does not coincide with a joist and that there is no pipework or electrical wiring immediately above it. Then mark a hole of the appropriate size on the ceiling with a pair of compasses, and cut it out with a keyhole-saw. Where the ceiling is lath-and-plaster, reinforce the cut laths with battens pinned between the joists. Then connect up the power supply to the fixture and clip it in place.

Rise-and-fall Fittings

Rise-and-fall fittings are basically pendant lights with a spring-loaded wire that it is drawn out or retracted to hold the light at any desired height below the ceiling. The cord is the curled type familiar on telephones, and the suspension wire is threaded through the center of the coiled cord. Their advantage is that they can be pulled down over dining tables, breakfast bars and the like during the meal, and then pushed up out of the way afterwards.

Fitting one involves installing an octagonal box in a recess in the ceiling, screwed securely either to a joist or to a bearer fixed on battens between the joists. The power supply cable and the switch cable (if a switch loop is being used) enter the box and are linked to the wires from the fitting itself. Connect black to black, white to white if no switch is being used. With a switch loop three connections are required.

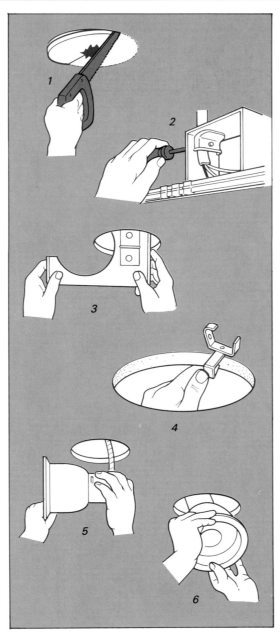

Downlighters in an existing ceiling. 1. Cut the hole. 2. Connect the cable. 3. Insert frame. 4. Clip into place. 5. Attach trim. 6. Push into place.

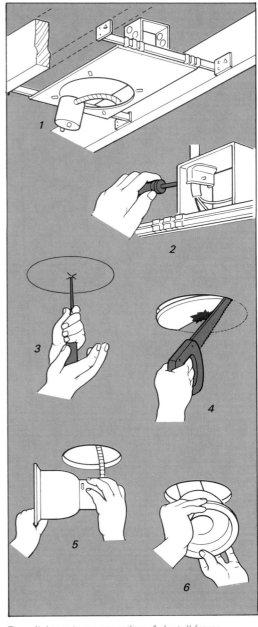

Downlighters in a new ceiling. 1. Install frame. 2. Connect the cable. 3. Install ceiling. 4. Cut the hole. 5. Attach trim. 6. Push into place.

1. Recode the outgoing white wire to the switch with a piece of electrical tape, making it essentially a black wire too. Join the recoded wire to the incoming black wire on the power cable. 2. Connect the returning black wire from the switch to the black wire on the fixture. 3. Connect the white wire on the fixture to the white wire on the incoming power cable. Remember to ground the fixture and the junction box.

Track Lighting

Track lighting is one of the most versatile types of lighting available, since it allows a range of different lighting effects from just one power source. The system consists of a length of special conducting track that is attached to ceiling or wall surfaces, and on which light heads of various types are mounted. The conductors within the track are safely shielded from touch, and each light picks up its power supply from special contacts once it is clipped into place. There is a wide range of heads — spots, floods and more diffuse beams can all be used from the same track. The only limitation is in the recommended maximum wattage the track manufacturer specifies, and the existing overall wattage on the lighting circuit you will use to power the track — remember that each 15 Amp circuit can supply a maximum of 1800W. Various track lengths are available, and you can butt several lengths together if you want a continuous lighting 'rail' across the room.

You can provide power to your lighting track either from an existing ceiling box — some

129

FITTING DECORATIVE LIGHTS

types are designed so that all you do is connect the track into the box in just the same way as fixing an ordinary pendant light. Obviously, in the case of an existing ceiling box you will have to mount the track's end over the box so that the wires can be connected up.

Once you have sorted out the power supply, you can start installing the track. Some systems use small clips that are screwed to the ceiling; with others you screw through the base of short stems that support the track. In either case, a firm fixing is necessary; either screw directly into joists (ideal if the track run coincides with a joist exactly) or fix bearers between the joists. With some track types you can drill fixing holes through the track to coincide with your joist centers.

Once the track is securely fixed in place, make the final electrical connection to your box, and clip the various light heads into place on the track.

Close-fitting bowl lights

There is a wide range of close-

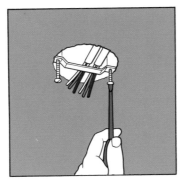

Installing a rise-and-fall fixture: 1. mount the hanging bracket onto the ceiling box.

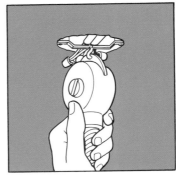

2. Hook the fixture onto the mounting bar and make the cable connections.

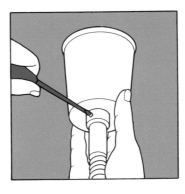

3. Slide up the canopy and secure by means of a small screw.

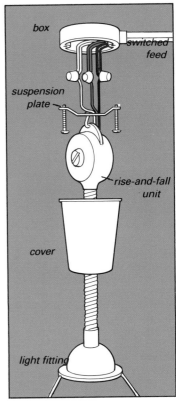

Exploded view of the components of a rise-and-fall fixture.

fitting bowl lights available, in round, square and oblong shapes with clear or translucent bowls in a great many styles and colors. They are useful where you want a diffuse light close to the ceiling — perhaps where headroom is limited, such as at the foot of the stairs, and are obligatory in bathrooms.

Most are mounted in a similar way, with a fixing bar being screwed to the outlet box first and then a base plate being secured to this. If you are fitting one in place of an existing ceiling fixture, you simply have to remove the

OPTIONS

TYPES OF LAMP

There is an enormous range of lamps and tubes you can use in your light fixtures. The most familiar are the everyday pear and mushroom-shaped opaque bulbs available in clear and colored in a wide range of wattages. Decorative bulbs, widely used in wall lights, include candle lamps, decor round lamps in various sizes (intended to be seen through decorative shades) and pigmy lamps — small low-wattage bulbs often used in festoons. All these give off light in all directions unless the fitting itself modifies the beam. Reflector lamps have a special inner coating which reflects the light in a particular direction. Internally silvered lamps are silvered round the base and sides and so give a broad beam in a 'forward'-only direction. CS (crown silvered) lamps have the top of the lamp silvered to control glare, and rely on the fixture to direct the beam outwards. They produce a narrow beam suitable for spotlights. PAR (parabolic aluminized reflector)

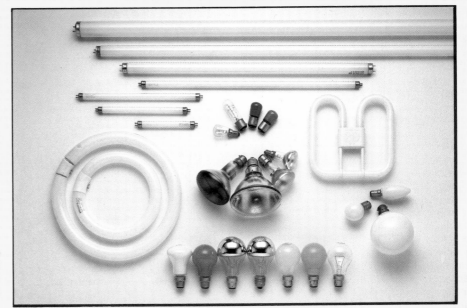

lamps have armored glass, and provide a broad beam; they are intended for outdoor use.

Fluorescent tubes (circular, straight and U-shaved), piginy lamps, PAR and reflector spots, GLS and decor lamps.

old fixture; there is generally no need for a new box. Screw the new bar to the box that supported the old fixture, then connect up the existing circuit cable to the terminal block on the fitting's baseplate. You can then attach the baseplate (which carries the bulbholder) to the fixing bar, and offer up the bowl after fitting a bulb of the recommended type and wattage. Some are held in place with small screws or spring-loaded clips; with others a sliding level locks the bowl in place.

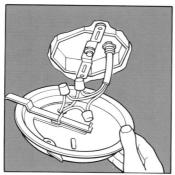

1. Screw the mounting bar into the outlet box and make the wire connections.

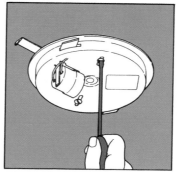

2. Screw the fixture base to the mounting bar.

3. Hold the bowl in place and secure by pushing in the lever or by tightening the supporting screws, depending on type of fixture.

Eyeballs and Wallwashers

Apart from straightforward downlighters, there are several variations on the recessed lighting theme that can perform more varied lighting functions. The downlighter simply casts a uniform beam straight down at the ground beneath the fixture — a virtual pool of light. Wall-washers are basically directional downlighters, and are usually installed near to one wall of the room so that the light from the fixture literally 'washes' the wall with light. The fixture is adjustable, allowing the angle of incidence to be varied to achieve precisely the desired effect. Several wallwashers installed in a line can be used to wash an entire wall with light, and if colored bulbs are used some very attractive and dramatic color scheming effects can be achieved — literally changing the room's day-time color schemes at the flick of a switch.

Eyeball fixtures are another type of downlighter, and literally work like an eye — the bulb itself is housed in a spherical mounting which can swivel within the main body of the fixture to almost any angle. If fitted with a spotlight it can be used to highlight individual features in the room in a far less obtrusive manner than an ordinary ceiling — or track — mounted spotlight.

Installation and electrical connections are much the same as for a downlighter — power for the light can be taken as a spur from a nearby junction box unless the fitting is replacing one already in that position.

Many of these fixtures can generate quite a lot of heat. Make

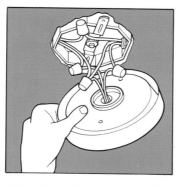

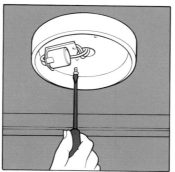

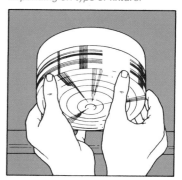

Follow the first two steps described above, but then secure the bowl by twisting into position.

sure that you allways purchase a fixture that is correct for the location in which you are using it. Also make sure that your fixture has a U.L. mark and follow the manufacturer's instructions regarding fire protection.

WARNING

Only use materials and fixtures that are clearly labelled with a U. L. mark.

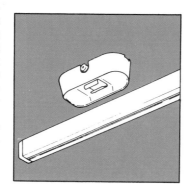

Methods of fixing lighting track to a ceiling: Surface-mounted clips connected by flex to a nearby ceiling rose.

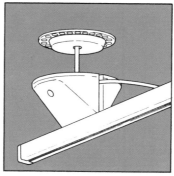

Mounting canopy fitted over an existing ceiling rose; the canopy also conceals the slack flex necessary for making connections.

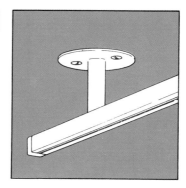

Mounting stems screw directly to a BESA box; both this and the surface-mounted clip can be used for fixing track to a wall also.

Trick

ELECTRICIAN'S

FITTING A FLUORESCENT LIGHT

Fluorescent lights are undoubtedly more efficient than filament lamps in terms of light output per watt of power consumed, but the light they emit is usually felt to be rather flat and unsympathetic to the eye. However, they are excellent task lights for rooms like kitchens, bathrooms and workshops, and can be very effective when used as concealed lighting — behind a pelmet or baffle, for example, casting light downwards over drawn curtains or a kitchen worktop, or flush-mounted behind opaque diffusers in a suspended ceiling.

Most fluorescent lights are linear tubes, ranging in length from 150mm (6in) up to 2400mm (8ft) and in diameter through three main sizes — 15mm/⅝in (miniature), 25mm/1in (slimline) and 38mm/1½in (standard). The commonest sizes for domestic use are 1200mm (4ft) with a light output of around 40W and 1500mm (6ft) with an output of between 65 and 80W. Circular tubes are also made, commonly in diameters of 300 and 400mm (12 and 16in). All types are made in several 'colours' — ranging from the cold white through to 'warm white', the best choice for most domestic use.

The simplest way of fitting a fluorescent light is to buy a complete unit containing all the controls required — starter and choke or ballast — housed within a baseplate that is fixed to the ceiling. These are available for both linear and circular tubes, and there's a range of diffusers available to suit all tastes.

To install the fixture, start by using the template provided (or the fixture's backplate) to mark the fixing holes on the ceiling. Ideally the fitting should be screwed directly to a joist (or to several if its position is at right angles to the joist line), but if this isn't convenient you will have to fix bearers between the joists. Screw the baseplate in position, feeding the circuit cable(s) and connecting them. If your lighting circuit has only live and neutral wires, you must run in a separate ground wire from the terminal block back to the main grounding point at the service panel.

Next, fit the backplate cover in place and add the spring-loaded clips at each end which hold the tube in place. Slot the tube into place, fit the starter in the side of the baseplate and test that the light works.

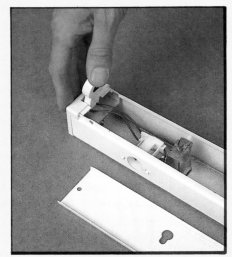

Fitting the end connectors to the ends of the fluorescent tube base; they may be fixed rigidly or spring-loaded.

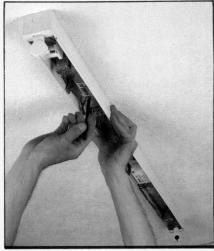

After locating a ceiling joist, marking through the fixing holes in the base of the fitting on to the ceiling.

Connecting the cable cores to the terminal block; make sure it is firmly clamped to the metal lug on the base.

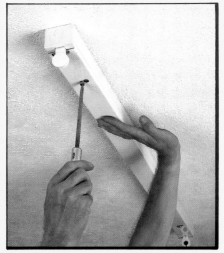

Securing the cover plate; this may have double fixing holes, one the size of the screw head which it fits over.

Fitting the tube into the end connectors by pushing in and twisting through 90°, or by springing out the caps.

Inserting the starter switch by pushing it into its holder until it locates in the sockets, then turning clockwise.

Improvements to your power circuits are generally far more of a necessity than those to your lighting arrangements. Less-than-perfect lighting may be a nuisance and a disappointment, but inadequate provision for your electrical appliances can actually lead to situations that are dangerous. If you don't have enough electrical outlets in the right places, you are likely to make extensive use of potentially overloaded adaptors and extension cords plugged into the few electrical outlets you have got. The end result is an increased risk of electrical accidents caused by short circuits, poor contacts between plugs and outlets leading to overheating, and overloading of the circuits causing persistent fuse-blowing and the risk of fire. What you need is more outlets.

As a guide to how many outlets the experts reckon a well-equipped home should have, the Electrical Code requires that electrical outlets should be placed no more than 12ft. apart, as a general guide outlets should be placed 10ft. apart with a minimum of three per room. Kitchen outlets should be spread at about 4ft. apart.

You may well find that you need more outlets than this in some rooms, fewer in others; the best way to find out is to make a room-by-room plan of the house and mark in what appliances you keep in a particular position (and which therefore need an outlet full-time) and which appliances you tend to take out and use occasionally (these can share an outlet). Mark the positions of existing outlets, noting whether they are singles or doubles and then add on outlets you need. This will help you to plan how best to carry out the extension work and give you an idea of the scale of the work too — you may need just one or two extra outlets, which can probably be added to the existing wiring or you may require so many that new circuits will be called for.

What's There Already

Once you have worked out what your requirements are, you must examine your existing wiring to find out where the circuits run, what type they are and what condition they are in.

Let's take the first point. To establish which circuit your various outlets are on, turn off the power on the main switch, remove one power circuit fuse and plug an appliance you know works into each outlet in turn. Mark on your plan those that are controlled by fuse 1, and repeat the process for as many power circuit fuses or breakers as you have in your service panel.

Lastly, you must check up on the condition of the system, to see whether it is safe to extend it. The cables are the most important factor here; inspect them at the service panel and where they run into individual outlets. Check as many as you can, with the power switched off for safety, in case parts of the system have been extended since the original installation. What you are on the lookout for is woven fabric sheathed cable. This has been obsolete for years, and will probably be well past the end of its safe working life — especially if you intend adding to the load a circuit is carrying. If you find this cable, you should seriously consider completely rewiring the circuits concerned. Not to do so may invite the risk of fire in the near future. If in doubt call in a licensed electrician to check the wiring.

If you find that your circuits are well wired in modern plastic sheathed cable and feed modern outlets, then you can probably carry out all the extension work you require with the minimum of rewiring. However you need to understand the principles behind each type of circuit, to understand the limitations placed on each by the requirements of your local electrical code, to which all new wiring work should conform.

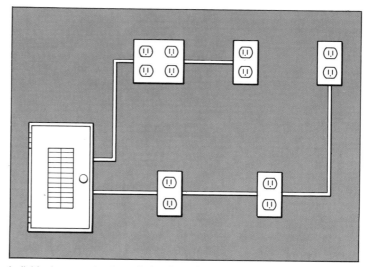

Individual power circuits radiating from the service panel.

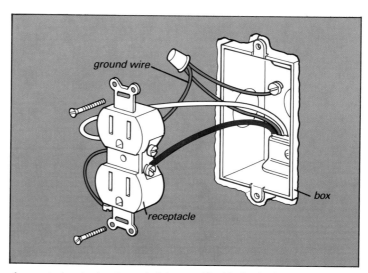

A receptacle wired at the end of the run. The black wire is attached to the brass screw and the white wire to the silver screw.

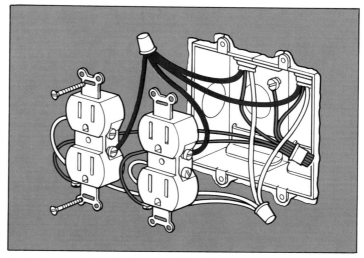

A pair of receptacles wired in the middle of the run.

133

ADDING A RECEPTACLE

As we have seen there are limitations placed on the number of electrical appliances and fixtures we can use on any one circuit, based on the cable size and the fuse or circuit breaker protection offered. Generally a 20 amp circuit of number 12 wire should take care of about 500 sq ft of floor area, or a 15 amp circuit 375 sq ft. However, to offer some reserve in the case of circuit failure and to help distribute some of the load, two or more circuits will supply outlets in any given room.

Almost all of the outlets and light fixtures on these circuits could serve as a power source for the installation of a new electrical outlet. What matters most is that you select a power source that is convenient to the position of your new receptacle and one that is on a circuit with enough reserve capacity to suit your needs. (see p 122)

Selecting a Power Source

There are three main possibilities:

1. End-of-the-run receptacle
This is the simplest location to make a power hook-up. Only one cable comes into the box and a black and white wire are connected to the receptacle, two of the terminal screws remain vacant. To tap off power bring in a new cable, attach its black wire to the vacant brass screw and attach the neutral white wire to the vacant silver screw. Finally splice together the ground wires.

2. Middle-of-the-run outlet
In this case two cables enter the box and all four terminal screws on the receptacle are occupied. To tap off power remove one pair of black and white wires from the terminals on the receptacle and replace with two short jumper wires about 4 inches long, a black jumper wire on the brass screw and a white jumper wire on the silver screw. Bring in the new cable, join the two black wires and the black jumper wire with a wire nut, join the two white wires and the white jumper wire with a wire nut. Finally splice together the ground wires.

3. Middle-of-the-run switch
In this case two cables enter the

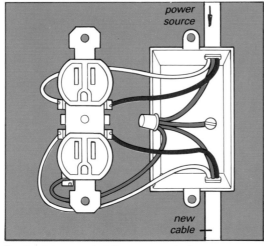

Tapping into an end-of-the-run receptacle.

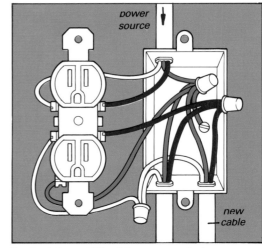

Tapping into a middle-of-the-run receptacle.

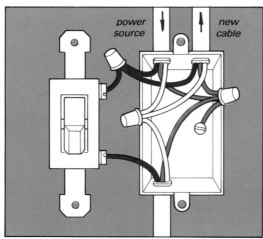

Taking power from a middle-of-the-run switch.

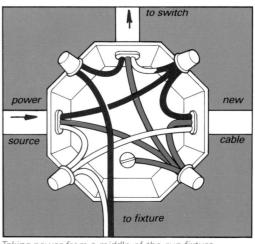

Taking power from a middle-of-the-run fixture.

box, the white wires are spliced together and the two black wires go to the switch terminal, and it is necessary to determine which of the two black wires is the power feed. This must be done by use of a voltage tester and entails switching the power on again after the switch has been removed. Remove the black wires from the switch terminals, have an assistant return the power, then using a voltage tester touch one of the tester probes against the metal junction box. Use the other probe to touch the two black wires in turn — the black wire that lights the tester is the power source. Turn off the circuit before continuing. Once you have identified the 'hot' black wire reattach the other black wire to the switch terminal. Cut a short black jumper wire about 4" long and attach this to the remaining

switch terminal. Bring in your new cable, splice together the three white neutral wires with a wire nut. Splice together the two black wires and the black jumper wire from the switch with a wire nut. Finally splice together the ground wires.

Middle-of-the-run fixture

Again it is necessary to identify the 'hot' wire by the use of a voltage tester. Several cables may enter the box and there will be at least two splices containing black wires. The black wire coming from the fixture itself will be connected into one splice — this splice is unlikely to contain the 'hot' wire. In order to identify the 'hot' wire in the other splice, turn off the power to that circuit, remove the wire nut and separate out the black wires, making

sure that they don't touch anything. Have an assistant return the power, then using a voltage tester touch one of the probes against the grounded junction box, touch the other probe to the black wires in turn — the one that lights the tester is the 'hot' wire from the service panel. Switch off the power before continuing. Bring in the new cable and splice the black wire together with all the black wires that were under the wire nut containing the 'hot' wire. Add the new white wire to the splice containing all the white wires. Finally splice together all the ground wires.

ELECTRICIAN'S

Trick

FIXINGS TO WALLS

The two tricky parts to extending your power circuits, once you have decided where the extra outlets are going to be are in running in the new cables (dealt with on page 120) and mounting the new outlets on the wall. Exactly how you go about the second part of this job depends on whether you are installing surface-mounted or flush outlets, and whether you have walls of solid masonry or of stud partition construction. Let's look at surface-mounted outlets first.

Surface-Mounted Outlets

Mounting your new outlet on the wall surface is certainly the easier option, whether you are running the new cables on the surface too (clipped in place or run in raceway) or hiding them beneath plaster and floorboards. The outlet faceplate is in this case screwed to a plastic mounting box (usually about 35mm/1⅜in deep) which is itself screwed to the wall. The cable is fed into the box from the side if it is run on the wall surface, from the back if it is concealed.

Flush Outlets

Mounting outlets flush with the wall surface is the neater solution. There is less risk of the outlet being damaged accidentally, and it is certainly less obtrusive. Rather more work is involved in fitting an outlet in this way, since the mounting box — in this case of galvanised metal — has to be fixed in a recess cut in the wall.

The cable enters the box through a hole knocked out of the side or base of the box. Then the outlet and its faceplate are connected up and screwed to the box to complete the job; now some adjustment is possible because the receptacle mounting screws are positioned in slots which allows it to be positioned vertically.

With hollow walls under construction the box is usually mounted on a batten fixed between the studs, and a hole is cut in the drywall over it. With existing walls it is possible to mount the box in a cut-out in the drywall by using small lugs clipped to the box sides, but it is an extremely fiddly job and the fixing is not particularly secure. A better and easier solution is to use a plastic cavity mounting box, which has a flanged edge and two spring-loaded clips that grip the back of the drywall or panelling when the box is pushed into place within the cut-out. The cables are fed into the box through a knockout before the box is positioned.

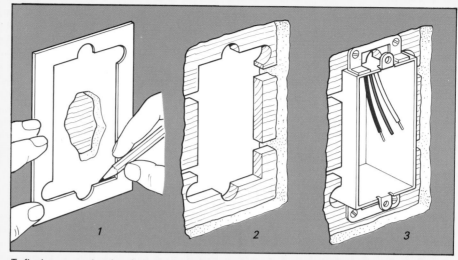

To flush mount a box in a lath and plaster wall: 1. Mark the box outline. 2. Cut the hole. 3. Fish the wires through and connect into the box, then mount the box and secure to the lath with screws.

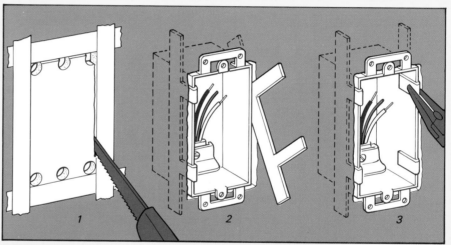

To flush mount a box in a gypsumboard wall: 1. Mark the box outline and cut out the hole. 2. Fish the wires through and connect into the box; push the box into position. 3. Bend the clips into position with a pair of plyers.

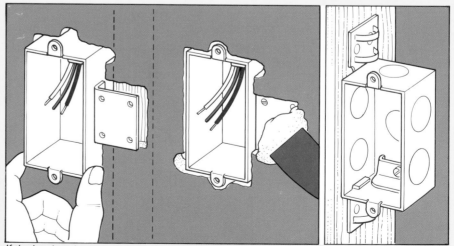

If the box is to be mounted close to a stud, the box shown above can be nailed to the stud by means of a metal flange. In new work (as shown on the right), the box can be nailed directly to the side of the stud before the drywall is installed.

CHANGING SINGLE OUTLET TO DOUBLES

An obvious way of increasing the number of outlets you have available without having to tamper with the fixed wiring in any way is to remove them and fit two outlets in their place or even three or four!

In principle, all you have to do is turn off the power, remove the fuse protecting the outlet, unscrew the existing single outlet and attach another one alongside. The obvious complication is with the mounting box; that will have to be changed and here you have several options.

Surface-to-surface Conversion

If your existing single outlet is surface-mounted and you want the new one to be mounted in the same way, buy a new double outlet with matching surface box, then unscrew and disconnect the old cover plate from the outlet, and unscrew the old single mounting box from the wall. Lift it away, leaving the circuit cable protruding from the wall (or from raceway alongside if this has been used). Remove an appropriate knockout from the new double box, feed in the cables and put the box against the wall to mark the positions of the fixing screws. Drill and plug the holes and fix the box in place, checking that it is truly level. Finally reconnect the wires to the terminals on the outlet and screw it to the box.

Flush-to-flush Conversion

If the old single outlet is flush-mounted and you want the new one to be flush as well, you have a little more work to do. Let's have a look at what's involved where the wall is solid masonry.

As before, begin by removing the original cover plate. Then unscrew the fixings holding the single box in its recess, and prise it out — you may need to use an old knife to cut round the sides of the box to free it first. Now check how much play you have on the circuit cables; if there is very little, you will have to enlarge the recess at each side, but if there is a fair amount of slack you can chop away the brickwork at one side only — the cable should still be able to reach the new terminals easily.

Place the new double box against the wall in the required position and mark its outline over the existing hole. Within the outline, drill a series of holes in the brickwork to the same depth as the box using a depth stop on your drill, and then cut away the honeycombed masonry with a sharp mason's chisel and a light sledge hammer. When the hole reaches the right size and depth, test the box for fit, and then mark the position of the fixing screws. Remove the box, drill and plug the holes and fix the box securely in place after feeding in the circuit cables. Finish round the edges of the box with filler, reconnect the circuit cables to the new receptacles and screw them into the box, and finally install a double cover plate.

Where you are carrying out the job on a stud partition wall, exactly what you do depends on what you find when you remove the old single cover plate. If the box is screwed to a batten fixed between the studs, simply remove it, enlarge the hole in the wall to match a double box and screw this in place to the batten. Feed in the circuit cable and reconnect as before. If the box was secured with metal clips, you could re-use them to fix the new double box. However, as already explained, this is a fiddly job and does not give a very secure fixing; it's better in this situation to discard the clips and to fit a double cavity mounting box instead.

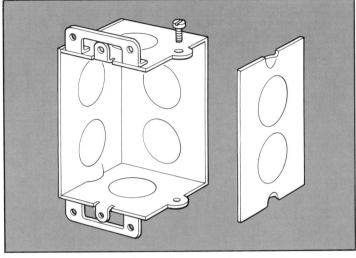

The side of the metal outlet box can be removed in order to join several boxes together.

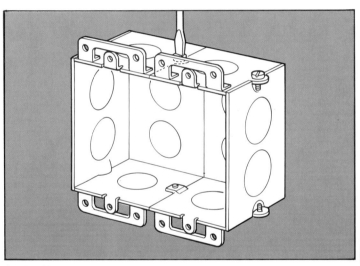

A pair of boxes joined to make a double box.

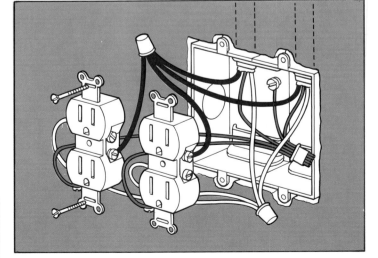

A pair of receptacles wired in the middle of the run.

WARNING

Always turn off the power at the service panel before beginning any work. Double check that the circuit is dead by means of a voltage tester.

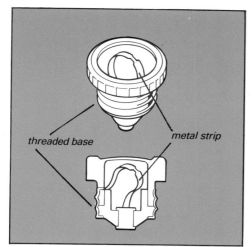

The standard plug fuse has a base similar to that of a light bulb and screws into the fuseway. The metal strip is visible through a window on the front of the fuse.

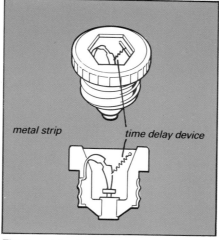

The time delay fuse allows for temporary circuit overloading, useful on circuits containing electrical appliances which draw a heavy initial current.

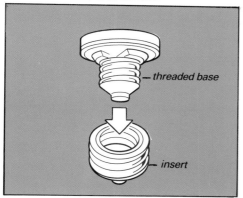

The Type S fuse allows only the fuse of the correct rating to be inserted into the fuse holder.

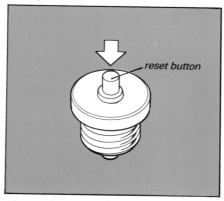

A screw-in type breaker can be inserted into the fuse holder to replace a standard fuse. A red reset button pops up in case of a fault.

The purpose of a fuse or circuit breaker is to protect you and your home in case of a fault in the electrical system. A fault may be due either to a 'short circuit' (a live wire coming into contact with a ground or neutral wire) or due to overloading of a circuit. It is necessary to determine the cause of any fault before replacing a blown fuse, or re-setting the circuit breaker. If a fuse blows when a particular electrical appliance is switched on then it is probable that there is a short circuit within that appliance. Alternatively, there may be several other appliances already on that circuit and the additional appliance may have caused an overload. A black or discolored window on the fuse indicates a short circuit; if however the metal strip is broken it is likely that the circuit was overloaded. In the case of a tripped breaker a red indicator square is uncovered to help identify the faulty circuit.

Types of Fuses

It is advisable to keep a supply of fuses of the correct rating and type close to the fuse panel. Never replace a blown fuse with another of a different rating; fuses of 15 amp, 20 amp and 30 amp are the most common in domestic circuits.

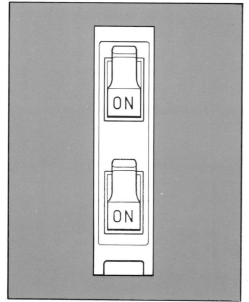

The tandem circuit breaker allows two circuits to be taken off in the space of a standard size breaker.

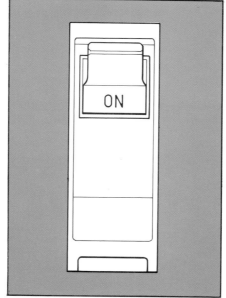

The standard circuit breaker. To reset a tripped breaker push the switch fully to the off position before pushing to the on position.

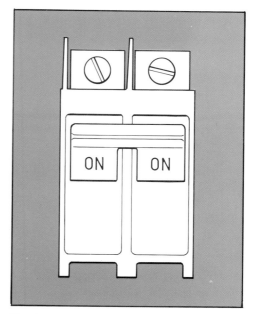

The double pole breaker is for use with 240 volt appliances and ensures that both phases of the supply to the appliance are tripped in the event of a fault on one phase.

137

TYPES OF FUSES AND CIRCUIT BREAKERS

The **standard plug fuse** has a base similar to that of a light bulb and screws into the fuseway in the fuse panel. A metal strip shows through the clear mica panel on the front of the fuse and indicates whether the fuse is good or not.

The **time delay fuse** is almost identical to the standard fuse except that it allows temporary overloading on the circuit which is useful to allow for the power surges in such appliances as washing machines and dish washers.

The **Type 'S' fuse** prevents use of a wrong size fuse by means of an insert which screws into the fuseway and which will only accept a fuse of the correct rating.

To replace a screw-in type fuse, first shut off the power by withdrawing the main fuses, identify the fault on the circuit and make the necessary repairs, unscrew the blown fuse and screw in a new one of the correct type and rating, finally restore the current. The screw-in type fuse can be replaced by a small screw-in type breaker, a red button pops out in the event of a short circuit, the breaker can be re-set upon correction of the faulty circuit.

Some fuse panels may be equipped with **cartridge type fuses**. It may be difficult to detect which of these fuses may have blown. To replace a cartridge type fuse first shut off the main power, remove the fuse by means of a fuse puller and check the fuse with a continuity tester to see if it has blown. If it is faulty replace with a new fuse of the correct type and rating.

Circuit breakers do the same job as a fuse by means of a small electro-mechanical switch which trips to the off position in the event of a short circuit or an overload. A red rectangle is exposed on the breaker when it is in the tripped position which helps to identify the faulty circuit. To reset a breaker, first identify and correct the fault, push the breaker fully to the off position which will re-set the switch, then push fully to the on position.

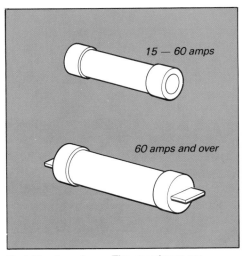

Cartridge type fuses. The round type are rated from 15 to 60 amps. The knife edge types are rated from 60 amps and over.

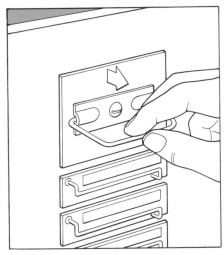

To remove a main fuse pull out the plastic fuse carrier from the fuse panel.

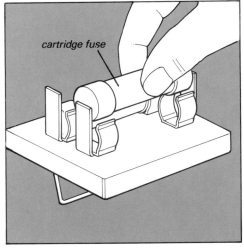

To replace a main fuse, pull the fuse carrier from the fuse panel, remove the fuse from the carrier and replace with a new fuse of the correct rating.

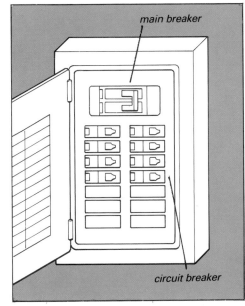

Circuit breaker panel. To shut off the power turn the lever handle to the off position.

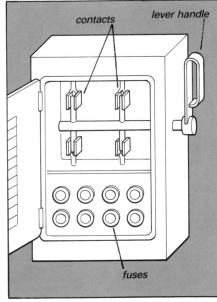

Lever type disconnect. To shut off the power turn the lever handle to the off position.

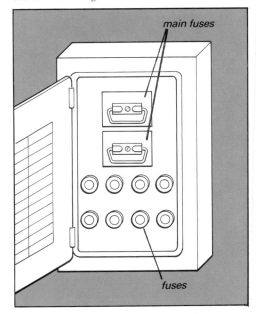

Fuse panel. To shut off the power pull out both of the main fuse carriers.

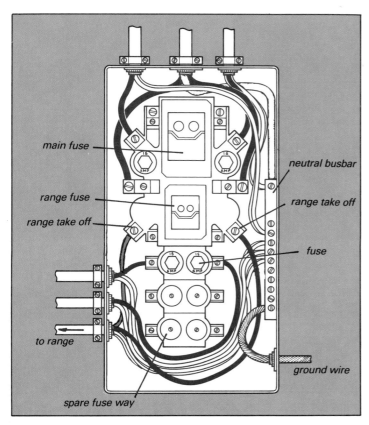

main fuse

range fuse

range take off

to range

neutral busbar

range take off

fuse

ground wire

spare fuse way

Circuit breaker panel with a main disconnect at the top.

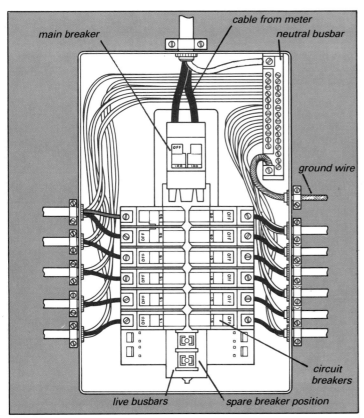

main breaker

cable from meter

neutral busbar

ground wire

circuit breakers

live busbars

spare breaker position

Typical fuse panel with a pull-out main fuse and a pull-out fuse for the range.

Extensions and additions to your existing lighting and power circuits may go a long way towards alleviating the problems of an inadequate electrical system, but there are sometimes circumstances where you have no alternative but to add a completely new circuit. One of the most common is where you want to install a high-rated electrical appliance such as a cooker, washing machine or dryer that cannot be run off an existing power circuit. Another is where you want to upgrade your lighting provisions and your existing circuits already have their full quota of lighting points.

The simplest way of doing this is to make use of an existing spare fuseway in your service panel. You will be unlikely to find a spare in any but a recent electrical installation — most electricians are loath for obvious financial reasons to install a bigger panel than the installation requires, but this is actually a false economy. If you are having rewiring work done that involves fitting a new service panel, choose a size that allows one, two or even three spare fuseways so that you can extend the system if you want to in the future with the minimum of upheaval.

What Type of Circuit

The new circuit, whether for lighting or to feed an individual appliance, will be wired up as a radial circuit. If it is for extra lighting, it should be run in number 12–2 wire in Romex or BX (always use what's already in your home. If you have BX use BX, if you have Romex use Romex) and the circuit fuse or circuit breaker should be rated at 15 or 20 Amps.

Connections at the Service Panel

It is customary to range the circuit fuses in modern service panels on the live busbars in such a way that the highest-rated fuse or circuit breaker is nearest to the main isolating switch and the lowest-rated one is furthest away. You may therefore have to alter the position of some of the existing breakers to allow the new one to be placed in the right position. In modern service panels it is easy to unclip individual breakers and simply move them along the busbar after turning off the system's main isolating switch. The new circuit breaker is then clipped into place on the busbar, ready to receive the new circuit cable.

The Circuit Cable

Strip enough from the cable so that the wires will reach the most distant connection point — (usually the neutral busbar); fit a two point clamp and feed the cable into the panel through a convenient knockout, cutting overlong wires to the correct length if necessary. Connect the live wire to the terminal on the fuseholder or circuit breaker, the neutral wire to the neutral block and the ground to the main grounding terminal, usually the neutral busbar. Check that all the connections are secure and correctly made.

The last stage is to refit the protective cover over the panel and to turn on the main isolating switch again so you can test the new circuit.

WARNING
ELECTRICITY CAN BE
DANGEROUS

Allways turn off the power at the service panel before beginning any work. Double check that the circuit is dead by means of a voltage tester.

APPLIANCE CIRCUITS

It is recommended that the following appliances are installed on a separate circuit:

Appliance	Watts	Voltage	Wire size	Fuse/ breaker size
Air conditioner	1200	120/240	12	20 Amp
Clothes washer	700	120	12	20 Amp
Dish washer	1200	120/240	12	20 Amp
Dryer	5000	120/240	10	30 Amp
Freezer	350-500	120	12	20 Amp
Furnace or boiler	800	120	12	20 Amp
Garbage disposer	300	120	12	20 Amp
Range with oven	1200	240	6	50-60 Amp
Range top (separate)	5000	120/240	10	30 Amp
Range oven (separate)	5000	120/240	10	30 Amp
Refridgerator	300-500	120	12	20 Amp
Water Heater	2000-5000	120	10	30 Amp

An appliance that draws a heavy amount of current must be wired to its own circuit. The wiring will be heavier than the normal house wiring and a special outlet is usually required. A whole range of outlets rated from 20 Amps up to 60 Amps is available. The arrangement of the slots in each varies according to the amperage, which is clearly marked on the front of the receptacle. Manufacturers of heavy household appliances supply the appliance with a power cord to match the relevant outlet. Never try to substitute a different plug or outlet than the one supplied with the appliance.

The following appliances do not need a separate circuit and can be used from a regular 20 Amp receptacle:

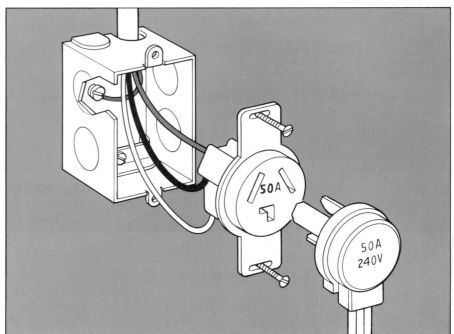

A heavy-duty appliance outlet. The receptacle will only accept a cord and plug of the correct rating. Both the receptacle and the plug are clearly marked.

Appliance	Watts	Voltage	Wire size	Fuse/ breaker size
Blender	300	120	12	20 Amp
Can Opener	150	120	12	20 Amp
Coffee maker	700	120	12	20 Amp
Deep fat fryer	1500	120	12	20 Amp
Dehumidifyer	300	120	12	20 Amp
Fan	300	120	12	20 Amp
Fryer	1200	120	12	20 Amp
Iron	1000	120	12	20 Amp
Floor lamp	300	120	12	20 Amp
Mixer	150	120	12	20 Amp
Radio	100	120	12	20 Amp
Room heater	1500	120	12	20 Amp
Sewing machine	100	120	12	20 Amp
Stereo	300	120	12	20 Amp
TV	300	120	12	20 Amp
Vacuum cleaner	600	120	12	20 Amp

POWER AND LIGHT TO AN EXTRA ROOM

If you have added an extra room to your house — as an extension or an attic conversion — you will naturally want to supply it with lighting and power circuits, perhaps even with special circuits as well if it's a kitchen or bathroom and you want to install equipment like an electric washer and dryer.

The first thing you need to establish is exactly what your requirements are. Use a copy of the plans for the new room to mark in exactly where you want light fixtures, switches, outlets and other special outlets. Then you can work out whether it is possible to extend your house's lighting and power circuits to supply the new room, or whether new circuits will be required.

In the case of existing circuits, each 15 amp circuit has a capacity of up to 1800 watts and each 20 amp circuit has a capacity of up to 2400 watts, so you need to check how much demand is on each circuit already, remembering to leave some reserve — see Extending Lighting Circuits on pages 122–125 for more details of exactly what is involved. If there is scope to extend the circuit, you can then work out the best point at which to connect

into it — at an existing junction box or at a new junction box cut into the circuit cable at a convenient point. Mark this on your plan, and then sketch in the likely cable routes to light fixtures and their switches, so you can estimate how much cable will be needed for this part of the job. Don't forget to include three-wire and ground cable too if you want any three-way switching arrangements. If your existing circuits already supply their quota of outlets, you will have to install a new circuit. The obvious way of doing this is via a spare fuseway at the service panel (if you have one) or by means of a new service panel (if you haven't) — see page 138 for more details. Each 15 amp circuit can serve an area of up to 375 sq feet, each 20 amp circuit can serve an area of up to 500 sq feet.

If the extra area of your new room(s) can be added to the area served by an existing circuit without exceeding these area figures, then you can extend this circuit as long as it has some reserve capacity. You can connect the new cable to it either from the last outlet on the circuit or at any convenient point along it. In this latter instance the con-

nection can be by means of a junction box cut in at a convenient point. Make sure you use cable of the same size as the existing circuitry.

You can extend a circuit in one of two ways — by adding spurs to the circuit, or by extending from the end but don't make it longer than 75 feet. You can add as many spurs to a circuit as there are outlets on the original circuit, and the actual connection can be via outlets or junction boxes cut into it. If your new rooms adjoin existing ones, it may simply be a matter of running spurs through the wall from the existing room to the new one.

Any other special circuits your new rooms need will have to be wired in as completely new circuits from the service panel.

WARNING

Allways turn off the power at the service panel before beginning any work. Double check that the circuit is dead by means of a voltage tester.

If the power requirements of the new room are small, you can wire the outlets by connecting into nearby power or lighting circuits.

For larger loads, such as in a kitchen, run new circuits from spare take-offs in the service panel or fit a sub-panel.

TAKING POWER OUTDOORS

More and more people expect these days to be able to make nearly as much use of electricity outside the house as within it — to have a power supply in the garage, garden shed, summerhouse or greenhouse, to be able to use the growing range of electrical gardening tools, to run a fountain or waterfall in the garden pond, or to provide garden/pool lighting. Of course it's very tempting to supply all these needs simply by plugging an extension cord into an outlet indoors and trailing it artistically across the lawn. The trouble is that such a set-up is safe only for temporary use — powering a hedgetrimmer or lawnmower, for example — and temporary arrangements have a habit of becoming permanent (and potentially dangerous) very easily. What is needed in all these cases is a proper permanent power supply.

Assessing Your Requirements

Once you have decided you want a power supply of some sort out of doors, it's best to work out exactly what you expect it to do. For example, you may want several outlets and good working light in a garage or garden shed, an array of fixed garden lighting, or a supply to a pond at the bottom of the garden; all of these must have new circuits, fed from individual fuseways in the house's consumer unit. You may on the other hand want just an outdoor outlet or a patio light on the back wall of the house, and these can usually be supplied by simple extensions of the existing house wiring — no need for extra circuits in this case.

Planning Cable Runs

Underground cables should be buried at least 500mm (20in) below ground level — deeper where they cross areas you dig over regularly but they can be down as little as 6in if it is protected beneath a concrete slab. If the cable is protected by conduit it can be laid 12in deep.

Check your local code to determine the required method in your area (conduit is usually preferred). You may use UF cable which is covered by a heavy plastic cover if conduit is not used. Use type TW in conduit. You can of course fix the cable to walls — boundary or building — but *not* to fences, which could blow down and cause the cable to rupture.

Choosing Accessories

Whatever type of outdoor power supply you are planning it is important to choose the correct type of fittings and accessories as well as installing the cable correctly. Obviously any light fittings must be designed for outdoor use. Outlet boxes out of doors must be the weather-proof type, while receptacles and switches within outbuildings need to be tough enough to withstand occasional knocks. The code now requires that all outdoor electrical outlets must be protected by a GFI device.

Making the Connections

With the cable run complete you can turn your attention to the ends of the run. If the cable is run to an outbuilding with its own sub-circuits, you must install a sub-panel there and connect the circuit cable to its feed terminals.

Within the house the circuit must start either at a spare fuseway or breaker in the existing service panel or at a separate sub-panel.

For extra protection when using electricity out of doors you must install a GFI circuit breaker at some point. You can either fit one in the sub-panel inside the house or outbuilding, or else use an outlet incorporating a GFI within it. The former arrangement has the advantage that the whole circuit is protected; whereas a GFI outlet receptacle only provides protection for the appliance plugged into the receptacle. The high-sensitivity type with a cut-off time of 30 milli-seconds should be selected.

Low-voltage Cable

If you want an outdoor power supply just to provide decorative lighting or to run a pump for a garden fountain, it is much simpler to opt for low-voltage equipment run from a transformer indoors. The low-voltage cable can be run on or near the

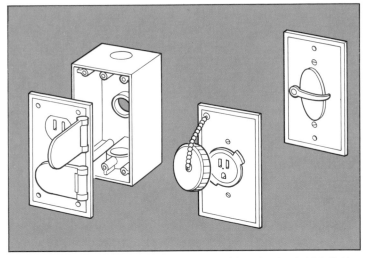

Weatherproof outdoor accessories: outlet box with spring-loaded lids (left), outlet box with screw cap (middle), and weatherproof switch box (right).

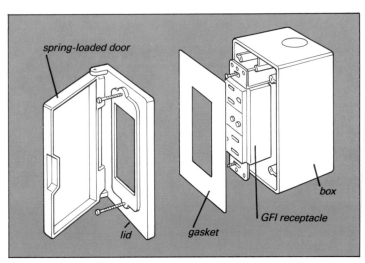

A ground fault circuit interrupter outlet and box for outdoor use.

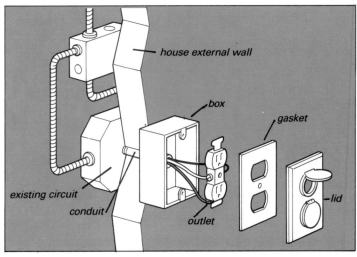

A simple way to bring power outdoors from an existing junction box, running connecting cable through conduit.

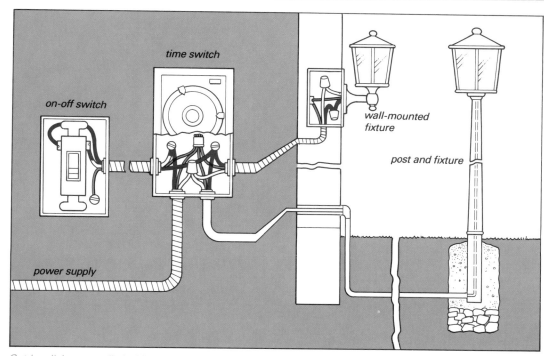

time switch

on-off switch

wall-mounted fixture

post and fixture

power supply

Outdoor lights controlled with an automatic time-switch which may be by-passed by a manual switch. Plastic-sheathed cable is used for underground installation.

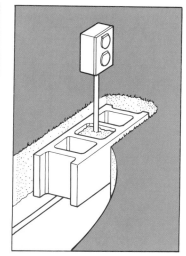

Set conduit to outdoor electric boxes in a concrete block, filling in the core with gravel.

surface of the ground with no danger; the transformer is simply plugged into a convenient outlet in the house or in an outbuilding with a power supply.

Voltage Drop
On long outdoor runs the voltage drop may exceed the maximum permissible figure of 6V — it all depends on the length of the run and the amount of current carried. Make sure that you keep your cable runs as short as possible — less than 75 feet if you are using number 12 wire. Longer runs will mean that you will have to use a large size wire.

TAKING POWER OUTDOORS FROM AN INSIDE JUNCTION BOX

With an underground supply, the cable will usually be run in conduit throughout the outdoor section. The first job is therefore to mark out and excavate the trench to take it. This should be laid out in straight runs; gentle elbows on the conduit will take care of abrupt changes of direction — for example, where the cable run leaves the house and heads underground.

With the run excavated to the correct depth, lay out the cable along it so that you can measure the precise length required to reach the end of the circuit. Add about 3 feet to allow for any slight errors and to enable the final connections to be made easily. If you are using plastic conduit start threading lengths of conduit onto the extended cable — this is easier than trying to thread the cable through each length of conduit already in position in the trench. Work from each end of the run back towards the middle, butting each length of conduit up against the next and adding elbows where necessary. When you have added the last complete length of circuit, work along the run bonding the lengths together with solvent-weld cement and lay the conduit in the bottom of the trench. At each end of the run, use elbows and short lengths of conduit to make up the above-ground sections where the run enters the house or outbuilding. Outlet boxes must be at least 12in above the ground. Anchor the conduit securely into the ground by lowering a concrete or cinder block over the conduit before installing the outlet box. Finish off by filling in the trench, covering the conduit in vulnerable areas with pieces of paving slab or roofing tile for extra protection.

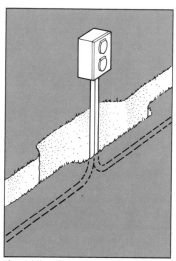

A middle-of-the-run outdoor electrical box with two conduit openings.

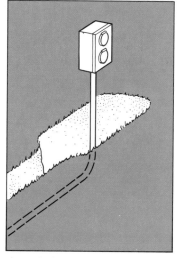

An end-of-the-run outdoor electrical box.

143

When electricity ceases to flow and an appliance stops or a light won't light, finding out what's wrong and putting it right is usually a matter of some logical detective work. As long as you have a reasonable working knowledge of your electrical system and you are prepared to trace faults systematically, it will only be a matter of time before you find out what is wrong. That's usually the hardest part; once you've found the fault a simple repair is often all that is needed to get the current flowing again.

Whatever the fault, always remember the golden rule and turn off the power before you start your investigations, whether it's at a light switch (to replace a failed bulb) or at the house main disconnect (to investigate an apparent circuit fault). Similarly, always unplug an electrical appliance from the main supply before working on it for absolute safety.

Here is a guide to tracking down the five major types of electrical fault you are likely to experience in your home.

A Pendant Light Fails to Work

1. The first thing to check is the bulb. Turn off the light switch controlling the light, remove the bulb and replace it with a new one — or one from another light that you know works, if you haven't got a spare. Switch on again; if the bulb fails to light, check point 2.
2. The next thing to suspect is a faulty connection between the pendant light cord and the main lighting circuit. To check this you must turn off at the mains, remove the lighting circuit fuseholder from its fuseway or fuse from its fuseway or turn off the lighting circuit breaker); you can then turn the main switch on again to restore power to the other circuits in the house. You may find when you go to do this that the circuit fuse has blown or the breaker has tripped off; this is a sign of a short circuit somewhere on the light circuit — probably on the cord, which is prone to chafing and wear because it can move about in the breeze, and which may disconnect itself from the lamp-

holder terminals as a result. Such a fault will stop the light from working; if in addition a loose wire touches another one, the resulting short circuit will blow the fuse or trip off the breaker.

Unscrew the lampholder first, and check that the wires are securely connected to their terminals. Remake any connections that are loose or broken, stripping off a little more insulation if necessary first. Most lampholders have small anchors to take the strain off the flex cores; make sure these are in use before replacing the cover.

Next, unscrew the ceiling rose cover and check the cord connections there too, again remaking any that are loose or broken and checking that the wires are hooked over the anchorages. Replace the canopy.

Now restore the power to the circuit by replacing the fuse or switching on the breaker. If the fuse blows again, check point 3.
3. The last fault you should check for on the pendant light itself is cord continuity; a worn or physically overloaded cord may have a fractured wire concealed within apparently sound insulation. Again working with the power to the circuit off at the panel, disconnect the flex from rose and lampholder and test each wire in turn with a continuity tester. If any wire fails to light the test lamp, replace the cord. If the circuit fuse still blows when you restore the power, there is a fault elsewhere on the Circuit (see Whole Circuit is Dead).

An Appliance Fails To Work

1. The first thing to check is that power is reaching the outlet you are using. Plug in another appliance you know works at the same outlet; if this fails to work here, the fault is at the outlet or on the circuit supplying it (see Whole Circuit is Dead). If it does work, check point 2.
2. Check the cord fuse on the first appliance; replace it with another of the correct rating for the appliance and test it by plugging it in again. Make sure the replacement fuse is sound by checking it with a continuity

tester.
3. Open up the plug and check all the cord connections, remaking any that are broken or loose by cutting the wires back slightly to expose fresh conductors and stripping away a little extra insulation to allow the new connections to be made. Replace the cover, and test the appliance once more.
4. Next, carry out a similar check at the point where the cord is connected to the appliance itself. Unplug it first, then open up the appliance so you can gain access to the terminal block. Remake any connections if necessary, as described in point 3.
5. Check the continuity of each core in the appliance power cord as described in point 3 under light faults, and replace the flex with new cord of the appropriate type and rating if you find any defects.
6. If these checks fail to restore power, there is a fault on the appliance that should be professionally repaired unless you are qualified to track it down and fix it yourself and you can obtain any necessary spare parts.

A Whole Circuit Appears To Be 'Dead'

1. If the circuit fuse has blown or the breaker has tripped off, start by switching off all lights or disconnecting all appliances connected to the the circuit concerned. Then replace the fuse with the correct rating, fit a new cartridge fuse of the right size or reset the breaker, and go round the circuit switching on lights or plugging in appliances one by one. If the circuit goes dead at any point, note which light/ appliance caused the fuse to blow and isolate it for repairs. Finally replace the fuse/reset the breaker again to restore the power to the circuit.
2. If the circuit is still dead, check all the wiring equipment on the circuit for signs of physical damage or faulty connections where the cable wires are linked to the equipment. Work with the circuit shut off, opening up each accessory in turn to check the state of the wiring at each one; remake any connections that are loose or broken, and replace any part that is

damaged.
3. If you know you have pierced a circuit cable during other do-it-yourself work, expose the damaged section and either replace it completely or cut the ends cleanly and reconnect them in a proper enclosure — a junction box in under-floor voids, a conduit box recessed into the plaster for buried cable. Remember to isolate the circuit at the mains before attempting this.
4. If the fault persists, call in a qualified electrician to check the circuit out thoroughly with professional fault-finding equipment.

The Whole House System Is 'Dead'

1. If the whole house system appears to have no power, the first thing to check is whether there is a power cut in your area. Remember that with three-phase supply, a fault on one phase only at your local sub-station will black out roughly half the circuits on the panel, and depending on the order in which the houses are connected to the three phases you may be without power while the lights are still burning next door. Report a power cut to your local 24-hour emergency phone.
2. If you have an earth leakage circuit breaker attached to your system, check whether it has tripped off and cut off the supply. If it has, reset it to on — it may have switched off because of what is called 'nuisance tripping'. If you cannot reset it, this indicates that there is an earth fault somewhere on the system. Tracking this down could be difficult, and it is probably best to call in a qualified electrician to trace it for you.
3. The power may have been cut off by the main service fuse blowing because of a major overload or other fault on the system. If you suspect this has happened, call a licensed electrician to check it and replace it for you if necessary.

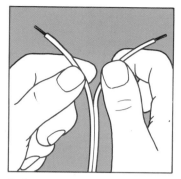
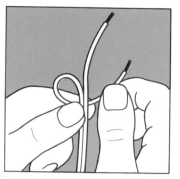
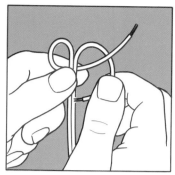
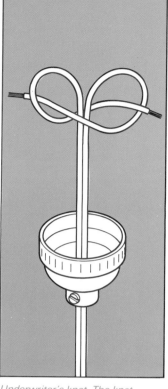

To tie an underwriter's knot:
1. Unzip the cord about two inches.

2. Make the first loop, passing the end behind the cord.

3. Make a second loop around the first free end.

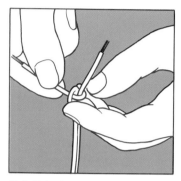
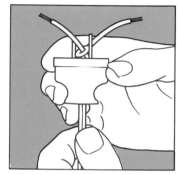

4. Pass the second free end through the first loop.

5. Pull the free ends tight.

6. Slide the cord through the plug or lamp holder.

Underwriter's knot. The knot protects the wires in a plug or lampholder from strain when they are pulled.

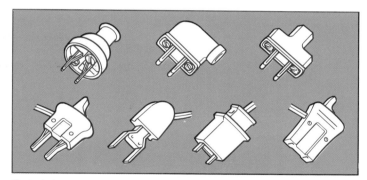

Typical plugs.

Some plugs attach to the cord without needing to strip wires. 1. Lift clamp, slide in cord, close clamp. 2. Hold prongs and remove case, slide cord through case. Open prongs, insert wire, close prongs and slide case back on. 3. Remove case, insert wire and push case back on.

Round wire plugs. 1. Slide wire through plug, tie underwriter's knot. 2. Pull wire tightly into the plug and twist free ends clockwise. 3. Attach ends of wire to terminal screws.

Grounded 3-prong plug. 1. Slide wire through plug and tie underwriter's knot with the black and white wires. 2. Pull wire tightly into the plug, twist free ends clockwise, and attach to terminal screws. 3. Tighten clamp on cord and replace the fiber cover over the prongs.

145

HEATING AND INSULATION

With prices what they are today, you would be forgiven for thinking that no matter what you do about heating your home it is bound to be expensive. But there are a number of simple, worthwhile improvements you can make, which, while they may mean dipping into your pocket now, can only leave you better off as fuel costs rise.

The first thing to consider is whether the heating system you've got really is the best one for your home and lifestyle.

Wet Central Heating

The majority of central heating systems are 'wet' systems — water, heated in a boiler, is pumped around the house through pipes and gives up its heat to the various rooms; normally via radiators. In most modern installations there will be two quite distinct sets of pipes. One takes hot water from the boiler to the radiators; the other takes cool water from the radiators and returns it to the boiler.

These are frequently run in ordinary 15mm copper pipe (equivalent to the old ½in pipe size), or there is another possibility, called 'microbore' types. Here the supply and return connections to the radiators are made with 10mm (⅜in) flexible pipes, which run back to manifolds near the middle of the house; these being connected by large diameter pipes to the boiler. The system's advantage is that it is a lot easier to install — the narrow pipes can be run as easily as electrical cable; see page 120.

One other wet system is like old-fashioned radiator systems that had a single pipe running from the boiler, through each radiator in turn, then back to the boiler. The modern version doesn't have radiators: sections of pipe are turned into radiators by the addition of metal fins, and the lot is hidden behind a metal casing which replaces your home's **base boards**.

Dry Systems

Where the heating was put in when the house was built, the most likely types are underfloor heating and ducted warm air systems. The former uses electric cables embedded in a concrete floor to turn the entire floor into a giant radiator. Not surprisingly, it tends to be very expensive to run. Warm air systems run on gas, oil or electricity, and comprise a central unit which heats the air and sends it to

Bleeding a radiator. Turn off the pump and turn the radiator key a fraction of a turn counter-clockwise; close again when water appears.

where it's needed along ducts. This too can be expensive to keep going.

Another common 'dry' system uses electric storage heaters. In the past these had a reputation for being unsightly, inefficient, expensive to run, and tricky to control. However, modern versions are a good deal better in all respects, and are well worth thinking about as replacements for existing storage heaters, and as new central heating.

Real Fires

Individual gas and electric fires are as popular as ever, though, as the sole means of heating a house, they are rather inconvenient and expensive to run Far better to use them as 'back-up' for central heating, but in that case solid fuel burning room heaters, stoves, and open fires could be a better bet, if only because it is often possible to arrange for them to contribute to the heating of the house as a whole, through the use of back-boilers which can be linked to a 'wet' heating system.

Efficient Improvements

You must ensure that your heating system works efficiently, and regular maintenance is a good first step in that direction. It's well worth taking out a maintenance contract to provide the central heating boiler, pump, and so on with an annual overhaul. Chimneys should also be kept in good condition. Sweep them regularly — and inspect the stack and chimney pots.

There are some maintenance jobs you can do yourself. Any radiators should be 'bled' regularly, to release the air that builds up in the system. As this accumulates, the top half of an affected radiator tends to become cool. All you do is insert a special key into the bleed valve at the top of the radiator, and turn it anti-clockwise, so opening the valve and allowing the air to escape. Close when water appears.

The central heating system's pump may also need bleeding if it seems sluggish in action. This is done in much the same way as for a radiator, except that the bleed valve can normally be operated with a screwdriver.

...

Another way of cutting heating bills is to improve the central heating system's controls — and the way in which you use them.

The system's most basic control is the boiler thermostat, controlling the temperature of the water in the system. This is generally best left as it is. Assuming it has been set correctly to begin with — your service engineer will advise you here — turning it up or down, can reduce the boiler's efficiency, and thus increase your heating costs.

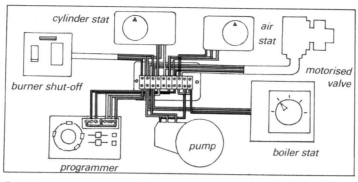

Control system for a pumped hot water and central heating system. Cylinder and air thermostats control the pump, and a motorised valve which allows flow through one or both systems; a programmer sets on/off times and hot water or heating; a boiler thermostat controls its temperature.

Time Clocks and Programmers

The system's time clock is another matter. This lets you turn the heating (and/or hot water where this is provided directly or indirectly by the central heating boiler), on or off automatically at pre-set times. For example, you can turn the heating on just before you get up, off while the adults are at work, and the kids at school, then back on again in the evening when everyone comes home, and finally off again a little before bedtime.

That's a fairly typical cycle and one any timer will handle. However, it may not be the best for you, so experiment. If you have a well designed, efficient system, and well insulated home, you may be able to reduce the heating periods without reducing comfort. Alternatively, a greater number of shorter heating periods may suit your lifestyle better. And don't forget weekends. Your heating needs are certain to be different.

The only snag is that you will probably reach a point where your existing timer is not capable of handling the program required, and when that happens, you should consider replacing it with some-thing more modern. You'll find many models on the market, varying in complexity (and price) from more sophisticated versions of the electro-mechanical timer you've probably got already, to electronic devices that are virtually miniature computers.

Fitting them into an existing system shouldn't be difficult. In principle it is simply a case of turning off the power at the mains, removing and disconnecting the old timer, and then connecting up the new programmer according to the instructions supplied by the manufacturer, before restoring the power. But remember that programmers are expensive, so if you run into difficulty at any stage, do seek expert advice.

Frost Thermostats

Having said all that, if reducing the length of time the heating system is active allows the house to become very cold, there is a risk of the central heating system freezing up. Admittedly, this is unlikely in the course of a day, but it could easily happen if you turn the heating off completely, say, for a weekend, or for a holiday. The answer is to fit a frost thermostat. This senses when your home's temperature is dangerously low, and turns on the heating automatically, until the danger passes. Unfortunately, these do not work on solid-fuel-burning systems.

Thermostatic Controls

The room thermostat is something else you should look at closely. It's job is to turn the heating on and off during the time clock or programmer's 'on' periods, in order to keep the house at a preset temperature, so, to begin with, experiment with the thermostat's setting to determine how far it can be turned down without affecting comfort. Changes of a degree or so, are rarely noticeable, except on fuel bills.

The thermostat's location is also important. Place it in a chilly hall or against a cold exterior wall, and the system will think the whole house is cold and react accordingly. Similarly, having it somewhere that is subject to frequent changes in temperature — a kitchen, for example — is also a bad idea. If you feel it could be better placed, try to compensate by adjusting its setting. Better still, consider replacing it with more effective thermostatic control — thermostatic radiator valves.

Thermostatic Radiator Valves

Fitted instead of the ordinary on/off valves, these control the flow of hot water to each radiator, and so can control the temperature of individual rooms — normally a hit-and-miss affair, since a room thermostat in, say, the living room, can hardly know whether a bedroom is too hot or too cold. They simplify alterations to the heating system, too, because you no longer have to rely on things like the size and number of radiators in a room to regulate its temperature.

If they have a drawback it is their cost. Fitting them to every single radiator in the house is rather expensive.

Trick

FITTING A THERMOSTATIC RADIATOR VALVE

Drain down the system (see overleaf) and remove the old on/off valve plus radiator tail pipe and coupling nut. Fit the tail pipe supplied with the new valve, binding its thread with Teflon sealing tape to ensure a watertight join, then connect the thermostatic radiator valve to this tail pipe, tightening up the coupling nut. Finally, connect the radiator supply pipe to the new valve, shortening it if necessary, and fitting it with a new olive (see page 93). Recommission the system, and set the new valve for the required room temperature.

EXTENDING YOUR HEATING SYSTEM

While you're looking at your central heating, think about radiators. Have you got enough? Are they in the right place? If the answer to either question is no, given basic plumbing skills, you should be able to tackle the necessary alterations yourself.

Draining Down the System

Before doing repairs and alterations, you must drain the system of water, and it is worth knowing how to do this in any event, in case the system springs a leak.

The first job is to turn everything — especially the boiler — off and stop fresh water entering. Most systems are supplied from a small storage tank called a feed and expansion tank, filled from the main via a ball valve. It might be in the attic near the main cold water storage tank, or in the basement itself near the boiler. To isolate it, look for a stop-valve on the main supply to the tank, or on the pipe leading from it, and turn it off. If there isn't one, tie up the ball-valve's float arm, or turn off your home's main stop-valve.

Now drain the pipework. There should be a drain-cock for the purpose. All you do is connect a hosepipe to the drain cock's spout, then turn the square boss on the top with a wrench. As water flows out, it can be directed, via the hose, into the garden, or into a sink. And where do you find the drain-cock? The short answer is: at the lowest point in the system — usually the boiler. Most freestanding models have a drain cock inside the casing at the front. If not, try along the pipes between boiler and radiators, bearing in mind that a system with two or more distinct radiator circuits, may have a drain-cock for each.

Can the System Cope?

The second thing to consider is whether the system can cope with extra radiators, and this involves some rather complicated calculations. Even if the pump can get water to the new radiator — which it may not if this is in an attic — the boiler may not be up to heating it properly.

One way out is to contact a firm specializing in 'central heating parts'. True, these are geared to supplying complete systems, but they may be willing to plan extensions, and supply the materials you need. Alternatively, you may prefer to trust to luck. Since most systems are installed with some spare capacity, if adding only one or two radiators, you stand a good chance of being successful.

New Pipes for New Radiators

If the existing system is run in standard copper pipe, installing new radiators should be fairly easy. Begin by tracing the feed and return circuit pipes supplying existing radiators, and decide where to tap into them. If you are adding only one radiator, any convenient point will do. Break into each pipe with a compression or capilliary tee fitting, and run branch pipes to the new radiator connection.

To create what amounts to a new radiator circuit, tap in at the end of an existing circuit, or close to the pump on the side farthest from the boiler. Using tees to break into the feed and return pipes, run a pipe from each along the shortest practical route between new radiators, teeing branch pipes off for connection to the new radiators.

Connections

Radiators come with a hole at each corner. The bottom two take an on/off valve and a balance valve, controlling the rate at which water leaves the radiator. Of the top two, one is merely plugged, while the other houses the bleed vent.

Both valves are fitted to the radiator using tail pieces (often supplied with the valve). Wrap their threads in teflon tape to ensure a watertight join. Tape is also needed around the thread of the radiator plug, but here you may have trouble tightening up, since the plug will normally have only a square or octagonal recess by which it can be **gripped. A 'lever bar'** is needed here. However, before going to the expense of buying one, try using a large screwdriver.

Finally, the bleed vent. How you fit this depends on its design.

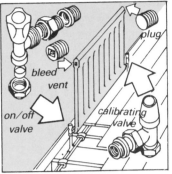

Components needed for a radiator: bleed vent; blanking plug; on/off (or thermostatic) valve; balancing valve.

After marking the center line of each hanger on top of the radiator, transferring the marks to the wall as a guide to fixing.

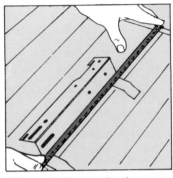
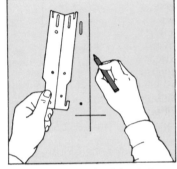

After positioning one bracket on a hanger, measuring from the top of it to the bottom of the radiator; add to this the floor clearance.

Marking through the fixing holes on to the wall with the bracket positioned the calculated height above the floor.

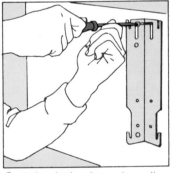

Screwing the bracket to the wall, using 50mm (2in) screws and wall plugs, with the corner of the bracket against the center line.

Lifting the radiator on to the two level brackets; plastic sleeves pushed on to the bracket lugs will prevent expansion noise.

If the part turned by the vent key is encased in an outer sleeve, bind the sleeve's thread with teflon tape, then screw it into place with a wrench. If, you have a one-piece vent, the whole of which screws in and out of the radiator, use the vent key to drive it home. Do not use tape or jointing compound on its thread.

You can now hang the radiator. It hooks on special brackets screwed to the wall, but make sure the wall fixings are firm — a full radiator is heavy. In solid masonry, ensure wall plugs expand in the body of the wall;

not in the plaster. On stud partition and lath-and-plaster clad walls, don't use cavity fixings. Screw into the wooden studs or into battens screwed to bridge two or more studs.

Care is also needed when positioning the brackets, if the radiator is to be in the right place. Measure the distance between the centers of the fixing lugs on the back of the radiator, and the distance between the lugs and the radiator's top and bottom edge. From these you can work out where the brackets should go for any given radiator position, and so long as you check that the brackets are vertical all should be well.

Finally, connect the feed and return branch pipes to the radiator valves. This is normally done using compression joints (see page 93). Connect the feed pipe to the on/off valve; the balance valve to the return.

Moving A Radiator

Moving an existing radiator is another job you can do yourself.

If the old and new positions of the radiator are fairly close, just extend the existing radiator branches of the feed and return circuits to the new position using standard plumbing fittings. Where the two positions are widely separated, cut the branch pipes back as far as they will go, then seal them off with stop-end fittings. The radiator can then be fitted in its new site, in the same way as if it were new.

Recommissioning the System

After such major changes to the central heating, it's necessary to recommission the system, and the first job is to refill it with water by reversing what you did to isolate the feed-and-expansion tank during the draining process. Leave the drain-cock open with hose attached for several minutes so that the fresh water will flush out any debris, then close it and let the system fill. Once full, bleed the pump plus all radiators to release.

If you have added a new radiator, the system will now need rebalancing. This may also be necessary if you have moved a radiator some distance. It's basically a matter of ensuring all radiators give out just the right amount of heat, and this is done by adjusting the balance valves using a special key (you can buy one cheaply). the more open the valve, the faster water

will pass through the radiator, and the less heat it will lose.

You will have to rent special thermometers which can be clamped to the pipes for this. To balance the entire system, fully open all balance and on/off valves, turn on the boiler and allow about half an hour for the system to reach temperature. With the aid of the thermometer, note the temperature of the return pipe on each radiator and compare it with the temperature indicated by the boiler thermostat.

One radiator — the index — will have a far lower reading than the others, and this should be left alone. For the rest, work round the system gradually closing down the balance valves, and renoting the temperatures, until all are within a degree or so of each other. Finally, check the temperature of the index radiator, if this is wildly different from the rest, try adjusting the water pressure ('head')

provided by the pump, assuming this is of the variable head type.

If you think all that sounds like a lot of hard work, just for the sake of a fairly minor alteration to the system, your right. What's more, it requires a fair amount of experience to balance a system properly, within a reasonable time — it could take you days. So, is there a short cut? Why not just balance the radiators you've added or moved?

Well, if you have simply moved a radiator, or added only one or two, it's certainly worth a try. By closing down the balance valves on the new additions and opening the valves on any existing radiators farther along the feed and return circuits, there is no reason why you should not achieve acceptable results. However, as a final test, do carry out a temperature check on all radiators in the system, just to make sure everything works.

Trick

GETTING READY FOR WINTER

Before turning on your central heating at the start of the winter, it's always worth giving the system a quick overhaul. The boiler and pump should certainly be serviced professionally, and it is well worth taking out a service contract for the purpose. There are however, a few checks you can make yourself.

Start with the feed and expansion tank. Because it has very little to do, even during the heating season, the ballvalve here is far more likely to stick than the one on the main cold water storage tank, and this can lead to overflows as well as a failure to top up the system effectively. To prevent this, simply move the valve's float arm up and down a few times to make sure it operates smoothly. At the same time, check that lowering the arm really does allow water into the tank, and that raising it shuts off the supply.

If the arm does have a tendency to stick, turn off your home's main stopvalve, and disengage the arm for the valve body by removing the retaining split pin.

Greasing float arm of expansion tank.

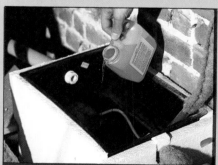
Adding corrosion inhibitor to tank.

Clean off any corrosion at the valve end of the arm with wet and dry abrasive paper, grease the surfaces lightly with a little vaseline, then refit the arm, and double check that it works.

Next turn your attention to the system's valves — both the on/off radiator valves, and any stop-cocks on the pipe runs. These, too, tend to stick if left unused for any length of time, so turn them all fully off, then fully on to make sure they work. If they are stuck, try freeing them with a little oil.

Finally, double check the settings on timers/programmers and thermostats, turn the system on, and go round checking for leaks. The radiators are the most likely to fail. This is because the combination of steel radiators, copper pipes and water turns the system into a sort of electric battery, which is powered by literally dissolving the steel. Small leaks can be plugged with solder or with a suitable epoxy resin-based filler; badly affected radiators should be replaced. To prevent further 'electrolytic' corrosion, consider adding a corrosion inhibitor to the water in the feed and expansion tank.

INSULATION

Although improving your heating system can go some way towards reducing your fuel bills, you can make even bigger savings simply by taking steps to keep the heat produced where it's needed — inside your home.

And it really is amazing just how much of the heat you've paid so much to get, does escape. Take a fairly modest window as an example: on a typical winter's day it can easily waste a couple of kilowatts of energy. In other words, if you heat your home with electricity, that window is about as wasteful as running ten hundred watt light bulbs for two hours . But it's not just windows that let heat out of your home. It can escape through the doors, walls, floors, and roof as well.

What can be done about it? The answer is: insulate. Insulation won't eliminate the heat lost completely, but it will reduce it, substantially in most cases, and with fuel costing what it does these days, any saving has to be worthwhile. At least, that is almost true: the insulation itself costs money, and you must therefore weight its cost against likely savings.

The simplest way to do that is to work out how long it will take for savings to cover the initial cost. Armed with those figures, it's easy to work out an insulation strategy for your home, with those forms of insulation that represent the best investment at the top of the list. Run through the following list of priorities.

Draft Prevention

In a typical one-family house drafts account for around 10 per cent of the total heat loss; a lot more if the place is old and unusually drafty. But it's not the size of heat loss that makes draft prevention so worthwhile. Rather it's that it is such an easy, relatively inexpensive job.

Even if you use the very best weather stripping on all external doors and windows, you should easily get your money back within a couple of years. With cheaper materials, the pay back time can be reduced to less than a year, but don't try to cut costs too far. Very cheap weatherstrip will need replacing more often,

Nailing weather-stripping round a window frame; not all types are suitable for all windows, so check before buying.

and so, in a way, is a false economy.

Roof Insulation

Although more expensive than weather stripping, roof insulation is very nearly on a par in terms of its value for money. Taking the typical "single family" house as an example, an uninsulated roof would be responsible for about a third of the total heat loss. What's more, insulating the roof is something you can do yourself, and if you do it properly, you should get your money back in a couple of years.

Laying insulating matting in an attic space; unroll the matting and push it down between the joists, butt-joining lengths.

Insulating Walls

Walls are also great wasters of heat, accounting for roughly the same proportion of the total heat loss as the roof. Unfortunately, insulating them tends to be expensive. It all depends on whether your home has a cavity within the walls. If it has, these can be insulated by pumping plastic foam, styrofoam granules, or mineral fiber into the air gap. This is a job for a reputable specialist contractor willing to

give a worthwhile guarantee. If it isn't done properly, it can lead to penetrating damp, and with foam, it's vital to check the wall's construction, to eliminate the risk of harmful fumes filling the house. Even allowing for the cost of this, though, wall cavity insulation normally has a pay back time of usually less than five years.

Solid walls are trickier still. One way is to add insulation to the outside of the wall and cover it with rendering or cladding. Like wall cavity insulation, this is really a job for professionals, but it comes rather more expensive. It could be eight to ten years before you got your money back.

Alternatively, insulation can be added to the inside of the wall, and this you can do yourself. Either stick insulation backed gypsum to the surface using special adhesive, or put up battens to support styrofoam or glass fiber blanket, and finish off with ordinary wallboard.

Sticking thermal gypsumboard to a wall with bands of adhesive along all edges; use a board to apply even pressure when fixing.

Double Glazing

Given the amount of heat lost through windows — generally more than 10 per cent of the total — double glazing may strike you as an excellent idea, but the snag is it can be expensive to install; so much so that with some professionally installed systems, the pay back time can be twenty years or more.

This makes having the whole house professionally double glazed a rather bad investment, and even doing the job yourself does little to improve matters, unless you count lining window frames with transparent plastic film as double glazing. In fact,

Applying plastic film double-glazing; press the film on to the window frame and shrink it taut with a hair dryer.

the only time it is worth double glazing the entire house, is if all the windows need replacing. Here it adds little to the overall cost, and indeed, aluminium and plastic replacement windows are normally double glazed as standard. Double glazing is worthwhile in some rooms — bathrooms, bedrooms, and lounges, — for the comfort it provides, and in this case DIY secondary glazing kits are well worth looking into.

Insulating Floors

Finally, there is insulation for floors, and the problem here is the work itself is rather tricky. With solid floors, for example, all you can do is lay styrofoam backed particle board, which raises the floor level and so can present problems. Suspended wooden floors can also be given this treatment, or you can lift the boards and hang glass fiber blanket between the joists before replacing them. Clearly neither option is worth considering, unless you have to lift the floorboards away, or are laying a new floor, say, in an extension.

Laying floating floor insulation; lay styrofoam on a plastic membrane and cover with tongued-and-grooved plywood.

Of course, it's not just the heat loss from the house that can cost you money. There's also the heat loss from your home's plumbing system to be considered.

Hot Water Savings

The hot water system is the most obvious candidate for insulation, and you should start by fitting the hot water storage tank with as thick a jacket as possible. Don't skimp in the belief that too much insulation will ruin the effectiveness of your airing cupboard. No matter how much insulation you add, enough heat will still escape from the tank and associated pipework to meet your needs.

Insulating the hot water pipes as they run through the house is a rather less attractive proposition, for the simple reason that it can be expensive to do, yet yields little in the way of tangible savings of heat. For this reason, the best advice is to insulate only selected hot water pipes. Choose those that run in the attic or against outside walls, plus any really long runs elsewhere in the house. Insulating the latter helps cut the time taken for hot water to appear at the faucet.

Cold Water Lagging

The idea that heat lost from the cold water system can cost you money may strike you as odd at first. But think about it. Isn't that what causes pipes to freeze and burst in winter? So it's absolutely vital to thoroughly lag every bit of pipework that's at risk.

That means every single pipe in the roof or attic, including overflows and vent pipes from the central heating and hot water systems. The cold water storage tank, and feed and expansion tank will also need protection, and do remember that, even if tanks and pipework already have some lagging, if you intend to improve the insulation in the roof, lagging may need to be increased. After insulation, the roof will be a good deal colder, and that increases the risk of a freeze-up considerably.

And what about pipework

elsewhere in the home? Any pipes to garden hose bibs and so on obviously need rather more lagging than usual once outside the house, and there's a slight risk of freezing in pipes run against an exterior wall, so lag these too.

Insulating Pipework

Having decided which pipes need insulating, how do you set about it? Well, there are two main types of lagging available. Perhaps the easiest to use is plastic foam tubing, already split down the side so it can be clipped over the pipework. Seal chinks in the lagging with a heavy-duty (preferably fabric-type) adhesive tape. Apply this along the split in the side, as well as to butt-joins between individual lengths. Extra tape will be needed around bends to hold the lagging in place and give a snug fit.

A cheaper alternative is glass or mineral fiber bandage. Sold in rolls, you just wind it around the pipe. (Wear a filter-type face mask, gloves and a long sleeved garment for this — the fiber glass can irritate your skin and lungs.) Start at one end of the pipe, tie the end of the bandage in place (use string or adhesive tape) then begin winding. As you work, secure the bandage at intervals with more string or tape and again take extra care turning corners. For the lagging to fit snugly without gaps, tie or tape it in position right round the bend.

Insulating Tanks

Jackets for hot water cylinders are simply slipped around the tank and secured with straps. Since they're tailored to the job and supplied with fitting instructions, they shouldn't present any problem at all. Measure the height and diameter of the cylinder before buying the jacket and ensure that it is manufactured to British Standard 5615: 1978.

Cold water tanks, too, can be kitted out with pre-made jackets (often insulation blanket wrapped in tough plastic) but you can improve insulation for both the tank and its lid quite easily and quite

Starting at the tank, wrapping overlapping turns of insulating bandage round the pipe; tie the lagging at the start.

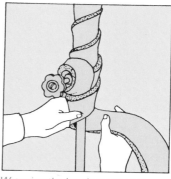

Wrapping the bandage round the body and neck of a valve; pay special attention to these as they must operate in an emergency.

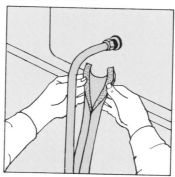

Slipping split plastic foam tubing over a pipe; choose the correct size for the pipework and butt-join lengths before taping together.

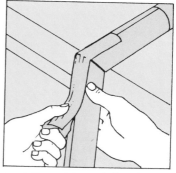

Insulating a right-angle bend; cut the ends of the insulation to 45° miters with a sharp knife and tape together with fiber tape.

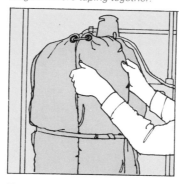

Fitting a cylinder jacket; ensure that there are no gaps between the segments and that the insulation does not slip down inside the cover.

Insulating a cistern with styrofoam slabs joined with cocktail sticks; join two slabs with the correct cement for a lid.

cheaply. There are three main ways in which this can be done. The first is to swaddle the tank with the sort of glass fiber blanket used for attic insulation (see page 152).

This is a messy job, however, and doesn't make it easy to get at the tank. A better method is to buy slabs of 25mm (1in) thick expanded styrofoam. Cut with a sharp bread knife, it's a relatively simple task to fashion a casing from this for the tank, and to hold it in place at the joins using adhesive tape or cocktail

sticks pushed through the corners of abutting panels. Simple, that is, if the tank is square.

If the tank is round, the simplest way out is to use a loose-fill material such as expanded styrofoam granules. Build an enclosure for the tank using hardboard or expanded styrofoam and pour the material in. For the lid, build a tray to take the insulant, or use an expanded styrofoam slab.

ROOF INSULATION

There are a number of materials available for roof insulation, but those suitable for do-it-yourself installation fall into two broad categories — glass fiber or mineral wool blankets, and loose fill materials.

Of the two, paper-backed glass fiber blanket is the better insulator, and a 100mm (4in) thick layer should be more than adequate. It comes in roll lengths of about 6 to 8m (20 to 25ft) various thicknesses — typically 80 and 100mm (3 and 4in) — so if you already have some insulation in the roof, you can choose the one that will top it up to the required level. You will also find rolls in different widths — usually 400 and 600mm (16 and 24in) — and although the wider material gets the job done more quickly, it's not as easy to lay as blankets that fit between the joists (which are usually spaced between 300 and 450mm (12 and 18in) apart), and since it covers the joists completely, it can make movement in an unboarded roof difficult in the future.

Loose fill insulation — commonly expanded styrofoam, gran-ules, loose mineral wool, cellulose fiber or vermiculite (based on the mineral 'mica') — is still easier to lay. You merely pour it on to the roof space floor and level it off. However, it's not as efficient an insulator as blanket types, so you need about two-thirds more thickness to achieve the same benefit, and if the joists in the roof are of relatively small section wood (likely in older houses), it may not be possible to achieve the required insulation without covering them.

Loose fill insulation also has a tendency to blow about within the roof, particularly around the eaves, and if this process is allowed to create gaps in the insulation, much of your hard work will be undone. For this reason, it is not recommended in drafty roof spaces of houses in exposed sites.

Loose-fill is sold in bags that typically contain 110 litres (4 cu ft) — sufficient to cover an area of about 1sq metre (12sq ft) to a depth of 100mm (4in).

Preparing the Ground

Whichever insulation material you choose, you will have to do a little preparation before you start to lay it. Firstly, check that the eaves of the roof are not blocked and that all plumbing in the roof space is adequately lagged against freezing.

Next, cover the floor of the roof space between joists with plastic sheeting, overlapping this at any joins by about 150mm (6in). This forms a vapor barrier: a certain amount of warm, humid air tends to percolate through the ceiling and into the roof space and ordinarily this disperses naturally. With the roof floor covered in insulation, however, it's quite likely to become trapped and produce condensation in the cooler top layers of insulant. The amount of condensation formed in this way, is unlikely to become very noticeable, but it does markedly reduce the insulation's ability to keep in heat.

Laying Loose Fills

Now to lay the insulation. Taking loose fill insulants first, all you do is empty the contents of the sack on to the attic floor, then — on shallow joists — run a wooden batten along the tops of the members to leave the insulation flush with their tops. Add more insulation as required to achieve the necessary thickness.

On deeper joists, make a spreader from stiff card or hardboard, with notches cut in the bottom corners, making a T-shape that spreads the insulation to the required 100mm (4in) depth.

Laying Blanket Insulation

Laying glass fiber or mineral wool blanket is also simple. Just roll it out between the joists, cutting it to length as necessary with scissors or a sharp knife. If you have trouble working into the eaves, use a broom to prod the blanket into place, but once again, ensure the eaves aren't blocked, and leave the space under water tanks clear.

But be warned. Glass fiber is unpleasant to work with. If it gets onto your skin, in your eyes, or you breathe in the fibers it's uncomfortable and could do real harm. So, wear protective clothing: you need rubber gloves, a filter facemask, and preferably goggles, too. To protect the rest of your body, buy a disposable overall, or wear old trousers and an old long-sleeved shirt. Do up all the buttons and seal yourself in by wrapping elastic bands around the cuffs and trouser leg bottoms. When you finish work, bundle these outer garments into a plastic bag, throw them away, and take a bath or shower to remove any fiber on your skin and hair.

Special Points

Don't carry the insulation to the point where it will block the eaves, though: these must be left clear to provide enough ventilation to prevent condensation. Place panels of hardboard between the joists near the eaves to prevent the granules falling into the cavity of the wall. You should also leave the area beneath cold water tanks free of insulation. The heat leaking through the gap, will stop the tanks freezing.

You can cover plumbing pipes with insulation as they run along the loft floor — it saves you having to lag them separately — but don't cover electrical cables: clip these to the sides of the joists or lay them on top of the loose-fill.

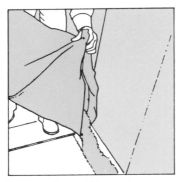

Emptying loose-fill insulation on to the attic floor after covering any pipes with building paper to prevent it from going beneath them.

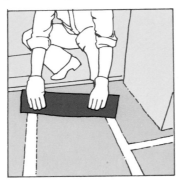

Levelling the insulation with a batten across the tops of the joists; on deep joists, notch the batten to give 100mm (4in) depth.

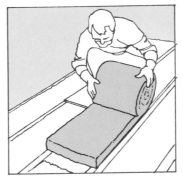

Unrolling insulating matting; work from the eaves towards the center, cutting where necessary with large scissors and butt-joining lengths.

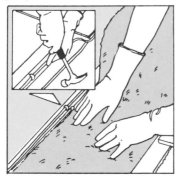

Tuck the insulation under cables or fix them to the joists with cable clips before tucking the insulation between the joists.

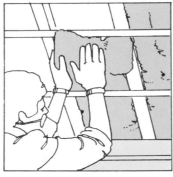

Insulating between the rafters with short lengths of matting tucked under thin battens nailed to the underside of the rafters.

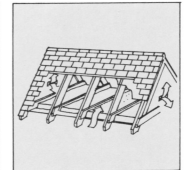

Ensure adequate ventilation to prevent condensation which reduces the effectiveness of the insulation and can cause the wood to rot.

If there is a key to successfully weather stripping your home, it's deciding where to seal, and which type of weather stripping is best suited to that particular situation. All external doors and windows — and that includes the trap door into the roof — should be sealed, while internal doors are generally best left alone unless they belong to rooms used very infrequently. Wasteful though they are, drafts also provide a lot of useful ventilation, so there's really no point in trying to stamp them out completely. If you do, you will simply have to provide some alternative means of ventilation, particularly in rooms containing fuel-burning appliances such as gas fires.

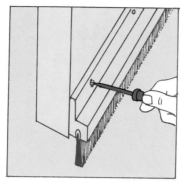

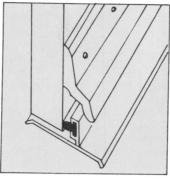

Screwing brush weather stripping to the bottom of a door; the bristles should just touch the floorcovering in the doorway.

Two-part threshold strip for use on external doors; as well as keeping out drafts, it also prevents water from dripping under the door.

Applying self-adhesive foam strip to a window frame so that it will be compressed when the casement is closed and fill any gaps.

Choosing Weatherstrip

With so many weather stripping products on the market, you're sure to be able to find something suitable at a price you can afford. Do try to match the quality of the product to the sort of wear and tear it is likely to receive.

For rarely opened windows and roof trap doors, look at the self-adhesive foam strips, sold in reels. These vary in price, but since none are very expensive, it is worth paying a little more for a fairly dense foam. It holds its shape better and so lasts longer than the very cheapest types. Remember, however, not to overpaint the foam, or it will be useless.

For the other windows, and most exterior doors, you need something more durable. Self-adhesive profiled foam strips (normally with a P-shaped cross section) should be suitable here, as are self-adhesive 'V-strips'. These are nothing more than strips of thin plastic which you crease down the middle to give the V-shape and stick around the frame so that, when the door or window is shut, the free half of the strip closes the gap.

This type of strip can also be used on entrance doors. However, entrance doors are rough on weatherstripping, and so it is probably worth looking for a strip that is both robust, and reasonably attractive. There are two main classes of product that fit the bill. Firstly there are the simple strips. Made from metal or plastic, these work in the same way as the 'V-strips' described above, except that, instead of folding them and sticking them in place, you pin them to the frame along one edge.

The alternative is what might be called "hard and soft" weatherstrip. Several designs are available for different situations, but basically, they consist of a flexible rubber tube which forms the seal, mounted on a strip of rigid plastic, which anchors the tube to the frame. Like the simple strips these are normally pinned in place, so they are not suitable for metal window and door frames.

Problem Solvers

Although, between them, the above will enable you to seal most of the gaps around the house, there are a few that are rather tricky to weatherstrip and here something special is needed.

Firstly, there are the gaps between window and door frames and the masonry of the wall. Filling these with ordinary internal and external fillers won't do much good, because such gaps have a habit of opening and closing. Instead, working on the outside of the house, run a bead of exterior silicon caulk right round all window and door frames: this remains flexible, accommodating any slight movement.

The gap at the bottom of a door is another problem, because with exterior doors, you have a step to cope with. This means that the simple brush-type weatherstrip designed for internal doors probably won't work. Instead, you need a strip that will automatically cope with the change in level caused by the step. Most of these are made from aluminum and rubber, and are generally available with a matching, rain deflecting weather strip for the outside of the door. However, they can be expensive so shop around.

Finally, fit key holes in external doors with a swing-down cover, and do something about the mail slot in the front door. Fitting a solid mail box to the door's interior is not a bad way to stop drafts getting in here. Alternatively, consider specially designed excluders consisting of two rows of brushes arranged so that while letters can be pushed between them, the bristles interlock to keep out drafts.

Trick

DOWNDRAFTS

A "downdraft" is caused by warm air striking a cold, single glazed window. As the air cools, it falls and gives the impression of a cold draft. There's only one cure for this and that's double glazing. So called secondary double glazing is easiest to install. Here a second pane of glass is mounted on its own frame within the window reveal to trap an insulating layer of air. You'll find several types on the market. Generally made of plastic or aluminum, they are readily available as kits for do-it-yourself installation, and come with full fitting instructions.

DECORATING

The purposes of decorating are two-fold: to protect interior and exterior surfaces and to bring color and character into the home. The arguments about where to start and what colours to use are many but, whichever room you may choose to decorate first, there's only one place to start and that's with the preparation. Having said that, time must be given to determining color schemes and choosing which area to tackle first.

A lot will depend on the state of decoration of the property. On moving house, you could easily find that the exterior is in severe need of attention. Despite the fact that the rooms may also be crying out for treatment, if the weather is suitable — warm and dry — it would be unwise not to get out there straight away and add some protection before the property has to face another damaging season of high winds, rain and frost.

Coming indoors, there is little point in decorating first a room or hallway that will have to act as a thoroughfare or storage area while you decorate the rest of the house. Work out a plan of attack and finish one room completely before starting another. This really is the only way to avoid schemes that have tremendous potential but achieve nothing special because the finishing touches are missing.

Preparation

Preparing surfaces thoroughly takes time, often much more than the actual decorating. But don't create work: sound surfaces need not be stripped at all, just cleaned. Loose paint must be removed though, as must loose wallpaper, all cracks and holes filled and certain surfaces sealed. This is also the ideal time to carry out any repairs.

Exterior surfaces need cleaning and preparing in exactly the same way. The brickwork or other fabric must be sound, with cracks and holes filled, mortar renewed where necessary, woodwork re-protected against damp and any metalwork checked for rust and brought up to a suitable state to accept new paintwork.

The ideal weather for exterior decorating is warm and dry: late summer usually provides the right conditions. Hot sun will cause new paint to blister; if the atmosphere is damp, the paint may peel. And it's not a good idea to be working up a ladder or from a scaffold in a severe wind. This can obviously be avoided, and valuable time saved, by working in protected areas of the property.

Interior Walls and Ceilings

To prepare a room for redecoration, clear out all the furniture if at all possible. Those items that must by necessity remain should be moved to the centre of the room and protected with plastic sheeting (cloth dust sheets allow paint drops to seep through). Take up the floorcovering completely or, if this is impossible, roll it back away from the walls and, again, protect with plastic sheeting. Protect varnished or polished floors with paper and plastic sheeting.

Before you start any preparation, turn off the electricity supply at the mains or, if you need the light to work by, carefully protect light fittings, sockets and switches from getting wet.

New Plaster

This has to be allowed to dry out completely before decoration. If the wall is to be papered eventually it needs at least 4–6 months for the moisture and salts in the plaster to come to the surface. The waiting period used to be considerably longer, with builders recommending a full 12 months, but modern plaster dries out more efficiently. It should then be primed with an alkali-resisting primer.

The only decoration that can be applied more or less immediately is latex emulsion paint; this is because it allows moisture through. Therefore, the plaster can continue its drying out process. Even then emulsion should not be applied until the plaster becomes lighter in colour, losing its dark, wet look.

Don't sand new plaster; the surface should be beautifully smooth and sanding will only create scratches that will still be apparent when painted. Simply wipe down new plaster walls or ceilings to remove surface dust immediately before painting with emulsion.

New Wallboard

The two sides of drywall sheeting are different: one side is grey, the other ivory-coloured. If it has been fixed with the grey side showing it will need to be skimmed with a thin coating of finishing plaster (see page 23). This must be allowed to dry before painting, as with new plaster. If the ivory side is showing and the joins between the sheets have been filled (see page 23), the drywall is ready for decorating. No priming is necessary: paint or paper can be applied direct.

Latex-painted Walls

There's no need to strip sound paintwork. Wash with detergent to remove all traces of grease and dirt, rinse from the top of the wall down to avoid streaks, and leave to dry overnight. Some scrubbing may be needed to shift heat marks on surfaces near radiators, boilers or light fittings, and to lift stains.

Particularly stubborn stains, which could show through new paintwork, can be concealed by painting the wall with aluminum primer. Household bleach will deal effectively with any sings of mildew.

Any areas of paint that are flaking or cracked should be scraped off and the surface sanded until quite smooth. Fill all holes, cracks and indentations (see overleaf). Wash down to provide an absolutely sound and clean surface, prime the wall (or ceiling) with a stabilizing or multi-purpose primer before painting or papering. This stabilizes any softness in the plaster, which would otherwise become powdery. It may not always be necessary; the condition of the plaster will determine this.

Gloss-painted Walls

Gloss paint is not a good decorative finish for plaster as it does not allow the surface to breathe and seals in the moisture. It used to be popular in kitchens and bathrooms where it was seen as a foil against condensation and could be washed down easily but, with today's washable latex paint finishes, there's no benefit in using gloss.

If you're faced with such a wall, don't attempt to strip the paint; it would take forever. (Blowtorches and hot air strippers, which speed the process of stripping gloss, are not suitable for use on plastered surfaces.)

Wash the wall thoroughly with water and detergent to rid it of grease and dirt, rinse, allow to dry then deal with any damaged areas. Scrape off flaking paint, using a flat scraper or shave hook, and sand until perfectly smooth. Fill any cracks, holes and indentations (see overleaf) then sand the entire wall to

provide a 'key' for new paintwork. Prime any areas of bare plaster.

Sanding an enamel-painted wall to provide a key for new paintwork; use medium sandpaper round a cork block or a foam-filled abrasive pad.

Whitewashed and Distempered Surfaces

The whole area must be stripped as these finishes are very unstable and new paint or paper will not adhere properly. Water and detergent used with a stiff-bristled banister brush and sponge will be effective if the paint has been applied direct to plaster. If it is backed with lining paper, then the paper will have to be stripped with it. Soapy water or wallpaper remover left to soak in will soften the paper sufficiently for it to be removed with a flat scraper. The surface should then be thoroughly cleaned to remove all traces of whiting and glue (the constituent parts of distemper) and effectively sealed with a coat of stabilizing primer, multi-purpose primer to ensure stability.

Removing whitewash with a stiff bristle scrubbing brush, water and detergent before applying a stabilising primer.

Papered Surfaces

If the wallpaper is perfectly sound and stuck firmly to the surface it will probably not need stripping. It's not a good idea to build up too many layers, though and stripping could prove advisable for this reason alone. Another instance when sound paper may need to be stripped is if the dyes in the pattern are not fast and the surface is to be painted rather than papered. This is easily tested: dab some paint on to the paper and if the colours show any sign of running, either strip the paper completely or apply a good covering of aluminium primer to seal it. Another alternative, if there are not too many layers of paper already, would be to cover the existing patterned paper with plain lining paper (see page 164). Small damaged areas of paper can be sanded smooth and lifting corners or torn pieces restuck with paste.

To clean wallpaper: brush down with a soft-bristled brush. The room must be left for at least 24 hours to allow dust to settle. (It's preferable to use a vacuum cleaner attachment for this job as it cuts down on dust.)

Stripping Wallpaper from Plaster

Unless the covering is vinyl, which just peels away from its paper backing, soaking and scraping are the techniques used here: the important thing is to leave the paper to soak thoroughly. Warm water works just as well by itself as when it's mixed with wallpaper stripper if it's allowed to penetrate and soften the paste on the wall.

To aid penetration, especially when the paper has been painted over or is heavily embossed, scratch the wallpaper with a wire brush or coarse glasspaper to allow the liquid through more easily. Sponge or spray on the water from a houseplant sprayer.

Work from top to bottom, doing one width of paper at a time. Use the scraper carefully, holding it at an angle that will lift the paper but not damage the plaster underneath. Special wall-

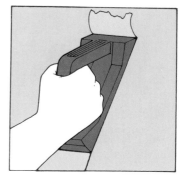

Removing wallpaper with a stripper; a roller in the base ensures that the blade does not dig into the plaster.

paper scrapers are available, which allow you to strip off old wallpaper easily without danger of scoring the wall surface.

When the wall is bare, scrub off any remaining paste and sponge the surface clean ready for filling and making good.

Steam strippers can be rented to facilitate stripping very thick paper or layer upon layer. They're not that much quicker and are tiring to use, as a metal sole plate from which the steam emerges has to be held against the wall until the paste and paper has softened. Again, scratching the paper in advance speeds the process.

Using a steam-stripper for stubborn paper; hold the sole plate against the wall and strip off the paper when saturated with steam.

Stripping Wallpaper from Wallboard

It's not advisable to strip paper from drywall, even if it has been primed beneath the paper, as the water could soak through and ruin the drywall itself, or the scraper cause irreparable damage. Restick any areas that may be lifting, sand smooth areas that are scratched or torn and coat with aluminum primer if the colors in the pattern show signs of running, or cross-hang with lining paper to cover all imperfections (see page 165).

Exterior Walls

Many people choose to paint only the woodwork ouside their house, leaving the walls in their natural state. Once painted, brickwork, stone, rendering or any other fabric will have to be maintained that way on a regular basis; to strip the paint completely would be an unthinkable task. The preparation for painting will depend on the existing condition. Start at the top of the wall.

Unpainted Brickwork/ Rendering/Stone

Scrub down with plain water but if there are signs of efflorescence (a white residue), which is the natural salts in the bricks, brush off with a stiff *dry* brush. Water will aggravate the problem. Do not use a wire brush as it will leave marks and if bits of wire break loose they will rust and spoil the finish.

Removing efflorescence; use a stiff bristle or plastic brush and no water as the salts will dissolve and the problem will recur.

Carry out any repairs that are needed (see below), then, if leaving unpainted, brush on a colourless water-repellent treatment. This will prevent rain penetrating the fabric of the walls without affecting their natural appearance.

If the wall is to be painted, prime with a stabilizing primer but only if the surface is powdery, alkaline or stained. Paint within days of priming.

Painted Brickwork/ Rendering/Stone:

If the surface is sound just give it a thorough brushing down with a banister brush; if dirty, scrub with detergent, rinse and leave to dry. Scrape away any loose or flaking paint. Deal with any repairs (see below) and apply a coat of stabilizing primer if the surface is at all powdery. If the wall is painted with a cement-based paint, which is unwashable, brush and scrape it clean. Having dealt with repairs, apply a stabilizing primer to give a solid surface on which to re-decorate.

Common Faults

Algae Remedy the cause, which is damp (see page 80). Apply a fungicide solution, following the manufacturer's instructions. Hose off the solution using a hand-brush attachment.

Moss/Mould Apply diluted bleach (1 part bleach: 4 parts water) and scrape off growth when dry. Apply bleach again and leave to dry. A fungicide solution can also be used.

Water stains Caused by defective guttering/leaders or dripping windowsills. Having remedied the defect, allow the stain to dry then apply an alkali-resistant primer to stop the stain coming through.

Cracks in surface or gaps by doors/windows Fill with an exterior filler.

Broken/cracked bricks For these larger areas, use a cement mortar as a filler. Rake out loose material. Undercut the edges of wider cracks and holes using a sledge hammer and cold chisel and brush away dust. Paint with

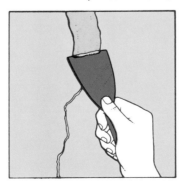

Filling cracks in plaster; undercut the edges to provide a key for the filler, brush out debris and fill with a filling knife.

a PVA bonding agent and press in the mortar. If the hole is deep, do this in two stages, scratching the first layer to give a grip for the second and leaving it to dry completely. Smooth off top layer with a builder's trowel or float.

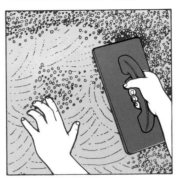

Repairing damaged pebbledash; after renewing the mortar, throw on the pebbles while it is still wet and press in with a wooden float.

Missing pebbledash Remove any loose material and hack back to bare bricks, undercutting the edges of the hole. Apply a PVA bonding agent to the hole. Spread on cement mortar. While still wet, throw suitably sized pebbles on to the surface, press in with a wood float and leave to set. If the wall is to be painted the color of the pebbles is immaterial.

Repointing brickwork The mortar between bricks will inevitably need renewal in some areas. Chisel out the mortar from the vertical then the horizontal joints. Brush away dust. Trowel mortar into the joints; uprights first. Apply a pointing profile to match the surrounding wall.

Repairing Interior Walls

When working outside, exterior grade filler must be used; inside, however, interior or exterior fillers are suitable. You can buy powder fillers for mixing with water, which is most economical, or ready-mixed types in tubs for convenient use.

Cracks Using the edge of a flat scraper, rake out any loose material. Mix the filler according to the manufacturer's instructions (or scoop straight from the tub) and press into the crack with the scraper. Overfill slightly, as most fillers tend to shrink and will leave indentations. Smooth

off with a wet blade and leave to dry. When hard, sand level with surrounding surface, using medium-grade and then fine-grade glasspaper.

Indentations Slight fluctuations in the surface will ruin the effect when exposed under lighting and should be brought up level using a fine-surface filler. Simply press in the filler, leave to dry and sand down.

Holes Small holes should be dealt with like cracks. Large holes should be filled with finishing plaster rather than filler. Having removed all loose material and undercut the edges with a cold chisel, wet the hole and then press in the plaster with a trowel. Do this in two stages if it's easier, scoring a criss-cross pattern on the plaster and allowing it to dry before adding a second layer. Filler can be used on top to bring it up to the general level of the surface. Sand smooth. With a really deep and wide hole some backing material may be necessary to support the filling substance. Crumpled chicken wire or dampened, screwed-up newspaper can both be used.

Corners Temporarily fix a wood batten to one edge of the corner with two nails. Dampen and fill in the other edge by scraping filler against the batten. When dry, release the batten, sand smooth the filled edge and nail the batten over. Fill in the second edge.

Uneven surface If the irregularities spread all over the wall and will be difficult to even out, hang a thickly embossed lining paper or use a textured paint (see page 176).

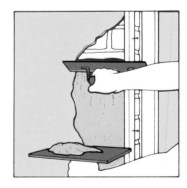

Repairing a damaged corner after fixing a temporary guide batten to one face; when the plaster is dry, repeat for the other face.

The techniques for preparing wood to give a firm surface for the new coats of paint are the same both inside and outside the house. Stripping wood takes a long time and, as it is unnecessary to strip sound surfaces, strip only the faulty areas. There'll be times when complete stripping is unavoidable: for example, to bring a built-in cabinet back to its natural finish when it's to remain unpainted. Several layers of paint are, in fact, an effective protector for the wood, so never strip it simply for this reason, although it could be preferable if the molded detail has been lost beneath the layers.

Once the damaged areas have been stripped, dust down and prime bare wood. Fill in any defects, prime the filling and sand down the whole surface to provide a key for painting. Always follow the grain of the wood when sanding to avoid scratching. The smoothest finish is achieved with the wet-and-dry abrasive paper used wet. A powered orbital sander will greatly speed up the sanding of large flat areas that need keying.

Stripping Interior Woodwork

The areas that will need attention are: doors, windows, base boards, stairs and banisters and decorative features such as architraves, picture rails, built-in cabinets, dado rails and wainscotting. There are three ways to strip paint or varnish from wood: dry scraping, heat stripping and chemical stripping.

Dry scraping Suitable for small areas only. Scrape the flaking paint off with a hook scraper or a shavehook (the combination shavehook, having a straight and a curved edge, is particularly good on mouldings). Sand the small bare patches level with medium- then fine-grade glasspaper.

Heat stripping There are two ways to apply heat to paint: with a blowtorch or an electric hot-air gun.

The second, a fairly recent innovation and although not quite as quick as a torch, is preferable for several reasons: some people are nervous of the

Stripping paint from a windowsill with a hot air gun; direct it ahead of a shave hook and scrape the paint as soon as it blisters.

flame of a blowlamp, but with a hot-air gun there's no flame, and there's far less likelihood of scorching the wood, which is important if you want to leave the surface bare. When used outdoors there is no danger of it being extinguished by a sudden gust of wind (although the cord does limit where you can use it; a blowtorch is still hard to beat when working aloft on soffits and fascia boards).

Using a Hot Air Gun

Allow the stripper to heat up before starting. Holding it about 25mm (1 inch) from the surface, wave it over the area to be stripped. Watch for the softening of the paint — blisters and bubbles — then draw a shavehook firmly down, removing the layers of paint and undercoat in one go. Move the stripper just ahead of the shavehook and always use this in a downward motion.

The paint hardens quickly on cooling, so scrape it off immediately. Catch the hot paint droppings on newspaper, ready to be bundled up for disposal. A flat scraper can be used on flat expanses of wood, with an upward movement, but the shavehook is best as it prevents any gouging of the wood.

Most undercoats will lift off with the top coat but any residue, or any slight scorching that will occur with a stripper that is handled without care, can be sanded down when stripping is complete.

To avoid scorching the wood at all, never hold the stripper over one area continuously. The paint needs only to melt. Deal with mouldings first, as they're

the most intricate part, and shield adjacent areas from the heat. This obviously applies particularly to the glass in windows. A piece of board secured in place will suffice. Most hot air guns come with a selection of optional nozzles for concentrating the jet of hot air: a wide, narrow mouth is ideal for use on thin glazing bars.

Using a Blowtorch

With a blowtorch, the process is much the same, but take particular care to turn it away from the surface while doing the scraping. Keep the flame about 150mm (6in) away from the surface and wave it to and fro, to melt the paint while not affecting the surface beneath. This requires skill and charring and scorching are inevitable for the less practised. Sand down any scorches that do occur, after the blowtorch treatment is completed.

Working with a blowtorch; the process is similar except that it must be directed away when scraping off. Do not use close to glass.

Chemical Stripping

There are two ways to strip paint chemically; with liquid or with paste. The liquid is best for windows as there's no danger of damaging the glass. Wear protective rubber gloves and follow the instructions on the can carefully.

Dab the stripper on, leave for 15–20 minutes and scrape off the blistering paint. Be particularly careful where the shavings fall and protect any floor-covering efficiently. Wash down the stripped wood with water or white spirit (according to the maker's instructions) and leave to dry overnight. Smooth all over

Using paint-stripper round a window; brush on and follow with a scraper as soon as the paint surface blisters.

with medium-grade glasspaper.

Chemical paste is particularly useful on mouldings (which are fiddly to strip by any other method) and for overhead use, where liquid would drip. Trowel the paste on and leave to do its work. Test its efficacy at intervals and lift off in a complete 'sheet' when it has worked through all the layers of paint. Scrub clean and leave to dry overnight.

Chemical stripping is best for areas that are to retain their natural finish as there's no danger of scorching.

Priming the Wood

Priming of bare wood should be done before any filling is carried out. Acrylic or multi-purpose primers are both acceptable for interior woodwork. Aluminium wood primer should be used where stains or preservatives could cause discoloration in the final decorative finish. It is also used on oily or resinous woods such as teak and cedar, for the same reason. A second application of primer is needed on damaged areas once any defects

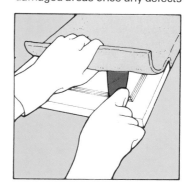

Stripping paint from moldings with a paste stripper; apply with a trowel, leave as recomended and peel off with the paint.

have been filled and knots treated.

Filling Defects

For interior woodwork a plaster filler is acceptable but if the filling is in an area that is likely to be affected by the weather (window frame) or damp, exterior-grade filler or one of the many proprietary brands specially devised for woodwork would be better.

The damaged area having been stripped and primed, press the filling agent into the hole and smooth over with a filling knife. Leave to dry then sand smooth. Prime the filled area.

Any visible nail or screw heads should be punched down using a nail punch or countersunk respectively, primer applied, then a dab of filler used to fill the small holes before a final coat of primer is applied.

Knotting

Knots are immediately obvious on new wood, being the circular dark patches. If left untreated

they will ooze resin and cause any paint covering to lift. This is what makes knots apparent in a painted surface.

Strip any coating away. Applying heat to the knots will

Applying shellac knotting to a knot in bare wood to prevent the resin from oozing out and staining the paintwork when applied.

draw out the resin, which can be wiped away with white spirit.

Apply two coats of shellac knotting with a small brush or cloth before priming: this will stop any remaining resin from seeping out and discoloring the decoration.

Stripping Other Finishes

Not all interior woodwork is painted; it could have been varnished, oiled or waxed as an alternative.

Varnish is stripped in exactly the same way as paint, with heat or a chemical stripper speeding the process.

Oil or wax is best removed with white spirit and steel wool, following the grain of the wood. Wipe clean with absorbent paper and keep repeating the process until all signs of the coating are gone. Paint will not adhere to oil or wax. Scrub thoroughly with detergent and dry before priming. Any discoloration in the wood can be remedied with wood-colour restorer.

Exterior Woodwork

Wash sound surfaces with a sugar soap solution. To achieve a good key for fresh paint, rub down while still wet with wet-and-dry abrasive paper, used dry. Rinse down to remove dust,

and leave to dry overnight.

It is far more likely that the exterior woodwork will be in a generally poor condition, in which case all flaking, peeling, chipped or split paint must be removed back to the bare wood. The methods of stripping are as for interior woodwork. The hot air stripper or blowlamp will be the quickest and most efficient on large areas. Reserve the chemical stripper for windows or where a natural finish is wanted and scorching would spoil the effect (say on a front door).

Bargeboards, Fascias and Soffits

Apart from the obvious doors, window frames, wall cladding and any decorative features, the areas to be dealt with include: bargeboards, fascias and soffits. As all this woodwork is above eye level the principal purpose is protection rather than appearance. Clear away all debris, including the occasional bird's nest, and scrape clean. Use a flat scraper and hot air stripper with an extension cord, or a blowtorch, (being particularly careful near the eaves as fire is a genuine hazard) to remove flaking paint. If this can be avoided, simply sand the entire surface of the board and prime any bits that need filling. Use an exterior grade filler or waterproof stopping and smooth it with a filling knife. When dry, prime the entire surface.

Wall Cladding

This will be the single largest area of exterior woodwork on any house. If it is new and is to be left with its natural finish, it must be coated with a water-repellent wood preservative for protection against damp. Coloured preservative can also be bought as an alternative.

If the wood is varnished or painted, sand down following the grain. Prime and fill holes and other defects before priming the entire surface ready for redecorating. If you are painting new wood cladding that has been treated with a preservative coating, use an aluminum wood primer to prevent any discoloration to the final decoration.

DECAYED WOOD

While stripping the exterior paint keep an eye open for irregularities in the surface. Although the paint coat may look sound, the wood beneath could be soft and crumbling. Probe gently with a knife. If the wood is soft it will need repair or replacement. For lesser damage, hack out the soft wood and use a wood repair system.

One available system is used in three stages: firstly, a chemical wood hardener is painted on to give a sound, firm base. A high performance wood filler is used next to make the repair, which will expand and contract with the wood and special pellets of preservative are then fitted into pre-drilled holes surrounding the repair. These act on the basis that once the moisture content in the wood rises to a level when rot can start, the pellets dissolve and release preservative before any damage can be done.

Applying high-performance wood filler to a rotten windowsill after treating with hardener; finally insert pellets.

REGLAZING A WINDOW

When you're redecorating windows it's likely that you'll have to repair defective, crumbly putty seals and even replace panes of glass that have been cracked.

The normal thickness of glass for a window is 3 to 4mm (⅛in). When ordering the new pane, measure 3mm (⅛in) less each way than the space inside the rebate to allow for fitting tolerance. It's unlikely that a wood frame will be exactly square, so as well as measuring all four sides, measure the diagonals before buying the glass. Buying the right sized glass will save a lot of time as trimming, even using a glass cutter, is not easy.

If there is beading on top of the putty remove this first by prising it away from the centre. Stick strips of adhesive tape across the broken pane in criss-cross fashion then, wearing thick gloves, tap out the fragments, letting the glass fall carefully onto many layers of newspaper, which can be parcelled up and put into a box for safe disposal.

Hack out the old putty with an old wood chisel or a glazier's hacking knife, taking care not to gouge the frame. Pull out the glazing sprigs (small triangular nails which retain the glass in a timber frame) and set aside for re-use. Clean down the exposed rebate, scraping away any flaking paint, and prime it.

Use linseed oil putty for a wood frame (or an all-purpose type). Knead the putty until it is pliable. Roll the putty into long sausage-shapes and press into the rebate with your thumb.

Lift the glass into place, pressing it into the putty at the bottom, around the edges, then at the top. Don't press the centre of the pane or it may crack. Replace the sprigs (or use panel pins), knocking them into the frame with the cross pein of a pin hammer (or use the back of a hacking knife). If the hammer head or knife is slid against the pane all the time the glass is far less likely to be broken accidentally. Press another sausage of putty all round the glass, then smooth to a neat bevel with a putty knife; trim off excess both inside and out. Make a mitred joint at each corner then run a paintbrush over the smoothed putty to make sure it adheres to the glass and has formed a watertight seal. Leave the putty to harden for 48 hours before cleaning the glass with methylated spirit. Paint the putty after two weeks.

For metal windows use special metal casement putty. Glazings clips are used in place of sprigs and, again, can be re-used. Note their position in the frame for replacement. Scrape away any rust to base metal and treat the frame with a rust-inhibiting sealer. Secure the new pane with putty and glazing clips.

Removing the glass from a broken window; criss-cross with masking tape to prevent pieces from falling out and wear gloves.

After removing all fragments of glass, chiselling out the old putty; pull out glazing sprigs with pliers and retain.

Applying a bead putty to the rebate in the frame after first coating it with a suitable primer.

After pressing in the glass round the edges, tapping in the sprigs; slide the hammer across the glass.

With the glass secured in the rebate, applying a covering bead of putty to seal it in.

Mitering the corners after smoothing with a putty knife; finally brush over with a clean paintbrush.

PREPARING METALWORK

The prime purpose of decorating metalwork is to protect it against tarnish and corrosion, especially outside the home. Ferrous metals (iron and steel) are particularly prone to rusting. Both new and tarnished metal surfaces must be carefully prepared before painting. Rust is a particular problem which can be dealt with in several ways.

Heat strippers are ineffective on metal; the metal absorbs the heat and the paint does not soften but instead becomes baked on. Use a wire brush to scrape off the flaky paint and rust and if necessary, a chemical stripper.

Priming of bare metal is essential, as primers contain a rust-inhibitor which protects the metal against further corrosion.

Cast Iron/Steel

New Clean thoroughly with white spirit used with emery paper to remove grease. Remove any rust particles with a wire brush. Apply a zinc chromate primer.

Tarnished Scrape down thoroughly with a wire brush to remove all loose paint and rust, right back to 'bright' metal (this doesn't mean that the metal must shine, however). An electric drill wire cup brush attachment will greatly speed this process (see facing page). Dust off and treat with zinc chromate primer.

Small items such as door knobs, letterplates and other decorative pieces are easily stripped of paint by immersion in a solution of caustic soda (tie lengths of wire to them for retrieval). Use a plastic bucket and wear protective rubber gloves and goggles. When stripped clean, rinse well and dry quickly or rusting will occur. Pour the used soda down the drain outside, flooding it through with lots of water.

Galvanized metal

This is coated with zinc to protect against rust but the galvanizing can chip or wear off, exposing the steel. When cleaning take care not to remove or damage this coating.
New Clean to remove grease with a rag dipped in white spirit.

Treat with a calcium plumbate primer.
Tarnished A chemical stripper would harm the zinc coating, so brush down with a wire brush to remove loose paint. Brush lightly, taking care not to scratch the surface. Remove grease with white spirit and treat with zinc chromate primer.

Aluminum and Other Non-Ferrous Metal

New Aluminum (windows, for example) need not be decorated. If it is to be, rub down with fine emery paper, clean with white spirit applied with a rag and treat with a zinc chromate primer.
Tarnished Scrape or brush away any signs of corrosion, being careful not to scratch the metal surface. Dust off and prime with a zinc chromate primer.

Indoor Metalwork

Central Heating pipes With many installations the pipework is concealed beneath the floorboards and it's only where solid floors intervene that the pipework is commonly surface-mounted. It can be left as it is or painted to match the decoration on the supporting wall.

A thorough rub down with abrasive paper will remove any loose surface material and any corrosion that may have appeared where water has dripped onto the pipes (when bleeding radiators, for example — see page 146). Any bare areas should be primed with a zinc chromate primer prior to painting.
Radiators These should be treated in the same way. All signs of rust should be removed. New radiators (and window frames) are supplied ready-primed but, where this has been chipped and the primer removed, clean the area and prime again or paint will not adhere well.
Windows Scrape and rub down to remove all rust. Check condition of the putty and, if necessary, renew (see glazing a window, page 159). Prime any bare metal with a rust-inhibiting primer prior to painting.

Rubbing off loose rust with steel wool before treating the area with rust remover; follow manufacturer's guide for surface preparation.

Coating the surface with metal primer immediately after treatment; with some rust removers, the enamel paint can be applied direct.

Removing flaking rust with an abrasive disc and an electric drill; a flap sanding attachment works equally well.

Using a wire brush attachment in an electric drill to remove rust from intricate shapes; a cup-shaped brush is also available.

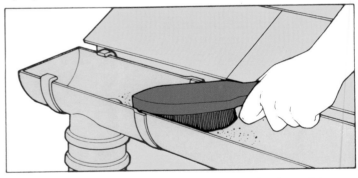

After removing debris with a masonite scraper cut to the shape of the guttering, rubbing down rust with a wire brush.

Using abrasive paper wrapped round a sponge to rub down curved areas; a flexible sanding block is a useful alternative.

Exterior Metalwork

When preparing metalwork for decoration, some faults in existing guttering systems will probably be uncovered.

Badly corroded cast iron guttering and downpipes can be quite easily replaced with plastic systems (see page 102). These need no painting and very little maintenance. If you don't like the color (black or grey), a simple cleaning with white spirit is all that's necessary before painting with gloss; no priming or undercoating is necessary.

Guttering

Blockages Clear all leaves and debris from gutters before attempting any other preparation. Clear out hopper heads and replace mesh guards in the tops of downpipes.

Cracks Having cleaned the pipe or length of guttering and removed all rust, fill the cracks with a waterproof caulk.

Leaking joints These will be instantly obvious as they will have caused corrosion of the surrounding area. Lengths of guttering are joined by being overlapped, the joint sealed with caulk then bolted. The bolts can be released and the caulk seal renewed. Alternatively, apply caulk to the join on the inside of the gutter without releasing the bolts. Seal leaking joints in downpipes with caulking.

Gates and railings Undoubtedly, the most common problem here is rust. The mouldings and lack of flat surfaces will make stripping painfully slow, so the simplest course of action is to remove paint and loose rust from the affected areas either mechanically or with a wire brush, then treat as shown on facing page.

Trick

REMOVING/ NEUTRALIZING PAINT

To strip a metal surface that is liberally covered with flaking paint and heavily corroded back to clean, sound metal, would be an awesome task. Fortunately, several manufacturers are of the same opinion and there is, on the market today, a wide selection of products for dealing with rust.

As well as looking in hardware stores, look at the shelves in automobile accessory shops. The products are designed to work on rust wherever it may be, and that includes autos, bicycles and lawnmowers as well as guttering, gates, railings and other areas connected with the house.

Rust Removing

When using a rust remover, the uppermost, loose layer is best removed mechanically with a wire brush attachment to an electric drill. These come in various shapes: a cup brush of 50 to 75mm (2 to 3in) diameter will cope in most situations. A hand-held wire brush can be used on small areas.

Daub the rust remover liberally onto the rusted areas only, not the entire surface and leave for about 15 minutes. Apply a second thin coat of remover and wipe dry with a clean cloth. In about another 30 minutes the patches will be ready for a coat of primer and this should be applied to the entire surface to protect the metal against further corrosion.

Chemical Neutralizing Agents

As well as rust removers there are chemical rust neutralizing agents, which actually act on the rust itself, converting it into an inert metallic coat ready for redecoration. There's no need to brush away the loose rust. Apply a thick coat of the agent all over the rusted area. Leave it to harden slightly for about an hour and then wipe away any excess from the surrounding areas with white spirit.

After 24 hours wash the area with water and leave to dry. No priming is necessary before painting but, if the entire metal surface is to be redecorated, the rest of the metal will need to be primed with a rust-inhibiting primer.

Special rust neutralizers are available for use on chrome, where no paint is to be applied.

After treating ironwork with rust remover, wash off well and prime with a general purpose primer.

This rust converter requires no priming; it changes the rust into an inert compound which can be painted directly.

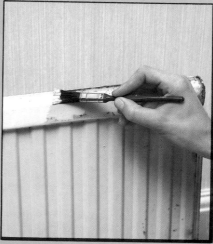

Ideal for central-heating radiators, this treatment dries to a smooth flat white finish suitable for repainting.

WALLCOVERING

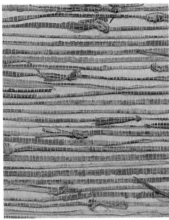

A selection of the more extravagant wallcoverings available: (from left to right) grasscloth, flock, textile and foil with matching border.

Decorative wallcoverings can be applied to any flat surface in the home. This includes not only all walls but also ceilings and, for example, the panels in wooden doors. All that is required is that the surface is properly prepared (see page 155).

There are various different types of wallpaper, not to mention fabric finishes, and certain types are obviously more appropriate in different rooms. Nearly all come in a standard (27in) width. Bathrooms and kitchens nearly always pose a problem with condensation, however good the ventilation in the rooms may be. If the walls are not smooth enough simply to be painted, a lining paper could be used to disguise the unevenness. Vinyl emulsion would then provide a washable finish in the same way as vinyl wallpaper.

The more expensive hand-printed papers and fabric finishes are best restricted to areas such as living rooms, dining rooms and bedrooms. Hallways tend to suffer a lot of wear and tear simply because they are thoroughfares and they also include the most inaccessible part of a house for papering: the stairwell. It is advisable, therefore, to select a covering that is straightforward to hang.

One thing to remember with a stairwell, is that a patterned paper, once hung, needs no more attention. Lining paper, on the other hand, has to be painted with two or three coats.

Concealing a Poor Surface

● **Lining Paper** Lining paper is invariably used on bare walls that are to be painted and it also gives the perfect face on which to hang decorative wallpapers, evening out any small imperfections in the surface. It comes in several weights — that is, thicknesses — the heavier paper being most useful in concealing a very uneven surface and as a base for heavyweight wallcoverings. Where it's being used under paint, hang it vertically as for wallpaper; if it's to be used under wallcoverings, hang it horizontally around the room so that the butt joins don't coincide with those of the wallcovering.

With unbacked fabric wallcoverings, it's essential to use lining paper and paint it in a color to match the top covering. Whereas standard wallpaper paste is normally sufficient for hanging lining paper, with a heavy decorative covering it may be necessary to use heavy-duty paste so that the weight of the covering does not pull the lining paper from the wall.

● **Woodchip (ingrain) papers** Woodchip is a relief lining-type paper coated with small woodchips then covered with another sheet of paper to seal in the chips. There are various textures of woodchip according to the size of the chips. Coloured woodchip can be bought but it is generally used as a lining on walls with minor imperfections and is then painted. It is hung, like ordinary wallpaper, vertically. One problem is in cutting the paper, due to the presence of the wood chips.

● **High Relief Papers** These are particularly heavy coverings, some designed to be painted over, others already finished, which are very efficient in concealing the defects in cracked and uneven surfaces. One made from thick paper, is embossed on both sides: another is made from cotton fibers; another is made from vinyl. The embossed patterns come in a range of designs, from sculpturally classic to geometrically modern, and can thus look appropriate in several styles of home.

● **Embossed covering.** This heavy, embossed covering with a flat paper back comes plain, to be painted, or ready decorated, and includes finishes such as tile and brick simulations. The edges as well as the ends of each length need to be trimmed, using a straight-edge and sharp trimming knife. The paper is extremely durable but once up is extremely difficult to remove. Bear this in mind when considering its practicality for the situation.

Coverings for Decorative Effect

● **Surface-printed papers** These are the most familiar of wallcoverings; what you'd call 'ordinary' wallpaper. They vary in thickness and the thinner ones can give problems in hanging with overstretching and tearing. However, if hung with care, they're perfectly simple to handle. Ordinary papers are also made in a vast selection of printed patterns. They are not washable (although they can be wiped over), so are not suitable for areas likely to suffer heavy wear and tear.

Hand-printed papers are much more expensive. They do not all come in the standard width and some are sold with edges that need trimming in order to match patterns.

● **Washable papers** As the name implies, these papers, which have a thin plastic (PVA) coating, can not only be wiped clean, but washed, so are ideal for use in areas such as the kitchen where grease deposits, for example, are inevitable, or the bathroom where condensation is likely. Don't confuse washables with vinyls (see below); unlike the latter, these papers should not be scrubbed too vigorously or the washable coating could be damaged.

Some washable papers come ready-pasted. These are cut to length, each length is soaked in a special water trough then positioned on to the wall. They are easy to hang but, like vinyls, need special paste where any overlapping is unavoidable as the paper will not stick to itself.

● **Borders** Where an overall pattern would be too fussy, but a plain paint colour looks disappointingly unoriginal, a border can add an effective point of interest. They come in various widths from about 50 to 150mm (2 to 6in), and are often colour co-ordinated with a range of wallpapers.

Use a border at any height: around the top of the wall, butting the ceiling; at base level, continuing around door-frames; at about 1m (3ft) up the wall to create a dado effect; around the edge of the ceiling; or simply around the features that deserve particular definition — a recessed fireplace for example.

TYPES OF WALLCOVERING

Some delicate, some particularly practical and hardwearing, there are many finishes other than paper or paint that can cover the walls of a house.

Vinyl Wallcoverings

Regarded almost as familiarly as wallpaper, vinyl coverings are particularly durable. The vinyl layer, fused with a printed pattern (not only washable but also scrubbable), is backed with paper and is no more difficult to hang than ordinary paper. The only slight complication is that paper will not stick to vinyl so, where overlapping is unavoidable, a special adhesive must be used. Also, to prevent mould growing in the paper behind the impervious vinyl layer, a fungicidal size and paste must be used. The paste is applied to the covering as with ordinary paper.

Expanded (Blown) Vinyl Wallcoverings

These are thicker than ordinary vinyl and are especially suitable in rooms such as kitchens or bathrooms where there might be condensation problems. They must be left to soak after pasting and extra paste on the wall will be needed at joins. All joins are butted and rolled, but pattern-free papers can be joined like furnishing hessian (see page 168) where the edges are overlapped and then cut through for a matching butt join.

Flock Wallcoverings

These are made by sticking the fibres of a fabric or wood to paper, creating a raised velvety pile effect, usually in two-tone colouring. Care must be taken not to get any paste on the front of the paper. They do not clean well. However, vinyl flocks are both tough and washable. It does not matter if paste gets on the surface of these as it can be sponged off. Flock paper is hung like other textile wallcoverings.

Hessian

Hessian can be bought either paper-backed ready for hanging or unbacked, as a furnishing fabric. The paper-backed variety — usually in 889mm (35in) or 914mm (36in) wide rolls — is by far the easier to hang and can be treated like any other paper-backed textile wallcovering. It comes in several shades and can also be painted over.

Furnishing hessian is a different matter. It comes in broad rolls, and is usually sold by the metre. As it is unbacked the condition and colour of the wall behind are of great importance. Always line the walls, as any patches of the old colour could show through the hessian weave. Check that furnishing hessian is color-fast, shrink-resistant and moth-proof.

Felt and Suede

Coverings rich in color, felt and imitation suede are heavy (usually paper-backed) fabrics made from dyed compressed wool. Not really feasible for a single person to undertake hanging, the roll — typically 700mm (28in) wide — can be supported on a batten spanning two step-ladders, which eases the weight problem. With the wall pasted, the felt is pressed on from the bottom upwards, a paint roller being used to smooth it into place. It can be butt-joined or overlapped and trimmed but the joins should not be rolled or they will appear unnaturally flattened. Roll the whole length of the felt instead.

Grasscloth

This luxurious material is made by weaving natural grasses with a fine cotton weft. Not a hardwearing covering. So long as the paste is kept off the grass itself, it's not difficult to hang. A special ready-mixed paste is needed, applied to the back of the covering, not the wall. The joins are not so important as the vertical lines of the grasses and their rough texture form a pleasantly random effect. The seams should not be rolled, or the effect will be flattened.

Rolls are normally about 914mm (36in) wide. The material is often sold by the metre.

Textile wallcoverings

There are many different patterns and effects created by fabrics and fibres being fixed to a paper backing. As with paper-backed hessian, this makes the hanging much more staightforward.

Silk cloth is probably the most expensive, and great care must be taken not to soak it with paste or crease it.

Wool, tweed and Rayon effects are no more expensive than some ordinary surface-printed papers but offer a softening, cosy appearance.
Roll widths are typically: silk, 762mm (31in); wool, 690mm (27in) or 750mm (30in); tweed, 690mm (27in).

The method of hanging varies; with many, the paste is applied to the wall and seams are usually butt-joined, though some can be overlapped and cut (see page 168).

Never use water on these coverings as this can cause shrinkage. Dust down with a brush to clean and remove any stains with a dry upholstery cleaner.

Foil

A metalized plastic film on a paper backing, the reflective surface of foil is ideal for covering a small, dark room. However, it also shows up any imperfections in the surface, so should not be used on a poor wall. It is hung like ordinary wallpaper, using a fungicidal paste, but must not be tucked under light switches/ sockets, as it can conduct electricity.

Foamed polythene (Novamura)

This unique wallcovering is ideal for kitchens and bathrooms. It's made from foamed polyethylene (with no paper backing) and, being warm, helps to reduce condensation. It is extremely light to handle as there is no paper in its manufacture, making it easy to hang, but rather prone to damage if knocked. It comes in standard-sized rolls and in a wide variety of designs and colours.

Fabric

Lengths of furnishing fabric can be used as a covering for walls but should be reserved for areas where the effect can be appreciated and where cleaning is not a problem. Vacuuming is the best method of cleaning.

The fabric can be stuck directly to the pasted wall or stapled to a series of battens around the room at ceiling and skirting height.

Cork-faced Fabric

Thin veneers of natural cork stuck onto a paper backing make an interesting textured wallcovering that's warm to the touch and subtle in tone. Some types have the coloured backing showing through for a random-patterned effect.

Tiling on a roll

Quicker to put up, and warmer than ceramic tiles, tiling on a roll is also scrubbable, easy to hang and strips off like vinyl wallcoverings, leaving its backing paper on the wall. It is a paste-the-wall type of covering and is smoothed into place with a sponge.

HANGING WALLPAPER

The preparation for surfaces to be papered is given in detail on pages 154 to 156. The walls must be cleaned of all grease and dirt, damaged paint or paper either stripped or repaired and cracks and holes filled and smoothed. Unstable (powdery) surfaces must be sealed with a primer and paint finishes sanded to provide a key for the paste.

New plaster must be left for four to six months to dry out before papering. If you want a temporary decorative finish, the wall can be painted with emulsion. This allows the plaster to continue its drying out process.

All the woodwork in the room should be painted prior to papering. It must be allowed to harden for at least seven days or the finish might be knocked and spoiled while the next stage in decorating is under way.

The order of work in any room is: ceiling, woodwork, walls. If it's necessary to paper the ceiling with lining paper prior to painting, do this first, following the instructions on page 169. The painting of the ceiling can then be done in unison with the painting of the woodwork as it is unlikely that one will interfere with the other.

Sizing

Before hanging any paper, lining or otherwise, on any wall, the surface should be sized.

This treatment prevents the wall drawing out the moisture from the paste used to hang the paper enabling it to be slid on the wall during hanging, to form good butt joints between strips.

Size can be bought or wallpaper paste diluted with water as instructed on the packet. Apply the size with a large paintbrush and allow to dry.

If a fungicidal paste is needed for hanging then a fungicidal size must also be used.

Equipment

Pasting table The ideal size is 1.8m × 600mm (6ft × 2ft) but any kitchen or work table will do.
Pasting brush A large paintbrush, at least 100mm (4in) wide, is best.
Pasting bucket Any plastic bucket that will hold at least 4 litres (1 gal) of water will do. Tie a piece of string across the top, from one end of the handle to the other, on which to rest the brush when not in use and scrape off excess paste.
Scissors paperhanger's scissors have extra-long blades but a large pair of household scissors can be used instead.
Paperhanging brush This is a flat-handled brush with long bristles, used for smoothing down the paper once it has been pasted to the wall it will squeeze all the air out from behind the paper and prevent air pockets or bubbles forming. A sponge should be used with washable papers.
Seam roller With either a wooden or plastic roller, this is used to flatten the joins between the lengths of paper ensuring they stick.
Plumbline A plumbline or spirit level that can be used vertically is needed to ensure that the first length of paper is hung straight.
Stepladder To reach the top of the wall. A hop-up or strong box may be easier to work from, in which case an apron with a large pocket will be useful as there will be nowhere to rest the hanging brush and scissors while the paper is being manoeuvred.

Paste

In general the heavier the paper, the thicker the paste.

There are two types of cellulose paste, one for lightweight papers, the other for heavyweights. Certain types are suitable for all coverings and are mixed, to be thicker or thinner.

The paste used to hang vinyls and washable papers must contain a fungicide to prevent a growth of mold behind the paper. Fungicidal paste should also be used if, during preparation, the wall was treated for mold, or showed signs of damp. Use a fungicidal size (or diluted fungicidal paste) also.

Certain special wallcoverings (see page 168) need particularly strong adhesive and this will be given in the manufacturer's instructions for hanging. Ready-pasted papers, of course, need no further pasting.

Trick

PASTING

Mix the paste with water in a plastic bucket or bowl. Having cut several lengths of paper, place these face down on the pasting table, with the first length on top. To allow the paste to soak in (some heavyweights need about 10 minutes), paste several sheets before you start hanging. Allow about three minutes soaking for the average weight of paper. This not only allows the paper to become more supple and easier to hang but also to expand to its fullest extent. If paper is hung too quickly it will expand on the walls and, being constricted by the paper on each side, will either spread out at the joins or bubbles will form in the middle.

Spread the paste over the entire surface of the paper. Position the paper so that one edge runs along the far side of the table, one end square with one end of the table, the other overhanging and retained by string looped round the

Folding the pasted paper back on itself to prevent it from drying out; support the hanging end in a loop of string.

table legs. Stroke the paste along the paper, then centre, being careful to paste right up to the edge away from you and the end. When this part of the paper is fully pasted, pull the top strip towards the near edge of the table and repeat the procedure. Fold the paper back on itself, pasted sides together, move it along the table to hang over the edge and paste the other end. Fold this back in the same way, remove from the table and leave to soak (drape over a broom handle spanning two chair backs). Any paste that went over the edges will have gone on the second length, which can now be pasted.

Always try and make the first fold the longer one, indicating the top of the paper. If in any doubt about which edge is the top, mark it lightly with pencil when cutting it or snip the trimming excess.

How much Paper to Buy

Most wallpapers are sold in rolls 10m (33ft) long and 686mm (27in) wide. Measure right round the room. If the door or window space is particularly large (wide French windows for example with little wall space above) make an allowance for this in the measurement; if not, ignore them. The number of drops of paper needed is this figure divided by the width of the paper. To estimate how many 'drops' can be cut from each roll

● Measure the height of the room from base board to ceiling.

● Divide this figure into the length of the roll. For example, in a room that's 2.4m (8ft) high, four lengths can be cut from a single roll. The number of rolls needed to paper the whole room is the number of drops needed divided by four.

These calculations must take into account pattern matching and pattern repeats. Matching a pattern always creates waste and this must be allowed for. It cannot be measured absolutely accurately, so if the pattern repeat is large it's probably best to allow an extra roll of paper. Never buy too few rolls: to be certain of the colours being the same on every roll of paper they must all come from the same batch. If you run short, an extra roll may not match perfectly. Always check batch numbers when buying paper.

Pattern Matching and Repeats

Measure the height of the wall for the first drop and cut a piece of paper this length plus 50mm (2in) top and bottom for trimming. Lay this sheet on the pasting table face up, and unroll the paper from which the second length is to be cut next to it.

Slide the roll along until the pattern matches (there will be more waste at the top) and cut it to match the first length. Follow this procedure for each length of paper, always matching the new length to the one before it.

Some papers have a pattern that matches straight across the wall, others have what is called a 'drop pattern'. With drop match papers, alternate lengths begin half a repeat further on the roll,

so that length one and all odd-numbered lengths will match, and all even-numbered lengths will match length two.

All pattern matching sounds more complicated in theory than it is in practice: with the pattern to look at, the matching becomes obvious. You may save on wastage by cutting lengths from two rolls of paper alternately.

Hanging Lining Paper

If lining paper is to be painted over it can be hung vertically like any other paper. If it is being used as a backing for a decorative paper, it should be hung horizontally.

The finish does not have to be quite so perfect, as any mistakes will be hidden; a slight gap between joins, for instance, will not matter, but an overlap between two strips will show.

Cut the paper to cover the length of the wall, allowing about 50mm (2in) top and bottom for trimming. Paste and fold the paper concertina fashion and start at the top of the wall.

Do not paper right round corners. Allow about 12mm (½in) to go over on to the adjacent wall and make a butt joint when papering that wall. Trim close to doors and windows. Cut around light switches, sockets and wall lights as explained below. Finish one wall before going on to the next.

Where to Start Papering

If there are four flat walls, start on the wall with the door. Work right round the room from the opening side of the door, ending by hanging the final sheet of

Hanging lining paper; fold it into a narrow concertina for ease of handling and hang in horizontal strips, starting at the top.

After marking the starting position on the wall, hanging a plumb line to one side of the mark and drawing a line through the mark.

Smoothing the paper on to the wall, from the center outwards to avoid trapping any air pockets, using a hanging brush.

paper behind the door.

In a room with a chimney breast, hang the first drop in the centre of the breast and work back on each side towards the doorway. By this method, any pattern loss (final length meeting first length) will be in the least conspicuous part of the room.

Finding the Vertical

When starting from the door, measure out at the top of the frame about 25mm (1in) less than the width of the paper. Make a pencil mark. If using a spirit level with a vertical bubble, put it to this mark and draw a continuous line down the wall: extend it using a long straight-edged batten. If using a plumb-line, drop it from this point and make pencil marks at intervals down the line, then correct them using a straight-edged batten.

This gives the true vertical on that wall: the first length of paper is placed to this line and waste trimmed at the edge of the door frame. Check that at no point does the distance from the line to the door measure more than

Hanging the first length of paper in a corner; position the outer edge along the marked line and brush into the wall/ceiling angle.

After creasing the paper into the wall/ceiling angle with the back of the scissors, pulling it away from the wall to trim the top edge.

the width of the paper. If it does, draw a second vertical slightly closer to the door, so that there is always paper to be trimmed.

If the first length of paper is to be hung from a corner of the room, trim the waste to allow 19mm (¾in) to overlap the corner on to the adjoining wall.

To find the vertical on a chimney breast, measure the width and divide in half to find the center point. Mark this and measure back 343mm (13½in) or half the width of your roll. Mark the vertical from this point and paste the first length of paper in the centre of the breast, with one edge to this line.

Hanging Straight Drops

Position the stepladder alongside the starting point. Carry the folded paper to the wall, hold it by the top edge so that the fold falls away and offer it up to the marked vertical. Align the edge of the paper with the vertical.

Smooth the paper on to the wall at the top with the paperhanging brush. Brush it straight down the centre of the paper then with outward strokes, pressing any air bubbles out towards the edges. Align the edge of the paper with the marked vertical all the way down the wall, smoothing the paper and using the bristles of the brush to work it into the ceiling and base board at top and bottom, making a crease line.

Crease the overlaps at top and bottom with the back of the scissors, gently peel the paper back, trim then smooth back into position.

At sides of doorframes and windows, brush the paper into the angle to make a crease. Define this with a pencil line or scissors, peel back, cut away the excess and smooth down again. At the corners of frames, cut diagonally into the paper at this point to make it easier than to trim the two verticals. If the cut is slightly too long, don't worry: when the paper is smoothed flat, the cut will not show.

With light switches and sockets, first turn off the electricity supply. Smooth the paper down to the obstruction and then cut a cross in the paper over the centre of it. Mark the

After making angled cuts in the paper, creasing the flaps along the edges of an electrical outlet with the back of the scissors.

After removing the circuit fuse, tucking the trimmed flaps within the perimeter of the plate; trim foil paper along the creases.

outline of the switch or socket and extend the cross cuts back just past these lines. Trim the excess and smooth down.

With flush outlets, turn off the power at the mains, loosen the screws holding the faceplate of the outlet, then smooth the paper underneath and screw the facing back, hiding the cut edge of the paper. Follow the same procedure for wall light fittings removing shades and bulbs first.

The drop of paper abutting a mantelpiece should be trimmed flush with the top then cut in carefully round the sides, following the moldings — you'll find small nail scissors handy here. Again, small diagonal cuts can help stop the paper tearing and will not show when smoothed flat.

Chimney breasts and recessed windows both create extra angles to paper around.

On an internal corner measure into the corner from the last-hung drop and cut a length of paper to this width, plus 19mm (¾in). Paste the paper, allow to soak then hang into the corner, smoothing the excess onto the adjoining wall. Find the true vertical on this wall, using a plumbline or spirit level, at a distance from the corner to match the offcut paper. Paste this to the wall, taking it right into the corner. Any loss of pattern will not be apparent.

Chimney breasts create both internal and external corners. The center of the chimney breast will already be papered. Measure from here to the side of the breast and add on 19mm (¾in) to take the paper round the corner on to the side. Paste the paper on to the wall, butting it to the piece already in position and smooth the excess around the corner. Find the true vertical. The width of paper on the side of the chimney breast should cover the overlap from the front, but be set slightly back from the edge, and continue into and around the internal corner by 19mm (¾in). Continue as for internal corners. With window reveals, paper the insides of the reveal first, overlapping on to the main wall by 12mm (½in). The paper on the main wall should be trimmed to fall just short of the edge but covering the overlap.

Papering an internal corner; hang the first length to turn the corner by 19mm (¾in) and hang the second with its edge in the angle.

Papering an external corner; hang the paper on the face of a chimney breast to wrap round the corner, and overlap with the strip on the side.

After trimming wallpaper to overlap a door frame by 25mm (1in), making diagonal cuts 6mm (¼in) beyond the frame at the corners.

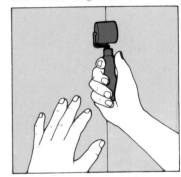

Smoothing the paper into the angle of the frame before creasing into the angle, pulling away from the wall and trimming.

Tearing the paper above and below a windowsill or obstruction to make the join less noticeable; take care as wet paper tears very easily.

Using a wallpaper edge roller to ensure a smooth butt join between lengths; do not use on embossed wallcoverings.

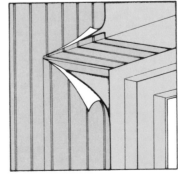

Papering the corner of a recess; hang an offcut to lap up the wall and down the recess and cut the length along the top of the recess.

Hanging the second length of paper; hang from the wall/ceiling angle, smooth under the recess and trim against the frame angle.

Trick

PAPERING A STAIRWELL

A rather complicated system of ladders, scaffold planks and boxes is needed to gain access to a stairwell. But stairwells vary in design and the system will have to be structured to suit the location.

Basically, you'll need a long ladder placed on the stairs and leaning against the head wall. Wrap the ends of the ladder with cloths so that they don't damage the wall. Position a stepladder on the half-landing, leaning against and facing out from the well wall. If there's no carpet, this ladder can be wedged firmly in place by a length of wood screwed to the floor against it. If this is not possible, secure the ladder by jamming a length of wood between it and the next flight of stairs.

Place a hop-up or strong box at the top of this short flight and lay a scaffold board from it back to the stepladder. Another board can then be positioned at right-angles to this one, and supported by it, running back to the long ladder. If the gap is more than 1.5m (5ft) use two boards for extra strength.

Lash the boards to the ladder rungs using strong rope; it's preferable to bolt the boards to the rungs of a ladder, or attach two stout battens to the underside, spaced so they straddle a rung. (If you've hired the boards, however, you won't be able to drill bolt holes.)

It is advisable not to work alone when papering a stairwell. Quite apart from the fact that an accident is more likely, the lengths of paper needed can be extensive (often up to 6m/19ft.) and will be much heavier. The heavier they are, the more likely they are to tear and it's useful to have a second person to support the folded length of paper.

Start papering at the longest drop, where the well wall meets the head wall. Find the true vertical with spirit level or plumbline and pencil in the line, allowing the first length of paper to turn 12mm (1/2in) round the corner onto the adjoining head wall. Measure up and find the vertical on the head wall as well.

Measure up and cut the paper to length. If using decorative paper, measure up for the second piece, pattern-match it against the first piece from the top and cut to length. Remember to continue matching the pattern for each length of paper.

Paste the paper, fold concertina style, allow to soak for the recommended time and then walk on to the platform with the drop draped over your arm. Unfold the top piece and brush onto the wall; the folds will unfold as the paper is smoothed out on to the wall, controlled by your helper just below you. Keep the

After nailing battens to the underside of the scaffold board to prevent slipping, lashing it to the ladder rung.

Carrying a length of paper, folded into a concertina, over one arm to leave the other arm free for hanging.

edge against the pencilled vertical, brush well into the corner and flatten down the 12mm (1/2in) overlap.

Continue papering the well wall, butting the joins and working back along the scaffold board to the half-landing. When this wall is finished, with 12mm (1/2in) overlapping at the other end on to the adjoining wall, remove the boards and ladders. Paper the head wall from a stepladder on the landing.

It may be easier to hang the first drop (in the far corner) from the scaffold boards but it will not be possible to decorate the whole wall from there, as the ladder will block your access.

Decorate the wall at the other end of the stairwell last, as it's the easiest to reach. Work from the stepladder on the half-landing and the hop-up or box on the upper landing.

Nailing a batten to the stair tread to secure the foot of the ladder after pushing it into the tread/riser angle.

After securing the top edge, brushing the paper on to the wall while an assistant supports the weight.

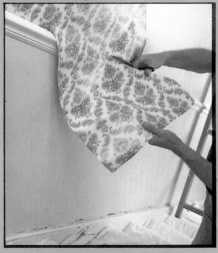

Trimming the bottom of the length to overlap a dado rail before creasing into the angle and cutting along the crease.

HANGING SPECIAL WALLCOVERINGS

The normal way to hang wallpaper is to paste each length and press it onto the wall, working from top to bottom, butt-joining the lengths and rolling the joins. With many special wallcoverings there's some variation in this method. The prime consideration is usually to avoid smearing adhesive on the front of the wallcovering. It cannot easily be washed off and will undoubtedly leave a noticeable mark.

Textile Wallcoverings

The coverings that have a textile finish but are paper-backed can be easier to hang than ordinary wallpaper. Most, but not all (check manufacturer's instructions) are hung with a heavy-duty pre-mixed adhesive which is applied to the wall.

Paste one width at a time. Don't stretch the covering but smooth it on from top to bottom, using a wide paint roller to dispel any air pockets. Butt-join the lengths, being careful to avoid paste stains. Don't seam-roll the joins or you may flatten the pile.

High Relief Papers

The basic approach is as with ordinary wallpaper. Paste the back of the paper, being careful to get paste into the indentations and leave to soak for 10 to 15 minutes to become supple. Butt-join the lengths but don't flatten the joins with a roller; use a paperhanger's brush instead, wielded gently.

To reduce the thickness where overlapping occurs (in corners), feather the edge that is underneath by tearing it straight down. Flatten this rough edge with a roller and paste the adjoining length over it.

Because the wallcovering is heavy, the wall preparation must be particularly painstaking; loose paint will simply be pulled away. The wall must be well sized.

Heavily embossed papers have to be sponged with warm water prior to pasting with a special glue. Each length is hung immediately up to each other. This makes pattern matching difficult at corners, where the walls are likely to be out of line. Overlapping is impossible.

After applying paste to the wall with a roller, smoothing the unbacked fabric on to the wall with a clean roller.

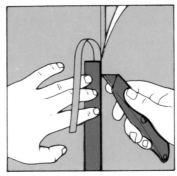

Cutting along the middle of an overlapping join between lengths before peeling off the offcuts and refixing.

Smoothing the fabric into a corner; wrap the first length round the corner, overlap the second, cut through the overlap and refix.

Papering a corner with a relief wallcovering; tear along the turned length, edge-roll the feathered edge and overlap the next length.

Applying a fungicidal adhesive to the wall before hanging vinyl wallcovering; pasted width should be slightly wider than the wallcovering.

Smoothing the vinyl wallcovering on to the adhesive with a damp sponge; do not cut lengths but trim off the roll at the bottom of each drop.

After rolling unbacked hessian on to a pole, right side inwards, hanging it on the pasted wall in overlapping lengths.

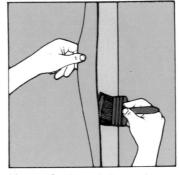

After cutting through the overlap and peeling off the excess, pasting under the edges with a small brush before lightly edge-rolling.

Supporting felt wallcovering; roll round pole, right side inwards, and support between step-ladders with wrong side towards pasted wall.

Hessian

Unbacked hessian as opposed to the paper-backed variety, is liable to shrink, so allow an extra 50mm (2in) on each length. As with ordinary papering a plumbline is used to find the true vertical. Paste the wall with a heavy-duty paste applied with a paint roller.

Hang the hessian to the marked plumbline, smoothing it from top to bottom, taking care not to stretch it. Smooth it with a clean paint roller. Overlap each length by about 25mm (1in) and leave to dry. This allows time for any shrinkage before trimming.

Trim at top and bottom with a sharp trimming knife and, using a straight-edge and sharp knife, cut through both layers at the centre of each join. Remove the waste strips, peel back the edges and re-paste the wall. Press the edges back into place to achieve a perfectly matched butt join.

PAPERING A CEILING

Papering a ceiling may seem like a daunting task, but — given the correct access to the surface — there's no reason why one person alone shouldn't make a professional job; the techniques are similar to papering a wall.

To reach the ceiling you can make a 'walkway' from two stepladders with a scaffold board between them, or else rent special decorator's trestles, which enable you to span the room at the correct working height.

It's best to hang the paper across the ceiling working back from the window so you're not in your own shadow. Measure out from the window wall the width of the paper less 12mm (½in). Stretch a stringline across the ceiling, fixing it with drawing pins, then draw a pencil line along it, using a straight-edged batten. Remove the pins and string. Alternatively, chalk the string and snap it against the ceiling to make a chalked guideline.

Cut the paper to length, allowing extra for trimming. Paste it as described on page 166, folding it concertina style with the folds not being more than about 450mm (18in). Support the folded length on a roll of paper and mount the walkway. Hold the folded paper in one hand and apply the free end to the ceiling, keeping the edge on the pencil line. Smooth the paper into place.

Step along the platform, unloop a concertina fold, smooth it up on to the ceiling then continue along until the whole strip is hung. If the walls are to be lined or otherwise papered, smooth the extra 12mm (½in) at the side of the paper onto the wall; do the same at each end. If the walls aren't being papered, mark the creases and trim into the angle between ceiling and walls in the usual way. Butt the following lengths to the first one.

Where the paper covers a ceiling-mounted light fixture, cut a cross over the fixture, slot the lamp-holder through then trimming round it. With a decorative ceiling rose, paper up to it, mark the moulding in pencil, peel back the edge of the paper and trim to fit as closely as possible.

Setting up a scaffold-plank walkway between two step-ladders to give about 150mm (6in) headroom below ceiling.

Snapping a chalk-line on to the ceiling, parallel to the window wall and paper-width less 12mm (½in) into the room.

Pasting a cut length of paper; start at one end and fold the paper concertina-fashion as you progress along it.

Supporting the concertina on a spare roll of paper and brushing the paper on to the ceiling, parallel to the line.

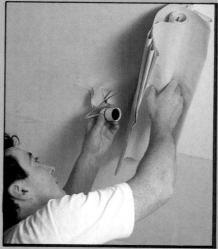

Pulling a light fixture through a cross cut in the paper before trimming round the ceiling rose.

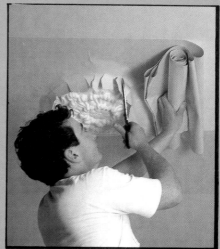

Making a series of cuts round a molded ceiling centerpiece before hanging the rest of the length.

PAINTING WALLS

With the extensive range of paints available to use today, it's extremely easy to decorate an entire house imaginatively and colourfully simply by painting it. Pattern could be introduced with one of the special effects detailed on pages 172–173 and texture with one of the textured effects shown on page 176.

Painting is not difficult and the painting of interior walls one of the simplest tasks. Be prepared to use several coats, though, as many as are necessary to give some depth to the finish.

Equipment

Brushes Several sizes are needed, the ideal width for painting large areas being 100 to 150mm (4 to 6in). Narrower 25 and 50mm (1 and 2in) brushes will be needed for woodwork. Two useful extras are a cutting-in brush, with bristles angled to cut in on narrow window glazing bars, for example, and a radiator brush, for painting behind radiators and pipes and in awkward corners.

Clean brushes immediately after use, in water for latex paint, with white spirit for gloss. A brush can be stored overnight without cleaning by being suspended in water or white spirit; the bristles must not touch the bottom of the container. Shake and wipe dry before use the following day.

Rollers Come in different sizes, including one for painting behind radiators, and different fabrics. They are often interchangeable. They are quicker on large areas than brushes, often giving a better finish, but use more paint and tend to spatter. Foam-covered rollers are the cheapest; they are also the worst spatterers. Cleaning is more difficult than with brushes and cleaning oil-based paint from a foam roller is probably not worth the trouble. The tray also has to be cleaned. To prevent it rusting, grease it lightly before storage but wash well before future use. Gadgets designed for cleaning rollers thoroughly and without mess are available and may be worth the investment where you're doing a lot of painting.

Paint pads Comprising a pile stuck to a foam back, pads don't spatter and give a good smooth finish. Various sizes are available, plus extension handles and replacement heads. Pads are good on textured papers and woven surfaces.

Paint kettle Useful when doing a lot of painting. An old paint can with a handle will do; fix a strip of wire across it against which to wipe the brush.

Ladders Two step-ladders with a scaffold plank between are the ideal arrangement when painting up high, as it avoids having to go up and down the ladder all the time. Hop-ups are also very useful. Remember that such equipment can be rented.

Using and Storing Paint

Coverage is given in square feet and varies between manufacturers. To find the quantity needed, multiply the height of the room by the perimeter measurement (in feet). Make deductions for doors and windows if large.

Stir all liquid paints well before use. Turning the can upside down for some hours will help redistribute the paint particles. If a skin has formed, never mix this in. Cut round it to remove it and strain the paint through stocking fabric to rid it of solid bits.

An innovation in paint storage and packaging is the paint box — like the familiar wine boxes — where paint is always on tap in a sealed container, meaning skin won't form and therefore less wastage.

OPTIONS

TYPES OF PAINT FOR INDOOR USE

Latex Paint

Latex paint comprises particles of synthetic resin — acrylic or vinyl — mixed with pigment (which gives the paint its colour) suspended in water. When the water evaporates a film forms on the surface, which is permeable, allowing moisture to pass through.

Quick-drying, latex is also easy to apply (and wash off brushes and equipment) to interior walls and ceilings and a number of materials — plaster, gypsumboard, wood, synthetic boards, brick and cement render. Two finishes are available: flat and satin (semi-gloss) both of which are tough, hardwearing and easy to clean (especially the latter). The flat finish is better on surfaces that have been filled and repaired, as the non-shiny finish helps to conceal irregularities.

Non-drip thixotropic latex combines good one-coat coverage, excellent spreadability and largely splash-free application.

Solid latex in white and tinted tones offers non-drip, non-spatter application by roller or brush, making it ideal for use on ceilings or where you can't (or don't want to) remove a floorcovering but don't trust your ability to avoid splashes and drips.

Latex paints can be thinned with water as a priming coat for porous surfaces, such as new plaster. Unlike gloss (see below) latex does not emit the same unpleasant smell when drying.

Gloss Enamel paint

Solvent-based (oil) paints comprise pigment, binder (which makes it stick to the surface you're painting and resists damp), and a drier to speed up the rate at which the paint dries. These ingredients are suspended in a solvent or 'thinner' such as white spirit. A compatible oil-based undercoat is needed as a flat, obliterating matt base for the shiny top coat (which dries to give a water-resistant finish that's durable enough to withstand day-to-day knocks). Enamel paint is commonly used for woodwork and isn't really suitable for decorating walls. Non-drip thixotropic enamel needs no undercoat and, applied thickly, gives better coverage; only one coat may be needed. It avoids the problems of runs and drips that can occur with liquid enamel. There's a wide selection of colours and tints to choose from.

Eggshell/Semi Gloss

If a floss-type finish is required on walls, this resin-based paint is the one to choose. It's steam resistant, like enamel and therefore particularly suited to use in kitchens and bathrooms. It can be used on both walls, ceilings and woodwork.

Textured Paint

Extremely efficient in masking general unevenness in a wall or ceiling surface, or a mass of hairline cracks, textured paint comes in two types: ready-mixed and powder form. The former needs no over-painting and is available in a range of colours.

The powder form has to be mixed with water and comes in white only; it's designed to be painted over. Both types can be applied using a short pile or foam roller or paintbrush for a random effect, or you can impress it with a variety of interesting patterns (see page 176).

It's important to work in good light, preferably natural, to ensure even coverage of the paint. If you have to work in artificial light, remove the shade and use a high-wattage bulb.

In all rooms, paint the ceiling first. If using two stepladders and a scaffold board, set these up across the window wall. With a single ladder, set this up at one end of the window wall.

Using a Brush

Apply the paint with a wide 100 to 150mm (4 to 6in) brush: dip only the first third of the bristles into the paint and wipe off excess on the edge of the kettle. Work across the ceiling, back from the window, in strips 600mm (2ft) wide. Turn the brush on its edge to paint a band round the edge of the ceiling, working right into the wall. The overlap will either be covered by paint on the wall or by wallpaper. Then turn the brush full face and proceed to paint in strips. When you're applying latex, you're not governed by a strict painting pattern, as it does not readily form solid lines.

Using a roller

A paint roller will speed the operation considerably, which is always welcome, as painting a ceiling is tiring.

Paint a band around the room using a brush: the roller cannot reach into the ceiling/wall angle. To avoid spatters, load the roller with paint and remove the excess by rolling it on the ribbed end of the tray, out of the paint. Keep the roller close to the surface all the time and apply the paint in criss-cross strokes, picking up the wet edges of adjoining

Using a compressed-gas-powered paint roller; thinned paint in the canister is fed to the roller by a carbon dioxide capsule in the lid.

star shapes formed to coat the whole area. 'Lay off' by rolling in one direction, parallel to one wall, in very light strokes.

Use a brush on any moldings, and use a brush to apply paint around them.

Walls

If you're using two ladders and a scaffold board, work in bands across the room, from the top of the wall to the bottom. If using only one ladder, work in strips down each wall. Keep the strips about 450mm (18in) wide in order not to lean out dangerously from the ladder. Don't keep the edges of the strips straight or they will be more difficult to blend.

Never leave painting a wall incomplete: the paint will dry and it will be obvious where it was taken up again by a hard ridge. If you're using more than one can of paint, stir the second can thoroughly and mix some of it in the paint kettle with the remains of the first can. There should not be an obvious variation in colour but any minor difference will be minimized.

After cutting in at the wall/ceiling angle with a small brush, brushing in horizontal bands working from the top downwards.

After cutting in at corners with a small brush, applying paint with a roller; start at a corner, with the handle away from the side wall.

Semi gloss enamel paint needs more careful application than latex. Paint it on in downward strokes and lay off in light strokes, without reloading the brush with paint, horizontally. Always lay off from one strip to the next carefully to ensure even coverage.

As with painting ceilings, a roller is speedy on walls, except where textured paint has been used previously. When using a brush on such surfaces, it will be necessary to stipple the paint into the deep indentations.

Spray Painting

For exceptional swiftness when painting walls, you'll find a spray gun supreme. Guns can be bought or hired, are either electrically-powered or work by pump action and can be used with latex or gloss paints.

What slows the spraying down is the need to mask off anything not to be painted with plastic. This is why it's only worth considering spraying on large areas: you'll have to mask off the base boards and floor, taping the sheets down with masking tape. The same must be done with switches, sockets and

Covering the horizontal strokes at the top of the wall with vertical strokes, before the paint dries, to ensure good coverage.

Overlapping with criss-cross strips; paint 1 sq m (10sq ft) at a time and make angled strokes off the edges to start the next patch.

light fixtures. Newspaper around the floor close to the walls (over the polythene) will soak up any flying spray.

Apply the paint in horizontal bands but spray the two sides of an interior corner separately; mouldings and external corners should be given an initial coat then painted again with the whole wall for sufficient depth of colour. For an even coverage, keep the nozzle at right angles to the wall, 150mm to 200mm (6 to 8in) away, and don't swing it from side to side.

After cutting in round the edges of a ceiling, covering the area with diagonal strokes in alternate directions.

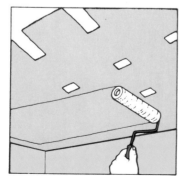

Finishing the ceiling by working towards the window with straight strokes of the roller parallel to the side wall.

Making horizontal sweeps with an electric sprayer before following up with vertical sweeps; adjust for even coverage without splutter.

SPECIAL PAINT EFFECTS

There are numerous patterned effects that can be created with paint. Basically, they all involve using one or more colors on top of another. The overall effect is determined entirely by the choice of colors. Combining several shades of the same color or closely related pastels leads to a soft, gentle finishing. Using the same painting technique but choosing contrasting bold colors will create a more dramatic finish.

Sponging On

This is the simplest of techniques, creating a speckled effect. Two or more colors can be used. Having applied a solid base coat of color to the entire surface, the other colors are dabbed on to it, using a natural sponge. The base coat will always be the dominant color.

The base coat can be either latex or semi gloss. Using flat latex produces the softest build up of color, but enamel is preferable in a bathroom. Allow to dry for 24 hours.

The paint to be sponged on can be used as it is or thinned for a more delicate, translucent effect. Thin latex with water, oil based semi gloss with white spirit, 50:50 to start with, adding more thinners if preferred.

Spoon a little of the paint into a bowl. Dampen the sponge with water and squeeze it out. Press the flat side into the paint to absorb most of it. Test the effect on a piece of lining paper. Place the sponge on it. The impression will not be very effective at this point but as the paint is dabbed off, a speckled effect will appear.

Now move to the prepared wall. Dab the sponge on, being careful not to skid across the surface. The speckled look will lessen as the paint runs out. Refill the sponge with paint, test as before and continue. When the wall/room is finished, leave the sponged-on color to dry for 24 hours. A second color can be sponged on in exactly the same way after this time.

Try to apply the second color so that it fills the gaps between the first set of sponge marks, slightly overlapping to create a random effect.

If it appears that too much color has been sponged on, this is easily remedied by sponging some of the base color over the sponged color when it has dried.

Ragging On

This looks particularly effective when a dark color is ragged on to a lighter base coat. The technique is much the same as sponging on but the result, a crinkled look, is more like that achieved with rag rolling (see page 174). Using a rag is not quite so easy as using a sponge.

Allow the base coat to dry. Dilute the color to be ragged on, if you prefer, and spoon some into a bowl. Testing the impression created by the rag in order to gain the desired effect is the most important stage of the operation.

Crumple up a piece of rag. Dab it into the paint until it is fairly saturated then press on to a piece of lining paper. If you don't like the pattern bunch up the rag again and see what impressions can be made.

When you're happy with the pattern, and the paint has been dabbed off to create the required crinkled look, press the rag gently on the wall. Raise your hand from the wall, turn it slightly and press the rag on to an adjoining area. The spaces between pressings should be kept fairly even.

As the paint runs out, the impression will fade. Refill the rag with paint, keeping it bunched as it is to continue the same print or crumpling again for a more random effect. As with sponging on, too much sponged color can be concealed by ragging on a little of the base color.

Dragging

Dragging is a popular treatment for woodwork as well as walls, and is one of the paint effects that is best achieved by two people working together. Latex or semi gloss enamel can be used on walls, semi gloss only on woodwork.

The effect is created by painting a thin glaze of color over a base coat then using a dry brush to drag off this color, allowing the base color to show through: the result is finely graduating lines. They can be dragged vertically or horizontally, even one on top of the other, but with woodwork the dragging looks better when it follows the grain of the wood.

Dilute the color to be dragged at least 50:50. Mix enough to drag a complete wall. Mix any remainder into the next batch. Don't try to join two batches in the middle of one wall.

The work progresses in strips about 600mm (2ft) wide, one person brushing on the color, the second person dragging it off while it's still wet (remember that latex dries more quickly than

Ragging on; when the base coat is dry, dab on the covering coat at regular intervals with a crumpled rag.

enamels).

Brush the paint on thinly and evenly, so that it completely covers the base colour. When a complete strip has been painted, one person moves on to paint the second while the other drags the first strip.

Hold the dragging brush (a proper one is expensive — a long-bristled wide brush will do) firmly and draw it steadily down through the wet paint. Your touch should be firm but light, not hard like scrubbing. Wipe the brush on rags after two or three strokes so that it does not become so loaded with paint that it puts it on rather than taking it off. Relax the grip at the end of a stroke — at the bottom of the wall, round light switches and other obstacles as this is where paint tends to build up.

The edge of each strip of paint being brushed on must remain wet if the strip

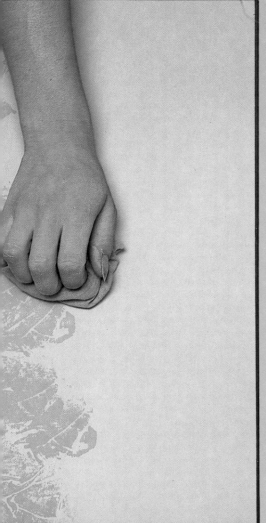

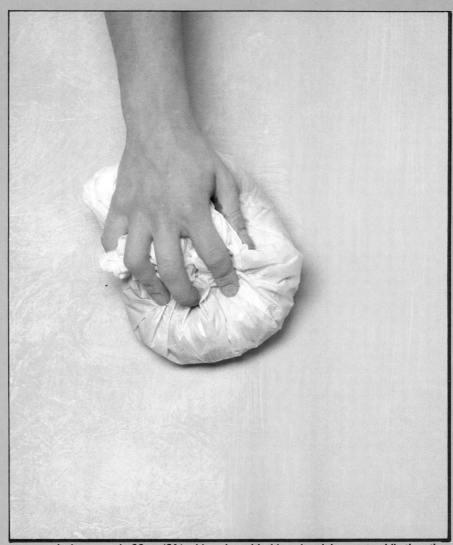

Bag graining is best carried out by two people; one covers the base coat in 60cm (2ft) wide strips with thinned graining coat, while the other presses a plastic bag, half filled with rags, into overlapping areas of the wet paint. Rag rolling; after coating the base coat with thinned latex paint, roll the rag into a sausage shape and, wearing rubber gloves, roll it in overlapping strips over the surface. Re-roll the rag when it becomes soaked with paint.

next to it is to merge properly. Any build up of drying paint between strips will be obvious and will ruin the delicate effect. The painter should start applying the second strip while the dragger works on the first; the dragger follows the painter along the wall.

It may not be necessary to have two people working on woodwork as the area to be covered is not so large and enamels do not dry as quickly as latex paint.

Bag Graining

This crushed velvet type of finish using two colors is best achieved with two people working in tandem. The graining coat is diluted as for dragging (again, latex or enamel) and a sufficient quantity must always be mixed for a wall: (a slight variation in color between walls will not show but on one wall it will).

The bag for the graining is simply a plastic bag, half-filled with rags and secured by a knot. Paint on the diluted graining coat exactly as for dragging, in strips about 600mm (2ft) wide, thinly and evenly to cover the base coat.

The person doing the graining can start work on the top half of the first strip while the painter works on the bottom half. There'll be little danger of paint drying too quickly if this rhythm is maintained.

Press the graining bag on to the surface, lift and place on an adjoining area. Wipe excess paint off the bag. Overlap the bag impressions slightly to create the crushed and crinkled impression. If the grained coat of paint appears too dominant, go over it again with the bag, continually wiping off the excess paint with a rag.

Sponging Off

This is identical to bag graining except that the paint is sponged away with a natural sponge rather than grained with a bag of rags. See Bag Graining above for details.

Rag Rolling

A particularly attractive and impressive finish for walls, although it is more difficult to apply. Satin enamel is best for this, resulting in a wrinkled effect with a soft sheen rather like silk. The patterning is more marked than that achieved with the other techniques and there's greater surface variety.

The process is similar to bag graining. The top coat of color (diluted with white spirit) is painted over the base coat in strips 600mm (2ft) wide by one person, then rolled off with a bunched up rag by the second person. Make sure there's a good supply of rags cut to about 300mm (1ft) square before starting work.

Roll the rag into a sausage shape about 150mm (6in) wide. Hold between two hands (wear rubber gloves), then roll up the painted strip, lifting off the paint to reveal the base coat. When the rag becomes paint-soaked, re-roll it to produce a clean surface or use a new rag.

Overlap the vertically-rolled 150mm (6in) strips slightly. Leave an edge of about 50mm (2in) next to the second strip of paint being applied so that the rag rolling can run right up the join, making the two painted areas merge completely.

Always apply the top coat of paint with vertical strokes from the top to the bottom of the wall and rag-roll the paint off working from the base board upward.

Marbling

True marbling is a highly skilled effect and amateurs can really only aim for the faster impressionistic finish, which still imitates the broken color finish of the real thing. Study some examples before starting, to see how the veins interlink and change direction. The process involves several stages and some specialist equipment is necessary: an artist's brush and artist's oil colors in raw umber and black. Use enamel paint for the base colors.

First, a diluted glaze of white enamel tinted with a little black artist's paint is applied over a base coat of white and sponged off (see Sponging Off and Bag Graining for details). Allow to dry thoroughly.

Apply veins to this surface by painting on, with an artist's brush, strokes of grey-brown color (a mix of black and raw umber). The paint strokes should be fidgety and form a pattern of diagonals, one stroke meeting another. Sponge lightly to remove excess paint and soften the lines by stroking a paintbrush or a feather along them. Mix up a darker grey and paint in some fine darker veins, joining them to the originals and, again, working diagonally. Sponge the veins to soften them and agitate the sponge on the areas between the veins to imitate the spots of color in real marble.

Soften the whole effect again with a dry paintbrush, drawing it along each diagonal. Repeat until the effect is suitably softened.

Leave the surface to dry and then paint in some veins and blotches of diluted white satin enamel paint. For a richer effect, repeat the veining with a second color that can be found in real marble.

To achieve a sheen like real marble, varnish with matt or satin coat varnish. When dry, sprinkle over French chalk and rub off with a duster.

Stencilling

A patterned paint effect for walls, floors and furniture, the designs should be kept simple, combining two or more basic patterns for a more intricate effect. Two or three colors is also the best combination, applied on a neutral background.

Ready-made stencils can be bought

Marbling; after painting glaze and light veins over the base coat, add darker veins before softening with a dry brush.

from artist's suppliers and some decorator's merchants. Originals can be cut very easily by drawing the design on ordinary paper and tracing it on to acetate paper. This is the best stencil material to use as it can be wiped clean and used many times. Use a craft knife for the actual cutting. If the stencil is to be used over a large area, it's sensible to cut several at the same time. They can then be compared to make sure they have been identicallly cut.

If several stencils form part of the pattern, each being painted a different color, cut them all and line them up in advance, making holes which can be matched up when they are put on the wall.

Mark guidelines for the width and height of the stencil on the wall in chalk so that as the stencil is moved along the wall it matches the previous pattern

Trick

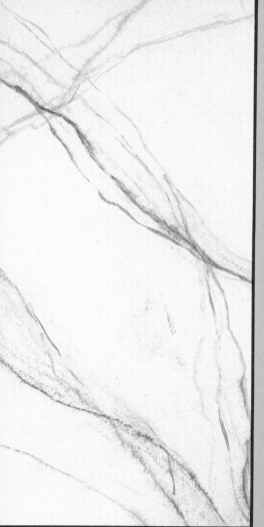

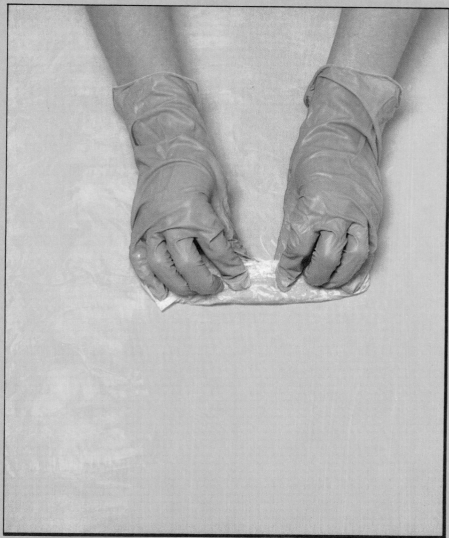

(Above right) Rag rolling; after coating the base coat with diluted eggshell paint, roll the rag into a sausage shape and, wearing rubber gloves, roll it in overlapping strips over the surface. Re-roll the rag when it becomes soaked with paint. (Below) Stencilling; buy ready-made stencils or cut them from acetate sheet, and fix them to the surface with masking tape. Apply the paint with a stippling motion using a stencilling brush which has a broad, flat end for even coverage.

exactly. Fix it in position with masking tape. Apply the paint with a special stencil brush, stippling it through the holes in the stencil card. Leave to harden for a few minutes, then release the card and place it in the next position. Continue until this stencil is complete. Allow to dry completely before using the second stencil and the second color on top, matching it up by the holes as was done when the stencils were originally cut. Color in this stencil in exactly the same way as the first.

Stencilling is best carried out with enamel paint, as it dries quickly. However, on floors or furniture some protection will be necessary. When the paint is completely dry, use polyurethane varnish, in several coats on floors, and flat, satin coat or high gloss finish as preferred.

USING TEXTURED PAINT

After applying textured paint, creating swirls in the surface with a comb.

Creating a block pattern with a piece of batten; sand off sharp points when dry.

Forming a regular diamond pattern with a contoured roller.

Walls and ceilings that are in bad condition, that is, they have been prepared properly but are covered with cracks and holes that have been filled and the surface is impossible to make perfectly smooth, are best covered with a textured finish. Textured paint is easy to apply and is much quicker to use than textured paper. Its only drawback is that it is difficult to strip, should you fancy a change in the future. But used judiciously, this should not be necessary and will not, therefore, be a problem.

Surfaces to be textured must be sound. Although the paint conceals defects very efficiently it will not adhere to unstable surfaces, to paper or to polystyrene tiles. It cannot be used to cover areas that should be replastered and a recommended stabilizing primer should be used on porous or powdery backings. If being applied over paintwork, this should be sanded down to provide a key.

If the background color is very deep. it is a good idea to paint on one coat of white before using the textured paint. This, of course, is not necessary if the textured paint is to be painted anyway. It can be used directly on ceramic tiles if the grout lines are filled in and a PVA adhesive primer applied first.

The paint does tend to spatter and, apart from protective clothing, goggles and a facemask are advised. When painting ceilings, a bath cap to protect the hair may look funny but will not come amiss.

Tools for Patterning

Textured paint is not just a cover-up; it can be patterned in several ways with accessories or home-made tools and

With a coarse foam roller, creating an overall stippled effect.

may be preferred to a flat finish. Large-toothed combs cut from a piece of firm plastic (an old ice cream carton, for example) can be swept over the wall to create swirling designs or used in short, straight lines to create structured squares. The teeth could be cut raggedly for a random effect or evenly for a measured pattern effect.

A sponge in a plastic bag pressed onto the wet paint will create small swirls. The accessory tools available include a swirlbrush and patterned rollers with diagonal, diamond and bark-effect designs cut in their surface.

Painting

Of the two types of textured paint available, the powdered version dries too slowly for patterning, but the ready-mixed variety can also be patterned

successfully and needs no overpainting.

Use either a roller (not a patterned one) or a large distemper brush to apply the paint. As only one coat is used it must be thick enough to conceal any defects and provide a good thick base for patterning. Work in bands up and down the wall (across the ceiling from the window backwards) until the whole surface is covered. Pattern this area before painting the next wall.

Patterning

There will usually be plenty of time to pattern the paint before it dries but check the manufacturer's instructions. If in doubt, and a structured, more detailed pattern is planned, pattern each strip as you finish painting, being careful to match the pattern from strip to strip.

Random patterns do not need this consideration and are quick to effect. In fact, applying the paint with a plain foam-covered roller creates a small stipple effect and needs no patterning. Brush strokes are usually too random and need some smoothing out with a roller or patterning tool.

When the paint has dried, knock off any sharp points, especially on walls. Sand to smooth slightly if still sharp enough to hurt someone brushing against the wall.

Maintenance

The powdered textured paint finish will need painting. Both this finish and the ready-mixed variety are easily maintained by repainting. The surface should be cleaned of dust and dirt by detergent and water applied with a paintbrush.

Getting a good smooth finish with gloss, the paint normally reserved for woodwork, is much more difficult than with latex. Because latex is absorbent, the brush strokes will always merge and blend to nothingness; not so with oil-based gloss. If the results are not to be disappointing, great care must be taken over the way the paint is applied.

Having followed the instructions as to the preparation of woodwork (see page 157), the surface should be sound, smooth, primed and undercoated ready for painting. Special undercoats may be recommended with certain gloss colors, so check the paint chart or the can. One coat of primer and one of undercoat is normally followed by two coats of gloss.

Doors

The entire door must be painted in one session. Wipe down to remove dust immediately beforehand and arrange newspaper on the floor to catch any drips.

Panelled doors. There is a sequence that must be followed when painting panelled doors, affected slightly by whether it opens towards or away from the painter. Opening towards the painter, the top edge and opening edge should be painted first; away from the painter, the hinged edge is painted first. From then on, the sequence is the same.

Paint the mouldings and the panels in the top of the door then those at the bottom. Follow these with the central vertical section and the three horizontal cross sections (top, middle, bottom). Finally, paint the two outer vertical sections. When the door itself has been finished, move on to the frame and architrave.

The paint cover on the closing edges and the mouldings should be kept thin as it is easier for paint to accumulate on these narrow areas and for runs to occur.

Flush doors. Quick confident painting is the answer. Divide the door mentally into four. Paint the top two sections first, then the bottom two. Speed is essential to avoid a hard edge forming

Applying enamel paint along the grain of a panelled door; blend together adjacent strokes as you proceed across the door.

After completing the horizontal strokes, painting across the grain with a loaded brush to ensure full and even coverage.

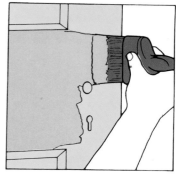
Painting towards the edge of the door to prevent paint from being scraped on to the edge and forming a ridge at the corner.

between the sections as the paint dries. The correct application of paint to large flat areas like the flush doors is particularly important (see below).

Glazed doors. The glass should be protected from the paint. Either stick masking tape around the edge or use lengths of double-sided tape with newspaper stuck on top to cover all the glass. Don't leave either tape too long or it will be difficult to remove, especially if the sun has been shining on to the glass from behind.

Using Liquid Gloss

The paint shouldn't just be slapped on. There's a sequence of laying on, cross-brushing, smoothing out and laying off. First of all, stir the paint using a length of wood to blend in the solvent.

The brush should not be heavily loaded. Holding the brush in a pencil grip — fingers on the ferrule (metal band), thumb hooked behind the stem — dip about one-third of the

length of the bristles into the paint. Press the brush against the wire over the paint kettle or can to remove the excess. Lay on the paint with vertical strokes.

Without reloading the brush, cross-brush the adjoining section. Smooth the two sections together, again with horizontal strokes and without reloading the brush. Lay off with light vertical strokes, drawing the brush upwards away from the wet edge.

Move down the door and follow the same sequence, laying off the paint into the top section. When painting wood, always lay off the paint in the direction of the grain.

Sags and runs are caused by an overloaded brush or the paint being applied unevenly and not cross-brushed, normally by painters in a hurry. After the first coat, when the paint is completely dry, smooth down the faults with fine glasspaper. A second coat of gloss will cover these areas completely. To ensure a really smooth finish and good adhesion between coats of

paint, give a light key to the entire surface with fine glasspaper and wipe down to remove dust and grit after each coat, using a tacky rag. Don't attempt this until the paint is thoroughly dry. Check the paint can for the manufacturer's instructions on drying times.

Using Non-Drip Gloss

This paint has a thick consistency, like jelly, and needs no brushing out. Load the brush. Paint with vertical strokes; do not cross brush and do not try to make the paint spread. The paint is designed to be painted on thickly and only one coat should be necessary. It will not drip from the brush and, although the brush strokes show alarmingly while the paint is wet, they disperse to a smooth finish. This type of paint is obviously useful when painting overhead. You don't need to stir non-drip paint, but if the paint shows signs of the solvent separating, stir it to blend it in again, but leave the paint until it has assumed its jelly-like consistency again.

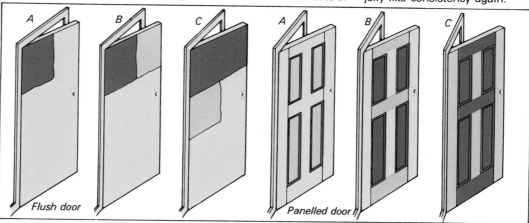
Paint a flush door is a series of squares, laying off each one as it is completed and blending them together. Start with the moldings and panels of a panelled door, then paint the horizontal rails, outer rails and edge.

WINDOWS

There will be no large flat expanses of paint here, so achieving a smooth finish is rather easier. However, as there are a lot of narrow edges and moldings where paint can accumulate, be particularly careful not to overload the brush.

The glass should either be masked with masking tape or double-sided tape and newspaper. Alternatively, buy a metal or plastic paint shield or cut one from cardboard: hold close against the rebate where it meets the glass as you apply the paint. Carry the paint film onto the glass by about 3mm (⅛in) so a watertight seal is formed.

If spots of paint do get on to the glass, leave them to dry and then scrape off with a razor blade: wiping wet paint will simply cause smears.

As with doors there's a sequence to follow for painting each type of window.

Sash windows Open the window, raising the lower sash almost to the top and bringing the upper sash as far down as possible. Paint as much of the upper sash as is now accessible and the bottom edge (that closes down on the frame) of the lower sash. Then move to the top of the window and paint the soffit and 50 to 75mm (2 to 3in) of the outside runner on each side, being careful not to get paint on the sash cords.

Reverse the position of the sashes. Paint 50 to 75mm (2 to 3in) down the inside runners at the top and the same distance up both inside and outside runners at the bottom. There's no need to paint the full length of the runners as they're protected by the tight fit of the sashes. They only need the paint at top and bottom for protection when the window is opened.

Paint the rebates next, applying a thin coat with a cutting-in brush and masking or shielding the glass. The cross bars and stiles come next followed by the frame and the architrave.

Casement windows Fasten the window open slightly. The sequence of painting is much the same as for sash windows. Paint all the rebates and inside edges, which close against the frame, first, protecting the glass from the paint. Move on to the cross bars and the cross rails.

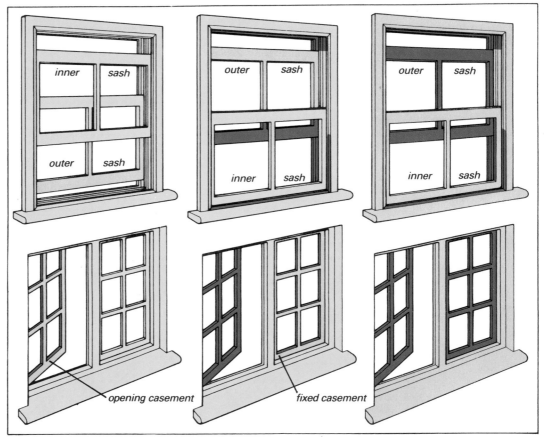

Sequence for painting sash windows (top): with inner sash raised and outer sash lowered, paint outer sash meeting rail, part of vertical rails, inner sash bottom edge, soffit, outer runners; reverse positions and paint runners, rebates, cross bars, stiles, frame and architrave. Painting casement window (bottom): paint rebates, inside edge, cross bars, cross rails, hanging stile, meeting stile, frame and architrave.

Paint the hanging stile next and then the meeting stile. Finally paint frame and architrave.

Pivot windows If using the same color and paint finish inside and out paint both sides at the same time. Open the window as far as it will go in order to paint the outside first. Paint the bottom half, which will be pivoted out slightly at the top, first. Don't forget the edges and top and bottom, as this is where the weather will penetrate. Then paint the top half of the outside which will be pivoted inward and easy to reach. Bring the window back to a semi-closed position in order to paint the inside.

Stairs

Stairs require the same careful preparation as doors and windows. Worn woodwork, on the treads, for example, is better filled with exterior-grade filler as this will stand up well to the heavy wear. Paint the stairs in the following sequence: banisters, handrail, skirting and treads.

DECORATOR'S

Trick

GRAINING WOOD

The purpose of graining is to make a plain surface look like a piece of wood. The decorative element is the important thing with graining at this level, not producing a perfect copy of nature.

Color

The effect is created by spreading a colored transparent glaze over a solid base color then brushing out the glaze to acquire graining and knots.

Two shades of color look better in combination than contrasting colors, but they need not be brown. For a truly dramatic and original effect choose a color that fits the decorative scheme of the room but will stand out: shades of grey in a basically white or cream room; deep raspberry in a room of pastel pink. Green, blue, yellow, red can all look spectacular in the right setting.

The lighter of the two shades should form the base, as this will be the dominant color; the deeper shade, used to paint in the wood grain and knots, will never then appear too heavy.

Materials

The base color must have a non-porous finish so that the glaze can be worked on without being absorbed into the base. Satin Enamel paint, with its mid-sheen finish, is ideal; latex can be used but should be sealed with satincoat varnish. The transparent glaze, sometimes called 'scumble glaze', can be brought ready-mixed but it has to be colored: artists' oil colors offer the widest range of colors. It can be used like this but a subtler effect will be created if the glaze is diluted with white spirit and it will retain its slight sheen.

Method

The base coat must be completely dry. Brush on the glaze with a small decorator's brush. Use either an old decorators' brush with clumps of bristles cut away or a comb made from plastic or cardboard with unevenly spaced teeth to mark the grain.

Drag the brush or comb along the surface, keeping a loose wrist, so as to achieve gently rippling lines rather than dead straight ones. Soften the grain by stroking the surface with a soft-bristled brush, following the line of the grain.

Paint in the heartwood, joining the graining and curving it, using an artists' brush. Having a piece of wood to copy will make this stage much easier. Make knots in the 'wood' by dipping a rag-covered finger into the glaze and then pressing it to the surface, turning it at the same time.

Applying the base coat of latex paint to the surface.

When the base coat is dry, applying the colored glaze with a small decorators' brush.

Marking the grain in the glaze with a cardboard comb.

Softening the grain by brushing lightly with a soft bristle brush.

Painting in the heartwood with a fine artists' brush.

Making knots with a rag-covered finger dipped in glaze.

SANDING FLOORS

One of the greatest expenses in decorating a house is the carpeting. If it is to give an efficient service it must be good quality but, by the time the entire floor area has been measured and the quality of carpet needed calculated, the financial outlay can sound alarming.

If the figure you arrive at is prohibitive, consider re-using carpet brought from a previous home (full details for fitting carpet are given on pages 186 to 188). Some rooms may be better without carpet — the obvious example being the kitchen, although there are special carpets for this very purpose.

There are plenty of other floorcoverings that can be used but the alternative, which can really cut the cost and look as good, if not better than a fully-fitted carpet, is the soft sheen of floorboards that have been sanded and sealed. This treatment is in keeping with any age or style of property and costs no more than the rental of the sander, the abrasive papers and the floor seal.

The final flourish can be provided by a colorful rug, which can be anything from a genuine Persian (expense again) to a plain-coloured square bought cheaply at a carpet warehouse.

Preparing the Floor

Sanding floors is one of the messiest of all decorating tasks and should be done before anything else. The dust gets everywhere, however carefully you prepare the room in advance. It's also very noisy, so a warning to neighbours never goes amiss, especially if windows are to be left open.

Having emptied the room of absolutely everything, go over the floor board by board to see if any repair work is called for and to prepare the surface for sanding. It may be necessary to renew an entire board which has been badly damaged (details for replacing the floorboards are given on page 45).

Nail heads Any nail and screw heads left sticking up above the surface of the boards will rip the abrasive papers. This is obviously not only a waste of money but also an annoying interruption, as the paper will have to be changed. Using a hammer and nail punch, sink all exposed nailheads to about 3mm (⅛in) below the surface of the board. Any old tacks left over from a previous floorcovering should be removed with pincers.

Some boards may be secured with screws: remove these and increase the depth of their countersink holes then replace them.

Loose Board If punching down the nails has no effect, drive an extra nail into each joist. If the board is beginning to split, screw it down rather than nailing it, with a countersunk screw.

Warped Board This can be a problem with square-edged boards, where the edge of one board is sticking up higher than the one next to it. Don't rely on the sander to flatten it but plane it smooth, following the grain of the wood. If a board is particularly badly warped, it may be possible to lift it and turn if over, using extra nails to help flatten it to match those on either side.

Knots These can stand proud of the surface, especially in old boards. Either plane to be level or chisel off the excess. Loose knots may be stuck back in using PVA woodworking adhesive.

Gaps between boards These are not only unslightly, but extremely draughty with square-edged boards. In most cases the gaps can be filled but in an older property, where the gaps have developed over the years and are now wide and appear between virtually every board, re-laying could be the solution (see page 45).

There are several methods for filling gaps, according to their size. Small gaps can be filled with a wood filler, which will expand with the boards. Work it well down into the cracks but leave it standing proud of the boards. When it is hard, sand it level and smooth. Choose a filler that's close in color to that of the boards.

Another filler for cracks is a home-made papier-maché, based on newspaper and wallpaper paste. Shred the paper and leave it in a weak solution of wallpaper paste (like a size) until it is well-soaked and porridge-like. Press it into the

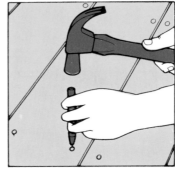

Punching nail heads well below the surface of the boards as any left protruding will tear the abrasive sheet on the machine.

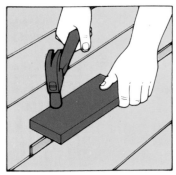

Filling gaps between boards with fillets of wood glued and hammered into place; plane flush with the boards before sanding.

Starting the sander with the drum held above the level of the floor by tilting the machine backwards on to its wheels.

Making the first pass, diagonally to the boards; continue parallel to the first pass until most of the floor has been covered.

Sanding across the ends of the boards; allow the machine to pull you forwards then drag it backwards for a second pass.

Using a scraper or shavehook to scrape stubborn areas at the edges; any low areas which the machine has missed must be sanded by hand.

Vacuuming the floor clean after allowing plenty of time for the dust to settle; use a crevice nozzle between boards.

Applying a sealing coat of varnish; dilute it 3 parts varnish to 1 part white spirits and apply with a clean lint-free cloth.

Fitting a sheet of coarse abrasive paper to the drum; ensure that it is taut on the drum before screwing down the clamping bar.

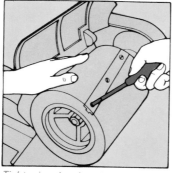

Tightening the clamping bar screws; make sure that they are fully home otherwise they will cause extensive damage to the floor surface.

Making the second pass at right-angles to the first one; the sanding will flatten out any warped or twisted boards.

Making the final pass parallel to the boards; repeat the process with medium and fine grades of abrasive, depending on the surface.

Changing the abrasive disc; unplug the machine, turn it upside down and remove the locknut and washer; replace in reverse order.

Using a heavy-duty disc sander to level areas which are inaccessible to the drum sander; again use decreasingly coarse abrasives.

Applying the sealing coat with a long-handled roller is easier over large areas; wear socks or clean indoor shoes.

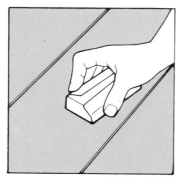

Between coats, sanding with medium sandpaper to provide a key for the next coat; wipe clean with a cloth dampened with white spirits.

cracks with a filling knife and level it off while still wet.

If the gaps are rather more than cracks, any filler that is inserted will simply fall through. If this happens, cut narrow fillets of wood to fit, glue each side then hammer them into place; allow them to stand slightly proud of the surrounding boards then plane them level.

Stripping Old Varnish In some older properties, where rugs were used, the boards around the edge of the room were coated with a varnish stain, or thick wax polish. Both simply clog up the sanding disk and must be stripped first. Neither reacts well to heat, simply becoming sticky, so they're best stripped chemically.

Daub on the stripper liberally and leave it to do its work, then scrape off with a shave hook, flat scraper or wire wool. The sander can cope with the stain left by such coatings, so all traces do not have to be removed, just the thick gummy surface.

Sanding the Floor

Sanding machines can be rented from tool stores. A drum sander is used for the main area of the floor, a heavy-duty disc sander for the edges. The rental company will supply different grades of abrasive sheets — coarse, medium and fine — and charge for them as used.

As the rented equipment costs money, do all the preparatory work in advance so that the machines can go straight into use and be returned as soon as possible. To speed the operation, one person should sand the main floor area, the other the edges. As well as the sanding equipment a dry hook scraper is useful to get right up to the base board beneath radiators and into corners where the disc sander cannot go.

Protecting the House

Most of the dust is collected into the bags on the sanding machines but a large amount still manages to coat every surface in the room. Protective gauze facemasks can be bought and are well worth while. If it's possible to seal the door with masking tape while doing the sanding to protect the rest of the house, do so. Open the window and have a vacuum cleaner handy to periodically suck up the dust.

Drum Sander

Start with the roughest grade abrasive paper — it's commonly held around the drum by a screw-down clamping bar — and sand diagonally across the floor. To start, drape the cable over your shoulder to prevent it becoming entangled in the machine, and tilt the sander so that the drum is raised. Switch on: don't be alarmed at the great noise caused by the whirring drum — it's quite normal!

Slowly lower the drum onto the floor and in the same movement, allow the machine to roll across the room. Keep the machine on the move for even sanding, and always turn it off when stationary, even if only momentarily: if you don't you'll gorge a deep indent in the floor.

Sand again diagonally from the opposite direction, then follow the grain of the wood, running parallel to the boards. Repeat for the medium-grade paper and finish with the finest-grade. The amount of sanding necessary depends on the floor: two sandings may be sufficient on newer boards.

Disc Sander

To use the disc sander, fit an abrasive disc — usually secured with a central bolt — and grasp the two top handles. Stand with legs apart with the sander between and forward. Switch on and run the sander along the edges. It is not easy to get a smooth finish with a sanding disc attachment to an electric drill.

After sanding, allow at least 24 hours for the dust to settle; the air will be heavy with it. Vacuum the room clean; do not sweep it as this will simply raise the dust. Wash down any ledges, door frames and other obstructions so that dust will not fall on to the floor before the sealant has dried.

Trick

DECORATOR'S

VARNISHING WOOD

Applying a sealing coat of thinned varnish on a clean rag along the grain; work backwards towards the door.

When the sealing coat has dried, keying the surface by rubbing lightly with medium sandpaper.

Applying the second coat with a brush, working across the grain, after cleaning off all dust with a tack rag.

If wood is not be painted, it must be protected with another form of sealant, such as varnish. The easiest sealant to apply is a ready-mixed polyurethane varnish and this is commonly used on floors that have been sanded.

Types of Varnish

That most commonly found in Hardware Stores is the ready-mixed, ready to use, polyurethane varnish (some brands are called floor sealers). It often comes in three types of finish: flat, mid-sheen (satincoat) and high gloss. Each is as tough as the other. They are all resistant to stains, heat and scratches. They are all equally easy to apply but the high gloss and satincoat will show up odd bits of dirt and uneven sanding more than the flat finish, just as paint does.

All varnish, even though it is transparent, darkens the wood. Today, though, varnishes can be bought in almost any color, some mixed at the store, as are many paints. They're available in all three finishes and are still transparent so the wood grain shows through.

Some people argue that a better finish is achieved by combining a straightforward wood stain and a clear uncolored polyurethane varnish. The stain penetrates the wood more efficiently and can be wiped down to reveal the wood grain more clearly. However, the colored varnish is obviously labor saving as both jobs are done in one go.

According to the surface being varnished, use a brush or lambswool roller. The varnish should always be applied soon after sanding so that new dirt does not become ingrained.

Brushing out the second coat along the grain; use light strokes of the brush and avoid over-spreading.

Remember that it is much easier to clean brushes with white spirit than it is rollers.

When varnishing a floor, work from the far corners back towards the door. Don't wear shoes as they will simply bring in dirt. Keep a rag handy to wipe away any loose dirt.

Dilute the first coat with white spirit in the ratio 3 parts varnish: 1 part white spirit. Apply this coat with a cloth pad. It will dry quickly, sealing the wood, and the following coat can be applied within hours.

Brush or roll the varnish on across the grain and then smooth out with the grain (if using a roller, fit a handle extension so you can work by standing). Allow at least six hours between unthinned coats. Ideally, each application should be sanded before the next is applied but this quality of finish is not necessary on a

Using a lambswool roller with an extension handle to coat a large floor, working backwards towards the door.

floor.

Use at least three coats on a floor, preferably five for a really tough, resistant finish. A wax polish can be used over the varnish if you prefer. Remember though, that this would have to be completely removed before a new coat of varnish could be applied.

Plastic coating can be used on all interior woodwork, including furniture and floors. It is particularly tough finish, reinforced with melamine. It is like plain polyurethane varnish in that it is clear, has no color in it and comes in the three finishes of flat, satin and gloss.

Once mixed it stays workable for two to three days. It is extremely quick drying and is touch-dry within the hour. Brush on, following the grain of the wood and leave to harden to a heat-resistant finish that will not chip or crack.

Finishes other than varnish can add both color and a shine to wood.

Staining

Wood stains, or dyes as some are called, are available in a huge range of colors, not just shades of brown. They have various uses: all are for application on clean, well-sanded wood only. A natural colored stain is useful in matching new wood to old, perhaps in furniture repairs and also in display floors, where several boards may have had to be renewed. The stain will make the color difference less obvious. A stain in a primary color can enhance an attractive feature.

Not all wood has a naturally attractive finish, especially when it has suffered heavy wear and tear. You may realise on stripping an item of furniture that a simple coat of varnish or polish will not be sufficient to hide its defects. Applying stain can improve the finish by giving added depth in color and distracting the attention from marks that were glaringly obvious before.

Types of stains Stains can be made by mixing colored pigment with water, but the stains and wood dyes most commonly found are mixed and ready to use. They are spirit-based, dry quickly, can be lightened with methylated spirit and are best for use under polish or varnish. Check that the stain is compatible with the finish that is to be applied. This will be confirmed by the manufacturer's instructions for polish or varnish.

Application Always test the color of the stain on an inconspicuous part of the wood: once applied it can't easily be removed. Remember, too, that polish or varnish will darken it further: it's worthwhile making a test strip on scrap wood to familiarize yourself with the various likely effects.

Apply the stain with a soft smooth cloth or brush, to give an even liberal coat, always following the grain. For greater grain definition wipe with a dry cloth, again following the grain, while the stain is still wet. Only one coat is needed; avoid going over already-applied stain or a

harsh line may show. Work quickly so that the stain does not dry before the entire surface has been covered. Allow to dry for the recommended time then wipe over again with a clean dry cloth before applying the finishing coat of varnish or

Applying wood stain with a cloth; the stain will be absorbed more readily by end grain, giving a darker color.

polish.

Oiling

Oil can be used as a finish on sanded wood, over a stain or over previous oil finishes. Old wax and varnish finishes must be stripped — varnish chemically, wax with white spirit and steel wool. Oils of all types penetrate the wood to seal it and there is no surface film that can be chipped or cracked. Oils, in fact, do three things; prime, seal and finish the wood, all in one go.

Grain filling For a really smooth surface, the grain of the wood can be filled in prior to oiling. Grain filler is mixed with white spirit to form a paste and then rubbed firmly into the wood against the grain. When all the pores are full, leave overnight to harden. The filler can be stained first if necessary. Before oiling, seal the wood with a thinned coat of varnish, allow to dry then sand with flour paper.

Types of Oil. Linseed oil was traditionally used to finish wood, and is still readily available; but takes longer to dry than the brands that now abound and tends to darken.

Teak oil is one proprietary finish which is easier to apply than linseed oil: the wood should be sealed then sanded first.

Remember, though, if you are oiling wood that's naturally oily, greasy or resinous (teak is one example) that you should wipe over the surface with methylated spirit before oiling.

Application Wipe on a liberal coat of oil with a cloth pad. Rub

Wiping on teak oil liberally with a cloth pad before rubbing into the surface with fine steel wool; buff with a soft cloth.

the liquid well into the wood grain with 100–400 grit silicon carbide abrasive paper or 000 grade steel wool, wipe off excess with a clean rag and leave to dry for the recommended time. Repeat the process about three times then buff with a soft cloth to improve the luster. New wood may need several coats of oil before sufficient depth of sheen is achieved. The details with the different proprietary brands regarding drying time and buffing do vary, so always check the instructions on the container at the point of buying. Burn all cloths outdoors after use, as they're highly flammable.

Polishing/Waxing

This is probably the most sympathetic treatment for wood but it does involve more work. Labor is an important ingredient and a good rub will always produce a better shine.

Types of Wax The traditional wax polish always used was beeswax mixed with turpentine, although carnauba, cerestine and paraffin waxer were also popular; with these the addition of turps and beeswax was necessary to achieve a workable material. Today's prepared wax polishes contain silicones and driers. These aid the application, speed the hardening and

produce a tougher finish.

There are several brands of wax polish available but a beeswax polish can be prepared as follows: grate a lump of wax into a roughly equal proportion of pure turpentine in a boil-proof jar or can. Immerse the container in

French polishing; saturate a wad of cotton wool, wrap in a cloth, press out excess, apply a blob of linseed oil and rub in a figure of eight.

a pan of boiling water until it has melted than leave to cool a little, until soft but no longer liquid.

Application Wax polish can be applied direct to the wood but an initial coating of thinned polyurethane varnish will seal the wood, making the finish more durable and a sheen easier to achieve. Sand the seal following the grain of the wood. Polish can also be applied over a previous oil or wax finish.

Modern wax polishes are easy to apply. Use a soft cloth or pad made from cotton wool wrapped in a rag to spread the wax thinly. Leave to dry then use a soft cloth or brush to buff up a shine. According to the brand chosen, drying times will vary and several coats may be needed.

Beeswax polish should be rubbed thinly into the surface with a soft brush (a shoe brush is ideal) or cloth pad. Leave to harden completely; this will be several hours. Rubbing to a shine will be a long slow job and hard work. (The brush will need cleaning frequently as it becomes clogged with polish.) The harder waxes (carnauba, for instance) should be burnished 24 hours after application using steel wool along the grain, then buffed with a cloth. However, there is no other finish to rival the sweet smell and rich gleam of beeswax.

183

FLOORCOVERINGS

More often than not floorcoverings constitute the greatest expense in the decoration of a home. Unlike paint, which can be changed at the touch of a brush, they're expected to give both lasting pleasure and good durability for a number of years. A mistake can be an expensive one; one that has to be lived with and be much regretted.

Although a single covering continuing throughout a house, especially fitted carpet in one color, looks impressive, most householders will take one room at a time. A combination of textures — carpet, wood, hard tile, soft tile — and colors can look equally well thought-out and pleasing. The nature of the sub-floor, solid or wooden may also make different floorcoverings more suitable.

Consider not only durability but also comfort. Cold, hard surfaces are tiring and not gentle on the feet. Carpet tiles, sheet vinyl or cork could be a choice where carpet is impractical but softness is still a virtue. The kitchen, where almost all the work is done standing up and children often play, is one example. Thermoplastic tiles and uncushioned vinyl — which do not have the same 'give' — are better reserved for hallways and other thorough-fares.

Fitted carpet is the obvious choice for bedrooms. Although the wear is not as heavy as that dished out to floorcoverings in rooms that are in use all day, it is very uneven.

A cheap, light-wear carpet will soon show up the track that develops round the bed and and which is hard to avoid. Pastel shades look good in bedrooms but will stay looking good longer if more importance is given to their durability.

Children's bedrooms, in particular, should be viewed rather as living rooms when it comes to choosing a carpet and considerable attention given to the wear quality of the carpet. There are also ranges designed specially for kitchens and for bathrooms where water spillage, cleanliness and condensation are particular problems.

If there is any question of a surface being damp, or not having a waterproof membrane, the choice of floorcovering will be restricted. Thermoplastic vinyl tiles (check the manufacturer's instructions) and quarry tiles can be used here.

OPTIONS

TYPES OF FLOORCOVERING

Carpet

The classification of carpets is vast and fraught with confusion for the would-be-purchaser, but basically they can be categorized as 'woven' or 'tufted'. Woven types, notably dense-pile Wiltons and multi-hued Axminsters, are made by weaving the pile with a jute or hessian backing; tufted types comprise continuous strands 'needled' into a ready-woven backing and secured with adhesive — a foam backing may be stuck to the main backing, obviating the need for an underlay.

'Bonded' carpets describe another method of production, in which synthetic fibres are bonded to an impregnated woven backing with adhesive: carpets are made face-to-face then sliced down the middle to make two carpets.

Although you should always aim to buy the very best you can afford, pile length and its treatment are important considerations when buying. There are two main types:
● Looped pile.
Made by leaving the continuous strands long and uncut, giving textures that are either firm, short twists or knobbly, thick ribs.
● Cut pile.
Made by cutting the tops off the loops; the pile may be short and stubbly or long and silky (shag).

Fiber content is another factor to consider: although the best types are made from wool, they're costly and carpets containing a percentage of man-made fibers are a cheaper alternative, which doesn't compromise quality. Wholly synthetic-fiber carpets, too, need not be cheap, interior substitutes: modern production methods offer wool-lookalikes with the benefit of stain resistance and durability. Typical fibers include hard-wearing nylon; soft, fluffy polyester; tough polypropylene (good for 'cord' effects); wool-like acrylic.

Carpets are usually sold in various widths from about 1m (3ft) to 5m (16½ft) — although made in metric sizes, Imperial is often quoted in the shops. 'Broadloom' describes carpets of 1.8m (6ft) width and more; 'Body' refers to carpets usually 700 to 900mm (27 to 35in) wide and intended for halls and stairs (although some can be seamed to cover larger areas). 'Carpet squares' (not tiles) are large rectangles with bound and finished edges, which are intended as loose-laid rugs.

To avoid excessive wastage, take a plan of the room with measurements to the supplier. He will work out the most economic method of fitting the carpet and advise on different ranges accordingly. Woven-backed carpets will always require an underlay (felt or rubber); carpets with built-in foam backing are laid over a lining paper to stop them sticking to the floor.

Carpet Tiles

Soft and warm underfoot, and with a good resistance to dirt and stains, carpet tiles score over roll carpet in many ways: because they're loose-laid they can be lifted and rearranged to distribute wear and have the advantage that you can wash them under the faucet; damaged tiles can be replaced with a spare (you should keep a supply of these to hand and regularly swap them with laid ones so color changes aren't a problem); by mixing and matching different colors, checkerboard effects uncommon with roll carpet can be created.

Loop and twisted piles are available in tile format in wool or natural fiber. Tiles should have a thick rubber backing, which produces a quiet surface to walk upon. Sizes are typically 400mm sq (16in sq), although larger versions are also available.

Sheet Vinyl

Soft and warm underfoot, sheet vinyl (the successor to linoleum) is unbeatable for ease of cleaning and durability in areas of heavy wear where spillages are likely — the kitchen or bathroom, for example (although some are susceptible to heat — a lit cigarette or dish straight from the oven, for instance). It's usually available in 2, 3 and 4m (6ft 6in, 9ft 9in and 13ft) widths, making it ideal for covering an average-sized room without the need for seams. Most vinyl sheet is laid loose, although where joins are unavoidable the seams can be stuck down with special adhesive.

There are two main types of sheet vinyl:
● Unbacked vinyl.
This is made from a PVC backing printed with a pattern then protected by a thin

transparent PVC layer. Solid vinyl has the color running through the whole thickness of the material.
● Backed vinyl.
This has a backing layer or 'cushion' of foamed PVC (sometimes felt).

Many sheet vinyls have an embossed pattern, frequently imitating a tiled or brick effect, complete with surface texturing.

All but the largest roll widths are straightforward for one person to lay.

Vinyl Tiles

Extremely tough and hardwearing:
● Cushioned vinyl tiles.
Exactly like sheet vinyl but could save on wastage in an awkwardly shaped room or a very small area. They're soft, warm underfoot and easy to clean. They are sold in packs and are self-adhesive.
● Plain vinyl tiles.
Very resilient but colder and harder underfoot than the cushioned ones.

A selection of floor tiles, soft and hard, warm and cold, for any situation.

They are an obvious choice for hallways and other areas where resilience is more important than comfort. They also come in packs; some are self-adhesive.
● Thermoplastic tiles.
Tough and inexpensive. They are not so easy to clean as other vinyl tiles. Some of these tiles may be suitable for use where there is the slight possibility of damp (although this isn't to be recommended). They are stuck down with adhesive.

Vinyl tiles typically measure between 200 to 300mm (18 to 12in) sq.

Cork Tiles

Available polyurethane-sealed or unsealed, both with a pleasing natural appearance created by compressed cork granules glued together then sawn to produce tiles typically 300mm (12in) sq (the unsealed variety must be sealed after laying). Cork tiles are also good insulators and a good treatment for a bathroom, where they're warm underfoot.

Cork tiles are sold in packs and easy to lay, being stuck with adhesive to an even sub-floor; self-adhesive tiles are available, too.

Ceramic Tiles

Available in an enormous range of colors and patterns, with a smooth, usually shiny finish, glazed ceramic floor tiles differ from their wall-hung counterparts in that they're thicker due to the wear they're likely to receive —

typically 10mm (⅜in). They're tough, ideal for use in kitchens and bathrooms, where there's likely to be a lot of water and if you want to tile a path or patio outside, frost-resistant versions are made.

Although square tiles are most popular, (measuring from about 100mm (4in)) there are rectangular units of these squares — plus a range of octagons, hexagons and interlocking styles.

Most tiles are square-edged and unglazed but some may have two glazed edges for use as steps. Some tiles are made with spacer lugs (most aren't) but you can use plastic spacers instead.

Quarry tiles

Quarry tiles are unglazed ceramic tiles that are particularly useful where the floor is subject to heavy wear; they can also be used outdoors as a surface for a patio. They come in various sizes — commonly 75, 150 and 228mm (3, 6 and 9in) sq — and thicknesses (typically 12, 16 or 30mm/½, ⅝ or 1¼in) and in subtle browns, reds and yellows. There are also rectangles and octagons and specially-cut tiles are available to form a base. Smooth-surfaced, uniform-size quarries, or rough-textured, uneven-sized types are available. They have to be laid in a bed of sand/cement mortar which is smoothed out between battens. They are grouted when dry like ceramic tiles.

Mosaic and Wood Block Flooring

Parquet tiles — or mosaic floor panels — are 8mm (⁵⁄₁₆in) thick 'fingers' of wood stuck side by side to a bituminous felt backing or wired together to form a square, the squares are arranged as panels about 300mm (12in) or 450mm (18in) sq in basketweave design. The panels are usually glued to a suitable subfloor.

Traditional wood blocks, usually about 255mm (10in) long and 70mm (2¾in) wide by 20mm (¾in) thick, are laid in basketweave, herringbone or stretcher bonds to create a tough, resilient timber floor surface. Some blocks have a tongue along one edge and a groove along the opposite so they can be slotted together. Normally bedded in hot pitch, blocks aren't easy to lay, although special flooring adhesive can be used.

Wood Strip Flooring

Strip flooring is made up from separate strips of solid or laminated hardwood. They measure between about 400mm (16in) and 1.8m (6ft) long, between 70 and 200mm (2¾ and 8in) wide and 9.5, 19 or 23mm (⅜, ¾ or ⅞) thick (solid) or 6 to 20mm (¼ to ¾in) thick (laminated). Strips are usually tongued-and-grooved for slotting together; some strips also come in tile form, resembling long wood planks when laid — the thickest strips can be used as replacements for ordinary floorboards.

Laminated strips are made pre-finished, as are some solid versions, although the latter must usually be sanded and sealed after laying.

LAYING CARPET

The average householder isn't likely to spend hundreds of dollars on a new carpet, then save comparatively few by fitting it himself: mistakes can happen, and you'd have no one to blame but yourself if you ruined the floorcovering. Knowing how to fit a carpet does come in useful, though, when you've moved house and you have old but perfectly good carpets to be re-used, or perhaps you'd risk laying a cheaper quality carpet yourself. The carpet must, of course, be larger than the room for which it's intended. It may be entirely the wrong shape and neces-sitate a lot of trimming. Lay it down in the room and trim it down to 75mm (3in) larger than needed all round. This will make fitting more manageable.

When making joins, the pile must always face the same way. If a strip is cut from the length and turned at 90 degrees to make up the width, the change in the direction of pile will show. This may be acceptable where, for example, an alcove is to be filled or most of the strip will be hidden by furniture.

The carpet should be arranged so that the pile faces towards the door and away from the main source of light. If a join must be made, try to avoid the area of heaviest traffic and always make the join along the traffic area rather than across it. Where a join is used to make up the width of a room, it should be on the side away from the door. Do not attempt to lay carpet on an uneven floor: the edges of boards will soon rub away at the underlay or woven backing and will create lines in the carpet. Nail down loose boards, turn warped ones or plane down the edges against the grain and fill any large cracks (see page 41).

Solid floors with a mortar screed can be carpeted but there must be a waterproof membrane and the surface must be absolutely dry and smooth.

Foam-backed Carpet

This is much easier to lay than the woven variety: it needs no underlay, no stretching and no gripper rods or tacks. It's stuck to the floor around the perimeter of the room with double-sided tape. To prevent the foam backing sticking to the floorboards under friction, and tearing away when the carpet is lifted, a paper lining is arranged over the boards. Special paper can be bought or strong brown paper can be used.

Firstly, cover the floor to within 50mm (2in) of the wall with the paper underlay. Join it if necessary with single-sided adhesive tape and fix it round the edges with double-sided tape. Stick lengths of double-sided adhesive tape all round the room.

Spread out the carpet on the floor so that it laps up the base all round. Roughly trim off the excess carpet with a sharp trimming knife — cut through the foam backing not from the pile side — leaving about 75mm (3in) all round.

At chimney breast alcoves, push the carpet up against the face of the protrusion, the excess folded back on itself. Measure off the depth of alcove then make a cut this length parallel with the side of the chimney breast — allow 75mm (3in) for trimming. Cut off the end of the piece that fits into the alcove, again allowing a margin for trimming, then cut along the face of the chimney breast.

To fit the carpet into a corner, grasp the overlap and push your thumb deep into the baseboard angle. Pull away the carpet with your thumb still in place and cut off the corner of carpet just beyond it.

Trim the edges of the carpet all round, by pressing the overlaps well into the baseboard angle with a paint scraper or flat chisel. Pull back the carpet and trim along the score mark.

Peel the backing off the double-sided tape, smoothing the carpet down on to it.

Woven Carpet

There are two ways to lay woven carpet: by tacking or with tackless fittings. Whichever you choose an underlay is needed. A knee-kicker, which can be rented, is essential for stretching the carpet into the place.

Tackless fittings give a better fitting as no tacks are used through the face of the carpet. The fittings, or gripper strips, are thin wood laths with barbs, which are nailed in a continuous line around the room with a gap between them and the wall slightly less than the uncompressed thickness of the carpet. Punch down the nail heads. Cut the strips to length using pruning shears or use a sharp knife. Arrange short lengths to fit round obstructions.

Position the underlay right up to the inside edge of the gripper rods and tack it, staple it, or stick it to the floor with double-sided tape. Join any seams with adhesive carpet tape (plus a latex adhesive if the underlay is felt).

The carpet has to be stretched over the gripper rods to be held firm and flat by the barbs. Roll it out in the room, leaving the surplus riding up the walls all round. Trim off the surplus, leaving about 50mm (2in) overlap. Use the knee-kicker to stretch the carpet taut over the barbs on the gripper rods: set the tool's pins to the correct depth, press the head into the carpet pile to pierce the weave then nudge the padded end with your knee to stretch the carpet.

'Kick' the carpet to one of the adjoining corners and again, hook it into position. Work back along the wall to the first corner, stretching the carpet on to the gripper with the knee-kicker, leaving the surplus sticking up all along.

Work from the first corner to the other adjoining corner and back along this wall. Repeat from this corner to the final corner, stretching the carpet across the room and hooking it onto the strips. Trim down the surplus to about 10mm (⅜in) and turn this down into the gap between the strips and the wall. Use a flat chisel to push the cut edge into the gap. Leave the surplus at the doorway to be fitted into a special edging strip or binder bar.

Fitting around Pipes

You'll probably have to cut the carpet to fit round central heating and plumbing pipes emerging from the floor. To do this, fit the carpet up to the wall on which the pipe is located then make an incision in the edge parallel with the center of the pipe; measure from the baseboard to the pipe then cut out a small circle of carpet this distance from its edge.

Laying foam-backed carpet: After fixing the threshold strip, unrolling the carpet with the pile sloping away from the window.

After stretching the carpet and creasing into the floor/baseboard angle, cutting along the crease for an exact fit.

With the carpet trimmed to lap up the walls 75mm (3in), sticking double-sided tape to the floor alongside the paper-felt underlay.

Peeling off the backing strip of the double-sided tape before pressing the carpet on to it; keep the carpet taut as you proceed.

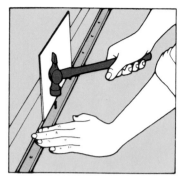

Laying woven-backed carpet:
Nailing gripper strip one carpet-thickness away from the baseboard; protect with a piece of card.

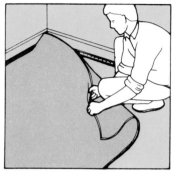

Laying the foam-rubber underlay; butt one end of the first length up to the gripper strip and cut to fit the same way at the other end.

Using a knee kicker to stretch the carpet on to the grippers; adjust the teeth to grip the woven backing, press down and knee-kick the pad.

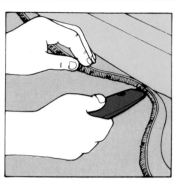

After fixing all round the room, trimming the edges of the carpet with a sharp knife to leave 10mm (⅜in) lapping up the baseboard.

With the carpet held taut with the knee kicker, pushing the surplus into the gap behind the gripper strips with a chisel.

Cutting to fit round a hearth; fold back the carpet over a piece of board and cut to a loose fit through the backing.

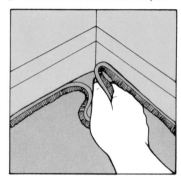

Fitting to an internal corner; press the thumb firmly into the angle, grip the carpet and lift it away from the corner.

Making a cut just beyond the tip of the thumb before cutting diagonally across the corner of the carpet and pressing back into position.

Trick

SEAMS AND DOORWAYS

Foam-backed carpet is easily joined with adhesive carpet tape. Fit it to one edge and roll the other on to it, butting the two edges neatly.

Woven-backed carpets are joined with latex glue and carpet seaming tape. Brush the adhesive up the pile to prevent fraying.

At doorways, carpet should extend under the centre of the closed door: there are aluminum edging strips for both foam-backed and woven carpets. Where two carpets meet in a doorway, use a special strip which incorporates two barbed flanges and a common edge strip. Screw the bar into position (use glue on a concrete floor), stretch the carpet into place, trim and hook over the barbs. Where the carpet meets a smooth floor-covering, use an edging strip that incorporates barbs one side for the carpet and a retaining flange for the vinyl (or whatever is used).

Joining woven-backed carpet; brush latex glue on to backing, edge of pile and tape, allow to dry then press together.

At a doorway, using a chisel to push the edge of the carpet under the center bar of the threshold strip.

LAYING STAIR CARPET

Stairs can be carpeted with fitted carpet or what's called a runner, that is a strip. This is the easier of the two methods. A woven carpet runner also allows the carpet to be moved from time to time to equalize wear. Old-fashioned stair rods with side clips can be used to hold a runner in place and form part of the stair decor, but it is now more usual to use gripper strips. Special pinless grippers are available for use with foam-backed carpets: the carpet is held in tight jaws. The wooden strips are used in pairs, one at the back of the tread, one at the bottom of the riser, or you can buy a metal version that's already formed into a right angle.

Cut the strips to length, if necessary, 38mm (1½in) shorter than the width of the carpet using tinsnips or secateurs for wooden strips, a hacksaw for the metal type. Nail them into place, omitting the bottom riser. The gap between each pair of wooden strips should be just big enough to squeeze the carpet down into. Cut the underlay to fit between the rods and tack close to the rods, omitting the bottom tread. No underlay is needed with foam-backed carpet.

Fitting a Woven Carpet

With a runner, an extra length of carpet is included so that it can be moved up to even out the wear taken on the treads; this is folded underneath the bottom step. The pile should run down the stairs to prevent uneven shading and promote longer wear.

Start at the bottom of the stairs. Tack the end of the carpet face downwards to the bottom tread, at the back, close to the gripper. Run it down over the tread to the bottom of the last riser, fold it back and tack the fold to the riser and tread. Run the carpet up the stairs, stretching it over the gripper rods and pushing it down between them with a flat chisel. It should join any landing carpet at the top of the last riser. If there is no carpet on the landing take the stair runner over the top of the final riser, turn under the edge and tack down.

Fitting on Winding Stairs

Where the stairs go round a bend, gripper rods cannot be used in the usual way. The carpet need not be cut but can be folded to fit the turn.

Woven carpet Fit the gripper rods only to the treads on winding stairs. Fold the surplus carpet, with the fold falling downwards, and tack it to the bottom of the riser at 75mm (3in) intervals. Stretch the carpet over the next rod up and repeat the folding and tacking process.

Foam-backed Omit the pinless rods altogether on winding stairs. Tack the carpet to the tread, right at the back so that the tacks are not too noticeable. Fold down the surplus and tack neatly at the bottom of the riser.

Fitting Stair Carpet

The fixings for a fitted stair carpet are as for a runner. The extra length of woven carpet is not needed at the bottom, though, and underlay should be fitted to all the steps. The gripper rods should be the full width of the stairs. Fit the carpet from the top of the flight. The landing carpet should overlap on to the stairs and down to the bottom of the uppermost riser. The stair carpet must be stretched over the gripper rods as usual and pushed down between them. In addition it will have to be trimmed to fit at the edges. No fixings are needed at the edges.

Winding Stairs

The treatment on winding stairs will depend partially on the type of carpet. However, whatever the carpet, a simple fold on the riser will not do. Each tread and the riser below it must be fitted individually, the carpet cut to size each time.

With a woven carpet, fit rods to both the treads and risers as on a straight run and also along the outside edge of the tread. Cut the carpet to fit over the rod at the back of the tread and down on to the rod at the bottom of the riser below. Cut and fit the underlay to lie in between the rods. Stretch the carpet over, trimming it at the edges and pulling it over the rod at the outside edge. Repeat on each stair not part of a straight run.

With a foam-backed carpet, gripper rods cannot be used. The carpet must be cut to fit each tread and the riser below, allowing a turn-under at the bottom. The pieces are tacked into place. Fit the lowest piece first, turning under the bottom edge, tacking it to the riser, pulling it up over the tread and tacking it flat right at the back of the tread. The next piece, its end tucked under and tacked to the riser, will conceal the tacks on the tread below, giving a neater finish. The side edges need not be turned under or fixed.

Tacking gripper strips to the back of the tread and the bottom of the riser, leaving a gap into which the carpet can be pushed.

Fixing underlay to the treads and risers with a staple gun to butt up to the gripper strips; continue the landing underlay to the top riser.

Tacking down carpet on an open landing; fold under the edge and tack through both thicknesses by each baluster.

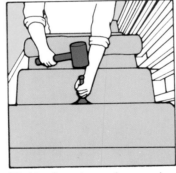

Working from the top downwards, stretching the carpet and pushing it between the gripper strips with a chisel; take care not to cut it.

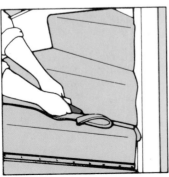

Cutting off surplus carpet on a winder; cover each tread separately, cutting off along the crease at the gripper strips.

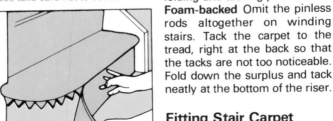

After tacking through zig-zig flaps turned under a bullnose tread, fitting a covering strip; tack through the top edge and both ends.

Pushing foam-backed carpet between tackless grippers with a chisel. (Gripper shown for clarity).

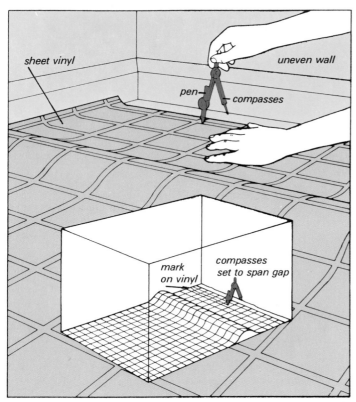

Scribing along an uneven wall; mark where one end of the sheet meets the wall and pull the sheet back squarely until the end lies flat, set the compasses to span the gap between the wall and the mark, and run the point of the compasses along the angle with the pen on the vinyl.

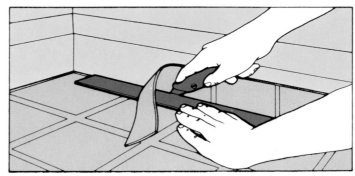

Trimming along a straight wall; push the end of the sheet firmly into the wall angle with a metal straight-edge, making sure that the rest of the sheet is lying flat, and cut along between the straight-edge and the wall with a sharp knife to remove the surplus.

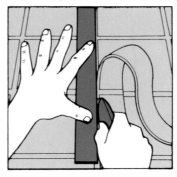

Joining lengths of vinyl by overlapping the two sheets until the pattern matches and cutting through both thicknesses.

Joining the cut edges with double-sided tape; after removing the offcuts; butt join the edges along the tape and press down firmly.

Sheet vinyl is the successor to linoleum, but combines the virtues of linoleum and carpet. It is extremely durable and completely waterproof but is also soft and warm underfoot. The cushioning makes it less tiring to stand on than hard vinyl tiles, ceramic tiles or quarry tiles, making it a prime contestant for kitchens and utility rooms. Its warmth makes it equally suitable for bathrooms.

Manufacturers are only too aware of the popularity of tiles in these situations and many sheet vinyl floorcoverings come in tile patterns. The advantage with sheet vinyl is that being available in three widths: 2, 3 and 4 metres (6ft 6in, 9ft 9in and 13ft), it is usually possible to cover a floor without any joins.

Preparation

Sheet vinyl can be laid on both wooden and solid floors, provided that they are both absolutely smooth and the solid floor has a waterproof membrane. Check the condition of the airbricks under a wooden floor and, if necessary, increase the number to ensure efficient underfloor ventilation (see page 40).

Plane down any raised board edges on a wooden floor. If it is very uneven, and the lines will show through the vinyl, level off the entire floor with sheets of hardboard (see page 45).

An uneven solid floor can be levelled with a self-levelling compound (see page 46).

The roll of vinyl should be left in the room in which it is to be used (lying down, not stored on end) for at least 24 hours before any fitting commences so that it will acclimatize.

Fitting and Trimming

Unroll the vinyl and cut it roughly to fit, leaving about an extra 50 or 75mm (2 or 3in) all round. If any joins are to be made and a pattern matched, take this into account when bringing the two sheets roughly to size.

It is unlikely that any one wall will be perfectly straight, but if one looks straight, butt the edge of the vinyl up to it. Stand in the doorway and assess the appearance. If the pattern looks straight and central on the floor then work from this straight edge. If it does not look absolutely right, it is better to trim this edge as well.

Pull the vinyl away from the wall by about 25mm (1in), keeping the vinyl straight to the room as a whole, not the wall. Use either a pair of compasses or a short block of wood and a felt-tipped pen to mark a line on the vinyl exactly following the line of the wall.

Run one leg of the compass along the base board, the pen on the vinyl, or move the block or wood along the base board, holding the pen close against the other side all the time.

Cut along this line with a sharp trimming knife and push the vinyl into place against the base board. It will be a perfect fit, overlapping at each end on to the adjoining walls.

To trim the next straight edge, use a block of wood to push the vinyl into the angle between the floor and base board. Either cut along the crease with a trimming knife freehand or mark the line in pen, then cut along the line.

Joining Sheets of Vinyl

If two sheets are to be joined, cut both roughly to size. In doing this allow extra on the length in order to match the pattern. The tile designs on sheet vinyl are arranged so that the sheets can be butted together and the pattern is continuous, like wallpaper.

Having fitted one sheet, move the second sheet along to match the pattern exactly. Trim to fit as with the first sheet.

Some sheet vinyls may be liable to shrinkage (check the manufacturer's instructions for laying); if shrinkage is likely, any joins will have to be overlapped and left for whatever time is recommended — before the final trimming can be done. The join is then made by cutting through both sheets of vinyl, through the mid-point of the overlap. Such vinyls will not have a pattern that continues across the sheets, as pattern matching would be impossible.

All joins should be secured (see adhesives below).

LAYING SHEET VINYL

Fitting Round Obstructions

At an internal corner where surplus vinyl runs up both walls, trim away the corner of the vinyl bit by bit until it can lie flat on the floor. The two straight edges can then be trimmed in the usual way.

At an external corner, cut down through the vinyl following the line of the protruding corner. It may be necessary to cut a narrow V-shape if the line is not straight. The two straight edges can then be pressed against the base board and trimmed in the usual way.

At door frames or other obstructions, make vertical cuts down through the surplus vinyl, keeping the blade of the trimming knife close to the contour of the obstruction. When all the vertical cuts have been made down to floor level trim away the surplus by joining the vertical cuts with horizontal ones.

Making a Template

In a Powder Room or small bathroom where the obstructions are numerous and awkwardly shaped, it will be simpler all round to make paper templates for cutting the vinyl to fit. Fit the vinyl roughly to the walls first, making incisions from the edge where it meets a basin pedestal or toilet base, so it will lie almost flat.

Take a sheet of stiff paper that's about 25mm (1in) larger than the obstacle and gently tear it to fit roughly round half the pedestal or toilet base. Fit another sheet at the other side of the obstacle. Use a pencil and a block of wood to scribe the profile of the obstacle on the template.

Lay the template on top of the vinyl and secure it with adhesive tape. Transfer the profile to the vinyl by running the pencil and block along the scribed line. Cut the vinyl to shape then fit around the obstacle.

Adhesives

Check the manufacturer's instructions for the recom-

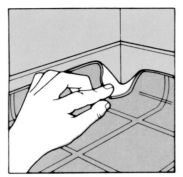

Fitting sheet vinyl to an internal corner: With the sheet flat on the floor, bending back the surplus to form a crease mark in the corner.

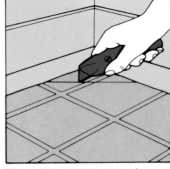

After pulling back the sheet from the corner, cutting diagonally through the crease; push into corner and trim along the walls.

With a straight-edge along one side of an external corner and across the vinyl, cutting along it before sliding the sheet into the corner.

Fitting at doorways; leave a flap overlapping the threshold and make a series of vertical cuts down the contours of the architrave.

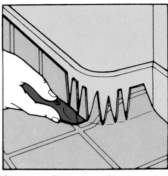

At a curved corner, making a series of vertical release cuts to allow the vinyl to lie flat before trimming round the curve.

Fitting round a pedestal: Making a paper template by tearing two halves to a rough fit, taping together and scribing round against a block.

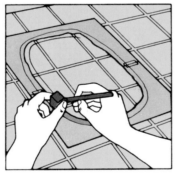

After sticking the template in the correct position on the vinyl, scribing on to the vinyl by running the block inside the line.

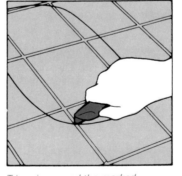

Trimming round the marked contour; to fit the vinyl round the pedestal, make a straight cut to the edge and join the edges after fitting.

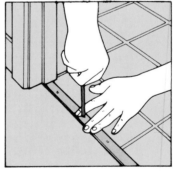

Fitting a threshold strip in a doorway to secure the edge and prevent tripping; choose a type to suit the adjoining floorcovering.

mended method of fixing the vinyl. Some can be laid loose, others secured with a double-sided tape or liquid adhesive.

The double-sided tape can be stuck to the floor prior to fitting the vinyl, leaving the backing on. When the vinyl has been trimmed, remove the backing and press the vinyl on to the sticky band.

Liquid adhesive can be applied in a strip all round the room or to cover the entire floor. Roll back the vinyl, weight it lightly and apply a band of adhesive about

100mm (4in) wide with a notched spreader. Release the vinyl on to it and press down.

Secure joins between sheets in the same way, but spread the adhesive in a band 200mm (8in) wide. Press the edges of the vinyl together over the adhesive, using a broom to work along the seam.

If the whole floor area is to be covered with adhesive, do half at a time: roll back the vinyl, spread the adhesive, release the vinyl on to it. Treat the other side of the floor in exactly the same

way. Use a broom to flatten down the vinyl and squeeze out air bubbles.

Edging Strips

As with carpets, a neat edge is achieved at a doorway with a binder bar. Buy one to suit the thickness of the vinyl, cut to length if necessary and fit with the screws provided or nails, slotting the edge of the vinyl in under the metal rim. Knock the rim flat with a hammer, protecting it with a block of wood.

Ceramic tiles made for use on the floor are thicker than those designed for walls. They often do not have spacer lugs (the little notches on the edges, which set the tiles the correct width apart for grouting), nor are they usually available with rounded edges as these are not needed. Those designed for outdoor use will be frost-resistant. This makes them extremely strong but unfortunately hard to trim and shape.

Preparing the Floor

The ideal base for ceramic floor tiles is solid concrete. This should be level, dry and free from grit, dirt and grease. If it is uneven it can be levelled with a self-levelling compound (see page 46). Seal the floor with a diluted coat of PVA adhesive or a primer recommended by the manufacturer of the adhesive to be used.

A wooden floor can be tiled with ceramic tiles but it must be able to take the added weight and be firm enough not to flex underfoot and thus lead to tiles cracking and joins parting. The floor can be strengthened with covering sheets of plywood (see page 44).

Marking the Square

Ceramic floor tiles should be arranged so that they are square with the doorway rather than a straight wall. This keeps the pattern effect regular, especially in a room that is an odd shape. If the tiles are not square to the door, it's immediately apparent on entering the room — the effect will be lopsided. A preliminary marking up process is essential.

Stand in the doorway. Draw a line across the doorway, against which the tiles will fit. Find the centre point on this line and measure out from it a 90 degree angle into the room. Set a batten to this point and extend it in pencil or chalk across the room to the opposite wall.

Place a tile into the right angle at the centre of the door. Allowing a 3mm ($\frac{1}{8}$) gap between tiles for spacers, move the tile up the line, marking where each tile will be. At the

opposite wall stop when the mark for the last complete tile has been made. Secure a batten across the floor, its inner edge to this point, making sure it is fixed at right angles to the drawn line from the doorway and regardless of the wall behind it. Fix a second batten at right angles to the first at one end of the room. This creates a perfect square in which the first tile can be fixed.

To see how the finished effect will look and where tiles will have to be cut, you can lay out all the tiles dry, starting from this corner.

Remember to allow for spacers between the tiles. If it seems that some awkward cutting will be necessary and can be avoided by moving the side batten a little further into the room or out, do so.

Laying out all the tiles will also bring to notice any variation in the color — batches can vary in tone. If this is apparent anywhere, move the tiles around to lessen the effect. Keep any damaged tiles (unlikely except in the case of 'seconds') for cutting round the edge.

Laying the Tiles

The adhesive for all ceramic tiles is applied to the floor or wall, not the tiles. Use an adhesive intended for ceramic floor tiles, not wall tiles, as this is likely to be more flexible and will accommodate any small movement in a wooden floor, for example. On a solid floor, a cement-based adhesive is usually used; on a wooden floor use the same mixture if the surface is primed, otherwise apt for a cement-rubber type.

Mix the adhesive following the manufacturer's instructions — it's usual to add water to make a creamy paste — and spread it with a trowel across an area of about one square yard, in the starting corner. Adhesive is usually spread on in a 3mm ($\frac{1}{8}$in) thick layer but some 'thick bed' types are spread to 12mm ($\frac{1}{2}$in) thickness for uneven floors. Using the grooved spreader sold with the adhesive, draw ridges through the adhesive: these create suction when the tiles are pressed on.

Press the first tile into position

Fitting temporary guide battens for laying ceramic floor tiles; after marking on the floor the position of the last full row of tiles to give equal-width cut tiles at each end, nail the battens to the floor, square to each other, outside the marked lines.

Spreading adhesive with a notched spreader over an area of 1sq m (10sq ft); ensure the notches are the correct depth for the tiles.

Positioning the first tile in the corner of the guide battens; push it tightly against the battens and press down firmly and evenly.

Continuing laying tiles along the first row; use a piece of card or spacer pegs to leave equal gaps between the tiles for grouting.

Completing the tiling over the first area of adhesive before spreading a further 1sq m (10sq ft); check that the tiles are level.

with a slight twisting movement; do not slide it into place. This ensures that the entire back of the tile is bedded in the adhesive. Plastic spacers can be bought that fit on the corner of the tiles to hold them the required width apart. Put one on the protruding corner of the tile to make sure the two adjoining tiles are the correct distance apart. The spacer pegs lie flat in the adhesive and do not have to be

removed prior to grouting.

Alternatively, simply use off-cuts of thick card as spacers. Continue fitting tiles and spacers until the adhesive has been covered. Wipe away the excess adhesive from the edges and between the tiles and spread a second square yard ready for tiling. Continue in this way until all the whole tiles are in position, then remove the battens.

LAYING CERAMIC FLOOR TILES

Cutting Border Tiles

Each border tile must be cut individually to fit the space between the whole tiles and the base. To make the cuts you can use either a tungsten carbide-tipped tile scorer or a cutting tool; the easiest to use works like pliers to snap the tile along a scored line. Other, more complex (and costly) devices feature a marking, scoring and cutting jig — this may be worth the investment if the room is large and there's a lot of tiles to cut.

To mark the tile for cutting or breaking, hold it face down in place against the wall, over-lapping the tile already stuck down. Allowing for the spacer peg between the two tiles, mark in pencil on each edge, the overlapping amount that must be removed. Turn the tile face up and using a straight edge and a scorer, cut through the glazed surface, joining the two pencil marks.

Kneel on the floor, grip a spare tile between the knees, hold the tile to be cut with one hand on each side of the score line and bring it down on to the edge of the outer tile. It should break cleanly. If it does not break at all, use one of the stronger tile cutters available. You can even buy a special tile-cutting blade — either a round-section 'rod saw', or a flat blade — to fit a hacksaw and this is useful with parti-cularly stubborn tiles or where you have to cut out curves and notches.

Smooth the cut edge with a carborundum stone, rubbing it along the edge not across it. Check the fit, putting the tile in position with the cut edge to the wall. Apply adhesive to the back of the tile and stick it down firmly. Don't forget the spacers.

Where tiles need more than one edge cut it will be better to use a tile cutter or saw for the job. If the amount is small, use a pair of pincers to nibble off the surplus, bit by bit. The resulting cut will not be clean but, once in position and grouted, the unevenness will not be notice-able.

To mark up for an external corner and in order to keep the cut edges to the wall, put the tile to be cut face up on top of the adjacent whole one, on one side of the corner. Put a spare tile on

Marking the width of edging tiles; position over the last full tile, and mark against its edge, allowing for grouting.

After scoring a straight line across the tile through the mark with the tile cutter, snapping the tile between the jaws.

top of this, but with its edge to the wall, and mark a line across as though for a straight cut.

Do not turn the tile, but move it to the whole tile adjacent to the other side of the corner and use the spare tile to mark a line across for a straight line at right angles to the first. Cut out the surplus area between the two lines and the remaining bit of tile will fit exactly — cut edge to the wall.

For an internal corner, put the tile to be cut face down on the whole tile central to the corner. Use a spare tile held against the wall to mark the two lines to be cut. When flipped over to face the right way up, the cut edges will be to the wall.

Where a more complicated cut has to be made, such as round a curving architrave, treat as an external corner with the tile to be cut face up on the adjacent whole tile. Use a spare tile to mark the cutting lines and join any curving ones by freehand. A tile-cutting rod saw is useful for cutting such intricate lines.

Finishing Off

Leave the floor for at least 24 hours for the adhesive to set firm (check the manufacturer's in-structions on this point). Don't walk on the floor during this time. Make sure that any surplus adhesive is wiped off while still wet as, once dry, it is extremely hard to remove and will spoil the finish of the tiles.

Grouting

To finish off the tiled area neatly, the gaps between each are filled with grout, which — traditionally white, but also colored — comes in powder form to be mixed with water. Grouting can be done as soon as the adhesive has set. Mix the grout to a thick paste. Do not mix too much at one time as it hardens quite quickly. Have a bucket of water and a sponge handy to wipe off excess grout.

Apply the grout with a flat spreader — there's usually one provided with the grout — taking it over the tiles and forcing it into the joins. Clean off the spreader

and scrape it over the tiles to remove the excess grout. Use the blunt end of a pencil or just your fingertip to press the grout in between the tiles and smooth it. As the grout starts to dry, dampen the sponge and smooth it lightly over the tiles to clean them. Rinse the sponge fre-quently in the bucket of water or the grout will just be smeared back on to the clean tiles.

Continue until the whole floor has been grouted. Check the lines of grout and run a finger or pencil over them again where necessary to get a good clean line. Wipe off any excess and leave to harden. When com-pletely dry, give a wipe all over with a dry cloth, buffing up a shine where the tiles have a highly-glazed finish.

If the tiles form a lip in the doorway, a piece of angled beading or strip of hardwood will protect the edge and give a neat finish. Varnish it or paint it before pinning and sticking in place. Touch in the pin heads if painted. Alternatively, shaped quadrant tiles are available for finishing off this edge.

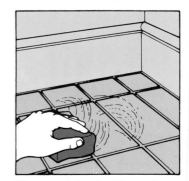

After completing the tiling and allowing the recommended drying time, sponging a slurry of grout into the joints to seal them.

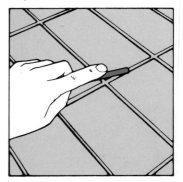

Using a pointed piece of wood or a grouting tool to round off the grout in a slight curve downwards.

A professional-type tile cutter will save time and ensure good results.

QUARRY TILES

Quarry tiles are unglazed ceramic tiles. Like glazed ceramic tiles they are hardwearing and easy to clean. They can be laid with flooring adhesive but it's more usual to bed them in mortar.

Quarry tiles are difficult to cut so plan a simple layout, avoiding awkward cutting and very narrow spaces. Calculate the quantity needed by multiplying the length and width of the area and dividing by the size of the tile. Round up the number and allow an extra five to ten per cent for breakages.

Clean sound concrete thoroughly. Stabilize powdery concrete with a priming coat of PVA adhesive. For a wooden floor to be suitable there must be no movement in it, loose boards must be nailed securely and the surface levelled with plywood (see page 44). Loose-laid floorcovering must be lifted but existing fixed tiles can be left in place.

To fix tiles it's necessary to create a bay into which the mortar is spread; you can then arrange the tiles on top. When one bay is completed, the battens are removed and set up again alongside. Starting on a straight wall in one corner, (preferably away from a door) fix two battens — they should be twice as thick as the tiles — at right angles to each other. Make a tiling gauge to plot the positions of the tiles on the floor: plot four tile-widths away along the wall and fix a third batten in this position at right-angles. Check that the battens are horizontal with a spirit level and pack them up with cardboard.

Fill the bay with a fairly crumbly mortar mix (3 parts sand: 1 part cement) and level off by dragging across it a board cut to span the battens and notched at each end the thickness of a tile. As you draw the board along the sides of the bay, the lower edge, recessed between the battens, will level off the mortar to the correct depth. Use the tiling gauge to position the tiles on the mortar. When the 16 tiles are in place, tap them down into the mortar with a block of wood. Check their evenness with a spirit level. Lift the third batten and reposition it to form another bay — four tiles wide — next to the tiles already laid.

As a section is finished the edging tiles can be cut to fit. Score deeply along the cutting line with a tile cutter. Tap with a pin hammer on the underside of the tile on the scoring line to break the tile. Bite away small pieces at a time for an angled cut, using pincers.

Fix base by buttering the back of each tile with mortar. Press into place, lining the files up with those already positioned on the floor.

Grout the tiles after 24 hours with a flooring grout, rubbing it in well.

Drawing a levelling batten across the crumbly 3:1 mortar; notch the ends to the depth of one tile thickness.

Tamping the tiles level in the first bay with a block of wood; check in all directions with a level.

After moving one side batten four tile-widths along, levelling the second bed across the batten and the laid tiles.

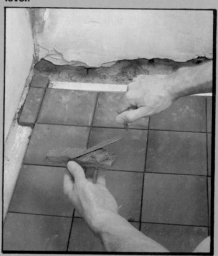

Buttering the back of a cut tile with mortar to fill in the gaps round the edges left after removing the battens.

Pressing the cut tiles into position; then refix the original baseboard or fix quarry tile base in the same way.

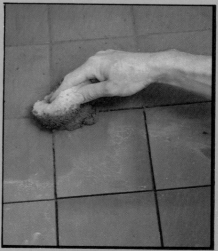

After 24 hours, grouting with flooring grout mixed to a creamy consistency; rub well into the gaps with a sponge.

LAYING SOFT FLOOR TILES

There are several types of soft floorcoverings that come in tile form. These include: carpet tiles, cork tiles, vinyl tiles and rubber tiles. Their general qualities are described on page 184.

There are various methods for laying these tiles: some are self-adhesive, some are laid loose and some are laid on a bed of adhesive. They all require a sound, dry, clean, level surface beneath them. Wood floor boards can be covered with hardboard, rough side up unless otherwise directed (see page 44). An uneven solid floor can either be filled laboriously or screeded over with self-levelling compound (see page 46).

Generally, old coverings that are stuck down can be left in situ, provided they are un-damaged. Broken tiles may need to be screeded over and all surfaces will need to be thoroughly scoured with steel wool to rid them not only of dirt and grease but also of old polish finishes. Existing materials laid loose must be lifted and the surface beneath treated accordingly.

Many floorcoverings, especially cork and those with cushioned or rubber backing, are unsuitable for use on floors with under-floor heating. The manufacturer's instructions should be checked for this point.

Setting out the Floor

Whether the tiles are laid loose or stuck down, the marking out of the floor is the same.

First, find the centre point of the floor. Do this by finding the centre point on each of the walls, measuring straight along and ignoring bay windows and doors. Take two lengths of string, coat them with chalk and pin them from one wall to the opposite. The two strings will cross in the middle of the floor at right angles to each other; the centre of the cross is the exact centre of the room. Snap each string against the floor to leave a chalk line then remove the strings. Leave the pins for the time being.

Set out a row of tiles dry from the centre point to one wall. See what size border will have to be cut. Continue the line of tiles to the opposite wall to see the width of border on that side of

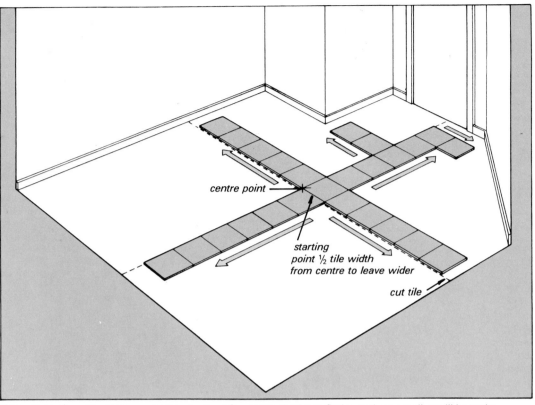

When laying floor tiles it is important to dry-lay a few strategic tiles to find out where cut tiles will be and to adjust their widths to give a balanced look to the final job. Starting from the measured center point of the floor (X), work outwards in a cross shape in the direction of the arrows and adjust the starting point as needed.

the room. Move the tiles a little either way to even up the borders — aim for a margin no less than half a tile wide — it will avoid some awkward trimming. Move the pins on each wall to the same distance.

Do the same with a row of tiles between the other two walls. Again, slight adjustments to give symmetrical, substantial borders may be necessary. Move the pins to compensate.

Remove the dry tiles, refit the strings and chalk two fresh lines. The cross will mark where the first tiles are to be laid.

Removing the dry-laid tiles after snapping chalk lines on to the floor to mark the adjusted starting point; work to these lines.

Loose-laid Tiles

Carpet tiles are laid loose. Most have a non-slip back but may require strategic spots of latex adhesive if slipping is a problem.

From the chalked cross, lay a row of tiles across the room from one wall to the opposite one. Each tile has an arrow on the back, which refers to the pile direction; these should be laid at right angles to each other to avoid a mish-mash of piles. Butt the tiles closely together. Cut and fit the border pieces (see below). Cut the tile from the

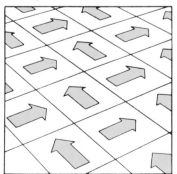

Direction of pile may be marked on the reverse side with an arrow; lay the pile in alternate directions for a subtle chequerboard effect.

back.

This gives a firm line to work to. Arrange another row going across the room at right angles to the first. Cut and fit the border tiles. Now simply build up a pyramid shape across both halves of the room, butting the tiles tightly and always cutting and fitting them to fit borders or other obstructions as they appear. This ensures that each completed row is a good tight fit.

Self-adhesive Tiles

Check the color matching between the boxes of tiles and leave in a warm room for 24 hours before laying. Porous sub floors (concrete, hardboard or other wooden overlays) must be primed. Check the manufacturer's instructions for a recommended brand. The tiles are laid while the primer is still tacky.

Self-adhesive tiles should not be used on wooden floors that have been treated with a wood preservative but some can be used on solid floors incorporating underfloor heating: these are usually the vinyl tiles with no cushioned backing.

Self-adhesive tiles are laid out like other soft floor tiles. Peel off the backing and press each tile into place. Fit all the full tiles first and fill in round the walls at the end (see directions below). Check the pattern match between the tiles, turning each one before sticking it to judge the best way. Self-adhesive tiles can be lifted two or three times without spoiling the adhesive.

The floor is ready for immediate use but do not wash it for at least seven days.

Tiles bedded in Adhesive

Cork tiles and the non-self-adhesive vinyl ones are stuck down using a special flooring adhesive.

Apply the adhesive with a notched spreader to cover an area of about one square yard at the centre point on the floor. Leave to become tacky then press the tiles into place. Wipe off excess adhesive while still wet. Fit all full tiles first then cut the borders and shape to fit around other obstructions.

Seal uncoated cork tiles as soon as the adhesive is dry.

Peeling the paper backing off a self-adhesive tile; arrows may be printed on the back to indicate the direction of laying.

After determining the center of the floor area to give equal width tiles round the border, laying the first tiles at the center.

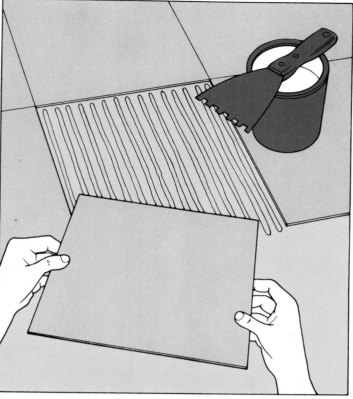

Laying a regular tile on a ridged bed of adhesive; a notched spreader may be supplied with the adhesive but over large areas a notched trowel will save effort. Ensure that the notches are the recommended depth and that you spread the adhesive thickly enough.

Trick

BORDERS

To cut a tile to fit a border, lay it face up squarely on top of the adjacent whole tile. Take a spare tile and, with one edge butted up to the wall, overlap the tile you're going to cut: draw along the edge of the top tile, remove the tile below and cut along the line with a sharp knife. The offcut of tile will fit the border exactly, cut edge to the wall.

Where tiles have to be cut from the back (carpet tiles), either measure the gap carefully and transfer these to the tile or position the tile to be cut face down. Place a spare tile on top of the whole tile next to it, overlapping the tile to be cut. Mark the line and cut through from the back. Flip the tile over and it will fit exactly with the cut edge to the wall. This is the way to fit all internal corners if the cut edges are to the wall.

Make paper templates (see page 190) of intricate shapes, or draw in curved lines freehand.

Marking border tile; lay over last full tile, lay second tile on top butting up to baseboard and mark along its edge.

Marking tile for external corner; follow procedure for straight border tile but repeat on second face of corner.

PARQUET AND WOOD STRIP FLOORING

Wood-block flooring, once regarded as a rather luxurious floorcovering, is also available in easy-to-lay tile as an alternative to the individual blocks. The individual pieces come in a variety of sizes and are already laid together in a pattern, and either tongued-and-grooved or bonded to a paper backing, ready to be stuck to the floor with the recommended adhesive. Parquet tiles, as they're known, come ready-sanded and some ready-sealed.

An acrylic seal makes the tiles particularly hardwearing. The sanded ones can be finished with several coats of poly-urethane varnish. They can be stuck to both solid and wooden floors provided they are firm, level and dry. No special preparation is necessary.

If you'd prefer the more substantial individual wood blocks, which can be used to create more elaborate patterns such as herringbone and basket-weave, in addition to the traditional parquet design, these are also available. Blocks are thicker than the parquet tiles and are generally used only on solid floors. Again, these are stuck to the sub-floor with an adhesive recommended by the manu-facturer.

Wood strip flooring comes in long strips, which are tongued-and-grooved to slot together. Some come with fixing clips which are driven into the adjacent boards; others are

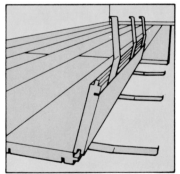

Floating wood strip flooring; metal clips fit between grooves under adjacent boards, joining them to each other but not to the floor.

secret-nailed through the tongue so that the nails do not show on the surface and yet others are fixed with adhesive. The strips can be used on solid

and wooden floors and in a thicker form.

An uneven wooden floor will have to be levelled with hardboard (see page 44) and an uneven solid floor with a self-levelling compound (see page 46). Any sub-floor where there's a possibility of damp is not a suitable surface for any type of wood block covering.

Laying Parquet Tiles

Set out the floor as for soft floor tiles. Loose-lay some tiles and adjust the fit as necessary. Spread the adhesive on the floor and, when it is tacky, lay the first tiles. At the sides of the room leave an expansion gap of 10mm (⅜in). Some manufacturers recommend fitting a cork strip in this gap to acommodate the slight movement, although a quarter round beading nailed to the base (not the floor) will effectively conceal the gap without looking at all incongruous. To trim tiles, cut through the backing between the strips. Cut intricate shapes with a saw, using a template for accurate measurement.

Laying parquet panels on masonite; spread enough adhesive for four panels. Work from the corner outwards, leaving an expansion gap.

Laying Wood Strip Flooring

Some manufacturers recommend laying plastic under the boards, others provide a special underlay.

The base can be removed or not; if it is, when it is replaced, it will cover the expansion gap that must be left at the sides of the room. This gap can be filled with special cork strips and quarter round beading used to conceal the gap, Door frames will need trimming at the bottom.

Begin laying the strip flooring

Putting down the underlay for wood strip flooring; this takes up any unevenness in the sub-floor and provides heat and sound insulation.

Tapping the groove on to the tongue of the previous board using a block of wood to protect the tongue; align end joints in alternate rows.

parallel to the longest wall bearing in mind that on wood floors the strips must run the opposite way to the boards underneath. Lay complete rows with the tongue out on tongued-and-grooved boards. Don't rely on the wall being dead straight.

Chalk a straight line across the room from the door and another at right angles to this. This forms a set square for the room on which further guidelines can be drawn. To determine the expansion gap, fit wooden wedges of the correct thickness between

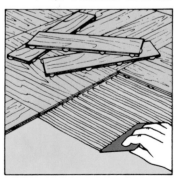

Spreading adhesive on a solid floor with a notched spreader; to fix the strips to a wood floor, nail through the lugs with panel pins.

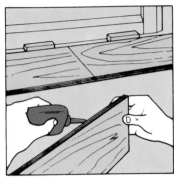

Applying woodworking adhesive to the groove of next board; maintain the expansion gap round the edges with wedges against the baseboard.

Covering the expansion gap with quadrant molding; pin the molding to the baseboard only, so that the boards may move beneath it.

the wall and the first board.

Join the strips by whatever method is recommended by the manufacturer: secret nailing, gluing, fixing clips. Where lengths have to be cut to complete a strip, try to stagger the joints across the floor.

When the floor has been covered replace the base or fit beading to conceal the expansion gap. A pre-finished floor will need no sealing. An unsealed floor may need sanding and sealing (see page 180).

Fitting the groove of the next strip over the lugs of the previous one; the strips may also be laid in herringbone pattern.

In certain areas of the house tiles may be preferred as a wallcovering to paint or paper: for example, around a shower, bath, basin or sink ceramic tiles will provide a waterproof background. Cork provides added insulation. It keeps warmth in and cold out, feels warm to the touch and is useful where condensation is a problem. Mirror tiles, too, have several virtues, reflecting the light in dark rooms, the space in small rooms.

Ceramic Wall Tiles

Ceramic tiles for walls are available in a wealth of colors and patterns. They can vary in price so much as to make tiling an inexpensive treatment or an extravagant luxury. Plain tiles are usually cheaper than patterned, hand-printed being the most expensive.

Standard tiles come as either 'field' or 'edge' (or border) tiles: the former are glazed only on their faces, their edges being concealed by the surrounding tiles; the latter have an exposed edge rounded off and glazed. Each range normally offers RE (rounded edge) tiles with one rounded glazed edge and REX (rounded edge external) tiles with two rounded glazed edges. However, these tiles are rapidly becoming obsolete, as manufacturers are turning to the 'universal' tile, which has all four edges glazed: it can be used as a field or an edge tile.

Ceramic tiles are available in various sizes: from 54mm (2in) sq to 300mm (12in) sq. The most common sizes are 152mm (6in) sq and 216 x 108mm rectangles. Tiles vary in thickness from 4 to 6mm (³/₁₆ to ¼in).

Some ceramic wall tiles have spacer lugs on the sides so that they can be set at an equal distance apart for grouting. If the tiles don't have lugs, plastic spacers can be bought to fit on the tiles. They sit flat on the wall and do not have to be removed prior to grouting. Alternatively you can use matchsticks.

Fix the tiles with ready-mixed or powdered filing adhesives (choose a waterproof type for use in a bathroom or shower cubicle).

Cork Wall Tiles

Cork tiles are usually used on one wall or, because of their decorative quality, on a particular feature such as a chimney breast. Various effects are available in tile form, from neat even-grained finishes to a rough, bark-effect finishes, in honey colors through to deep brown.

Some cork tiles are sealed, others not; some that are not sealed are specially designed this way and should not be sealed. In areas where a washable surface is preferred, sealed cork tiles or those that can be sealed should be used. The tiles are usually sold in packs of 9 to 20, and measure 300mm (12in) sq by 3, 5, 8, 12 or 20mm (¹/₈, ³/₁₆, ³/₈, ½ or ¾in) thick.

Cork tiles are stuck to the wall using a special spirit- or water-based cork adhesive.

Surface Preparation

As with any decoration, the surface behind tiles must be properly prepared. Previous coats of wallpaper must be stripped, holes filled and the wall thoroughly cleaned to remove old paste and dirt. Sound painted walls must be washed down to remove grease and dirt and sanded to provide a key for the new covering. A flaking paint surface must be scraped and sanded. If the plaster is powdery, the simplest way to get a firm backing for the tiles is to paint it with a stabilizing primer, some manufacturers recommend hanging lining paper (see page 165) behind cork tiles.

Ceramic tiles can be applied to an existing layer of tiles. Make sure the old tiles are stuck firmly to the wall and that they are clean. If a half-tiled wall is now to be fully tiled, a piece of varnished or painted wood beading can be fixed at the top of the double layer of tiles, with the new tiles continuing above it. Alternatively, the old tiles can be hacked away and the plaster wall dealt with as above.

Adhesives

Use the recommended adhesive with cork tiles, as it varies from manufacturer to manufacturer. Ceramic tiles should be applied with a waterproof adhesive specially formulated for ceramic wall tiles. There are several proprietary brands. A combined adhesive/grout is also available.

Sorting Ceramic Tiles

The coloured glaze on tiles differs slightly and it is advisable to get all the tiles out of their boxes and check them. Also, take out those tiles to be used for edging and corner edging. If plain and patterned tiles are to be mixed, arrange them on the floor to assess the effect of the design. Mix them around until the desired effect is created. It is much easier to do this in advance on the floor, rather than trying to visualize the effect on the wall.

Setting out Ceramic Wall Tiles

This is the correct procedure for all ceramic and other small tiles, mirror or metal. The tiles are fixed to the wall, working upwards from the bottom, whether this be the base board, the edge of a shower tray, a bath, sink or basin. It is essential that the first row of tiles be absolutely straight and it is unlikely that any of these fixtures is that, so battens are used to set them squarely and support them while the adhesive sets (if applicable).

First of all make a gauge from

Trick

TILING ROUND FEATURES

On a wall with a big feature, such as a window, the ideal arrangement is to have the equal cut tiles on each side of the feature rather than at the ends of the wall. Use the tiling gauge to find the centre point of the feature and offer up the wood, positioning it so that the center point of a tile fall on the center point of the window.

Moving to the edge of the window, mark on the wall the outer edge of the tile that will have to be trimmed to fit round the window. Move the marked length of wood back towards the end of the wall and mark where the last full tile will fall. Drop a plumbline through this point and nail a batten to the outer edge. Check the angle between the horizontal and vertical battens.

TILING WALLS

a long length of wood by striking off in tile width increments (plus any grouting gaps necessary). Use the gauge to plot how many whole tiles you'll be able to fit in the wall height: aim for borders at top and bottom that are no less than half a tile wide. Mark the wall to indicate the perimeter of the 'field' of whole tiles.

Plot the tile positions across the width of the wall, mark suitably wide borders. Next, temporarily nail a straight-edged length of 50 × 12mm (2 × ½in) softwood batten horizontally to the wall with its top edge level with the field perimeter mark. Place a spirit level on the batten (into which you should first drive nails at 300mm/12in intervals so they just break through on the opposite side for easier fixing) to check the level. Tap in the nails so the batten is held against the wall. The first row of tiles is fitted along this batten, the tiles beneath being trimmed to fit the profile of the base board, or whatever you're tiling against.

Having set the horizontal support, the vertical must be marked. A plumbline is used for this; drop a plumbline through this point and nail a batten to the outside of the line. It should be at an exact right angle to the horizontal batten. Check the angle with some loose tiles.

Fixing Ceramic Wall Tiles

Fix all the full tiles first, cutting in at the ends of walls and around features afterwards when the tiles are set firmly and the battens can be moved. With careful cutting one tile can be used to fill two gaps that are each less than a tile width in size.

Apply the recommended tiling adhesive to the wall with a notched applicator (there's usually one in the adhesive container). Do not attempt to cover an area greater than one square metre (1 square yard) at a time.

Press the tiles into the adhesive with a slight twisting movement to form suction with the ridges of adhesive. Work across the wall in horizontal rows, setting the tiles lug to lug if

they have them, fitting spacers if they have not. Wipe off any excess adhesive that squeezes through the joins with a damp cloth.

When all the field tiles are stuck up, allow about 12 hours for the adhesive to set firm and then remove the battens. Cut and fit tiles to fill in the borders.

Tiling Around Fitments

On reaching the basin, for instance, fix a batten above it, its top edge level with the line of full tiles to the side. Tile from this horizontal upwards. Cut in the tiles to fit round the basin later.

Cutting Ceramic Wall Tiles

Ceramic wall tiles are not too difficult to break. Once the glazed surface is scored through with a tile cutter, the tile can be snapped along that line. The scoring must be done firmly to ensure a clean break.

To measure the tiles for filling a straight border, lay the tile over the tile nearest the edge, offer up

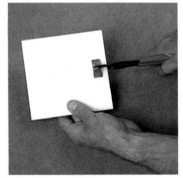

Cutting tiles by scoring a line along a straight-edge and breaking between the jaws of the tile cutter; also score rounded edges of tiles.

a spare tile to overlap it and score down the line lightly. Score again firmly before breaking the tile over a matchstick. Smooth the rough cut edges with a carborundum stone or file.

If you have a lot of tiling to do, invest in a tile-cutting jig, of which there are several prototypes on the market: with these, you're able to measure and mark the size of cut and hold the tile securely while the cutter is operated.

Pincer-type tile cutters are a fairly cheap and accurate means

After determining the best starting point, fitting horizontal and vertical guide battens to the wall, crossing at this point.

Spreading adhesive on the wall over 1sq m (10sq ft) with a notched trowel; use waterproof adhesive in potentially wet areas.

Starting in the corner, laying the first tiles; press them firmly into the adhesive and insert spacers if the tiles are square-edged.

After removing battens, mark the width of an edge tile; hold it over the last full tile and mark along another against the side wall.

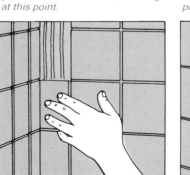

After spreading adhesive in the gap (or on the back of the tile if the gap is too narrow), pressing the cut tile into position.

Tiling an external corner; lay the edge of one tile flush with the side wall and overlap its edge with the tile on the other wall.

Cutting out a corner from a tile; after scoring the cutting line with a tile cutter, nibbling away the corner with pincers.

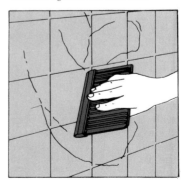

After allowing the recommended time for the adhesive to dry, filling the gaps between tiles with grout using a sponge.

of cutting tiles: they usually incorporate a wheel scoring disc and jaws into which the tile is placed, then snapped using scissor action.

As ceramic tiles have to be cut from the front, it is easier to mark the cut lines on the front, always using the spare tiles to indicate these lines. If a tile is offered up face down, mark the cut lines in pencil and extend them round to the front of the tile. Shapes such as an L to fit round an obstruction should be scored and then bitten away little by little with a pair of pincers. A tile-cutting hacksaw blade is useful for curving cuts. A hole in the middle of the tile is cut by scoring a line through the centre of the hole, breaking the tile along the line, then pincing or sawing out the two half circles.

On external corners, the tile on one wall is cut to fit the space exactly. The tile on the facing wall, which will be one of those with a glazed edge, is cut to overlap this raw edge, giving a neat finish.

In recesses that are greater than one tile in depth, the full tiles are placed around the front of the recess, butting over those on the surrounding wall, and cut tiles are positioned at the back. Where it is awkward to apply adhesive to the wall, it can be put on the back of the tile.

Grouting

Once strictly white, grout now comes in several colors. It is always mixed with water, adding the powder to the water to avoid over-watering, to form a thick paste. It is applied after all the tiles have been firmly adhered for several hours.

Spread it over the joins between the tiles with a flat spreader (usually one edge of the adhesive applicator is intended for this), wiping it off the tiles and into the joins. Scrape off surplus and use on the adjoining tiles. Wipe down with a damp sponge or cloth. When beginning to harden, pull the blunt end of a pencil along the lines of grout. (If using a finger to push the grout into the joins, be careful not to cut it on the edge of a cut tile.) When completely dry, wipe over with a clean dry cloth.

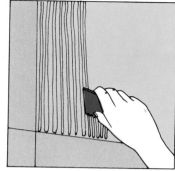

Working from the center of the wall outwards, spreading adhesive over an area slightly larger than the cork tile with a notched spreader.

Setting out Cork Tiles

Cork and other larger tiles are treated in a similar way. It is not necessary to use battens, though. On a plain wall measure horizontally and vertically to find the center point. Mark the lines with a chalked stringline (as in setting out for floor tiles; see page 194), using a plumbline for the vertical drop and a spirit level for the horizontal.

The center point can be moved slightly sideways or up or down if this will significantly reduce the number of tiles that need trimming. Positioned as it is, it ensures equal trimming at both sides and top and bottom.

On a wall with a feature, the tiles radiate out from the center of the feature so that, as with ceramic tiles, the cut tiles to either side will be equal. Thus

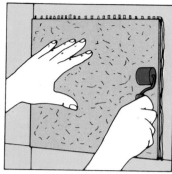

After carefully positioning the first tile square to the guide lines, firming it into the adhesive with a wallpaper edge-roller.

one tile is placed centrally over the cross made by the vertical and horizontal plumbline, rather than four tiles being placed in the right angles.

To mark its position, measure down from the horizontal exactly half the width of a tile and chalk in another horizontal. This will be the starting point for the first row of tiles across the wall. Measure on either side of the vertical line half the width of a tile. Make two small marks. This will be the exact position of the first tile.

Fixing cork wall tiles

The tiles are fixed either with an adhesive that is applied to the wall or with a contact adhesive that is applied to both the wall and the backs of the tiles. Follow the tile manufacturer's instructions. Before fixing, take the tiles

out of the packs and spread out to check any colour variations between packs. Sort them out and if creating a pattern with more than one type, work this out in advance on the floor.

With contact adhesive, stick up one tile at a time, working in horizontal rows from the central position of the first tile. With adhesive that is applied only to the wall, spread on about 1 square metre at a time, butting the tiles closely from the centre point outwards.

Press the tiles flat against the wall, being careful not to slide them out of line. Any adhesive which gets on the front of a tile should be wiped off with a cloth dampened with white spirit.

Cut the tiles as for floor cork tiles, putting the tile to be cut face up on the last whole tile in the row. Butt a spare tile against the wall to overlap the tile to be cut and mark the line in pencil. Put the tile on a firm surface and, using a straight edge as a guide, cut through cleanly with a sharp trimming knife. Wherever possible, put the cut edge into the angle with the wall. On an external corner, the cut edges of the butting tiles can be lightly sanded.

Edging strips can also be bought to fit over external corners. They fit over the edges giving a neat finish and protection against knocks in this exposed position.

Trick

GROUT RENOVATOR

White grouting can become discolored, particularly when it gets constant splashings of water. Bleech will restore it for a while, but there's a special renovating substance on the market, which comes in white and five colors and is simply painted over old sound grouting.

After an hour it is soaked with water and, in a few minutes, the surplus color that has gone on to the surrounding tiles can be washed off. It is not only a good way to restore brilliant white grout but is a simple way of changing from white to a color.

Trick

BRICK AND STONE

The appeal of brick and stone is in their naturalness: their natural color and rough textures impart a wholesome, very warm feeling. But to strip a wall back to bare brickwork inside a home is an awesome project — both time consuming and messy. The easy way to bring brick and stone inside is to use cladding tiles.

Brick Tiles

Brick tiles not only look real but feel it too as they are genuine brick slips — thin slivers sliced from real kiln-produced bricks. The colors vary from reddy brown to sand and grey, intended to imitate the popular types of bricks. The textures vary too: you'll find smooth-faced new-looking types and cracked, chipped versions that resemble old bricks. There are even special bricks to go round external corners, comprising one header and one stretcher face.

Unlike real bricks which have to be built up in straight courses, tiles can be arranged in a variety of ways: vertically, herringbone style, diagonally. Many patterns are possible. The more conventional bond is obviously the most realistic and causes fewer problems at corners.

Brick tiles are usually approximately brick-sized — 215 × 65mm (8½ × 2½in) — but only about 15mm (⅝in) thick. They usually come in boxes containing typically about 30 tiles, which is enough to clad an area about 1m × 500mm (3ft × 1ft 8in).

Stone Tiles

Made from reconstituted stone, these tiles are shaped in molds to resemble blocks of natural stone. The irregular shapes can be used for a thoroughly natural random effect, the rectangular ones for a more structured, coursed finish. Sizes range from about 100mm (4in) to 300mm (12in) across. Try various designs in advance, laying the stones out on the floor.

Fixing Brick Tiles

The wall must be clean and sound. Strip off wallpaper and scrape away flaking paint. Wash well to remove dirt and grease and allow to dry. Sand lightly to produce a key.

Surface Preparation

Battens are needed to ensure coursed

After nailing a horizontal guide batten to the wall, applying adhesive over 1 sq metre (1sq yd) with a notched spreader.

Cutting a brick tile with a masons chisel and hammer; rest it on a flat surface, score both sides then tap the chisel sharply.

bricks (and stone) run horizontally. Measure the height of the wall to ensure that a number of whole tiles, plus mortar joints, will fit the space. If necessary, remove the skirting board and replace it afterwards, overlapping the bottom row of tiles. It may be possible to use the existing skirting as the bottom batten but check that it is horizontal first. You can then fit new skirting on top.

Apply adhesive to the wall to cover about one square metre by spreading it on with a notched applicator. Press the first brick tiles into the adhesive, resting them on the batten with spacers between them. On the second row, place spacers between each brick and that below it. Wherever tiles have to be cut, scribe both sides and tap with a bolster chisel and hammer. A pincer-type tile cutter can also be used.

Working upwards from the guide batten, pressing brick tiles into the adhesive; cut up the packing to make joint spacers.

Fitting a corner tile to an external corner; the tiles have stretcher and header faces to match the bond pattern.

Fixing Stone Tiles

Fix coursed stone tiles as for brick tiles. For a random stone effect, however, it's usual to spread on a base coat of special adhesive then, when it's dry, apply more adhesive to the back of the stones, to the edges and in the middle. Press each stone to the wall, starting at the bottom. Use small stones to fill gaps between large ones. Shape stones to fit corners simply by snapping pieces off with pliers. On external corners, saw a large stone in half and use one half on each face of the corner, mitering the join.

Pointing

Courses, brick and stone, must be pointed. Point the joints as for a real wall.

Small quantities of ready-mixed mortar can be bought.

Strategically placed mirrors can play a great part in a decorating scheme. Placed opposite a window they will reflect light into the darker areas of the room, while in a small room or a long, dark hallway, they can give the illusion of greater space. They can also be used to reflect interesting objects or to highlight a decorative effect. For example, potted plants standing in front of a large mirror will appear to double in number. Translate this into a mirrored alcove with a selection of plants both large and small and suddenly you have a miniature conservatory.

Mirrors are heavy though, awkward to hang when large, and expensive. Mirror tiles, on the other hand, are light, easy to hang and can be used for a small feature area or to cover a complete wall. They come in several sizes, typically 106, 150, 225 and 300mm (4, 6, 9 and 12in) sq. Oblong tiles can be bought too, and some with a bronzed or smoked finish rather than the traditional silvered. These give a quieter, more subdued effect.

To find the number of tiles needed, measure the width and height of the area to be covered. Divide both these figures by the size of tile chosen, counting any fraction as a whole tile, and multiply the two figures.

Surface Preparation

The surface must be as level as possible, sound and free from damp. A significantly uneven wall should be levelled with plywood or hardboard screwed to battens or the reflections (which will never be perfect, even with a flat wall) will be uneven and the effect disjointed. Hold a long straight-edged batten across the wall to check for obvious dips and lumps. Fill any minor defects with fine-surface filler.

Mirror tiles applying must be stuck on a non-porous surface; this means applying enamel paint (latex paint will not do). Paint the wallplaster, gypsumboard, plywood, hardboard — with at least two coats of enamel paint. Allow to dry for three days then wash down well.

Fixing sheets of plywood or masonite to the battens after packing out any low spots with shims of wood.

Pinning a guide batten to the board after marking horizontal and vertical guidelines on the enamel painted surface.

With one edge in contact with the guide batten, tilting the first tile into position with its bottom edge on the horizontal guideline.

Scoring a line on the mirror face of the tile against a straight-edge; a single swift, light stroke gives best results.

After screwing horizontal battens to the wall to coincide with the edges of the board, checking them for level with a straight-edge.

Peeling off the protective backing from the adhesive pads; use extra pads to level a mirror tile over an uneven area.

Pressing the tile firmly on to the wall with a soft cloth; press only over the area of the adhesive pads or the tile may break.

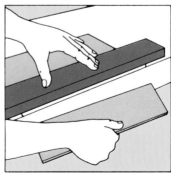

Breaking the tile by laying it on a flat surface, mirror side up and with the score line over the edge, and pressing downwards.

Setting Out

Half-way up the area to be covered, draw a horizontal line across, using a spirit level as a guide. Draw a vertical line through the half-way point, making sure it runs exactly at right angles to the horizontal.

Make a tile gauge by striking off a long batten in tile-width increments then plot the positions of the tiles across the area. Adjust the central guidelines if necessary so that the border tiles will not be too narrow. This could mean reducing the number of whole tiles used by one and running the first row of tiles positioned centrally over this original guideline rather than fitting a row to either side. Pin a batten to the vertical guideline.

Fixing the Tiles

The tiles will either have adhesive tabs already fixed to them or will be supplied with the tabs to be fixed on. The tiles must be positioned accurately as, with lifting off and replacing, the tabs will lose their adhesion.

Position the first tile against the batten, with its lower edge running along the horizontal guideline. Pivot it up into place.

Butt the next tile to the vertical batten above the first tile. Make sure it will butt the first tile closely but not too tightly, and fix in place. Press over the surface of the tiles gently with a soft cloth to ensure good adhesion. Stick up all the full tiles first.

Unevenness Extra adhesive tabs are supplied with the tiles and where there's a slight irregularity in the surface these can be used to level up the tile. Simply stick them on top of the existing tabs.

Cutting Tiles

Cut tiles from the front. Mark the cut by placing the tile over the last full one in the row and butting a spare tile to the wall, overlapping the tile to be cut. Use a metal straight edge as a guide when cutting and moisten the line with water or white spirit.

Use a wheel glass cutter to score the line and then break it cleanly over the edge of a table or workbench. Fix on some extra adhesive tabs and press the tile into place.

CEILING TILES

May be it is because they are above eye level that ceilings do not often get their fair share of the attention when decorating schemes are being planned. More often than not they are painted — and white still seems to be a popular choice. It is only when they are in bad condition and a simple coat of paint is not enough that they get a little more consideration.

Ceiling tiles are a clean and efficient way of concealing a badly cracked or discolored ceiling. They are a good choice where sound insulation is a consideration and bring an extra decorative element into a room with little trouble as they are easy to install, whichever method is chosen.

If ceiling tiles are a householder's choice on a bad ceiling, there is no reason why they should not be used on a perfectly good ceiling. If a textured rather than a flat surface is desirable, then ceiling tiles could be the answer.

Types of Tiles

Polystyrene tiles are the type most frequently used. They are extremely lightweight and easy to secure, being stuck to the ceiling with a recommended adhesive. They come in a variety of sizes and with different textured effects, to be unobtrusive or more dominant in a room scheme. There are some with classical designs, making them more in keeping with older-style properties.
Safety Polystyrene tiles are inflammable and, for this reason, should *never* be painted over with an oil-based paint. Any ceiling that is painted the same color as the walls, or a lighter shade of that colour, creates a prettier picture than one painted a bald white, and the same is true of ceiling tiles. It is perfectly safe to paint them, provided latex — a water-based paint — is used.

A second point of safety is on the method of fixing. The adhesive must be applied to the whole of the back of the tile, not just in five dabs, as was common practice, to ensure firm adhesion and to prevent fire from spreading rapidly through the gap between tiles and ceiling.

Fiber Tiles There are various types of fiber tiles, most of which are more familiar in a business environment than in the home. Some are intended for use in a suspended ceiling, being fixed with special clips, others can also be stuck to the ceiling like polystyrene tiles or fixed to a system of battens. All types of fiber tiles have one distinct advantage over polystyrene tiles in that they are not flammable. They come in various sizes and with different textured effects.

Methods of Fixing

Where a suspended ceiling is not being considered, the tiles can be stuck to the ceiling or nailed or stapled to a series of battens fixed across the ceiling. There is also a kit available which includes everything needed to build a new ceiling just below the level of the old one.

Where the height of the room is a factor and you're considering installing a suspended ceiling, refer to page 48.

Access to the ceiling

To avoid climbing up and down a ladder all the time it's best to fix up an access system. It only needs two ladders, one at either side of the room, and a scaffold plank running between them. Fix the plank at a level that makes both reaching the ceiling and stepping up from the floor straightforward.

Fixing Polystyrene Tiles

Like most floor tiles, these are fixed from the center-point of the surface, working outwards. This is important if a symmetrical effect, with an equal border on each side of the room, is to be achieved.

To find the center of the ceiling, measure along each wall and mark the exact center. Fix a nail at this point, tie a piece of string across to the wall opposite and tie it to the nail there. Snap the two strings against the ceiling to make two chalked lines. Where the lines cross is the exact center of the ceiling. Make sure the lines are at right angles to each other.

Offer up a tile to see what width of border will be created if the tiles are arranged from this point. If the border will be narrow it's best to position the first tile with its centre over the chalked cross, rather than four tiles butting the four lines of the cross, so reducing the number of whole tiles in the row by one and making a much wider border. The border on the opposing wall will still be equal. Minor adjustments in either direction can be made if this will avoid some awkward fitting or to accommodate a central light fitting that is slightly off-centre.

Spread adhesive over the back of the tile and press it into place. To avoid denting the delicate face of the tile, use a piece of wood or other material and press against this. Continue to stick up the tiles, working around the first one, until only the border is left. Mark the border tiles for cutting by placing them over the last whole tile in the row, butting a spare tile to the wall and marking the line of the overlap. Cut the tile then stick the offcut in place with the cut edge to the wall.

To conceal the raw edge, you can stick polystyrene or fibrous plaster coving around the edge of a plain ceiling.

Sticking Fiber Tiles

Fiber tiles that can be stuck to the ceiling should always be used with the recommended adhesive. Prime a piece of each tile, near the corners, with a coat of diluted adhesive. Then dab on four whirls of adhesive. Take the tile to the ceiling and slide it into position in one movement, applying pressure at the same time. Fit the tiles from the center, as with polystyrene tiles, for a symmetrical finish and cut border tiles to fit in the same way.

Pinning/Stapling Fiber Tiles

The tiles are fixed with panel pins or staples to a series of battens. These do not need to be sustantial as the tiles are not heavy. Battens of 50×12mm (2 × ½in) planed softwood are

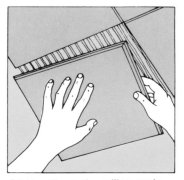

Sticking tiles to the ceiling; apply adhesive to the back of the tile or use a finely-notched spreader to apply it to the ceiling.

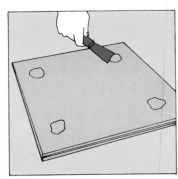

Applying a dab of adhesive to each corner of a fiber tile with a filling knife after first priming with thinned adhesive.

Fitting the cut tiles round the edges before finishing off with coving; use a square of masonite to press the tiles into position.

Sticking the tile to the ceiling; place it about 25mm (1in) from its final position, then apply pressure and slide it into position.

Nailing parallel battens to the ceiling to support fiber tiles; hold a spacer between the battens when nailing them to the joists.

Working diagonally outwards from the corner of the ceiling, nailing through the edge grooves of the tiles into the battens.

Fixing tongued-and-grooved fiber ceiling tiles to battens from one corner diagonally across ceiling. Staple through edge of grooves.

suitable. Cut these to length and nail to the ceiling, using 25mm (1in) panel pins running in the opposite direction to the joists. (Look at the floorboards in the room above; the joists run at right-angles to them. In an upstairs room, look in the attic to see which way the joists run.)

Firstly, though, find the center point of the ceiling and snap chalk lines. Work out, by offering up a tile, how they will run and what width of border there'll be. Adjust the center point if necessary to allow an equal border of quite substantial

width.

Pin the first batten to the ceiling butted up to the edge of the wall. Fix the second batten on the line where the border tile will be fixed. Work across the ceiling, pinning battens where the edges of the tiles will meet. At the other side of the room space the battens to accomodate the border tiles.

Fix the tiles with staples (fired from a heavy-duty staple gun) or 25mm (1in) panel pins, securing them to the battens. Measure up and cut border tiles as described for polystyrene tiles.

Cutting Round a Ceiling Rose

A central ceiling light should always fall in the centre of a tile or between the corners of four tiles, or it will spoil the symmetry of the arrangement. The chalk lines may have to be adjusted, to take account of a light fixture that is just slightly off center. Where the ceiling light is not positioned centrally, or there's more than one light, these can be accommodated at any point on the tile.

Turn off the electricity at the mains. Remove the bulb and

lampholder then unscrew the cover of the rose and remove it. On the reverse side of a single tile, find its center point, place the rose over it and draw round. Where the light fixture does not fall in the center of the tile, take accurate measurements on the ceiling, transfer these to the back of the tile, mark the point of the center of the fixture, position the rose over this and draw round it.

Where the fixture falls between four tiles, butt the tiles together upside down on the floor, position the rose centrally over the four corners and mark round it.

Cut with a sharp knife, just inside the penned line, so that the hole is very slightly smaller than the rose. Stick the tile to the ceiling, pulling the cables through, and screw the rose cover back in place. It should cover the raw edge of the hole.

Lowering a Ceiling Rose

With a fiber tile ceiling fitted to battens or a suspended ceiling the light fixture will have to be lowered to fit onto the new ceiling. (See page 123.)

Trick

FIBRE TILE KITS

Kits that are specifically designed for handyman installation are as easy to work with as the two methods described here. A 'tight-up' system is fitted just below the existing ceiling, so no height is lost. The measurements are given to the manufacturer who supplies everything, including the tiles, to fit the ceiling exactly, together with detailed fixing instructions.

Suspended ceiling kits consist of metal channels on which the fibre tiles are supported. First secure the wall angles horizontally round the room at the required height. Then, after cutting to length the suspension channels, lay them across the shorter dimension of the room and suspend them from screw eyes in the joists, checking for level. Slot in the short channels and fit the tiles.

Hanging suspended ceiling channel on its support wire; secure to ceiling eye, pass through channel hole and twist round.

After slotting in the short cross pieces and passing the fiber tile through at an angle, lowering it on to the channels.

PANELLING WALLS AND CEILINGS

Take one very ordinary room and panel the walls with wood. The change is really quite dramatic. It takes on an elegance and a feel of refined luxury that is difficult to achieve with any other wallcovering. And the same goes for ceilings. Of all treatments, wood panelling has to be one of the most attractive — and the most commented upon. Wood has a natural beauty and a certain charm that make it feel right in any style or age of property.

Planning

Consider the shape of the room. Panels arranged vertically will increase the apparent height, arranged horizontally they will seem to lengthen it. They can be used on all the walls or just one wall, the ceiling or just a chimney breast. They can also be arranged in more flamboyant patterns, for example diagonally or in a zig-zag design.

Buying the Panelling

Buy tongued-and-grooved matchboarding; knotty pine — which contains too many knots for joinery construction — is the most popular, although lumber merchants may well produce an alternative, such as mahogany, cedar or ramin.

Standard T & G boards give a flush surface when the tongues are slotted into the grooves; tongued, grooved and V-jointed (TGV) types have a bevel cut on their top edges to creak a fine V-shaped recess when the boards are connected, highlighting the panelled effect. Other boards have complex routed profiles for a more decorative effect.

Matchboarding is sold in various lengths up to 3m (10ft) in nominal widths of 100m (4in) and a thickness of 12mm (½in). Actual sizes (due to planing) may be 10mm (⅜in) less all round.

Wood panelling can also be bought in kit form from some lumber supply houses. The shrink-wrapped wood comes in 2.4 (8ft) or 2.7m (9ft) lengths, 100mm (4in) wide and 12mm or 16mm (½in or ⅝in). Packs commonly contain 16 lengths. Some come with special clips for fixing. The various moldings needed for finishing off at corners, ceilings

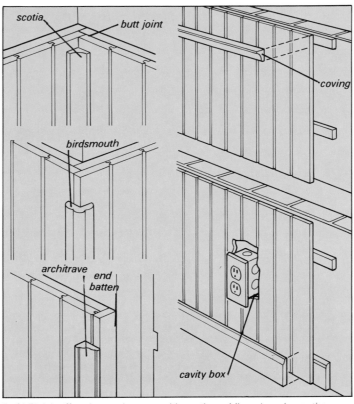

(Left) Finish off an internal corner with scotia molding pinned over the butt-joined boards and use birdsmouth molding at an external corner; at a window frame, pin on an end batten and cover with architrave.
(Right) Fix coving at ceiling level and mount electrical outlets in cavity boxes.

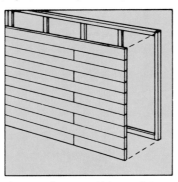

An outer frame and intermediate vertical battens support horizontal panelling; butt join the ends of boards over a batten.

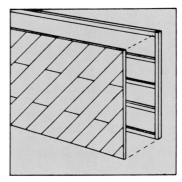

For diagonal panelling the battens run horizontally; stagger the ends in adjacent rows and align them in alternate rows.

and baseboards can be bought in separate packs.

Buy the panelling at least two weeks in advance so that it has time to acclimatize to the warmth of the room: the wood will shrink a little.

When buying, examine the boards for warps, splits and loose knots. Take the room measurements to the lumber yard to confirm the number of boards required: basically the width (or height) of the wall divided by the width of the board, taking into account the length of the boards required and allowing

for joins. Buy a few extra to allow for wastage and mistakes.

Methods of Fixing

The panelling is either pinned to battens or, on a hollow partition wall, can be pinned direct to the vertical studs and horizontal bracing; find the position of the framing by tapping the wall and mark them as a guide for the pinning of the panelling.

When battens are being used added insulation can be incorporated by fitting polystyrene sheet or mineral fiber blanket

between the battens. To protect against condensation it's advisable to hang a sheet of plastic flat to the wall behind the battens; they will hold it in place.

The battens should be 50 × 25mm (1 × 2in) sawn wood (their finish is unimportant as they don't show). They should be fixed at 600mm (2ft) intervals, running in the opposite direction to the panelling and must be absolutely horizontal (or vertical). The arrangement of the battens will be affected by the way the panelling is to be arranged (see diagram). They must be nailed or screwed to the wall at the point where joins in the panelling are to be made, in order to support them.

The panelling is secret-nailed through the tongue at an angle into the batten so as not to be visible on the surface: the groove of the adjoining board conceals the fixing. If the panelling has been bought in kit form special clips may have been provided which obviate the need for secret nailing — they also lessen the chances of splitting the tongues of the boards.

Existing architraves and base boards can be panelled over with batten-mounted panelling, if the battens are thicker than the obstructions. Alternatively they can be removed. Electrical fixtures may need to be remounted flush with the panelling (see page 128).

Fixing the Battens

Fix the battens vertically or horizontally, according to the choice of panelling, with 63mm (2½in) masonry nails or 63mm (2½in) No. 8 countersunk woodscrews. Drive in the nails so that they just break through the wood before positioning the batten against the wall. Check that it is level (use a spirit level) and drive the nails fully home. With screws, pre-drill pilot holes in the batten, mark the wall, drill for plugs and then screw into position. If incorporating insulation, remember to fit the plastic sheet now.

Not only must the battens be level but also their faces must lie flat. Check this with a straight-edged plank of wood and pack out any irregularities with offcuts of hardboard. An existing base board can act as a horizontal batten and may also need padding out.

At an external corner, butt the end of one batten to the face of another. Fit extra battens at obstructions such as windows and doors, fixing them around them. Cut slabs of insulation material to fit between the battens. They'll need no other fixing.

Fixing the Panelling

Cut the first board to length and offer it up to the wall, tongue outwards. Check that it is straight with a spirit level or plumb line. If not, it can either be scribed to fit or a slight gap left which can later be concealed with a length of molding.

To scribe the board, fix it temporarily to the wall, absolutely straight. Place a small block of wood on the board, one edge pressed to the side wall, and hold a pencil against the outer edge: it's useful to tape the pencil to the block. Run the two down the board to mark the wall profile and saw along the pencil line with a rip saw.

Fix the first board in position tongue outermost and secure it to the battens with 25mm (1in) long panel pins knocked through the tongue at an angle of 45 degrees. (On wood-framed walls, use 35mm/1¼in long nails.) Offer up the next board, slot the groove over the tongue. Tap it in close, at the top, middle and bottom, protecting the edge of the board with an offcut. Nail the board then continue fixing the panelling across the wall.

At an external corner, plane off the tongue and/or cut the board down to overlap the corner by the thickness of the panelling. Butt the grooved edge of the board on the other side of the angle up to it. Conceal the joint with right-angled molding.

Fit the panelling close to doors and windows and nail on new architrave to conceal the edges.

To avoid difficulty in fitting the last board into an internal angle, don't secure the previous two boards, but instead slot the three together, position the groove of the first one over the tongue of the last board on the wall and snap the three into place together for a tight fit. Butt the

first board on the facing wall into the corner and conceal the join with molding.

Fit ceiling molding and new base board to conceal cut edges at the top and bottom of the wall.

Using Fixing Clips

Where clips are supplied with the panelling, the boards should be fitted with the groove outwards. Slot the clips on to the lower edge of the groove and nail

to the battens through their small fixing holes. The tongue of the next board slots into the groove, concealing the clip.

Wainscotting

This is wood panelling fitted vertically to a height of about 1m (3ft). It is fitted in exactly the same way as full wall panelling, a top edge of molding being fitted to conceal the cut ends of all the boards. A wide lipping can also serve as a narrow shelf.

Panelling Ceilings

The principle is the same as that for walls, with battens being fixed at intervals across the ceiling. A special ceiling molding can be fitted all the way round to conceal both cut ends of boards and any slight gaps where the room is not square.

Sealing the Panelling

The wood must be sealed or it will quickly become dirty. Varnish gives it a tough finish, and you can apply stain or wood dye first to alter its color. The panelling can also be painted: semi gloss paint gives a pleasantly soft sheen to the surface while for a shiny finish choose enamel. Any of the special paint effects — grainy, marbling, rag rolling — described on page 172, can be applied to the match-boarding for a dramatic effect.

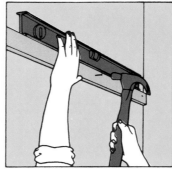

After hammering masonry nails into the batten, nailing it horizontally to the wall over a vapor barrier of plastic sheeting.

Before hammering the nails fully home, inserting shims of wood to pack out low areas; check for level with a straight-edge.

Fitting cut slabs of styrofoam between the battens to provide thermal insulation; no fixing is needed.

Holding the first board vertically, groove against an uneven end wall, and scribing on to the board; cut and pin in place, tongue outwards.

Knocking the groove of the second board over the tongue of the first by hammering against an offcut; check that the board is vertical.

Pinning the board to the battens by hammering 25mm (1in) long panel pins through the tongue at 45° and punching below the surface.

After locating the ceiling joists and nailing battens to them at right-angles to the panelling, fitting the tongued-and-grooved boards.

Although painting the exterior walls of your house is primarily meant to revive a shabby appearance, the treatment is equally important to protect the structure from the effects of the weather; paint deteriorates more rapidly outside a house than inside because of the harsh treatment it receives. Not only does it have to contend with severe variations in temperature but also a regular dashing with rain and wind, which, at best, will leave it looking dirty at worst, will cause problems with damp, rot and a general breakdown in the structure.

The most important thing to remember when contemplating painting walls that have previously been left plain is that, once decorated, the finish will have to be maintained on a regular basis.

The answer for brick walls that look good as they are is to paint them with a clear water repellant. This prevents the penetration of moisture, preserving the condition of the brickwork without altering its natural appearance (see page 81).

Planning to Paint

It is not necessary to paint the entire house at one time. Adopt a regular cycle, by treating one or two elevations one year, then dealing with the others the next, then repeating the process every four or five years. The weather should be warm but the sun not too hot: a calm, dry day between late spring and early autumn is ideal.

When redecorating, it is quite likely that one wall will be in far worse condition that the others, because it is in a more exposed position. It could even be that this wall will need redecorating on a more regular basis than the rest of the house. Don't create work: don't paint sheltered walls that are in good condition, unless of course a change in color is planned.

It's sensible to carry out a regular check on the condition of the exterior paintwork; here is a some guidance as to the regularity with which certain checks should be carried out. A house in a city or town is likely to need more regular treatment than one in the country.

For all houses, clear the gutters of debris each year and check the condition of leaders. Check over and clean ledges and sills every two years. Nothing will ruin the paintwork more rapidly than leaking gutters, leaders and window sills with clogged drip grooves, which allow water to trickle onto the wall surface instead of throwing it clear.

On a city house a paint finish should last for at least five years, if it has been properly applied; in country areas it could last twice as long.

Never leave paint until it reaches the point of cracking and lifting. If it is caught before this stage the preparation will be much easier and quicker.

Industrial pollution is a major hazard in towns and cities and, although the paintwork may be in good repair, it will be dirty: a rigid policy of washing down annually will keep it looking in trim.

Preparing to Paint

Adequate preparation of exterior paintwork is vital, even though the finished appearance may not be as important as interior finishes: the protective qualities are paramount. Full details on preparing exterior walls and some common repairs that may be necessary are given on page 156.

Carry out all preparation first, of walls, woodwork and metal, so that there is no danger of paint chippings or cleaning agents falling on newly painted surfaces. Work from the top of the house down for the same reason.

Aids to Decorating

The main problem is access to the upper areas of the house. An option to a ladder is scaffolding, which you can rent: towers of different heights, ending in a wooden platform and ones fitted with castors for mobility (without having to dismantle the sections) are a good choice. When erecting the tower; beware of positioning it too close to the wall, making it difficult to reach the area immediately in front of the scaffolding. Don't forget to lock any castors before you mount the tower. When using a ladder, choose an extension type fitted with a ladder stay, which clips over the top rung of the ladder and supports it away from the wall and the guttering: the stay is wider than the ladder and has a much better grip, so it's not likely to slip sideways. It also makes it much easier to attach a paint kettle to an upper rung; this can hang in front of the painter, making it easy to reload a brush or roller while keeping one hand on the ladder all the time for safety.

The painting of large areas is greatly speeded by using a roller and many rollers can be fitted with an extension pole, allowing the painter to work without a ladder in lower areas and extending the reach of a ladder in upper areas.

Exterior Wall Finishes: Some Special Considerations

Brick New brickwork must be allowed to dry out for at least three months before any painting is attempted.

If in any doubt of the stability of

Painting a pebbledash wall using a dustpan brush, after masking drainpipes with newspaper, to ensure that the mortar also is painted.

After filling a wide bucket ⅓ full with paint, pulling the loaded roller over a board to ensure uniform coverage.

Starting at the top right-hand corner (if right-handed), cutting in under the eaves with a brush, taking care not to overstretch.

Again working from the right if right-handed, painting a row of vertical, slightly overlapping strips with the roller.

After completing one width of the wall, painting a second series of strips, working in easy-to-reach stages across the wall.

Near ground level, using the roller with an extension handle to avoid having to dismount and remount the ladder for each strip.

old brickwork, painted or plain, paint it first liberally with a stabilizing solution; this will give a sound base on which to decorate. One coat of primer is sufficient. If you're going to use resin-based paint, apply an all-surface primer instead.

Rendering Always looks better painted. If the finish is fairly smooth it will be possible to use a roller. Rough cast rendering, which tends to hold more dirt than smooth surfaces, will need particularly thorough cleaning before being painted with a large distemper brush.

Pebbledash This tends to deteriorate more rapidly than other wall finishes because any movement in the mortar, shrinking or expansion, causes cracks which lift the pebbles which eventually fall off leaving bald patches. Paint will conceal many of the defects very effectively, sealing small cracks and preventing further deterioration. It makes repairs a little simpler too, as the color of the pebbles used to fill bald patches will not matter if they are to be painted over. To ensure good paint coverage, particularly to the mortar between the pebbles, it is best to use a lambswool roller or large distemper brush.

Stone The easiest surface to paint, being the smoothest. Use a roller for speed. If the surface is at all powdery or stained, use a stabilizing solution as a primer.

Painting the Walls

Follow the sun around the house, starting on the wall it has

Masking off windows with large sheets of paper or plastic before painting walls with a spray-gun; lay dust-sheets on the ground.

Mask drainpipes with newspaper. Work from the bottom upwards; stick joints between sheets, and edges with masking tape.

After thinning the paint as recommended for the equipment, spraying towards breaks in the wall, such as drainpipes.

Continue downwards in horizontal strips; spray over edges of all masked-off areas and keep gun at right-angles to wall.

Removing the masking tape from masked-off areas before the paint has dried, otherwise the paint may peel away with it.

Painting the remaining areas with a brush; use a small brush to cut in round door and window frames and to paint behind drainpipes.

just left, so that it has time to dry out the surface before you reach it. The positioning of the ladder is important. For right-handed people, erect it at the right side of the wall, about 600mm (24in) from the end. Point the wall to the right only; do not try to paint from both sides of the ladder. When this area is finished, move the ladder to the left and paint the next area. This way, the ladder is always being moved

onto unpainted areas. If you're left-handed, reverse the process.

Always start at the top of the wall. Aim always to have a wet edge of paint to brush into the next area being painted; dried edges will show and exterior wall paint dries very quickly.

Paint the whole wall in one go or stop only at an obvious break-off point: where a downpipe divides a wall, it is acceptable to

paint the two halves of the wall separately, so long as the same paint mix is used. The joining line will be concealed by the pipe. Likewise, paint definite 'bays' formed by corners of walls, windows and door frames.

Always apply the paint generously and wash off splashes promptly as the paint dries quickly.

OPTIONS

PAINT FOR EXTERIOR WALLS

The various special paints suitable for all types of masonry are:
● Exterior grade latex.
Similar to the indoor type, a water-based liquid that dries to a smooth, matt finish. More durable than its indoor counterpart, it comes in a wide range of colors and contains a mold-resisting additive. It's usual to apply a thinned

priming coat on porous walls, followed by one or two full strength coats.
● Reinforced latex.
A water-thinnable, spirit-based liquid with added fine aggregate (such as mica) for a finely textured finish. Two coats are necessary and the paint will cover hairline cracks.
● Cement paint.
The cheapest exterior wall paint, comes as a dry powder which you mix with water in the proportions 2:1. There's a limited range of colors, but clean sand

can be added to give extra protection on an exposed wall.
● Stone paint.
A durable treatment for any type of masonry, capable of filling minor cracks in walls.
● Masonry paint.
A resin-based paint which dries to a tough, semi-gloss finish. It should be applied in a thinned first coat (using white spirit) to prime the surface for two full strength coats.

Exterior woodwork suffers deterioration more rapidly than any other part of the house. This is basically because wood is extremely sensitive to moisture. Rising moisture content in the wood is stronger than the paint film covering it and will break through, lifting the paint.

Obviously, exterior woodwork is subject to constant attack by moisture, from rain, early morning dew and, possibly, at lower levels, damp from the soil. Thorough preparation is essential if a decorative paint finish is to last.

Preparing to Paint

Details of preparing wood for painting is given on page 157.

Remember always to prime bare patches and prime areas that are to be filled both before and after filling. Make sure the primer is absorbed well into the wood.

Never paint in full sun: the heat will accelerate the drying process unnaturally and the paint may wrinkle, flake off or blister. Don't be tempted to start painting too early in the morning either, as dew could easily ruin a smooth coat of paint, thinning and streaking it.

Paints for Exterior Woodwork

Ordinary gloss paint, like that used inside the home, is suitable for external use but it has a major drawback: it provides an impermeable seal on wood, which prevents the penetration of moisture from the outside but equally does not let any moisture inside escape. So pressure of

moisture builds up and finally breaks through, lifting and cracking the paint. Internal moisture can now escape but that from outside can also get in. This is how the rot sets in.

This problem can be overcome by buying one of the brands of paint specially formulated for exterior wood. These allow the wood to 'breathe': the moisture escapes in the form of water vapour.

Several brands are available, some having the added advantage that they need no primer or undercoat. The paint is applied direct to the prepared wood and dries to a smooth sheen rather than a high gloss. Specially formulated gloss paint is also available but this does require the usual primer and undercoat.

An alternative to paint is varnish — ideal where you want to retain the natural graining of the wood. Again there are specially-formulated brands for exterior use (such as yacht varnish). Another finish that maintains the natural appearance of the wood is a decorative wood preservative combining a water repellent with a wood preserver and a color pigment. This will restore the color to wood that has been bleached by the weather and has become rather grey, while protecting it from further attack by both moisture and insects.

Painting Soffits, Bargeboards and Fascias

Being at the top of the house, these are the areas of wood to paint first. According to the choice of paint, apply one coat of

undercoat after the wood has been sanded down, filled and spot-primed. Although primer can be left uncovered for a few days, undercoat cannot. The first application of top coat should follow within 48 hours.

The finish of the top coat is unimportant from an appearance point of view as these areas are well above eye level. Make sure a good covering of paint is applied, though, for protection purposes. Being high up and, therefore more exposed, these areas are particularly vulnerable to the elements. Although two coats of enamel should be sufficient, an extra one could be worthwhile. Apply the paint more generously than on interior surfaces.

Painting Windows

Paint the upper windows first, following the same sequence as for painting the inside (see page 178). Use a paint guard or masking tape to protect the edge of the glass (be very careful that the masking tape does not become baked on in hot weather as it's then difficult to remove). Any paint drips on the glass can be scraped off when it has dried. There are special scrapers but a razor blade is just as effective.

Don't overload the brush: too great a build-up of paint on the edges will cause the windows to stick. Paint both the top and bottom edges of the sashes as this is where rain penetration is most likely. When painting over the putty, extend the paint on to the glass by about 3mm (⅛in) to provide a waterproof seal against damp, protecting both the putty and the wood frame.

Windowsills: wooden sills have a drip groove on their underside, running the length of the sill, designed to prevent rainwater dripping over the edge of the sill and running back along the underside into the wall. Keep this clear of debris and excess paint. The underside should be painted for protection.

Painting Cladding

The largest area of wood likely to be found on a house is wood cladding. It is essential that the edges and end grain are thoroughly protected to prevent

moisture penetration.

For a natural finish, a decorative wood preservative, which will maintain its color as well as protect it, is a good choice. This type of finish is also available in non-wood colors, still let the grain show.

A large brush can be used to speed the operation slightly. Do not bother rubbing down between coats. If the paint is applied as directed on the can, observing the drying times, this will be unnecessary.

Spot-priming chipped paintwork; when the primer has dried, fill the chip level with the surface, smooth, reprime and paint.

Painting Exterior Doors

The exterior doors should be the last area of wood to be painted. Whereas the window frames and other areas are quite likely to be painted white, this is one area where color can be introduced quite confidently. It will not be interfering with neighboring schemes and makes a strong focal point for the exterior.

Follow the sequence for painting that is given for painting the inside (see page 177), according to the type of door being painted. The highest level of finish is needed, particularly on the front door, and the work should not be hurried. See page 177 for the correct application of enamel paint. Remember to paint both the top and bottom edges and that at the bottom of the door. If necessary, take the door off its hinges to do this. This end grain is susceptible to penetration by dampness and the bottom of the door is the most vulnerable part.

Painting a soffit with a brush; spot-prime any chips, undercoat and apply at least two liberal coats of enamel paint.

Protecting shiplap wood cladding with an oil-based exterior varnish; don't use polyurethane varnish as it breaks down in sunlight.

The painting of exterior metalwork is often the final bit of decorating to be done. For those with no metalwork on the house itself it can be tempting to put the brushes away after the final touch has been given to the doors. But even a single gate needs the protection that sound paintwork provides and there is little point in having a property to be proud of when the entrance is an eye-sore.

It is only too obvious when metal is deteriorating, rust being the noticeable effect. Although extensive corrosion can look alarming, with today's special treatments even the worst areas can be dealt with.

Preparing to Paint

This has been made much easier with the rust-neutralizer treatments that are now available. However, these are not always necessary and, where the rust is not extensive and is easily brushed away, a rust-inhibiting primer will be sufficient. Do apply this liberally; it is the most important stage in the decorating procedure.

Paints for Exterior Metalwork

Gloss enamel paint is that most commonly used. There are now enamel paints that are particularly formulated for metal, although they can be used on woodwork too.

These paints are very tough and will transform a pitted surface into one that is smooth and glossy: one brand gives a beaten metal effect, particularly attractive on railings and gates. The surface must be sanded to provide a key and all loose rust removed, but it is not essential to remove all the old paintwork and firm dry rust. Old paint should be cleaned thoroughly to remove all traces of grease and dirt.

Most ordinary paints are applied with a brush, spray or roller. Only one generous coat is needed but it may be easier with vertical surfaces to apply two thinner coats and thus avoid sags and runs in the paint. The paint is touch-dry in 30 minutes so the waiting time between coats is minimal.

Rubbing down a steel window frame with steel wool to remove any rust and to provide a key on the painted areas for the new paint.

After wiping off all traces of rust and debris with a clean cloth, appyling a coat of primer over the bare metal areas.

Brushing off rust from a cast iron soil or rainwater downpipe using a wire brush; check that all fixings are securely in the wall.

Protecting the wall behind a downpipe with masonite to prevent paint splashes; pay particular attention to the back of the pipe.

Drying guttering with a cloth after removing all rust and debris and washing out thoroughly with a hosepipe or plenty of water.

Painting the inside of cast iron guttering with black bitumen paint after sealing any leaking joints with bitumen cement.

The thicker the finish the better. It should be the equivalent of four coats of ordinary gloss paint.

Painting Guttering

Cast iron guttering needs regular maintenance. Common faults that can be easily remedied are given on page 113. The best treatment for new or repaired lengths of guttering is to paint the inside with a bituminous paint. This resists the corrosive effects of rain and there's no need to prime the metal first.

For the decoration of the outside of the guttering and the downpipes, having primed the metal with a zinc chromate primer, apply one undercoat and two top coats of enamel. Protect the wall behind the downpipes with a piece of card. Splashes of enamel paint on the wall are difficult to remove and look awful. A small paint pad on a long handle can be useful for getting round the back of pipes that are set close to the wall.

When the condition of the guttering is such that replacement is a consideration, the type requiring least maintenance is plastic. It comes in either black or grey and needs no paint protection. Should the color be changed though, clean the plastic with white spirit or turpentine and apply two coats of enamel paint. There is no need to prime or undercoat plastic.

Painting Metal Doors and Windows

These require the same careful protection as wooden doors and windows and should be painted in the same sequence as the insides. Be careful to protect the top and bottom edges with a good coating of primer and paint. Although the paint coat needs to be thick, several thin coats applied one on top of the other will be more satisfactory and the problem of sags and runs will be avoided. On windows and glazed doors, remember to continue the paint over the putty to form a watertight seal on the glass.

Painting Gates and Railings

These will inevitably be awk-ward and the simplest way to deal with an iron gate is to remove it from its hinges and lay it flat on a large piece of cardboard (an opened-out cardboard box will do). Paint the gate with a large brush, using the paint generously, turning it to paint the other side when the first is completely dry.

Railings, unfortunately, are not so easy to remove. Make sure the angles between uprights and horizontal bars are well brushed to remove loose rust and that both primer and all coats of paint are applied well into the crevices.

Painting an iron gate after lifting it off its hinges and laying it flat on cardboard; paint one side, allow to dry, then paint the other.

HOME SECURITY

Many people may feel that it is the job of the police to fight crime — after all that is what they are paid to do. But in reality taking steps to defeat the criminal is something we all have a duty to do, not just by doing all we can to help the police catch criminals but by doing our best to prevent crimes occurring in the first place.

A major contribution that all householders can make to this fight is to ensure that their homes are well protected against burglars and intruders of all kinds. Developing a security conscious attitude and investing a relatively small amount of money in security devices will provide a high degree of protection for you, your family and your possessions.

How Vulnerable is your Home?

It's surprising just how many people believe that they would never be burgled, that they don't have anything worth stealing. The fact is that just about every home — be it a grand mansion or a lowly studio — has something of value in it. Stereo systems, TV sets, video recorders, jewellery, even small amounts of cash can be found in most places and it is this fact that encourages the opportunist thief (who commits a high proportion of burglaries) to take the chance when he can see an easy way in.

Some houses are more vulnerable than others; those that stand on their own in secluded grounds or those surrounded by tall hedges or fences are prime targets since they allow the thief to work unseen at breaking in. Closed-in porches, side gates and bushy shrubs by windows provide similar cover.

The last thing a thief wants is to be seen at work, or risk an encounter with the householder, so he will take steps to check that the house is empty first. At night he will look for a house showing no lights, and during the day a build-up of newpapers will indicate that the family is away. He may even knock on the door, giving a bogus story if anyone answers.

Most people will take the trouble to provide strong locks and bolts on their front door, but the back door is probably at greater risk of attack since it will probably be more secluded. Back doors often have pathetically inadequate locks that would give way under a shoulder charge and they are usually glazed, allowing the thief to break the glass and reach the latch inside. Often the householder will conveniently leave the key in the lock. Many back doors open outwards making the hinges vulnerable; all the thief has to do is drive out the hinge pins and lift the door from its opening.

Windows, with their large areas of easily broken glass and usually wooden frames, are really at risk. The catches can often be jarred free by simply pounding on the window frame, or a knife blade can be slipped between the opening and fixed frames to flip the catch. Many householders conveniently leave a transom open, allowing the thief to reach the catches inside, or to pass his junior assistant through.

Even upstairs windows are at risk if there's a means of climbing up to them: a drainpipe, large tree or a ladder left in a conveniently unlocked shed.

Once in, a burglar will arrange an easy escape route, usually the front or back door, and again keys are often left handily in the locks they operate or close by. Some locks do not even need a key to open them from inside. Yet if the burglar is denied this easy exit, he may leave empty handed since carrying bulky objects like TV sets through small, broken windows is often impossible.

Working out just how vulnerable your house is can be achieved by putting yourself in the burglar's shoes and imagining that you have locked yourself out. How would you get back in? A burglar knows all the tricks you would use and a lot more, so if it is not too difficult for you, think how easy it will be for him.

The best method of all for working out your security needs, however, is to contact your local police and ask their Crime Prevention Officer to call. He will inspect your house from top to bottom, show you its weak points and advise you on the steps to take to improve it — all at no charge.

The locks fitted to the doors of your house by the builder are usually woefully inadequate, so a major step forwards in providing greater protection is to replace them with something more substantial. Any improvements should not be limited to the front door only; the back door is just as much at risk, if not more so since it will probably be of inferior construction compared to the front door and may well be in a more secluded position. Always treat the front and back doors in the same manner, fitting the same type of locks to each. And don't forget any sliding patio doors or French windows either.

Before investing money in strong locks, however, examine the condition of the doors and frames. If the doors are warped or rotten, or the frames loose in their openings, put this right first. Many thieves are not averse to levering out a door and frame (or a window frame for that matter) to be able to get in. Make sure the doors are soundly made and at least 38mm (1½in) thick.

Rim Latches

Most front doors are fitted with a spring-loaded cylinder latch, also known as a rim latch or night latch. This is screwed to the inner face of the door so that it shoots its bolt into a staple mounted on the adjacent frame. The bolt is operated by a key from outside and a knob on the inside. One side of the bolt is curved so that as the door is pushed closed, it rides over the edge of the staple and springs out again to latch the door. A sliding catch

is provided for holding the bolt in the extended or withdrawn positions.

This type of latch is very weak by virtue of the fact that it is surface mounted, relying purely on the strength of its fixing screws for security. On a glazed door, all the thief has to do is break the glass and reach in to turn the knob, or he can often slide a piece of flexible plastic such as a credit card between the door and frame to push the bolt back.

Such a lock should either be replaced with something stronger or be supplemented with a second, stronger lock. A security version of the rim latch is available and will often fit directly into the space occupied by the old lock. At most, you may only need to do a little paring of the door edge with a chisel to make it fit. Instead of a spring-loaded, curved bolt, this version has a square-edged bolt operated from both inside and out by a key. This is known as a deadlock and it cannot be sprung back.

Some versions have a spring-loaded bolt as well which is withdrawn by handles on each side of the lock. This is ideal for securing the door when you are home and going in and out of the house a lot.

However, such locks still have the basic weakness of being secured to the surface of the door by ordinary screws.

Mortise Deadlocks

A much more secure lock is the mortise deadlock, the body of which actually fits inside the door, shooting its bolt into a

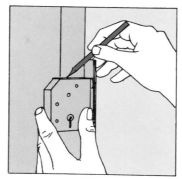
Fitting a mortise deadlock: Marking the height of the lock body on the edge of the door; then mark the depth on both faces.

After chiselling out the mortise and checking for fit (with bolt extended to assist removal), mark the keyhole with a bradawl.

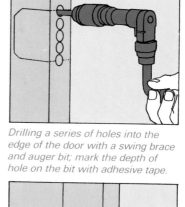
Drilling a series of holes into the edge of the door with a swing brace and auger bit; mark the depth of hole on the bit with adhesive tape.

Cutting the keyhole with a padsaw after drilling right through the door into a block of wood to prevent the surface from splitting.

recess cut in the edge of the door frame. In order to overcome such a lock, a burglar would have to destroy the door around it.

Fitting a mortise lock is more difficult than a rim latch, since you must cut a slot in the door for its body, and that slot must only just be wide enough otherwise you run the risk of weakening the door. Normally, the bulk of the slot is cut by boring a series of holes into the door edge with a brace and bit, or flat bit in a power drill, then cleaning up the sides with a chisel.

Will they Fit?

An important point to consider when buying locks is whether they will fit the doors. You will need to know the width of the vertical door stile and also the thickness of the door. Mortise locks, for example, cannot be fitted to doors less than 38mm (1½in) thick, and even then it would have to be a special narrow version.

Fitting a deadlocking rimlatch: Drilling a hole through the door for the cylinder using a flat bit in an electric drill.

After slipping the latch-pull (if fitted) over the cylinder barrel, pushing the cylinder into its hole from the outside of the door.

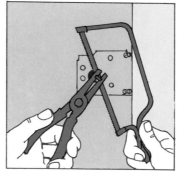
After screwing the backplate to the inside face of the door, holding the connecting bar with pliers and cutting to length with a hacksaw.

Screwing the latch case to the backplate after securing the cylinder; some types need rebating into the edge of the door.

SECURING DOORS

Other forms of Protection

Fitting strong locks is fine, but there may still be other areas of the door at risk, particularly the corners where a crowbar can be inserted to lever it out. Additional protection can be provided by fixing stout bolts to the top and bottom of the door so that they slide into the frame above and the sill below. However, on a glazed door, it may be possible to reach these after breaking the glass and a better idea is the rack bolt (see below).

Outward opening doors should be protected by fitting hinge bolts to their back edges next to the hinges. These hardened steel studs fit into holes in the door frame when the door is closed, preventing removal of the door even if the hinge pins are removed. They can be fitted to inward opening doors, too, for extra protection.

Protecting Sliding Doors

Sliding patio doors are particularly vulnerable to attack

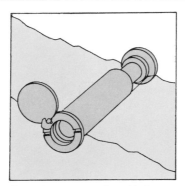

Door viewers are adjustable in length; use a broad-bladed screwdriver to tighten the eyepiece on to the outer section.

Fitting the locking plate of a rack bolt to the door frame; mark the position by closing the door and operating the bolt.

since they can be levered from their tracks and removed to provide easy entry. To prevent this a patio door lock should be fitted. This is fixed to the edge of the inner door or fixed portion with self tapping screws. When operated, it shoots a bolt into a hole drilled in the outer door, preventing it from being levered upwards or sideways. Most are set by pushing a button and unlocked with a key.

Protecting Outbuildings

Outbuildings such as garages and garden sheds should not be ignored since they often contain a useful selection of tools and equipment which the burglar can use to break in with. And, of course, they may contain valuable items in their own right.

The favourite method of securing outbuilding doors is with a hinged metal flap known as a pad bar and a padlock. The pad bar fits over a staple on the door frame, and the best

examples cover the fixing screw or bolt heads when closed.

Padlocks should always be sturdy with short, thick shackles that cannot be easily cut with bolt cutters. One particular example has a strong steel cover that fits over the shackle when closed.

Door Viewer

It is always a wise precaution to see who is calling before you open the door, and the easiest way is with a compact door viewer. Depending on the type, this has a wide-angle lens which gives a field of view between 160° and 190°, so you can see a caller even if he or she is standing to one side of the door.

Fitting is simple, you just push the outer section through a hole drilled in the door at eye level and screw on the eyepiece to secure it.

Trick

Fitting a lock bar into a recess cut in the door frame; make sure that the screws grip firmly into solid wood.

Fitting a rack bolt into a hole drilled in the edge of a door; only a small escutcheon is visible on the closed door.

LOCK BARS & RACK BOLTS

An alternative to the traditional door chain which prevents a bogus caller forcing the door open, but allows you to open it sufficiently to identify him, is the lock bar or door limiter. The pivotting, cast metal bar screws to the door frame and engages with a bracket screwed to the door. When connected, the bar limits the amount by which the door can be opened. To open the door fully, you must first close it so that the pegs on the door bracket can be disengaged from their slots in the bar.

The rack bolt is a more secure alternative to the ordinary surface-mounted bolt. It fits into a hole drilled in the edge of the door and is operated by a splined key from inside, the bolt shooting into a hole in the door frame. Smaller versions are made for windows.

Fitting dual screws to sash windows: With the sashes fully closed, drilling through the inner into the outer meeting rail.

Screwing the locking plate to the outer meeting rail after recessing it; some types have a barrel which is hammered in instead.

Screwing the threaded barrel into the inner meeting rail until it is flush with the surface; easy-fit types are hammered in.

Locking the sashes by passing the screw through the threaded barrel into the outer rail; ensure that it turns freely before using the key.

Fitting good strong locks to the external doors of the house is important, but it is just as essential to lock up the windows as well, even those upstairs. Windows with their large, breakable panes of glass and weaker frames are much more vulnerable than doors, providing an easy means of entry for the burglar. Fortunately, there is a wide range of window locks to choose from, all of which are designed for home handyman installation. Most are reasonably priced.

Before buying window locks, consider carefully your needs, bearing in mind the type of windows you have and the materials from which they are made. Some locks are universal in their application, while others are intended for specific types of window or a particular frame material — you must get the right type.

Windows can have wooden, steel, aluminum or even plastic frames and their opening portions may be side hung, top hung, pivotting, horizontally sliding or vertically sliding. Often locks which appear the same are intended for one particular type of frame material with a particular style of opening light.

Another important consideration is the ease of use of a lock. Some locks operate automatically when you close the window, whereas others have to be set by turning a knob, pushing a button, or turning a key. In each case they must be released by turning a key. Yet another, simpler type has to be screwed down with a special key and unscrewed to allow the window to be opened.

To be effective, window locks must be set every time you go

out and if they are too difficult or time-consuming to use, you'll end up not using them at all, which will defeat the object of having them. There may be windows which you open regularly and others which are seldom opened and here you may be able to economise by fitting the simpler and cheaper screw-down types to the latter and the more expensive automatic, or semi-automatic types to the former.

Whatever you do, you should fit at least one lock to every opening window in the house and preferably two on tall windows, spacing them so that they hold the corners of the opening frame tightly in place. This will prevent a burglar forcing a crowbar between the two portions of frame to lever them apart.

Window locks may be opened by conventional keys or often by specially shaped keys; hexagonal or splined for example. Often it is possible to buy several different types of lock to suit different types of window, yet they can all be

opened by the same key. This is useful since you don't have to carry a large bunch of keys around with you when you are opening the windows in summer. You should always keep the keys where they are easily accessible — you may need to use the window as an escape route in the event of a fire — but never near the window they control. Otherwise, a burglar might be able to break the glass, reach the key and let himself in.

Locks for Wooden Windows

The advantage of wood is that it is easily cut and drilled and this has led to the greatest range of locks being available for wooden windows. Not only that but often the locks on wooden windows are stronger than on other materials because rebates can be cut in the frame for the lock body and for its bolt. Locks on all other materials must be surface-mounted with screws.

Without a doubt, the strongest form of lock for a wooden

Fitting a push-lock to a casement window: mark the position on frame and casement, screwing backplate to the casement.

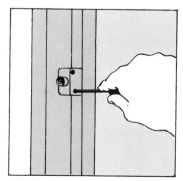

After fitting the lock body over the backplate, screwing it to the frame; fit the wedge supplied if the side of the frame is bevelled.

window is a smaller version of the door rack bolt. This is set in a hole in the edge of the opening frame and shoots its bolt into the fixed frame. It can't be seen from outside and can't be tampered with. The only point to watch with this type of lock is that the frame is thick enough for it to be fitted without actually weakening the wood. Ideally, the hole bored in the frame edge for the lock body should not be more than a third of the total thickness.

If you have doubts about the frame thickness, you will have to use a surface-mounted lock, and the easiest to operate is the automatic type. With this the lock body is screwed to the fixed portion of the frame and a metal stud screwed to the opening portion. As the window is pulled to, the stud snaps into the lock body and is held fast until released with the key. This type of lock is ideal for windows which are opened often.

In terms of strength, however, it is probably better to fit the type that shoots a bolt into a rebate cut in the fixed portion of the frame. These may be either push-button operated or set by turning a small knob. The rebate is either a round hole or a narrow slot cut with a chisel, depending on the type of bolt.

The simplest type of window locks are the screw-down type and they come in various styles. One has a hasp for the opening frame and a staple for the fixed portion. To lock it, the hasp is flipped over the staple and a threaded stud in the former tightened against the latter. Another type comprises a threaded stud in a bracket on the opening frame which screws

213

SECURING WINDOWS

into a hole in the fixed frame.

A variation on the theme is the dual screw: a long stud which screws into a threaded ferrule in the opening frame and extends into a receiver ferrule set in a hole in the fixed frame.

All of the above mentioned locks are suitable for hinged or pivotted windows, but sliding sash windows present their own particular problems. The usual method of locking them is to fit something that will prevent one sash sliding past the other. The dual screw is ideal for this, the receiver being fitted in the upper sash; and if two receivers, the window can be locked partially open for ventilation.

Purpose-made sash window locks usually have a surface-mounted lock body for the lower sash, which shoots a bolt into a bracket fixed to the upper sash or into a hole drilled in it. There is also a rack bolt which is set in a rebate in the upper sash to stop the sashes passing each other.

Locks for Metal-framed Windows

Locks for metal windows are invariably held in place by self-tapping screws, but make sure the locks you buy have the right screws for the frame material — steel windows will need a different type of screw to aluminum ones.

There are fewer choices of lock for metal framed windows because it is not possible to cut rebates in the frames. Many of those available are intended to be screwed to the opening frame and shoot their bolts across the face of the fixed frame. Often these are universal types which can also be fitted to wooden windows. Since they are surface-mounted they can be seen and may be tampered with. Some types fit inside the window opening rebate, key-operated through a hole in the frame.

The largest selection of locks for metal windows comprises devices for preventing the cockspur handle turning or for clamping the stay to its rest. These are also suitable for wooden windows, too. They are not the most secure of fittings but are better than nothing, and in some cases may be your only choice.

Cockspur handle locks are usually in the form of a sliding bolt screwed to the fixed frame. When the cockspur handle is in the closed position, the bolt is slid up beneath its nose and locked to prevent the handle being turned.

Stay locks may be in the form of a clamp that fits round the stay and rest or a sliding bolt which attaches to the stay and can be locked beneath the rest. The latter type occupies some of the holes in the stay.

If you have horizontally sliding, metal framed windows you can fit a smaller version of

Fitting a pivoting lock to a metal casement window: marking the fixing positions for the staple on the fixed frame with the lock closed.

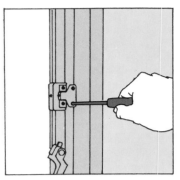
After opening the lock and drilling pilot holes, screwing the staple to the frame with self-tapping screws; cover the heads with plastic plugs.

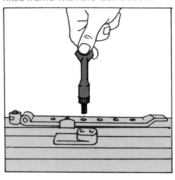
Securing a casement stay with a screw stop; the socket fits in place of the existing pin, and a clamp is used on an undrilled stay.

A sliding cockspur-handle lock, screwed to the casement below the handle, restrains the handle when pushed up and is released by a key.

the patio door lock mentioned previously. French windows can be fitted with many of the locks mentioned above, depending on whether they are wooden or metal framed.

One important point to consider with all surface-mounted locks is that they are only as strong as their mounting screws, so make sure they are substantial. For extra security, plastic plugs are often supplied to blank off the screw heads, or you can blank them off with car body filler, or drill to distort the screw heads so they can't be unscrewed.

OPTIONS

ACCESSORIES

Automatic Light Switches

Unlit houses at night are a dead giveaway that no one is at home — just what a burglar wants to know. However, you can give the impression that someone is in with automatic light switches. These are disigned to replace standard light switches and can be programmed to switch lights on and off at preset times every night or in a random fashion to give a more realistic impression.

Outdoor Lighting

At night darkness is on the side of the burglar, providing plenty of shadows near the house for him to work in. Fitting porch lights and wall lights round the house and lights in the garden will prevent him lurking unseen. Such lighting should be left on throughout the night and can be controlled automatically by a photocell switch which reacts to dusk falling.

This digital timeswitch has three on/off settings; versions are also available with random switching.

Alarm Systems

There is no doubt that an alarm system can be a considerable deterrent to a burglar; even the sight of the sounder box high on the wall can be enough to send him on his way empty handed. Though an alarm may be considered a luxury, the ready availability of systems designed for installation at reasonable cost makes this form of protection well worth considering.

Usually alarm systems come in the form of a basic kit which can often be extended and modified with accessory packs to meet your needs and property exactly. Most are of the perimeter type; that is they rely on sensors detecting someone breaking in through a door or window to trigger the alarm. Some have sensors that detect movement inside the house.

In addition to door and window sensors — usually in the form of magnetic switches — an alarm kit will include the control unit, alarm sounder (a bell or siren) and the necessary wiring. Some kits may even provide mounting screws, wall plugs and cable clips as well. If movement detectors are offered, they usually take the form of pressure mats which can be laid under the carpet in doorways, in front of the TV set or at the foot of the stairs.

The system will operate from the mains supply but a good kit will also provide a standby battery in the control unit in case the mains power is cut off. The sounder should also have its own battery so that it will operate if the wiring between it and the control unit is cut.

Sensors are screwed to wooden window frames or stuck to metal ones with self-adhesive pads, then the wires are run back unobtrusively to the control unit (mounted out of the way but still within easy reach). The sounder must be mounted high on a wall outside where it is plainly visible.

Safes

Most people have small items of value — both monetary and sentimental — that they would never want to lose, and it makes sense to keep such possessions locked away; a small safe is ideal and not as expensive as you might think.

There is quite a range of small safes and strong boxes to choose from, many of them relying on clever camouflage rather than great strength for protection. Although freestanding safes are available, these do tend to be expensive and a better bet is to choose a wall safe or floor safe, particularly if you only want to protect small items like cash or jewellery.

Wall safes usually come in a size equivalent to a whole number of standard bricks, although their depth is limited to that of one brick. However, at least one company has produced a safe that projects into the cavity of an external wall.

To fit a wall safe, all that is necessary is to remove sufficient plaster and chop out the bricks behind. Then mortar the new safe into place and re-plaster. You can either leave the safe door exposed or disguise it by the traditional method with a picture.

One or two types of wall safe come ready disguised — as double convenience outlets, the face plate being removable. However, care must be taken when using this type of safe in case you encourage young children to push keys into the real thing.

Floor safes can be fitted in concrete floors or suspended wooden ones, the former being the most secure. To install a safe in a solid floor involves breaking through the concrete and making a hole large enough for the safe. The hole should be lined with a plastic waterproof membrane, linked to the floor waterproof membrane, and then the space around the safe filled with concrete reinforced with steel rods. This type of safe can be quite roomy, but many have round lids and necks which restrict the size of items you can keep in them.

Safes for suspended wooden floors are designed for bolting between two adjacent joists. Obviously an access panel is needed and it is probably best to make this from particle board held to the joists with magnetic door catches.

After rolling back carpet and underlay, screwing a pressure mat to the floor; conceal the cables and connectors under the carpet.

Window and door contacts can be surface mounted but it is better to recess them and conceal the cables in raceway beneath the sill.

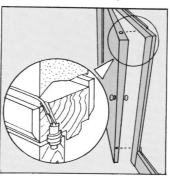

Flush-mounted versions should be positioned so that there is a gap of no more than 6mm (¼in) between them and the magnet.

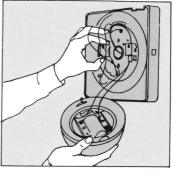

Connecting the circuit cable to the bell high on a wall and seal behind it with mastic.

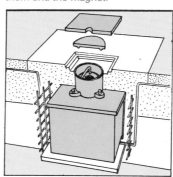

After cutting the hole for a floor safe, instal a DPM to link with the existing one and set the safe in reinforced waterproofed concrete.

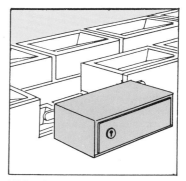

Wall safes are made in brick sizes and may extend into the cavity of a cavity wall; they may be fixed with swivel lugs, screws or bolts.

Drilling the hole for a cartridge safe; choose a concealed position away from mains services and hammer in the barbed housing.

After screwing the escutcheon to the face of the wall or making good round the housing, inserting the cartridge into the housing.

MAKING MORE OF YOUR GARDEN

The amount and nature of the work you do in your garden depends largely on what you want from it. If you simply want the garden to serve as an extension of the house, you'll not be so concerned with dealing with the levels of the lawn and the drainage of the flower beds. You will want to ensure that there is a solid surface on which garden furniture can rest, and you'll want to guarantee an element of privacy with fences or walls. On the other hand, if you want to create a wonderful display of plants and foliage you're likely to be concerned with the overall design of the garden and so be more involved in work which will fundamentally change its appearance, rather than simply adding practical features such as patios and paths.

There are no hard and fast rules about choosing a style for your garden, although you are likely to be influenced by its size. A general guide would be that the smaller your garden, the less formal it should be. After all, a formal garden relies on the visual effect of lines and shapes over a fairly large area. This is impossible in a small town garden. And of course, your choice of style is going to be influenced tremendously by the state of the garden when you take it over. The chances are that you're never going to be able to start entirely from scratch, and to do so would in any case entail a great deal of work before your garden was anywhere near finished.

At the same time, though, if you want your garden to continue the themes of your house, then whether or not it is small or large will be irrelevant — its style will be determined by what lies inside and by the appearance of your home.

Whatever style you choose for your garden, there is one thing you will want — privacy. In the same way that you don't want people staring into your house, so, if the garden is, weather permitting, to become an extension of the living area, you won't want intrusions all the time.

There's a vast array of walling materials easily available and most are fairly straighforward to erect. A simple brick wall can be particularly attractive in its own right as well as being a perfect background on which to grow climbing plants.

Low walls to divide up sections of the garden can be swiftly built from concrete blocks or reconstructed stone, and these can be used in boundary walls as well. You could consider building a dry-stone wall to add a rural touch to your garden, but these are not really suitable for boundary walls and are better used as retaining walls if you want to create a raised bank or emphasize a change in level in your garden.

The important thing is to make sure that textures and colors harmonize. Many materials come in a variety of colors, but do be careful when choosing them. As a rule, black, white and natural stone colors will look good in just about any sort of garden. But don't choose a bright green in an attempt to blend it with the foliage: it will probably clash with all the natural greens. If you want to use colored stone or wood stains, then go for a contrasting color such as deep reds or russet colors.

Concrete will prove a very useful material for your work in the garden. You'll need foundations for any walls you build and if you need a floor for a shed, or garden steps then these can be cast with concrete. You can even cast a very basic path from concrete, but you'll probably prefer to use crazy paving or slabs. Concrete screen blocks are particularly useful if you want to build a wind break round a patio. You can use concrete, paving slabs, stone, timber or brick. The important thing to remember is that it will provide a visual link between the home and the garden. Make sure it does this in a smooth fashion without violent clashes of colour and material. And of course you'll have to make sure that it's large enough to accommodate furniture for at least four adults.

If you are a keen gardener or just enjoy sitting outside, poor drainage could prove to be the bane of your life. Waterlogged soil will result in poor plant growth and cause roots to rot or be attacked by mildew. And what's more, a sodden soil will remain cold and hinder further growth.

Most gardens will have a few puddles after a particularly heavy rain storm; this is nothing to worry about. However, if puddles stay put and do not drain within a couple of hours, you should think about improving your garden's drainage. First make a couple of tests.

Dig a hole that is about 600mm (24in) deep and about 250mm (10in) square, then fill it with water. If the drainage in your garden is satisfactory, the hole will have emptied within about 24 hours. However, if your drainage is really poor, there will still be some water present after more than 48 hours. The fact that your garden drains poorly doesn't mean that you'll automatically have to dig it up to lay down a complete drainage system. Depending on the nature of your soil, you can dig it over or add things to it to lay down a complete drainage system.

Poor drainage is most often associated with clay soils that are frequently impervious. Simply digging the soil over will break it up, adding more air and so improving drainage. If you do this just before the winter, you should then leave the soil untouched as the frost will also serve to break up the soil. Mixing in organic substances such as compost will increase porosity, while the actual texture of the soil can be improved by digging in sand. The texture of a clay soil can also be improved by the addition of ground limestone. Allow about 250g (9oz) per square metre (sq yd) and leave the soil untouched for a couple of months so that it's thoroughly washed in.

You could also create small but effective draining holes by using a tining fork in the soil and then filling the deep holes with a fine gravel.

If you find after trying all this that the drainage of your garden has not really improved, then you'll have to consider putting down land drains to solve the

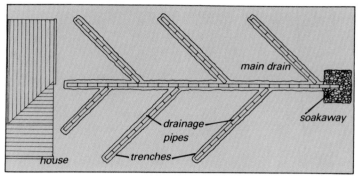

Layout of a land drainage system; excess ground water soaks into the herringbone pipes and from there to the main drain and soakaway.

After digging trenches to a slight fall, laying the pipes in them on a bed of gravel; leave 12mm (½in) between unperforated pipes.

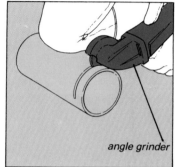

Cutting unglazed clay pipe with an angle grinder; lay the pipe in a hollow in soft earth to prevent it from rolling while cutting.

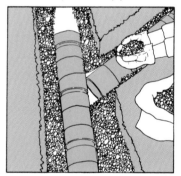

After covering the joins between pipes with plastic sheet or tiles to prevent soil from blocking them, sprinkling gravel over the pipes.

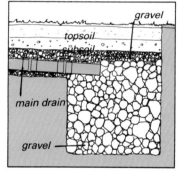

Section through a soakaway; the main drain ends half way across the hardcore which is covered with gravel, then subsoil and topsoil.

Shovelling broken brick hardcore into the soakaway up to the level of the main drain pipe; tamp it down with a sledgehammer or post.

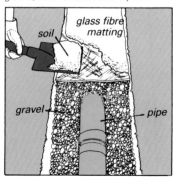

Backfilling the trenches with the excavated soil after covering the gravel with glass fiber matting to prevent silting.

problem.

You'll have to lay down a run of pipes that will drain the water from the garden into a soakaway.

The best way to do this is to lay the drains in what is called a herringbone pattern — a central drain running the length of your garden with several drains branching off on each side.

The pipes themselves come in a range of different materials. They are available in the traditional unglazed clay, pitch fibre, concrete or plastic. You'll probably find perforated plastic ones the easiest to use.

A herringbone pattern requires only a very slight gradient, otherwise it won't work effectively. However, the main drain can be put down on a steeper gradient such as 1:40.

Mark out where you want the pipes to run and dig out trenches that are about 300mm (12in) wide and about 750mm (30in) deep. Incorporate the gradient and line the bottom with 50mm (2in) of gravel. You can then position the pipes. If you are laying the perforated type, make sure the holes are on the top, so that water can seep in and be carried to the soakaway. Unperforated pipes should have a 12mm (½in) gap between them for this reason. Cover each joint between the pipes with a piece of roof tile or thick plastic to prevent the pipes from getting clogged up with soil. At the start of each run the end of the pipe should be blocked with another piece of tile. Cover the pipes with more gravel then back-fill the trenches with earth.

The drainage system will have to take the water into a soakaway. This consists of a pit that is about 1.2m (4ft) square and deep enough for its bottom to be 1m (3ft) below the level of the incoming drainage pipe. It should obviously be at the lowest point in your garden. Fill the hole with coarse gravel or broken brick to the level of the pipe, which should project about 300mm (12in) into the pit. Tamp down the gravel using a sledgehammer or stout post and then add a layer of pebbles to prevent silting. Alternatively put down a double sheet of heavy-duty plastic or a piece of blanket insulation. You can then replace the sub-soil and top soil.

MODELLING THE GROUND

Choosing a particular style for your garden is all very well in the abstract, but what should you do if the actual contours of the ground don't entirely suit what you have in mind?

If you want to put down a large patio and then create a fine lawn for the rest of your garden, you'll face problems before you start work if your ground slopes away into the distance.

From a practical point of view slopes in the garden can be irritating. Access will inevitably be poor — try pushing a fully-laden wheel barrow up even the slightest slope — and you'll soon be longing for the levellest of plots.

Similarly, creating terraces in a very flat garden will be a problem. Raised banks and changes of level can look very attractive and will be eye-catching features in any garden. With a certain amount of hard work, it is possible for you to achieve this.

Before you start re-modelling your garden — and this should obviously be the first task of all in the garden — it is nevertheless important to have a completed plan for the rest of the garden. You should have worked out where you want to build your patio, where you want your path to run and where you want to build your steps. Otherwise you could be letting yourself in for a lot of wasted effort.

You should draw a scale plan of all the features of the garden — trees, existing flower beds and so on — and add to it the additions you plan to make.

But remember, whatever you decide to do, the final outcome is what you are going to have to live with. A garden must look natural. Complete remodelling will involve a lot of hard work and you'll probably find it best to use existing contours as a guideline.

You shouldn't be put off levelling steep slopes and creating terraces, however. And in some cases, removing an existing slope that is steeper than 30% can only be a good thing. After all, not only will it be awkward for access, but the top soil could be in danger of being eroded, or washed away in torrential rain.

Whatever work you do in

Levelling ground for a lawn or patio: After knocking in the prime datum peg to the required level, driving in a second peg.

Levelling the second peg to the prime datum peg by resting a level on a straight-edge resting across their tops.

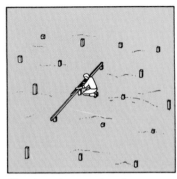

After inserting a series of pegs over the area at 1.5m (5ft) spacing, checking the levels from one to another and adjusting if necessary.

Redistributing or adding soil until it is level with the tops of the pegs; check for low areas between pegs with a straight-edge.

remodelling your garden, you must take care of the soil you are digging up. Top soil is a valuable commodity and you should make sure that whenever you have to remove it you keep it separate from any dug-up sub-soil, and that you preserve it so that it can be put back at a later stage. And, of course, the same applies to any turf that you have to lift. You should cut rectangles of turf measuring about 300 × 400mm (12 × 16in). They should be about 75mm (3in) thick. After you've lifted the turfs, they should be rolled up with the grass facing inwards and set aside. If you have to keep the turfs for more than a few days, unroll them and keep them in a cool place, watering them from time to time. Otherwise the grass will die.

You might find that you have just a few mounds or lumps in what is otherwise a perfectly acceptable lawn. In this case, you won't have to go in for extensive remodelling, but for some rather more straight-forward work. All you have to do is cut a cross over the middle of the rise and cut other parallel lines to mark out rectangles of

turf. Use a spade to lift the turf and fold it back to expose the soil. Then dig away what soil is necessary or even just rake over the exposed area and reposition the turf. You should then sprinkle fine soil in the small gaps between the turfs. Fill in any hollows that are more than about 25mm (1in) deep by exposing the soil by the same method and simply adding a mixture of soil and sand.

Obviously dealing with your lawn this way is only suitable for very localized treatment. To

Removing mounds in turf: Making a series of rectangular cuts about 75mm (3in) deep over the raised area with a spade.

After rolling back the turf, levelling the soil with a fork or rake; roll back the turf and fill between strips with fine soil.

establish a level for the whole lawn requires more work.

However, if you are actually starting from scratch with a lawn or planning to build a patio, then the chances are that you're going to want a reasonably level and well-drained area on which to work.

You can establish a level for this area using a series of pegs driven into the ground and corresponding to the level of what is called a prime datum peg. This is the first peg that you'll drive into the plot. It should be about 30cm (12in) long and at least 25mm sq (1in sq). Fix it into the soil so that its top is at the level you want the soil to be. Once this is established, you can drive in a second peg 1.5m (5ft) away from the first. The idea is to use the first as a guide from which to set the level of other pegs. You can check this by laying a straight-edged length of wood on the tops of the two pegs. Then all you do is put a spirit level on the wood to see if the two pegs are at the same level. If not, adjust the second one until its level is correct. Once this has been achieved you can drive in more pegs, again with a distance of about 1.5m (5ft) between them. Do this over the whole site then adjust the level of the soil so that it lies flush with the tops of the pegs.

If you don't have a ready source of soil in your garden, you can easily buy some from your local garden center. Once you've spread the soil to the correct level you should compact it lightly (taking short, overlapping steps on it should prove adequate) to reveal any hollows or rises. You can then make

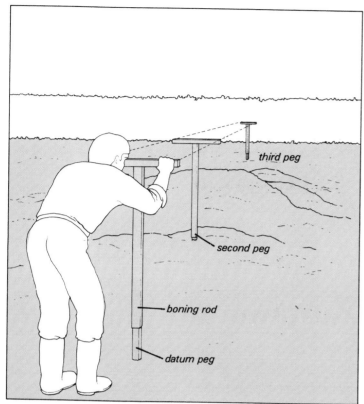

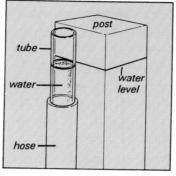

A hose pipe water level; fill nearly to top of plastic tube, remove all air bubbles, hold tops of pegs level and mark water level on both.

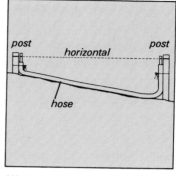

Water level in use; position datum peg and adjust other peg until level of water coincides with marked line. Take care to avoid spillage.

Setting levels with boning rods. Drive in a datum peg to the required level and then a second about 600mm (2ft) away; level this with a spirit-level. Sight across boning rods on the two pegs and adjust the height of a third peg until the boning rod on top of it aligns.

further adjustment, then rake the whole site to give it a flat finish.

There are other methods of establishing whether a site is level and marking it out so that it can be adjusted to a particular level.

Over large areas you might find it easiest to establish your level by sight. To do this you'll have to make what are usually called boning rods. These are basically T-shaped rods that sit on top of the pegs and serve as a sight-guide for the level of the ground. You'll have to drive a peg the same size as used in the prime datum levelling method into the ground at the highest point. Drive in a second peg about 600mm (24in) away and a third at the far end. Adjust the level of the second peg so that it's at the same level as the first. You'll have to make your boning rods from 900 × 50 × 25mm (3ft × 2in × 1in) lengths of wood and then nail a 300mm (12in) cross-piece at the top.

Stand one of these boning rods on each of the first two pegs and then get a helper to hold the third on the peg on the far side of

the site. You should then crouch down so your eye-level corresponds with the level of the T-bar of the first two boning rods and sight across that to the third. Your helper should adjust the position of the third peg until all the boning rods appear to be

level when sighted across.

The third method of establishing the level of a piece of ground is by exploiting the principle that water will always rise to its own level. This method is particularly useful if you want to level pegs over a long distance or round a corner. You'll need a length of clear plastic piping or a garden hose with a length of clear tubing fitted in each end.

Fill the hose with water and fix one end of it to a datum peg so that the water level sits level with the top of the peg. Then all you have to do is align the tape at the other end with the top of the second post and adjust the height of the peg until it's the same as at the other end.

Establishing a level for a particular site is very important, but you might find that you want to level a sloping section of your

garden or simply adjust the shape of existing levels.

The easiest way to do this is to employ a technique that is known as cutting and filling.

In effect what you have to do is remove the soil from the high area and use it to build up the low area. That way you can simply ease the angle of a slope, level it completely or create a terrace effect.

You'll have to start by cutting away the turf using a half moon cutter and a spade, and then dig away the top soil to a depth of about 150mm (6in). Remember to keep it carefully so it can be repositioned. Then all you have to do is excavate the sub soil to the required depth and add it to the sub soil at the lower level. Spread it over the area, roll it or trample it and then rake it, then finally replace the top soil.

Trick

SETTING A GRADIENT

Setting a gradient usually involves some measurement. One end of a spirit level can be lifted with a shim to give a fall of the shim thickness over the length of the spirit level; with a water level a second mark could be made on the peg, spaced to give a certain fall over the distance between the two ends.

To set gradient directly, an angle-finder can be used which sits on top of a spirit level (or straight-edge). A chart is supplied to work out the gradient in degrees which is set on the dial. A concave-edged blade is available for use on top of pipes.

USING CONCRETE

Concrete is an ideal material for use in the garden: it is extremely versatile, easily available and fairly cheap. What's more it is straightforward to work with.

The chances are that whatever sort of building work you do in the garden — a simple path or an extension to your home — will demand the use of concrete.

It's important to know exactly what concrete is and how it works. The constituent materials are cement, sand and aggregate — stone or gravel. When water is added, a chemical reaction occurs within the cement causing it to bind together all the materials into what becomes a very hard and solid material. Provided you use the right mix for strength, and as concrete is a plastic material, it can be molded into just about any shape — hence its versatility.

There are several ways of buying the materials for concrete. If you're going to do the mixing yourself you'll probably want to get the materials separately. Concrete is also available in a dry-mix form and all you have to do is add water. Obviously for small jobs you'll find this way the most convenient. Finally it is possible to get ready-mixed concrete delivered to your home. However, this is only worth doing if you need a large amount of concrete — for laying a drive or large patio.

There are a number of precautions you should take when buying the materials separately. Remember, concrete comes in large bags and is heavy to lift: take care not to injure your back. Don't buy the materials too far in advance. If you have to store make sure you keep the cement in a dry place — otherwise you'll find that it gets hard in the bag and you might not be able to use it. Cement should be kept under cover and preferably off the ground — on a couple of lengths of wood, say, and away from other materials. Sand and aggregate should be kept on a hard, flat, dry area and covered by plastic sheeting.

You should avoid direct contact with the skin: cement contains materials that will be an irritant.

There are several types of concrete mix which are suitable

Ready-mixed concrete being channelled on to the job site for foundations.

for a variety of different jobs. The important thing is to get the proportions right.

General-purpose concrete lives up to its name being suitable for just about everything except foundations and exposed paving. This should be mixed in proportions of 1:2:3 — cement/sand/20mm (³/₄in) aggregate. If you want to use all-in aggregate, a combination of sand and stone, substitute a proportion of 4 for the sand and aggregate.

To obtain one cubic metre (35.3cu ft) of this concrete you'll need 7.6 94lb bags of cement, 680kg (1490lbs) of sand, 1175kg (2590lbs) of aggregate or 1855kg (4080lbs) of all-in aggregate. For ordering ready-mix you should specify a medium- to high-workability of 'C20P to BS 5328'.

Foundation concrete should be mixed to the proportions 1:2½:3¼ or 5 if you're using all-in. For one cubic metre (35.3cu ft) of concrete you'll need 6.7 94lb bags of cement, 720kg (1580lbs) of sand, 1165kg (2550lbs) of 20mm (³/₄in) aggregate or 1885kg (4150lbs) of all-in. The exact proportions of the mix for concrete may vary according to your local Building Code. Allways check with your local building Department before beginning any job.

For drives it's best to use ready-mix because you'll need a

lot of concrete. If you decide to mix your own the proportions are 1:1½:2½ or 3½ for all-in For one cubic metre of concrete you'll need 9.5 (94lb) bags of cement, 600kg (1320lbs) of sand, 1200kg (2640lbs) of 20mm (³/₄in) aggregate, or 1800kg (3950lbs) of all-in. Discuss what you need with the ready-mix supplier and he'll suggest a suitable mix.

To calculate the amount of concrete you need is simple: just measure the area to be concreted and multiply by its depth to obtain the required volume.

Inevitably there are certain tools that you'll need for working with concrete. The chances are that you'll have most already — the floats, shovels, wood, string and spirit level. However, there are one or two items which are absolutely vital. First you must have a decent wheelbarrow in which to cart the concrete. It should be a strong builder's-type barrow with a thick rubber tyre. These are by far the easiest to manoeuvre when full.

It is also wise to make yourself a builder's square for obtaining true right angles when setting out. This consists of three lengths of wood fixed together in a triangle in the proportions 3:4:5. If this is correctly done, the angle at the point where the two shorter sides meet will be a right angle.

Remember that concrete will

stick to anything it comes in contact with, so you should clean your tools as you go along. If for some reason concrete has set on any first rub it down with a piece of brick or old concrete then complete the cleaning with a wire brush. And remember, never flush slurry or cement-dirtied water down a drain, where it could cause a blockage.

Concrete is ideal for creating a stable base on which to undertake any building project. In the case of a simple freestanding garden wall you'll have to lay down strip foundations — a 150mm (6in) thick strip of concrete in a trench on sub-soil.

A ground-supported concrete slab will be an adequate foundation for something as light as a garden shed; it'll also serve as a floor. Where a slab is to support walls its edges will have to be doubled in depth, while for a more substantial extension a raft can be reinforced by steel mesh. Alternatively trench-fill foundations can be used.

The plasticity of concrete is its major advantage and its use is not exclusively for foundations. Creating moulded steps from concrete requires careful preparation and strong formwork — the mould. But the finished product will serve you well.

And, of course, you can change the colour of the concrete if you want. Liquid and powdered pigment is available through builders' merchants. However, if you do decide to colour the concrete remember to follow the instructions very carefully: as concrete dries so its colour changes therefore you'll have to make sure you use the correct quantity of colourant.

But using concrete doesn't always mean having to cast it. Pre-cast concrete slabs are available for use in paths, patios and drives. These come in a huge variety of shapes and sizes. Concrete block paving is simple to put down — it only requires bedding in sand — and looks extremely attractive.

Concrete masonry for a variety of walls comes in a number of different shapes and sizes and in a vast array of finishes.

The form in which you buy your concrete depends largely on the size of the job you're planning. You have three options: dry mix, separate materials, or ready mix.

Dry-mix Concrete

Dry-mix concrete is easily available from hardware stores and consists of ready-bagged, correctly-proportioned amounts of cement, aggregate and sand. It comes in bags ranging in weight from under 5kg (11lb) to about 38kg (94lbs) and when you mix in water you'll produce a specified quantity of concrete.

Dry mix comes in various types of mixes, so if you decide on it — and the chances are that for a small job you'll find it easier and cleaner — make sure you choose the right one for what you have in mind.

Using dry-mix concrete can prove slightly more expensive than if you were to mix your own concrete from separate materials but you'll probably find its convenience outweighs that extra expense.

For larger jobs such as the laying of paths buying all the materials separately is probably your best bet.

The standard-sized bag of Portland cement is 38kg (94lb), which is equal to one cubic foot of cement although smaller quantities can be obtained. Similarly sand and aggregate are available in such bags but it's more common to get these both loose from builders' merchants in measures of cubic metres (cubic yards). All-in aggregates — consisting of a mix of sand and coarser aggregate — are also easily available and you might find these more convenient.

Ready-mix Concrete

If you're doing a really large job that requires a considerable amount of concrete you might find buying it ready mixed the best way. You'll have to estimate fairly accurately the amount of concrete you're going to need and then make sure the supplier will deliver that amount: most ready-mix contractors have a minimum amount that they deliver — usually one cubic metre (35.3 cu ft) — and if you

want less then it will work out quite expensive.

You'll also have to provide good access to the site for the truck as well as specify a precise delivery time. Make sure that you have everything ready when the delivery is due. It's always a good idea to have assistants with barrows ready to help you shift the concrete if it can't be deposited exactly where you want it: preferably on your prepared foundations.

An alternative to ready mix is the use of a mix-on-site truck, which will arrive with all the materials, including barrows. Mix the amount you require and no more, although most firms have a minimum charge. it allows you time to unload the concrete and get it to your work site if access is limited.

Mixing Concrete

Obviously if you plump for dry mix or separate ingredients then you are going to have to mix the concrete yourself. If you are mixing by hand make sure you work on a hard, smooth surface such as a drive or a sheet of plywood. Remember, it is crucial to get the proportioning correct, if not the actual quantities, so use equal-sized containers throughout. However, you should use a separate shovel and bucket for the cement; otherwise moisture from the aggregate could cause the cement to set on the tools.

As hand mixing is hard work, you might prefer to rent a mixer. These come in several sizes, the standard one being that which produces a barrow-load of concrete. This is usually referred to as a 4/3 — four cubic feet of material goes in and three cubic feet of concrete emerges. Mixers are easy to rent, quite cheap and save you a lot of tiring work. They usually have gasoline or electric-powered engines. On delivery make sure the mixer stands level and is firmly held in position so it won't move around as it works. Check that it can discharge conveniently into a barrow (or directly onto the foundations) otherwise lay down a sheet of plywood onto which it can deposit its load. Tip in half the aggregate and half the water and turn it over for a few minutes. Add most of the sand

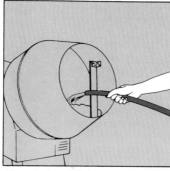

After tipping half the aggregate into the mixer, adding water from a hose-pipe; turn on the mixer and run it for a couple of minutes.

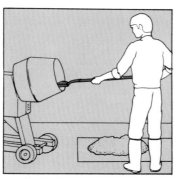

Shovelling in the cement while the mixer is running, then the rest of the aggregate (and sand if used) and more water.

Tipping out the mixed concrete with the drum turning slowly; when it is of the right consistency it should fall cleanly off the blades.

and cement. Add materials alternatively after this and keep the concrete wet to enable it to be properly mixed. Keep the mixer going for a further couple of minutes. When it's ready the mix should fall readily off the mixer blades but should not be crumbly or too wet. Finally clean the mixer by turning it over with a small mixture of coarse aggregate and water in the drum. Finish off by cleaning the blades by hand. Never leave the mixer empty for too long without cleaning it.

Mixing concrete by hand: after mixing the cement and aggregate to a uniform color, forming a crater in the top of the heap.

Adding water to the crater; take care not to overfill the crater – more water can be added later. Mix dry-mix concrete in the same way.

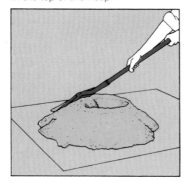

Carefully knocking material from the sides into the crater; quickly stop any overspills of water or cement will be washed away.

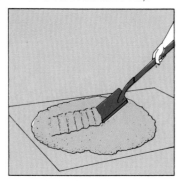

After turning over the heap several times for a uniform mix, testing with a shovel; the surface should be close knit and just moist.

MAKING FOUNDATIONS

Strip Foundations

If you're planning any sort of building work — be it just a simple garden wall or an extension to your home — you must give careful consideration to its foundations. All walls need foundations to give them a stable, solid base.

Foundations serve their purpose by dispersing the load directly above them to the stable sub-soil below. And in the case of freestanding walls they provide vital lateral stability.

There are various types of foundations: which you use depends on what you're building and the nature of the sub-soil. Strip foundations consist of a strip of concrete laid at the bottom of a trench; trench-fill foundations are literally a deeper and wider trench than is used with strip foundations that is then filled with concrete. Raft foundations consist of a concrete slab set on the ground. The slab then serves not only as a stable base for the walls of the structure (although the thickness of the edges of the slab where the walls will sit will have to be thickened to support them) but also as a floor.

If you're only building a small garden wall then you'll need only a fairly shallow strip footing. This should prove perfectly adequate to take the loading and provide stable support for the wall. If you want a base for a carport or shed then a slab is ideal, some structures are subject to Building Code approval (see page 251) and will probably require quite deep trench-fill foundations, however, always consult your local Building Code to determine what type of footings are required in your area.

Preparing the Base

Crucial to the success of any type of foundation you use will be the sort of ground on which it is being built. Therefore, before you start you must prepare the site for the foundations.

As foundations have to be set on firm and stable ground, all top soil and vegetable matter will have to be dug away until you reach a solid sub-soil. You'll probably reach the sub-soil at a depth of about 150mm (6in) but

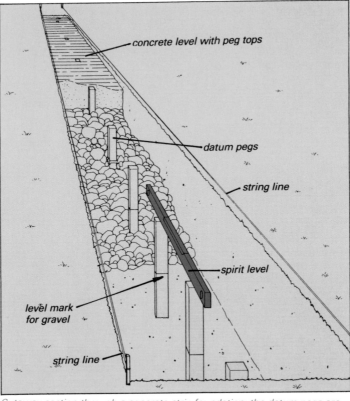

Cutaway section through a concrete strip foundation; the datum pegs are hammered in to the level of the concrete after marking on them the finished level for the compacted gravel. Tamp the concrete with a board to ensure that there are no trapped pockets of air.

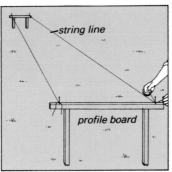

Marking out the foundation trench with string lines stretched between profile boards; tie the string to nails in the horizontal battens.

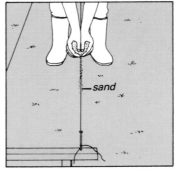

Sprinkling a guide line of sand on to the ground before digging so that the string lines can be removed for ease of working.

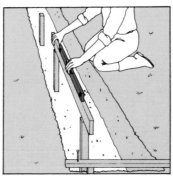

After excavating the trench to the required depth, setting out datum pegs with their tops at the level of the finished concrete.

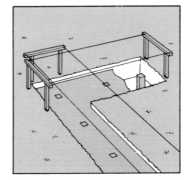

Where the foundation trench turns a corner, set up two pairs of profile boards with the string lines at right-angles.

this varies and you might have to dig deeper. Top soil is always soft, contains vegetable matter that will leave soft spots, and will not provide an adequate base. However, you should keep the soil you dig up; it can be used elsewhere in the garden. Never be tempted to lay even a small slab on ground where the top soil has not been removed.

When laying strip foundations, start by marking out the area of your trench so you can dig it accurately. As the strip is laid so that its top will be below ground level, you'll have to make the trench a minimum width of about 450mm (18in) to allow you space to work. The strip should be twice the width of the wall and if the wall is going to be higher than 750mm (30in) it will have to be three times as wide.

Start by driving two pegs into the ground at each end of the projected trench. Make sure they sit outside the area of the actual trench and that their tops are level with each other. Then cut two lengths of 50 × 25mm (2 × 1in) slightly longer than the width of the trench. These are called profile boards and should be nailed across the top of the two pegs — one at each end. From these profile boards you'll run stringlines to provide a guide for the line and width of the trench. Attach the lines to nails fixed in the profile boards in line with the width of the trench and make sure they're kept taut.

Now that you've established the exact lines of the trench, transfer the dimensions to the ground to aid accurate digging by sprinkling sand along the ground in line with the stringlines.

The concrete will have to be at least 150mm (6in) deep and its bottom should be about 350mm (14in) below the top soil so it sits firmly on the sub-soil.

Dig out the trench, making sure that the bottom is firm. Check that there are no soft spots and check the depth at 1m (3ft) intervals. You'll then have to drive in a series of pegs at 600mm (24in) intervals to serve as level pegs for the top of the strip. Fix them in the center of the trench and use a spirit level to ensure they are all level. Make sure that the length of peg protruding from the base of the trench is the exact depth of the strip.

You can now start filling the trench with concrete. Make sure the concrete fills it to just above the top of the pegs. Compact the concrete with your shovel. Finally you'll have to tamp the surface so that it finishes level with the top of the pegs. Use a stout length of wood as a tamper and work your way lengthwise along the trench. Then check the level of the strip using a spirit level on a straight-edged plank. Don't worry if there are slight irregularities; they can be compensated for when laying the first course of masonry.

If you're working on a slope then the strip foundations will have to be stepped. Work in an uphill direction. You'll find it easiest to make each step equal to a certain number of bricks but make sure that the step is not deeper than the strip itself. Ensure that the two levels overlap by an amount at least equal to the depth of the strip.

As a rule foundations are made of concrete, usually to the following proportions: 1:2½:3½ — cement:sand:20mm (¾in) aggregate. If you intend to use all-in aggregate then you should use the proportions 1:5. To gain one cubic metre (35.3 cu ft) of this concrete you'll therefore need 6.7 bags of cement, 720kg (1580lbs) of sand and 1165kg (2560lbs) of 20mm (31in) aggregate. Alternatively you can buy 1885kg (4150lbs) of all-in aggregate. Using just one bag of cement and mixing the concrete to these proportions will yield you about 0.18 cubic metres (.23cu yd).

With strip and trench-fill foundations the concrete will be held in place by the edges of the trench until it has set. However, a slab will need extra support and restraint both when you cast it and when the mix is setting. This is where formwork is so vital. It consists of straight, firm edges that will support the concrete as well as provide a level-guide when you lay it.

Use lengths of 25mm (1in) thick sawn wood for the form edges and ensure that they're as wide as your slab is deep; otherwise you'll have set them into the earth slightly. For a neater finish to your slab edges

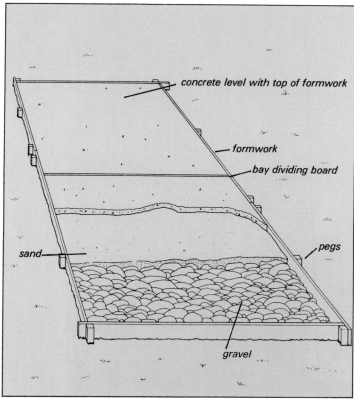

Cutaway section through a concrete path; the compacted gravel is blinded with builder's sand and the concrete is levelled with a tamping beam resting on top of the formwork. To allow for expansion of the concrete in hot weather, a softwood board is set across the path every 3m (10ft).

After knocking in pegs at the corners and along the sides of the path to support the formwork, setting them to the finished level.

Securing the formwork at the corners of the path; butt the boards end-to-face and nail through them into the pegs.

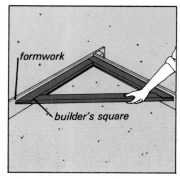

Checking the corners with a builder's square; adjust the pegs or insert packing between them and the formwork if necessary.

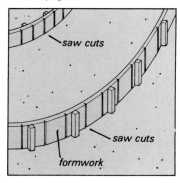

To form curves, make saw cuts through half the thickness of the formwork on the outside of the curve and space the pegs more closely.

and greater ease when stripping and cleaning for re-use you might prefer to use planed wood, but this will prove more expensive.

The edges are held in place by being nailed to 50mm sq (2in sq) pegs that are driven into the ground to a depth of between 300 and 500mm (12 and 20in). The pegs should be positioned at the edge of the slab area at centres not exceeding 1 metre (3ft). They should not stick out over the top of the formwork as this would hinder you when tamping the slab.

You may well find that you have to join together two lengths of wood in order to create an edge the length of the projected slab. Butt the two ends together and make sure there is no step in the top edge of the join. Reinforce the joint on the outside with a short length of the same size wood. It's a good idea to tape the joint on the inside face to prevent any concrete oozing through.

Corners of the framework should be constructed carefully. Ensure they are a right angle by using a builder's square. Butt the wood tightly together at the corners and make sure that one length extends beyond the joint by about 150mm (6in) so the corner can be supported by an extra peg. Again, tape the inside angle to prevent oozing. You might, of course, need to lay a slab that does not have only straight edges. To make curved formwork you'll first have to soak the wood and then bend it round pegs that have been previously driven into position. In the case of curved formwork the pegs should be fixed at centers closer than 1m (3ft).

However, if your curve is quite severe, you'll have to make saw-cuts halfway through the timber on the inside face. The interval between the cuts depends on how sharp the curve is.

You might find it easier to hire steel rod forms — especially if your slab is a one-off and you're unlikely to need the timber again. Both rigid and flexible forms are usually stocked by hire firms and they come in 3m (10ft) lengths and depths ranging from 100 to 250mm (4 to 10in). When you hire this you'll also get steel fixing pegs to support it.

223

FOUNDATIONS

Raft Foundations

Raft foundations or a concrete slab have a variety of uses — for shed floors, patio bases and drives.

As they usually take up a fairly large area it's wise to use ready-mix concrete; it'll save you a lot of hard work.

If you're going to mix the concrete yourself, a general-purpose mix will be suitable for slabs protected from the weather and with only light use. Mix the concrete to proportions of 1:2:3 — cement:sand 20mm (¾in) aggregate or substitute 4 of all-in aggregate. If the slab is to be used for a carport or drive then it's best to use a stronger mix with proportions of 1:1½:2½ or 3½ with all-in aggregate.

The thickness of the slab depends largely on its intended use, its size and the nature of the sub-soil on which it will stand. If it's going to be lightly loaded and rest on a firm base of hardcore and a stable sub-soil and not exceed 2m (6ft) sq then it need be only 75mm (3in) thick. If it is to sit on a clay sub-soil then its depth should increase to 100mm (4in). If the base is going to take the weight of vehicles or serve as a workshop floor then it should be 100mm (4in) thick provided it's set on a firm sub-soil; otherwise it should be increased to a depth of 125mm (5in).

There are various guidelines to follow concerning the other dimensions of the slab — especially if you want to be able to lay it in one go.

As a rule the slab should not be longer than twice its width — ideally only one and a half times — and the maximum dimension should not exceed 40 times the slab thickness or more than 4m (13ft). However, if you find that you can't follow these rules then you'll have to lay the slab in sections.

Mark out the area for the slab using stringlines running from pegs driven into the ground just outside the area to be concreted. You can then dig away the top soil, making sure you leave yourself enough space in which to work.

Exposed slabs that are close to buildings should have a slight gradient running away from the building to allow for drainage: 1:40 should prove sufficient. If you're intending to use the slab as a garage floor or shed then incorporate a 1:60 slope towards the door. You can allow for the gradient when setting the level for the slab: either measure down from the pegs on the low side of the slab and mark a working level or use a piece of wood — a shim — of the correct thickness under the spirit level on the low side pegs to establish the slope. Establish the level and depth of your slab in much the same way as for strip foundations. Drive in 50mm (2in) sq pegs at 1.5m (5ft) intervals in the slab area. The first peg you fix will be the one from which you set the level of the others. You can then measure down to get the correct depth of slab and dig

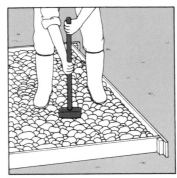

Compacting the gravel using a punner; use graded gravel for close packing and ensure that there are no voids against the formwork.

Blinding the gravel with builder's sand by spreading a thin layer over the surface; this fills any voids which could cause sinking.

Tamping the concrete with a beam across the formwork; work slowly forwards, pushing the beam from side to side in a sawing motion.

After filling and tamping any low areas on the surface, settling the concrete round the edges by hammering along the formwork.

out accordingly. Allow for a 100mm (4in) base of 'gravel or broken brick hardcore.

Once you've dug out the site, fix the formwork in position. Add the gravel and compact it firmly in position. You can then start to add the concrete.

Shovel it in and spread it so it sits about 10mm (⅜in) above the edges of the formwork. You'll then have to tamp it down. Use a

length of 175 × 25mm (1 × 3in) wood that is slightly longer than the slab is wide. Tamp the concrete with an up and down motion moving the wood forward half its width with each stroke. Tamping is very important to the compaction of the slab so resist any temptation just to scrape it over the concrete. Once you've tamped completely it's a good idea to go round the slab

Trick

STEEL ROD FORMWORK

You might find it easier to rent steel rod forms — especially if your slab is a one-off and you're unlikely to need the wood again. Both rigid and flexible forms are usually stocked by rental firms and they come in 3m (10ft) lengths and depths ranging from 100 to 250mm (4 to 10in). When you hire this type of formwork you'll also get steel fixing pegs to support it.

Joining lengths of steel formwork with a connecting strip.

Securing the formwork to steel pegs by hammering in wedges.

Forming a non-slip surface by brushing with a stiff broom after tamping; work from both sides, or from a board above the surface.

After allowing the concrete to cure for at least 14 days, remove formwork by first tapping downwards then away from the slab.

tapping on the outside of the formwork to settle the concrete further.

Finally run the edge of a steel trowel along the perimeter of the slab to prevent crumbling when the formwork is removed. If your slab is too large to be made in one go you'll have to divide it into bays — preferably of the same size and square. Use lengths of softwood or hardboard that is about 12mm (½in) thick to

separate the sections. These are called expansion joints and stop any cracking when the slab expands or contracts. Treat the wood with preservative and hold it in place with extra formwork or small heaps of concrete. Cast each section separately but when you come to tamp it make sure you do so towards the joint but without knocking the wood out of line. Remove extra formwork before filling the

adjacent section, but leave the joint itself in position.

You can finish off the surface of the slab in a number of ways. Obviously you can leave it as tamped but if you want a non-slip surface brush over it with a stiff broom to give it a corduroy-like texture. Going over the surface with a wooden float will leave a fine sandpaper-like surface while for a completely smooth finish run over the slab with a steel float.

You must ensure that your slab doesn't dry to quickly. This could cause weakness and possible shrinkage cracks. As a rule concrete needs moisture and time to set to its full hardness.

Ensure that the surface is hard enough not to be marked and cover it with plastic sheeting, taped at any joints. Weigh it down round the edges to prevent it blowing away and sprinkle sand on top to stop it ballooning in wind. Alternatively you can use damp hessian, but you must

make sure that it remains damp while the concrete cures.

If you are laying the slab during cold weather you should take precautions against potential damage through frost (although you should'nt really attempt to lay it during frosty weather). Insulate the slab with a layer of straw between weighed-down sheets of plastic. Alternatively use a layer of earth or sand. Never lay concrete on a frozen base or use frozen materials.

Leave the plastic sheeting on the slab until it has cured — usually about four days but up to ten in the winter. Leave the formwork in place for a further ten days before removing it by first tapping it downwards and then knocking it away from the slab.

Fins of concrete at the edges can be cleaned away with an arrissing tool made from a small piece of sheet metal bent to a right angle and fixed with a wooden handle.

Trick

USING READY-MIX

If you're laying a slab for a drive you'll probably find it easiest to order your concrete from a supplier of ready-mix. This will require a certain amount of organization. You'll have to know exactly how much concrete you're going to need and exactly when you'll need it. You'll have to provide easy access for the truck either to the actual site or to a point that is convenient for unloading. Most ready-mix trucks have extendable chutes for depositing the concrete so if you can only provide access to within about 3m (10ft) of the slab that should be enough. If the truck is going to deposit its load elsewhere, make sure it's on a solid surface and lay down a plastic sheet to make clearing up that much easier. As you're likely to be taking delivery of a large quantity of concrete try to get some assistance; after all one cubic metre of concrete is about 40 barrow loads.

Make sure you have prepared the base, erected the formwork and constructed any expansion joints necessary before you take delivery. The sup-

plier should know what you're using the mix for: that way he can make suggestions about the type of mix you use. But if it can't be discharged directly into the form-work you should specify a high-workability load to give you extra time. It might be a good idea for the supplier to incorporate a 'retarder' in the mix.

Laying a drive is much the same as a simple slab. However, you'll probably need a stronger mix, the slab might well have curved edges and you could be

working on a slope.

If the drive slopes down to a garage you'll have to ensure that its lowest point is about 75 to 100mm (3 to 4in) below the level of the garage floor. You can then insert a length of drainpipe across the drive to mould a run off and slope the final couple of metres up towards the garage. On a sloping drive it's best to work uphill and as you progress check that levels are accurate.

Never lay your ready-mix over an existing cracked concrete drive: all that will happen is that the new one will crack in the same places. Break up the old one and use it as a hardcore base.

If your drive is likely to incorporate an inspection chamber try to make sure it's at the edge or alongside a joint. Failing that it should be 500mm (20in) away from the edge. Before laying the drive you should box out the top of the chamber and concrete round it to bring it to the level of the drive. Remove its form once the concrete has hardened and replace it with expansion joint **before laying the slab.**

PATHS AND PAVING

Types and Materials

Making a path in your garden requires careful planning. After all, a path is a functional line of communication from one point to another. But it is also vital to the overall aesthetic appeal of your garden. A path contributes significantly to the shape of a garden and helps to determine its tone.

A path should be made from a suitable material to allow it to take a reasonable flow of traffic and withstand the vagaries of the climate. But it must enhance the whole style of the garden be it formal or informal. That's why it's so crucial to choose the right material.

A well designed hand-constructed path will not only provide years of good service, but also will help the draining of your garden.

As a path is primarily a functional construction it's important that it is the right size. Even if it is of secondary importance, the path should never be too narrow. A width of 600mm (24in) is the minimum while double that is probably the ideal size. A path should be able to accommodate two people walking side by side and should not hinder somebody pushing a fully-laden barrow. But if you feel you've made your path too wide it can always be disguised by shrubs and flowers at its edges. Most path surfaces are available in a whole range of shapes, sizes and colors so you're going to have to plant carefully. Start by making a scale drawing of your garden — it's best to use graph-paper. You can then plan the path's route and get an idea how useful it will be. It's no good laying down a path that takes a

Trick

LAYING AN ASPHALT DRIVE

Hot asphalt, or macadam or blacktop as it is often called, will give a good surface finish to a drive and is easy to lay. It's available in black but sometimes in red or green, from specialist suppliers.

First of all you'll have to work out how much you'll need. Asphalt is usually sold by weight, by the tonne, and one tonne (1000kg) (2,200lbs) will be enough to give about 25 sq metres (28 sq yds) coverage to a depth of 25mm (1in). You can arrange to collect the material yourself, but you'll find it a lot easier to get your supplier to deliver it although you will have to pay an extra delivery charge.

There are certain tools you'll need to lay a drive of hot asphalt. An eight-pronged fork is important not only for loading your barrow, but also for ensuring that the macadam is kept loosely packed and therefore easily workable. A wide rake is essential for spreading the asphalt over your existing drive and levelling it off, while a special tamper called a 'punner' is useful for compacting the asphalt at edges and in corners. You'll probably already have a good barrow and shovel, but you'll have to rent a motorized plate vibrator to compact the asphalt as it is put down and a heavy-duty (preferably motorized) roller to finish it off with.

The secret to the successful laying of a drive is to be well organized and to have everything ready for when the asphalt is delivered.

Make sure that the surface of your existing drive is suitable for taking the asphalt. Rid the surface of weeds and moss using weedkiller or fungicide to

ensure they don't grow back through the new surface. Check, too, that the surface is relatively smooth. If there are obvious potholes these will have to be filled before you lay the asphalt (although they can be compensated for at a later stage). There will have to be a slight gradient on the new drive for drainage purposes, so your best bet is to follow that of the old surface.

Make sure you protect any manhole covers or drains. The former should be masked with a sheet of weighted-down hardboard while the latter can be plugged with rags to prevent any asphalt getting into them.

Bear in mind that your new drive will end up being about 25mm (1in) higher than the old one. If it runs up to garage doors you should check that this won't prevent them from opening. One solution is to flatten the asphalt enough to allow the doors to open, but this way you risk creating a slope that will let rainwater run in. Perhaps the easiest solution is to trim the bottom of the doors.

Finally, check the edges: asphalt is self-supporting to a certain extent and so needs no complex formwork and can be safely butted up against the home walls — provided it is lying at least 150mm (6in) below the flashing. However, where it is to butt up against kerbs or such like you'll have to make sure they are solid. Only where the drive abuts a lower level will there be need for edging. The best arrangement is to build a permanent edge by bedding a series of concrete kerbstones in concrete. The top edge of the stones should finish level with the top of the asphalt.

Finally, on the day the asphalt is to be

delivered thoroughly sweep the surface on which it is to be laid. Get the macadam dumped at one end of your drive and immediately cover it with a sheet of thick-gauge plastic to slow down cooling. The material starts to set as it cools, so it is never a good idea to use hot asphalt on a very cold day.

Fill the barrow and wheel it to the far end of the drive. Tip it out and start raking it using the wide rake. Use the back of the rake to level out the asphalt to a depth of about 38mm (1½in). It's a good idea to have some help at this stage so you can continue raking out the asphalt while others keep you supplied.

Proceed until you have covered a quarter of the drive. If you want to give it a finish of gravel, scatter some over this section (using a shovel) before going over it with the plate vibrator. Alternatively, leave the asphalt bare. The vibrator will compact the asphalt as well as revealing any depressions, which should be promptly filled in and further compacted. Avoid high spots as well — they'll eventually lose their chippings and give the drive a worn and patchy appearance.

Continue over the rest of the drive, working back towards the main pile. Where the drive joins the road you should then tamp it down using the punner to avoid an obvious ridge. Apply more chippings of gravel and vibrate, especially over the joins between the sections. You should then go over the whole surface with the roller to ensure it is well compacted. Finally you can apply more gravel and distribute it with a brush to gain an even covering. Allow 24 hours for the asphalt to set completely.

Granite blocks, also used here for low retaining walls, lend themselves well to curved patterns and are extremely hard-wearing.

circuitous route that in the end people won't use.

Once you've planned your path you'll have to consider exactly what material you want to use for it. Don't choose something that would clash dreadfully with the existing style or tone of your garden: as a general rule brick paths go best with brick houses and stone with stone houses.

If you are in any doubt it's sensible to visit your local garden center or builder's suppliers. That way you can see for yourself the type, quality, color and texture of material that is available.

Herringbone pattern breaks up the regularity of bricks, enabling curved drives to be laid without looking awkward at the edges.

Of course, you could just use grass for your path, although it would have to be a particularly tough seed.

A simple concrete raft can serve quite effectively as a path although in laying one you would be giving little consideration to the path's aesthetic appeal. However, provided the slab is finished with a stiff brush to give it a non-slip surface it should be perfectly satisfactory: and concrete finishings are available to give a more decorative treatment.

At the other extreme perhaps the most attractive path is likely to be one made of natural stone. However, while this would be a way of obtaining a very durable path it would also prove very expensive.

One of the most popular surfaces for paths is concrete slabs. There are two kinds — pre-cast, which are set in a mold, and the more expensive; more durable, hydraulically-pressed concrete slabs.

The most common shapes are square and rectangular and their dimensions are usually multiples of 225mm (9in) or 300mm (12in) up to 675 × 450mm (26½ × 18in) and 600mm (24in) sq. Other shapes are hexagonal — useful for paths which turn corners, these

are usually about 450mm (18in) wide, circular, and ones with special cut-outs to allow you to pave round trees. They are normally about 38mm (1½in) thick.

Slabs are finished with a wide variety of surfaces, textures and colors. Some are designed to look like natural stone, while others are pressed to have surface patterns that look like brick or mosaic. And there are many colors available ranging from an off-white, through buff tones, pinks, browns, reds or greens.

Concrete paving blocks are usually 200 × 100mm (8 × 4in) in size and either rectangular or else shaped to interlock. Used in a path they will require some form of edging and can be laid by hand, although you'll get much better results if you rent a plate vibrator to set them securely in a bed of sand. The blocks come in different thicknesses, but 60mm (2½in) will be adequate both for paths and patios. A variety of colors is available and the blocks can be laid in a number of patterns.

Bricks will give a particularly warm and rustic look to a path and should harmonize nicely with their surroundings. However, not all bricks can be safely used for paths — common house bricks will eventually crumble — so it's best to use tough paving

bricks. They can be bedded on a layer of sand or mortar and like concrete blocks can be lain in different patterns.

Gravel is a very traditional and comparatively cheap material for use on paths. While it is very easy to lay it is not necessarily the best surface. Its advantages are that it will last a long time, it is very easy to repair — all you do is add more gravel — and it can be easily put down on a surface that isn't level. However, in wet weather gravel paths tend to be slippery and somewhat sticky — you'll find that plenty of the chippings will stick to your shoes. If you do plump for gravel make sure your path runs on porous soil so it drains quickly. The other disadvantage of gravel is that it won't keep to its level and so will require frequent raking as well as occasional treatment with weedkiller — although the latter usually applies to all paths.

One slightly unusual material you might not have considered for your path is wood. You would have to cut cross-sections of logs about 150mm (6in) long and bed them in soil or a mortar base. If you have a log with a large diameter you could create a stepping-stone effect. You'll have to soak the wood in preservative — a non-toxic one — so it can withstand constant exposure.

Wood decking has a rural appeal but needs regular maintenance to prevent rotting, and algae can make it very slippery when wet.

LAYING SLABS

If you decide to use concrete paving slabs you'll find these simple to use and your path quick to complete.

Once you've planned where you want the path to go you'll have to decide whether you want to use plain or colored paving slabs. There are plenty of patterns you can create, but it's a good idea not to be too flamboyant: You don't want your path to take attention away from the rest of the garden. You can get an idea of what the path will look like by drawing it to scale on squared paper, then by coloring in the squares as if they were the slabs. Doing this might prevent you from making a terrible mistake which you would come to regret. Some builder's suppliers or garden centers will have leaflets offering suggestions for designs and even offering pre-selected slabs for sale.

You would be wise to order your slabs well in advance, especially if you want some unusual colors or finishes. And always allow a few extra for any breakages that might occur.

It is important to store the slabs correctly — otherwise you risk unnecessary breakage. Keep each size and color separate so they're easily reached when needed. They should be stacked face-to-face on edge and resting on lengths of wood to avoid chipping. Lean them up against a wall at an angle to make sure they're stable.

How to lay the path depends on what it is going to be used for and the nature of the soil underneath. If the path is only likely to be used by people walking on it then simply bedding the slabs on sand

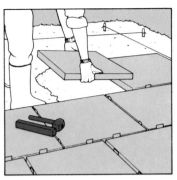

Laying paving slabs on mortar; a full mortar bed gives extra strength where needed, otherwise bed each slab on a box of mortar.

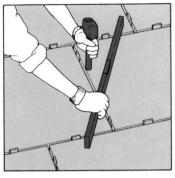

Tapping down the corners of a slab with the handle of a light sledge hammer; check the level across adjacent slabs with a long spirit level.

Filling the gaps between slabs laid on sand with a soil/sand mixture; point slabs laid on mortar with a pointing trowel and crumbly mortar.

should suffice; if, however, the path is to carry heavy traffic such as mowers and barrows then, it's probably better to bed the slabs in mortar. Either way preparation of the site is similar.

Mark out the exact area by putting down the corner slabs. Drive in pegs and attach stringlines to give a guide to the trench to be dug and allow a little extra space in which to work.

In the same way as if you were laying a concrete slab you'll have to dig away the top soil and any vegetation. Then compact the base using a small garden roller or a strong wooden post. Check that the base is level using a spirit level on a wooden straight-edge.

If you are working on soft ground — clay or peaty soil — you'll have to dig down a further 75mm (3in) or so and fill in with a layer of gravel. Compact this using a club hammer so that it is firmly bedded and cover with a blinding layer of sand. The level of both the hardcore and soil base should be calculated by allowing for the depth of the slabs plus an extra 25mm (1in)

or so for a layer of bedding sand or mortar.

If you are going to lay the slabs on a simple bed of sand you should make this about 25mm (1in) thick. You can then start laying the slabs at one end and work towards the other.

Remember, if you are laying a path on a flat surface you'll have to allow a slight gradient to facilitate drainage. This can be worked out either by driving in extra pegs in the trench and fixing them so that one side is lower than the other and using these as a guide for the level of the slabs, or by putting a 25mm (1in) thick block of wood under the spirit level when you check the path as you lay it. Either way you should allow a cross fall of about 25mm (1in) in each metre of path. Adjust the stringlines so that they mark out the exact width of the path.

Lay the first slabs and check that they are level. When abutting slabs to others offer up the edge first and then ease the full slab into position. You can then tap it into place with a block of wood. With several slabs down check the level across them all by resting your spirit level on a straight-edged plank. Finally, fill the the gaps between the slabs by brushing in a mixture of soil and sand.

For laying on mortar you'll have to mix a bedding material using the proportions of 1:5 Portland cement to sharp sand. Simply spot-bedding the slabs — dabs of mortar at each corner — is not ideal. Adopt a technique called 'box-and-cross' bedding, which will give the benefits of adjustment allowed by spot-bedding and some of the strength of a full mortar bedding.

Make a rectangle of mortar slightly smaller than the slab itself then lay a strip of mortar across it. Omit the cross strip for small slabs but use two for larger ones.

Again firmly bed the slabs in position using a wooden block or mallet and check that they are level with a straight-edge.

You should aim to allow a 13mm (1/2in) gap between adjacent slabs. Some will have this moulded in at their edges but with others you'll have to ensure a consistency of space by cutting wooden spacers and slotting them into the spaces. These will also prevent newly-laid slabs from closing up on each other. Continually check the level across the path to be sure of the correct drainage fall.

With all the slabs in position, you'll have to point the gaps. Use a dry, stiff mix and force it home using a pointing trowel. The crumbly nature of the mix should prevent any staining of the surface but you should wipe away any on the surface with a wet cloth. Finish the pointing to just below the surface of the slabs to make draining easier.

Finally you can finish along the edges of the path with soil and let the grass grow back. Alternatively lay down soil and strips of turf.

It is possible that you'll have to cut some slabs during the course of making the path.

Mark the line of the cut right round the slab with a piece of chalk, guiding your hand with a straight-edge. Then score along the line using a flat masons chisel. It's best to place the slab on a soft surface that will absorb the shock as you cut a groove. Continue cutting the groove until the slab breaks.

Scoring along the marked cutting line, all round the slab, with a masons chisel and light sledge hammer; rest the slab on a bed of sand.

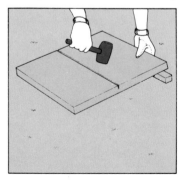

After raising one end of a the slab, bottom face upwards, on a batten, tapping along the score line with a light sledge hammer to break it.

Types of Surfaces

A patio is literally an extension of your home, so the materials you use should not clash violently with the house. At the same time, the patio surface must suit the garden as well. It should be sound, flat, quick to dry after rain, and easy to sweep. But building a patio is not just a matter of buying the right materials. Careful planning is necessary.

Make a scale drawing of your garden and mark the area of the intended patio as well as all other features in your garden and the neighbouring houses. Make sure you have chosen the area which gets most sun if this is a priority. After all, it would probably defeat your purpose were you to build a patio only to find it always in the shade.

Size is also important. A patio is likely to be used by more than one person, and for more than just sitting on. It's wise to make it large enough to accomodate garden furniture for four people, as well as permit passage through to the garden. The minimum practical size is about 3.7m sq (40ft sq).

After size, you'll have to consider drainage: you don't want to cause a flood every time it rains. If you're building on a flat surface then you'll have to incorporate a slight fall, say 1:72 (25mm every 1.8m/1in every 6ft) towards the garden or a flower bed. If you are building on a slope that runs down towards the house, dig away the area on which you'll lay the patio, from a fall away from the house, incorporate a drainage channel at the end of the patio and build a retaining wall.

Alternatively, if the garden slopes away from the house, build edging walls on which to lay the patio so that it has the appearance of a stage. Infill the area with gravel.

And you'll have to make allowances for any inspection chambers in the area on which you want to build the patio. Either build them up to the new surface level or cover them with loose-laid slabs to allow easy access.

The most strking character-istic of your patio will, however, be its surface, and there is an

Patchwork of colors and shapes.

Hexagonal backdrop for a shrub.

abundance of suitable materials for you to choose from. Don't mix too many surface materials; using two or three together can be eye-catching but unless done with care it can look messy. Try to use materials with flat surfaces; while a patio built entirely of cobbles may look very attractive, it is difficult to walk on, let alone set out garden furniture on.

Preparing the base for any type of surface is much the same, although depth depends on the thickness of the surface material to be used. You'll have to set a marking or datum peg at one side of the patio. Its top should sit at least 150mm (6in) below the flashing. Position another at the other side, making sure the levels are the same. Use pegs and stringlines to mark out the perimeter of the patio and dig down to about 225mm (9in), saving top soil. Compact the earth and drive in more datum pegs at 1.5m (5ft) centers. Put down a 100mm (4in) layer of gravel and compact it. Then add a 50mm (2in) layer of sand and roll it.

The easiest sort of patio to build is one that uses a concrete slab as its surface and is laid in the same way as raft foundations. However, an expanse of concrete won't look terribly attractive.

Natural stone, such as York

Soft but contrasting textures of wood decking and cobblestones.

stone, will provide a very attractive surface, although it will prove expensive. An alternative is to use slabs which are given a natural split-stone finish. With stones or slabs there are three methods of laying. You can spot-bed them or lay them on a full layer of mortar. Ensure an even space between slabs and use a dry mortar mix watered in. However, if you've laid the slabs on a mortar bed you should wait a week before doing this.

Bricks are particularly suitable for a patio surface if it abuts the house or if you have a walled garden. It's important to use frost-resistant ones. You can lay the bricks in a number of different patterns.

Bricks should be laid on a 50mm (2in) dry bed of mortar mixed to proportions of 5 parts sand: 1 part cement. Leave positioning any cut bricks until last and ensure that there is a 9mm (3⁄8in) gap betweeen each for pointing. When all the bricks are down, sweep more of the dry mix into the gaps and water using a can fitted with a fine rose — otherwise you risk washing the mix away.

Granite setts are very hard-wearing — they used to be used in road-building — and provide a striking patio surface. However, they would probably prove a bit too dark for the whole surface

and are not particularly easy to walk on. They are ideal for edges or in conjunction with a lighter patio surface for creating patterns and are laid in the same way as bricks.

Cobblestones can be safely used in patios but not for areas which are to be walked on. There are three methods of laying them. They can be bedded in a mix of 5:1 sand to cement mortar, making sure they are tightly packed with no mortar between the stones; bed them in dry mortar then water, or simply lay the cobbles loose on top of one another.

Finally, you could use wood for your patio. You would have to lay a 50mm (2in) concrete layer over the gravel then lay a line of single course brick sleeper walls to carry the supporting wooden members. Top the bricks with bituminous felt strips to ward against rising damp. Support members should be spaced about 400mm (6in) apart then the decking — exterior grade hardwood — fixed on top at right angles with rust-proof counter-sunk screws. Ensure that there's a 9mm (3⁄8in) gap between the wood and build a single skin wall round unenclosed edges.

Trick

BLOCK PAVING

Apart from their durability, the advantage of block paving, is that they are simply laid on a bed of sand — no mortar is required — making them quick and easy to lay, and just as easy to lift for alterations or access to underground drainpipes in event of maintenance.

Block paving is available in several different thicknesses and shapes — although 65mm (2½in) thick is ideal for patios and paths. The commonest types are roughly brick-sized rectangles, with a bevelled top edge to outline their shape in an overall design. Irregularly-shaped blocks — typically S-shaped or zig-zag shaped — are interlocked to form a complete pattern.

The other advantage of pavers is that they can be laid in several different patterns. A running or stretcher bond is the most simple pattern, though this is not really suitable for curved or irregular paths or patios. It can only be laid at right angles to the line of the paved area. A herringbone pattern will give the strongest bond but requires more careful work, while a basketweave pattern is the easiest, provided the area to be paved is in units of 200mm (8in). However, it is also the bond most likely to be disturbed.

Wherever you're laying the paving blocks, they will require a firm edging. Butting them up against a wall is perfectly suitable, but if it is the house wall, the level of the stones will have to be at least 150mm (6in) below the flashing. Existing paving will suffice as an edging; otherwise, you'll have to lay down kerbstones in concrete or else use lengths of 38mm (1½) wood dipped in preservative and fixed securely to pegs in the ground outside the area to be paved.

Two extra pieces of equipment you'll certainly need are a plate vibrator to bed the pavers firmly in the sand and an hydraulic stone splitter for cutting the stones. Each can be easily hired.

Prepare the base as if you were laying a slab and only put down hard core if you are working on a clay or peat soil, or if the area is to be used for cars. Make sure the base is level. You'll have to lay a bed of sand as you proceed. This should be about 50mm (2in) thick after being compressed, so make sure you're generous with it. About 1 tonne (1ton/1000kg) of sand is sufficient for 10square metres (11.19 sq yd). Arrange the sand at intervals across the site and start spreading it from close to the pile of blocks. Lay the sand about 2m (6ft) ahead of where you're laying the blocks (which you should also the position to hand). Use a kneeling board to distribute

To provide a firm edging for the pavers, bedding kerbstones in concrete after excavating the site.

Levelling the bed of sand with a straight-edge across two 50 × 25mm (1 × 2in) guide battens laid on edge.

Cutting a paver by scoring round with a masons chisel and hammer, then hitting the bolster sharply.

Positioning the pavers, working forwards over the levelled sand; tap down any pavers which are obviously proud.

your weight and adjust individual blocks if they are obviously proud or lower than the others. Leave gaps for half blocks that will have to be cut and fill them later. When 4 or 5m (12 or 15ft) of paving have been laid, bed them securely using the plate vibrator. Make sure it is fitted with a rubber sole plate, or lay down an old carpet to avoid marking the blocks. Traverse the area two or three times with the vibrator but keep it at least 1m (3ft) away from the unfinished edges. When all the blocks are down, spread dry sand on the surface and run over it with the vibrator to force it into the joints, further firming the base.

Blocks for small areas can be laid without a vibrator. Use a firmer and moister sand and bed each block using a wooden mallet or a light sledge-hammer over a block of wood.

Compacting the pavers into the sand with a plate vibrator; a piece of carpet prevents the pavers from being marked.

It's no good having a terrace in your garden if you can't get to it. Similarly, if the garden slopes steeply in the middle or is on two levels, access to the far end can be awkward. However, it's fairly straightforward to put in some garden steps that will solve all your problems.

There are two types of steps you can build and which you choose depends on exactly what you want access to. If you have a terrace surrounded by a retaining wall, then the most suitable flight of steps would be a free-standing one. This can be 'toothed' into the wall and so become part of the terrace.

However, if you simply want access to another level or want to make the passage over a steep bank that much easier, your best bet would be to set the steps in the slope itself.

While steps have a specific function, there is no point treating them as merely an unimportant feature in your garden; they can be attractive and eye-catching. As with the materials for a patio or path, the materials for steps should blend in with the rest of the garden. If you're building steps up to a terrace, use the same material for both.

There are many materials you can use in building steps, whether formal or not.

If you're building the steps fairly close to the house, then it's best to use brick, stone or moulded concrete. In some cases you'll want to combine these, perhaps using bricks for walls and risers and concrete slabs for the treads.

If you're making steps at some distance from the house, and not connecting to a terrace, other materials can be used. For example, timber steps can be very attractive. Use logs stripped of their bark and supported at the front by stakes driven into the bank at each end. Obviously you'll have to treat the timber with a suitable preservative but when the area behind the steps is infilled with soil you'll have a sturdy, natural-looking flight of steps.

Natural stone is very suitable for garden steps (although as mentioned previously it is rather expensive). Again, it can be used in combination with other

materials. Brick is the obvious choice as a partner for stone.

Brick can also be used on its own, and it is particularly suited to a town-style garden. With brick, you can create steps without a nosing projecting over the treads. Engineering bricks are the most suitable, being durable and designed to withstand frost.

People often think that narrow steps — taking up less room in the garden — will make the rest of the garden look bigger. This is not the case. And it is as much of a mistake to build the steps so that they are too steep. The depth of the risers should not be so shallow that people will simply trip on them and find them awkward to adjust to. The ideal height is between 125 and 150mm (5 and 6in).

Similar rules apply to the front-to-back depth of the tread. It should never be less than 450mm (18in) and of course the wider and deeper the treads, the more the steps become a feature in their own right. There's nothing to stop them from being used as extra seating or for carrying pots for plants. The front of the treads can overhang the risers by about 25mm (1in): this 'nosing' defines the step.

Steps require considerable planning and as with paths, it's wise to work out exactly where you're going to run them and plan carefully. Placing steps down the middle of a garden is not always a good idea; the result tends to give the impression that both sections of the garden are smaller than they really are. Steps built at the side of entrances or banks will give much more of a feeling of space.

It's important to make allowances for drainage. When positioning treads you should ensure that you build in a slight fall towards the front to allow rainwater to run off. An alternative method for steps adjacent to walls is to create a small concrete channel at each side to funnel off the water.

It's quite simple to work out how many steps you'll have to build. Measure the difference in height between the level at the top and that at the bottom then divide it by the height of the riser (and tread) to give you the number of steps.

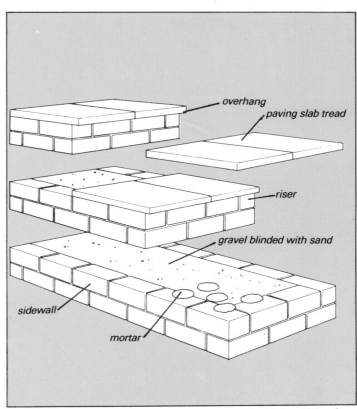

Construction of freestanding steps; paving slabs are bedded on blobs of mortar and supported on the sidewall and, in the middle, compacted gravel blinded with sand. To avoid cutting slabs, step the sidewalls the length of the slab less 25mm (1in) for the nosing or overhang.

Building up the brick sidewalls, using string line guides for height and drainage fall; build the riser across gravel in the 'box' below.

Filling between the walls with gravel; level it off flush with the tops of the bricks and blind it with sand.

Checking the height of the brick courses with a gauge rod; it is important that each step has the same rise to prevent tripping.

Bedding the paving slab treads on blobs of mortar, overhanging the risers; check that there is a slight fall to the front.

231

BUILT-IN STEPS

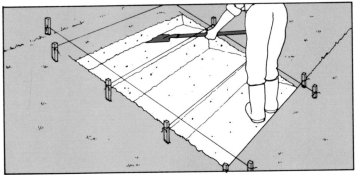

After marking out the sides of the flight with string lines and setting out lines at right-angles to these for the nosing of the treads, digging out the treads, working from the bottom upwards; dig within the lines of the nosings to allow for the thickness of the risers and treads.

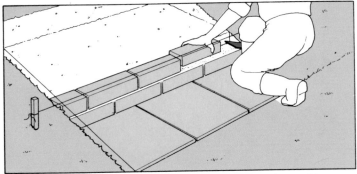

Building the first riser; after laying paving slabs up to the riser position as a continuation of a path, compact gravel behind them as a footing for the riser and lay the blocks on a bed of mortar with their front faces 25mm (1in) behind the string line.

The idea behind built-in steps is to employ the shape and structure of the slope as a base for the steps. If the soil is stable and compacted enough it can form the base of the steps, but it's more usual to put down a layer of gravel to provide stable foundations. Plan your steps carefully and make sure you have enough material. The method for working out how many steps you'll need and the constituent parts of the steps are described on the previous page.

The first thing you'll have to do is mark out the course of the steps on the bank. Fix pegs at the top and bottom of the slope marking the width of the steps. Run stringlines from between the pegs and make sure the lines are parallel and that the flight they are marking is lying straight on the bank.

You'll then have to set up horizontal stringlines to mark the nosing of each step, making sure that each line is at right angles to the main stringlines. With all the lines in position, start digging out a rough shape of the steps. Work from the bottom up. You'll have to dig out to a depth sufficient to take a gravel filling and the depth of the rise and tread. Dig behind and below the stringlines, taking care not to dislodge them. Compact the soil base with a length of strong wood or a sledgehammer then start on the next step to be dug. Work your way up to the top of the bank ensuring that you do not disturb the edges of the bases you have already cut away.

You should start building the steps at the bottom and work up. If the soil is soft you'll have to put down a 100mm (4in) deep concrete footing on which to lay the first riser. However, on small flights and where the soil is stable, this is not really necessary.

Lay a gravel base at the bottom for the first riser then compact it using the post or sledgehammer. Then put down a dryish mortar mix made up to the proportions of 1:5, cement to sand. You can then lay the bricks, stone or blocks for the first riser, making sure that each course sits level and square. Tap them into position with a wooden mallet or with the handle of a club hammer.

Carefully fill the gap behind the riser with hardcore, without disturbing the newly-laid riser. Push the hardcore down then further compact the risers. You'll then have to put more hardcore on the exposed soil base to bring it up to the level of the top of the riser. As you compact it make sure that you have allowed a slight fall towards the riser to allow water to drain off the steps when they are completed. Bed the first treads on mortar. Position them so that their top edges line up with the stringline running across the flight of steps and make sure they overhang the riser by about 25mm (1in).

The next riser stones will have to be set in mortar on the back of this first tread. Take care not to get any mortar on the surface of the tread as it will stain. Proceed up the slope, laying the risers and treads in the same way. The top tread will have to be laid so that it sits level with the top of the slope. Finally, brush a dry mortar mix into all the gaps and point the joints. Don't use the steps for at least seven days so that the mortar will set fully.

Taking care not to disturb the blocks of the riser, compacting gravel behind it with a post or punner; the gravel should be level with the top of the riser and rise slightly away from it to allow for drainage. Check that the riser is still square to the sides and the top horizontal.

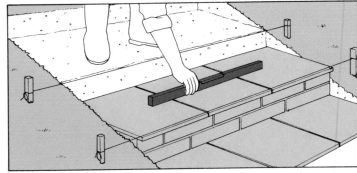

After laying the slabs for the first tread on rectangular boxes of mortar, overhanging the riser by 25mm (1in), checking that they are level across the tread; there should be a slight fall to the front of the tread and the top edge should be against the string line. Adjust with a mallet.

After building the next riser on the back of the first tread, continuing up the flight in this way; the final tread should be level with the ground at the top of the slope. Finally point between the slabs by brushing in a dry mortar mix; leave for seven days before using.

(Top) Screen walling blocks used as a backdrop for a barbecue setting. (Above) Modular stone walling blocks come in a range of soft colors.

Formal brickwork sets off the decorative wrought-iron gate.

If you're planning to build a wall in your garden, it's likely to be for one of three purposes: it could be a boundary wall to divide your property from that of your neighbor; a retaining wall to restrain a bank of earth or higher ground; or a partition wall, dividing small spaces or enclosing and disguising certain unattractive areas of the garden such as a compost heap. There is a great variety of materials you can use for your garden wall.

Brick is probably the most common, and will look particularly attractive with plants trailing over it. There are three types of clay bricks. Common bricks have no particular finish and are used in the main where they are likely to be covered with plaster, render or paint.

Facing bricks are designed to be displayed and so are given a variety of textures and colors. They are suitable for use both inside and outside where they are capable of bearing quite heavy loads. However, it is worth nothing that these bricks are susceptible to damage from damp and frost and should be protected by a flashing and coping stones.

The third type of clay brick, the engineering brick, is particularly strong and doesn't absorb water readily. It is therefore ideal for using on foundations.

These three types of brick are available in three qualities also. They can be classified as interior, ordinary and special quality. The first category implies the usage of the brick, the second is suitable for most jobs and the third is particularly frost- and damp-resistant. Calcium silicate bricks are also available and are particularly suitable for

decorative purposes, being made in a number of different colors.

The average brick size is 215 × 102 × 65mm (8½ × 4 × 2½in). But for the purposes of calculating necessary amounts of bricks, what is called a format size is used. This adds an extra 10mm (⅜in) on to each dimension to allow for the mortar joints between the bricks.

Bricks are laid in overlapping bonds to provide strength for the wall. There are a number of different bonds — stretcher, English, Flemish, for example — but the principles behind them are the same. The idea is not to place one vertical joint directly above another, as this would weaken the wall. The type of bond used determines the thickness of the wall as well as the pattern of the finished product.

Reconstructed stone, another walling material, consists of concrete mixed with an aggregate of crushed stone. There are two types. Split-faced is made when a large block is riven to give two straight and textured edges, while pitched is specially

shaped to look rugged. Another variety is designed to look like dry stone walling, each block appearing to consist of a number of stones complete with recessed false joints. Reconstructed stone is suitable for most garden walls.

Concrete screen blocks are not suitable for retaining walls nor ideal for boundary walls. However, they are perfect for partitioning the garden. The units are usually square, blocks pierced with geometric patterns. As they are made from a dense concrete they come in a natural greyish color or white. The most common size is 305mm sq (12in sq), with a thickness of about 102mm (4in).

Before starting on your wall, there are certain regulations that may have to be considered. Check with your local Building Code before building.

And of course you'll have to make sure that boundary walls are built entirely on your property — otherwise you could encounter some disagreement with your neighbors.

All walls, be they brick or screen block, will require extra supports on long runs. In brick

walls these are called piers and pilasters and have to be built in by altering the bond. As a rule, a half-brick-thick wall will need a pier every 1.8m (6ft) and if the wall is higher than 900mm (3ft) it will have to be a one-brick-thick pier. A one-brick-thick wall will need fewer piers; only if it is higher than 1.3m (4ft) will it need them at 2.8m (10ft) centres.

Screen blocks are designed for stack-bonding — one laid on top of the other — and so piers are vital. Most ranges include special pier blocks which are given vertical support by reinforcing rods that run in the center of piers and are bedded in the foundation concrete. The central hollow is itself filled with concrete as the wall is built up.

BASIC BRICKLAYING

The principles of bricklaying apply to any kind of brick wall. What differs is the kind of bonding you use. The chances are that for a simple garden wall you'll only need to build a half-brick thick one using stretcher bond. First dig a trench and lay your foundations (see page 222). You'll have to adjust the string-lines to give you the building lines for the wall. Make sure the wall is to run centrally on the footing by moving the nails an equal distance from the sides.

These lines will give you a guide but you'll have to transfer the line to a thin screed of mortar on the footing. Transfer the line down to the screed using a spirit level held against the string-lines. This same technique can be used if the wall comprises just a straight run or corners.

There are various tools you'll need but of most importance is a builder's trowel for applying the mortar to each brick. One with a 225mm (9in) blade will be perfectly adequate.

You'll also have to be able to cut bricks. Resist the temptation to use a trowel for this (a common method that's hard on the tool); instead mark a cut line with chalk then use a bolster chisel to cut a groove before striking the chisel firmly with a hammer to sever the brick. A brick cut in half is called a 'half-bat'. If you need a 'three-quarter bat', this has had a quarter removed, while a 'quarter-bat' has three-quarters cut away. A 'closer' is a brick cut in half length ways.

One other piece of equipment that will prove useful is a gauge rod. This consists of a length of 50 × 25mm (1 × 2in) wood marked clearly at 75mm (3in) intervals which will let you see if the wall is being built with consistent mortar courses.

Make sure you mix a mortar that doesn't set too quickly and so crack or pull away from the bricks. Use 1 part cement: 5 parts soft sand and include a measure of plasticizer as well.

Spread a 10mm (⅜in) thick layer of mortar on the foundation and position the first bricks, making sure they are correctly aligned and level. As a rule, you should build up the corners or stop ends first then fill in the course between. In stretcher bond a corner is made by butting up the bricks at right angles to each other. As you work your way upwards, check the corner with both the gauge rod and the spirit level. Reposition the stringline with each course.

If your wall is to be built between two stop ends you should start with these after you've laid the complete first course. You'll have to cut bricks in half for every other course to give you a neat finish without interfering with the bond. The cut side of the brick wall should be buried in the mortar of the joint. For a stronger stop, end lay the last brick in every other course at right angles to the wall face and lay a half bat next to it.

If your wall needs supporting piers, start them in the first course. Where the pier is to lie, bed two bricks header on. This pattern is repeated in alternate courses. On the next course, though, you'll have to prevent any aligning vertical joints by spanning the joint between the headers with a half-bat and laying a three-quarter-bat on each side of it to preserve the bonding. Behind the half-bat and the two three-quarter bats, lay a brick across the two headers.

You should step the corners and stop ends so that they have the correct overlay. Complete six or seven courses then start filling in, adjusting the stringline with each course.

You can adjust the position of individual bricks by tapping them down with the wooden handle of the trowel or by removing it and renewing the mortar underneath to bring it to the correct level. It is possible that dry bricks will suck the moisture out of the mortar and this could lead to a weakening of the joint. To avoid this, dip the bricks in water before laying them.

Finally you'll have to tidy up the exposed mortar joints. There are two reasons for pointing. First, to make sure all the joints are solidly filled and second, to provide a decorative finish that will shed rainwater from the face of the bricks and the joints. You can use the edge of your trowel to create flush joints or slightly recessed ones. Recessed joints are made by raking out about 10mm (⅜in) of mortar using a shaped piece of hardboard.

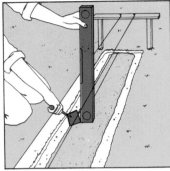

After setting up profile boards and string lines to thickness of wall, transferring edge line to mortar bed with trowel and masons level.

Laying first brick on mortar bed with face of brick against guide line; wiggle to bed it down then scoop up excess mortar for reuse.

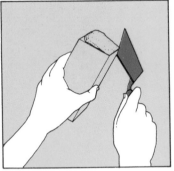

Buttering one end of second brick; scrape mortar off trowel in wedge shape, furrow with point of trowel and butt up against first brick.

After laying one complete course of bricks, checking for level and alignment with masons level; tap high bricks with trowel handle.

Strengthening wall with simple pier. Lay two headers then one stretcher alternately; use two ¾ bats and one ½ bat to keep bond in wall.

After building up corners and checking for square, filling in middle of wall; use string line in mortar joint as level guide.

Check brick courses with a gauge rod; mark batten at 75mm (3in) intervals – one brick height plus 10mm (⅜in) mortar joint.

Checking a corner with a builder's square made from three lengths of batten so that the triangle sides are in the exact ratio 3:4:5.

Trick

DECORATIVE BLOCKS

While the use of bricks for walling is probably the most popular and natural method of building, there's a vast array of materials available which can be loosely bracketed under the term 'decorative blocks'.

Basically these blocks are made from reconstituted stone. This is crushed to form a natural aggregate that is mixed with concrete and, when necessary, coloring pigment, before being compacted together under a great deal of pressure.

The result is hardwearing, easy-to-use blocks that provide an attractive alternative to brick.

Once the crushed sections of stone and concrete have had time to set fully, they're split to give a rough-hewn finish to the block that is provided by the natural stone aggregate. Therefore the blocks look very similar to stone, yet are available at a considerably cheaper price.

While the splitting of the blocks gives a natural quality, the blocks are available in two types of finish. An ordinary split finish has a relatively smooth surface; the pitched face has a distinctly rugged profile.

The type of stone used in decorative blocks varies and depends largely on where it has been made, and will vary greatly across the U.S.

As a rule, there are no standard sizes for blocks of reconstructed stone. Sizes vary from manufacturer to manufacturer and there are usually many to choose from, allowing you to use a random course in the walls if you want. Indeed, most manufacturers produce at least two different sizes of each particular stone, some even being available in up to nine different dimensions.

Some decorative blocks are designed purely and simply for low garden walls and the like. They are not therefore suitable for use in load-bearing walls.

The colors of reconstructed stone blocks vary a great deal. A natural buff or stone color is probably the most popular but some stones are available in a whole array of reds, greens and greys.

Reconstructed stone is also made in special modular units. These are large blocks that are designed to give the impression of a random-coursed wall but which don't require any complicated building work. They are similar to the imitation dry-stone walling blocks previously mentioned (see page 233).

Most decorative walling blocks are sold by the square metre (yard) of single thickness wall. The easiest way to order

Building a garden wall with pitched-face stone blocks: Buttering on mortar mixed with soft sand and plasticizer.

Cutting a block using a masons chisel and light sledge hammer; after scoring a line all round the block, break it with a sharp blow.

After setting out the line of the wall with string lines and casting a strip foundation, laying the blocks along it.

Finishing off the wall with copings; they should overhang the wall equally on both sides and are bedded on mortar.

the stone is to visit your local garden center or builder's supplier to see exactly what is available, then consult the manufacturers' leaflets. These will almost certainly give you detailed figures of how many stones will be required to build a square metre (yard) of wall, allowing for a 10mm (⅜in) mortar joint between each block.

It's wise to get all the blocks you need at the same time, as slight differences in color may be apparent between different manufacturing batches. Store the blocks on a hard dry surface and cover them with plastic sheeting to protect them from the weather. However, you should allow air to circulate. Finally, it's best to use a mortar that uses soft sand and incorporates a plasticizer; that way it will be less likely to crack.

Pointing the completed wall, taking care to keep mortar off the faces; recess the joints about 6mm (¼in).

RETAINING WALLS

If you want to create a raised bank, terraced flower bed or simply divide up a sloping area of your garden, you'll have to build a retaining wall. This is designed to hold back the earth at the change of level and therefore must be stronger than an ordinary garden wall.

While brick is probably the easiest material to use, there are plenty of others available. You could cast a concrete retaining wall, use concrete blocks, or for a low wall, use decorative concrete blocks. If you want to give a particularly rugged look to your garden, a dry-stone garden wall would be particularly apt, while there's nothing to stop you using preservative-treated **wood** if you want.

Whichever material you go for, the planning of the wall and the building of its foundations are very important.

A brick retaining wall must be one brick thick. You can choose between a number of bonds such as English, English Garden or Flemish. You must make sure you choose a type of brick that does not absorb much water. Choose special quality bricks or engineering bricks. Mix a mortar to the proportions of 1 part cement: ½ a part lime 3 parts sand.

Foundations

The first step is to build the foundations for the wall. These can be strip foundations, which must be twice the width of the wall. With normal strip foundations it's sufficient to lay the concrete at the bottom of a well-compacted trench. However, a retaining wall demands that its foundations are set on a 100mm (4in) bed of gravel or broken brick and stone hardcore set at the bottom of a trench. The concrete strip should be 150mm (6in) deep and its top should be about 500mm (20in) below the soil level.

If you're working in particularly loose soil you might have to put a 'key' at the outer edge of the footings to prevent the wall being pushed forward. This consists of a deeper strip of concrete at the outside edge of the foundation. This shouldn't be necessary if your wall is going to be less than 900mm (3ft) high as

For walls above 1m (3ft) high a keyed foundation (with the key facing away from the raised level) gives greater strength. This can be further increased by sloping the wall inwards towards the higher level at a gradient or 'batter' of not more than 1 in 5.

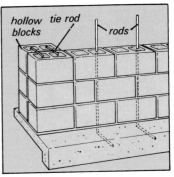

Vertical reinforcement for long, high walls: piers tied in with mortar cramps and rods through hollow blocks filled with concrete.

the push of the earth behind it won't be a crucial factor.

If you're incorporating a corner in the wall, start laying the bricks there — as in an ordinary wall. Otherwise start at one end. As the wall will be one brick thick, lay the outer lengthwise leaf first and then the inner, making sure that there's the correct bond. Check that the bricks are level and that the corner is at right angles. Work your way up out of the trench making sure that you follow the correct bond pattern. Continually check that the bricks are level and the wall vertical.

Providing Drainage

You will have to provide some drainage for the wall as ground water can exert a dangerous pressure on it. You can either leave vertical joints open every 1m (3ft) just above ground level or build in lengths of 75mm (3in) diameter plastic pipes. The latter are likely to be more efficient as the joints could easily get blocked. You'll have to bed the pipes on mortar and at a slight angle so the water will drain through the wall.

Continue the wall up to its final height then top it off with a course of bricks laid on edge to serve as coping. Alternatively, lay concrete coping stones on top to give further protection.

Before filling in behind the wall with well-compacted soil, it's a good idea to paint the back face of the wall with bituminous paint to protect it from further damp.

Laying the header course of English garden wall bond on top of three stretcher courses set on a trench foundation.

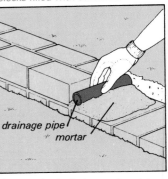

Setting plastic drainage pipes into the course above ground level on a generous bed of mortar; cut the bricks to maintain the bond.

An alternative to drainage pipes is to leave weep-holes every 1m (3ft) in the course above the lower level and cover with a stretcher course.

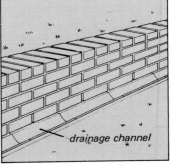

To prevent ground water flowing on to the lower level, set a drainage channel of half-round section into mortar below the weep-holes.

After allowing the mortar to cure and painting the inside face of the wall with bituminous paint, backfilling the soil.

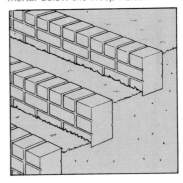

Unless a high retaining wall is necessary, a series of lower walls is preferable in terms of strength and ease of construction.

Building a screen block wall: After setting a bent rod into the foundation, filling the first pilaster with concrete.

Removing excess mortar from the channel in the pilaster after setting the first screen block on a bed of mortar.

Setting coping stones on the top course of blocks; cap the pilasters and piers also and point all joints.

SCREEN WALLING

A screen wall is particularly suited to partitioning sections of the garden without forming a solid, ugly-looking barrier.

As concrete screen blocks are square and cannot be cut, they cannot be given a conventional bonding. They are used in 'stack bond', which means that vertical joints align. This requires precise work because inaccuracies will show up very clearly in the finished wall. It also requires extra reinforcement.

Manufacturers produce a range of pilaster blocks, which are grooved on one, two or three sides to allow the blocks to slot into position as running piers or stop-ends. These blocks are hollow to allow them to be given extra reinforcement provided by a steel bar bedded in the footings and surrounded by concrete.

As a rule, piers should be set at 3m (10ft) centres and strengthened with a 16mm (⅜in) steel bar or 50mm sq (2in sq) angle bar. If your wall is likely to be more than 600mm (24in) high, then it should also have some horizontal reinforcement. This usually consists of 50mm (2in) wide galvanized steel mesh bedded in the horizontal joints.

As many screen blocks are white, it's best to mix a mortar using white cement and a light, soft sand. The usual grey color of Portland cement does not look particularly attractive in a finished wall. Alternatively, when you come to the pointing stage you could rake out the joints and fill them with a colored mortar.

You'll have to lay conventional strip foundations for a screen block wall. As stack-bonded masonry is likely to be damaged more by settlement than properly bonded walls, make sure that the foundation is on really solid ground. For low walls, a footing of 100mm (4in) on a bed of 100mm (4in) of gravel will be adequate. If your wall is to be highter than 900mm (3ft) the footings will have to be 125mm (5in) deep, 200mm (8in) wide and sit on a 125mm (5in) deep layer of gravel. Increase the width of the strip where there are piers.

Starter Bars

To provide vertical reinforcements for piers and pilasters you should bed what are termed starter bars in the concrete footings. These consist of 10mm (⅜in) steel rods that are bent at right angles and set in the concrete so that 500mm (20in) projects. Further steel reinforcement can then be tied into place using galvanized wire, provided the bars overlap by about 500mm (20in). Eventually the joints will be anchored by infill concrete.

Your wall will look better if it starts above ground level and doesn't sit directly on the foundations. To achieve this you'll have to construct a plinth which is wider than the blocks themselves. You can either cast a concrete plinth, in which case starter bars will have to project through this as well, or build a brick or concrete masonry plinth, incorporating the bars. Obviously the vertical joints won't align with those of the wall, in which case you might want to render the plinth, and you should top the plinth with flat coping

stones to provide a suitable surface on which to lay the first course of blocks.

Start by building up the first pier or corner. First tie on the angle iron or steel rod and cut it to finish some 50mm (2in) below the top of the pier so it will be completely protected by the infill. Bed the first block on mortar and make sure it's square and level. Lay a bed of the mortar round its top rim and bed the second block. Proceed in the same way until you've completed the pier.

You can now start building the wall out towards the next pier or corner. Put down a bed of mortar extending from the pier and about the equivalent of three blocks in length. Butter one side of a block with mortar and place this edge in the groove of the lowest pier block. Put more mortar on the opposite side of the block and place the second block in position. Continue in the same way until you reach the position of the next pier. Make sure that the course of blocks is level and that you scrape off any mortar that might have found its way on to the face of any of the blocks.

Continue to build up the wall, but don't lay more than four courses in one day: you must allow time for the mortar to set fully.

The next day, continue building up the wall and fill in the piers with a general-purpose concrete mixed with 10mm (⅜in) aggregate. Tamp the concrete round the steel using a length of small-section wood. Alternatively, fill in the piers as you build them up. Finally, bed bevelled coping stones on top of the final course of blocks to protect them from frost and rain and sit caps on top of the piers and pilasters.

TYPES OF FENCING

Erecting a fence in your garden is likely to prove cheaper than building a wall and can in certain circumstances be more attractive. You can decide whether you want the fence to provide you with complete privacy or simply serve as a boundary marker. However, allways check with your local Building Department regarding the siting and construction of a proposed fence. There's a great variety of fencing available and it is usually made of wood, plastic or metal.

The most common wooden fencing is close-boarded vertical or horizontal. The former consists of vertical posts and horizontal arris rails to which are nailed vertical boards. These can be square-edged, in which case they usually butt up to each other, or feather-edged, in which case they overlap slightly. The boards are available between 900mm (3ft) and 1.8m (6ft) in length, and between 100 and 150mm (4 and 6in) in width. As a rule, they're fixed to the arris rails so there's a gap between them and the ground. This is then filled by a 'gravel board' to protect them from damp. The

board can easily be replaced if rot should set in.

The latter type comprises feather-edged boards that are nailed directly to the posts and which overlap each other to provide protection against the rain. Horizontal close-boarded fencing also comes in panel-form. These are simply nailed to the side of the posts. Close-boarded fencing will give you almost complete privacy and serve as a perfect wind-break.

Interwoven fencing is the cheapest of the solid types of fencing and has a basketweave appearance created by the interweaving of thin wooden slats. It is sold in panels 1.8m (6ft) wide and 600, 900, 1200, 1500 and 1800mm (2, 3, 4, 5 and 6ft) high.

Paling fences are made up of vertical wooden pickets which are fixed to arris rails. The height of the pickets and the interval at which you nail them to the rails is entirely up to you. While it's most usual to make the fences up from the various components, kits are available. They come in panels which are simply bolted to the posts. The tops of

the pickets are usually given some sort of ornamental shaping.

Ranch-style fencing was originally used for penning-in livestock or surrounding paddocks but is increasingly popular in domestic situations. It consists of wide horizontal rails nailed directly to vertical posts with a gap left between them. This type of fencing is also available in a plastic form.

Wooden trelliswork can form fences on its own or be fixed to the top of closeboarded fencing or a wall. It is made up from 25mm (1in) battens that are fixed together to create either a diamond or a square pattern. It can be made up to size or comes in panels. However, it's worth remembering that trelliswork is not strong and is at its best when serving as a framework for climbing plants.

Where appearance is unimportant, you might consider using chestnut paling to serve as a fence. It consists of split chestnut pickets that are linked together by galvanized wire. It is sold in rolls of between 4.5 and 9m in length, in heights of be-

tween 900mm and 2m (3 and 6ft).

Plastic fencing has the advantage of being durable and requiring little maintenance. The most common form is plastic ranch style, although plastic paling and plastic boards for closeboarded fencing are increasingly common.

The cheapest type of metal fencing is chain link made from galvanized wire. A more decorative type is plastic coated. Both types are fixed to vertical posts and come in rolls about 25m (80ft) long, in various heights. The actual mesh size and wire thickness varies and welded mesh can also be bought quite easily.

Spiked chains are specifically designed to mark out borders, especially in front gardens. These are loose-hung between wooden or concrete posts. A plastic variety also exists but is easily broken.

Also suitable for low surrounds is hooped wire which is not very strong but which can be fixed directly into the ground. If you use a higher version then you will, of course, have to provide vertical support posts.

Trick

ARRIS RAILS

Arris rails are normally fixed to the fence post with a simple mortise and tenon joint. Occasionally the arris tenon will break. Rather than buy a new arris, it's easier to use a special galvanized metal extension bracket, which will enable you to fix the old arris back into position. First nail the bracket on to the arris. Then offer up the arris to the post and fix it in position using either galvanized nails or rust-proof screws. An alternative method is to cut four lengths of 25mm sq (1in sq) wood and fix three of them round the mortise to form a support for the arris. Lay the rail in the slot and then fix the fourth length of wood on the top so the rail can't slip out.

A special bracket is also available for repairing arris rails that have snapped in two. First attach the bracket to one half of the rail and then force the two sections tightly together before fixing the bracket to the other half.

Repairing a broken arris rail; nail a straight bracket to one half, force the two together and nail into the second.

Nailing a splayed-end bracket to a fence post after nailing the straight part to the arris rail with a broken tenon.

All wooden fences will require some sort of maintenance or repair during their lifetime. This might consist of dealing with rotten wood or stabilizing the fence. Whatever, it should be dealt with promptly.

On the most basic level, it is vital to ensure that your fence is given treatment against the weather. All wood used should be pressure-impregnated with preservative and you should make sure that you re-apply preservative to existing fences every two years.

On most wooden fences it is the posts that determine stability and the chances are that the bulk of repairs will have to be made to these. As fence posts are bedded in the ground, a relatively common occurrence is rotting. However, this doesn't necessarily require that the whole post is replaced. You can secure the sound wood to a concrete fence spur that serves as an anchor and is fixed in the ground in the same way as a post (see page 80). Check that the spur is upright, and that its longer face is against the post. Use the pre-drilled holes in the spur as a template and transfer them on to the post. You'll then have to drill holes in the posts and bind the two together using carriage bolts.

Perhaps the simplest method of stabilizing a rotted post is to refix it using a special metal spike. All you do is drive the spike into the ground then fix the post into its socket, after trimming away the rotten section.

It's important that rain should not penetrate the end grain at the top of the post. If the top of your posts have been cut off square then you should fit either a hardwood cap or a metal cap. Each is toe-nailed into place. Alternatively, shape the top so that water will simply run off.

If you have a gravel board that has rotted, then replace it without delay to avoid the danger of the vertical boards being attacked by the damp.

First you should remove the rotten boards then clear away the soil that will hinder you from fixing the new ones in position. Some gravel boards are fixed into recesses cut in the fence posts; others are nailed to blocks called 'cleats' fixed to the bottom

After cutting off the base of a rotten wooden post, setting a spur post vertically into a 600mm (24in) deep hole alongside it.

After marking through the holes in the spur and drilling through the post, bolting them together with coach bolts before concreting in.

Nailing new cleats to a fence post after removing old gravel board; set them back from the face of the fence by the thickness of the board.

Nailing the new gravel board to the cleats after cutting it to fit between the posts; treat it with preservative and clear away soil.

Removing a rotten fence board by punching the fixing nails through into the arris rail; support the rail from behind.

Using a spacer gauge to set the overlap of boards; lay the thick edge over the previous thin edge and nail through the overlap.

of the posts. If necessary, cut new cleats from 50mm sq (2in sq) wood. These should be 150mm (6in) long and you'll have to nail them to the inside faces of the posts. Use 150 × 25mm (1 × 6in) wood for the new gravel board. Nail to the blocks and check that there is no soil piling against the board.

Your fence might have concrete posts in which case you'll have to cut longer fixing blocks, about 600mm (24in) in length. Drive these into the soil so that they butt up tightly against the inside face of the post. Make sure that only 150mm (6in) of the pegs project from the ground then nail the board in position.

It is possible that on a close-boarded fence individual boards will have to be replaced. Start by removing the old one and extracting the old nails. If this is impossible, drive them into the arris rail. Then punch through the nails holding the thicker, outer edge of the adjacent board before slipping the thinner edge of the new board under it. You can then nail through the two boards and through the thick edge of the new board where it

overlaps the previous one.

With panel fences, repairs are not quite so simple especially with interwoven fencing. It is not easy to obtain individual slats to fit into a panel and to do so you'll probably have to remove a slat from a damaged panel. If you don't have any damaged panels ask at a local garden centre.

To replace a slat, lay the damaged panel on firm dry ground. Remove the central vertical support band on the upper side and one of the two

batten at each end. Carefully remove the damaged slat and replace it with the new one, taking care not to disturb the position of the other slats. You can then replace the vertical battens and fix the panel back into position. A simpler method would be to replace the entire panel: proceed as if you were erecting a new panel fence.

A damaged board in a panel of horizontal closeboarded fencing can be replaced.

Refixing a broken post by hammering a metal post spike into the ground; set an offcut of wood into the socket and insert to ground level.

After cutting the end of the post square, setting it into the socket before drilling pilot holes and screwing through the slots.

ERECTING A PANEL FENCE

As with any type of fencing, you should start off by marking its run. Drive pegs into the ground and run a taut line between them. The first step is to fix in the first fence post. You should use 150mm sq (6in sq) wood for this and make sure that it is pressure-impregnated with preservative. As the post has to sit securely in the ground you'll have to dig a hole 300mm sq (12in sq) and a minimum of 500mm (20in) deep. To make the job easier, hire a post-hole borer. This works in a similar way to a cork screw. Turn it first one way, applying a certain amount of pressure which will dig it into the ground. Then turn it the other way, which removes the blades and the earth at the same time. You'll be left with a neat hole that has the right dimensions to take a fence post. Ensure that you bore on your garden's side of the stringline.

Fill the bottom 150mm (6in) of the hole with hardcore and compact it using the end of a sledgehammer or a stout length of wood. Don't be tempted to use the post itself: you might damage it. Before placing the post in the hole, paint the part that will be buried with a coat of bitumen paint to give it extra protection against damp.

Drive the post on to the bed of gravel then knock a couple of lengths of batten into the ground next to the post but at right angles to each other to support the post. Check that the post is vertical and then nail the battens to the post keep it level.

You can then start to fill the hole. Don't just cram it with concrete. If the post shrinks at all then it will not get adequate support. The best thing to do is to fill the hole with alternative layers of earth and gravel, making sure that you ram it down well. Fill the hole to within about 150mm (6in) of the surface. Now you can use concrete. Fill the rest of the hole and then shape it up around the base of the post so that water will run quickly off it.

If you are using concrete posts, or for that matter setting up a concrete spur to support a post, you can fill the entire hole with concrete.

With the first post in position, you can mark the position of the others. The easiest thing to do is to cut a length of wood that is the same length as the panels. Then simply hold this against the first post and mark the point on the ground at which it ends. Dig the hole for the second post, fill the bottom with gravel and secure the second post. Don't as yet put in the concrete as you might have to make slight adjustments.

Now fix one end of the first panel to the first post. There are a couple of ways of doing this. You can either nail it into place using galvanized nails — in which case you should drill pilot holes first in the frame of the panel to avoid splitting it — or you can use special brackets which should be nailed to the fence posts with 50mm (2in) nails. All you do then is slot and drive nails through the pre-drilled holes at the sides of the brackets and into the framework of the panel.

It's a good idea to set each panel on a brick at each end. That way when it's fixed in position and the bricks are removed it will sit clear of the ground and so be protected slightly from damp. Never let soil build up against the panel sides.

With one end of the panel in position, you'll have to check that the second post is upright and that it is at the same height as the first post. This will make the final appearance of your fence much more attractive. Lay a level on a length of wood and place the timber on the tops of the posts to establish this. Finally, when you're satisfied with the position of the second post, fill in the hole with the collar of concrete and fix the other end of the panel to it. Proceed in exactly the same way with the rest of the fence.

If you are using concrete posts the technique is slightly different. The panels fit into slots that are pre-cast in the posts and held in place with special brackets.

If you are running a fence in line with a slope it's best to fit it in steps. You'll be left with some gaps at the bottom but these can easily be filled in with cut panels.

Using a post hole borer as an alternative to digging holes; turn clockwise to bore into the earth and anticlockwise to remove.

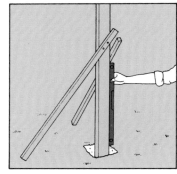

After digging or boring the hole, propping the post on gravel in the hole with temporary supports; check that it is truly vertical.

Carefully packing gravel round the post to within 150mm (6in) of ground level; ram down and check that the post is still vertical.

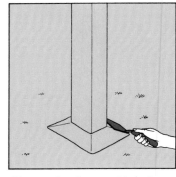

After topping the gravel to just above the ground level with concrete, smoothing the surface to a drainage fall away from the post.

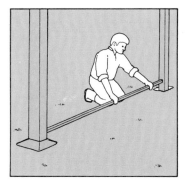

Using a batten the same length as a fence panel to position posts the correct distance apart; check each is vertical as you proceed.

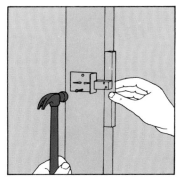

Nailing a proprietary fence panel clip to the post, make a simple T-shaped gauge to set the clips the correct distance in from the face.

Nailing a fence panel clip to the post; make a simple T-shaped gauge to set the clips the correct distance in from the face.

After sliding the panel in between the clips, nailing through the clips into the face of the panel, using galvanized nails.

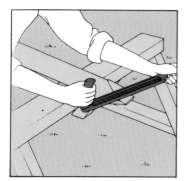

Shaping the ends of an arris rail; after cutting the ends to the rough shape of the tenon, smooth them with a planer file.

After concreting in the first post, and slotting the arris rails into it and the loose second post, checking that the rails are level.

After concreting in the second post, nailing through the face of the post and right through the tenon to secure it in the mortise.

When the run of posts and rails is complete, nailing blocks of wood to the bottom of the posts to hold the gravel boards.

The preliminaries of erecting a vertical closeboard fence are much the same as for a panel fence: you start with the first post. It is possible that you'll want to run the fence right up to your house wall, in which case the first post will have to be fixed securely to it. You won't have to set the post in the ground, but you'll have to secure it to the wall, using two or three 6mm (¼in) expanding anchor bolts.

The skeleton of fence posts and arris rails is most important to closeboard fencing and it's best to complete this before fixing on the individual boards. Start with the first and last posts — this way you'll get a better appearance, with the arris rails all level. This is especially important if you are intending to use rough-cut mortise and tenon joints to hold them in place. So you should run taut stringlines between the tops and bottoms of these two posts.

The arris rails consist of square wooden members that are sawn diagonally in half. If you have pre-cut mortises on the posts then you'll have to cut the tenons on the rails in order to fit them. It's best to saw the ends to gain the rough shape of the tenon and then finish them off using a planer file or wood rasp.

Prepare several rails in one go and treat the newly cut tenons with preservative. You can then use the cut rails as markers for the position of the posts. Dig out the holes using a post hole borer and fill the bottom 150mm (6in) with hardcore. Place the second post in its hole and put in enough earth and gravel around it to hold it upright.

Place the end of the rails in the mortises of the first post so that the flat face of the rail faces away from your garden. Hold the second post upright and slot the arris rails into its mortises. You should use a spirit level to check that the rails are level before securing the second post in position with a collar of concrete. Secure the tenons in the mortises by driving 75mm (3in) galvanized nails through the posts and into the rails. You'll probably find it easier if you have a helper holding the posts steady.

(If you find that your fence posts don't have pre-cut mortises you should use arris brackets to secure the rails in position. See page 238).

Proceed in this fashion until you have a skeleton of posts and arris rails. The next step is to fix the gravel boards which will protect the vertical boards between the bottom of the posts (see page 239). Ensure that the boards sit flush with the posts.

Once you've fixed all the gravel boards in position you can start attaching the feather-edge boards. You should use 50mm (2in) galvanized nails to secure them to the arris rails. Sit the boards on the gravel boards and fix the first one so that its thick edge butts up tightly against the first post. As the boards will overlap each other, it's a good idea to cut a gauge from a piece of scrap wood: this will enable you to measure an equal overlap throughout the length of the fence. The ideal overlap is 13mm (½in). Position the second board so that its thick edge overlaps the first board's thin edge by this amount and then nail it to the rails. It's best to drive the nails in

at a slight angle. That way if the fence is buffeted by strong winds the nails won't pull straight out.

Drive in the top and bottom nails first and finish with the nail in the middle arris. Each of the boards should be vertical. Check them with a spirit level; this will probably only be necessary every four or five boards.

Although an overlap of 13mm (½in) is to be recommended, you won't necessarily be able to make every board overlap by exactly this amount. You may find that as you approach the second post you'll have to increase or decrease the overlap slightly, since the important thing is that the final board butts up tightly against the post. And you should reverse the last board to allow its thicker edge to sit against the post.

When you have completed the fence, give it a thorough application of preservative. To further protect the posts, you should fit hardwood or metal caps — unless you've already shaped the tops so water runs off the end grain — and nail a coping strip on top of the boards.

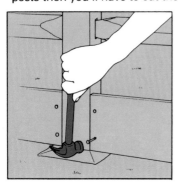

Nailing the treated 150 × 25mm (6 × 1in) gravel boards to the blocks, flush with the posts; clear away all soil from the board.

After nailing the first board to the arris rails, thick edge to the post, fixing subsequent boards to overlap by 12mm (½in).

Checking that the boards are vertical after nailing; the bottom of the boards should sit squarely on the gravel board.

Nailing coping strip to the thick ends of the boards to prevent rain from entering the end grain; cap the posts for the same reason.

PROJECTS

KITCHEN UNIT

There is no doubt that a fitted kitchen is a pleasure to look at and to work in, but fitted kitchen units can be expensive if you buy them ready made. Fortunately, the availability of melamine-faced particleboard in various widths, ready-made worktops and cabinet doors means that you can make your own units at a fraction of the cost.

The unit shown here is a basic two-door cabinet, but there is no reason why it cannot be adapted to accept drawers made from drawer kits or be varied in size to suit the kitchen and particular fittings. Multiples of the unit can be bolted together to make long cabinet runs and in this case it is best to fit one-piece worktops, upstands and plinths to give a unified look to the assembly.

The basic carcase is made from 19mm (¾in) thick melamine-faced particleboard which is easy to use and has the added advantage of providing an easy-clean finish — essential in the kitchen.

The side pieces are cut from this material and are 543mm (21in) wide and 889mm (35in) high (although this is variable if you want the work surface lower or higher).Right-angle cutouts are made at the corners for the plinth, upstand,worktop support rail and rear lower rail.

Make the cutouts using a fine toothed saw or circular saw. The top two are each 2in deep, the front one 19mm (¾in) wide and the back one 16mm (⅝in) wide.

The plinth cutout at the front corner is 100mm (4in) deep × 56mm (2¼in) wide and the cutout for the rear rail measures 75mm (3in) × 25mm (1in).

Next cut the upstand, worktop support rail and plinth from melamine faced particleboard. The upstand is 150mm (6in) deep × 750mm (30in) long, the worktop support rail 50mm (2in) deep × 750mm (30in) long and the plinth 100mm (4in) × 750mm (30in). If the cabinet is to stand on its own, the exposed cut ends of these pieces can be finished with iron-on facing strip to match the finish. The rear lower rail is made from 750mm (3in) × 25mm (1in) planed wood such as pine.

Screw a length of 25mm (1in) square batten to each end panel to act as a support for each end of the bottom shelf. Screw a similar piece along the upstand as a support for the back edge of the worktop. If fitting a center shelf — it can be made from a length of 450mm (18in) wide melamine faced particleboard — mark its position on each end panel and fit plastic joint blocks up against the line to act as shelf supports.

Plastic joint blocks are also used for the assembly of the carcase. Use them to fit the plinth, worktop support rail, upstand and rear lower rail to the end panels. Cut a piece of 520mm (21in) wide melamine faced particleboard for the lower shelf and screw this down to the top edges of the lower rear rail and

plinth using countersunk particleboard screws. Also screw the ends down to the support battens. Then fix the center shelf.

Pin a sheet of 3mm (⅛in) plywood to the back of the unit, cutting it so that it is flush with the end panels.

Fix the worktop in place using plastic joint blocks attached to the end panels and back of the worktop support rail. You can also screw up into the worktop through its rear support batten or simply leave it resting on this. If using a ready made worktop, you may have to trim it down using a circular saw so that it projects about 50mm (2in) beyond the support rail.

Finally, you can fit a pair of ready-made doors measuring 750mm (30in) high × 375mm (15in) wide. These should be mounted on concealed hinges that prevent the door opening beyond the thickness of the carcase material. Screw these to the rear faces of the doors and inner faces of the end panels.

A wide range of door pulls and handles is available — choose some that fit in with the door style. They usually either screw into the face of the door or bolt through it. To retain the doors when closed fit a magnetic catch to the bottom shelf behind the leading edge of each door.

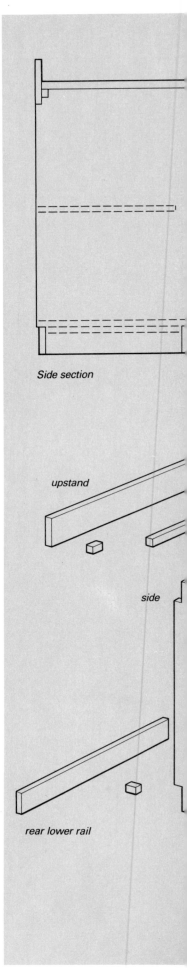

Side section

upstand

side

rear lower rail

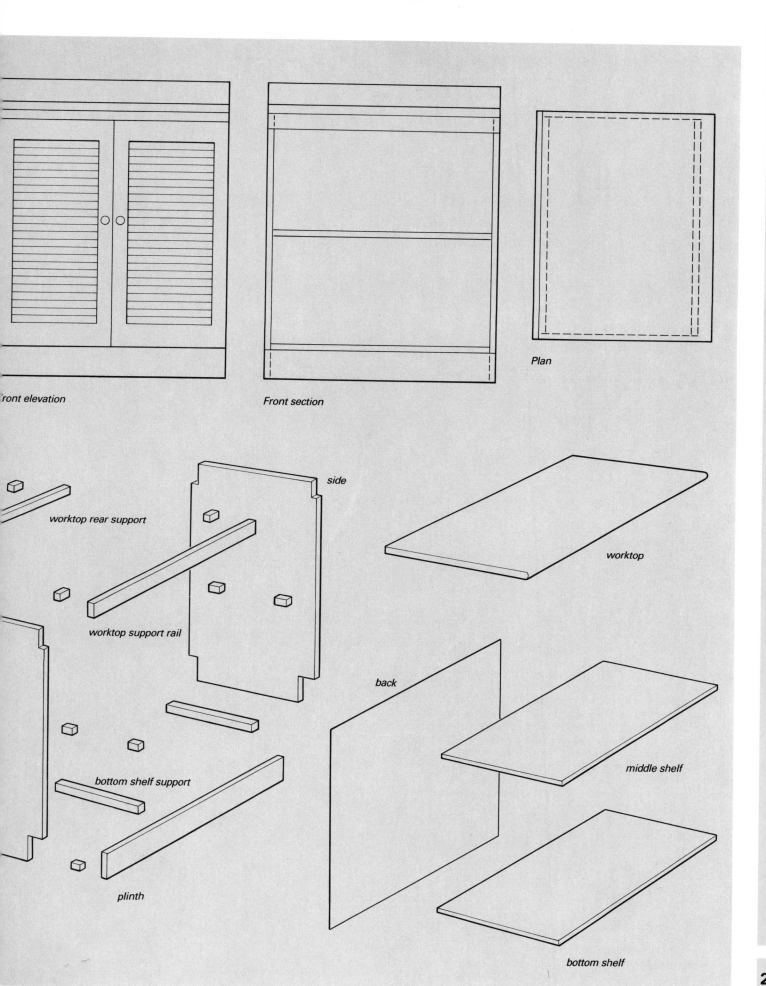

Front elevation

Front section

Plan

worktop rear support

side

worktop support rail

worktop

back

bottom shelf support

middle shelf

plinth

bottom shelf

243

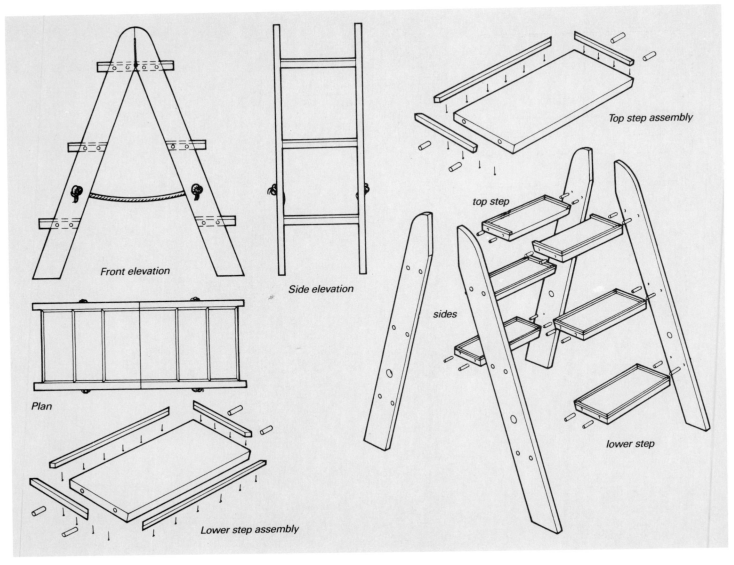

Front elevation

Side elevation

Plan

Lower step assembly

Top step assembly

top step

sides

lower step

PLANT LADDER

Pot plants will do a lot to brighten a room, but rather than stand them on window sills — where they will be hidden when the curtains are closed — or balancing them on top of the TV or odd shelves, why not make a feature out of them with this plant ladder. If trailing plants are used, it will create an attractive visual feature in the corner of a room.

The plant ladder is simply constructed from prepared softwood such as pine and can be finished with a clear or tinted polyurethane varnish, or it can be stained first, using one of the many colorful wood stains available.

Cut the sides from 100mm (4in) × 25mm (1in) pine, making sure they are all identical by marking out one and clamping all four together before finally cutting them to length, 130cm (52in) in one go. The foot of each side piece must be cut at an angle of 80° and top at an angle of 170°. These cutting lines are marked out with a bevel gauge which has been set against a protractor. Mark the large angle first since the gauge can be left at 80° for marking the 'step' positions. Mark the rounded top edge freehand and cut it to shape with a jig saw. The bottom step is fixed about 200mm (8in) from the foot of the side, the middle one about 500mm (20in) from the bottom and the top one level with the angled cut.

Each step is a 300mm (12in) wide piece of 150mm (6in) × 25mm (1in) pine, and to ensure accuracy when cutting, cut them roughly so size, clamp them together and mark all round using a trysquare. Then either cut them individually or in a batch. In addition cut leengths of 12mm sq (½in sq) beading to fit round the steps to prevent pots slipping off them. No beading is required on the back edges of the two top steps, which make one large platform. Before assembling the ladder, drill a hole in each side for the retaining ropes — you can use any rope you like or even sash cord. The holes should be about 350mm (14in) from the floor. You'll need about 150cm (5ft) of rope.

The steps are held in place by glue and dowels driven through the sides and into the step ends. However, if you wish you could glue and screw them using brass screws with screw cups for a decorative effect.

If fitting dowels, use the 6mm (¼in) size and mark their centres on the side pieces. To transfer the marks to the step ends either use proprietary dowel pins or drive 12.5mm (½in) panel pins into the sides so that their tops are just protruding. Snip off the heads with pliers and gently tap the steps down on to the pins. Pull out the pins with pincers and drill the dowel holes in all the pieces.

Assemble each half of the ladder by applying glue to the dowels and driving them through the sides into the steps. Hold each assembly together with sash cramps while the glue dries, making sure they are square by measuring the diagonals which should be equal.

Pin the beading round the step edges, having first mitred the ends. Then mark the hinge flap positions on the mating edges of the two halves and pare away the wood to the depth of the flaps. Fit the hinges and check that the two halves align properly. Then remove them, thoroughly sand the wood and finish in the desired manner.

Finally reassemble the ladder, inserting the rope through the pre-drilled holes, knotting it and cutting off the surplus.

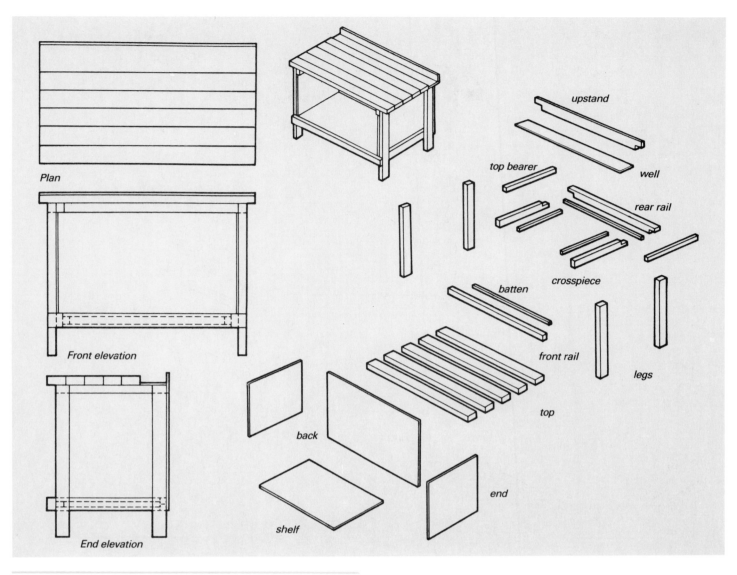

Plan

Front elevation

End elevation

upstand

well

top bearer

rear rail

crosspiece

batten

front rail

legs

top

back

shelf

end

WORKBENCH

A sturdy workbench is a valuable asset to have for many jobs, but a ready-made example will cost you a lot of money. This simple design uses readily-available wood and is easy to make. If you wish you can make it longer, or shorter, narrower or wider and as tall or as low as you wish, depending on your own particular needs.

The main structure of the bench is made from pine because this is easy to obtain and cheap — you could even use second-hand wood. Most commercially made benches will be constructed of something like beech which is harder wearing but much more expensive which explains their high cost.

The bench top is made by glueing four 120cm (48in) lengths of 100mm (4in) × 50mm (2in) prepared pine together edge to

edge. Use woodworking glue and cramp the pieces together with sash cramps. You can rent these from good tool rental shops. Use at least three cramps, fitting two across one face and the third across the opposite face between the first two.

Meanwhile you can make the rest of the framework. The legs, front and rear rails and lower crosspieces are cut from 75mm (3in) × 50mm (2in) prepared wood. The legs are 700mm (28in) long, the front rail 110cm (44in) long, the rear rail 100 cm (40in) and the crosspieces 600mm (24in). In addition you'll need two 600mm (24in) lengths of 50mm (2in) square pine.

Cut the ends of the crosspieces and the rear rail to make halving joints, then assemble the leg frames. Glue and screw the lower crosspieces across the

legs, setting them so that they are 150mm (6in) up from the bottom of the legs with the halving joints at the back. Then glue and screw the two lengths of 50mm (2in) square wood across the tops of the legs.

Glue and screw the front rail across the front edge of the legs and the rear rail between the two lower crosspieces. Upend the top and glue and screw the legs assembly underneath so that the top overlaps by 50mm (2in) at the front and at each end.

The top well is made by glueing and screwing a length of 150mm (6in) wide 19mm (¾in) thick plywood across the tops of the legs so that it butts up against the back edge of the worktop. An upstand of 150mm (6in) × 25mm (1in) pine is then screwed across the back. Before doing this, however, you can plane off any unevenness in the worktop, working the plane across it diagonally from each edge. Next screw lengths of 25mm (1in) square batten

around the inside of the front and rear rails and lower crosspieces to support the bottom shelf. These should be 19mm (¾in) below the top edges of these pieces so that the 19mm (¾in) thick plywood shelf sits flush with their top edges. Screw the shelf down to the battens.

To strengthen the bench and keep it square and upright, screw a panel of 19mm (¾in) plywood to the back of the legs and lower rear rail. If you wish you can fill in the ends with similar material, fitting the panels inside the legs at each end.

Any finish you choose for a bench is bound to get knocked about, so it is probably better — particularly since the bench is likely to be kept in a garage or outbuilding — to treat it thoroughly with a good quality wood preservative instead.

FITTED CLOSET

The closets shown here incorporate a small dressing table and provide plenty of hanging space and storage on top. Simple to construct, they make use of ready-made louver or panel doors.

The wardrobes are designed to span the end wall of a room or an alcove and there is no reason why you should not increase the width of the doors or increase the number of doors if you want a really long run of wardrobes. Since they will run the length of a wall, there is no need to worry about putting backs or ends on the units — the walls of the room provide these. Closing panels are only needed on either side of the dressing table and these are taken care of very simply by rigidly mounting a pair of doors in the opening. Alternatively, you could fill the spaces with plywood or T & G boarding.

The most important part of the construction is the framework that supports the doors. This is mainly constructed from 50mm sq (2in sq) square planed pine although the two uprights at the front corners of the dressing table section are 75 × 50mm (2 × 3in) for extra rigidity.

The framework comprises a ceiling rail which should be screwed through to the joists or to battens nailed between the joists if the latter run in the 'wrong' direction; an upright at each end screwed to the wall and an upright on each side of the dressing table. A second horizontal rail runs across the uprights just above the tops of the wardrobe doors. Both ceiling and horizontal rails are glued and screwed to the uprights at halving joints, inserting the screws from the back so they won't show. Two additional 50mm sq (2in sq) uprights are screwed to the back wall in line with the back corners of the dressing table.

At floor level lengths of 50 × 25mm (1 × 2in) batten are screwed down to provide a support for a plywood floor inside each wardrobe and to locate the bottoms of the two 75 × 50mm (2 × 3in) uprights. The ends of the inner battens are cut to fit round these and screws are driven through into the uprights from behind. At the front and dressing table sides, the battens are set back sufficiently to allow the doors to fit flush with the uprights.

A framework of 50 × 25mm (1 × 2in) battens is made up level with the horizontal cross rail for a floor for the top row of cupboards. Lengths of batten are screwed back to the back and end walls level with the cross rail and more sections screwed to the rear face of the rail. Crosspieces are fitted between the long rails, using halving joints to locate them properly; these can be pinned and glued. A double crosspiece is fitted on each side of the dressing table space to provide a support for the top of the closing panel.

Once the framework has been assembled, cut section of 12mm (½in) plywood or chipboard to make the shelves of the top cupboards and the closet floors — pin and glue them in place; note that the upper shelf also acts as a door stop. If using ready made doors for the closing panels, fit these into the opening using joint blocks and metal plate brackets at the top. Before installing the doors, fit hanging rails in each closet. Fit the doors so that they fit flush within the openings, using a chisel to pare out the recesses for the hinge flaps. Allow about a 3mm (⅛in) gap all round the doors for clearance. Screw suitable handles to the doors and fit magnetic catches to the framework level with the tops and bottoms of the doors.

Finally, assemble the dressing table section. The top is cut from a section of pre-glued pine boarding about 600mm (24in) wide. Cut it so that it fits snugly in the opening and round off the front edge with a plane. Screw 50 × 25mm (1 × 2in) battens to the back wall and closing panels to support the top which should be attached to them with jointing blocks for a concealing fixing. A front panel should be cut and shaped from a length of 75 × 25mm (1 × 3in) pine and simply fixed to the underside of the top with jointing blocks. Another length of 75 × 25mm (1 × 3in) is fixed across the top of the dressing table opening with jointing blocks and can be used to conceal a light tube.

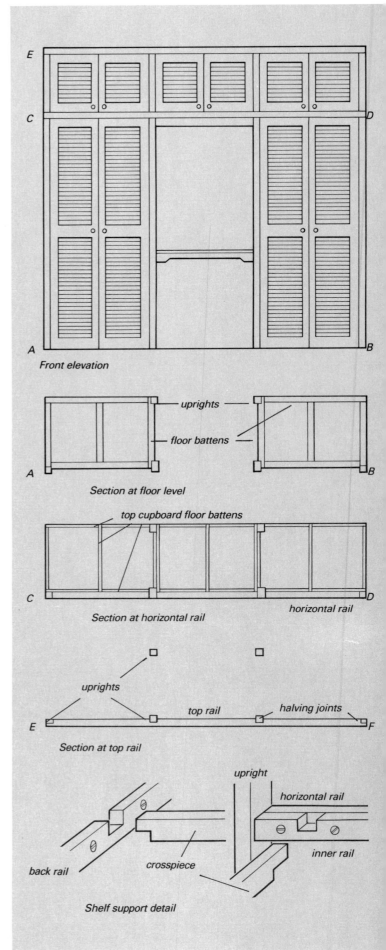

Front elevation

Section at floor level

Section at horizontal rail

Section at top rail

Shelf support detail

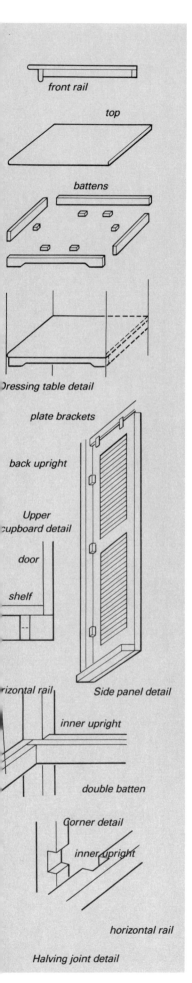

front rail

top

battens

Dressing table detail

plate brackets

back upright

Upper cupboard detail

door

shelf

horizontal rail

Side panel detail

inner upright

double batten

Corner detail

inner upright

horizontal rail

Halving joint detail

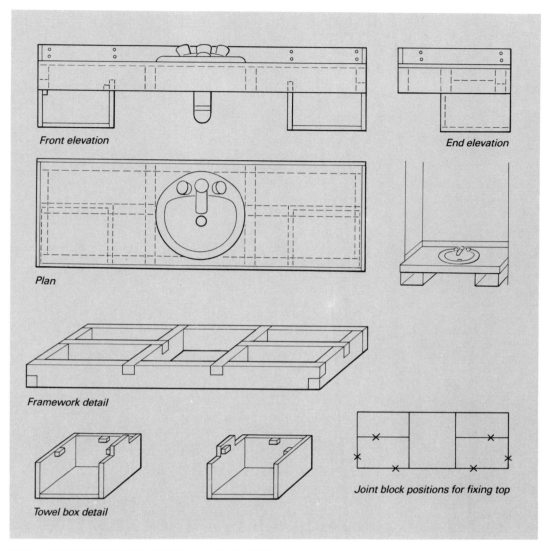

Front elevation

End elevation

Plan

Framework detail

Towel box detail

Joint block positions for fixing top

VANITY UNIT

A hand basin in a bedroom is a useful addition and when teamed with a dressing table top to make a vanity unit it is particularly handy. This example is intended to fill an alcove up to 180cm (6ft) wide and incorporates a couple of useful towel storage boxes too.

The actual size of the unit's top will vary with the alcove width and size of the basin chosen although 600mm (2ft) is probably the maximum width you could get away with. However, there is no reason why it should not project forwards beyond the alcove if this was particularly shallow.

The main supporting framework is made from 4in (10cm) by 2in (5cm) planed pine, the back and end rails being screwed to the surrounding walls and the front rail being supported with halving joints where it joins the end rails. These joints are glued

and reinforced with countersunk screws. Additional crosspieces are also installed using halving joints in the perimeter rails. The two middle crosspieces should fit close to the basin position to provide plenty of support to the top when the basin is full of water.

The towel boxes are made from 25mm (1in) thick pine boarding, the sides being 175mm (7in) deep, the back 150mm (6in) deep and the bases 300mm (12in) square. The boxes are assembled with simple butt joints between the various panels which are glued and reinforced with 6mm (¼in) dowels driven through the sides into the edges of the base and back and through the base into the lower edge of the back. Note that the inner panel of each box is shaped to fit between the sections of framework.

Fix the boxes to the framework using three joint blocks for each, screwing into the end rails, front rail and box support rails.

The top of the unit is made from 18mm (¼in) laminated particleboard and this should be cut to size so that its front edge flush with the edge of the front support rail; use the template supplied with the inset basin to make the basin cut out. Then fix the top to the framework using jointing blocks.

To hide the edge of the top and the detail of the frame's halving joints, cramp and glue a length of 125mm (5in) × 18mm (¾in) planed pine around the back and end walls to make an upstand. Use brass screws with screw cups for a decorative effect. You can finish the upstand, front trim panel and towel boxes with stain and varnish or just a varnish for the full benefit of the wood's natural color. Finally, install the basin and its pipework as described on page 97.

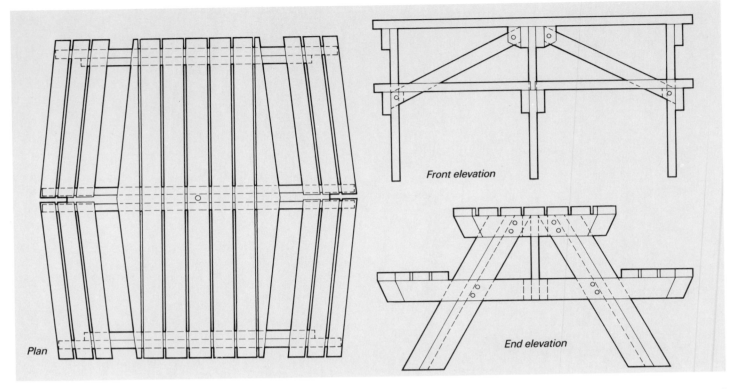

Front elevation

End elevation

Plan

PICNIC TABLE

Eating out in the garden during the warm days of summer can be a lot of fun, especially if you have a barbeque. A decent size table is essential though if you are to be able to lay out the meal and eat in comfort. This sturdily-built picnic table and benches will seat four people with ease and it can be unbolted for stacking against a garage or shed wall during the winter.

Since you will want to leave the table outside during the summer, it should be constructed of a wood that will stand up to the weather — something like redwood or beech would be ideal. However, if you are unable to obtain any of these woods locally, you could use pine instead, but it may not have such a long life. Whichever wood you choose, it is essential to treat it well with a good quality preservative. The best way to do this is to immerse the various pieces in the preservative so that they can soak it up. For this you'll need an old bath, or you can dig a trough in the garden, line it with thick plastic and pour the preservative into it.

Practically all of the table is made from lengths of 100mm (4in) × 37.5mm (1½in) wood but the bench slats and diagonal braces are of 75mm (3in) ×

37.5mm (1½in) and the brace supporting blocks are of 50mm (2in) × 37.5mm (1½in). You'll need a good quality waterproof wood glue and some 75mm (3in) galvanised nails for the bulk of the assembly. You'll also need 16 100mm (4in) carriage bolts with washers and butterfuly nuts and 12 6in (15cm) carriage bolts with washers and butterfly nuts.

As shown, the table top is 150cm (5ft) long and 750mm (2ft 6in) wide at the center, tapering to 600mm (2ft) at each end. The benches are 250mm (10in) wide and each just under 750mm (2ft 6in) long. However, there is no reason why you should not alter these dimensions to make the table longer if you wish, or wider.

Begin by making the top. This has seven 100mm (4in) wide slats, the outer slats being tapered from the center to a width of 25mm (1in) at each end. You can do this with a circular saw, planing and standing off the cut edges to smooth them. Cut the horizontal supports from the same size wood, making the two end pieces 600mm (2ft) long and the two center pieces 750mm (2ft 6in) long. For appearance cut the ends back at an angle.

Nail and glue the top slats to

the horizontal supports so that the ends of the slats overhang by 50mm (2in) at each end and the center supports are 37.5mm (1½in) apart and an equal distance from the top center line. Space the slats evenly. Drive the nail heads down below the top surface by at least 3mm (⅛in). If you wish you can bore a hole in the center of the top for a sunshade.

Next assemble the bench sections. Cut the bench supports, making the two end sections 130cm (4ft 4in) long each and the two center pieces 145cm (4ft 10in) long. Cut their ends back at an angle for appearance. Then cut the bench slats, making them slightly overlength to allow for trimming their ends at the required angle. Mark the slat positions in from the ends of the supports, spacing them at 12mm (½in) intervals. Then glue and nail the slats to the supports so that the latter are spaced exactly as the table top supports. It is a good idea to assemble the benches on top of the upturned table top so that the supports coincide exactly.

When the glue has dried, punch the nail heads well below the surface and use a circular saw to trim the slat ends parallel with the support pieces and so that they overhang by 50mm (2in) at the outer ends and by 12mm (½in) at the inner ends.

Cut the brace support blocks and nail and glue them to the

central table top supports and outer bench supports, making sure they are spaced equally on either side of the center line, and a total of 37mm (1½in) apart.

Now cut the legs — you'll need six all exactly the same size, so it is best to mark one and use this as a master to transfer the marks to the others with a trysquare. Each leg should be 900mm (36in) long but note that the ends are cut at an angle of 60° which should be marked using a bevel gauge set against a protractor.

When the legs have been cut, drill two bolt holes on the center line, one 25mm (1in) from the top, the other 75mm (3in) from the top. Offer the outer legs up against the end table top supports, so that they meet on the center line and mark and drill through the bolt holes. Bolt the legs in place with the top inverted. Then lift the bench assemblies over the top and prop them up so that the tops of the slats are 350mm (14in) from the ground. Drill through the outer legs and the bench supports and fit the bolts. Then offer up the middle legs and drill through the bench supports on either side for the fixing bolts. Fit all the bolts and turn the table right way up.

Check that the legs are vertical and the table top level, then measure between the brace support blocks and cut the braces. Line them up and drill through the blocks and brace ends. Fit the securing bolts.

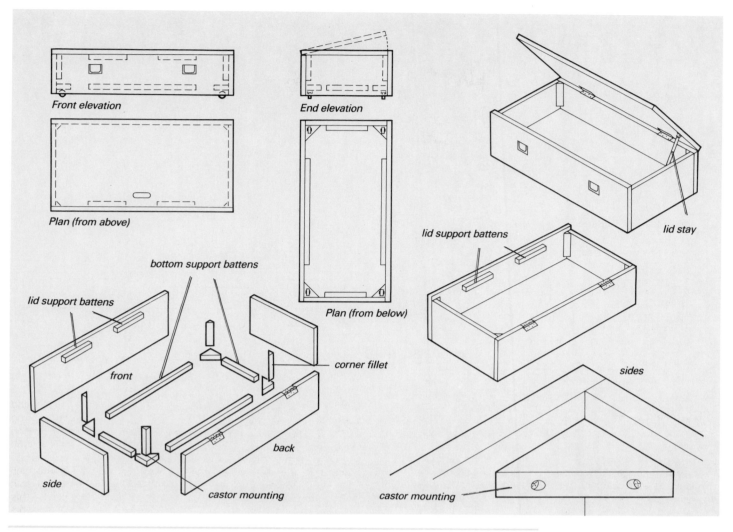

Front elevation

End elevation

Plan (from above)

lid support battens

lid support battens

lid stay

bottom support battens

lid support battens

front

corner fillet

side

back

Plan (from below)

castor mounting

sides

castor mounting

UNDERBED STORAGE BOXES

No matter how many closets, shelves and wardrobes we have there always seems to be a shortage of storage space in any house. Invariably the space under the bed is pushed into service, concealing a motley collection of cardboard boxes, old suitcases and the like to meet all of our storage needs. Unfortunately this not only looks unsightly but it makes life very difficult when you want to get something from under the bed or when you want to sweep or vacuum beneath it. The solution is a system of purpose made storage boxes that not only make the best use of available space underneath the bed, but look good and can be easily moved when required.

They are made from pine to fit in with the very popular pine beds of today, but there is no reason why they should not be stained or painted or even covered with material to match bedroom decor or the bed itself.

The dimensions given are nominal and you will probably want to adjust them slightly to suit the available space.

The front, sides and back of the box are made from 25mm (1in) thick prepared pine, the front panel being 225mm (9in) deep and the remaining three pieces 200mm (8in) deep — you should be able to get four boxes, each measuring 900mm (36in) long by 450mm (18in) wide under a normal size double bed.

Assemble the basic box shape from the front and back panels and two ends, glueing the butt-joints and reinforcing the corners by pinning and glueing 25mm (1in) by 25mm (1in) triangular fillets of wood in place. These should be 125mm (5in) long and fitted flush with the tops of the end and back panels. Check that the boxes are square by measuring the diagonals, which should be equal.

Cut a piece of 6mm (¼in) ply-

wood for the bottom of the box and set it aside while you cut four 150mm (6in) × 150mm (6in) triangular sections of 25mm (1in) thick pine to reinforce the lower corners and provide mountings for the casters. Turn the box upside down and drop in the plywood bottom. Glue and screw the triangular pieces into the corners, setting them 25mm (1in) up from the bottom edges of the front, back and sides; cut or drill pockets in the edges of the triangular blocks so that you can drive the screws squarely into the box sides. Next screw lengths of 25mm sq (1in sq) batten around the sides of the box level with the triangular fillets; pin the plywood bottom down to these supports and the triangular fillets. There is a wide range of drawer handles you can use for the boxes, but if fitting flush types, cut the recesses for them now, using a chisel or power router. The box top is

made from 1in thick pine, too. You can either make it yourself by glueing two or more lengths of pine edge to edge, using sash cramps to hold them while the glue dries, or you can cut it from a section of ready-glued board which is now available from many hardware stores. Cut the board so that it fits flush with the end panels and back edge of the box. Cut the hand hold by drilling a hole near the edge and saw it out with a saw. Round off the edges with sandpaper.

To provide extra support for the top, pin and glue two short lengths of 25mm sq (1in sq) batten to the rear face of the front panel level with the tops of the side panels. Then fit the top in place, using two brass hinges, cutting recesses for their flaps in the box top and rear panel with a chisel. Finally, fit a lid stay to the top and side of the box so that it holds the lid open at a comfortable angle.

Finish the box as desired and then screw four casters to the triangular fillets.

COFFEE TABLE

Coffee tables are always useful to have around the house; they serve a number of useful purposes — from providing a home for a TV set or record player to providing a handy surface for serving afternoon tea. This particular example is simple to make, attractive and can be varied in size to suit your own particular needs. Being made from pine, it can be varnished, stained and varnished or even painted.

As shown here, the table is 600mm (24in) square, but you can make it larger or smaller or oblong if you wish.

The top is made by glueing 11 pieces of planed 50mm sq (2in sq) pine together; for a 600mm (24in) square table each should be 560mm (22in) long. Glue them together using woodworking adhesive and hold them with sash cramps while the glue dries. You will need three cramps — you can rent them from good tool rental companies — and they should be fitted so that two span one face of the top and the third spans the opposite face between the two others. Fit scraps of wood between the jaws of the cramps and the top to prevent it becoming bruised or damaged as you tighten them up.

When the main part of the top has dried, cut lengths of 50 × 25mm (1 × 2in) pine to fit round the outside, simply overlapping their ends since these will eventually be cut off. Glue and cramp these edging pieces in place.

When the glue has set you may have to plane off any unevenness in the top surface — work the plane diagonally over the battens and inwards from each edge to prevent splintering.

The four corners of the top are cut off at an angle of 45° and each angled cut must be exactly the width of each leg. You can do this quite simply with a bevel gauge or combination rule set to 45°; if using a bevel gauge mark the leg width on it with chalk.

Cut off the corners with a **back saw, taking great care to** keep the cuts square; otherwise use a circular saw which will produce a square cut automatically.

Finish off the top by sanding it well and if you intend using a coloured stain to finish the table, apply it now to prevent uneven colour build-up at the junctions with the legs.

Cut the legs from 100 × 37mm (1½in × 4in) planed pine, making them 330mm (13in) long and rounding off the tops with a spokeshave or plane and sandpaper. Each leg is held to the top by glue and a 75mm (3in) long, 25mm (1in) diameter wooden dowel.

To fit the legs, first make a pencil mark across each one 25mm (1in) down from the top using a trysquare. Then mark the center of the dowel position 25mm (1in) below this line. Fit a dowel pin or drive in a 12mm (½in) panel pin at this point, snipping the head off the latter with pliers. Offer up the leg to the table top, aligning the pencil mark with the top's upper surface and pressing it home so that the dowel pin or panel pin makes a mark on the edge of the top. Remove the dowel pin or panel pin with pincers and drill both leg and top for the dowel, the latter to a depth of 50mm (2in).

Spread a little glue around the inner edge of the hole in the leg, push the dowel through from the outer face until it just protrudes from the inner face. Then spread more glue on the table top edge and the inner face of the leg and fit the latter to the former, tapping the dowel home with a wooden mallet.

Fit two diagonally opposed legs at a time, cramping them tight while they dry — you many have to combine two cramps to get a long enough span for this.

When all four legs are fitted, plane down any protruding dowels, sand and finish the table as required.

If the legs are uneven, set the table on a flat, level surface and wedge it so that its top is horizontal (check with a spirit level). Then hold a pencil on top of a thin block of wood; hold this on the surface and mark round the base of each leg for trimming.

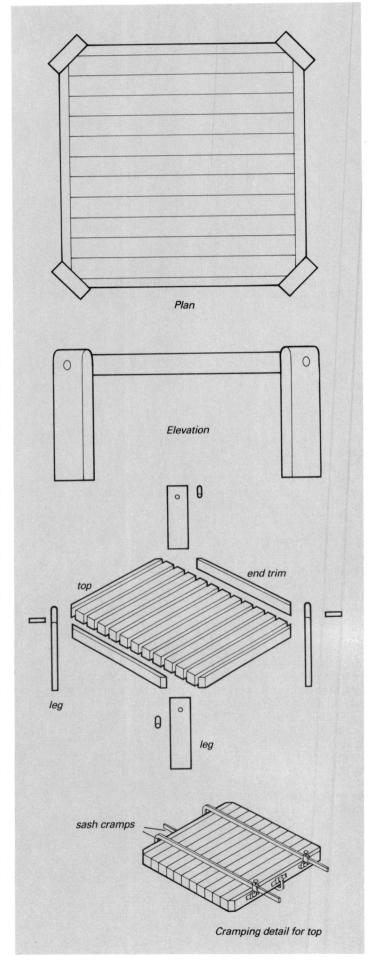

Plan

Elevation

top

end trim

leg

leg

sash cramps

Cramping detail for top

THE BUILDING CODE

Whatever you plan to build or alter in your home it is likely that you will need to apply for a building permit before commencing the work. All new construction, remodeling or renovation work in your area is bound to certain rules and regulations known as the Building Code. The purpose of the Building Code is to provide minimum standards of construction and to make sure that your home is safe for occupancy.

All communities have adopted the Federal Building Code as a minimum standard, to this has probably been added any additional State or County Building Codes which apply to the community. Finally the town or village may have adopted its own regulations which take into account local building standards, local building practices, materials or preferences in addition to the minimum standards set down by the National Building Code. This entire body of regulation makes up your local Building Code, before starting any work in your home make sure you pick up a copy of the Code from your local Building Department at the town hall, at this time you may be able to discuss your improvement plans with the Building Inspector himself or at least an assistant. Codes are frequently up-dated so be sure to obtain a current copy.

Zoning

You will find that all property in your community is divided into lots, each lot has a number and a record of all the lots is kept at the town hall. The lots are further grouped into zones set aside for specific purposes which have been determined by the local community. The zones may be designated as either residential, commercial or manufacturing. Residential zones will probably be broken down into several different types such as zone A, zone AA and zone B or maybe zone R1, zone R2, zone R3 etc. It is important to determine in which zone your property lies as each zone may have separate requirements under the local Code. Depending on which zone your property is located in the Code will cover such items as minimum lot size; front side and rear yard setbacks; height restrictions; positioning of wells and sewage systems; accessory buildings and occupancy requirements.

Additional Restrictions

In addition to the Building Code your house may be part of a residential community or association which also places restrictions or limitations on the type of alterations that may be made to the property. Generally this extends only to the type and style of fences or a ban on blacktop driveways, but in some areas — a neighborhood of Victorian gingerbread houses for example — it may restrict the architectural style of any new work. Further restrictions to the type of alteration you may make to your home may be made by the mortgage holder or by the house insurer. Allways check with your insurance agent to make sure that your home owners policy is not invalidated by the construction work. Some insurers will insist that at least part of the work — usually the electrics or plumbing and heating — is carried out by professionals.

Houses built before the Building Code took effect are not required to comply to the Code unless they are altered.

Building Permits

A building permit will probably be required if you plan to do the following:

1. Alter or change the external appearance of your house. For example if you: add a porch; add a screen in a porch; add or remove a window or door, or if you build a fence or wall.
2. Any electrical work.
3. Any plumbing work.
4. Add or remove any structural element.
5. Build an addition to your house.
6. Build a separate building on your property.

You probably will not need a permit to perform regular maintenance work, for example: painting the exterior of your house; replacing or repairing a shingle roof; replacing a toilet or tub on existing pipework, etc.

Applying for a Building Permit

To obtain a building permit a set of plans showing your proposed alterations must be submitted to the local Building Department where they will be checked for compliance with the National and local Building Code. If the plans are up to code a permit will be issued, usually for a small fee. The permit will be valid for one year after which time a new application must be made if the work has not started. The permit must be displayed prominently at the job site for inspection by any interested authority.

At various stages of the construction work you may be required to call in the local building inspector to check the work for compliance, for instance, before and after any footings have been poured. This checking procedure ensures that the work is indeed being carried out according to the approved plans and that the method of construction and the quality of the materials is up to the standard set out in the Building Code. This procedure may not be necessary on your job, however, the Building Inspector may call by at any time to check on the progress of the work.

Allways be sure to complete the job according to the approved plans, if in doubt call the building inspector and ask his advice, never try to guess. Work not covered by the approved plans or not up to the standards of the code may be condemned.

Seeking a Variance

If your plans are rejected by the building department for non-compliance you will receive a notification of the reasons given. In some cases this may be simply dealt with by altering the plans and re-submitting them. In other cases the layout of your property may make it impossible to comply with the requirements of the code. In this case you may seek an exception to the law by filing an application with the Zoning Board of Review. When filing for an exemption, evidence supporting your position must be presented with your application, together with a block plan showing all lots within 200 feet including all buildings and marked with owners' names and addresses. A plan of your lot showing the proposed and existing structures, and plans and elevations of the proposed work, must also be submitted. A decision will be made after a public meeting of the Board during which any interested member of the public may speak for or against the project.

INDEX

alarms, 215
asphalt drive, 226
attics, 52-53; 69-71;
    access, 52; conversion, 69-71;
        ladders, 53

ball-valves, 114
baseboards, 75
basin, fitting and removing, 97
bath, fitting and removing, 98
beams, 27, *see also* lintels
bidet, plumbing, 112
blocks, decorating, 235
blockwork wall, 18
bricklaying, basics, 234
building code, 251

carpets, 186-88
ceilings, 48-51
    cracks, 48
    joints, filling, 51
    new ceiling, fitting, 50
    plastering, 48; finishing
        plastering, 51
    removing, 49
    sagging, 48
    suspended, 50

chimneys, 61
concrete, 220-221 ff.
    readymix c., 225

damp, 80-83
    indoors, 83
    pointing, 81
    sealing, 81
decorating, 154-209
    ceilings, tiling, 202-3
    floorcoverings, 184-96
    graining wood, 179
    joinery, exterior, 208; interior 158
    metalwork, exterior, 209;
        interior, 160-61
    oiling, 183
    panelling, 204-5
    polishing, 183

sanding floors, 180-81
varnishing wood, 182
wallcoverings, 162-68
wallpaper, hanging, 164-69
walls, exterior, 206-7; interior,
    155-56; interior brick and stone
    walls, 200; painting, 170-76;
    tiling, 197-99, 201
waxing, 183
windows, 178
woodwork, interior, 157
doorways, 28-31
    external ds., 31
    fitting frame, 29
    lintel, 29
    needles, 28
    opening, cutting, 28
    redundant ds., filling in, 30
    stud partitions, ds. in, 29
    temporary support, 28
dormer windows, installing, 66-68
drainage systems, 90
    correcting, 217
    single stack d., 103
    two pipe d., 103

electricity, 118-145
    appliances, 140
    eyeball light fittings, 129
    bulbs, types, 130
    cables, 120
    ceiling lights, 123
    circuits, extending, 138, 141
    distribution, 120
    downlighters, 129
    faults, 144
    fittings, 123
        decorative fs., 129-131
    fluorescent lights, 132
    fuse panel, 119
    individual circuits, 119
    lighting circuits, extending, 122,
        123, 141
    lights, 123; 129-131
    outdoors, 142-3
    outlets, 134
        changing singles to doubles, 136
    pendant light, 124
    plugs, 145
    power circuits, 133-135; 138;
        extending, 133-135; 138
    service panel, 119
    switches, 126;
    three way s.s, 127
    track lighting, 131

wall lights, 122, 125
wallwashers, 129
wiring, 145
extensions, 76-79
    drainpipes, 78
    foundations, 77
    planning requirements, 76
    roofs, flat, 79
    types, 76

fencing, 238-241
floorcoverings, laying, 189-196
    types, 184-185
floor tiles, laying, 191-195
flooring, 40-47
    damaged boards, 41
    floorboards, creaking, 41
    plywood, 45
    joists, sagging, 41; renewing, 42
    levelling, 44
    relaying, 43
    sanding, 180-181
    solid concrete f.s, 40, 46; casting,
        47; damp, 46; unevenness, 46
    suspended f.s, 40
foundations, 77, 222-3
    concrete raft f.s, 77
    raft f.s, 224
    sloping ground, 77
    strip f.s, 77, 222
    types, 77

girders, 27
ground, modelling, 218-219
guttering, 115
    cast aluminum g., 115
    downpipe, 117
    installing new g., 117
    leaks, 115
    overflow, 115
    plastic system, 116
    sagging, 115
    surface rust, 115
gypsum board, 23

heating, 146-149
    draining the system, 148
    dry systems, 146
    fires, real, 146

frost thermostats, 147
pipes, 148
programmers, 147
radiators, 147, 149
thermostatic controls, 147
time clocks, 147
high suction walls, 21
hot water cylinder, 91, 106
fitting 106
removing 106

insect attack, 88-89
insulation, 150-153
attics, 152
blanket insulants, 152
double glazing, 150
draftproofing, 150, 153
floors, 150
glass fiber insulants, 152
lagging, cold water, 151
loose-fill insulants, 152
pipework, 151
plumbing, 151
tanks, 151
walls, 150

joinery, exterior decorating, 208
fitting and replacing, 75
painting, 177
preparing for painting, 158

kitchen units, 242-243

lighting circuits, extending, 122
lintels, 27

masonry, plastering, 24
mesh arch formers, 35
metalwork, exterior decorating, 209

oiling wood, 183

panelling, ceilings and walls, 204-5
parquet, 196
partitions, 15
blockwork p.s, 18; services in
blockwork p.s, 20
dry p.s, 16
electricity, 20
plumbing, 20
stud p.s, 15; bracing studs, 16;
erecting framework, 15; services
in stud p.s, 20, trimming doorway,
16
pass-throughs, 28
paths, 227
patios, 229
paving slabs, 228
penetrating damp, 80
pests, 88-89
picture rails, 75
pipes, 92, 102
copper, 92-93
plastic, 102
plaster, 21
bonding, 21
browning, 21
cement based, 21
finish, 24
grounds, 22
gypsum based, 24
metal beads, 22
mixing, 21
screeding method, 22
thistle board finish, 23
plugs, 145
plumbing systems, 90
bursts, 114
draining, 114
faults, 113
leaks, 114
polishing, wood, 183
power circuits, extending, 133

rainwater systems, see guttering
reglazing, windows, 159
rising damp, 80
rising main, 91
roofs, 54-68, 79
access, 55
extensions, 79
flashings, 63
flat roofs, 54; refelting, 62;
repairing, 62
hips, 60
pitched r.s, 54
rainwater systems, see guttering
slates, 56-7
verges, 60
windows, installing, 64-65
rot, 84-7

safes, 215
security, 210-215
alarms, 215
doors, 211-12
windows, 213-14
sheet vinyl, laying, 190-191; see also
'floorcoverings'
showers, 107-11
cubicle, 111
fitting the rose, 109
installing mixer, 109
pressure head, 107
shower tray, 110
temperature, 107
thermostatic shower, 109
types, 107
sinks, 94
staining wood, 183
staircases, 72-74
banisters, repairs, 74
styles, 72
treads, repairs, 73
types, 72
steps, 231-32

terraces, 231-232
through rooms, 32-5
tiles, 58-60; 191-99
brick t.s, 200
ceiling t.s, 202-3
ceramic floor t.s, 191-2
eaves t.s, 60
gable t.s, 60
laying t.s, 58
mirror t.s, 201
quarry t.s, 193
removing, 59
replacing, 59
ridge t.s, 60
soft floor t.s, 194-5
types, 58
valley t.s, 60
wall t.s, 197-99

vanity unit, 247
varnishing, wood, 182
vinyl, laying sheet v., 189-90

w.c., high to low level, fitting and
removing, 99
walls, 26; 170-75; 197-99; 206-7;
233-237

exterior decorating, 206–7
load-bearing, 26
non-load-bearing, 26
outdoor walls, types, 233
painting, 170–175
retaining, 236
screen walling, 237
tiling, 197–99
wallcoverings, 162–63

wallpaper, hanging, 164–69
wardrobes, 246
water supply, 90
waxing wood, 183
wet rot, 84–5
windows, 36–39
  decorating, 178
  enlarging, 36–39
  fixings, 39

  sub-sills, 39
  types, 36
wiring, 145
woodworm, 88–9
workbench, 245
washing machine, 96
waste disposal unit, 95
waste runs, 103

The following suppliers lent materials, tools and equipment for the projects in this book:

APPLE ELECTRICAL SUPPLIES (HACKNEY) LTD, London, lamps & electrical fittings, pp. 120–143; BLACK & DECKER LTD, London, paintmate roller p. 171; BURGESS POWER TOOLS LTD, Leicester, Model 969 paint spray p. 171; BUTTERLEY BUILDING MATERIALS LTD, Derby, brick tiles and adhesive p. 200; COLLINS & CHAMBERS LTD, London, safety equipment p. 49; CROWN LEA PLANT HIRE London, plate vibrator p. 230; DH SUPPLIES, Middlesex, radiator p. 161; EDISON HALO LTD, Middlesex, eyeball & downlight wallwasher fittings p. 129; HAIGH ENGINEERING CO LTD, Herefordshire, Tweeny 125 waste disposer p. 95; JACKSON & CO (BARKING) LTD, Essex, plastering tools p. 21; LONDON & LANCASHIRE RUBBER CO LTD, London, Fibatape p. 23; PECKS PLANT HIRE, Essex, scaffold tower, ladders and ladder-stay pp. 55, 206, 208; PLASPLUGS LTD, Derby, pro-tiler tile cutter p. 192; RFJ PRODUCTS, Devon, Jenny Twin slate clips p. 56; REDLAND ROOF TILES LTD, London, roof tiles and fixing clips p. 58; RYTON'S VENTILATION EQUIPMENT LTD, Northants, plastic cavity-wall ties p. 78; TEK MARKETING LTD, Cambs, plug–in digital security timeswitch p. 214 TRANSBYN MARKETING, London, Saniflo WC shredder system p. 100; ZEBRA TOOL CO LTD Hants, angle–finding indicator p. 219.

The photograph on p. 84 (above) is reproduced by permission of the Buildings Research Establishment's Princes Risborough laboratory.